Human Communication

Human Communication

Seventh Edition

Stewart L. Tubbs

Eastern Michigan University

Sylvia Moss

McGraw-Hill, Inc.

New York   St. Louis   San Francisco   Auckland   Bogotá   Caracas
Lisbon   London   Madrid   Mexico City   Milan   Montreal   New Delhi
San Juan   Singapore   Sydney   Tokyo   Toronto

HUMAN COMMUNICATION

34567890 AGM AGM 90987654

ISBN 0-07-065487-5

This book was set in Sabon by Ruttle, Shaw & Wetherill, Inc.
The editors were Hilary Jackson and Scott Amerman;
the production supervisor was Kathryn Porzio.
The cover was designed by Tana Kamine.
The photo editor was Elyse Rieder.
Arcata Graphics/Martinsburg was printer and binder.

Cover photograph: Dominique Sarrante/The Image Bank.

Library of Congress Cataloging-in-Publication Data

Tubbs, Stewart L., (date).
    Human communication / Stewart L. Tubbs, Sylvia Moss.—7th ed.
        p.   cm.
    Includes bibliographical references and index.
    ISBN 0-07-065487-5
    1. Communication.   I. Moss, Sylvia, (date).   II. Title.
P90.T78   1994
302.2—dc20   93-35432

About the Authors

Stewart L. Tubbs is Dean of the College of Business and Professor of Management at Eastern Michigan University. He received his doctorate in Communication and Organizational Behavior from the University of Kansas. His master's degree in Communication and his bachelor's degree in Science are from Bowling Green State University. He has completed post-doctoral work in management at Michigan State University, the University of Michigan, and Harvard Business School.

Dr. Tubbs has also taught at General Motors Institute, and at Boise State University where he was Chairman of the Management Department, and later Associate Dean of the College of Business.

He has been named an Outstanding Teacher three times, has consulted extensively for Fortune 500 companies, and is former Chairman of the Organizational Communication division of the Academy of Management. Dr. Tubbs is the author of *A Systems Approach to Small Group Interaction* and co-author, with Sylvia Moss, of *Interpersonal Communication*. He is also listed in *American Men and Women of Science, Contemporary Authors, Directory of American Scholars*, the *International Who's Who in Education*, and *Outstanding Young Men of America*.

Sylvia Moss is a professional writer with a strong interest in the behavioral sciences. She received her undergraduate education at Barnard College and the University of Wisconsin and holds graduate degrees from Columbia University and New York University. She is the author, with Stewart Tubbs, of *Interpersonal Communication* and has contributed to several college texts in the social sciences.

A writing consultant, Ms. Moss has also taught writing workshops. Her poems have appeared in the *Grolier Poetry Prize Annual* as well as in *New Letters, Helicon Nine,* and other literary journals. A collection of her poetry, *Cities in Motion,* was selected for The National Poetry Series in 1987. She has twice been a Yaddo Fellow and in 1988 was the recipient of a Whiting Writer's Award. She teaches at the College of New Rochelle.

To
Gail, Brian, and Kelly
Harry, Michael, and Sara

Contents

Preface

Human Communication is designed for introductory communication courses. Since it was first published twenty years ago, it has been used by over 125,000 students—a figure that makes us feel both humbled and encouraged. As in earlier editions, our commitment is to present students with a comprehensive theoretical base, an understanding of how modern communication has evolved and continues to change and grow, and a grasp of its immediate and long-term applications to their own lives.

Once again we focus on the traditional concerns of speech communication and link together contexts as various as two-person communication and mass communication. Our approach is to fuse current and classic communication theory, fundamental concepts, and important skills. Despite its complexities, we believe we can present our subject to introductory students without over-simplification, in language that is clear, vivid, and precise.

We have tried, as in previous editions, to create a text that is sensitive to diversity, one that reflects our long-term interest in gender and cultural issues. Thus, throughout our book we integrate examples and references that represent a wide variety of backgrounds, ages, and ethnic and cultural groups.

New to This Edition

The seventh edition of *Human Communication* encompasses many changes. The first is the addition of a new chapter on ethics, a subject of increasing importance to communication scholars and students and of great concern to educators. For example, a recent national survey of university deans and faculty members reports that 95 percent of those polled feel it is important to provide students with a framework for ethical decision-making. The new chapter introduces basic ethical principles and then addresses the significant ethical issues encountered in virtually every communication experience.

This seventh edition has also been thoroughly updated, with over 250 new citations, and revised to present a range of new issues, theory, and communication research. In addition, the book has been redesigned and includes numerous new photos to reflect the diversity of our communication encounters and to illustrate key points.

There are also structural changes. As before, the six chapters of Part I introduce the principles of communication. Part II devotes a chapter to each of the seven communication contexts laid out in the introduction: two-person, interviewing, small-group, public, organizational, mass, and intercultural communication, which occurs in any number of contexts. In response to suggestions by reviewers, however, we have revised the chapter on relationship processes (formerly Chapter 3, now Chapter 6) and moved it so that it forms a natural bridge to Chapter 7 on two-person communication. The change creates a more meaningful sequence between two chapters that together encompass so much information about fundamental interpersonal relationships. Part III, new to this edition, explores the vital connections between ethics and communication.

Plan of the Book

Chapter 1 addresses the process of human communication. It has new material on people's reports of communication after near-death experiences, Kiazen or continuous improvement in organizational communication, mass communication's influence in the 1992 presidential campaign, intercultural communication, new communication technologies, and communication ethics. There is also a new simplified model of communication.

Chapter 2 on person perception has a new expanded section on how we perceive ourselves: it examines self-concept, self-esteem, shyness, feedback, and competence. The chapter then examines how we form impressions of others as well as stereotyping, perceiver accuracy, and the influence of social roles. There is also new material on the stereotyping of homosexual persons and on physical appearance.

Chapter 3 on the elements of verbal communication has new material on connotation, designations of cultural groups, communication between cultures, as well as recent studies suggesting gender differences in the use of language.

The structure of Chapter 4 on nonverbal communication follows that of the sixth edition, moving from the interpretation of nonverbal messages to spatial, temporal, visual, and vocal cues. Among the changes are new cross-cultural material on proxemics and the expansion of the final section on deception, currently a research area of high interest.

Chapter 5 on listening has new material on male-female relationship communication, the importance of listening for executives, as well as information on the millions of dollars saved by American Airlines from their corporate program to improve listening.

Chapter 6 on relationship processes has been thoroughly revised, reorganized, and expanded. In addition to sections on attraction, defining characteristics of relationships and their life cycles, and conflict, this chapter has two new sections—on relationship maintenance and family communication (the latter moved from Chapter 9 and thoroughly expanded).

Chapter 7, the first to focus on a communication context, sets forth the elements of two-person communication from the most intimate to the most formal. Changes here include a new discussion on sibling relationships as well as new material on intimacy and power; the chapter also consolidates the book's coverage of self-disclosure.

Chapter 8 on interviewing has new material on television interview shows such as *Larry King Live* and their significance in the 1992 presidential election.

Chapter 9 on small-group communication has new material on the importance of small groups in finding and implementing educational innovations, material on Self-Directed Work Teams (SDWT), revised treatment of the autokinetic effect, and a revision of the coverage of group roles (i.e., task roles, group-building and maintenance roles, and individual roles). There is also new material on group conformity pressure as it relates to the movie *A Few Good Men*.

Chapter 10 on public communication has a new section on persuasion theory and several new excerpts from outstanding speeches as examples.

Chapter 11 on organizational communication has new material on total quality management (TQM), on Work-force 2000, on the importance of communication skills to employers, and on teamwork and empowerment.

The revised survey of mass communication in Chapter 12 incorporates new research and examples on media ethics, presidential elections, and attitude influence. It includes a new section on women and minorities as gatekeepers in the mass media, as well as new material on media violence and new communication technologies.

Chapter 13 treats the essentials of intercultural communication and relates back to the other six contexts discussed. In addition to many new examples, its numerous revisions include material on high- and low-context cultures, language differences, synchrony, ethnocentrism, and the effects of new communication technologies in bringing together people of diverse cultures and background—the effect of a true global village.

Chapter 14 introduces representative ethical principles and goes on to examine a broad spectrum of ethical issues as they emerge in communication contexts as varied as two-person and mass communication.

Like past editions, this text incorporates a number of teaching aids, of benefit, we hope, to both students and instructors: In addition to the lists of student objectives that introduce the chapters, *Human Communication* includes end-of-chapter summaries, review questions, and exercises. Annotations for all the end-of-chapter Suggested Readings, which include popular and scholarly readings as well as selected other media, have been updated; and these may provide the basis for further study and exploration. To encourage other forms of student participation, the text has an appendix with exercises and role plays. There are also two sample speeches to complement Chapter 10 on public communication. For this seventh edition the Instructor's Manual and Test File has also been revised and updated.

Reviews and critiques of the sixth edition have been of great value, and for these we thank: Jerry Allen, University of New Haven; Nick Backus, Washburn University; Jack Bain, Michigan State University; Leonard Barchak, McNeese State University; Marvin Cox, Boise State University; Monte Koffler, North Dakota State University; Rebecca Parker, Western Illinois University; Janice Schuetz, University of New Mexico; and Shirley Willihnganz, University of Louisville.

We also wish to express our gratitude to our editors: Hilary Jackson, whose commitment and contribution to this book are longstanding, and Scott Amerman, who skillfully guided our manuscript through the intricacies of editing and production.

Stewart L. Tubbs
Sylvia Moss

Human Communication

PART I
PRINCIPLES

CHAPTER ONE

*T*he Process of Human Communication

CHAPTER OBJECTIVES

After reading this chapter, you should be able to:

1 Define the term "communication."

2 Describe what is referred to by the term "input" as it is used in the communication model.

3 List four types of messages and give an example of each type.

4 Distinguish between technical and semantic interference and give an example of each.

5 Describe the impact of feedback on behavior.

6 Identify six different contexts of communication and explain how each is distinctive.

7 List and describe three characteristics of two-person communication.

8 Define effective communication in terms of five possible outcomes of human communication.

*F*or many years it has been thought that the speech function was unique to modern Homo sapiens. However, just within the past few years, evidence has been found that indicates that the first creatures to use spoken communication were Neanderthals, or more ancient Homo sapiens dating back 60,000 years. Garrett (1989) reports: "Now an international research team has found what it believes is the Neanderthal version of a bone that is a key to modern human speech. . . . Baruch Arensburg of Tel Aviv University and his team unearthed the hyoid bone while digging in Israel's Kebara cave. . . . The hyoid is a U-shaped bone that supports the tongue and its muscles" (p. 560).

Begley and Gleizes (1989) report this additional evidence:

> Early Orators: Although Neanderthal's brain was bigger than ours, ever since his discovery "he was considered dull-witted and inarticulate," says neuroanatomist Terrence Deacon of Harvard University. Now that prejudice is yielding. Fossil brain casts show a well-developed language area, says Dean Falk of the State University of New York at Albany. His speech was only slightly inferior: using skull fossils to infer the position of the voice box in early humans, . . . Neanderthals had a more restricted vocal range than we do. They had nasal voices, but could probably pronounce every consonant and vowel sound except "oo" and "ee," adds Deacon. "They were articulate, intelligent humans we would be able to understand and interact with" he says. (p. 71)

Fast forward. One modern marketing forecaster has labeled the nineties as finding "Americans huddled in high-tech caves. Cocooning . . . was in full spin. Other predictors of cocooning . . . were: the skyrocketing of VCR purchases and tape rentals; . . . comfort food for the couch; . . . home microwave popcorn sales were a $300 million business" (Popcorn, 1991, pp. 27–28). It seems we have come full circle back to the cave man and woman existence. These changes in life-styles have major implications for the communication patterns of the twenty-first century.

For over 60,000 years men and women have been communicating. Yet we still feel the need, perhaps more than ever, to find ways to improve these skills. This book is dedicated to that end.

THE IMPORTANCE OF HUMAN COMMUNICATION

According to numerous research studies, for your entire life you have spent about 75 percent of each day engaged in communication. Therefore, you may be wondering why you need to study communication in the first place. There is a good reason: Quantity is no guarantee of quality. Given the number of divorces, unhappy workers, and ruptured parent-to-offspring relationships, quantity and frequency of communication are clearly no measure of how effectively people communicate with each other.

Despite the difficulties inherent in ordinary communication, some researchers are attempting communication with an unborn child. Laitner (1987) reports that in Hayward, California, the Prenatal University (PU) was founded by obstetrician-gynecologist Dr. Rene Van de Carr. His work involves teaching babies in the uterus, thus giving them a head start on verbal ability and social skills. Parents talk to their children through paper megaphones (called "pregaphones") directed at the mother's abdomen. Research conducted on PU graduates showed that they "were communicating significantly earlier, and they used compound words earlier, and the mother felt they understood things earlier." However, a warning about pushing children too fast has been issued by the American Academy of Pediatrics. Dr. Robert Sokol, chairman of the Department of Obstetrics and Gynecology at Wayne State University in Detroit, says that "there is no evidence that (fetuses) can process language" (p. 2B).

At the other end of the life spectrum, Morse and Perry (1990) report on the near-death experiences of several dozen people who have survived death and come back to tell about their communication experiences. Reading their book is like watching the movie *Ghost:* It extends the boundaries of our knowledge of communication even beyond death.

Among other things, communication has been linked to **physical well-being.** Stewart (1986) indicates that socially isolated people are more likely to die prematurely; divorced men die at double the normal rate from cancer, heart disease, and strokes, five times the normal rate from hypertension, five times the normal rate from suicide, seven times the normal rate from cirrhosis of the liver, and ten times the normal rate from tuberculosis. Also, poor communication skills have been found to contribute to coronary heart disease, and the likelihood of death increases when a marriage partner dies.

Communication is also closely associated with one's **definition of self.** Rosenberg (1979) relates the story of the "wild boy of Aveyron" who was raised by wolves. He developed no identity as a human being until he began to interact with humans. Individuals gain a sense of self-identity by being paid attention to and getting feedback from others. Also, a sense of identity and worth develops from comparing ourselves with others.

Social needs are also satisfied through interaction with others. Haslett (1984) found that infants and children have a strong motivation to communicate, and an innate capacity to understand interpersonal interaction, because they recognize that communicating is a means of establishing relationships. The child learns primarily from the mother how to interact and to adapt.

On-the-job communication is constantly cited as one of the most important skills in "getting ahead." King (1987) compared rankings of college-educated employees' and employers' lists of required on-the-job skills. He found that out of twenty-eight possible job skills, the following were the top-ranked skills (p. 37):

	Employer Rankings	College Graduate Rankings
Listening	1	3
Written communication	2	1.5 (tie)
Leadership	3	4
Informal oral communication	4	1.5 (tie)
Analytical thinking	5	6

In this book we shall be exploring each of these aspects of human communication—all the way from the first impressions we form of one another to how human relationships are maintained and sometimes terminated.

WHAT IS HUMAN COMMUNICATION?

What do you think of when the word "communication" is used? Students answering this question may mention anything from the use of electric circuits to prayer (that is, communication with God). Communication is a subject so frequently discussed that the term itself has become *too* meaningful—that is, it has too many different meanings for people. Agreeing on a working definition is the first step toward improving our understanding of this complex phenomenon.

Communication has been broadly defined as "the sharing of experience," and to some extent all living organisms can be said to share experience. What makes human communication unique is the superior ability to create and to use symbols, for it is this ability that enables humans to "share experiences indirectly and vicariously" (Goyer, 1970, pp. 4–5). A **symbol** can be defined as **something used for or regarded as representing something else.** For the time being, though, let us say that **human communication** is *the process of creating a meaning between two or more people.* This is at least a partial definition, one we shall want to expand in discussing communication outcomes.

A MODEL OF HUMAN COMMUNICATION

Since human communication is an intangible, ever-changing process, many people find it helpful to use a tangible model to describe that process. Actually, a motion picture would be a better form for modeling communication. As you read this book, think of the model that follows as one frame of a motion picture—a momentary pause in an ongoing process. The model is not an end in itself; it is only a means to help explain the ways in which the various component parts interact.

Figure 1.1 is a model of the most basic human communication event; it

FIGURE 1-1   The Tubbs Communication Model

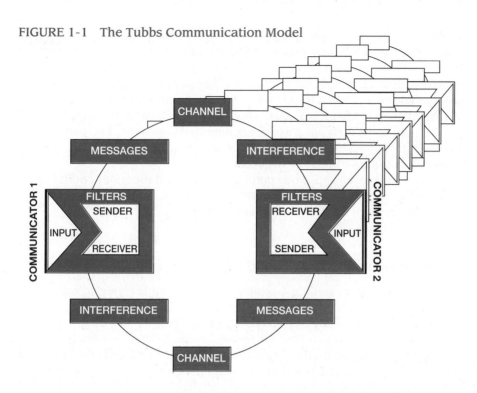

involves only two people. Initially, we shall call them Communicator 1 (the sender/receiver) and Communicator 2 (the receiver/sender). In actuality, both are sources of communication, and each originates and receives messages simultaneously. In addition, both parties are simultaneously being influenced by one another in the transaction. Communicator 1 may originate the first message, and Communicator 2 may be the first person to perceive the transmitted stimuli, but most of our daily communication activities are spontaneous and relatively unstructured, so that these are overlapping roles.

Thus, as represented in the present model, a great many transactions can be initiated from either the right or the left side. For example, when you got up this morning, did you speak to someone first, or were you spoken to first? You probably don't even remember because who spoke first was a matter of chance. In an important sense, it is arbitrary to call yourself either a sender or a receiver: You are both. Even while you are speaking, you are simultaneously observing the other person's behavior and reacting to it. This is also true of the other person as he or she interacts with you.

The transactional view also emphasizes that *you change* as a result of the communication event. Have you ever been drawn into an argument so intense that the more you told the other person how angry you were, the angrier you became? The reverse is also possible. If a man tells a woman how much he cares for her and goes out of his way to do something thoughtful for her, what is the result? Typically, he increases his feeling of closeness to her, even though she may not respond well to his gesture. The research on self-persuasion shows that when you give a persuasive presentation to others, you are often the person who is most persuaded by it. Alcoholics Anonymous has worked with this principle for many years. The people who get up at meetings and try to persuade others to stay sober are also doing a lot to keep themselves persuaded. The transactional viewpoint, then, emphasizes the simultaneous and mutually influential nature of the communication event. The participants become interdependent, and their communication can be analyzed only in terms of the unique context of the event.

As you read more about our model, keep in mind the *transactional* viewpoint with its emphasis on the extent to which the two or more people involved *create* a relationship as part of their communicating.

Communicator 1: Sender/Receiver

Let's take a closer look at Communicator 1, who is trying to transmit a message. Keep in mind that both people are simultaneously sending and receiving all the time. What characteristics of this person would be important in the communication process? Obviously, mental capacities are of central importance. Inside the human brain are millions of nerve cells that function together to store and utilize knowledge, attitudes, and emotions. We want to know what makes Communicator 1 distinct from any other. Like those of any other human being, Communicator 1's senses are continually bombarded by a wealth of stimuli from both inside and outside the body. All that he or she knows and experiences—whether of the physical or the social world—comes initially through the senses. Borrowing from computer terminology, we call these raw data **input**—*all the stimuli, both past and present, that give us our information about the world.*

From the accounts of explorers, castaways, and prisoners of war, we can learn what it is like to experience a long period of isolation, but even in these extreme situations there has been some sensory stimulation. The effect of radically decreased input—in solitary confinement, for example—is more difficult to imagine. You can get some notion of how dependent you are on a steady flow of stimuli by supposing that your senses were shut off one by one. Imagine what it would be like without them for a day or just an hour or even fifteen minutes.

Messages

Looking again at the model in Figure 1.1, we can think of the message that Communicator 1 transmits as being conveyed. These messages may be verbal or nonverbal, and they may be intentional or unintentional. Thus four types of messages are possible: (1) intentional verbal, (2) unintentional verbal, (3) intentional nonverbal, and (4) unintentional nonverbal. As we examine these categories individually, keep in mind that most messages contain two or more types of stimuli and that they often overlap.

Verbal messages   A **verbal message** is *any type of spoken communication that uses one or more words.* Most of the communicative stimuli we are conscious of fall within the category of **intentional verbal messages;** these are *the conscious attempts we make to communicate with others through speech.* Undoubtedly, the most unique aspect of human communication is the use of verbal symbols. It is somewhat of a miracle that we can look at ink marks on a piece of paper or listen to sounds carried on air waves and be able to create images in each other's brains. In fact, the process works so well that we often are surprised when problems occur.

For example, a friend once commented to her mother (who came to this country from Europe) that she had just received a new VISA card. Her mother responded by saying, "Oh really, I didn't know you were planning a trip." To the mother, the term "visa" referred to a permit used to travel to foreign countries. In fact, this "visa" was a charge card. This example serves to illustrate the common principle that words themselves do not contain any meaning. Haney (1992) calls this the "Container Fallacy." In other words, it is a fallacy to believe that meanings are carried or contained by words. If it is possible to have misunderstandings using words that refer to such tangible objects as charge cards, imagine how difficult it is to be able to communicate to another person what we mean by such abstract terms as "truth," "justice," and "fair." Many labor contracts state that if a dispute arises, it must be resolved "within a reasonable period of time." Imagine how much confusion could potentially occur trying to agree on the meaning of "reasonable."

Unintentional verbal messages are *the things we say without meaning to.* Freud argued that all the apparently unintentional stimuli we transmit—both verbal and nonverbal—are unconsciously motivated. We cannot discuss the merits of this argument here, but we can cite an amusing example of a slip of the tongue described by one of Freud's colleagues: "While writing a prescription for a woman who was especially weighed down by the financial burden of the treatment, I was interested to hear her say suddenly: 'Please do not give me *big bills,* because I cannot swallow them.' Of course, she meant to say *pills*" (Brill, quoted in Freud, 1938, p. 82).

Everyone makes slips occasionally. During an interview with the director of admissions at Lafayette, a candidate was asked why he thought that particular college would be suitable for him. His response was, "Well, I don't want to go to a real big college or a real small college. I just want a mediocre college like Lafayette" (Moll, 1979).

Sometimes it's only when we get feedback from others (laughter, for instance) that we become aware we have transmitted such messages. Even in mass communication, which generally involves a great deal of planning and control, such unintentional messages make their appearance. On a television program, the moderator of a network panel discussion on the safety of nuclear power plants voiced her agreement with one of the panelists. Two days later letters started arriving from all over the country; viewers were incensed by her lack of objectivity. In general, unintentional stimuli, both verbal and nonverbal, tend to increase in number if the person is a poor communicator.

Obviously, those people who represent the mass media are expected to be skilled communicators.

Nonverbal messages   **Nonverbal messages** cannot be described as easily as verbal messages, probably because the category is so broad. They include all the nonverbal aspects of our behavior: facial expression, posture, tone of voice, hand movements, manner of dress, and so on. In short, *they are all the messages we transmit without words or over and above the words we use.*

Let us first consider **intentional nonverbal messages,** *the nonverbal messages we want to transmit.* Sometimes we rely exclusively on nonverbal messages to reinforce verbal messages. For example, you can greet someone by smiling and nodding your head, or you can say "Hello" and also smile or wave. At times we deliberately use nonverbal messages to cancel out a polite verbal response and indicate our true feelings: The verbal message may be positive, but the tone and facial expression indicate that we mean something negative.

Much of what we are as a person "communicates" itself every time we behave. Much of this behavior is unintentional. Some writers on the subject go so far as to assert that what we communicate is what we are. **Unintentional nonverbal messages** are *all those nonverbal aspects of our behavior transmitted without our control.* For example, one of the authors once told a student speaker to relax. "I am relaxed," the student replied in a tight voice, trembling, and speaking over the rattling of a paper he was holding. A problem frequently raised in management classes is that store managers unintentionally communicate anger or impatience to their customers.

What nonverbal messages is this speaker conveying?

Controlling nonverbal messages is a very difficult task. Facial expressions, posture, tone of voice, hand gestures—what some writers have called "body language"—often give us away. Ralph Waldo Emerson phrased it well when he remarked to a speaker, "What you are speaks so loudly that I cannot hear what you say." And of course the better a person knows you, the more likely he or she is to pick up your nonverbal expressions—even if you don't want that to happen. Lest we paint too dark a picture, however, we should add that as your communication skills improve, you may find that the number of unintentional messages you transmit will decrease significantly.

Channels

If you are talking on the telephone, the channels that transmit the communicative stimuli are the telephone wires. The **channels** of face-to-face communication are the sensory organs. Although all five senses may receive the stimuli, you rely almost exclusively on three: hearing, sight, and touch. For example, you listen to someone state an argument, or you exchange knowing glances with a friend, or you put your hand on someone's shoulder. In addition to the sensory organs, the channels of organizational communication include company newsletters, bulletin boards, and memoranda. In mass communication the primary channels would be newspapers, films, radio, and television.

In the less formal contexts of communication we rarely think about communication channels. Usually, a person becomes aware of them only when one or more are cut off or when some sort of interference is present. For example, if there is a large vase of flowers between two people trying to talk across a dinner table, both lose a lot because they are unable to see each other's faces. They may even find it too unsettling to carry on a conversation without the presence of facial cues. In other words, face-to-face communication is a multichannel experience. Simultaneously, we receive and make use of information from a number of different channels. In general, the more channels being used, the greater the number of communicative stimuli transmitted.

Interference

After initiating a message, the sender almost always assumes that it has been received. The sender is puzzled or annoyed if he or she is misinterpreted or gets no response. The sender may even have taken special pains to make the message very clear. "Isn't that enough?" the sender asks. In effect, he or she wants to know what went wrong between the transmission and reception of the message.

The communication scholar would answer, **interference**, or **noise**—that is, *anything that distorts the information transmitted to the receiver or distracts him or her from receiving it.* In communication theory, "interference" and "noise" are synonymous terms. "Interference" is probably a more appropriate word, but because "noise" was the term first used in studies of telecommunication, you should be familiar with it too.

Remember that there are many kinds of noise, not just sound. A smoke-filled, overheated classroom, a student who has made abundant use of a very strong perfume, and a lecturer dressed in weird clothing can all become sources of interference.

We can distinguish between two kinds of interference: technical interference and semantic interference. **Technical interference** refers to *the factors that cause the receiver to perceive distortion in the intended information or stimuli.* And the sender too may create the distortion: A person who has a speech impediment or who mumbles a great deal may have difficulty making words clear to someone else. At a party one person may not be able to hear the response of another because the stereo is blaring or because other people standing nearby are speaking so loudly. In this case, the interference is simply the transmission of the sounds of other people in conversation.

The second type of interference is **semantic interference,** which occurs when *the receiver does not attribute the same meaning to the signal that the sender does.* For example, a city official and a social worker got into a heated argument over the causes of crime. The city official argued that the causes were primarily "economic," and the social worker maintained, quite predictably, that they were largely "social." Only after considerable discussion did the two begin to realize that although they had been using different terms, essentially they were referring to the same phenomenon. Bear in mind, however, that no two people will attribute exactly the same meaning to any word and that it is also possible to attribute different meanings to nonverbal messages.

As we have seen, interference can exist in the context of the communication, in the channel, in the communicator who sends the message, or in the one who receives it. Some interference will always be present in human communication.

Communicator 2: Receiver/Sender

Traditionally, emphasis has been given to the communicator as message sender, but equally important to any viable model of human communication is an analysis of the communicator as receiver. For most communication, visual perception will be an essential aspect of message reception. Another critical aspect of message reception is **listening.**

Listening

Listening and hearing are far from synonymous. When Communicator 2 (the receiver/sender) listens, four different yet interrelated processes will be involved: attention, hearing, understanding, and remembering.

Thus far we have discussed the transmission and reception of a single message. At this point, however, our model departs from several current models that create the illusion that all human communication has a definite starting point with a sender and a termination point with a receiver. When the second communicator in Figure 1.1 has received a message, we have come only halfway through the continuous and ongoing process that is communication. For each receiver of a message is also a sender of messages—hence, the term "receiver/sender." Moreover, that person's uniqueness as a human being ensures that his or her attempts to communicate will be very different from those of the other person in the model. For example, Communicator 2's cultural input may be quite unlike that of Communicator 1. His or her filters, both physiological and psychological, will be different. The stimuli he or she transmits will be different. Even the selection of channels and sources of difficulty, or interference, may differ.

The present model includes these differences as inherent parts of the communication process. Although the left half of the model lists the same elements as the right half—input, filters, messages, channels, interference—and these elements are defined in the same way, they are always different in content from those in the right half. The transmission and reception of a single message are only part of our model. Face-to-face communication in particular is characterized by its interdependent participants and the explicit and immediate feedback between them. Even in organizational and mass communication, where the sender/receiver may represent a social organization, the receiver/sender is still able to supply feedback. It may take any number of forms, from a union slowdown in response to the visit of a time-study analyst to an angry letter to the editor of a major newspaper.

Feedback

Luft (1969) calls **feedback** *"the return to you of behavior you have generated"* (p. 116). When we examine feedback solely in interpersonal terms, we can be more specific and say that feedback reinforces some behaviors and extinguishes others. For example, one story has it that a psychology instructor who had been teaching the principles of instrumental learning was actually conditioned by his own class. The students decided to give him reinforcement by taking lots of notes, looking attentive, and asking questions whenever he moved to his right. Whenever he moved to his left, they tried to extinguish this behavior by not taking notes, being inattentive, and not asking questions. He was just about teaching from the right front corner of the room when he realized what was happening.

More recently, Knapp (1984) has observed,

many times we talk about our relationships with people as if we had no *relation* or connection to them—as if our behavior had nothing to do with what the other did. In actuality, however, we have a lot more to do with our partner's responses than we may wish to acknowledge. The reason we often fail to acknowledge this interdependence is that it means we have to accept more of the responsibility for our communication problems. It is much easier to describe your partner's behavior as independent of your own—e.g., "He never listens to me"; "She is never serious with me"; "He doesn't tell me the truth." Acknowledging interdependence forces you to ask yourself what you do to elicit such responses and what you can do to get the responses you desire. Communicators who recognize their interdependence also recognize that communication problems are the result of mutual contribution. One person can't be entirely clean and the other entirely dirty. (p. 11)

Thus, feedback is an essential characteristic of relationships as well as an important source of information about yourself.

Time

Once Communicator 2 responds to Communicator 1, their interaction can be represented by a circle. But as their exchange progresses in time, the relationship between them is more accurately described by several circles. In fact, all but the briefest exchanges entail several communication cycles. Thus **time** itself becomes the final element in our model.

We have tried to convey the presence of time in Figure 1.1 by representing communication in the form of a spiral, like an uncoiled spring. Some writers prefer to symbolize time as a helix; the only difference between these forms is that the spiral is usually regarded as two-dimensional whereas the helix is thought of as three-dimensional. We shall treat them as identical.

Spiral (or helical) models emphasize the effect of the past on present or future behavior. Dance (1967) sums up this emphasis in the following way:

At any and all times, the helix gives geometrical testimony to the concept that communication while moving forward is at the same moment coming back upon itself and being affected by its past behavior. . . . The communication process, like the helix, is constantly moving forward and yet is always to some degree dependent upon the past, which informs the present and the future. (p. 295)

The spiral also illustrates that participants in the communication process can never return to the point at which they started. The relationship must undergo change as a result of each interaction.

Throughout this text we shall try to point out the effects of time on communication. Implicit in this emphasis is our belief that time is one of the most relevant variables in the study of human communication. If it does nothing else, the spiral or transactional model should remind us that communication is not static and that it thus requires different methods of analysis from a fixed entity. Dance (1967) sums up the problem so well that we simply quote his statement here:

The means of examining something in a quiescent and immobile state are quite different from the means of examining something that is in constant flux, motion, and process. If communication is viewed as a process, we are forced to adapt our examination and our examining instruments to the challenge of something in motion, something that is changing while we are in the very act of examining it. (pp. 293–294)

One author (Conner, 1993) has written that an overwhelming majority of those recently surveyed indicate that the pace of life seems to be changing at a more rapid rate than ever before. Thus, the pressures of too much to do in too little time would also appear to be influencing both the quantity and the quality of modern-day communication.

The model identifies some of the major elements that exist in all human communication. We have discussed such communication only in its simplest form. As we add more communicators, change the kind or amount of interference, or vary the messages transmitted, our subject increases in complexity. We shall see this especially when we turn to the study of communication contexts. As you read on, you may want to look at other models, some of which are mentioned in the books listed at the end of this chapter. You may even want to try your hand at developing a model of your own. In either case remember that each communication event you will study has something unique about it, and no model can be used as a blueprint of the communication process.

COMMUNICATION CONTEXTS

It seems clear that human communication occurs in several kinds of situations. Six different contexts seem to be widely agreed upon in the communication literature. These are (1) two-person, (2) interviewing, (3) small-group, (4) public, (5) organizational, and (6) mass communication. Keep in mind that while each of these contexts has some unique characteristics, all six share in common *the process of creating a meaning between two or more people.* And all six sometimes involve intercultural communication, another variable we will be examining.

Two-Person Communication

Two-person, or **dyadic, communication** is the basic unit of communication. For this reason, our communication model depicts this context rather than another. Two-person communication events include most of the informal, everyday exchanges that we engage in from the time we get up until we go to bed. While a lot of very informal and superficial communication may occur in dyads, this is also the context that includes the most intimate relationships we ever experience. Think about communication between loved ones as typical. Bochner (1984) states, for example:

Interpersonal bonding refers to the process of forming individualized relationships—affinities that are close, deep, personal, and intimate. . . . The importance of communication seems obvious, even axiomatic. (p. 544)

Interviewing

Interviewing is often defined as *conversation with a purpose*. It usually involves two people and so it is considered a special form of dyadic communication. Whether it is talking to a physician to help diagnose an illness, to a prospective employer for a job, to a professor for help in a course, to a market researcher to identify strengths in a product, or to a prosecuting attorney on the witness stand, interviewing is more targeted toward accomplishing a specific purpose than most two-person communication. Since interviewing is such a stylized form of communication, specific techniques have been developed that can be used to best accomplish the interviewer's purpose. These techniques, along with specific types of interview questions, and so on can be observed on such television programs as *60 Minutes* and *Meet the Press*.

Small-Group Communication

Small-group communication is defined as "the process by which three or more members of a group exchange verbal and nonverbal messages in an attempt to influence one another" (Tubbs, 1992, p. 5). Since this context involves three or more people, the degree of intimacy, participation, and satisfaction tends to be lower than in two-person communication. Small-group communication occurs in churches, in social situations, in organizations, and in therapeutic settings, to name a few examples. Group dynamics is a well-researched field of study and tends to focus on small groups that engage in problem solving and decision making. Small-group communication, therefore, tends to focus on the ways to improve the work that can be accomplished in groups. Self-directed work teams are but one example of small groups dedicated to improving organizational performance (see Fisher, 1993).

Public Communication

This context is often referred to as "public speaking." It is a distinct context in a number of ways. First, it occurs in public rather than private places—that is, in auditoriums, classrooms, ballrooms, and so on. Second, public communication is relatively formal as opposed to informal, unstructured communications. Usually, the event is planned in advance. Some people are designated to perform certain functions (such as introducing the speaker).

In a commencement exercise, for example, there may be several speakers, as well as a prayer and a ceremony in which degrees are awarded. And third, there are relatively clear-cut behavioral norms (Lucas, 1992). For example, questions are usually addressed to the speaker *after* the speech is completed. Thus **public communication** usually requires that the speaker do significantly more preparation, and he or she should expect a more formalized setting than in two-person or small-group communication.

Organizational Communication

Organizational communication is defined as *"the flow of messages within a network of interdependent relationships"* (Goldhaber, 1990, p. 11). This definition fits not only businesses but also hospitals, churches, government agencies, military organizations, and academic institutions. Here we are concerned not only with the effectiveness of the individual communication but with the role of communication in contributing to or detracting from the effective functioning of the total organization.

The nature of organizations is radically changing. For example, Wall and associates (1992) state:

> The old hierarchy is ending. Your company's future depends upon leadership, trust, and participation. The only way to build them is through vision. Welcome to the visionary leader.

Greater emphasis than ever is being placed on "continuous improvement." In Japan, this is known as *kaizen* (*kai* means "change," and *zen* means "good" or "for the better") (Imai, 1986). An example of this is the story about several customers who are waiting in line for service (it could be anywhere). One person at the front of the line gets mediocre service, and everybody else gets mad. They say, "Who do you think you are getting mediocre service—you are supposed to get lousy service like the rest of us!" This is just one indication of why organizations need to be striving toward *kaizen*.

Mass Communication

This sixth context involves communication that is mediated. That is, the source of a message communicates through some print or electronic medium. And mediated encounters differ from personal encounters (Avery and McCain, 1982). In addition, the message is intended for masses of individuals rather than for only a small number of individuals. Of the six contexts of human communication discussed in this book, **mass communication** is the most formal—and the most expensive. Television advertisements during the Super Bowl each January will cost millions of dollars per minute! In addition, the

Call-in talk shows have dramatically changed the nature of mass communication, as was evident by the scrambling of the 1992 presidential candidates to be interviewed for *Larry King Live.*

opportunities for feedback are severely limited, especially when compared with two-person or small-group communication. The audience in mass communication is relatively large, heterogeneous, and anonymous to the source. Finally, communication experience is characterized as public, rapid, and fleeting.

Willing (1992) states that the 1992 presidential election campaign was different from any other because of the complex interplay between mass media and Bill Clinton's skillful use of his own media. He excels in question-and-answer formats, such as on the *Larry King Live* show, and is able to bypass the networks "filters." (B1, B5). In addition, the frequent use of polls became an important tool in shaping the outcome of the election. As the results became known, they were fed back to the voters, which in turn influenced future polls, and so on. This is a perfect example of the helical communication model referred to in this chapter.

Intercultural Communication

In our analysis of human communication, another category we shall be exploring is **intercultural communication**—that is, *communication between members of different cultures (whether defined in terms of racial, ethnic, or socioeconomic differences, or a combination of these differences).* **Culture** is *a way of life developed and shared by a group of people and passed down from generation to generation.* Gudykunst and Kim (1992) offer the following example of intercultural communication:

Consider a visit to North America by strangers from a culture with a communication rule requiring that direct eye contact always be avoided. . . . If the strangers do not look them in the eye when talking, the North Americans will assume that the strangers either have something to hide or are not telling the truth. (p. 35)

This dimension of experience cuts across all communication contexts: It may occur in two-person communication, interviews, small groups, or any of the other categories we will examine in Part 2. Thus intercultural communication will be discussed not only in Chapter 13 but also in many other chapters of this text—for example, in relation to person perception, human attraction, and verbal and nonverbal communication. In a society such as our own, with its rich mix of cultures, intercultural communication will be especially relevant.

COMMUNICATION TECHNOLOGIES

We are all becoming increasingly familiar with what was once considered complex communication technology. For example, personal computers have become a daily tool for many. Students walking across campus are often listening to their Walkman. Fax machines are so popular that fast-food restaurants like McDonald's use them to take orders.

Another technological wonder that has swept the country is the cellular car phone. DiPaolo (1989) reports that "nationally the industry is attracting

How have cellular phones changed human communication?

customers at a rate of 75,000 per month—a growth rate faster than [that of] VCRs" (E1). Southwestern Bell Telephone reports in its 1988 annual report that "the number of cellular customers industry-wide at the end of 1988—two million—is expected to increase 10 times by 1994." The saturation point is projected to be at an unbelievable 64 million units by the year 1998 (p. 9). Thousands of people have even bought fax machines for their car phones.

Even farmers have gone high tech. Kageyama (1992) reports that some farmers in Japan have outfitted their cattle with beepers. He reports that "he dials the cows' number on a portable phone to get their attention, and 'they look up immediately from eating the grass.' Usually they head for the feeding station, but sometimes they ignore the beeps and continue grazing" (A3).

With all this high-tech communication potential, human communication is at once more possible and perhaps less human. Regardless of your sentiments regarding these innovations, there is no question that they are having a profound and permanent impact on human communication.

Communication Ethics

In this edition we have added a chapter on ethics in communication. It seems that hardly a day goes by without some scandal being reported, whether it's Senator Packwood from Oregon being accused of sexual harassment or Stanford University being accused of misusing overhead expense accounts from research grants. In any case, the chapter on communication ethics should provide you with some helpful insights and guidelines on how to avoid difficulties.

WHAT IS EFFECTIVE COMMUNICATION?

Earlier in this chapter we said that we would be concerned not only with human speech communication but with the concept of **effective communication.** But what are the criteria that make for effective communication? Students sometimes say that communication is effective when a person gets his or her point across. This is but one measure of effectiveness. More generally, communication is effective *when the stimulus as it was initiated and intended by the sender, or source, corresponds closely with the stimulus as it is perceived and responded to by the receiver.*

If we let S stand for the person who is the sender or source of the message and R for the receiver of the message, then communication is whole and complete when the response S intends and the response R provides are identical (Goyer, 1970, p. 10):

$$\frac{R}{S} = \frac{\text{receiver's meaning}}{\text{sender's meaning}} = 1$$

We rarely reach 1—that is perfect sharing of meaning. As a matter of fact, we never reach 1. We approximate it. And the greater the correspondence between our intention and the response we receive, the more effective we have been in communicating. At times, of course, we hit the zero mark: There is absolutely no correspondence between the response we want to produce and the one we receive. The drowning man who signals wildly for help to one of his friends on a sailboat only to have her wave back is not accomplishing his communication objective to say the least.

The example of the drowning man is extreme. By now you may be wondering just how important effective communication is on a day-to-day basis. A long-term study of MIT graduates who were interviewed several times over a fifteen-year period has revealed that even for those very talented, technically competent people, graduates of a prestigious school, effectiveness in communication was one of the most important skills in achieving a successful and fulfilling life, if not *the most* important. On the basis of his research, the author of this study stresses the increasing importance of interpersonal competence as a skill critical "not only for dealing with self and family development, but for career advancement as well" (Schein, 1978, p. 77).

But how do we measure our own effectiveness? We can't judge our effectiveness if our intentions are not clear; we must know what we are trying to do. What makes that first definition of effectiveness inadequate ("when a person gets his or her point across") is that in communicating, we may try to bring about one or more of several possible outcomes. We shall consider five of them here: understanding, pleasure, attitude influence, improved relationships, and action.

Understanding

Understanding refers primarily to *accurate reception of the content of the intended stimulus.* In this sense, a communicator is said to be effective if the receiver has an accurate understanding of the message the communicator has tried to convey. (Of course, the communicator sometimes conveys messages unintentionally that are also quite clearly understood.)

The primary failures in communication are failures to achieve content accuracy. For example, the service manager of an oil company had a call one winter morning from a woman who complained that her oil burner was not working. "How high is your thermostat set?" he asked. "Just a moment," the woman replied. After several minutes she returned to the phone. "At 5 feet 3½ inches," she said, "same as it's always been." This confusion is typical of a failure to achieve understanding. Most misunderstandings of this kind are relatively easy to remedy through clarifying feedback and restatement.

As we add more people to a communication context, it becomes more difficult to determine how accurately messages are being received. This is one of the reasons that group discussions sometimes turn into free-for-alls. Comments begin to have little relation to one another, and even a group with an agenda to follow may not advance toward the resolution of any of its problems. Situations such as these call for more clarifying, summarizing, and directing of group comments.

With respect to public communication, much has been written about how to improve understanding when speaking to inform—with "understanding" often being referred to as "information gain." What the public speaker must remember is that the feedback he or she receives is often quite limited; the speaker should therefore make a concerted effort to be as objective and precise as possible in explaining his or her subject. The use of supporting materials—examples, analogies, and the like—helps clarify an explanation of almost any subject.

Within an organizational setting, accurate understanding is one of the most basic desired outcomes. It is not possible, for example, for an organization to function efficiently unless employees understand what they are expected to do at their jobs. This may involve understanding not only verbal directives from immediate superiors but also information disseminated through interoffice memos, employee handbooks, and other restatements of company policies.

In mass communication the dissemination of information is also a primary objective on many occasions. (Newscasts, documentaries, and videotape programs immediately come to mind.) Presumably, those who work in the mass media have developed their communications skill to a high degree so that they are able to organize, present, and interpret information in a way that promotes understanding. For example, in a single hour a television special can present a program on depression: its symptoms, causes, and possible treatment. Because feedback is so limited in this setting, however, it is difficult to assess the level of information gain within the audience.

Pleasure

Not all communication has as its goal the transmission of a specific message. In fact, the goal of the transactional analysis school of thought is simply to communicate with others in a way that ensures a sense of mutual well-being. This is sometimes referred to as a **phatic communication,** or maintaining human contact. Many of our brief exchanges with others—"Hi"; "How are you today?"; "How's it going?"—have this purpose. Casual dates, cocktail parties, and rap sessions are more structured occasions on which we come together to enjoy the company and conversation of others. (Some think that the word "rap" comes from the word "rapport," which refers to a positive relationship between people.) The degree to which we find communication pleasurable is closely related to our feelings about those with whom we are interacting.

The purpose of public communication can also be pleasure; the after-dinner speech and the speech intended to entertain fall into this category. Much of the informal communication within an organization takes place during lunch hours, coffee breaks, company picnics, and management club dances. And certainly in movies, situation comedies, and televised sports events, we see entertainment provided on a grand scale.

Attitude Influence

Suppose that five politicians meet to determine the best way to reduce cost overruns on military contracts and that they reach a stalemate because of their extreme differences of opinion. Such situations are often erroneously referred to as "communication breakdowns." If the disputing parties understood each other better, it is assumed, their differences would be eliminated and through negotiation an agreement would be reached. As Acuff (1993) puts it, at no time in history has there been so great a need for international negotiation skills—that is for each negotiator to influence the other in positive, constructive ways (p. 3). But understanding and agreement are by no means synonymous outcomes. When you understand someone's message, you may find that you disagree with him or her even more strongly than you did before.

Influencing attitudes is a basic part of daily living. In many situations we are interested in influencing a person's attitude as well as in having him or her understand what we are saying. The process of changing and reformulating attitudes, or **attitude influence,** goes on throughout our lives. In two-person situations, attitude influence is often referred to as "social influence." In the counseling interview, it might be called "gentle persuasion." Attitude influence is no less important in the small-group or the organizational setting. For example, consensus among group members is an objective of many problem-solving discussions. And industries often try, especially through the mass media, to influence public attitudes toward big business by presenting themselves in a flattering light. (For example, Exxon commercials about ecology suggest that the fuel industry is greatly concerned about the pollution problems caused by industrial waste.) When applied to public and mass communication contexts, the process of attitude influence is usually referred to as "persuasion." Studies of mass communication are particularly concerned with the persuasive impact of the message on various opinion leaders within the larger mass audience.

In determining how successful your attempts to communicate have been, remember that you may fail to change a person's attitude but still get that person to understand your point of view. In other words, a failure to change someone's point of view should not necessarily be written off as a failure to increase understanding.

Improved Relationships

It is commonly believed that if a person can select the right words, prepare his or her message ahead of time, and state it precisely, perfect communication will be ensured. But total effectiveness requires a positive and trusting psychological climate. When a human relationship is clouded by mistrust, numerous opportunities arise for distorting or discrediting even the most skillfully constructed messages. Voters may well be suspicious of their mayor's promise that if reelected, he will fulfill all the campaign promises he failed to keep during his first term in office. A young man will probably discount a young woman's assurances that she is very interested in him after she breaks a date for the third or fourth time. A professor may begin to doubt the excuses of a student who is holding court at the student union an hour after the student was too sick to take the midterm.

We mentioned that the primary failures in communication occur when the content of the message is not accurately understood. By contrast, secondary failures are disturbances in human relationships that result from misunderstandings. They stem from the frustration, anger, or confusion (sometimes all three) caused by the initial failure to understand. Because such failures tend to polarize the communicators involved, they are difficult to resolve. By acknowledging that the initial misunderstandings are a common occurrence in daily communication, we may be able to tolerate them better and avoid or at least minimize their damaging effect on interpersonal relationships.

Still another kind of understanding can have a profound effect on human relationships: understanding another person's motivations. At times each of us communicates not to convey information or to change someone's attitude but simply to be "understood" in this second sense. Throughout this text we shall discuss various facets of human relationships: motivation; social choice; confirmation, self-disclosure, trust; group cohesiveness; and source credibility in public and mass communication. We hope to show that all these concepts are bound together by a common theme: the better the relationship between people, the more likely it is that other outcomes of effective communication in the fullest sense will occur.

Action

Some would argue that all communication is useless unless it brings about a desired action. Yet all the outcomes discussed thus far—understanding, pleasure, attitude influence, improved relationships—are important at different times and in different places. There are instances, however, when action is an essential determinant of the success of a communicative act. In the sales interview, an automobile salesman who wants you to think more favorably of his car than his competitor's also wants you to act by buying a car; his primary objective is not attitude change. A math tutor is far from satisfied if the student she is coaching says he understands how to do a set of problems but fails to demonstrate that understanding on his next exam. And we might question the effectiveness of a finance committee that reaches consensus on how to balance a budget yet fails to act on its decision.

Eliciting action on the part of another person is probably the communication outcome most difficult to produce. In the first place it seems easier to get someone to understand your message than it is to get the person to agree with it. Furthermore, it seems easier to get that person to agree—that he or she should exercise regularly, for example—than to get the person to act on it. (We realize that some behaviors are induced through coercion, social pressure, or role prescriptions and do not necessarily require prior attitude change. Voluntary actions, however, usually follow rather than precede attitude changes.) If you are trying to promote action on the part of the receiver, you increase your chances of getting the desired response if you can (1) facilitate understanding of your request, (2) secure agreement that the request is legitimate, and (3) maintain a comfortable relationship with the receiver. The desired action does not follow automatically, but it is more likely to follow if these intermediate objectives have first been accomplished.

The difficulties of eliciting action on the part of the receiver are further compounded in organizational and mass communication settings. The plant manager's sharp memo on absenteeism, for example, may trigger more absenteeism, or the sick calls may taper off and some form of sabotage appear in the products turned out on the assembly line. Certainly, the mass media are often concerned with promoting audience action—whether it be promoting a particular brand of detergent, getting mothers to immunize their children against rubella, or changing audience voting patterns. Yet researchers have questioned the effectiveness of mass communication in changing behavior. It has been found, for example, that political campaigns conducted through the mass media have little direct influence on changes in voting behavior.

In short, the five possible outcomes of effective human communication are understanding, pleasure, attitude influence, improved relationships, and action. At different points in this book, we shall give special attention to each of them. For example, the concepts of attitude similarity, status, social influence and consensus, and persuasion all have some bearing on attitude influence. Similarly, the concepts of trust, cohesiveness, and source credibility are all relevant to improved human relationships.

The five outcomes we have discussed are neither exhaustive nor mutually exclusive. Thus a look at the relationship aspects of communication in Chapter 6 will illustrate that defensive behaviors distort understanding, that the so-called disconfirming responses are not pleasurable. In the chapters that follow we hope to show some of the many ways in which communication outcomes are interdependent and to demonstrate that this is true for many different communication contexts, or settings.

SUMMARY

In this book we view human communication as the process of creating a meaning between two or more people. Today many communication scholars emphasize the transactional nature of the communication process, so that one person's communication can be defined only in relation to some other or others.

In this chapter we presented a model to help us conceptualize the relationships between the elements of human communication. Like all human beings, both communicators in our model originate and perceive messages. Both depend on the steady flow of physical, social, and cultural input, and both select from the total input through their perceptual filters and sets.

We then discussed the components of a message in terms of the types of stimuli transmitted: verbal and nonverbal, intentional and unintentional. We learned that though all five senses are potential channels for receiving stimuli, face-to-face communication relies primarily on hearing, sight, and touch and is usually a multichannel experience. The channels of organizational communication would extend to newsletters, memos, and the like, whereas those of mass communication would include newspaper, films, radio, and television. Anything that distorts the information transmitted through the various channels or that distracts the receiver from getting it would be considered interference.

We saw that all the elements in Communicator 1's half of our communication cycle—input, filters, verbal and nonverbal messages, channels, and interference—are different for Communicator 2 because of his or her uniqueness as a human being. Emphasis was given to the receiver as listener. We examined the importance of feedback, and we examined the effect of time, represented in the model by a spiral, as a crucial variable in all studies of communication.

Much of the time people spend communicating involves two-person communication. But in studying human communication, we are also concerned with contexts in which a great many parties are involved, feedback is limited, and messages are transmitted through such media as newspaper, radio, and television. We are interested therefore in the principles of human communication as they apply not only to the two-person setting and the interview but to small-group, public, organizational, and mass communication. We are also interested in communication behaviors that are ethical.

After a brief discussion of each of these six communication contexts, we turned to an examination of what constitutes effective communication. It was established that communication is effective to the degree that the message as it is intended by the sender corresponds with the message as it is perceived and responded to by the receiver. We learned that effectiveness is closely linked with intention and that in communicating, we usually want to bring about one or more of several possible outcomes. Five of the major outcomes— understanding, pleasure, attitude influence, improved relationships, and action—were considered here, with emphasis on their application to the various communication contexts. Another area of interest is intercultural communication, which cuts across all the contexts we shall be discussing.

REVIEW QUESTIONS

1. Provide you own personal definition of "communication." How is it similar to, or different from, the definitions given in this text?

2. What is input, and how does it influence a person's communication?

3. Name the four types of messages. Give a specific example of each from your own experience.

4. Explain the difference between technical and semantic interference and give an example of each.

5. Discuss the influence of various kinds of feedback.

6. List six different communication contexts. Explain the distinctive characteristics of each.

7. State three characteristics of two-person communication. How does such communication differ from other types of human communication?

8. What is effective communication? Think of arguments for and against the types of communication effectiveness that have been described in this chapter. Are there some that the text has not included? Are there some it has discussed that you think should not be included? What do you think is the most important outcome of face-to-face communication?

EXERCISES

1. Start a personal log in which you record your daily reaction to perhaps ten members of your class. Only some will impress you (favorably or unfavorably) at first. Note details of their behavior. Describe your own responses as candidly as possible.

2. a. Draw and label a model of human communication. If possible, include components that can be appropriately labeled as Communicator 1 (sender/receiver), Communicator 2 (receiver/sender), input, filters, messages, channels, interference, and time.
    b. Examine the model carefully and formulate five statements that describe how two or more components of the model may influence communication effectiveness as defined in this chapter.

3. Select a group of about ten students, and ask them to discuss one of the case problems listed in the appendix. Observe the group and, if possible, tape-record the discussion. Analyze the group's communication in terms of intentional, unintentional, verbal, and nonverbal stimuli.

4. Write a short paper in which you analyze the strengths and weaknesses of the communication model in this chapter. Compare and contrast it with some other models, which may be found in the books in the suggested readings.

5. Divide the class members into groups of five or six; then have each group member discuss a personal problem in communication. Have each group select its "best" example of a communication problem as well as a spokesperson to present the example to the entire class. Then analyze each example in terms of the communication model given in this chapter.

6. Observe several communication events and keep a record of their outcomes. Which outcomes occurred most frequently? Under what conditions did these outcomes seem to occur? How can you explain these results?

7. Write a one-page case study of a communication failure that you have experienced or observed. Then write an analysis of its causes, and suggest a way to resolve it.

8. Think of two people you know, one an excellent communicator, the other quite ineffective. Write a highly specific description of each; then write a comparison of the two in which you contrast and evaluate their communication styles. On the basis of this analysis, set yourself three specific objectives for improving your own communication behaviors.

SUGGESTED READINGS

Acuff, Frank L. *How to Negotiate Anything With Anyone Anywhere Around the World.* New York: American Management Association, 1993.

This excellent book helps explain how to apply communication principles in forty-one countries. It is a very valuable resource.

Fisher, Kimball. *Leading Self-Directed Work Teams.* New York: McGraw-Hill, 1993.

This book gives an outstanding overview of the ways in which group communication within organizations can improve organizational functioning as well as employee satisfaction.

Griffin, Em. *A First Look at Communication Theory.* New York: McGraw-Hill, 1991.

This book is an excellent introduction to communication theory. It goes into much greater detail on many of the subjects discussed in this chapter.

Murphy, Kevin J. *Effective Listening.* Salem, NH: ELI Press, 1992.

This brief book covers the receiver side of the communication model discussed in this chapter.

O'Hair, Dan, and **Gustav W. Friedrich.** *Strategic Communication.* Boston: Houghton Mifflin, 1992.

This is an interesting book that covers many topics related to this chapter.

Popcorn, Faith. *The Popcorn Report.* New York: Doubleday, 1991.

This book is a remarkable view of life in the future. It has many implications for communication as our living patterns change.

Trenholm, Sarah. *Human Communication Theory.* 2d ed. Englewood Cliffs, NJ: Prentice-Hall, 1991.

Intended for the advanced student, this book parallels many of the chapters in our book but at a purely theoretical level.

Watzlawick, Paul, Janet Beavin, and **Don Jackson.** *Pragmatics of Human Communication.* New York: Norton, 1967.

Using an interactional approach, the authors present an excellent explanation of several basic communication principles.

Williams, Frederick. *The New Communication.* 3rd ed. Belmont, CA: Wadsworth, 1992.

Here is a comprehensive text that takes a mass communication slant. It includes some unusual chapters such as "Political Communication" and "Information and Public Opinion."

CHAPTER TWO

Person Perception

CHAPTER OBJECTIVES

After reading this chapter, you should be able to:

1 Explain the difference between a perceptual filter and a psychological set and discuss the selective nature of all perception.

2 Describe how person perception differs from object perception and explain the implications of such differences for communication.

3 Discuss the development of self-concept and some of the variables that influence self-esteem, and state two current research findings about shyness.

4 Identify the major difference between how we perceive our own behavior and that of other people.

5 Describe the concepts of private personality theory, trait centrality, and primacy.

6 Discuss several variables including perceived traits and physical attractiveness that influence our impressions of others.

7 Distinguish between personal generalizations and stereotypes, and discuss the effects of stereotyping.

8 Discuss how work, student, sex, and marital roles influence person perception.

9 Describe several variables involved in forming accurate perceptions of others, and identify three ways to improve person perception and communication effectiveness.

*T*ake a good look at the illustration in Figure 2.1 by Al Hirschfeld. This master of caricature has drawn most of the legendary stars of stage and screen, so you can probably identify the subject—Meryl Streep. But can you see any words in her portrait?

Hirschfeld has become known for concealing NINA, his daughter's name, in his drawings, and if you look again, you should be able to find three NINAs. Since 1960, the artist has added the precise number of NINAs in each drawing to his signature (Hirschfeld, 1991). Hirschfeld's caricatures play games with our perceptions, showing us how context can limit and shape what we perceive.

Like our perceptions of letters, words, and objects, our perceptions of other people are often bound by context, and as such these perceptions are

FIGURE 2.1 Caricature by Al Hirschfeld (*Source:* Al Hirschfeld. Copyright © 1991 Al Hirschfeld. Drawing reproduced by special arrangement with Hirschfeld's exclusive representative, The Margo Feiden Galleries Ltd., New York.)

fallible, subject to error. In exchanging impressions of others, there are times when it is difficult to believe we are talking about the same person. Yet, as communicators, we depend on these perceptions in almost every aspect of daily life. And the way we perceive another person determines the kind and quality of communication that will take place between us.

Thus our impressions of others form the basis for numerous decisions throughout our lives, whether it be choosing one professor's course over another, buying a car from a reliable sales agent, choosing a roommate, or selecting a business partner. The list is virtually endless. In the following pages we will be examining the initial process by which all such impressions of other human beings are formed.

PERCEIVING PEOPLE AND OBJECTS: A COMPARISON

Our total awareness of the world comes to us through our senses. Thus all our perceptions—whether they be of drawings, household objects, or other people—have a common basis. Yet, as we've seen countless times, two people often disagree sharply in their judgments about a third. Have you ever been "fixed up" with someone described to you as just your type, only to be thoroughly disappointed from the very beginning of the evening? You might have even asked yourself whether the person who arranged the date perceived you or the other party with any accuracy. The reasons for such varying perceptions should become apparent as we consider similarities between interpersonal perception and perception in general.

Two Kinds of Filters

Your capacity to register sensory stimuli is limited. You cannot take in everything. Nor do you always want to. You choose certain aspects of your environment over others. What you are aware of at any time is determined in part by what you as a receiver *select* out of the total input. "You hear what you want to hear," mutters the irritated father to his teenage son, "This is the third time this afternoon I've asked you when you're going to get around to washing the car." Later that day the same man may sit at the dinner table reading the Sunday paper, oblivious to a family quarrel that is taking place across the room. *The ability to process certain of the stimuli available to us while filtering out others* is called **selective attention.**

The American philosopher and psychologist William James explained the process of selection at work here in terms of interest: "Millions of items of the outward order are present to my senses which never properly enter into my experience. Why? Because they have no *interest* for me. *My experience is what I agree to attend to.* Only those items which I *notice* shape my mind—without selective interest, experience is an utter chaos" (James, 1950, p. 402).

Each of us, then, perceives only part of the available stimuli while filtering out other stimuli. There are two kinds of filters through which all input or sensation will pass: physiological and psychological.

Perceptual Filters

Among the inherent structures of our sense organs are our **perceptual filters,** *physiological limitations that are built into human beings* and cannot be reversed. Such limitations on our capacity to perceive exist whether we are experiencing an object or a person. And they vary considerably from one individual to another so that we differ in the degree to which our various senses are accurate.

To the human communicator one extremely troublesome perceptual filter is the limit on one's ability to hear. Sometimes we think we hear a person say one thing when actually he or she said another. We then act on the basis of what we think that person said. Or we may act without hearing what a person said at all. Many communication difficulties are rooted in this kind of mis-understanding. For example, one woman found out through a third party that she had antagonized her next-door neighbor by "cutting her dead." It turned out that the neighbor had walked by and said hello while the woman was standing at her front door anxiously awaiting her young son. This was the first day she had allowed him to walk home by himself from his first-grade class, and the boy was late. She was staring in the direction of the school and never even heard the neighbor's greeting. The neighbor, who was new to the community, interpreted the woman's unresponsiveness as a snub.

Psychological Sets

The other kinds of filters influencing our perceptions are psychological. You may not have been able to distinguish the NINAs in Figure 2.1 because they are concealed in the drawing of Meryl Streep. Once you are aware that there are words within the drawing, you still may not be able to see both the words and the human figure at the same time. Our **psychological sets**—that is, our *expectancies or predispositions to respond*—have a profound effect on our perception of objects.

Similarly, psychological set affects your perception of other people. If asked, for example, to interpret what is happening between the man and woman in Figure 2.2, what would be your answer? And what are the people like? Is the seated woman attracted to the man behind the sofa—or is she being aloof, or just indifferent? Is the man a reassuring figure, or is his presence somehow threatening? And what is the relationship between the two people? Are they friends, relatives, lovers—or possibly business associates? An infinite number of interpretations can be evoked by an ambiguous illustration such as this one. Each of us has a story for this picture; with a little prodding, each of us could elaborate on it.

Whatever the story, it reveals much about our own expectations and past experiences. If we are defensive, for example, we are more likely to perceive at least one of the people in Figure 2.2 as hostile, or critical, or menacing,

FIGURE 2.2

because we have come to expect and anticipate such behavior—perhaps out of past experience. As you read on, you will see that past experience is a strong influence on what you select from all the available stimuli; and often you are judging another person, at least initially, by the group or context in which he or she is first seen. This will certainly be apparent when we discuss stereotyping.

Culture and Perception

One of the most powerful determinants of psychological set is culture. Consider the two parallel straight lines in Figure 2.3. Which would you say is longer? Chances are that if you live in a Western culture, you will perceive the bottom line as being the longer of the two. If you measure them, though, you will see that they are actually the same length. This is a well-known phenomenon called the *Müller-Lyer illusion*. It is an illusion in visual perception that Western peoples are particularly likely to experience and one to which certain non-Western peoples are much less susceptible.

One explanation for the Müller-Lyer illusion is that people who live in a visual environment in which straight lines and right angles prevail—a "carpentered world" constructed with tools such as the saw, the plane, and the plumb bob—learn to make certain visual inferences. For example, they tend to interpret acute and obtuse angles as right angles that are extended in space. This is what happens when Westerners look at Figure 2.3. From the two-dimensional drawing they make inferences about perspective, thus seeing the two lines as unequal in length. People who live in a culture that has very few structures made up of straight lines and corners—people from Ghana, for example—are not likely to experience the Müller-Lyer illusion because they do not tend to make such inferences about perspective (Segall et al., in Price-Williams, 1969). This is just one way in which culture influences our perception.

We have sets not only about objects and words but about other human beings—what they should look like, how they should act, and what they will say. In our culture a business person expects people to be on time for appointments, and in turn those people do not expect to be kept waiting for long periods of time. When such expectancies are shared by all involved, they are often useful in facilitating communication. Other sets interfere with our ability to perceive accurately and respond appropriately. For example, some people—especially in telephone conversations—are so accustomed to being asked how they are that after saying "Hi" or "Hello," they answer "fine" to whatever the other party has just said.

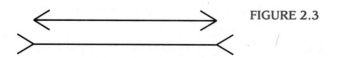

FIGURE 2.3

A great deal of interpersonal conflict stems from people's unawareness of the limits on their perceptual capacities. If they do realize the fallibility of their senses, they may be too defensive to acknowledge their mistakes. There is now convincing evidence that in some situations, if such a person is pressed, opposition to our point is likely to be reinforced instead of reversed, even though the person appears to be agreeing with us.

As two people communicate, each formulates ideas that become the content of the communication event. How accurately a message is received depends on the other person's perceptual filters and sets. Remember that psychological and physiological characteristics will influence which stimuli are selected and how they are perceived.

Selective Perception, Organization, and Interpretation

Today we don't believe, as early philosophers did, that the human mind is a blank tablet on which impressions are imprinted. We know that perception is not a passive state in which stimuli are received and automatically registered. Quite the opposite. Perception is an active process: Each of you **selectively** perceives, organizes, and interprets what you experience.

In general, you perceive stimuli that are intense, repetitious, or in the process of changing. Nonetheless, each person actively chooses what to attend to depending on personal interests, motivations, desires, and expectations. Entranced by a young woman's appearance, a man sitting next to her at a party may notice what great legs she has and pay little attention to what she's saying. Someone else in the group may be more interested in her remarks about working in the personnel department of a large company because *he* is looking for a job.

In addition to the selective perception of stimuli, we tend to organize stimuli selectively—that is, we order the stimuli with which we are presented into a "whole," a complete, sensible picture. The test from which the ambiguous picture in Figure 2.2 derives is based on this notion. Take a very simple example of how people organize stimuli. Dan Williams goes into an office supply store to buy cartridges for an electric typewriter:

Dan: Do you have two cartridges for the Smith Corona? I need a correctable film ribbon.

Clerk: What number is that?

Dan: I think it's seventy twenty.

Clerk: (from the back of the store) No. That's not right. But I've got what you need.

Dan: I'm pretty sure that was the number, seventy twenty. See—there it is on the box. I was right.

Clerk: No. This order number is seven zero two zero.

As this brief dialogue should make clear, even a simple array of numbers—7020—must be organized by the individual perceiver. And it's very unsettling to consider someone else's method of organization simultaneously with your own. People organize stimuli according to different schema and expectations: they attribute cause and effect uniquely. A quarrel between husband and wife in which he claims to withdraw because she nags while she claims to nag because he withdraws is such an example: The differences in organizing the sequence are at the heart of their different perceptions. Asked to explain, the husband maintains his withdrawal is his sole defense against his wife's nagging. She, in turn, sees his explanation as a deliberate distortion of "what 'really' happens"—that the reason for her critical attitude *is* the husband's passivity (Watzlawick et al., 1967, pp. 56–57).

After stimuli are selectively perceived and selectively organized, they are selectively interpreted—that is, the stimuli are assigned meanings unique to the perceiver. Personal interpretations are based on the perceiver's past experiences, assumptions about human behavior, knowledge of the other's circumstances, present moods/wants/desires, and expectations.

Perceiver/Object/Context

Like perceiving objects, perceiving other people may be thought of in terms of three elements: the perceiver, the object of perception (in this instance, another human being), and the context within which the object is viewed. As the perceiver, you are of course influenced by your own attributes. For example, people seem to have predispositions to make generally negative or positive evaluations of others; certainly we have all met someone who feels that "people are no damn good" or, at the other end of the spectrum, someone who would say that there's good to be found in all of us (Kaplan, 1976). It is through the eyes of the perceiver that all the attributes of that second person (the object, if you will) are filtered. Remember, though, that because person perception is a transactional process, those attributes do not always remain constant. If early in our first conversation you act as if I'm a terrible bore, you might find that my behavior changes from mildly friendly to downright obnoxious. As for the third element, the context or setting within which the process of interpersonal perception occurs is both physical and psychological, as we shall see.

To some degree, however slight, we assume that the other person shares some of our characteristics, that we resemble each other in some ways. We are—or so we think—familiar with some of the other person's experience. Such assumptions may help us perceive more accurately. For example, if I know that you have just returned from a funeral, on the basis of my own experiences I will probably interpret your silence as depression rather than indifference. On the other hand, we often misinterpret what we perceive precisely because we assume other people are like us. If I assume that your taste in music is like mine, when I offer to play some hard rock, I may interpret your remark "Oh, great!" as genuinely enthusiastic though it is clear to most people from your facial expression that your reply was sarcastic.

Another way in which perceiving people differs from perceiving objects is that our perceptions and misperceptions influence and keep on influencing our interactions with others—because they keep responding to these perceptions. Sometimes people correct our misperceptions. But occasionally one misinterpretation leads to another, and we get further and further afield. Even if an initial misperception is corrected, it may persist because of the psychological sets we have about other people. Vine Deloria, a Native American who was director of the National Congress of Americans, recalls his visit to the home of a congressman whose wife wanted to meet some Indians. With him were Helen Schierback (a Lumbee) and Imelda Schreiner (a Cheyenne River Sioux). Throughout the afternoon, the congressman's wife repeatedly asked them their names when she addressed them. When they left, she asked them again for their names so that she could say goodbye. "As we went out the door," writes Deloria, "she thanked us for coming and profusely apologized for not remembering our names. 'Indian names,' she said, 'are so peculiar and hard to remember.' It had completely escaped her that we all had European names" (Deloria, 1970, p. 27).

Person perception then is a special form of perception. As we go on to examine how impressions of others are formed, we will also give some attention to how members of other cultures tend to be perceived.

FORMING IMPRESSIONS

Our concern with the process of forming impressions involves the discussion of many variables, but it begins with you, the perceiver, and how you view yourself.

Looking at Yourself

If you were to describe yourself, what information would you give—a physical description, your age, gender, membership in an ethnic group? Perhaps you would define yourself by certain traits or by what you do. You might say you are a student, that you are outgoing and interested in politics, or that you are athletic and somewhat shy. People define themselves very differently, and for some self-description is an uncomfortable process. For example, one college application asks prospective students to describe themselves by using ten adjectives. One reason college applications can be so difficult to fill out is that they often require statements about self-concept.

Self-Concept

Your **self-concept,** *your relatively stable impressions of yourself,* includes not only your perception of your physical characteristics but your judgments about what you "have been, are, and aspire to be" (Pearson et al., 1991, p. 54). Self-concept develops partly out of the feedback you receive from the people around you. In fact, some early theorists believe that there is a "looking glass self" that develops out of our relations and interactions with others. In other words, you evaluate yourself primarily on the basis of how you *think* others perceive and evaluate you. Such a view gives great weight to your social experiences as a child.

If, for example, Maria's parents, relatives, and school friends all come to think of her as "the good student," she may learn to regard herself in the same way and strive even harder to do well in classes. Academic performance may become an essential aspect of the way she thinks of herself. Conversely, if Jon is viewed by his parents, relatives, and neighbors as "the black sheep," he may come to see himself in this light.

Self-concept also has a comparative dimension. For example, Kagan writes: "Although a particular child is a female, Canadian, Catholic, with brown eyes, she is also prettier than her sister, smarter than her best friend and more fearful of animals than her brother" (1989, p. 244). So a good part of how you think about yourself may have to do with how you judge yourself in relation to others.

Self-Esteem

One of the chief measures of self-concept is **self-esteem,** *your feelings of self-worth.* Your self-esteem might be linked with your physical appearance, intelligence, work, any number of qualities, traits, and affiliations, but self-esteem may be entirely subjective. There may be no direct relationship between your actual traits, achievement, or competence, and your feelings of self-worth (Sternberg and Kolligian, 1990). For example, research on exceptionally bright students shows that academic excellence does not necessarily make for high self-esteem. One high-achieving college student recalls:

> Everyone in 7th grade hated me, with some exceptions. My friends were the "out" class. The popular kids looked down on me. I felt dirty, un- classy, unfeminine. It was worse in 8th. The one thing my ego was based on was being smart. (Janos, 1990, p. 108)

Many studies of children report differences in self-esteem between boys and girls. In general, boys have a tendency "to inflate their sense of compe- tence" while girls usually play down their own abilities. Traditionally, our culture has handed down different behavioral norms and role models for male and female children. Consider this example:

A boy in a mass communication research project is asked what he would like to be when he grows up if he were a girl. "Oh," he exclaimed, "if I were a girl, I'd have to grow up to be nothing." (Lazier-Smith, 1989, p. 247)

Current research suggests that such patterns are cultural and conveyed through what parents believe and expect concerning their children's capabilities (Bandura, 1990, pp. 344–345). For example, studies by Gilligan and others (1982; 1989) propose that because most women are brought up to emphasize caring and responsibility for others rather than autonomy and independence, they tend to develop different moral value systems than men.

A summary of research on self-esteem includes these differences between men and women:

+ Men have a higher expected success rate on non-social skills than do women; even when men do not perform better, people perceive that they do.

+ Single women have higher self-esteem than do married women.

+ Older children score higher on self-esteem than do younger children.

+ Similarity in self-esteem appears to be a factor in selecting someone to date or have a relationship [with]. (Pearson et al., 1991, p. 67)

Feedback

Feedback often has a direct effect on level of self-esteem. When people are asked to predict their own performance on a test—whether it be of social, intellectual, or physical competence—and are later given feedback on how well they scored, they revise their predictions for the next experimental task in the direction of that feedback. This is true regardless of whether the feedback is accurate or not.

Numerous studies of speech communication feedback suggest that this common-sense hunch is correct: When you get positive feedback, you gain in self-confidence. Negative feedback can make you flustered and cause disruptions in your delivery, whether this is indicated by the loudness of your voice, rate of speech fluency, nervousness, stage fright, eye contact, or body movement.

Current research on how we *perceive* our own abilities supports the view that our relationships with others make up the foundation out of which we develop a sense of self and competence (Schaffer and Blatt, 1990, p. 244). Some researchers believe that earlier theories about self-concept are still useful as a base for further studies on how the self develops in social contexts (May, 1991, p. 492).

Shyness

"Do you consider yourself to be a shy person?" This is one of the questions with which Zimbardo began his pioneering studies of shyness over twenty years ago. According to Zimbardo, "the average person you meet is either shy, used to be shy, or is easily shy in certain situations." In fact, "only about 10 percent of Americans say they've never felt shy" (Kutner, 1992; Jones et al., 1986; Zimbardo, 1990).

Today much is known about shyness. For example, researchers have found that some people have a "temperamental bias," or genetic predisposition, toward shyness; interestingly enough, this includes some physical traits such as light-colored eyes. Shyness has many physical symptoms, and these vary from one person to another—trembling, rapid heartbeat, dry mouth, sweating, blushing. Shy people date less frequently, have fewer friends, "tend to have low-esteem and are preoccupied with the thought that they are socially inadequate" (Cheek and Cheek, 1990, p. 15).

Because they have lower self-esteem, they also tend to apply for jobs beneath their level of skills and to settle for the first job offer that comes along. In general, they earn less and advance less in their work because, as researchers explain, "shy people self-select themselves out of high-paying careers" (Cheek and Cheek, 1990, p. 176).

A growing body of research and case material shows that shyness is sometimes outgrown and that it is treatable.

Self-Fulfilling Prophecies

For artists, writers, and scientists, early rejection has usually been "the rule rather than the exception"—the careers of architect Frank Lloyd Wright, composer Igor Stravinsky, and novelist James Joyce offer just a few examples. We know that people who have the same set of skills "can perform poorly, adequately, or extraordinarily" and that often one's sense of competence and self-esteem can contribute to success (Bandura, 1990, p. 315).

Our expectations also have an influence on our impressions of other people. People who expect to be accepted by others and who perceive others as friendly are often outgoing and congenial; and their behavior accounts in good measure for their popularity and the positive way in which others respond. On the other hand, people who expect to be rejected often are (Adelmann, 1988). Perceiving others as hostile or unfriendly, they often act defensive or superior; this behavior may very well set in motion the rejection they fear.

Because of their psychological set, these people help to confirm their own expectations so that a favorable self-concept may lead to success, an unfavorable self-concept to failure. This phenomenon is called a **self-fulfilling prophecy.**

Behavior Attribution

Still, there is a major difference between the way you perceive yourself and the way you perceive other people. A series of studies on behavior attribution suggests that you see your own behavior as a sequence of responses to the demands of a given *situation,* but you view the same behavior in others as generated by their *disposition,* that is, their stable traits or needs. Lee, for example, sees himself as cutting down on his expenses and living more economically because he's saving up for a car; but he tends to think of Adam, his roommate, as cheap. Or "She is arrogant," but "I was provoked." In addition, a consistent finding in attribution research is that we tend to attribute the causes of our success to ourselves and the causes of our failures to external factors (Nurmi, 1991).

Two reasons for these perceptual differences have been proposed. First, the information available to the actor (the one who performs the action) and the observer may be different. The observer sees the actor at a particular point in time. Generally, he or she does not—cannot—know firsthand the actor's history, experiences, motives, or present emotional state; these can only be inferred. Thus if we see a person overreact to a mildly critical remark, as observers, we may not know what events preceding this episode made it the straw that broke the camel's back. A second possibility is that even when the same information is available to both actor and observer, they process it differently because different aspects of it are salient to each of them.

Storms (1973) suggests that these information differences may exist in actor and observer because their points of view are literally quite different. You do not see yourself acting; under ordinary circumstances you cannot be an observer of your own behavior. And while as an actor you watch the situation in which you find yourself, the other person spends most of his or her time observing you, not the situation.

But suppose we reverse the viewpoints of actor and observer. Storms found that he could change the orientation of actor and observer by showing them videotapes of their own interaction. Videotape offered the actor a new perspective, that of an observer, and often changed his or her inferences about why he or she had behaved in a particular way. After seeing ourselves on tape, we are much more likely to explain our behavior as a reflection of personal disposition than as a response to the environment.

While a change in visual orientation seems to heighten self-awareness, the prospect of viewing videotapes of all our behavior is neither appealing nor feasible. Nor is it perhaps desirable. Storms mentions, for example, that when videotape is used in therapy, patients sometimes take undue responsibility for their behavior, overlooking genuine elements in the environment that have influenced their actions. Videotape is not the answer. What we need is a more balanced view of ourselves and of others, a view that enables us to interpret behavior in terms of both disposition and environment.

Research on behavior attribution has several implications. The most important for our purposes is that by combining information about ourselves that is available only to us with an awareness of how other human beings perceive us, we may begin to see ourselves in sharper perspective.

Yet we must still bear in mind the fallibility of our own perceptions. In reviewing attribution studies, Ross and Fletcher (1985) caution:

The bottom line is this: both actors and observers can only infer the causes of the actor's behavior. When there are differences of opinion, actors are more likely to be correct, because they have more information. There is no reason to assume, however, that the actor's judgment will necessarily be valid. (p. 113)

Looking at Others

In many situations we find ourselves making several judgments about others—and all at once. For example, Matt Philips was at a Christmas party. Mixed in with the old crowd were four people he didn't know. But by the end of the evening he had, at least to his own satisfaction, sized up all the newcomers. The young woman in the red dress was lively and pleasant; he liked her right away. But her husband was a terrible snob—and so self-involved. The tall blonde was too nervous, but the older man seated next to her was easygoing with a great sense of humor. And Matt noticed how confident he was—they spent quite a bit of time talking.

Like Matt, most people form impressions of others quite easily; yet they find it difficult to explain the process. In fact, many feel that they make their judgments intuitively. One recent study of dating "shows that dates are rapidly defined as promising or not (in the first 30 seconds!)" (cited in Duck, 1991, p. 33).

"Impression" is a word we use about our judgments. We speak of being "under the impression," or of someone making a "lasting impression," a "false impression," or a "good impression." Even our legal system reflects the degree to which we rely on snap judgments. Before a trial begins, prospective jurors are screened by the defense and the prosecution. In addition to raising specific objections to certain candidates for the jury, both the defense and the prosecuting attorneys are allowed to reject a certain number of would-be jurors without stating their reasons. Attorneys often make their decisions rapidly, though they are complex ones and are probably based on several considerations. They will probably take into account their perception of the potential juror and the client and the impression they feel that the client will make upon that juror. And, of course, the attorney for one side might be more than willing to accept a juror whom opposing counsel finds objectionable.

Attorneys usually seem to be rather skilled perceivers, accustomed to formulating judgments about others very quickly. But think of the members of the jury. They will be meeting and evaluating many people for the first time—and presumably doing this entirely on their own. In a short time each juror will probably have formed an impression of most if not all of those involved in the case—including the witnesses, the defense attorney, the prosecuting attorney, and even the judge.

Research by Barge and his associates (1989) on person perception in legal

Do you think this lawyer is credible to all members of the jury?

settings confirms that a juror's perception of an attorney's credibility and of the defendant's guilt will be influenced not only by the attorney's opening statements but by various nonverbal cues in delivering those statements.

Because a juror's final judgment about the person on trial can have dramatic consequences, it is important to consider how he or she forms initial impressions and whether those impressions will have any effect on later perceptions. Our own evaluations of people also have important if less dramatic consequences, so we might all benefit from looking more closely at how an impression of another person is formed.

The First Impression

One of the major uses of evaluating personality is to explain and predict behavior on the basis of very limited information. How do we put this information together and come up with a first impression? Actually, each of us seems to hold a **private theory of personality** (sometimes known as "implicit personality theory"). Essentially, the term refers to *how we select and organize information about other people on the basis of what behaviors we think go together.*

Suppose you are given the following list of words describing a man you have never met and are then asked to write a personality sketch of him:

energetic   ironical
assured   inquisitive
talkative   persuasive
cold

In a classic experiment Solomon Asch (1946) used this list to learn more about how impressions of others are formed. He read the list to a group of students and asked them to write a full impression of the person described by these adjectives. There were two important findings.

Unity   First, all the students were able to organize the scanty information they received and create a consistent, unified impression, though there was a great deal of variation in their personality sketches, and they all went beyond the terms of the original description. Here are two samples:

> He seems to be the kind of person who would make a great impression upon others at a first meeting. However, as time went by, his acquaintances would easily come to see through the mask. Underneath would be revealed his arrogance and selfishness.

> Possibly he does not have any deep feeling. He would tend to be an opportunist. Likely to succeed in things he intends to do. He has perhaps married a wife who would help him in his purpose. He tends to be skeptical. (p. 261)

Central traits   Second, Asch found that certain traits are more **central**, more influential than others in forming impressions of personality. When one of the adjectives on the list was replaced by its opposite, the personality descriptions were radically different. Can you guess which of the seven adjectives was the crucial one? It was "cold." The list, with the trait "warm" substituted for "cold," was read to half the students. In another experiment Asch substituted the pair "polite-blunt" for "warm-cold," but these traits had relatively little effect on the way personality impressions were formed. Whether a person is warm or cold was more important than whether he is blunt or polite.

Students in an economics course at MIT were unwitting participants in a related study. Before the first class meeting, they were all given a brief biographical note about a new lecturer on the pretext that they would later be asked to fill out forms about him. Half received the following information:

> People who know him consider him to be a rather warm person, industrious, critical, practical and determined.

The other students received the same note but with a single word change: "cold" rather than "warm." After the lecturer spoke, the students were asked to describe him and rate him on fifteen characteristics. Those who read the "warm" biographical note usually described him as social, popular, and informal. Those given the "cold" description felt he was formal and self-centered (Kelley, 1950).

Do we like people who argue less? A recent study of argumentative situations (Onyekwere et al., 1991) reports that those who rank higher in argumentativeness and are more committed or attached to the issue being debated are perceived more positively than those who argue less and are less committed to the topic. When highly argumentative subjects were less involved about issues they were debating, they were viewed less favorably, so it appears that being partisan is significant. In essence, the researchers speculate, "when people like what they are doing, they may be perceived as more trustworthy because their enthusiasm, excitement and confidence may be interpreted as more sincere and dependable behaviors" (p. 45).

For a long time theorists believed that impressions of others were interpreted on the basis of the "halo effect," the tendency to extend a favorable or unfavorable impression of one trait to other traits. Thus you might think of Donna as honest and polite, just because you consider her intelligent. Or if you feel Paul is cheap, you might attribute several other undesirable traits to him. This explanation sounds reasonable, but we now know that the halo effect is too simple a concept to account completely for the way we interpret our perceptions.

Indirectly, experiments such as those described above tell us that certain traits carry weight and are clearly more decisive to our judgments than others. Somehow we manage to make all the information we have about a person— all those distinct verbal and nonverbal cues—fit together (Asch and Zukier, 1984). If they don't seem consistent, we build in an explanation. In looking at others we assume a certain stability in the traits we see. That's why, for example, it is so difficult to think of the martinet in the office as a loving family man and doting father. It will take some doing, but most of us will find a way to reconcile those two kinds of behavior.

Bruner (1986) illustrates how we invoke circumstances to explain away behavior that violates our theory about what people are like. He and his colleague Henri Zukier were trying out a variant of the Asch experiment with a group of college-age subjects:

> To begin with, we gave them a short list of consistent trait names characterizing an imaginary person, like spiritual, introverted, religious, to which they would respond by describing him as "a saintly kind of person." Then we added to the list practical and money-minded. One subject: "Sure. A good man, but he's probably in one of those cut-throat businesses." Another: "I've known them like that—like those Amish or Men-

nonite farmers where I grew up, good in his own group and drives a hard bargain outside." (p. 38)

People seem more reliable, more knowable, when we can predict some aspects of their behavior. Perhaps that explains our need to perceive another human being as a "personality"—to see that personality quickly; to see it vividly, with certain dominant or central traits; and most important, to see it as a unity.

The Primacy Effect

Time is one of the most significant variables in our communication model. Thus it seems natural to ask what effect the first impression you form will have on your future perceptions of another communicator. Ideally, as you learn more about someone, you continually revise or refine your impressions in the light of new information. But is this in fact so? Does a first impression enhance or interfere with later knowledge, or does it have no effect at all?

Among studies of impression formation, those of Luchins have been very influential. In one of his experiments, subjects read two paragraphs describing a young man named Jim. One paragraph described actions of Jim's that were predominantly introverted, the other described actions that were predominantly extroverted. All subjects read the same paragraphs; only their order varied. Luchins found that a **primacy effect** did exist—that *the first information we receive about a person is the most decisive in forming our impression* (Luchins, in Hovland et al., 1957). So first meetings—especially the very first minutes of those meetings—are important.

Primacy has a clear-cut effect on communication. If you look once more at the model in Figure 1.1, you see that each communicator should be receiving input and feedback. The primacy effect blocks both. It is, in our terms, a source of technical interference, and this time the interference is within the communicator. If Sandra, after spending five minutes with her roommate's brother Bill, is sure that he is overbearing and phony, she is not going to be very interested in getting any feedback about her impression of him. Most of you have been in Bill's place at least once. It's as though you suddenly had become invisible. No matter what you said or did, the other person no longer seemed to respond; you couldn't change that first impression of you.

Rightly or wrongly, most people feel quite confident about their judgments. For example, in Luchins's experiment almost all the subjects were very willing to answer questions about Jim's behavior that were totally unrelated to the information they had read about him. Given information about some of his behavior, they inferred several other things about him and confidently predicted how he would behave in other social situations. Only a few asked how they were expected to know such things (Brown, 1986). But as we will see in Chapter 3, all inferences involve some measure of risk, and this is true of inferences about personality.

We all know how often first impressions can be mistaken ones, and we also know how often decisions depend on first impressions. Imagine that you are being interviewed for your first job after graduation. You look very nervous and were ten minutes late for the interview. Then you make an obvious grammatical mistake in speaking. What is likely to be the outcome?

It's disturbing to think that first impressions can have such dramatic effects on judgment. But Luchins found that if people were warned not to make snap judgments, the primacy effect was reversed or eliminated completely. Several other studies confirm that the primacy effect is not inevitable.

Physical Attractiveness

In some ideal world we will all be beautiful. Until that time, however, it seems likely that those of us who are physically attractive will have a slight edge—at least initially—on those of us who are not. Among scholars there is general agreement: Physically attractive people are considered by others to be more sociable, more popular, more sexual, more successful, and more persuasive. And frequently they are thought to be happier and to have more appealing personalities (Berscheid and Walster, in Berkowitz, 1974).

In our culture being attractive is often associated with thinness so that one of the unpardonable sins—at least for women—is becoming "fat." Witness the alarming number of women suffering from such eating disorders as anorexia and bulimia: One writer on anorexia places "the number of anorexics at 5 to 10 percent of all American girls and women. On some college campuses . . . one woman in five is anorexic" (cited in Wolf, 1991, p. 182).

We take many of our images of beauty from the mass media. One researcher reports the most common body type in women as average (77 percent); next came thin (15 percent) and overweight (7 percent) and obese (1 percent). Despite these numbers, a study of body images that appear in ads for women's magazines reveals the following:

+ The proportion of thin models increased each decade since the 1950s, reaching a high of 46 percent in the 1980s.

+ Thin models were featured as most attractive and successful of all body types.

+ The combined ratings of attractiveness, success, and happiness yielded a "Yendex," or desirability index, that showed thin models to be the most desirable of all body types. (Gagnard, 1989, pp. 261–262)

We can bear this out just by looking at a few current ads. Gagnard suggests that women's magazines are increasingly emphasizing an unrealistic message and that the mass media play "a major role in perpetuating cultural definitions of attractiveness and success."

Recently there has been a great surge in the popularity of dating services and the number of people placing personal ads in newspapers and magazines. In summarizing research on this phenomenon, Duck (1991) notes the finding that "men 'offer' their status and height when describing themselves, while women 'offer' physical attractiveness" (p. 33).

Aside from liking physically attractive people because they are good to look at, we sometimes like them because we feel that by being seen with them, we will enhance our own image. The college man who consistently dates beautiful women is very likely to improve his own image among both his male friends and his prospective female acquaintances. The woman who dates handsome men is also increasing her own self-esteem.

Attractiveness may also be linked with perceptions of power and status. One study reveals that American women perceive men dressed in formal attire as more attractive than men who are informally dressed (Hewitt and German, 1987).

It also turns out that subjects differing in their level of attractiveness are distinguishable on the basis of their attitudes toward relationships (Erwin and Calev, 1984). Attractive subjects view their friendships in terms of personal rewards and being liberal and "easygoing": those of average attractiveness viewed them in terms of personal reward and involving commitment; unattractive subjects emphasized social and commitment aspects of their relationships. The authors of the study believe their findings may support the matching hypothesis—people of like levels of attractiveness stay together—because like levels of attractiveness may reflect similar attitudes toward friendship.

Despite the association of beauty with talent, however, career success for women is not furthered by their good looks. In fact, studies point to a bias against good-looking women in executive positions (Heilman and Stopeck, 1985). Attractive women who run for public office, unlike their male counterparts, also seem to be at a disadvantage (Dullea, 1985). The so-called beauty backlash applies only to women.

In general, researchers tend to agree that the influence of physical beauty is most powerful early in a relationship (Knapp and Vangelisti, 1992). As we acquire more and more information about a person, the effects of physical appearance diminish considerably. It seems, after all, that "you can't live on looks."

Personal Generalizations and Stereotypes
Your private theory of personality is in large part based on generalizations, many of which derive from personal experience. If Jane favors boys of Fraternity XYZ, for example, then she may be attracted to Phil simply because he is a member. Similarly, if she thinks math students are nerds, then she may refuse a first date with one regardless of whether he fits her personal definition of math students. If your luggage is stolen while you are traveling in Italy, you may come to feel that Italians are dishonest. If you have seen several Swedish films starring beautiful actresses, perhaps you have come to believe that all Swedish women are beautiful.

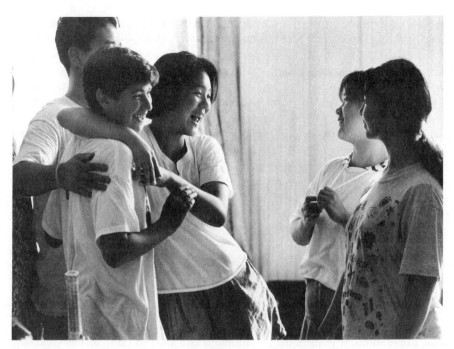

This lively exchange is clearly being enjoyed by all parties.

In saner moments we realize that although generalizations are necessary to the organization of any perceptions, generalizations based on very limited personal experience are often inaccurate and misleading. Jane may find that the next member of Fraternity XYZ she dates is a nerd. You may get to know members of a wonderful Italian family who practically take you into their home. The first Swedish girl you actually meet may be unattractive.

But how we perceive other human beings also depends on generalizations derived from our shared experiences as members of a given culture or society. Earlier in this chapter, in discussing the Müller-Lyer illusion, we observed that culture is a determinant of visual perception. It is even more significant from the standpoint of human communication that culture can be a determinant of *person* perception.

Culture   The influence of a culture on the person perception of its members is most directly seen in its stereotypes. A **stereotype** is *a generalization about a class of people, objects, or events that is widely held by a given culture.* We cannot say categorically that all stereotypes are false. According to one hypothesis, there is a kernel of truth in all of them. Thus we can at least acknowledge that some are accurate enough to provide a very limited basis for making judgments about groups of people we hardly know. But when applied to a specific individual, most stereotypes are inappropriate and highly inaccurate—and many are false. Relying on stereotypes rather than on direct perceptions can result in embarrassing social situations.

There can be no doubt that race membership affects our perceptions of others. For example, we are better at recognizing pictures of members of our own race than pictures of members of another (Malpass and Kravitz, 1969). A lighthearted illustration of this phenomenon is suggested by a popular cartoon. The setting is a Chinese restaurant in the United States. All the waiters are Chinese; all the customers are Occidental. In the foreground a waiter holding a tray with a covered dish confers with several other waiters. "I can't remember which customer ordered this," he is saying, "They all look alike."

Even positive stereotypes can have damaging effects on intercultural communication. In this country, Asian Americans have generally been singled out as America's most "successful" minority. Since the 1960s, the mass media seem to have given special emphasis to the "success story" of Asian Americans. "Intelligent," "hard-working," "quiet," "soft-spoken," "well-mannered"— these were some of the all-too-predictable terms. The success story has another side, though, fostering resentment by others and subtle forms of discrimination.

In our culture, with its strong emphasis on youth, stereotyping by age is also quite common. Thus, many older people find that despite their professional experience, it is difficult to change jobs, and, in fact, some who have spent most of their working lives within a single company are passed over for promotions or even let go. Several books on finding jobs and changing careers advise those over fifty to consider eliminating their age, date of college graduation, and mention of early employment from their résumés.

Stereotyping by age is especially apparent in the mass media (Liebert and Sprafkin, 1988). Although about 15 percent of our population is now over age sixty-five, content analyses of television programming show that elderly people are represented in between no more than 1.5 to 3 percent of all roles and that they appear twice as often on talk shows or comedies as in dramatic representations (p. 192). Older people are rarely represented in romantic situations. In fact, they are often portrayed as unhappy and inept; they are seen as having difficulty solving their own problems and are often helped by younger adults.

The film industry has a long history of stereotyped portrayals. According to one critic, in American films homosexual villains are replacing drug dealers and investors from Japan as "the new bad guys," gay men and lesbians are portrayed exclusively in terms of their homosexuality, and "homosexuality seems invariably to signal that a character is either sinister or irrelevant" (Weir, 1992, p. 17).

Basic Instinct, a film with Michael Douglas and Sharon Stone, drew particular criticism for its negative stereotypes, as

> a movie with four sinister and seductive women who are, variously, cigarette smokers, fast drivers, or sexual adventurers. . . . Three of the

women are bisexuals; the fourth is lesbian. . . . [and] the women are characterized as vicious man-killers. (p. 17)

In 1992, gay activist groups protested that three of the five films nominated for Oscars had negative stereotypes of homosexuals: Jonathan Demme's *Silence of the Lambs,* Oliver Stone's *J.F.K.,* and Barbra Streisand's *Prince of Tides.*

Physical attributes   Stereotypes also extend to physical attributes. Think of the longstanding American stereotype concerning the advantages of being blonde. A wide variety of rinses and dyes are available to all who wish to cover even the earliest signs of gray hair or simply to choose the hair color of the moment.

In discussing attractiveness, we saw that physical attributes have considerable influence on our first impressions. Each culture emphasizes certain facial cues. It might be the amount of makeup a woman wears or how she wears her hair or even whether she wears glasses. For example, in some cultures, people are regarded as more intelligent, reliable, and industrious when they wear glasses (Kleinke, 1986, p. 79). No doubt you have seen people who are aware of the power of this stereotype and exploit it to create an impression. It's the same impulse that makes the budding "professorial type" sport a pipe or the femme fatale take to smoking little cigars.

Information about status differences also affects our perception of physical attributes. In one well-known study a speaker named Mr. England was introduced to each of five college classes by a different title—from "A student from Cambridge" all the way up the social scale to "Professor England from Cambridge." Students were later asked to estimate Mr. England's height; the higher his status, the taller students thought he was (Wilson, 1968). Today there is considerable evidence that we tend "to judge people of high status and people we like as taller than people of low status and people we dislike" (Kleinke, 1986, p. 74).

Some effects of stereotyping   In each of these examples of stereotyping, a person is considered to have attributes generally ascribed to the group of which he or she is a member. That person is not perceived as a unique human being but as a member of a certain category of human beings, whether it be actresses, Asian Americans, or college professors. In a sense, the person is judged in terms of context. Although some generalizations about categories are valuable to us in daily experience, generalizations about human beings— especially generalizations about how they think and how they are likely to behave—tend to distort our perceptions and to interfere with our ability to make accurate judgments. Unfortunately, personal generalizations or stereotypes cannot be eliminated simply by alerting the perceiver to their dangers.

A recent analysis of work on stereotypes finds at least four statements that seem warranted. First, stereotyping results from "cognitive biases stemming from illusory correlations between group membership and psychological attributes." Second, our stereotypes influence the way we process information—we remember less favorable information about out-groups and more favorable information about in-groups. Third, "stereotypes create expectancies (hypotheses) about others, and individuals try to confirm these expectancies." And last—and perhaps most significant from the standpoint of intercultural communication—our stereotypes operate as a constraint upon the communication behaviors of others, giving rise to behavior that then confirms our stereotypic expectations (Gudykunst and Ting-Toomey, 1988, pp. 136–137). (See Chapter 13 for a further discussion of stereotyping.)

Social Roles

Among the several social roles that influence how we perceive and are ourselves perceived by others are work roles, student roles, sex-linked roles, and marital roles.

A classic example of how our **work roles** may alter perception is Zimbardo's so-called prison experiment (1971) in which students randomly assigned to be "guards" and others designated "prisoners" quickly came to see and respond to each other in stereotypical guard-prisoner fashion: The guards became cruel and unjust, the prisoners rebellious. Although planned for two weeks, the experiment was stopped after only six days. Students no longer thought like students, but like guards and prisoners. They truly lived their parts.

More recently, research on Hispanics and whites (Jones, 1991) supports the view that perceived differences in social status (as defined by work roles) influence ethnic stereotypes and that "occupational status . . . is often used to make rather confident judgments of personal attributes." According to this study, "occupational title appears to be a more central trait than ethnicity in determining American students' perceptions of people" (p. 475).

As for **student roles,** research on perceptions in the classroom finds that teachers perceive the model student as a compliant communicator—"well-behaved, patient, controlled, and polite. He or she waits before speaking, listens intently and politely, sits quietly while others talk, and contributes clear and germane comments" (Trenholm and Rose, 1981, p. 24). Teachers describe the model student as one who willingly does all assignments, "never criticizes the teacher or gives way to frustration, and accepts and even welcomes criticism" (p. 24). According to these findings, compliance rather than inquiring behavior would be rewarded. This expectation is also born out by a study of beginning teachers, on both the elementary and secondary levels: They perceive classroom discipline, motivating students, and dealing with individual differences as among their greatest teaching problems (Veenman, 1984).

What a contrast with the way most students feel about unquestioning compliance. Years after he graduated from college, Peter Taylor could still recall the time he received an A for a paper he wrote for comparative lit while Nazik, the Iranian grad student sitting next to him, received only a B— for hers. Peter knew he had only summarized and "played back" Dr. Kiernan's views. Nazik had taken a more controversial stance, and in class Dr. Kiernan had questioned her about it. A published author in her own country, Nazik was having difficulty slipping back into the role of student. And Dr. Kiernan was more interested in compliance than originality. He was not at all pleased by a student who challenged his analysis even when she was able to defend her point of view.

Another aspect of student-teacher roles is the perception of power in the classroom. Although teachers and students generally agree on power bases, some important differences exist. Both groups see most power stemming from the teacher's ability to give rewards (e.g., high grades, approval), ability to make the student identify with the teacher, and the teacher's perceived expertise. But again students, as you might expect, have a less positive view of the teacher's *use* of power (McCroskey and Richmond, 1983).

That **sex roles** also influence perceptions is confirmed by several research summaries (Rosenthal and DePaulo, 1979, LaFrance and Mayo, 1979; and Pearson et al., 1991). The consensus is that women are perceived as more supportive than men, laughing more often, intruding less on others, and being more deferential. Men, on the other hand, are considered more dominant and achievement—and task—oriented. These descriptions reflect the more stereotypical views that women place a higher value on establishing and maintaining relationships while men tend to perceive the world more as a place to "win" or "achieve." A twist on this view is the old joke, "Behind every great man is a woman saying 'You're wrong. You're wrong.' "

Although in most studies males are perceived as more assertive in their communication style and females as more responsive, other research (Staley and Cohen, 1988; Bonaguro and Pearson, 1986) fails to find evidence of the latter. Staley and Cohen point out that little attention has been given to self-perceptions of male-female communication style, and their results indicate that for the most part, males and females tend to see themselves similarly. On the basis of their results, they suggest that future investigations of sex differences in communicator style concentrate on actual behavior.

Veenendall and Braito (1987) argue that a person whose self-concept is highly sex-typed may strive to maintain behavior that is consistent with various internalized standards for his or her sex role and to suppress behavior seen as inappropriate. They cite Bem's suggestion "that an androgynous self-concept might allow individuals to engage freely in both masculine and feminine behaviors and allow greater human potentiation . . ." (p. 32).

Perceptions of **marital roles** seem to have undergone considerable change in the last decades, particularly with the increased number of wives who have joined the work force. A study attempting to predict marital and career success among dual-working couples (Hiller and Philliber, 1982) identifies four major marital types: these are based on how the husband and wife perceive themselves.

In a *traditional marriage relationship,* the husband sees himself as masculine and the wife sees herself as feminine. For example, although both work outside the home, the husband is perceived as bringing home the proverbial bacon whereas the wife has sole responsibility for all the housework. Housework is her province, and he won't help with any of it.

In a *reluctant wife marriage relationship,* the wife views herself as feminine and her husband sees himself as androgynous (having both masculine and feminine characteristics). If the wife in this relationship does not perceive herself as furnishing most of the emotional support, she may perceive her husband as "too feminine." And if her husband helps with the housework, sharing these tasks because she is so busy as a result of her successful career, she may feel guilty—both because she neglects "her duties" at home and because her professional skills seem "unfeminine."

On the other hand, in a *reluctant husband marriage relationship,* the husband sees himself as masculine and his wife sees herself as androgynous: He may feel threatened by her broad range of activities if he defines her role more narrowly. Suppose, for example, that she wants to split all the housework while he believes that if she hasn't the time for all the domestic concerns, she should spend less time at the office.

In the *androgynous marriage relationship,* the fourth type, *both* spouses see themselves as androgynous: Both engage in so-called masculine and feminine behaviors, making adaptation easier. He may even do most of the cooking, while she does most of the cleaning and laundry. As you might expect, problems may still arise based on social expectations of appropriate or "proper" husband/wife roles.

It might be interesting to try classifying the marriages of those you know—relatives, friends, neighbors—and see whether you can discern any pattern related to age, work, and psychological makeup of the spouses involved. Or ask yourself which type of marriage you have or expect to have.

We've looked at several factors influencing our impressions of others. In addition to their physical attractiveness and social roles, our own self-perceptions, our notions of personality, and the stereotypes we hold and our own generalizations also come into play. So we turn in the final section of this chapter to questions concerning the accuracy of these impressions.

SOME VARIABLES INVOLVED IN ACCURATE PERCEPTION

Granted the selective quality of human perception, we must ask what are the other variables that will affect the accuracy of our perceptions. Studies suggest that at least three generalizations can be made. First, some people are easier to judge than others—perhaps because they are more open about themselves. Second, certain traits are easier to judge than others. For example, Zimbardo

(1990) has shown that it is much easier to identify people who are not shy than it is to pick out people who consider themselves shy. And third, people are better at judging those who resemble themselves.

Perceiver Self-Confidence

For a long time psychologists have tried to establish whether some people are indeed better judges than others. Certainly, we all know people who feel their perceptions to be extremely accurate. But is there a relationship between self-confidence and accuracy? Does self-confidence about our ability to judge others make a difference in how we see them?

In terms of our communication model, we might say that a person who forms impressions of others solely on the basis of personal expectations avoids the task of person perception. Researchers have found no correlation between confidence in our perceptions of others and the accuracy of those perceptions.

The Effect of Context

From what we know at present, it seems likely that the ability to judge other people may be quite specific to **context**. For example, students were asked to view a person bargaining, first in a very cooperative situation and later in a very competitive one. Group influence was so strong that when their perception of the bargainer did not correspond with the perceptions of other group members, subjects denied what they had seen with their own eyes. In fact, they came to believe the opposite of what they had seen (Tubbs, 1969). Majority or group opinion is just one instance in which context—the third element of perception—exerts its subtle influence.

Other Perceiver Traits That Affect Accuracy

Despite the fact that accurate person perception varies from one situation to another, theorists generally agree that certain characteristics are associated with sound perceptions of others.

First, *intelligence* is a prime factor. Second, the *ability to draw inferences* about people from their behavior seems related to accurate perception. Third, *people who score low on tests of authoritarianism* tend to be better judges of others. They are less rigid in their expectations, judging more from what they know about the person and assuming less that he or she is like themselves. And fourth, those with a *high degree of objectivity* about themselves tend to have insight into the behavior of others. Openness and awareness of our own shortcomings seem to play a part in this process.

How can this information be applied to improving our effectiveness as communicators? We certainly cannot improve our intelligence directly—and the ability to draw valid inferences about people from their behavior probably depends in part on intelligence. Nor can we simply tell ourselves to be less rigid or authoritarian. Research demonstrates that attitudes are rarely changed so easily. One thing we can do is become conscious of, and less defensive about, our own limitations. And the more sensitive we become to cues outside ourselves, the more we listen instead of projecting our own feelings onto others, the more accurate we are likely to be in our evaluations of others.

IMPROVING PERCEPTION AND COMMUNICATION

Failures in communication frequently occur because people have inaccurate perceptions of each other. If a man is told that a woman he knows only casually is snobbish and standoffish, he is not very likely to ask her out. If you feel that a particular instructor is stubborn and somewhat hostile, you probably won't consider questioning her about your low grade on the last exam. But how do you know you are right about your instructor? In many ways your perceptions of others can determine not only the kind of communication that takes place but whether or not you attempt communication at all.

It would seem then an easy matter to facilitate communication by simply improving the accuracy of our perceptions. Yet the three elements of perception—perceiver, object, and context—are so interwoven that one cannot be analyzed apart from the others. One of the most important things the perceiver can do is take into account the need to make perceptual adjustments as any of these three components varies.

The primary element in accurate person perception is empathy. **Empathy** involves *experiencing the other's perception—that is, seeing and feeling things as the other does*. We've already seen in the research on behavior attribution how people tend to view their own behavior as response to a given situation and to interpret the same behavior in another person as an expression of stable traits or needs. For example, you lose your temper and explain you've had a hectic and frustrating day, but when one of your coworkers loses his temper, you say he has "a short fuse."

Ideally, we work toward developing that sensitivity or responsiveness to others that actually extends perception. Floyd (1985) believes empathy is the key to effective listening and therefore to communication. In Chapter 5, the role of empathy in listening and in resolving conflicts should become clear: Perceiving something the way the other person perceives it—taking the other's perspective—provides insights and paves the way for effective relationships.

Another requirement of accurate person perception is an awareness that your own perceptions may be inaccurate. Improved perception and communication can occur only if you are willing to acknowledge that your perceptions are subjective. One of the authors remembers a conversation in which two people disagreed about their perceptions of a third. When one was asked whether she was sure of what she was saying, she replied, "Would I say it if it weren't true?" Her statement shows an obvious lack of awareness that human perceptions are subject to error. As long as she denied that possibility, there was little chance that an effective exchange of viewpoints could take place.

It would be utopian to say that more accurate person perception always makes for more effective communication. Nevertheless, communication in both long-term and short-term relationships is often enhanced when the participants perceive each other accurately. The same principles apply to marital and dating relationships and to many less intense interpersonal encounters.

Consider the interview, for example. It relies heavily on accurate person perception even though the relationship is relatively short term. Here is a situation in which two or more people meet to exchange information—ordinarily about a subject that has been decided on beforehand—and to formulate impressions of one another. In a selection or job interview, it is each person's intention to size up the other's attributes. Person perception is one of the prime objectives. In an evaluative interview an employee's work is appraised by a supervisor, and guidelines for improved job performance are discussed. Several studies have shown that two of the most important objectives of evaluative interviews are that the employee perceive the supervisor as helpful and constructive rather than critical and that the supervisor and employee perceive effective job performance in a similar way.

We have tried to suggest that interpersonal sensitivity is a requirement in both long- and short-term encounters. In the chapters that follow, we shall also see that although early impressions depend to a great extent on the perceiver's preconceptions and stereotypes and on the other person's physical appearance, as contact with a person continues, the content of his or her messages (both verbal and nonverbal) plays a greater role in modifying our perceptions of that person.

SUMMARY

In this chapter we demonstrated that person perception is an active process in which communicators selectively perceive, organize, and interpret what they experience. We also showed how person perception affects intercultural communication. We began by considering the physiological and psychological filters that affect all our perceptions. After suggesting some parallels and distinctions between person and object perception, we looked first at how we form our perceptions about ourselves. Thus we examined some of the many variables that influence self-concept and particularly self-esteem and looked at recent research findings about shyness. We then focused on how our impressions of other human beings are formed. We spoke of how we tend to view our own behaviors as opposed to those of others, trait centrality, and trait associations, primacy, and the effects of physical attractiveness. Personal generalizations and stereotypes and the influence of work, student, sex-linked, and marital roles were also discussed.

We saw that our impressions, while formed with relative ease, are not necessarily accurate. Some characteristics of accurate perceivers were mentioned, but judging ability itself was seen as specific to context. In concluding, we discussed inaccurate perception as a source of communication failures and how improved perception enhances communication. Empathy was seen to be the crucial element in this process.

REVIEW QUESTIONS

1. Distinguish between a perceptual filter and a psychological set.

2. Discuss two ways in which person perception is different from object perception. What are the implications of these differences for communication?

3. Discuss the formation of self-concept and two important influences on self-esteem.

4. Identify the single most significant implication of behavior attribution research for the study of person perception.

5. Explain the concept of central traits and its significance for person perception.

6. What is the primacy effect? How might it influence communication?

7. Give a brief summary of the major research findings on physical attractiveness and its influence on first impressions.

8. How do personal generalizations and stereotypes differ?

9. List four statements about stereotypes that are supported by recent research.

10. Describe the influence of work, sex, student, and marital roles on how we perceive and are ourselves perceived by others.

11. What three generalizations can you make from the research studies cited here about how various traits of the perceived affect the accuracy of person perception?

12. Discuss four perceiver characteristics associated with accurate perception of others.

13. What are two ways in which person perception and communication effectiveness can be improved?

14. Explain the concept of empathy and its significance for accurate person perception.

EXERCISES

1. Select one of the case problems listed in the appendix. Ask five people to read the same case problem and each to write a short paper supporting a solution to the problem. Examine the solutions offered in terms of differences and similarities in person perception. How do the following concepts relate to the similarities and differences:
   a. Psychological set
   b. Psychological filter
   c. Primacy effect
   d. Stereotype perceptions

2. Write a description of yourself in which you use ten adjectives. Then ask a person in your class to describe you in the same way, and compare the results. You might try this again with a close friend.

3. Write down some of the perceptions you have of your classmates. Then refer to your earlier comments in your personal log. Have you changed or confirmed some of your original impressions?

4. Reread your descriptions (in exercise 3) of people who really impressed you at first. Write a list of words describing each person. Then try to identify the specific verbal and nonverbal behaviors that led you to draw up each list. Now that you know each of these people better, what additional experiences have shaped your perception of each of them?

5. Write a paragraph describing someone you think is an effective communicator. List all attributes that seem to contribute to this effectiveness. Now think of a poor communicator. What characteristics seem to cause the ineffectiveness?

6. What characteristics do you possess that affect how you perceive these two people?

7. Have the class split up into groups of five. Your instructor will give you copies of the "Preliminary Scale of Interpersonal Perceptions." Fill out these forms, giving your perceptions of each of the other members in your group. Do not put your own name on the forms. When everyone has filled out all the forms, exchange them so that each person has a rating from every other group member. Then look at the ratings you received from the rest of the group. You might want to discuss these with others in the group

to gain additional feedback. Interview a person who does a lot of interviewing. Discuss communication and person perception with that person. Have the interviewer elaborate on how he or she perceives interviewees and selects cues in assessing them.

SUGGESTED READINGS

Brown, Roger. *Social Psychology.* 2d ed. New York: Free Press, 1986.

This is a revision of an outstanding text on social psychology. The section on how we form impressions of others is sophisticated and beautifully written.

Carroll, Raymonde. *Cultural Misunderstandings.* Translated by Carol Volk. Chicago: University of Chicago Press, 1988.

The author has written a fascinating analysis of many of the cultural differences between the French and the Americans that generate so much misunderstanding on both sides.

Cheek, Jonathan, and **Bronwen Cheek.** *Conquering Shyness.* New York: Dell, 1990.

The authors discuss shyness in the light of current research and outline a treatment program to overcome shyness and build self-esteem.

Gilligan, Carol. *In a Different Voice: Psychological Theory and Women's Development.* Cambridge, MA: Harvard University Press, 1982.

In this examination of moral development and the evolution of self-esteem, the author contrasts the different responses of men and women to various ethical dilemmas.

Gudykunst, William, and **Young Yun Kim.** *Communicating with Strangers: An Approach to Intercultural Communication.* 2d ed. New York: McGraw-Hill, 1992.

An up-to-date survey of studies in intercultural communication. Chapters 4 and 5 will be of special interest to students of person perception.

Kleinke, Chris. *Meeting and Understanding People.* New York: Freeman, 1986.

The subject of this book is how we "present" ourselves and form impressions of others, and the author's approach is thoroughly research based yet practical.

McCroskey, James C., and **John A. Daley,** eds. *Personality and Interpersonal Communication.* Beverly Hills, CA: Sage, 1987.

A valuable synthesis of important research and theory on personality and communication. Most suitable for advanced students.

Pearson, Judy Cornelia, Lynn H. Turner, and **William Todd-Mancillas.** *Gender & Communication.* 2d ed. Dubuque, IA: William C. Brown, 1991.

This is a timely analysis and survey of studies on the relationship between gender differences and communication.

Sternberg, Robert J., and **John Kolligan, Jr.,** eds. *Competence Considered.* New Haven: Yale University Press, 1990.

A group of eminent psychologists discuss how our perceptions of our own abilities influence our performance and development.

Zimbardo, Philip G. *Shyness: What It Is, What to Do About It.* Reading, MA: Addison-Wesley, 1990.

This is a classic on the nature of shyness.

CHAPTER THREE

*T*he Verbal Message

CHAPTER OBJECTIVES

After reading this chapter, you should be able to:

1 Explain what is intended by the statement "The word is not the thing," and distinguish between denotation and connotation.

2 Differentiate between private and shared meanings, and explain the concepts of overlapping codes and codeswitching.

3 Discuss two theories about how message encoding skills develop.

4 Summarize the Sapir-Whorf hypothesis and describe two ways in which language and thought are related.

5 Specify five problem areas in our use of language, and give an example of each.

6 Explain how one's cultural frame of reference influences communication and give examples from two different cultures.

7 Discuss the effects of sexist language on communication, how male and female language usage differs, and several language forms perceived by others as powerful.

8 Explain the concept of metacommunication and give an example.

*W*riting about American conversational style, Althen (1992) says:

> English lends itself to precise expression (except in the realm of emotions) and Americans use words, many of them, in order to communicate. They think it important to "spell things out," to "make things clear," by means of comprehensive verbal disquisition. (p. 416)

French conversational style is another story:

> Americans often expressed surprise in my presence at the fact that French people, "who claim to be very big on manners," are themselves so "rude": "they interrupt you all the time in conversation," "they finish your sentences for you," "they ask you questions and never listen to the answer," and so on. French people, on the other hand, often complain that American conversations are "boring," that Americans respond to the slightest question with a "lecture," that they "go all the way back to Adam and Eve," and that they "know nothing about the art of conversation." (Carroll, 1988, p. 23)

The word "conversation" is the same in English and French, but as Raymonde Carroll explains, "It is far from signifying the same thing in the two cultures." Words per se cannot be said to "contain" meaning. As we will see, even for people who share a common language, words often generate very different associations.

As we examine verbal messages in this chapter, we will take up four major concerns. The first is the relationship between words and meaning. Thus we will be talking about the symbolic nature of language, the descriptive and associative aspects of words (denotation and connotation), as well as private and shared meanings.

A second section takes up the complex process of formulating verbal messages and how we all learn to do this. As we examine the next issue, how language and thought are related, you will learn about a highly influential theory on the subject, the Sapir-Whorf hypothesis, and then look at several ways in which language use—abstraction, for example—affects your thinking.

In the concluding section, you will also learn about the influence of language usage on feelings and behavior. You will be looking at sexist language, gender differences in the use of language, and the linguistic forms considered more powerful or effective.

Let's turn first to a consideration of the nature of language.

WORDS AND MEANING

We saw in Chapter 1 that the communication process involves sending messages from one person's nervous system to another's with the intention of creating a meaning similar to the one in the sender's mind. The verbal message does this through words, the basic elements of language, and words, of course, are verbal symbols.

Symbols and Referents

In Chapter 1 we defined a **symbol** as *something used for or regarded as representing something else.* Thus the image of a lion can serve as a symbol of courage, a red and white striped pole as a symbol of a barber shop. In English the word "sun" is the verbal symbol used to designate the star that is the central body of our solar system; the French use another symbol, "soleil"; and the Germans a third, "Sonne." All three symbols represent the same star.

Consider the term "floppy disk." "Floppy disk" is the name given to the flexible, round magnetic recording medium or storage device. The term is arbitrary. It was assigned to the recording so that we could communicate about it without pointing each time we referred to it. "Floppy disk" might have been called "soft record" or "blank" or even "urg." So initially no real association exists between a word we agree to call something and its **referent,** *the object for which it stands.* Clearly, the word is not the thing. A word is merely a verbal symbol of the object it represents. Such words as "teletext," "modem," "digital information system," and "electronic mail" are but a few of those that have entered our language as a result of the new communication technologies.

Once we agree on a system of verbal symbols, we can use language to communicate. Of course, if all the words we used referred only to objects, our communication problems would be eased considerably. We could establish what referents we were speaking about with somewhat less difficulty. But words also refer to events, properties of things, actions, relationships, concepts, and so on. Take the words "white lie." Suppose one of your friends tells you something that is not true and you find out and confront her with your knowledge. Although she explains that it was just a "white lie," you may consider her action a form of "deception"—it's even possible that an argument will ensue. And if you can't reach agreement on relatively simple terms, what about terms that represent higher levels of abstraction? What are the referents of such terms as "ethics," "freedom," and "responsibility"?

The relationship between meaning and reference becomes especially clear when we encounter words in a foreign language. If we see **МИР**, the Russian word for "peace" and "world," for the first time, we have no way of determining what concepts that word represents simply by looking at the word itself. Even with new words in our own language, we have to learn what concepts they represent. Notice how we carefully avoided saying, "what the words mean." Meanings are not inherent in words. Words in and of themselves are meaningful only after we have associated them with some referents. It is human beings who assign meanings to words.

Denotation and Connotation

In discussing meaning, some students of language make the traditional distinction between "denotation" and "connotation," We have said that words are meaningful only after we have associated them with some referents.

When we speak of **denotation,** we refer to *the primary associations a word has for most members of a given linguistic community.* When we speak of **connotation,** we refer to *other, secondary associations a word has for one or more members of that community.* Sometimes the connotations a word has are the same for nearly everyone; sometimes they relate solely to one individual's experience or, more often, to the experience of a particular subgroup.

The connotations of words are often the occasion for disagreement and misunderstanding. Just a few years ago it was common to hear AIDS, or acquired immune deficiency syndrome, referred to even in the media as a "plague" of sorts. In spite of the popularity of this usage, there were many objections. For example, writer Susan Sontag (1989) argued that the word "plague" was not only inappropriate but had many moralistic connotations—historically, plague has often been associated with a punishment for sin.

Changing social mores have also demanded many changes in how we use language. The word "gay," traditionally a synonym for "happy" or "cheerful," is increasingly used as a synonym for "homosexual." For example, "gay rights" is a familiar term not only in popular conversation but in the media as well. In fact, "homosexual" has become one of the denotations of the word "gay." Similarly, when we say that two people "live together" the connotation is often—though not always—that they have a sexual relationship. One has to interpret from context.

Words used to identify different ethnic or racial groups have often been a source of heated controversy. Living in a nation long known as "the melting pot," what do we call ourselves? In *Latinos* (1992), a book about the culture and experiences of the Spanish-speaking peoples of America, Earl Shorris (1992) writes of how the desire for assimilation influenced the designations by which people wanted to be identified:

> When the theory of the melting pot still operated in the United States, artists said, in a flat-footed way, I am an American writer or painter or composer. They did not want to be Italian-American or Irish-American or Jewish-American, for the hyphen, that lonely segment of the great line of human society, separated them from the rest of the Americans; it cast them back into the inhospitable world from which they had so recently escaped. (Shorris, 1992, p. 381)

He adds:

> For one group of American artists, however, the hyphen had a different meaning; Latinos could not abandon the old country or its culture, for they were too close to home. (p. 382)

In the 1990 Census, over 22 million people living in the United States indicated that they were of "Spanish/Hispanic Origin"—the term used by the Census Bureau—yet many reject "Hispanic." Some say "Hispanic" is a term associated with colonization; others that it carries the connotation of "social striving, a desire to be accepted at any cost, even by using an 'English' word" (Gonzalez, 1992). Many younger people prefer "Latino," a word they feel connotes respect. And there seems to be a growing preference to reject those labels, and their stereotypes, entirely: According to a recent nationwide survey, "Most Hispanics/Latinos prefer to identify themselves as Puerto Rican, Colombian, Dominican or just plain American." (We should add that in textbooks such as this, the decision to use one term, "Hispanics," for example, is based on the need to describe research findings in the words used by the researchers cited.)

Negative-Positive Connotation

Because words can elicit such powerful emotional reactions, they are often said to have negative or positive connotations for people. Today many people prefer to be called "senior citizens" rather than "elderly." And though parents may take equal pleasure in hearing their children referred to as "brilliant" or "gifted," those with "retarded" children are sensitive to the many negative connotations of the word. Increasing efforts to avoid the stigma such a word seems to carry have resulted in terms with more positive associations—"slow learners" is an example as is "special education" students. The connotation

The word "pornography" evokes strong emotions—what about the term "adult store"?

of "special" has also changed with the use of such terms as "Special Olympics."

In research on word connotations, subjects were exposed to various words on a tachistoscope, and their galvanic skin responses were measured. Although there were nonsignificant differences between responses to "good" words ("beauty," "love," "kiss," and "friend," for example) and "aversive" words ("cancer," "hate," "liar," and "death," for example), some words caused significant reactions in both men and women. These were called "personal" words and included the subject's first name, last name, father's first name, mother's first name, major in school, year in school, and school name. Subjects were more physiologically aroused by the personal words than by either the good or the aversive words (Crane et al., 1970). [For a discussion of "What Makes Bad Language Bad," see Davis (1989).]

The Semantic Differential

Some of the most influential research on the measurement of meaning has been conducted by Osgood and his associates (1957), who developed an instrument called the **Semantic Differential.** With the Semantic Differential, a researcher can *test a person's reactions to any concept or term*—sex, hard rock, mother, political correctness, apartheid, ego, cigarettes, Madonna, capital punishment—and then compare them with those of other people.

The test itself is a seven-interval scale with limits defined by sets of bipolar adjectives. "The words used to anchor the scales," explains Griffin (1991), "are concerned with feelings (connotation) rather than a description (denotation)" (p. 32). Figure 3.1, for example, is a Semantic Differential for the word "commitment." The subject rates the concept by checking the interval between each pair of adjectives that best describes it. The researcher then draws a line connecting each point made by the subject, thus creating a profile of the subject's concept of commitment.

Statistical analysis of the work of Osgood and his associates suggests that our judgments have three major dimensions: evaluation, potency, and activity. Thus we say that commitment is good or bad and cruel or kind (evaluation), that it is powerful or weak and hot or cold (potency), and fast or slow and active or passive (activity).

Culture and Connotation

The subjects of Osgood's early research were Americans, but he was intrigued by the possibility of cross-cultural studies and went on to explore the dimensions of affective meaning in twenty-six different language communities (Osgood, 1974a; 1974b). According to Osgood, the major dimensions of affective meaning in all these cultures were the same: evaluation, potency, and activity.

From his cross-cultural research Osgood has compiled the *Atlas of Affective Meanings*. The 620 concepts in this atlas run the gamut from "accepting things as they are," "accident," "marriage," and "masculinity," to "master,"

FIGURE 3.1

Commitment

Sharp	_____ : _____ : _____ : _____ : _____ : _____ : _____	Dull
Courageous	_____ : _____ : _____ : _____ : _____ : _____ : _____	Cowardly
Dirty	_____ : _____ : _____ : _____ : _____ : _____ : _____	Clean
Hot	_____ : _____ : _____ : _____ : _____ : _____ : _____	Cold
Good	_____ : _____ : _____ : _____ : _____ : _____ : _____	Bad
Fair	_____ : _____ : _____ : _____ : _____ : _____ : _____	Unfair
Powerful	_____ : _____ : _____ : _____ : _____ : _____ : _____	Weak
Deceitful	_____ : _____ : _____ : _____ : _____ : _____ : _____	Honest
Fast	_____ : _____ : _____ : _____ : _____ : _____ : _____	Slow
Cruel	_____ : _____ : _____ : _____ : _____ : _____ : _____	Kind
Active	_____ : _____ : _____ : _____ : _____ : _____ : _____	Passive

"yesterday," "youth," and "zero." Although Osgood found certain definite cultural variations, many concepts were evaluated similarly by members of a great many different cultures. One such concept was "the days of the week." Monday was generally evaluated as the worst day in the week; things tended to improve after that, gathering momentum on Friday and reaching a peak on Sunday, the best day. For Iranians, on the other hand, the worst day was Saturday (comparable to our Monday), and Friday (the Moslem holy day) was the best (Osgood, 1974b, p. 83).

The great appeal of the Semantic Differential is its flexibility. The procedure is so general that it can be precisely tailored to the needs and interests of the experimenter, who can test the emotional valence of any concept at all.

Griffin (1991) offers this assessment of Osgood's work:

Of course, many anthropologists doubt the validity of Osgood's conclusion that evaluation, potency, and activity are universal dimensions of affect. Anyone who claims they've punched a hole in the language barrier is bound to draw fire. But a decade of rigorous cross-cultural testing with the semantic differential suggests that Osgood has made a quantum leap in understanding the meaning of meaning. (p. 36)

Private and Shared Meanings

In psychology and semantics much research is based on the distinction between denotation and connotation. The Semantic Differential, for example, is said to measure "connotative meaning." But when we examine it closely, the distinction between denotation and connotation seems to break down. All people who speak English are members of the same linguistic community; yet within that community certain groups exist for whom even the primary associations, or denotations, of a given word are different.

Take the case of the Americans and the British. In England you take a "lift," not an "elevator"; if you ask for the "second floor," you get the "third." You take the "underground," not the "subway." You "queue up"; you don't "stand in line." You go to a "chemist's," not a "pharmacy." The list seems virtually endless.

Private Meaning

We can all use language idiosyncratically, assigning meanings to words without agreement and in effect creating our own private language. We can decide, for example, to call trees "reds" or "cows" or "haves." Schizophrenic speech is often private in this way, but schizophrenics are unaware that they sometimes use language in a way that is not shared by others: they use the words they have re-created and expect to be understood. When one young patient was admitted to a hospital, she continually referred to her father, a lawyer by profession, as "the chauffeur." Everyone with whom she spoke found this reference bizarre. Only in treatment was it learned that when she called her father a "chauffeur," she meant that he was completely under her mother's domination.

Shared Meaning

Presumably, if we assign private meanings to words, we are aware that we can use them to communicate with someone only if we let that person know what the referents of these words are. **Shared meaning** requires *some correspondence between the message as perceived by the sender and the receiver.* Two friends, a husband and wife, an entire family, or a group of physicists may decide to use language in a way that makes little sense to others. Among themselves, however, they can communicate with no difficulty.

The same phenomenon occurs among members of many other kinds of groups. Actors understand each other when they talk about scenes being "blocked." Physical therapists refer in their work to "trigger points" and "jelling pain." There is an extensive vocabulary that describes the various moves possible on a skateboard. Skateboard enthusiasts talk about "ollies," "bonelesses," "720s," "thread the needles," and "slob airs." For the subgroup that uses this language, the meaning of "bonelesses" and "thread the needles" is always clear. Group members have no difficulty understanding one another when they use language in this way because they share a code. Communication difficulties emerge only when they expect meaning to be shared by those outside the group. This is a recurring expectation, especially in a country such as the United States, where so many different ethnic groups coexist.

Overlapping Codes and Codeswitching

In intercultural communication, the sender and the receiver often have **overlapping codes,** *"codes which provide an area of commonality but which also contain areas of unshared codification"* (Smith, in Samovar and Porter, 1972, p. 291). Even if the code they use at home is very different, members of minority groups are usually compelled to learn and make some use of the language of the majority because in education, business, and politics this language dominates.

Restricted codes of communication seem to be common among intimate dyads. A study of young lovers (Bell et al., 1987) found the number of personal idioms they used—that is, "words, phrases, or nonverbal signs they had created that had meaning unique to their relationship" (p. 47)—to be highly correlated with love, commitment, and closeness. This proved to be true for both premarital and marital relationships. The couples studied had private idioms, which they used only when they were alone, and public idioms, which they could use when others were present: the private idioms were usually sexual references or euphemisms and sexual invitations (for example, "Let's go home and watch TV."), whereas the public idioms were often nicknames, confrontations, teasing insults, and requests.

Shifts in codes occur in many different communication contexts. An analysis of such American television interviewers as Mike Wallace, Phil Donahue, and Tom Snyder (Scotton, 1988) argues that a pattern of frequent codeswitching within a single conversation can be used by a speaker for the purpose of negotiating power. **Codeswitching** is referred to here as *shifting to different styles* (casual, quasi-literary, and so on) *and introducing shifts in vocabulary or syntax.* There are many contexts in which codeswitching establishes or reinforces intimacy. Novelist Amy Tan (1991), author of *The Joy Luck Club,* writes of speaking to an audience about her life and work when suddenly her talk sounded "wrong." Her language was formal and literary, but her mother, who was born in China, was in the audience and had never heard her speaking this formally. Tan goes on to describe how later, when taking a walk with her mother, she once more became aware of the English she was using:

> We were talking about the price of new and used furniture and I heard myself saying this: "Not waste money that way." My husband was with us as well, and he didn't notice any switch in my English. And then I realized why. It's because over the twenty years we've been together I've often used the same kind of English with him, and sometimes he even uses it with me. It has become our language of intimacy, a different sort of English that relates to family talk, the language I grew up with. (p. 197)

The several "Englishes" used by Tan will also be familiar to children of bilingual families.

MESSAGE ENCODING: A CHILD'S USE
OF LANGUAGE

"You're lying," "I don't think you are telling the truth," "Fibber," "I don't believe you," "You liar"—these are alternate ways of formulating a single message, and there are many others. We use "Fibber" in one context, "You're lying" in another, and "I don't believe you" in a third, and we seem to make these distinctions without effort. Occasionally we wonder how to broach a delicate subject, but most of the time we speak without deliberation. Yet encoding a message is a complex process, however straightforward the message may be. Samovar and Porter (1988) define **encoding** as *"an internal activity in which verbal and nonverbal behaviors are selected and arranged according to the rules of grammar and syntax applicable to the language being used to create a message"* (p. 17). In short, when we encode a message, we must have some awareness of the receiver if we want to be understood. The other half of the process is **decoding**—that is, *"the [receiver's] internal processing of a message and the attribution of meaning to the source's behaviors that represent the source's internal state of being"* (p. 18).

A look at how children use language gives us a better understanding of what takes place in the encoding process. Children astonish adults with their verbal facility. The three-year-old can formulate sentences, repeat all sorts of long words and colloquial expressions, and use several tenses correctly. Some three-year-olds have a vocabulary of nearly 1,000 words. The five-year-old speaks in correct, finished sentences and even uses complex sentences with hypothetical and conditional clauses. At this age the structure and form of language are essentially complete. But what about the encoding abilities of the child?

Egocentric Speech

To study the functions of language in children, the Swiss psychologist Jean Piaget (1962) made exhaustive observations and analyses of the way children speak both when they are alone and when they are in the company of other children. He also devised a series of experiments to determine how objective children try to be in communicating information.

A typical Piaget experiment follows this pattern. A child is shown a diagram of a water tap—sometimes Piaget uses a diagram of a bicycle—and given a precise explanation of how it works. Once it has been established that the child understands the experimenter's explanation, he or she is asked to repeat it (with the aid of the diagram) to another child. Piaget found that though a child fully understood an explanation, he or she was not necessarily successful in communicating it to another child.

Why should this be? It is not that the child lacks the necessary vocabulary. Nor is he or she by any means inarticulate. Piaget's work led him to the conclusion that in the child under age seven or eight, language has two distinct functions and that two kinds of speech exist: egocentric and socialized speech.

As Piaget describes patterns of **egocentric speech** in the child, he gives us a perfect example of a poor encoder, someone whose *speech does not adapt information to the receiver:*

Although he talks almost incessantly to his neighbours, he rarely places himself at their point of view. He speaks to them for the most part as if he were thinking aloud. He speaks, therefore, in a language which . . . above all is always making assertions, even in argument, instead of justifying them. . . . The child hardly ever even asks himself whether he has been understood. For him, that goes without saying, for he does not think about others when he talks.

Piaget believes that until a child is seven or eight, egocentric language constitutes almost half of his or her spontaneous speech, and his book, *The Language and Thought of the Child,* is full of amusing "conversations" between children in which virtually no communication takes place:

L.: "Thunder rolls."

P.: "No, it doesn't roll."

L.: "It's water."

P.: "No, it doesn't roll."

L.: "What is thunder?"

P.: "Thunder is . . ." *(He doesn't go on.)*

In contrast to egocentric speech, **socialized speech** involves *adapting information to the receiver and in some sense adopting his or her point of view;* it involves *social rather than nonsocial encoding.* Piaget goes beyond his findings about language to argue that the adult "thinks socially, even when he is alone, and . . . the child under 7 thinks egocentrically, even in the society of others" (1962).

One team of researchers went on to a further examination of this discrepancy between the communication skills of children and adults. Their strategy was to create a communication problem in the form of a game called "Stack the Blocks." Pairs of children, separated by an opaque screen so that they could not see each other, were given sets of blocks with designs that had **low codability**—that is, they were *difficult to describe.* Describing the design of the block so that the listener could identify it and stack his or her blocks in the same order was the communication problem.

The children's descriptions showed little social encoding. For example, one block was described by different children as "somebody running," "eagle," "throwing sticks," "strip-stripe," and "wire." In the role of speaker, some kindergarteners and first-graders made comments such as "It goes like this," using one finger to trace the design in the air—which of course the listener could not see because he or she was behind a screen (Krauss, in

Walcher, 1971). In general, children tended to use private rather than socially shared images; as a result their messages were often idiosyncratic.

Variations of the Stack the Blocks experiment had been conducted with children of all grade levels as well as with adults. Although nursery-school children seem totally unable to complete this communication task, effectiveness in communication clearly increases with age (as measured by grade level).

According to Piaget's view, then, the speech of children, even at age seven, is of necessity egocentric. Thus they are unable to encode messages effectively for the benefit of others. Their competence in communicating is linked with physical and intellectual development.

Sociocentric Speech

In recent years, most theorists and researchers have come to look upon communication as developing through interaction—that is, as a social phenomenon. Elliott (1984) argues, based on a broad summary of research, that the child is not egocentric but rather **sociocentric**—that is, *centered on social interaction*—from birth. The development of competence in communication is seen as a three-part process: The initial interaction between infant and mother is described as *primordial sharing;* this leads to *proto-conversation,* which ultimately leads to *conversation.*

Primordial sharing refers to *the mother's exchanges with the infant—* through grimaces, glances, vocalizations, and so on—*and, soon after, the infant's responses.* This is a "you and me" stage of communication: Meaning and context are not differentiated; "you" and "me" are, in effect, both the context and the meaning. Exchanges between mother and infant convey mutual attention and recognition. Infant and mother appear to engage in a co-ordinated interaction: mutual attention, responsiveness, turn-taking, and synchrony of signals. If either mother or infant is unresponsive, there is no interaction, no context, no meaning.

Once mother and infant direct attention to some object outside their pair, **proto-conversations** begin. Infants as young as four weeks attend to objects in their environment. In the next few months, the mutual regard of other objects is supplemented by other actions—for example, alternate gazes to object and other, infant babbling, and development of interpretable gestures such as pointing. These proto-conversations can be characterized by "you, me, and it." The extension to objects permits a range of meanings and so, for the first time, meaning may be ambiguous (a child points and the mother interprets the possible object, the reasons for pointing, and so on). By the age of three or four, the child's proto-conversation has become pretty successful for taking communicative action. Proto-conversation is limited, however, by what can be pointed to or indicated.

Conversation, the third phase, begins when the context within which interactive meanings are generated includes references to entities and situations that are not present; these may be imaginary or even unknown. Although meaning is distinguished from context in proto-conversation, the context in conversation is far larger; now meaning and action may be generated within the interaction itself.

The child's development of conversational abilities has been traced by Haslett, who looks at four aspects of the child's "increasing understanding of how conversational exchanges take place" (1984, p. 107). Four areas of competence are developed out of social interaction. First comes the child's understanding of the value of communication. According to Haslett, human beings seem to have an innate grasp of interpersonal interaction; this sense that through communication we establish relationships may correspond to Elliott's notion of being sociocentric. Thus, children are motivated, perhaps innately, to communicate with others. The infant explores communication by interacting with an adult caretaker—in Western cultures, usually the mother.

The second stage is reached when the infant's behavior becomes less idiosyncratic and more conventional—that is, it takes on more of the characteristics of generally agreed-upon communication signals. Now infants communicate intentionally: They check adults for feedback, alter their signals when adult behavior changes, and shorten and ritualize signals so that they become more conventional. The effort, then, is to enter a world of shared meanings. Over time the child progresses from intent-to-act (usually on physical objects) to intent-to-convey (the expression of content). During the course of interaction, the infant's use of words becomes more accountable through the mother's responses—that is, the mother and child negotiate meaning.

The third stage of the child's development concerns understanding the nature of **conversation**. While many of the infant's first communications were monologues, dialogues (conversations) represent *a joint negotiation of meaning between two parties*. Before understanding the nature of conversation, the child must recognize four fundamentals:

1. Conversations have signals that indicate beginnings and endings.

2. Conversations require both speaking and listening.

3. Roles reverse during conversation; you listen sometimes and speak at other times.

4. Participants reverse roles by taking turns. (p. 113)

Thus children learn to appreciate the requirements of human dialogue.

A final step in acquiring conversational competence is learning to develop a conversational style. The particular style a child will adopt depends on his or her interaction with the mother. Mothers *interpret* what their children say and thus help them express intentions in conventional ways. They *model* and thus socialize children into culturally acceptable ways of communicating. They also *extend* what their children say by responding in challenging ways. They *provide opportunities for conversation*, thus helping children gain strategies for the topics and opportunities for interaction given them. And finally, mothers demonstrate *positive attitudes toward communication*. Thus, the caretaker has a critical role in developing the child's conversational abilities (Haslett, 1984, p. 120).

In contrast to Piaget's view, the sociocentric view is that message-encoding skills begin to develop when we are very young children and these skills evolve out of our exchanges with other human beings. So a child learns early on and is learning all the time, given favorable conditions, to participate in that world of shared meanings first introduced by the mother or some other adult care-taker.

As adults, we differ in our sensitivity to conversation. Some of us are particularly savvy, others take conversations pretty much at face value. Qualities of both attention and interpretation would seem to be involved. For example, not everyone you speak with can sense when you are trying to end the conversation. Recently a study (Kellerman et al., 1991) examined strategies people use to retreat when the decision to end conversation is not mutual. The researchers identified excuses, hints ("Well, . . . take care," "I wish I had more time to talk"), and departure announcements ("See you later," "I have to go now") as the most appropriate behaviors; excuses, departure announcements, and rejection as most efficient. Being unresponsive and changing the topic were least efficient. It seems that a person's ability to make it *appear* that the end of a conversation was arrived at mutually is particularly effective and involves skillful message encoding.

Another study of the components of conversational sensitivity finds that people high in sensitivity have a great capacity to remember what is being said, are perceptive in identifying deeper and sometimes multiple meanings, enjoy listening to social exchanges (even if they are not speaking), understand various kinds of power relationships in play, can sense patterns of affinity between people, are at ease with conversational word play, and can come up with extremely effective alternatives during conversation (Daly et al., 1987, p. 171). The researchers also report a correlation between high conversational sensitivity and high ratings for empathy, assertiveness, self-monitoring, and self-esteem.

LANGUAGE AND THOUGHT

In discussing message encoding, we've seen that language and thought are often said to be interrelated. But the nature of their relationship is far from clear. Is language a precondition of human thought? Is thinking simply inner speech? There are no easy answers. Students of communication have been particularly concerned with the question: Does language shape our ideas, or is it merely an instrument of thought?

The Sapir-Whorf Hypothesis

One version of the view that our thought is shaped by the language we speak is the **Sapir-Whorf hypothesis** that *the world is perceived differently by members of different linguistic communities* and that *this perception is transmitted and sustained by language.* Benjamin Lee Whorf (1956), whose work was shaped by that of the great linguist Edwin Sapir, regards language as the primary vehicle of culture. In short, the language we speak influences our experience of the world, while the evolution of language also reflects changes in the predominant modes of expression.

Whorf supports this theory with findings from studies of Native American languages. In English, he points out, we tend to classify words as nouns or verbs; in Hopi the words tend to be classified by duration. For example, in Hopi "lightning," "flame," "wave," and "spark" are verbs, not nouns; they are classified as events of brief duration. In Nootka, which is spoken by the inhabitants of Vancouver Island, categories such as things and events do not exist; thus it is said that "A house occurs" or "It houses."

Is it the case that differences in language reflect differences in perception? An Amazon tribe called the Bororo have several different single words for types of parrots. The Hanunóo of the Philippines have single words for ninety-two different kinds of rice. The Eskimos distinguish at least three kinds of snow in this way. We have only one word for parrot, one for rice, and one for snow. Does this mean that we are incapable of perceiving several types of each? Probably not. Social psychologist Roger Brown (1958, p. 236) suggests that the perceptual categories we use more frequently are merely more "available" to us.

Linguistic distinctions tell us something about priorities within a given culture. Eskimos have several words for snow because they need to make finer verbal distinctions than we do when communicating about it. By and large, we are unaffected by different kinds of snow and therefore expend little effort on making such distinctions. This does not mean that we are incapable of doing so. In fact, members of certain subgroups within our own linguistic community make more verbal distinctions about snow than the rest of us—weather forecasters, bobsled owners, ski resort managers, and so on. We can qualify the Sapir-Whorf hypothesis by saying that as a person learns the language of a given culture or subculture, his or her attention is directed toward aspects of reality or relationships that are important in that context, and this focus affects the category system in the memory.

Language does two important things. First, it serves as an aid to memory. It makes memory more efficient by allowing us to code events as verbal categories. Researchers have shown, for example, that we find it easier to recognize colors of low codability again if we named them for ourselves the first time we saw them (Brown and Lenneberg, 1954). It is now believed that an adult's memory is primarily verbal. And second, language also enables us to abstract indefinitely from our experience, which is especially important in communicating about abstract relationships (something animals are unable to do).

Language Problems

Ideally, language is a valuable instrument of thought; yet we know that language can sometimes interfere with our ability to think critically. Although

Whorf was best known for his writings on linguistics, he was trained as an engineer. When he became an accident investigator, he began to realize that a certain percentage of accidents occurred as a result of what might be called "careless thinking." For example, people would be very careful around barrels labeled "gasoline" but would smoke unconcernedly around barrels labeled "empty gasoline barrel," though the fumes in the empty barrels were more likely to ignite than the actual gasoline (Whorf, 1956, p. 135). There are many ways in which an imprecise use of language interferes with our thought processes. We shall examine several that have a direct influence on our communication.

Abstract Language

When people use **abstract** language, they frequently cause communication difficulties that have to do with the *vagueness* of words. As concepts become more vague, or abstract, it gets harder and harder to decode the intended meaning. S. I. Hayakawa has written several books on semantics, and in one he included the so-called abstraction ladder we see in Figure 3.2.

In general, the more abstract the term, the greater our chances of misunderstanding. Consider this exchange between father and teenage son:

Father: Have a good time, and don't stay out late.

   Son: Thanks, I will. Don't worry. I'll be home early.

The next day they may get into a disagreement because they were not thinking the same things when they used the words "early" and "late." Perhaps the son purposely did not clarify what the father meant by "too late" because he didn't want to be held to a strict time limit. And the father may have been vague intentionally so that his son would have a chance to exercise judgment and learn to become more adult. On the other hand, if the son came home at 4:00 A.M., both father and son would probably agree that he had indeed stayed out "late."

Speaking of being more adult, how old is an adult? Do you become an adult when you are allowed to drive? Is it when you are allowed to drink? Is it when you are allowed to see "adult" movies? Or is it when you become financially independent? In our society, the term "adult" is variously defined, and the age at which such privileges are granted varies.

Often, in an attempt to avoid ambiguity, we use very precise wording to clarify meaning. Legal contracts are such an example. But no amount of care is sufficient to avoid all ambiguity of interpretation. We need only look at the differences in how Supreme Court justices have interpreted the Constitution, or at the different ways in which the Bible has been interpreted, to see the inherent ambiguity in our use of language. Keep in mind the abstraction ladder, however, for some terms are considerably more abstract, and therefore more subject to misinterpretation, than others.

FIGURE 3.2   Abstraction Ladder

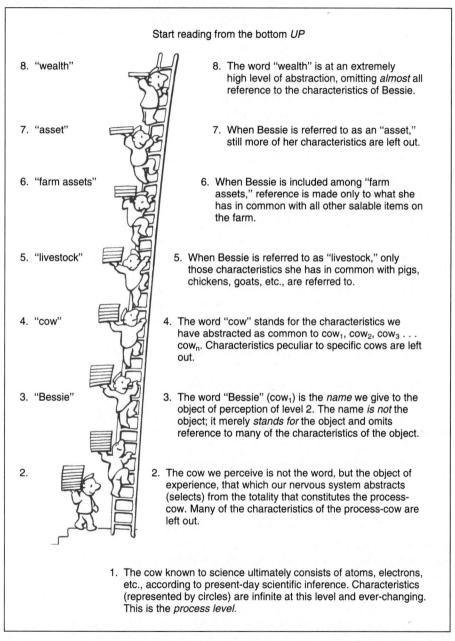

Start reading from the bottom *UP*

8. "wealth"

8. The word "wealth" is at an extremely high level of abstraction, omitting *almost* all reference to the characteristics of Bessie.

7. "asset"

7. When Bessie is referred to as an "asset," still more of her characteristics are left out.

6. "farm assets"

6. When Bessie is included among "farm assets," reference is made only to what she has in common with all other salable items on the farm.

5. "livestock"

5. When Bessie is referred to as "livestock," only those characteristics she has in common with pigs, chickens, goats, etc., are referred to.

4. "cow"

4. The word "cow" stands for the characteristics we have abstracted as common to cow_1, cow_2, cow_3 . . . cow_n. Characteristics peculiar to specific cows are left out.

3. "Bessie"

3. The word "Bessie" (cow_1) is the *name* we give to the object of perception of level 2. The name *is not* the object; it merely *stands for* the object and omits reference to many of the characteristics of the object.

2.

2. The cow we perceive is not the word, but the object of experience, that which our nervous system abstracts (selects) from the totality that constitutes the process-cow. Many of the characteristics of the process-cow are left out.

1. The cow known to science ultimately consists of atoms, electrons, etc., according to present-day scientific inference. Characteristics (represented by circles) are infinite at this level and ever-changing. This is the *process level.*

(*Source:* S. I. Hayakawa, *Language in Thought and Action,* 4th ed., Orlando, FL: Harcourt Brace Jovanovich, 1978.)

Inferences

An **inference** is *a conclusion or judgment derived from evidence or assumptions*. Every day you make dozens of inferences. When you sit down, you infer that the chair will support your weight. When you go through a green light, you infer that the traffic moving at right angles to you will stop at the red light. When you drive down a one-way street, you infer that all the traffic will be going in one direction. You may have good reason to expect these inferences to be correct, but there is also some uncalculated probability that events will not go as you expect. Drivers who have been involved in traffic accidents frequently say that the accident occurred because they inferred that the other party would act in a certain way when in fact he or she did not. Every year we read of people who were accidentally shot with guns they inferred were not loaded.

As students of communication, we are concerned with the inferences implicit in verbal messages. If you say, "It is sunny outside today," your statement can be easily verified. It is a factual statement based on an observed and verifiable event. If you say, "It is sunny outside; therefore, it is sunny fifty miles from here," you draw a conclusion based on more than what you have observed. You have made a statement based in part on an inference.

Consider a more complex situation. Sheila Waring has broken off a substantial part of one of her front teeth. Her dentist takes an x-ray, covers the tooth with a temporary, and gives her an appointment for the following week; she may, he mentions, need root canal work. The next week Sheila returns, and as she walks into the office, the dentist says "I'm sorry, Sheila, You do need root canal work. This calls for a heroic effort." Hearing this, Sheila is terrified and during the next hour sits in the chair awaiting the awful pain that never comes. "There. Finished—" says the dentist, "I've taken out the nerve." "But I didn't feel it at all. I thought you said I would have to be heroic about it." "No. I said 'a heroic effort,' " answers the dentist. "I didn't say *your* effort."

We make inferences in every imaginable context, and it is neither possible nor desirable to avoid them entirely. Nevertheless, to use language more precisely and to be more discerning when we hear others speak, we should learn to distinguish between factual and inferential statements. "You spend a great deal of time with my roommate" is a statement of fact. It involves a low level of uncertainty, it is made as a result of direct observation, and it can be verified. Add to it "I'm sure he won't mind if you borrow his coat," and you have an inferential statement that may well jeopardize a friendship. In becoming more conscious of inference making, we can at least learn to calculate the risks involved.

To compound the problem, our language is structured so that no distinction is made between facts and inferences. It is the verb "to be" that creates the difficulty: there is no grammatical distinction made between a fact verified through sense data (for example, "she is wearing a red coat") and a statement that cannot be verified through sense data and is merely an inference (for example, "She is thinking about her upcoming date this weekend").

FIGURE 3.3

SCALE OF DICHOTOMIES

Success	____	____	__X__	____	____	____	____	Failure
Brilliant	____	____	____	__X__	____	____	____	Stupid
Handsome	____	____	__X__	____	____	____	____	Ugly
Winner	____	____	____	__X__	____	____	____	Loser
Honest	____	____	____	__X__	____	____	____	Dishonest
Black	____	__X__	____	____	____	____	____	White

Dichotomies

Dichotomies, or *polar words,* are frequently responsible for another type of language problem. Some semanticists classify English as a "two-valued" rather than a "multivalued language." By this they mean that English has an excess of polar words and a relative scarcity of words to describe the wide middle ground between these opposites. Obviously, every person, entity, or event can be described in terms of a whole array of adjectives ranging from very favorable to very unfavorable. (Recall the Semantic Differential, discussed earlier in this chapter, which uses a seven-interval scale.) Yet we tend to say that a student is a "success" or a "failure," that a child is "good" or "bad," that a woman is "attractive" or "unattractive." Try, for example, to think of some words to describe the spots marked on the continua in the scale of dichotomies in Figure 3.3. As you search for words, you begin to see that there are a lot of distinctions for which we lack single words. The continua also illustrate how our language suggests that certain categories of experience are mutually exclusive, when in truth they are not.

Consider the first set of terms, "success" and "failure." Every human being undoubtedly meets with some success and some failure during the course of a lifetime. An insurance broker unemployed for many months and unable to find work may also be a supportive and much-loved father and husband. Yet our language suggests that he be classified as either a success or a failure. Similar difficulties crop up if we are asked to apply such adjectives as "brilliant" and "stupid" or "winner" and "loser" to other people. Is the math major with a straight A average brilliant or stupid if she can't learn to drive a car or ride a bike? If the author of a recent best-seller is divorced for the third time, is he a winner or a loser?

When polar terms are used in a misleading way, they suggest false dichotomies, reducing experience in a way that it need not be reduced. Differences are emphasized and similarities are overlooked, and in the process a great deal of information is lost. This is certainly true in our country at election time.

One way to avoid making false dichotomies, as Haney (1973, p. 374) has pointed out, is to make use of the questions "How much?" and "To what extent?":

How much of a success am I?

How much of a change is this from his former stand on gun control?

To what extent is he honest?

To what extent is her plan practical?

With the aid of such questions, perhaps we can keep in mind that we have many options, that we need not cast our messages in black-and-white terms, and that we need not accept these either-or distinctions when they are made by others.

Euphemisms

Through **euphemisms** we *substitute mild, vague, or less emotionally charged terms for more blunt ones*—"campaign of disinformation" for "smear campaign," "security review procedure" for "censorship," "discomfort" for "pain," "memory garden" for "cemetery," "powder room" for "bathroom," "attack" for "rape." "Portly," "stout," and "heavy-set" are ways to avoid saying "fat." Of course, they also lack the specificity of "fat" as well as the affect attached to the word. If we hear that a woman was "attacked," we don't know if she was assaulted or raped. Often the problem created by using euphemisms is that the intent may be conveyed but not the degree to which the intent is felt. So-called empty words are euphemisms because they are pleasant sounding yet indirect enough to avoid being blunt: "nice," "wonderful," and "pleasant" appear to be all-purpose euphemisms. They make for dull conversations. And on many occasions, euphemistic language is used to misrepresent what is being said. For example, one high school counselor revealed several phrases he used in writing student recommendations for college applications: describing a student with serious emotional problems as "having peaks and valleys"; saying a student "likes to take risks" when referring to a drug problem; characterizing an arrogant student as "pushing against the limits" (Carmody, 1989, B6).

In a study of encoding, Motley gives these examples of intentional ambiguity and euphemism:

[Thinking] *The (roommate's) manuscript is nonsensical.*
[Saying] *It's different.*

[Thinking] *The child is a brat.*
[Saying] *That's quite a kid.*
(Adapted from Motley, 1992, p. 309)

Equivocal Language

Misunderstandings often occur because people assume that a word, a phrase, or even a sentence is unequivocal—that is, it has only one meaning. Hayakawa refers to this as "the 'one word, one meaning' fallacy" (1978). But much of the language we use is **equivocal;** it has *two or more possible interpretations.*

We've seen the problems created by disagreements over the referents of such words as "peace," "truth," and "freedom." Misunderstandings are also quite common when the words and phrases in question sound far more concrete. If your date says "Let's get a drink after the show," the drink may refer to an alcoholic beverage, continuing the evening in a club, or simply a desire to stay together for simple conversation.

Newspaper columnist William Safire recalls receiving an invitation to the opera. "The time, date, and place were briskly and neatly laid out, and then, in the corner, a mysterious instruction about dress: '*Not Black Tie.*' What is that supposed to mean?":

> Profound motives aside, does *not black tie* mean business suit, which is what it says on the Turkish Embassy's invitation to a reception? Taking it a step further . . . does that mean today's American Uniform (blue blazer, beige pants) is out? Does *not black tie* mean "any old tie" or "no tie at all"? (1990, p. 84)

There seem to be two sources of confusion about words or phrases. First, people may assume that because they are using the same word, they agree, when in fact each interprets the word differently. In a comical incident a woman asks a pharmacist for a refill of her prescription for "the pill." "Please hurry," she adds, "I've got someone waiting in the car." Much humor is based on such double meanings. In daily communication this type of confusion may not be so funny. For example, one of the authors and spouse—and we're not saying which one—were drawn into a needless argument:

Husband: You know, the travel literature on Switzerland that I borrowed is still in the house. Since we're not going, I'd better return it to that fellow in my office. Could you get it together for me so I can take it in tomorrow?

Wife: I don't know where it is.

Husband: What kind of answer is that? If it's too much trouble, forget it.

Wife: What do you mean, "What kind of answer is that?" How can I do anything with it if I can't find it?

Husband: There's nothing to *do.* All I asked you to do was find it. You don't have to give me a smart answer.

Wife: But you said "get it together." I thought you meant put it in some sort of order.

Husband: I meant "find it." Don't you know what "get it together" means?

Wife: Well, I didn't know it meant *that.*

Husband: If you didn't know, why didn't you ask me?

Wife: Because I thought I knew. I speak English, too, you know.

For a time this misunderstanding created a lot of ill feeling. Both husband and wife were insulted—the husband because he felt his wife had refused to do something relatively simple for him, and the wife because she felt her husband had insulted her intelligence.

A second type of misunderstanding occurs when two people assume that they disagree because they are using different words when actually they may agree on the concept or entity represented by those words. That is, they use different terms that have the same referent. For example, a school psychologist and a guidance counselor were discussing a student who was failing several of her classes though she was of above-average intelligence. A disagreement developed when the counselor insisted that the girl definitely needed "help." "She certainly does not," countered the psychologist. "She needs psychological intervention." "That's what I'm saying," said the counselor. "She should be getting psychological counseling." "Well, then we agree," answered the psychologist. "When you said 'help,' I thought you were talking about tutoring." The psychologist and counselor were able to resolve their apparent differences because they did stop and redefine their terms.

Although our attention has been given to words or phrases, most messages take the form of sentences. "It's a rainy day," remarks Jack to Jill. What could be clearer than the meaning of that sentence? Yet Laing (1972) suggests five ways in which Jack might intend his statement. Perhaps he wishes to register the fact that it is a rainy day. If yesterday Jack and Jill agreed to go for a walk instead of going to a movie, he might be saying that because of the rain he will probably get to see the movie. He might be implying that because of the weather Jill should stay at home. If yesterday the two argued about what the weather would be like, he might mean that Jill is right again or that he is the one who always predicts the weather correctly. If the window is open, he might be saying that he would like Jill to close it. No doubt each of us could come up with several other interpretations. The point is that any message derives a great part of its meaning from the context in which it is transmitted. Our knowledge of the speaker and the speaker's use of language, our own associations with the words he or she chooses, our previous relationship, and the messages we have already exchanged should all play a part in how we interpret what is said.

Culture As Our Frame of Reference

Although all our behaviors have possible meaning for a receiver, language is by far our most explicit form of communication. In using it, our desire is to facilitate thought, not to obscure it. Language is potentially the most precise vehicle we have for human communication. Even if we grant the infinite richness of language and the precision it is capable of expressing, however, a look at intercultural communication makes clear that often people are divided not because of a failure to understand grammar or vocabulary but to understand rhetoric or point of view.

Kenneth Kaunda, the former president of Zambia, insists that Westerners and Africans have very different ways of seeing things, solving problems, and thinking in general. He characterizes the Westerner as having a "problem-solving mind." Once a Westerner perceives a problem, he or she feels compelled to solve it. Unable to live with contradictory ideas, the Westerner excludes all solutions that have no logical basis. Supernatural and nonrational phenomena are regarded as superstition. The African, on the other hand, allows himself or herself to experience all phenomena, nonrational as well as rational. The African has a "situation-experiencing mind." Kaunda believes that "the African can hold contradictory ideas in fruitful tension within his mind without any sense of incongruity, and he will act on the basis of the one which seems most appropriate to the particular situation" (Legum, 1976, pp. 63–64).

In ancient India, according to Kirkwood (1989) and other students of Indian rhetoric, truthfulness was considered the prime standard for speech. Emphasis was placed not only on the value of truthful speech to listeners but on the profound effects for the speaker as well. The practice of speaking truthfully was regarded as spiritually liberating, and the performance itself—the act of speaking the truth—brought with it self-knowledge as well as freedom, thus transforming the speaker. Such ideas date back to the tenth century B.C. and are an enduring aspect of India's culture.

On the other hand, a study of Chinese and Japanese attitudes toward speech communication in public settings offers several reasons for the lack of argumentation and debate in the Far East (Becker, 1991). According to Becker, social history contributed to an aversion to public debate. For example, in the Chinese and Japanese traditions, "taking opposite sides of an argument necessarily meant becoming a personal rival and antagonist of the one who held the other side. The more important concomitant of this idea was that if one did not wish to become a lifelong opponent of someone else, he would not venture an opinion contrary to the other person's opinions in public. Even the legal system was set up in such a way that it avoided direct confrontations" (p. 236).

In addition, various linguistic features of Chinese and Japanese (for example, Chinese lacks plurals and tenses) as well as great differences between Western and Eastern philosophy and religion all presented powerful barriers to the widespread use of debate and argumentation for considering new proposals or strategies for implementing social and political change (p. 242). Becker emphasizes that the Westerner's ideal speech situation requiring "equality of participants, freedom from social coercion, suspension of privilege, and free expression of feeling . . . [would be] both impractical and even theoretically inconceivable to traditionally educated Chinese and Japanese" (p. 242).

In looking at different cultural frames of reference, we seem to have come full circle, recalling elements of the Sapir-Whorf hypothesis. To some degree, linguistic traditions help shape our thought processes, but for members of different cultures, traditions can be a barrier.

We've considered several language-related problems that interfere with your ability to think and communicate clearly. Of course, there are numerous others. But just being aware of the *possibility* that language can be a source of misunderstanding should enable you to be more perceptive about verbal messages.

WORDS IN ACTION

In this final section of our chapter, we will examine some ways in which words influence human actions, both directly and indirectly. In ancient times, people of many diverse cultures believed that words had magical powers. For example, in ancient Egypt a man received two names: his true name, which he concealed, and his good name, by which he was known publicly. Even today many primitive societies regard words as magical. Members of some cultures go to great lengths to conceal their personal names. They avoid saying the names of their gods. The names of their dead are never uttered. Presumably, we moderns are far more sophisticated. Yet we have our own verbal taboos. And the euphemisms we've just talked about are part of our everyday vocabulary. Thus we often hear not that someone "died" but that he or she "passed away." And, a sudden drop in the stock market is often termed a "correction."

Some empirical studies of word power examine the ways in which a speaker's use of profane words affects our judgment of his or her credibility. (See Chapter 10 for a discussion of credibility.) Three classes of profanity were used: religious, excretory, and sexual. Although religious profanity was less offensive when circumstances appeared to justify it, sexual profanity—whether provoked or unprovoked—always seemed to bring the speakers significantly lower credibility ratings. These results are surprisingly consistent: They are the same for males and females, older and younger women, and freshmen and graduate students (Rossiter and Bostrom, 1968; Bostram et al., 1973; Mabry, 1975).

Writers on public communication traditionally refer to the effective use of language as "eloquence." In public speaking, eloquence describes a more dramatic, stirring use of language—often for the purpose of inspiring or persuading others. For example, recently Rev. James Forbes of Manhattan, a "preacher's preacher" who is known for his eloquence, spoke before a group of ministers on the need for compassion in preaching about AIDS. "In an existential sense," he said, "we all have AIDS, and the question is how *we* want to be treated as dying men and women" (Goldman, 1989, B3). One thinks also of the famous speech of Dr. Martin Luther King, Jr., "I Have a Dream," through which thousands were inspired to work for equal rights:

I have a dream that one day, even the state of Mississippi, a state swel-tering with the heat of injustice, sweltering with the heat of oppression, will be transformed into an oasis of freedom and justice. . . .

With this faith we will be able to hew out of the mountain of despair a stone of hope. With this faith we will be able to transform the jangling discords of our nation into a beautiful symphony of brotherhood.

With these words, Dr. King was able to move people's feelings more power-fully than he could have with more commonplace language. Lamenting the "eloquence gap" in contemporary politics, poet Michael Blumenthal ex-pressed his sense that "a nation that no longer expects and demands eloquence and statesmanship from its politicians no longer expects and demands gran-deur from itself—or precision of belief from those who lead it" (1988, p. 18).

Sometimes our decisions are based in part on how a thing is labeled. For example, certain words clearly have greater prestige than others. A "classic car" is better than an old one. "Vintage clothing" is more appealing than old secondhand clothing. The same desk commands different prices when it is called "used," "secondhand," or "antique." "Doctor" is another powerful word. In many situations, for example, it is undeniable that "Dr." Bradley will get more attention than "Ms." Bradley or "Mr." Bradley.

Sexist Language

Since the late 1960s many students of language, a good many feminists among them, have argued that our language is sexist, that it reflects a bias affecting how women are perceived and treated by others and sometimes how they regard themselves. For example, words associated with the descriptions of males often have positive connotations—"confident," "forceful," "strong," and the like—whereas females are more often described as "fickle," "frivo-lous," "timid," and so forth (Heilbrun, 1976).

In studies at three different universities, Pearson and her associates (1991) found that when students were asked to list all the terms for men and women, the list of words for women was longer and generally much less favorable than the one for men. (See Table 3.1.) It's the group in power, she points out, that "typically does the naming or labeling. In our culture men tend to name people, places, and things."

Of the differences in the labeling of men and women, she notes, "names for women are sometimes created by adding another word or a feminine marker to a name for men" (thus, "waitress," "actress," and so on). In ad-dition, terms for women tend to be more frequently sexual, often with con-notations that the women are the objects of sexual conquest.

New York Times columnist Anna Quindlen (1992) comments on another label:

At the time of Anita Hill's testimony, a waitress told me of complaining to the manager of the coffee shop in which she worked about his smutty

TABLE 3.1

Terms for Women and Men

Women			Men	
Chick	Wife	Honey	Gent	Boy
Girl	Old maid	Madam	Man	Stud
Old lady	Bitch	Whore	Guy	Hunk
Piece	Lady	Dog	Male	Bastard
Female	Broad	Cow	Husband	
Prostitute	Woman	Old biddy		

Source: From Judy Cornelia Pearson, *Gender and Communication* (Dubuque, IA: Wm. C. Brown, 1985), Table 3.2, p. 83.

comments and intimate pats. He replied, "You're a skirt." Then he told her that if she didn't like it, there were plenty of other skirts out there who would take the job—and the abuse. (p. 19)

The metaphors used for men and women also differ. Metaphors involving food are often used when referring to women—"tomato," "cookie," "sugar," "piece of cake," and so on. Sometimes animal names are used in referring to women, but these tend to be the names of baby animals ("chick" or "kitty," for example)—names which connote weakness or vulnerability. If men are linked with animals, it's with the names of far more powerful animals ("wolf" is an example). Pearson points out that the terms for men and women are often polar opposites, with the male term being positive, the female term negative—"bachelor" and "old maid" are a case in point.

Women tend to be referred to by euphemisms far more frequently than men are. And although men are not often called "gentlemen" or "boys," "ladies" and "girls" are terms still frequently heard by women as forms of address. Women use them too—hence such comments as "I'm going out for lunch with the girls."

A more subtle but extremely influential form of sexist language is the high frequency of familiar—or overly familiar—terms applied to women, terms which reflect lower social status. Although men are more frequently addressed formally ("Sir," "Mister," and so on), it is quite common for women to be called by their first names, or even to hear themselves called "honey," "hon," "baby," "sweetie," "dear," or the like—and sometimes by people they've never met before (Pearson et al., 1991, p. 100).

Despite many reforms, by far the most blatant example of sexist language is still the use of "man" as the generic term for "people" or "humanity," and along with this goes the frequent use of the personal pronoun "his"—especially in expository writing—as though women were pretty much an afterthought. In the last decade the use of such variants as "his or her," "he/she," "his/her," and "he or she" became more widespread. One critic writing on gender formulates the problem this way:

The abstract form, the general, the universal, this is what the so-called masculine gender means, for the class of men have appropriated the universal for themselves. One must understand that men are not born with a faculty for the universal and that women are not reduced at birth to the particular. The universe has been, and is, continually, at every moment, appropriated by men. (Wittig, 1986, p. 66)

The implication that men are the more important members of the human race can be changed in many ways. For example, "manhood" may be replaced by the term "adulthood," "firemen" by "firefighters," and so on. The use of such words as "chairperson," "business person," and "he/she"—for all their attendant awkwardness—attempts to address this problem.

The insistence of many groups on such changes is legitimate because, as we have tried to indicate, words shape perceptions and self-concepts. Linguistic changes evolve slowly, but they are taking place.

Male and Female Language Usage

Are there true differences between the way males and females use language? Most research supports the stereotypic view that in contrast to males, females are more submissive, affected by social pressure, and responsive to

How would you characterize individual communication styles at this business conference?

the needs of others. It has been found that although women seem to respond more to the remarks of other people, work harder at maintaining conversations, and give more "positive minimal responses," it is men who generally initiate as well as receive more interaction. Men also interrupt others more and ignore the remarks of others more frequently than women do. Such differences are often explained in terms of the greater social power men enjoy in most communication contexts (Haslett, 1987, p. 216).

Language differences that give rise to these perceptions have been described in this way: Females use more words, more intensifiers, questions, including tag questions ("That's great, isn't it?"), and affect words (that is, words implying emotion) than males use (Berryman and Wilcox, 1980). Male speech, on the other hand, shows more instances of incorrect grammar, obscenities, and slang (Liska et al., 1981). Apparently males and females both *expect* males to use more verbally aggressive strategies and females to use strategies that are more social and less verbally aggressive (Burgoon et al., 1983).

There are contrary findings worth noting, however. According to a study of college students, males and females differ little in the amount or quality of their talk about emotions, but males use more affect words when talking to females than to males; female speech does not vary this way (Shimanoff, 1983). A second study found that males and females used the same number of qualifiers ("maybe," "sort of," and the like) when talking to males, but males, when talking to females, decreased the number of qualifiers (Martin and Craig, 1983). Although language differences between men and women exist, such usage seems to be context-bound. As research in this area continues, it is likely that more and more conclusions will be qualified.

In *You Just Don't Understand,* a popular book that became a national best-seller, sociolinguist Deborah Tannen proposes that communication difficulties between men and women often originate in gender differences in conversational style.

She makes the distinction between "report talk" and "rapport talk." Tannen argues that most men use conversation primarily as a language of **"report,"** that is, "as a means to preserve independence and negotiate and maintain status in a hierarchical social order" (1990, p. 77). This conversational style emphasizes demonstrating knowledge and skill and in general having the right information. "From childhood," writes Tannen, "men learn to use talking as a way to get and keep attention" (p. 77). Thus in the world of many men, "conversations are negotiations in which people try to achieve the upper hand if they can, and protect themselves from others' attempts to push them down and push them around" (p. 24).

To most women conversation is, for the most part, "a language of **rapport,"** with which they have learned since childhood to establish connections and negotiate relationships, often for greater closeness. What women emphasize in their talk are their similarities with other people and their comparable experiences ("I'm just like that," "The same thing happened to me . . ."). Women also have interests in achievement or status goals, says Tannen, but they tend to go after them "in the guise of connection." Similarly,

Men are also concerned with achieving involvement and avoiding isolation, but they are not *focused* on these goals, and they tend to pursue them in the guise of opposition. (p. 25)

According to Tannen, it's these differences in style that account for so many misunderstandings. She gives a striking example:

Though both women and men complain of being interrupted by each other, the behaviors they are complaining about are different.

In many of the comments I heard from people I interviewed, men felt interrupted by women who overlapped with words of agreement and support and anticipation of how their sentences and thoughts would end. If a woman supported a man's story by elaborating on a point different from the one he had intended, he felt his right to tell his own story had been violated. (p. 210)

Feminist critic Deborah Cameron identifies two current approaches to the language styles of men and women. She contrasts theories of **difference**, such as Tannen's, with theories of **dominance**. In theories of dominance, "Women's style is seen as the outcome of power struggles and negotiations . . . played out under the surface of conversation" (1990, p. 25). This, for example, is how a theory of dominance would interpret research findings about questions:

Women ask more questions than men . . . not because insecurity is part of [their] psychology and therefore of [their] speech style . . . but because men in a dominant position often refuse to take responsibility for the smooth conduct of interpersonal relations. . . . Asking them a question is thus an effective strategy for forcing them to acknowledge and contribute to the talk. It can be argued that features like question-asking are not deferential at all. . . . (p. 25)

Theories such as these are a source of spirited debate and will be most valuable if they generate further research in language studies.

Powerful and Powerless Language

As we speak, many of us use tag questions—for example, "Let's go to the movies, okay?"—in making simple statements. We also use hedges—"kinda" and "I think"—or disclaimers such as "I probably shouldn't say this" and "I'm not really sure." In examining seven message types of differing **power**, Bradac and Mulac (1984) found that the language forms just described as well as hesitations such as "uh" and "well . . ." are perceived by other people as forms of powerless and ineffective speech; on the other hand, speech free of such usage is considered both powerful and effective.

A more recent study explored the relationship between language style and gender stereotypes (Quina et al., 1987). Researchers found that individuals using a so-called feminine style of speech characterized by politeness, exaggeration, hedging, and illogical sequence—one that was generally nonassertive—were perceived as having greater social warmth but less competence than those having a "masculine" style. The authors remind us that "a polite, warm linguistic style is not consistent with the popular image of American corporate success or achievement" (p. 118). Nonetheless, qualities associated with a feminine style included sensitivity, friendliness, and sincerity.

In general, communicators who use a powerful style are considered more competent and attractive. Legal situations are different, however; plaintiffs and defendants using a more powerful style are also considered more blameworthy, perhaps because they seem "in control" of themselves. Less powerful speakers are more often seen as victims (Bradac et al., 1981).

But it is not always the language itself that reveals who is powerful: the information provided by context as well as the personalities of those involved must also be considered. For example, the boss who asks the secretary to type something, by using several powerless forms such as hesitations, hedges, and tag questions, may appear polite and social—not powerless—even though he or she makes the request sound less like a demand (Bradac, 1983).

Metacommunication

In addition to trying to use a more powerful language, there's another very important way to increase the effectiveness of verbal messages. With practice, you can use language to change your relationship to others through **metacommunication**—that is, *communicating about communication*. This is a concept closely linked to the relationship level of human encounters. For example, if you say to your mother, "Tell him to mind his own damned business," and she replies, "I wish you wouldn't swear so much. You do it more and more, and I don't like it," she is responding not to the content of your remark but to your method of getting your point across. The content of her communication is communication itself.

Any comment directed at the way in which a person communicates is an example of metacommunication. For years the procedure in public speaking classes has been for students to give practice speeches and then have the instructor and class members give their reactions to the speaker and the speech. Such comments as "I thought you had excellent examples," "You could have brought out your central idea more explicitly," and "Try to be a little more enthusiastic" are all instances of metacommunicating.

Writing about families, Galvin and Brommel (1991) observe:

Metacommunication occurs when people communicate about their communication, when they give verbal and nonverbal instructions about how their messages should be understood. Such remarks as "I was only kidding," "This is important," or "Talking about this makes me uncomfortable" are signals to another on how to interpret certain comments, as are facial expressions, gestures, or vocal tones." (p. 18)

Metacommunication is not always explicit, even when it is verbal. Sometimes conversations that begin at the content level become forms of metacommunication. We can best illustrate with an anecdote. Craig and Jeanne, dressed for a night on the town, have just stepped out of a cab. As they stand at the corner waiting for the light to change, they rapidly become involved in a heated argument:

Jeanne: Next time try to pick me up earlier so we can be on time.

Craig: It's only a party. Next time tell me beforehand if you think it's so important to be there at eight sharp. And don't sound so annoyed.

Jeanne: But you're always late.

Craig: I'm not *always* late. Don't generalize like that.

Jeanne: Well, you're late a lot of the time. Why do you always put me down when I say something about you?

Craig: I don't "always" put you down. There you go again, generalizing.

Although they may well remember it simply as a quarrel about lateness, Craig and Jeanne are arguing about how they communicate with each other. He tells her not to sound so annoyed, he informs her that she makes too many generalizations, she counters that he puts her down, and so on. In effect, they are arguing about their relationship.

As we will see in Chapter 6, when there are serious conflicts about relationships rather than content, metacommunication is often especially difficult (Sillars and Weisberg, 1987). Two people may lack the skill to use metacommunication; and the source of the conflict may be "diffuse and selectively perceived. Attempts to communicate are therefore frustrated by a failure to agree on the definition of the conflict and by an ability to metacommunicate" (p. 151).

In a more supportive situation, the use of metacommunication might help people become aware of ways in which their communication practices are ineffective. For example, one teenage girl finally confided to her mother that she was embarrassed when the mother tried to sound "hip" in front of the daughter's teenage friends. It is sometimes awkward to provide such feedback. When given in a kind rather than a hostile way, however, it can be a valuable impetus to self-improvement.

SUMMARY

Our analysis of verbal communication began with a consideration of the concept of meaning. In discussing the symbolic nature of language, we saw that symbols and referents are associated with each other only by convention and that it is human beings who assign meanings to words. We reviewed the traditional distinction between denotation and connotation and went on to suggest that it might be more useful to distinguish between private and shared meanings. In this connection we discussed overlapping linguistic codes and codeswitching.

Our second subject was message encoding, which we approached through a comparison of the encoding abilities of children and adults. Piaget's research on socialized and egocentric speech made it clear that the message sender's perceptions and expectations about the receiver affect his or her ability to communicate accurately. While Piaget viewed the child's speech as predominantly egocentric, most theorists and researchers have come to view the child as sociocentric from birth with competence in communication developing through interaction that begins in infancy. In this alternate view, the adult caretaker (the mother, in most Western cultures) plays a critical role in developing the child's conversational abilities.

Our next concern was the relationship between thought and language, and after examining the Sapir-Whorf hypothesis, we considered several language problems created through abstracting, inferences, dichotomies, euphemisms, and equivocal meanings. We went on to observe that when people of different cultures communicate, they may be separated not so much by grammar or vocabulary as by frame of reference.

To study words in action, we examined sexist language, differences between males and females in their use of language (these seem to be context-bound), and the language forms perceived by others as powerful or powerless. In closing, we saw that metacommunication (communication *about* communication) is potentially a means of improving one's relationships.

REVIEW QUESTIONS

1. What is intended by the statement "The word is not the thing"?

2. What is the difference between denotation and connotation?

3. What is the Semantic Differential? Give an example of a differential.

4. Explain the difference between private and shared meanings.

5. What are the concepts of overlapping codes and codeswitching?

6. Explain Piaget's theory about how the child uses language.

7. Discuss the current view that the child is sociocentric from birth and that communication develops out of interaction.

8. What is the Sapir-Whorf hypothesis?

9. Discuss two ways in which language affects thought.

10. Describe the concept of abstracting and give examples.

11. Describe at least four problem areas in our use of language. Give an example of each.

12. What is the influence of viewpoint or frame of reference (as distinguished from grammar and vocabulary) on communication between cultures? Give two examples.

13. Discuss the use of sexist language and give two examples.

14. What are some of the differences between how males and females use language?

15. Specify the difference between the way males and females use language on the job.

16. Identify powerful and powerless language and explain its relationship to communication style.

17. What is metacommunication? Give an example.

EXERCISES

1. a. Construct a Semantic Differential consisting of ten bipolar adjectives. Assess the potential marketability of a fictitious product name by asking several classmates to react to two or more names using the Semantic Differential. The sample scale below shows two names for a perfume.

Bouquet	*Summer Nights*
Good X_____ Bad	Good _____X_ Bad
Sharp _X_____ Dull	Sharp _____X Dull
Active _____X_____ Passive	Active _____X_____ Passive
Pretty ___X_____ Ugly	Pretty _____X_____ Ugly

   b. How do the responses on the Semantic Differential reflect the difference between denotation and connotation; between private and shared meaning?

2. Construct a two-column list with proper names in one column and stereotypical occupations associated with those names in the second. Mix up the order of names and occupations in each column. Present the lists

to several people and ask them to match the names and occupations. A sample list appears below:

Miss Flora	Ballet dancer
Spencer Turnbull	Teacher
Harry Hogan	Car thief
Speedy	Banker
Dominique Dubois	Hairdresser
Ken Sharp	Wrestling coach

   a. To what extent do people agree in their responses? How do the results relate to the statement "The word is not the thing"?
   b. How do the results relate to the three factors that affect stereotype perceptions (see Chapter 2)?
   c. What implications do these results suggest about the relationship between language, stereotyping, and communication effectiveness?

3. Interview two people who are ostensibly very different—a local politician and an artist, for example. Ask each of them to make a list of adjectives describing (a) himself or herself and (b) a member of the other group. Compare the lists to see how differently each group member perceives himself or herself from the way he or she is perceived by the other person. Notice how the perceptual differences are manifested in the words chosen for the descriptions.

4. Prepare an oral persuasive message in two forms. Use the most tactful language possible in one and the most inflammatory terms you can think of in the other. Give the messages to two groups, and try to assess their reactions on an attitude scale. Which message is more effective? If the audiences are similar and your messages alike except for word choice (and assuming the nonverbal cues are similar), any difference in your results should be due to the difference in the language you use.

5. In a chance conversation deliberately assume that individual words have only one meaning and try to interpret them in a way that the other person does not intend. What are the results?

6. Prepare a short presentation in two forms. In the first, use words that are high on the ladder of abstraction (i.e., vague); in the second, use much more concrete, highly specific words. Discuss class reactions to these different presentations.

SUGGESTED READINGS

Bate, Barbara, and **Anita Taylor,** eds. *Women Communicating.* Norwood, NJ: Ablex, 1988.

An important collection of studies on women's talk.

Becker, Carl. "Reasons for the Lack of Argumentation and Debate in the Far East." In *Intercultural Communication: A Reader.* 6th ed. Edited by Larry A. Samovar and Richard E. Porter. Belmont, CA: Wadsworth, 1991.

One of several excellent articles about language and intercultural communication appearing in this popular reader.

Bruner, Jerome. *Actual Minds, Possible Worlds.* Cambridge, MA: Harvard University Press, 1986.

A collection of essays by an outstanding psychologist. Part Two, "Language and Reality," will be of special interest to advanced students.

Cameron, Deborah, ed. *The Feminist Critique of Language: A Reader.* London: Routledge, 1990.

In this anthology the editor brings together a range of feminist theories and perspectives on language as a social and cultural institution.

Haslett, Beth. "Acquiring Conversational Competence." *Western Journal of Speech Communication* 48 (1984):107–124.

The author discusses how a child develops the ability to communicate through language. Interaction with the primary caretaker—usually the mother—is seen as essential to this development.

Orr, Eleanor Wilson. *Twice as Less.* New York: Norton, 1987.

A thoroughly original analysis of how language differences affect the performance of black students in mathematics and science.

Tannen, Deborah. *You Just Don't Understand: Women and Men in Conversation.* New York: Ballantine, 1990.

A linguist looks at communication difficulties between men and women as differences in conversational style.

CHAPTER FOUR

*T*he Nonverbal Message

CHAPTER OBJECTIVES

After reading this chapter, you should be able to:

1 Describe four categories of communication, distinguishing between verbal and nonverbal as well as vocal and nonvocal, and give an example of each.

2 Discuss the relative weight we assign to verbal and nonverbal messages and the kind of information conveyed.

3 Specify three ways in which nonverbal messages relate to verbal messages and explain the concept of the double bind.

4 Discuss the concepts of interpersonal distance, personal space, and orientation.

5 Explain how we communicate through our use of time and how timing can interfere with intercultural communication.

6 Identify the major visual cues given by facial expression and head and body movements and discuss the kinds of messages they convey.

7 Describe how one's choice of physical objects, including clothing, communicates messages to others.

8 Explain the concept of paralinguistics and identify four kinds of vocal cues, giving an example of each.

9 Discuss deception cues and recent research findings on accuracy in judging deception and the mutual influence of deceivers and detectors.

*I*n October of 1991 millions of Americans spent several days watching television, almost mesmerized by the testimony given during the Senate hearings on the confirmation of Clarence Thomas as Supreme Court Justice. Anita Hill, who had worked for Clarence Thomas some ten years before, came forward with charges of sexual harassment; Thomas passionately and categorically denied them. Numerous character witnesses with conflicting testimony were also heard and questioned. Who was telling the truth, and what evidence was there to go on? Viewers were stationed at their televisions not only to listen to the dramatic testimony but to watch facial expressions, body movements—all sorts of subtle changes. Yet even among skilled observers, psychologists and others who study human behavior, there was no consensus about who was lying. Paul Ekman, a specialist in the psychology of lying, suggested that a person aware of lying before Congress would be terrified of being caught and that a person accused of lying would be "angry at their opponent, angry at the world . . . angry about being attacked." "From expression, voice and gesture, I can read anger," he said. "The problem is, both people show it" (cited in Barringer, 1991, A18).

Making inferences about nonverbal messages, then, is not always as simple as it might seem. In this chapter we begin by examining the relative weight people give to verbal and nonverbal messages. Thus we will consider how nonverbal messages are interpreted, what types of information we receive from them, and how they interact with verbal messages.

INTERPRETING NONVERBAL MESSAGES

The literal definition of nonverbal communication, communication without words, is something of an oversimplification, because written words are considered "verbal" although they lack the element of sound. Stewart and D'Angelo (1980) propose that if we distinguish verbal from nonverbal and vocal from nonvocal, we have four categories or types of communication. **Verbal/vocal communication** refers to *communication through the spoken word.* For example, Steve and his father discuss the new car Steve wants to buy and his plans for getting together the money. In **verbal/nonverbal communication,** *words are involved but no speaking takes place:* If Steve writes a letter to his father about the car, his communication is verbal but nonvocal. Or suppose that after Steve talks about the car, he asks his father for a loan and his father simply groans. Such *groans, or vocalizations, constitute a form of* **nonverbal/vocal communication.** A fourth kind of communication, **nonverbal/nonvocal communication,** *involves only gestures and appearance*—imagine Steve's father looking angry or pleased—or perhaps simply puzzled. Seen in these terms, **nonverbal communication** *conveys nonlinguistic messages.*

Such messages take any number of forms. You raise your hand to vote yes at a committee meeting, hail a cab, exchange signals with a bridge partner.

You sit on the edge of your seat in a dull seminar and keep twisting a lock of your hair. You touch the arm of a friend lightly to reassure her. You buy a red sports car because you think it's more your kind of car than a brown sedan. [One architect writes that the automobile now functions as a "portable facade that publicly expresses social standing" (Rybczynski, 1992)]. In this chapter we will be looking at nonverbal messages of all kinds, and one of the first issues we will explore is the division often made between meaning conveyed by nonverbal and verbal communication.

The Verbal/Nonverbal Split in Meaning

Nonverbal communication—indeed the entire communication process— must be viewed as a whole that is greater than the sum of its parts. Outside the laboratory we do not depend on isolated **cues,** or *hints.* In face-to-face communication, all cues, both verbal and nonverbal, are available to us. Mehrabian (1972) argues that 93 percent of all social meaning in face-to-face communication is conveyed through nonverbal cues, and Birdwhistell (1970) estimates that 65 percent of such communication is nonverbal. Although the percentages are disputable—Hegstrom (1979) believes talking in percentages is pointless since the studies have virtually no generalizability—no one contests the significance of nonverbal behaviors.

In their recent review of nonverbal research, Knapp and Hall (1992) conclude:

> It appears some people rely more heavily on the verbal message, while others rely on the nonverbal.
>
> We do not know all the conditions that affect channel preferences, but weighting of verbal, vocal, and visual cues probably changes in changing situations. (p. 22)

It has even been proposed that people have one of three preferences in how they make use of information from their senses:

Visual preference: People "see the world by constructing or remembering mental images."

Auditory preference: People "prize sound and can make decisions based on what they have heard or read."

Kinesthetic preference: People "handle the world through touch, taste, smell, or feelings. [For them] contact is communication." (Adapted from Madonik, 1990, p. 19)

It might be interesting to speculate about what your own preference is—and why.

Nonverbal Information

We learn most about the meaning of nonverbal messages by studying them in relationship to verbal messages. Essentially, a nonverbal message functions in one of three ways: It replaces, reinforces, or contradicts a verbal message.

A nonverbal message that substitutes for a verbal one is often easy to interpret. Our culture provides us with gestures and expressions that are the equivalents of certain brief verbal messages: "Yes," "No," "Hello," "Goodbye," "I don't know," and so on. Likes and dislikes can also be expressed without words—smiling, clapping, frowning, foot stamping, and so on.

When a nonverbal message reinforces a verbal message, meaning is conveyed quickly and easily, and with increased comprehension. Sometimes a single cue such as a hand movement or a long pause gives special emphasis to one part of a message so that we are able to discern what the speaker feels is most important.

Nonverbal cues predominate by sheer number. In general, if as receivers we are caught between two discrepant messages, we are more inclined to believe the nonverbal message. One reason for this is that nonverbal cues give information about our intentions and emotional responses. Thus, many busi-

Nonverbal cues can be important not only in giving directions, but also in learning whether they are clear to others.

ness people prefer face-to-face communication—whether it be meeting for lunch or in the formal setting of an office—to mail or telephone when solving problems or negotiating critical decisions. In negotiation, much is learned from "feeling your way," watching the other person's facial expression and gestures so that you can adapt your own responses. (In the future, teleconferencing, which would provide a wealth of nonverbal cues, might be another option.)

Another reason the nonverbal message seems to have greater impact is the popular belief that body movements, facial expressions, vocal qualities, and so on cannot be simulated with authenticity by the average person. Even children are quick to sense gestures or expressions that are not spontaneous.

Nonverbal channels convey primarily relational messages, messages about the feeling/emotional level of our communication, rather than the thoughts (best communicated by verbal communication); also, nonverbal messages are ambiguous for the most part, except perhaps for certain gestures (Ekman et al., 1984). Bernard Goetz, the New Yorker who shot four teen-agers on the subway, claimed that he did so because their behavior was threatening; he acted, he said, in self-defense. Yet there was no consensus among the other passengers as to whether the injured youths were menacing. Incidents such as this have increased, particularly with the escalation of racial tensions in many of our cities.

The skills involved in interpreting and displaying nonverbal cues are evident early in life and appear to be an integral part of social development. Recent studies of children demonstrate that the inability to interpret nonverbal cues of peers and teachers may be linked with poor grades and unpopularity, as well as defeatism and other emotional problems (Goleman, 1989, C1). For example, an unpopular child may unwittingly communicate overeagerness, which peers view as aggression, and thus isolate himself socially. Psychologist Stephen Nowicki has designed a new test that measures children's skills in decoding nonverbal behavior including how emotion is communicated through facial expression and tone of voice (Nowicki and Duke, 1989). He and his colleagues have successfully trained children deficient in these skills to read facial expressions and display the nonverbal cues that will strengthen their social relationships.

The Double Bind

Most of our problems in interpreting meaning arise when we receive a nonverbal message that contradicts a verbal message. Let us explore this subject briefly.

You are familiar with the word "bind" as used to describe a situation one cannot get out of. In 1956 the anthropologist Gregory Bateson and a group of his associates presented a theory of the **double bind** that revolutionized the study of schizophrenia. They proposed that schizophrenic comunication—

particularly within families—was characterized by the constant exchange of contradictory messages between two or more people, one of whom was designated the "victim."

The recurrent theme in the double bind is a sequence of three commands. The first says, "Do not do so and so, or I will punish you," or "If you do not do so and so, I will punish you." The second command contradicts the first and is often communicated nonverbally: "Posture, gesture, tone of voice, meaningful action, and the implications concealed in verbal comment may all be used to convey this more abstract message" (p. 254). (Note the multiple channels through which these commands may be communicated.) The third negative command makes the victim's position completely untenable by forbidding him or her to leave this paradoxical situation. Laing has given us this summary of a chilling example taken from Bateson's work:

> A mother visits her son, who has just been recovering from a mental breakdown. As he goes towards her
> a. she opens her arms for him to embrace her, and/or
> b. to embrace him.
> c. as he gets nearer she freezes and stiffens,
> d. he stops irresolutely.
> e. she says, "don't you want to kiss your mummy?"—and as he still stands irresolutely
> f. she says, "But, dear, you mustn't be afraid of your feelings."

Laing notes that the description does not include the patient's double-binding behavior toward his mother. "For instance, between steps (b) and (c) above, the patient in moving towards his mother may have succeeded by minute nuances in his expression and walk, in putting into his mother *his* fear of closeness with her, so that she stiffened" (1969, p. 127).

Bateson's double-bind thesis explains a great deal about contradictory messages and the breakdown of interpersonal relationships that may result from them. Although the theory applies specifically to schizophrenic communication, it is relevant to more general studies such as ours because normal and so-called abnormal, or deviant, behavior exist along a continuum. Suppose, for example, that a supervisor always cautions her employees not to postpone discussing problem areas in their work. "Don't wait till it's too late to remedy the situation. I want you to come and tell me when you run into problems," she repeats. Yet as one of the assistant managers enters her office, she looks up annoyed and gives him an icy stare. Then, as the employee starts to back out of her office, the supervisor says, "Well, don't stand there looking so frightened. Tell me what's on your mind."

Within the normal range of experience, Birdwhistell (1970) uses the term **kinesic slips** for *contradictory verbal and nonverbal messages.* Imagine this conversation between a married couple who have just had a bitter quarrel. The wife asks the husband, "Honey, are you still angry?" "No," he replies, "it's all right." "But you *sound* as though you're still angry," she says. "I'm telling you *I'm not angry!*" he answers. The husband's words give one message, his voice another. He may not even be aware of the second. Which message is his wife likely to believe?

Verbal/Nonverbal Interaction

For purposes of analysis we speak of verbal and nonverbal messages as distinct, yet in daily life we are rarely able to separate their effects. For example, what we say is qualified, modified, by *how* we say it—tone of voice, facial expression, eye contact, and so on—as well as by the almost instantaneous verbal and nonverbal responses of others. And this interaction is ongoing. We depend on it and are continually modifying our responses.

In the remainder of this chapter, we shall see how through their nonverbal messages people give us many cues, or intimations, about their emotions, their intentions, their personalities, and even their social status. Thus we shall look at several kinds of cues—spatial, temporal, visual, and vocal. In terms of our model, then, we are speaking about all nonverbal messages—both intentional and unintentional.

SPATIAL AND TEMPORAL CUES

Only when we interact with people of other cultures or subcultures do we begin to realize that some of our most cherished ideas about what is appropriate conduct are **norms,** or *rules, whether implicit or explicit, about behavior;* that is, they are relative, not absolute, values. Indirectly, our culture teaches us to communicate in many ways—through our voices, our gestures, and even our style of dressing. Yet each of us interprets and expresses these conventions somewhat differently.

Culture has an even more subtle and pervasive influence on nonverbal communication, however. Each culture continually provides its members with input about how the world is structured. (We saw this with respect to visual perception when we discussed the Müller-Lyer illusion in Chapter 2.) Slowly we develop preconceptions about the world. It is the cues derived from these preconceptions that we take most for granted and that imperceptibly set the limits for our style of communication. Our cues about space and time are among those most significantly influenced by culture and sometimes the source of many difficulties in intercultural communication.

Space

If you were to enter a restaurant with only one customer in it, chances are that you would not sit down right next to him or her. Edward Hall explains that though this behavior seems natural to an American, an Arab might have a very different notion of appropriate distance between strangers. Students of nonverbal communication are indebted to Hall for his cross-cultural studies of space.

Hall has given the special name of **proxemics** to the *study of space.* Social scientists make use of the Scale of Social Distance, an instrument that uses the term "distance" figuratively, to indicate degree of liking or preference. Hall (1959) goes a step further and speaks of measurable distances between people—one and a half inches, one foot, three feet, and so on. In fact, he offers a four-part classification of distances between people. There is nothing arbitrary about this classification, as he explains:

> It is in the nature of animals, including man, to exhibit behavior which we call territoriality. In so doing, they use the senses to distinguish between one space or distance and another. The specific distance chosen depends on the transaction, the relationship of the interacting individuals, how they feel, and what they are doing. (Hall, 1959, p. 128)

Very often our choice of spatial distance is an unmistakable reflection of attitude. For example, subjects who were interviewed by people (actually confederates) wearing "Gay and Proud" buttons chose to seat themselves a foot further away than they did from interviewers who were not wearing such buttons. Yet in a pretest, all subjects had indicated no intolerance of gays (Snyder, 1980). Clearly, their nonverbal behavior carried a very different message.

Hall describes human relationships in terms of four kinds of distance: intimate, personal, social, and public. Each distance zone is further differentiated by a close phase and a far phase within which different behaviors occur. Let us take a look at these four distances and Hall's findings about what they mean to most North Americans.

Intimate Distance

At **intimate distance,** *eighteen inches or less,* the presence of another person "is unmistakable and may at times be overwhelming because of the greatly stepped-up sensory inputs" (Hall, 1959, p. 116). In its close phase (six inches or less) intimate distance lends itself primarily to nonverbal communication. Any subject discussed is usually top secret. The far phase (six to eighteen inches) is often used for discussing confidential matters, with the voice usually kept to a whisper. Such close proximity is considered improper for public places, though dormitories seem to be exceptions to the rule. In general, Americans try hard to avoid close contact with one another on buses and other public vehicles.

Personal Distance

Hall compares **personal distance,** from *one and a half to four feet,* to "a small protective sphere or bubble that an organism maintains between itself and others" (1959, p. 119). Topics discussed would still be personal. The close phase (one and a half to two and a half feet) is still a distance reserved for very close relationships; the far phase (two and a half to four feet) is a comfortable distance for conversing with friends (see Table 4.1).

Social Distance

Social distance, ranging from *four to twelve feet,* is described as a psychological distance, "one at which the animal apparently begins to feel anxious when he exceeds its limits. We can think of it as a hidden band that *contains the group.*" The close phase (four to seven feet) is suitable for business discussions and conversations at social gatherings.

A study of plant managers (Gaddy et al., 1987) suggests that supervisors can prove their control by periodically stepping forward when talking to subordinates. One supervisor succeeded in moving the listener across the room because when the supervisor edged closer, the subordinate took a step back to maintain a comfortable distance from him (pp. 64–65). The far phase (seven to twelve feet) is appropriate for meetings in a business office. People who are in the room but outside the seven-foot boundary can be ignored without being offended.

Those who violate the seven-foot boundary tend to be surprised if we do not acknowledge their presence, unless we are very busy. Humans have extended social distance by means of the walkie-talkie, telephone, radio, and television.

Public Distance

The largest of zones, **public distance,** denotes *twelve feet or more* of space, and it exists only in human relationships. In fact, the public relationships and manners of Americans and Europeans are considerably different from those

TABLE 4.1

Social Distance Zones			
Distance	**Description of Distance**	**Vocal Characteristics**	**Message Content**
0–6 inches	Intimate (close phase)	Soft whisper	Top secret
6–18 inches	Intimate (far phase)	Audible whisper	Very confidential
1½–2½ feet	Personal (close phase)	Soft voice	Personal subject matter
2½–4 feet	Personal (far phase)	Slightly lowered voice	Personal subject matter
4–7 feet	Social (close phase)	Full voice	Nonpersonal information
7–12 feet	Social (far phase)	Full voice with slight over-loudness	Public information for others to hear
12–25 feet	Public (close phase)	Loud voice talking to a group	Public information for others to hear
25 feet or more	Public (far phase)	Loudest voice	Hailing, departures

Source: Table from *The Silent Language* by Edward T. Hall. Reprinted by permission of Doubleday & Company, Inc.

of other cultures. At the close phase (twelve to twenty-five feet) a more formal style of language and a louder voice are required. At the far phase (twenty-five feet or more) further accommodations to distance are usually made: Experienced public speakers exaggerate body movements, gestures, enunciation, and volume while reducing their rate of speech. Table 4.1 is a brief summary of how message content and vocal shift vary with distance between communicators.

Within a country as diverse as the United States, various subcultures develop their own proxemic norms. (A subculture is *a group having sufficient distinctive traits to distinguish it from other members of the same culture or society.*) A recent study (Albas, 1991) found that even for members of the same ethnic group, the comfortable distance they choose for interacting—in this case, during an interview—is negotiable. At the beginning of the interview the distance was 12.3 inches, but by the end of the interview it was 23.4 inches; when the interviewer retreated, subjects felt he "wished to have a greater distance between them and . . . they were attempting to accommodate him" (p. 701).

In research on intercultural communication, the distinction is often made between low-contact and high-contact cultures. One well-known study looked at the use of interpersonal distance by Venezuelans (high contact), North Americans (moderate contact), and Japanese (low contact). Researchers found that in speaking their own language, Venezuelans sit closest to each other, North Americans maintain an intermediate distance, and Japanese sit furthest from each other. When using English rather than their native language, people maintain interpersonal distances closer to North American norms so it seems that when we speak a foreign language, we tend to approximate the distance norms of that culture (cited in Gudykunst and Kim, 1992a, p. 178). And though there is a tendency to generalize about distance norms within Europe, it seems that people from northern European cultures—people from Sweden and Scotland, for example—require greater interpersonal distance than people from Mediterranean countries such as Italy and Greece (Samovar and Jain, 1991, p. 215).

Researchers are not saying that we calculate these differences while communicating. On the contrary, our sense of what distance is natural for a given interaction is so deeply ingrained in us by our culture that we automatically make spatial adjustments and interpret spatial cues. Latin Americans, Arabs, and the French, for example, stand so close to each other that if they exercise their own distance norms while conversing with an American, they arouse hostile or sexual feelings. If you want to test this concept in proxemics, the next time you converse with someone, keep inching toward him or her. See how close you can get before the other party starts backing away.

Personal Space

A somewhat different approach to space has been developed by Sommer (1969). His concern is with **personal space**, *"an area with invisible boundaries surrounding a person's body into which intruders may not come"* (p. 26;

italics added). In effect, he says that the concept of personal space can be thought of as a person's portable territory, which each individual carries along wherever he or she may go. Sommer is careful to distinguish his use of personal space from Hall's use of the term "territory":

> The most important difference is that personal space is carried around while territory is relatively stationary. The animal or man will usually mark the boundaries of his territory so that they are visible to others, but the boundaries of his personal space are invisible. Personal space has the body at its center, while territory does not. (Sommer, 1969, p. 248)

At least one investigator has suggested that personality variables such as need for affiliation influence the size of one's personal space (Rosenfeld, 1965). In his study of prison inmates who had committed violent crimes, Kinzel (1969) observed that these men had a personal space, or "body buffer zone," twice as large as that of nonviolent prisoners. Members of the violent group felt threatened when a person came close to them, as if the person were an intruder who was "looming up" or "rushing in" at them.

Other research on personal space focuses on the relationship between spatial arrangements (architectural elements, interior design, seating, and so on) and human feelings and interaction. For instance, it is estimated that college students begin to identify a particular seat in the classroom as "their chair" by as early as the second class period. Although you probably would not ask another student to give up what you considered to be your chair if you arrived a little late, you might feel annoyed to see someone else sitting in it. This feeling is somewhat reminiscent of the belief that there is a home court advantage for basketball teams.

In the study halls of college libraries, students tend to protect privacy by sitting as far away from each other as possible. One way of communicating this need is by occupying a corner position. Or students sprawl out, resting their legs on a nearby chair. If they get up from the table, they may "reserve" the place by spreading out books and papers or leaving clothing draped over the chair (Sommer, 1969, pp. 46–47). How far you go in defending your personal space will depend, of course, on both your personality and communication style. If you sit too close to me in the library, I may get up and move. But reverse our roles and you might glare at me and even spread out your notebooks and papers so that they take up a good part of the table.

Orientation

Orientation—that is, *the angle of your body as you interact with another person,* may also reflect the nature of the relationship between you. For example, some studies of British and North American seating patterns have shown that a 90-degree-angle orientation facilitates conversation, face-to-face orientations tend toward competitive behaviors, and side-by-side orientations are more often regarded as showing cooperation (Hargie et al., 1987, p. 27).

FIGURE 4.1   Seating Preferences at a Rectangular Table

Type of interaction	Position of Participants	Suggested Situations
Conversation		• Counseling interview • Employer interviewing an employee • Some progressive job interviews
Cooperation		• Friends meeting in a pub • Teacher helping a pupil in his work • Staff cooperating on the same project
Competition		• Some job interviews • Principal interviewing a pupil • Playing games such as chess, poker, etc.
Coaction		• Strangers in a public eating place • Unfamiliar students working at same library table • Strangers sharing a seat on the train

(*Source:* Adapted from Hargie et al., *Social Skills in Interpersonal Communication,* Cambridge, MA: Brookline Books, 1987, p. 128, Figure 2.1.)

In Figure 4.1 we see several preferences in orientation for sitting at a table. Notice how often situation determines choice of orientation.

Time

When we study *how human beings communicate through their use of time,* we are concerned with **chronemics.** For example, have you ever written direction, North Americans interpret such behavior as showing a lack of respect and a lack of "professionalism," but the reason may lie more in the culturally different treatment of time. (p. 111)

Thus, explains Condon, "it is not so much that putting things off until *mañana* is valued, as some Mexican stereotypes would have it, but that human activities are not expected to proceed like clock-work" (p. 111).

It has been pointed out that for the American business person discussion is simply "a means to an end: the deal" (Hall and Whyte, in Smith, 1966, p. 568). Moreover, it's a sign of good faith to agree on major issues, assuming that details will be worked out later on. But like the Latin American, the Greek business person engages in what seems to us prolonged discussion and is excessively preoccupied with details. For the Greek these concerns signify goodwill (Hall and Whyte, in Smith, 1966, p. 568).

Our assumptions about appropriate timing vary so much from culture to culture that they can make for all sorts of misunderstandings. The story is told of an Indian man who invited a visiting American and his family to come to his home. "Come any time," the Indian urged. After waiting several weeks, the Indian extended the invitation once more. But despite the American's assurance that he would like to come, he never did. He was certain that if the Indian really expected him to visit, he would state a time. The Indian, on the other hand, assumed that the American did not wish to pay him a visit. By the standards of his own culture, the Indian had indeed extended the invitation—for in India the polite host allows the guest to determine the time of the visit (Hall and Whyte, in Smith, 1966). Even for personal effectiveness with people of our own culture, we have to be more aware of time as an aspect of communication.

VISUAL CUES

The second category of nonverbal cues we will discuss is extremely broad, ranging from facial expressions and body movements to the clothing we wear and the objects we display. Let's begin with an anecdote.

At the end of the nineteenth century, a German horse named Hans was reported to know how to add. If you asked him to add 2 and 6, for example, he pawed the ground eight times. The curious thing was that Hans could do sums only in the presence of human beings. His mysterious talent was later explained rather simply: When he unwittingly reached the answer, he saw his audience relax, and he stopped pawing.

The people who came to see Hans perform would have been shocked to learn that they were, by their body movements, transmitting the correct answers visually. Yet they were probably leaning forward eagerly to take in every aspect of the spectacle before them, for we all know how much we gain by seeing a performer, a lecturer, or any person we are speaking to. In fact, members of discussion groups interact more frequently when seated facing

a letter to a friend only to wait what seemed to be an endless time for a rep
What inferences did you make about the strength of the friendship? Or h
you ever received a phone call at three in the morning? You probably thou
that it was a very important call, a wrong number, or a prank. How fai
advance can a first date be arranged? Must it be several days ahead, or
one call thirty minutes before? In each of these cases, timing leads to cert
expectations that influence the face-to-face communication that subsequei
occurs. A late entrance that violates standards of courtesy can have a dis
trous effect, not just a dramatic one. Much of the verbal communication t
ensues may be spent explaining away the nonverbal message that has alre;
been conveyed.

Conceptions of what is "late" or "early" vary from culture to cultu
Americans are "busy" people. We use our watches throughout the day.
like schedules and agendas. We value doing things "on time." It is sometir
jarring to see ourselves as others see us. Here, for example, is a Brazil
reaction to "Anglo-American" time:

> The rigid Anglo-Saxon attitude—"Time is money"—with an almost mys-
> tical cult of minutes and seconds on account of their practical, commercial
> value, is in sharp contrast to the Latin American attitude, a sort of "more-
> or-less" (*"mas o menos"*) attitude. It is easy to understand why a Nordic
> was so shocked in Spain to know that a Spanish or Latin American guest
> in a hotel asked the desk to call him next morning not exactly at ten or
> ten-fifteen, as an Anglo-Saxon or an Anglo-American would have asked,
> but at ten or eleven. (Freyre, 1980)

Hall (1984) distinguishes between monochronic and polychronic conc
tions of time. **Monochronic** *time is thought of as lineal and segmented.*
cultures with monochronic time, people like to do one thing at a time, ;
their preference is for precise scheduling. Making appointments and deadli
is highly valued. In cultures with a **polychronic** conception of **time**, on
other hand, *many things are going on at once.* Nor is there great surp
when delays or interruptions occur. Indeed, they seem to be expected.

In illustrating these differences, Condon (1991) compares North Am
cans with Mexicans. North Americans, whose culture is monochronic,
seen—even by members of other monochronic cultures—as far too gover:
by schedules. Mexican culture, on the other hand, is polychronic: Mexic
often conduct many activities at the same time and tend to take interrupti
in stride. When members of monochronic and polychronic cultures meet,
result can be misunderstanding:

> North Americans express special irritation when Mexicans seem to give
> them less than their undivided attention. When a young woman bank
> teller, awaiting her superior's approval for a check to be cashed, files her
> nails and talks on the phone with her boyfriend, or when one's taxi driver
> stops en route to pick up a friend who seems to be going in the same

each other rather than side by side (Steinzor, 1950). In other words, the greater our visibility, the greater our potential for communicating. And, as we saw in Chapter 1, the greater the number of channels the sender uses, the more information is received.

Visual cues add to the information transmitted through other channels and at times stand alone. Specific motions of the head, for example, give the equivalents of certain brief verbal messages such as yes and no, and these movements may vary from culture to culture. Even head orientation, the direction in which we turn our heads, communicates something. Mehrabian (1967) found that a person who gives more head orientation while speaking conveys more positive feeling. A study of how "warmth" and "coldness" are conveyed during an interview supports this conclusion: "Leaning toward the subject, smiling, and looking directly at him enabled the subject to judge the experimenter as warm. Conversely, looking away from the subject, leaning away from him, not smiling, and intermittingly drumming the fingers on the table impressed the subject as coldness" (Reece and Whitman, 1962, p. 250).

Knapp's (1978) summary of research in Table 4.2 indicates which cues

TABLE 4.2

Behaviors Rated as Warm and Cold

Warm Behaviors	Cold Behaviors
Looks into his eyes	Gives a cold stare
Touches his hand	Sneers
Moves toward him	Gives a fake yawn
Smiles frequently	Frowns
Works her eyes from his head to his toes	Moves away from him
Has a happy face	Looks at the ceiling
Smiles with mouth open	Picks her teeth
Grins	Shakes her head negatively
Sits directly facing him	Cleans her fingernails
Nods head affirmatively	Looks away
Puckers her lips	Pouts
Licks her lips	Chain smokes
Raises her eyebrows	Cracks her fingers
Has eyes wide open	Looks around the room
Uses expressive hand gestures while speaking	Picks her hands
Gives fast glances	Plays with her hair's split ends
Stretches	Smells her hair

Source: Adapted from "Judging Attraction from Non-verbal Behavior: The Gain Phenomenon." *Journal of Consulting and Clinical Psychology,* Vol. 43, 1975, pp. 491–497, 1975, American Psychological Association, as appeared in *Nonverbal Communication in Human Interaction,* 2d ed., by Mark L. Knapp. © 1972, 1978, by Holt, Rinehart and Winston.

are usually associated with warm or cold people. Notice that the nonverbal cues described include facial expression, eye contact, and body movements. We shall be discussing each of these sources of information. Bear in mind, however, that when you look at another person, you get a total impression: We separate various cues here only to examine the kind of information that each conveys. These are nonverbal cues associated with North Americans; other cultures would be described by other lists.

A pioneering figure in research on nonverbal communication, Ray Birdwhistell, believes that the entire communication context must be observed in all its complexity and that it is only productive to isolate individual variables if they can be integrated into "the general communicative stream, including verbal behavior" (Weitz, 1979). It was Birdwhistell (1952) who introduced the term **"kinesics"** to refer to *the study of body movements in communication.* "Body movements" is used in a broad sense and refers also to movements of the head and face. Birdwhistell has estimated that there are over 700,000 possible physical signs that can be transmitted via body movement. The first group of visual cues we will be looking at has to do with facial expression.

Facial Expression

A blank face is a riddle, troubling and open to interpretation. Garbo's director in *Queen Christina* attributed the film's success to his direction in the last scene: "Think of nothing," he told the actress. The film closes as Garbo, her face expressionless, stands on board a ship and stares into the turbulent water. This ambiguous ending allowed each viewer his own interpretation.

Most members of this culture could not maintain a blank face for very long. (That's why staring contests usually produce laughter after a short time.) Indeed, the human face is so mobile that it can effortlessly register boredom, surprise, affection, and disapproval one after another in a few seconds. *We constantly read expressions from people's faces.* In fact, **facial cues** are the single most important source of nonverbal communication. Comments such as "If looks could kill" and "It was all over her face" bear witness to the significance we give to facial expression. Often a child in trouble stares at the scolding parent, hardly listening to what is said.

Recent research confirms earlier work by Smith, Chase, and Leiblich (1974) and Dolgin and Sabini (1982) that compressing one's lips and displaying the tongue indicates a reluctance to interact with others and also discourages social contact. Two studies (Jones, Kearins, and Watson, 1987) done with college students found that "tongue showing had a significant deterring effect upon the willingness to interrupt [another person at work]" (p. 763). In one of the studies, students taking a test needed to speak to the teacher because a page of the test was missing. When there was a tongue show, however, the students took a significantly longer time to interrupt the teacher. And when the teacher and student were of the opposite sex, the delay in interrupting was even longer.

It has also been learned that we tend to describe faces in terms of a general evaluative dimension (good or bad, beautiful or ugly, kind or cruel, and so on) and a dynamism dimension (active or passive, inert or mobile, interesting or boring) (Williams and Tolch, 1965). And apparently some people are much more adept than others at interpreting facial cues.

So we like a face or we don't; we think it's animated or relatively inert. These are general impressions. But what do we see that makes us judge someone to be sad or happy or frightened or angry? Isolating which facial cues specify particular emotions is more difficult than simply judging a face. In one attempt (Harrison, in Campbell and Hepler, 1965) to decipher a facial code, subjects were shown simple illustrations (pictomorphs) such as those in Figure 4.2. A statistical analysis of the results led to the conclusions that half-raised eyebrows indicate worry; a single raised eyebrow, skepticism; half-closed eyes, boredom; closed eyes, sleep; an upcurved mouth, happiness; and a down-curved mouth, unhappiness. The smile button with its brief suggestion of a face—pinpoints for eyes and a single upcurved line for the mouth—is enough to suggest to most people a happy face.

The study of facial cues as expressions of specific emotions has a long history. One of the most eminent scientists to examine this subject was Charles Darwin. Darwin tried to find out whether the facial behaviors associated with particular emotions are universal. One method he used was to ask subjects to identify specific emotions from still photographs of people's faces. In *The Expression of the Emotions in Man and Animals,* published in 1872, Darwin presented some of his conclusions and speculations about expressive behavior. He felt that most of a human being's expressive actions, like those of other animals, are instinctive, not learned behaviors. For example, "We may see children, only two or three years old, and even those born blind, blushing from shame" (Darwin, in Loewenberg, 1959, p. 398).

Darwin's argument about the facial expressions of blind children is given further support by several studies done more than half a century after his book was published. Ekman and Friesen (1971) asked members of a preliterate New Guinea culture to judge emotions from the facial expressions of Westerners. The subjects had had virtually no exposure to Western culture. Yet they made the same identifications that Westerners made, with one exception: they were not able to differentiate between fear and surprise. The researchers conclude that, at least in some respects, expressive facial behavior is constant across cultures. They acknowledge that cultural differences exist but argue that the differences are reflected "in the circumstances which elicit an emotion,

FIGURE 4.2

in the action consequences of an emotion and in the display rules which govern the management of facial behavior in particular social settings" (p. 129).

According to anthropologist Melvin Konner (1987), smiling seems to be a human social display that is universal. For example, Eibl-Eibesfeldt's films from many remote parts of the world show smiling as a "consistent feature of greeting, often in combination with raising of the eyebrows" (p. 42). How our smiles are interpreted, however, will depend on many variables. Forgas (1987) found that the communicator's physical attractiveness can influence how cues of facial expression are interpreted: Smiles by unattractive subjects tend to be interpreted as reflecting submissiveness and lack of self-confidence; smiles by attractive subjects tend to be perceived as showing extraversion and self-confidence.

Other experts on nonverbal communication, including Ray Birdwhistell and Weston La Barre, have argued against the possibility of universal facial cues: They believe that the cues are culture-specific. The issue is far from settled. Experimental evidence is scarce and contradictory. Several researchers report negative results with such techniques as still photographs and illustrations that reveal only the face. For example, Motley and Camden (1988) found that in interpersonal communication settings, spontaneous facial expressions of emotions are far more difficult to identify than the posed expressions that have traditionally been employed in formal studies. Thus, they call into question the generalizability of previous research. "If we depend upon facial expression alone," they suggest, "we can 'read a person like a book' only if the person intends to be read" (p. 19).

A survey of research on the role of affect in interpersonal communication suggests that there may be two separate communication processes: "a spontaneous process based on changing emotional/motivational affective states of the interactions and a symbolic process involving intentional messages" (Sypher, Sypher, and Haas, 1988, pp. 377–378; Buck, 1984). Generally, our accuracy in identifying emotions seems to increase with the number of cues we see.

Eye Movements

Proper street behavior among Americans permits passersby to look at each other until they are about eight feet apart. At this point both parties cast their eyes downward so that they will not appear to be staring. The many other rules implicit in our culture about looking at others are a tacit admission that eye contact is perhaps the single most important facial cue we use in communicating. The *study of the role of eye contact in communications* is called **oculesics**.

Although the face has been called "the major nonverbal liar" (Ekman and Friesen, 1984), cues given in eye contact seem to reveal a good deal about personality. Apparently, we have greater control of the muscles in the lower part of our face than we do of the muscles around our eyes. (There are exceptions, of course. Machiavellian individuals and con artists are able to sustain good eye contact even when telling lies.) It has even been suggested that "the lower face may follow culturally transmitted display rules while the eyes may reveal the spontaneous or naked response" (Libby and Yaklevich, 1973, p. 203).

A broader study of eye movements began during the 1970s when a new form of therapy evolved that focused primarily on eye behaviors as clues to underlying problems. This approach, **neurolinguistic programming (NLP)**, is an attempt to change or "reprogram" patient behavior by discovering what patients are thinking. NLP therapists believe, for example, that eyes that move up and to the right indicate the individual is trying to envision an event that has never been seen; eyes that move up and to the left indicate the person is recalling an event that has been seen; eyes that are centered but glance to the right indicate the individual is trying to imagine a sound that has never been heard; eyes centered but glancing to the left indicate the person is recalling a sound that has been heard; eyes that move down and to the left indicate the person is carrying on an internal conversation; and eyes that move down and to the right indicate the sorting out of bodily sensations (Leo, 1983).

At the beginning of this chapter we referred to a related theory that people have preferred channels by which they transmit and receive information: visual (sight-related), auditory (sound-related), or kinesthetic (data related to touch, taste, smell, or feelings). According to this view, illustrated in Figure 4.3 by observing a person's eye movements, we can track which kind of information is being processed:

> Notice that eyes looking upward or defocussed typically indicate people accessing a visual system, eyes moving side to side or down to the left are usually seen with people seeking and retrieving auditory data, and eyes travelling downward and to the right side most times are tending to indicate people going for kinesthetic information (Madonik, 1990, p. 19)

At present, however, most of the research on eye movements has to do with eye contact. One study estimates that in group communication we spend 30 to 60 percent of our time in eye contact with others (10 to 30 percent of the looks last only about a second). Several of the unstated rules about eye contact are:

a. A looker may invite interaction by staring at another person who is on the other side of a room. The target's studied return of the gaze is generally interpreted as acceptance of the invitation, while averting the eyes is a rejection of the looker's request.

b. There is more mutual eye contact between friends than others, and a looker's frank gaze is widely interpreted as positive regard.

c. Persons who seek eye contact while speaking are regarded not only as exceptionally well-disposed by their target, but also as more believable and earnest.

d. If the usual short, intermittent gazes during conversation are replaced by gazes of longer duration, the target interprets this as meaning that the task is less important than the personal relation between the two persons. (Argyle, 1985)

FIGURE 4.3   Patterns of Eye Movements: A Theory about
Accessing Information

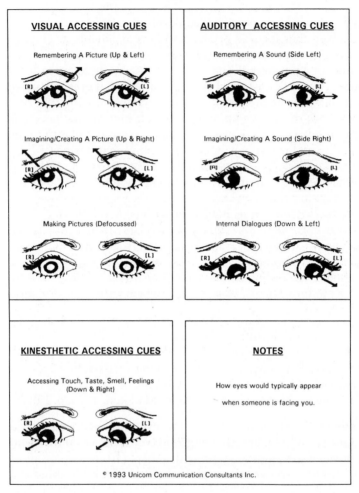

(*Source:* Barbara, Madonik ''I Hear What You Say, But What Are You
Telling Me?'' *Canadian Manager* 15 (1990), p. 19.

The second rule is corroborated by other researchers: Frequent eye contact
does seem to be a sign of affection or interest. And personality will affect the
degree of eye contact. For example, people who are high in their need to give
help and comfort maintain eye contact to a much greater degree than do
people who are rated low on this need (Libby and Yaklevich, 1973). Eye
contact with friends can also help us to cope with stress. A recent study
(Winstead et al., 1992) found that subjects who anticipated a stressful event
perceived greater social support from interacting with a friend rather than a
stranger. In this experiment the event was delivering an extemporaneous

speech. Researchers report the best nonverbal predictor of perceived social support and coping to be eye contact.

Even in public communication the frequency of eye contact affects the message sender. When an audience gives negative feedback (including poor eye contact), the speaker tends to lose fluency and to do poorly in presenting his or her message (Blubaugh, 1969). In turn, audiences prefer speakers who give good eye contact (Corbin, 1962).

Why is eye contact so rewarding to others? Perhaps it is because the eyes are considered such a valuable source of information. Hess (1965) found that Chinese jade dealers watch the eyes of their perspective customers for interest in a particular stone because the pupils enlarge with increased interest; similarly, magicians are able to tell what card a person is thinking about by studying his or her eyes. Hess's studies (1965; 1975) confirm that pupil size is indeed a sensitive index of interest.

There are several popular beliefs about what can be learned from watching someone's eyes. For example, two people who exchange knowing glances at a party seem able to communicate without words. Being able to look another person in the eye traditionally implies that you are being truthful and that your intentions are not to be questioned. Conversely, the person who averts his or her eyes is thought to be hiding something.

Norms governing eye movements and the interpretation of the implicit nonverbal message may be extremely clear in other cultures. For example, in the black township of Soweto in South Africa, a mother whose son had been killed in a violent confrontation with the police swore never again to avert her eyes or to bow her head in front of white people. In her culture, this was a major act of defiance (Rule, 1986, p. 57). (See Chapter 13 on intercultural aspects of eye contact.)

Body Movements

If during a party you were asked to record and classify all the body movements of two people in conversation during a five-minute period, you would probably think this an impossible task. Nothing short of a film captures the rapid, often subtle changes of the body. Much of what we know about kinesics has come to us indirectly, from such disciplines as anthropology and psychiatry.

The work of Scheflen (1965) is a case in point. He noticed that patterns of nonverbal flirting, or "quasi-courtship," between males and females emerged during psychotherapy. After studying films of a great many therapy sessions, he was able to classify some of the typical behaviors he observed. Signs of **courtship readiness** included preening hair, pulling at stockings, adjusting the tie, and so on. **Positioning** was another source of cues about interpersonal attraction. For example, two people might face each other and lean forward eagerly. Sometimes they sat with the upper half of their torsos turned in an open position so that a third person might enter the conversation

These two people are entirely dependent on nonverbal communication. What sorts of things have to be left "unsaid" until they emerge from the water?

but with their legs forming a circle and thus excluding the intruder. A third category, **actions of appeal,** included flirtatious glances and head cocking. Women signaled sexual invitation by crossing the legs, exposing the thigh, exhibiting the palm of the hand, and protruding the breast. Here is an example of these behaviors in context:

> At the beginning of the sequence . . . the therapist . . . turns to watch an attractive research technician walk across the room. The patient [female] begins to preen. . . . The therapist turns back to the patient and also preens, but he then disclaims courtship by an ostentatious look of boredom and a yawn. . . . Immediately afterward, the patient tells him she is interested in an attractive male aide. (p. 252)

Courtship behaviors occur in many other settings, such as business conferences, neighborhood parties, and other social gatherings. If we omit people's identities in the sequence just described, the scene could easily have taken place during a university seminar, an interview, or a committee meeting. Scheflen's observation that courtship behaviors tend to occur most often when a person feels he or she is not receiving enough attention can probably be extended to many interpersonal relationships.

Ekman (1965*b*) questioned whether the cues given by body movements are different from those given by head and facial movements. His findings indicate that cues from the head and face suggest what emotion is being experienced whereas the body gives off cues about how intense that emotion is. The hands, however, can give us the same information we receive from the head and face.

Hand Gestures

Anthropologists distinguish humankind from other animals by their use of language and their superior manual dexterity. Flexible hands enable human beings to use tools and to draw on a wide range of gestures in communicating. As a mode of nonverbal communication, **hand gestures** *rank second in importance only to facial cues.*

Although it is said that some people "talk" with their hands, it is not only broad, expansive gestures that communicate mood. Less animated people often communicate inadvertently by means of their hands. The rather reserved husband of a lawyer we know repeatedly drums his fingers on a table or chair whenever his wife speaks about her practice. This behavior is the only sign of his impatience with her deep involvement in her profession.

In his analysis of foot, head, and hand movements of mental patients under treatment in hospitals, Ekman (1965*a*) was able to distinguish more than a hundred different hand acts. Coding them along with the other body movements, he discovered that from the time of the patient's admission to his or her discharge, hand movements corresponded with various stages of treatment.

Hand gestures sometimes substitute for verbal communication. Deaf-mutes use a system of hand signals so comprehensive that it literally replaces spoken language. The signals themselves are arbitrary. Many of our hand movements are culturally determined. Thus the same gestures can convey different things to members of different cultures, and over time gestures change even within the same culture.

In *Bitter Lemons,* a book about the years he spent living in Cyprus, Lawrence Durrell (1957), an Englishman, is trying to persuade Mr. Sabri, a Turkish real estate agent with a reputation for cunning, to find him a cheap village house. Durrell announces that he has come to Sabri because of Sabri's reputation for being a rogue. In this part of the world, says Durrell, being a rogue can mean only one thing; being more clever than other people:

> I accompanied this with the appropriate gesture—for cleverness in the hand-language is indicated by placing the forefinger of the right hand slowly and portentously upon the temple: tapping slightly, as one might tap a breakfast egg. (Incidentally, one has to be careful, as if one turns

the finger in the manner of turning a bolt in a thread, the significance is quite different: it means to be "soft in the head" or to "have a screw loose.") I tapped my skull softly. (p. 49)

Such differences in meaning are a potential source of communication difficulty. To an American, for example, making a circle with one's thumb and forefinger and extending the other fingers means "okay," but to a Brazilian it is an obscene sign of contempt. Apparently, American visitors and even statesmen unwittingly offend their Brazilian hosts with this gesture.

Desmond Morris and his colleagues in England (1979) have identified what they call twenty key gestures used in Europe. They appear in Figure 4.4.

1. The fingertips kiss
2. The fingers cross
3. The nose thumb
4. The hand purse
5. The cheek screw
6. The eyelid pull
7. The forearm jerk
8. The flat-hand flick
9. The ring
10. The vertical horn-sign
11. The horizontal horn-sign
12. The fig
13. The head toss
14. The chin flick
15. The cheek stroke
16. The thumb up
17. The teeth flick
18. The ear touch
19. The nose tap
20. The palm-back V-sign

Some of these, such as the nose thumb, the forearm jerk, the ring, or the palm-back V-sign, are quite familiar to us. Others, however, such as the cheek

FIGURE 4.4   Key Gestures

(*Source:* D. Morris, P. Collett, P. Marsh, and M. O'Shaughnessy, *Gestures,* New York: Stein and Day, 1979. Copyright © 1979 by Stein and Day, Publishers. Reprinted with permission of Stein and Day, Publishers.)

screw, the horizontal horn-sign, the chin flick, or the fig are almost completely unknown in the United States. They found that different meanings were assigned in different countries. The fig (no. 12), for example, is interpreted in many different ways including as sexual comment, sexual insult, or protection. Similarly, the nose tap (no. 19) has several interpretations—among them, complicity, be alert, you are being nosey, I'm alert, he is clever, and awareness that a threat is present.

Haptics

The cues we receive from physical contact are especially revealing: Touch is one of our most important means of communicating nonverbally. **Haptics,** *the study of how we use touch to communicate,* has been receiving increasing attention among students of nonverbal behavior. Heslin and Alper (1983) indicate that in addition to conveying nurturance and caring, touch is also used to signify a professional relationship (being touched by a barber, for example); a social relationship (handshakes); friendship (for example, touching the upper arm); intimacy (hugs, for instance); and sexual arousal (for example, certain types of kisses). In each instance, touch is a bonding gesture.

Conversely, a limp handshake in our culture usually evokes negative feelings; Americans interpret it as a lack of interest or vitality. A moist hand is often considered a sign of anxiety, especially if the handshake precedes a potentially stressful situation such as an interview.

From summaries of research (Jones and Yarbrough, 1985; Montagu, 1971), we know that touch is essential for psychological and physical development in children and emotional well-being in adults. Being able to touch other human beings seems to be linked with high self-esteem and sociability.

We also use touch to influence others; in fact, touching increases self-disclosure and compliant behavior. The influence of touching on compliance has been demonstrated in several fascinating studies. For example, subjects touched lightly on the arm were more likely to sign a petition than those who were not touched (Willis and Hamm, 1980). Touch *avoidance* also turns out to be a good predictor of interpersonal distance, particularly when the other person is female—so in this instance, we see two nonverbal codes or messages interacting (Anderson and Sull, 1985).

Other work on touch (Jones and Yarbrough, 1985), conducted in naturalistic settings, found twelve different types of touches: *positive affect touches,* including support, appreciation, inclusion, sexual, and affectionate touches; *playful touches,* including those of playful affection and playful aggression; *control touches,* including touches of compliance, attention-getting, and signaling a response; *ritualistic touches,* including touches for greeting and departure; *hybrid touches,* including greeting/affection and departure/affection touches. *Task-related touches* include touches accompanying a verbal remark about someone's appearance (touching that person's clothing or hair, for example) and instrumental ancillary touches (those not really necessary to performing a task—e.g., touching hands when passing the telephone to someone) as well as instrumental intrinsic touches (those that are part of a task).

Besides the need for touch to establish and develop our relationships with others, some touch appears to have unambiguous symbolic content or meaning. Further, the codes of interpersonal touch encompass a far broader "range of meanings and degrees than previous research would suggest" (p. 51); so we use touch to convey many different things, some far more ambiguous than others. Touch is also *involving*; it is a form of approach behavior. And finally, context is critical to the meanings touch conveys (p. 51)—verbal behaviors as well as nonverbal behaviors *and* situation all influence the kind of meaning we attribute to a given touch.

Physical Appearance and Use of Objects

Clothes may not make the person, but dress, grooming, and general physical appearance are often the basis of first and relatively long-lasting impressions. As we saw in Chapter 2, even glasses affect the way the wearer is perceived by others.

Uniforms tell us a great deal about rank and status; many people believe that dress and personal grooming do too. In several studies people received greater help or compliance with their requests (signing a petition, for example) when they were formally or neatly dressed than they did when their dress was casual or careless (Kleinke, 1986, pp. 77–78). One study of beards suggests that women find a bearded man more appealing, that he has "more status in the eyes of other men," and that his beard may even create more social distance between him and another unbearded male (Freedman, 1969, p. 38). The popularity of beards seems to be cyclical (Kleinke, 1986, p. 78).

We sometimes dress to impress others, to be more like them, or—when we dress counter to prevailing norms—to express rejection of their values. Preppies tend to be associated with well-coordinated clothing, cardigans, Docksiders, argyle socks, and CB jackets (preferably with various ski tags left on the jacket). These days punks often wear lots of black clothing, and the favored footwear is a pair of Doc Martens (black "combat" boots). Yet the Docksiders and the Doc Martens have more in common than they appear to: both are part of carefully maintained dress codes.

A study of the relationship between dress and personality suggests that if you are highly clothes-conscious, you are likely to be compliant and anxious; if you have relatively little consciousness of what you wear, you are probably more aggressive and independent (Rosenfeld and Plax, 1977). (Men and women take note: This is a study of both sexes!) Through our clothing we often communicate our compliance or noncompliance with traditional values.

In general, people will tolerate a lot more deviation in dress if the person in question is rich or famous. Indeed, people often expect artists and performers to dress unconventionally. For example, we expect to see Tina Turner's wild spiky hair, short skirts, and super-high heels.

Elegant, expensive clothing can sometimes prove a barrier to communication, however—especially in a country such as ours with its democratic values. For example, we don't expect a politician to show up wearing a three-piece suit when he makes a speech in a working-class neighborhood.

Speaking on a recent talk show with David Letterman, Dustin Hoffman complained that he was never given roles in which he had to dress formally. Once, just once, he joked—or was he joking?—he'd like to do a film in which he had to wear an Armani suit. Given current trends, Dustin Hoffman may have to find that part very soon for there is a definite trend toward casual dress that is even filtering down to the workplace. At Alcoa, for example, employees are allowed the option of casual dress, where it seems to be improving morale *and* productivity. Citicorp's marketing department specifies days when employees can dress "outside the box," and at many companies employees dress more informally every Friday (Agins, 1992). One of the reasons for growing acceptance of the laid-back look may be "the rise of baby boomers—for whom blue jeans were once *de rigueur*—into positions of authority" (B1).

According to Marshall Blonsky, a specialist in the study of signs and symbols,

> the only type of offices that will be viable are those that are going to be less formal and hierarchic—those that allow more creativity in order to get the job done. That means getting rid of the rigid, fixed rules like dress codes. (Agins, 1992, p. B1)

The study of how we select and make use of physical objects in our nonverbal communication is referred to as **objectics**. Objectics is concerned with every kind of physical object from the clothing we wear to the food we serve to our dinner guests.

We communicate about ourselves by our choice of car, home, furniture, magazines, music, and many other things. A small pink triangle on an envelope conveys support for gay rights; wearing a red ribbon may draw attention to AIDS awareness; a nose ring may signal something about the wearer's unconventionality. In general, cosmetics, jewelry, and tattoos or decals—recently seen even on high-fashion models—often evoke strong responses from other people.

Whether we intend to communicate or not, the way we choose and display physical objects is taken by others as a source of information about us. It should go without saying that such information is not always accurate.

We have discussed a great many visual cues individually, but remember that as a communicator you are also taking in and interpreting cues about space and time as well as vocal cues, which we will look at in some detail.

VOCAL CUES

I cleared my throat and, to my shock, a hush fell over the room.—People were listening with an intensity that strangely emboldened me. It was as if their attentive silence allowed me to make contact with my own muffled self. I began to speak. A stinging point induced a ripple of agreement. I told a joke and they laughed. My voice got surer, my delivery rising. A charge passed between me and the audience, uniting and igniting us both. (Faludi, 1992, p. 29)

At the beginning of this chapter we spoke about communication that was verbal/vocal—that is, both verbal and vocal. The difference between the verbal and the vocal message is the difference between what is said and *how* it is said. Mehrabian put it well when he explained vocal information as "what is lost when speech is written down" (1968, p. 53).

Take the sentence, "I hate you." Imagine these words being said to show anger or in a much different way to sound seductive. The simple sentence, "I'm glad to meet you," can sound cold and insincere despite its verbal message. Or suppose you go to friend's apartment and she opens the door and says, "Oh, it's you." It is the vocal cues, perhaps in combination with several visual cues, that tell you whether your friend is really pleased to see you, or indifferent, or even disappointed. Of course, if she simply groans when she opens the door, this is an example of nonverbal/vocal communication.

The study of vocal phenomena, **paralinguistics** or **paralanguage,** refers to *something beyond or in addition to language itself.* Paralanguage has two components: *voice qualities,* such as pitch, range, resonance, lip control, and articulation control; and *vocalizations,* or *noises without linguistic structure,* such as crying, laughing, and grunting (Trager, 1958).

Several distinct emotions can be accurately identified solely on the basis of vocal cues, but the more similar the emotions—admiration and affection, for example—the greater our difficulty in identifying them (Davitz and Davitz, 1959*a* and 1959*b*).

Much research on vocal characteristics and emotions parallels the studies of facial expressions. Mehrabian (1968) found that people are easily able to judge the degree of liking communicated vocally. One team of researchers identified four categories of emotion: positive feeling, dislike, sadness, and apprehension or fear. The results confirm that "voice sounds alone, independent of semantic components of vocal messages, carry important clues to the emotional state of a speaker" (Soskin and Kauffman, 1961, p. 78). People can detect aggressiveness from a tape recording of a speaker's message, though not from a written transcript (Starkweather, 1956) and can judge intensity of emotion from vocal characteristics (Starkweather, 1961). We cannot assume, though, that vocal cues are similar across cultures.

A common problem in interpreting vocal cues is misunderstanding sarcasm. This is especially common in children and people with poor listening and/or intellectual skills (Anderson, 1984).

Vocal cues are sometimes the basis for our inferences about personality traits. If people increase the loudness, pitch, timbre, and rate of their speech, we think of them as more active and dynamic (Davitz and Davitz, 1961). If they use more intonation, higher speech rates, more volume, and greater fluency in their speech, we find them more persuasive (Mehrabian and Williams, 1969).

Despite wide agreement about certain relationships between voice qualities and personality traits, no conclusive evidence supports such inferences. They seem to derive from vocal stereotypes. Even if our beliefs have no basis in fact, however, they have striking effects on our response to others; we act on what we believe to be true. Thus when the talkies appeared, several stars of the silent films were ruined because the public expected their voices to sound consistent with their screen personalities. The great lover with the high-pitched voice was too great a disappointment.

Today in California, so-called accent therapists treat many people who want to rid themselves of their New York accents. For some, losing an accent is gaining status and acceptability. Status cues in speech are probably based on a combination of "word choice, pronunciation, grammatical structure, voice quality, articulation and several other observable features" (Harms, 1961). It's interesting that judgments about status can be made quite rapidly (for example, after listening to a sample of a person's speech for only ten or fifteen seconds). Apparently, we can make such inferences with a high degree of accuracy.

Volume

One precondition of effective verbal communication is adequate **volume.** If your voice is so low that you can barely be heard, people rapidly become too tired or too embarrassed to ask you to repeat your last remark. In this case, it is you, the message sender, who becomes a source of interference for the receiver.

According to Gaddy et al. (1987), in organizational communication vocal intensity is a "powerful communication tool for an influencer": it can reinforce or enhance a person's power base and convey a sense of confidence. For example, an employee who speaks loudly is more likely to enhance his or her expertise. Vocal intensity also enables one person to interrupt another and interfere with his or her efforts to speak.

Appropriate sound level varies considerably from one culture to another. At social distance, Hall observes that "in overall loudness, the American voice . . . is below that of the Arab, the Spaniard, the South Asian Indian, and the Russian, and somewhat above that of the English upper class, the Southeast Asian, and the Japanese" (1959, p. 121).

Most people link volume to certain personality traits: thus it is commonly thought that an aggressive person speaks in a louder voice than one who is reserved and shy. Volume, however, is not necessarily a function of personality. Our models in childhood also influence our volume level.

Feedback from the receiver is the best check on volume. If you are not getting through or if you're coming on too strong, adjust your voice accordingly.

Rate and Fluency

Your **rate of speech** is *the number of words you utter within a specified time.* The unit most often used is one minute, and the average speaking rate is about 125 and 150 words per minute.

Speech rates are highly stable for individuals. For this reason a faster rate (as well as shorter comments and more frequent pauses) seems to be linked to fear or anger and a slower rate to grief or depression (Barnlund, 1968, p. 529). Some people are able to control their rate of speaking despite their emotions, but the strain of maintaining this control is often expressed in other vocal or facial cues.

There is no optimum speaking rate. One speed may be appropriate for addressing an audience, another for talking to a foreign student, or a secretary taking dictation. Speech rate can have a definite effect on people's responses to a communicator. Like many other vocal qualities, rate of speech is more effective when adapted to the verbal content of the message and to the specific receiver.

The **fluency,** or *continuity,* of our speech is closely related to rate, and pauses, of course, affect fluency. The person who pauses continually, whose speech is full of vocalizations such as "um," "er," and "ah," may destroy his or her effectiveness as a communicator. Pauses that are frequent, long, and vocalized and that come in the middle of an idea are usually unsettling and undermine the sender's purpose. When used for emphasis and variation, pauses often enhance the verbal message—particularly if they are infrequent, short, and silent, and are used at the end of an idea.

Pitch

When, in *My Fair Lady,* Professor Higgins speaks with distaste about someone's "large Wagnerian mother with a voice that shatters a glass," he is referring to **pitch**—*the frequency level (high or low) of the voice.* Your pitch range is determined by the size and shape of the vocal bands within your larynx, or voice box, Optimum pitch, the level most comfortable for you, is usually one-third above the lowest pitch you are capable of producing (Eisenson and Ogilvie, 1977). Most untrained speakers use a pitch somewhat higher than their optimum pitch, but it has been found that lower pitches are most pleasant to listen to.

Pitch is an important element in people's judgments about a speaker. A voice with unvaried pitch is monotonous and usually disliked; in fact, a monotone seems to be as unpopular as a poker face. People sometimes derive information about emotions from changes in pitch (Weick, in Lindzey and Aronson, 1968). Pitch can even influence our judgments about a doctor's professional competence and social attractiveness. According to a recent study (Ray et al., 1991), when discussing serious illness with their patients, doctors with medium levels of pitch variation were rated highest in professional competence. Doctors with medium and high levels of pitch variation are also seen as more socially attractive than doctors with low variation in pitch.

Apparently, pitch level does not affect the amount of information you understand (Diehl et al., 1961), but it does influence your attitude toward the communicator and the content of the message. Exaggerated pitch changes are even more unpopular than the monotone (Eakins, 1969). A naturally expressive voice has a variety of pitch levels, which are spontaneous and unforced changes.

Quality

Think of a violin, a viola, and a cello. Each is a stringed instrument, but has a different size and shape. The same note played on each of these instruments will therefore have a different *resonance*—a distinctive quality of sound. Similarly, each of you has a distinctive voice **quality** because the resonance of your voice—which to a great extent determines its quality—is a function of the size and shape of your body as well as of your vocal cords.

There seems to be wide agreement in responses to vocal qualities. Judges could reliably distinguish voices described as shrill or harsh from those considered pleasant, or "resonant" (Bowler, 1964). Although it is common practice to refer to a pleasant voice as "resonant," "resonance alone does not make a superior voice" (Anderson, 1977).

In our culture, several voice qualities considered particularly unpleasant are *hypernasality* (talking through the nose), *denasality* (which sounds as though the speaker has a constant head cold), *hoarseness,* and *harshness* (or stridency). *Breathiness* is caused by air wastage, and like *huskiness* it occurs most often in women (Van Riper, 1984).

According to Pearson and associates (1991), differences in gender influence how vocal quality is interpreted. For example:

> A female speaker with a breathy voice is perceived as pretty, petite, feminine, highstrung, and shallow; a male speaker with a breathy voice is perceived as young and artistic. . . . Women with "throaty" voices are perceived as more masculine, lazier, less intelligent, less emotional, less attractive, more careless, less artistic, more naive, more neurotic, less interesting, more apathetic, and quieter. On the other hand, throatiness

in men resulted in their being perceived as older, more mature, more sophisticated, and better adjusted. (p. 144)

Through practice and training, almost all of us can improve our vocal quality. One of the best media available for studying communication style is the videotape recorder, though even videotape loses some of the nuances of vocal inflection, eye contact, postural cues, and the like. The audiotape recorder is another valuable aid and is even more accessible.

For discussion purposes, we have isolated three categories of nonverbal cues. But as we pointed out early on, people interpret messages on the basis of multiple nonverbal and verbal cues. This is certainly the case with *deception.*

DECEPTION

There are very few nonverbal behaviors that consistently differentiate liars from nonliars—for example, liars dilate their pupils more, shrug more often, hesitate and make more speech errors, and have a higher vocal pitch. In general, though, facial expressions are less revealing than body cues, perhaps because we have greater control over our faces.

The kinds of **leakage,** or *signals of deception,* that take place depend on whether the lie is spontaneous or rehearsed and whether we are concealing something emotional or factual. Deception cues are most likely to be given when the deceiver wants to hide a feeling experienced at that moment or feels strongly about the information being hidden. They also tend to occur when a person feels anxious, or guilty, or needs to think carefully while speaking (Cody et al., 1984; Zuckerman et al., 1981; Knapp and Comadena, 1979).

A more recent study found that deceivers delivering a prepared lie respond more quickly than truth tellers—mainly because less thinking is necessary (Greene et al., 1985). When they are unprepared, however, deceivers generally take longer than both prepared deceivers and truth tellers. Those telling the truth generally maintain more eye contact than deceivers. Deceivers also show less body movement, probably in an attempt to avoid leakage cues. At the same time, they laugh and smile more often, presumably trying to keep their faces from displaying other expressions that may turn out to be leakage cues. It's especially interesting that these people continue to behave "deceptively" even when telling the truth. They probably fear that they will lose control if the situation in which they need to lie should recur (Greene et al., 1985). We must note here the great potential for intercultural misunderstandings when cultural conventions of little gesturing and infrequent eye contact may be interpreted as deception.

Until recently, deception research focused on the nature of deception cues and on how information is leaked. Now new research by Buller and others looks at mutual influence in deception and the actual communication exchange between deceivers and detectors.

Do you think it would be easier to tell if your roommate was lying or if a total stranger was lying? And what about probing questions? By asking questions could you figure out whether someone was telling the truth? One recent study (Buller et al., 1991*a*) examines how effective probing is as a strategy for detection and whether knowing the source—that is, the deceiver—affects our ability to distinguish what is truthful.

Buller found that as receivers we communicate whether we accept or suspect a message and we also communicate our suspicion nonverbally through our increased vigilance. When receivers were suspicious they "spoke slower, were less fluent, and lacked clarity in their messages. When probing . . . [they showed] longer response latencies [delays] as the conversation progressed" (p. 18). In fact, they may have tried to conceal their suspicion by asking *fewer* probing questions—in effect, they themselves become less truthful. Deceivers, in turn, can judge our reactions to see how successful they have been and sometimes even modify their behavior to appear more truthful.

Another recent study (Buller et al., 1991*b*) compared the detection skills of those observing a conversation with those actually *participating* in it. (In past studies the "deceived" have usually been only observers.) Participants in conversations were less accurate than observers in detecting deception; in fact, participants showed a stronger *truth-bias*—a tendency to believe the deceiver. (Earlier research has shown that as we become involved in a relationship, the truth-bias tends to increase.) Observers made more accurate honesty judgments than participants, who seem to rely on different nonverbal cues. Researchers found that people participating in the conversation "relied more on facial and head cues when judging deceit—head nodding, smiling, head shaking, and facial animation—while observers relied more on vocal behaviors—interruptions, talkovers, and response latencies" (p. 37).

Most deception studies have used college students as subjects. Over the last twenty years of research, Ekman and Sullivan observe, "people have not been very accurate in judging when someone is lying," with average accuracy estimated as rarely above 60 percent (1991, p. 913). In a study of professional lie catchers, these researchers used seven groups of observers: members of the U.S. Secret Service, federal polygraphers, judges, police, psychiatrists, a diverse group of working adults, and college students. At first glance, the results seem surprising—most groups did no better than college students in judging when a person was lying; here lying involved concealing strong negative emotions. Secret Service people were the only ones who performed better than chance and had greater accuracy in detecting liars. The researchers conclude that Secret Service people are better lie catchers, that "more accurate lie catchers report using nonverbal as well as verbal clues to deceit, [and] that they are better able to interpret subtle facial expressions" (p. 920).

But what about the rest of us? Can we train ourselves to be more skilled in our judgments? Costanza (1992) has designed a training program to improve accuracy in interpreting both verbal and nonverbal cues. Although hearing a lecture on verbal and nonverbal cues did nothing to increase accuracy, practice in identifying relevant cues after viewing videotaped interactions—and then getting feedback about one's judgments—did improve decoding skills. This program emphasized several deception cues established as important from earlier studies; cues included greater speech disfluencies, greater delays in response, more pauses, briefer messages, and more hand gestures (p. 309).

This study also confirms other research that women are more skilled than men in interpreting both verbal and nonverbal cues. Costanza explains this as the result of socialization practices emphasizing "interpersonal skills in women" (p. 312). Although women had higher pretest accuracy scores, however, they were less confident than men that they had performed well. So again we see that greater sensitivity or competence is not always correlated with self-confidence.

The study of deception has much to teach us not only about individual nonverbal cues but about the interaction of verbal and nonverbal behavior. If at times in the last two chapters we have spoken of verbal and nonverbal messages as if they could be separated, this has not been our intention. Face-to-face communication is a total experience. No matter what a person is trying to say, you can see his or her face, body movement, clothing, and so on, and you are responding, whether you are aware of it or not, to all these cues.

SUMMARY

Nonverbal communication is going on all the time. In discussing the interpretation of nonverbal messages, we saw that a significant percentage of all social meaning is conveyed through nonverbal stimuli. We also saw that nonverbal channels convey primarily relational messages, messages about the emotional level of our communication, and that a nonverbal message can replace, reinforce, or contradict a verbal message. The source of most communication difficulties, double or contradictory messages, was considered in terms of double-bind situations and the kinesic slips common to daily experience. We suggested, however, that verbal and nonverbal responses qualify each other in so many ways that they are not totally separable.

Three broad categories of nonverbal cues were examined. First we discussed space and time, cues that have a subtle but pervasive influence on communication style and are, to a great degree, determined by one's culture. We saw that assumptions about nonverbal cues may create misunderstandings in intercultural communication. Visual cues from facial expressions, eye contact, body movements (particularly hand gestures), touching, and physical appearance and the use of objects were analyzed. We found that these cues give us information about human emotions and intentions; they are also the basis for some of our judgments about personality and social status. Vocal cues are another source of information, and we spoke about volume, rate and fluency, pitch, and quality.

In closing, we looked at an area of nonverbal behavior that cuts across all the individual nonverbal cues, the study of deception. We examined some conditions under which signals of deception are most likely to occur as well as new research findings about accuracy in decoding deception cues and the mutual influence of deceivers and detectors.

REVIEW QUESTIONS

1. Specify four categories of communication associated with verbal and vocal communication.

2. What is the relative weight we assign to verbal and nonverbal messages? What type of information does each convey?

3. What are three ways in which nonverbal messages relate to verbal messages?

4. What is a double bind? How does it relate to both verbal and nonverbal communication?

5. Specify four kinds of interpersonal distance. Give an example of each kind.

6. What is personal space? Give an example.

7. What is orientation? Give an example.

8. What is chronemics? Give an example of how timing might interfere with intercultural communication.

9. Explain the difference between monochronic and polychronic time, giving an example of each.

10. What is kinesics?

11. What are four unstated rules in our culture about eye contact?

12. Describe three categories of nonverbal courtship behavior. Give an example of each type.

13. What is the relationship between head and body movements in communicating emotion?

14. What is haptics?

15. Describe how touch might influence bonding, compliance, and self-disclosure.

16. Describe how one's choice of physical objects can communicate messages to others.

17. What is paralinguistics? Give some examples of paralinguistic cues.

18. What four categories of emotion are consistently identified by paralinguistic cues?

19. Identify the conditions under which signals of deception are most likely to occur.

20. Describe the possibilities for mutual influence between detectors and deceivers, and discuss recent research findings about accuracy in decoding deception cues.

EXERCISES

1. Form several two-person teams consisting of one male and one female. Have each team select a place where several people are likely to pass by. Have both members take turns asking strangers the time of day, or some other standard question. While speaking, slowly violate the stranger's proxemic norms until you are very close to him or her. The other member of the team should observe and record the stranger's reactions. When all the teams have collected data, discuss these questions in light of the data collected:
    a. In what ways did the strangers demonstrate nonverbal/vocal and non-verbal/nonvocal communication?
    b. How did the strangers respond to the questioner as he or she began to violate proxemic norms?
    c. Did male and female strangers respond differently to proxemic norm violation depending on whether a male or female did the violating?

2. Repeat the exercise just described, but this time have one questioner dress very neatly, and the other in a sloppy, unkempt manner. Discuss the differences in the strangers' reaction to the questioner.

3. Make a list of the various paralinguistic and vocal cues discussed in this chapter. Tape-record a series of short messages presented by a male and female that illustrate the various types of paralinguistic and vocal cues. Construct a Semantic Differential similar to the one suggested in exercise 1a in Chapter 3. Then ask a number of people to listen to the taped messages and rate the speakers using the Semantic Differential. How did the various paralinguistic and vocal cues affect the listeners' perceptions of the speaker? Relate the results to the concepts discussed in Chapter 2 on person perception.

4. The next time you get angry with someone, try to observe your own nonverbal behavior. Whom do you sound like? Whom do you remind yourself of? Most people look and sound like their parents or other members of their family. Facial expressions, posture, gestures, and vocal cues are often similar among family members. Do you notice similarities? What differences can you detect? Can you account for these similarities and differences?

SUGGESTED READINGS

Condon, John. "So Near the United States: Notes on Communication between Mexicans and North Americans." In *Intercultural Communication: A Reader.* 6th ed. Edited by Larry Samovar and Richard E. Porter. Belmont, CA: Wadsworth, 1991, pp. 106–112.

This is an excellent article on how cultural differences—many of them concerning nonverbal cues—have affected communication between Mexicans and North Americans.

Ekman, Paul. *Telling Lies.* New York: Norton, 1985.

A study of deception by an expert in the field.

Gudykunst, William B., and **Young Yun Kim.** *Communicating with Strangers: An Approach to Intercultural Communication.* 2d ed. New York: McGraw-Hill, 1992.

The critical role of verbal behavior in intercultural communication is the subject of Chapter 9 in this newly revised text.

Hall, Edward T. *The Dance of Life: The Other Dimension of Time.* New York: Doubleday, 1984.

The author views time as culture and explores how both consciously and unconsciously, time is formulated, patterned, and used in diverse cultures.

Hickson, Mark L., III, and **Don W. Stacks.** *NVC: Nonverbal Communication.* Dubuque, IA: Brown & Benchmark, 1992.

An introductory treatment of the subject with applications to nonverbal communication in the home as well as in social situations.

House of Games

A haunting and suspenseful film about a psychologist and a confidence man.

Knapp, Mark L., and **Judy Hall.** *Nonverbal Communication in Human Interaction.* 3rd ed. New York: Harcourt Brace Jovanovich, 1992.

An excellent and newly revised resource for the student of nonverbal communication. The authors have a readable and lively style and include a great deal of illustrative material.

Malandro, Loretta, Larry Barker, and Deborah Barker. *Nonverbal Communication*. 2d ed. New York: McGraw-Hill, 1989.

A thorough survey of present-day theories and research with many examples relevant to student life.

Pearson, Judy Cornelia, Lynn H. Turner, and William Todd-Mancillas. *Gender & Communication*. 2d ed. Dubuque, IA: William C. Brown, 1991.

For a survey of research findings on nonverbal communication and gender, see Chapter 6.

CHAPTER FIVE

*L*istening

CHAPTER OBJECTIVES

After reading this chapter, you should be able to:

1 Identify the most to least used modes of communication.

2 Identify the variables that influence arousal level.

3 Give examples of four different types of listening.

4 Identify four different methods of supporting a speaker's points.

5 Evaluate the various propaganda devices.

6 Differentiate between situations requiring critical listening and empathic listening.

7 Explain how "anticipatory set" can be used to improve listening.

8 Explain four ways in which "spare time" can be used to improve listening.

If I listen, I have the advantage: if I speak, others will have it.
ARABIC SAYING (ACUFF, 1993, P. 96)

*T*ed Koppel, host of the late-evening news program *Nightline,* isn't a sales-person, but he should be. Like most top salespeople, Koppel is a first-rate listener. Night after night, he interviews government officials, chief executives, and famous entertainers. He strokes their egos, and by striking a balance between attentive listening and incisive questioning, Koppel sells both his guests and his viewers on the idea that he is after the truth (Stettner, 1988, p. 44).

Listening is one of the reasons cited for the upset election results of 1992. Former President Bush was seen by many voters as out of touch with the country's economic problems, while President Clinton, having campaigned every two years since 1974, was seen by many as being more "tuned in" to the voice of the electorate.

WHY LISTEN?

Deborah Tannen's best-selling book *You Just Don't Understand* (1991) is a riveting explanation of many of the misunderstandings between men and women. In one example she writes,

> Eve had a lump removed from her breast. Shortly after the operation, talking to her sister, she said that she found it upsetting to have been cut into, and that looking at the stitches was distressing because they left a seam that had changed the contour of her breast. Her sister said, "I know. When I had my operation I felt the same way." Eve made the same observation to her friend Karen, who said, "I know. It's like your body has been violated." But when she told her husband Mark, how she felt, he said, "You can have plastic surgery to cover up the scar and restore the shape of your breast."
>
> Eve had been comforted by her sister and her friend, but she was not comforted by Mark's comment. Quite the contrary, it upset her more. Not only didn't she hear what she wanted, that he understood her feel-ings, but far worse, she felt he was asking her to undergo more surgery just when she was telling him how much this operation had upset her. (p. 50)

Tannen writes that Eve had wanted understanding, but Mark had given her advice. He was trying to act as a problem solver, when instead, she wanted him to confirm her feelings and give her support.

Communication between the sexes is just one very important reason why learning to listen more effectively is a valuable skill to learn in life. In fact, we spend more time listening than we spend at any other method of communi-cating. As early as 1926 it was found that we spend 70 percent of our waking

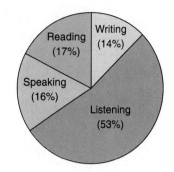

FIGURE 5.1 Waking Hours

(*Source:* Barker et al., "An Investigation of Proportional Time Spent in Various Communication Activities by College Students," *Journal of Applied Communication Research* 8, 1981, 101–109.)

hours communicating—that is, reading, writing, speaking, and listening. When the time spent on these activities was broken down, the results showed that we spend 42 percent of our communicating time listening, 32 percent talking, 15 percent reading, and 11 percent writing (Rankin, 1926).

In a more recent study, Barker and associates (1981) found that college students averaged 53 percent of their waking hours listening (see Figure 5.1). Given students' heavy reading and writing assignments, it seems plausible that the listening percentage for nonstudents is even higher. Research reported by Hargie and associates (1987) confirms the earlier findings. If we spend more time listening than talking, then why is listening a problem?

One study showed that of the four communicative behaviors—speaking, writing, listening, and reading—listening was second only to reading as the *least* arousing of the four activities. Speaking was the most arousing, then writing, then listening, then reading (Crane et al., 1970). In another study, those who talked most frequently in a small-group discussion were most satisfied with the group discussion, and those who participated least were least satisfied (Bostrom, 1970). It is obvious that, in general, talking is more enjoyable than listening to someone else talk. This is due to a number of factors including gaining social recognition, maintaining a topic of interest to you, and attracting attention to yourself.

Listening is like physical fitness or wearing seat belts: everybody knows it is desirable but finds it difficult to do on a regular basis. One psychotherapist we know observes that after a session with a patient he is drenched with perspiration and often feels exhausted, and he feels this is primarily the result of intensive listening. It would be hard to listen that intensively through much of every day, but most of us would agree that when it comes to listening, each of us has room for improvement.

Murphy (1992) cites several examples of how listening has saved American Airlines millions of dollars. He writes,

> Hold the olives please! A seemingly simple suggestion from an American Airline's flight attendant to eliminate the seldom eaten olives from first class salads saved this carrier over $40,000 a year.

In fact, American Airlines has achieved over $180 million in cost savings by tuning into ideas and suggestions of their employees. . . . In January of 1992, over 160 employees who made significant contributions to the IdeAAs in Action program were invited to take the maiden voyage on a new Boeing 757 that was purchased with $50 million of savings generated by employee ideas and suggestions. (pp. 1, 204)

IMPORTANCE OF LISTENING

Although it is somewhat of a truism that listening is important, it is worth documenting the various ways in which listening can help us. Floyd (1985) identifies three such areas of importance: job success, self-protection, and other affirmation (the very act of choosing to listen to someone is highly confirming).

Our listening behaviors can also determine our social and professional success. Think of the impression you get of a person who makes what he thinks is an original comment but is merely repeating what was uttered only moments before by another in the group. Similarly, many on-the-job mistakes result from the employee's not having paid attention to the instructions given by the supervisor. Even your self-concept may be affected by your listening ability.

McCormack (1984, p. 9) tells the story of how Pepsi-Cola had tried to get Burger King to use their product and had assumed that Burger King would never dream of dropping Coca-Cola. After approaching Burger King with a new product strategy concept, which linked Pepsi and Burger King, the Pepsi people were told, "We've been trying to tell you that for months. I'm glad someone finally listened."

On numerous occasions people have reported feeling inferior when, after attending a lecture, they hear their friends discussing issues that the group had "heard" but that they themselves had missed through inattentive listening. Whether the goal to be achieved is an education, social, or professional success, or even the maintenance of one's own self-esteem, as the situation increases in importance, the need to listen more effectively also becomes more vital.

In addition to the reasons stated above, Fisher (1992) has strong evidence that effective listening is associated with marital success. As an anthropologist, she feels that love relationships have evolved from when we were hunters and gatherers. Predictably, she offers the following counsel:

Women should wander side by side with their men, who are born to wander. . . . Men, on the other hand, should sit down with their wives and talk and listen—actively listen. (pp. 6–7)

In Chapter 1 we presented a communication model, and we also discussed the importance of active participation by the parties involved in the communication event. For the communicative cycle to be complete, the party receiving a message must respond accordingly. Without effective listening, the appropriateness of a receiver's response is severely diminished. Both from a practical and theoretical standpoint, then, effective listening becomes a vital element in human communication.

What Is Meant by Listening

One reason for misconceptions about "listening" stems from the ambiguity of the term. Listening is actually a complex process involving four elements: (1) hearing, (2) attention, (3) understanding, and (4) remembering. Thus, a suitable definition of listening would be "the selective process of attending to, hearing, understanding, and remembering aural symbols."

Hearing

The first element in the listening process is hearing, which is the automatic physiological process of receiving aural stimuli. It is at this stage that a defect in a person's physical hearing apparatus may cause difficulty in the listening process. Human speech frequencies range from 125 to 8,000 cycles per second; most words fall between 1,000 and 7,500 cycles per second, which is the critical range of auditory ability (Brooks, 1981, p. 82).

Typically, sound waves are received by the ear and stimulate neurological impulses to the brain. However, any physical defect that interrupts this normal chain of events can result in a hearing difficulty. Research indicates that very loud sound (measured in decibels) can and does produce both temporary and permanent hearing losses. For example, excessively loud rock music has been found to produce hearing losses in listeners.

The human ear can cope with 55 to 85 decibels. However, rock concerts can pose a problem because the noise level can reach as high as 100 decibels (the level of a plane taking off). Government regulations are now in effect in industry to ensure that workers are protected from hearing losses that might otherwise result from loud industrial noises. For the most part, if we assume that our hearing apparatus is functioning properly, problems in listening do not typically stem from problems in hearing.

Second, we place these sounds in a meaningful order or sequence so that they may be recognized as words. Third, we recognize words in a pattern that constitutes a language, which then helps to convey the message from the communicator to us.

Another factor in hearing is the speaker's rate. The average speaker's rate is between 100 and 150 words per minute. However, the research on compressed speech shows that most of us are able to comprehend rates up to 400 to 500 words per minute (Goss, 1982, p. 91).

Although the ability to process information four times faster than the average person speaks would seem to be an advantage, it turns out that it is instead a part of the problem in that three-fourths of our listening is "spare time." This means that we are able to comprehend what we hear much more quickly than a speaker is able to articulate his or her thoughts; thus we may get bored and begin to daydream. This fact tends to account for the findings that show speaking to be more interesting than listening. Later in this chapter we will look at ways of using our "spare time" to improve our listening ability.

Attention

Attending to stimuli in our environment is like focusing our conscious awareness on certain specific stimuli. In Chapter 2 we pointed out that our sensory receptors are constantly bombarded with so many stimuli that we cannot possibly respond to all of them at once. Specific cells in our nervous system (inhibitory neurons) serve to filter out some of these incoming sensations, keeping them from our conscious awareness. One writer stated that, were it not for these inhibitory neurons, we would experience sensations similar to an epileptic seizure every time we opened our eyes (Kern, 1971, p. 48). In spite of these neurological limitations, we still are not able to focus on a single event for more than just a few seconds at a time because of the other stimuli usually competing for our attention.

The phenomenon whereby *we attend to certain stimuli while filtering out others* is referred to as **selective attention.** In order to better understand this phenomenon, take out a piece of paper and a pen or pencil. Then, in a moment, stop reading and listen to the sounds around you. Now make a list of these

Selective attention is where we attend to certain stimuli while filtering out others, such as at a crowded party.

sounds. How many sounds did you write down? Were you aware of them while you were reading? Can you now focus on them or ignore them at will? Probably not, but perhaps you can better understand what we mean when we say that there are numerous stimuli competing for our attention most of the time. In fact, students who want to improve their study habits are often told to find a place that has the fewest distractions that could promote daydreaming (e.g., pictures of your girlfriend or boyfriend, windows, chairs facing doorways where people walk by, pin-ups). All of these stimuli are usually more pleasant to attend to than the study materials at hand. Based on this principle, how successful (from a learning standpoint) do you think a study date with a member of the opposite sex is likely to be?

A part of this selective attention process that has been experimentally studied is called the "cocktail party problem" (Bostrom, 1988)—namely, how do you listen to one voice when more than one person is speaking at the same time? Perhaps you have already tried this, but next time you are in such a situation try to focus on one voice at a time. Numerous studies have shown that a person will normally do this, rather than flitting attention from one person's voice to another (Broadbent, 1958). This is probably because we have a greater interest in a continuous message than in several interrupted messages. Another finding is that we are able to sort out a single voice much easier when it comes in only one ear while a competing message is coming in the other ear than if both messages are heard by the same ear. Research using headphones and tape-recorded messages indicates that selective attention from "*dichotic* presentation (when one message is presented to one ear, another to the other) was markedly superior to *monaural* presentation (where both messages were presented to the same ear)" (Moray, 1969, p. 17). The author concludes by stating that "it is clear that a listener *is* able to exercise considerable voluntary control over what he will hear" (Moray, 1969, p. 88).

An issue related to attention is the concept of **threshold.** A threshold is defined as

> the stimulus intensity at which the observer reports detecting a signal on 50 percent of the trials. . . . Threshold is determined by stimulus variables such as intensity, frequency (or wavelength), duration, size, and rate of presentation, as well as by subject variables such as adaptational state, training, age, motivation, and health; experimental procedures also affect thresholds. One of the most difficult problems is motivation and the subject's criterion for stating that he saw or heard something. (Moray, 1969, p. 18)

A threshold, then, is the minimum level of stimulus intensity that enables us to pay attention. The important thing to remember is that our attention thresholds vary depending on several things, including our own motivational state. Later in this chapter we will show how this fact relates to improving our listening behaviors.

One final element that affects attention is a person's **arousal level.** Arousal level is directly related to the thresholds we have for listening. Obviously, we do not listen well when we are asleep. Nor do we listen well when we are drowsy. General alertness, then, is related to our ability to attend aural stimuli and subsequently to listen more effectively. Not only is general arousal important, but specific arousal also has a bearing on our listening behavior. A mother may sleep through a loud noise only to awake at the cry of a small baby. A man in a noisy restaurant may "perk his ears up" when he hears his name paged, and a child alone in a house after watching a spooky movie on TV may hear many more creaks and sounds than she normally would. Our specific state of arousal, then, to some extent determines our threshold for paying attention to auditory stimuli. This concept will also be related to some advice later in this chapter on improving your listening.

Understanding

The third and most complicated element in listening is **understanding,** also referred to as *auditing*. Understanding usually refers to the process whereby we assign a meaning to the words we hear that closely corresponds to the meaning intended by the person sending the message. This process was discussed at some length in Chapter 1.

Since the process of understanding by definition requires us to associate a message with our past experiences, we also tend to accept or reject (i.e., evaluate) the message as we are trying to understand it. The famous psychologist Dr. Carl Rogers has written that "the major barrier to mutual interpersonal communication is our very natural tendency to judge, to evaluate, to approve or disapprove, the statement of the other person, or the group" (1961, p. 330). Thus, if we can focus more of our listening effort on trying to understand the meaning that the speaker was intending to convey, temporarily withholding our tendency to judge or evaluate that message, we should considerably improve our ability to listen more effectively.

Interpreting a message is literally *giving* it meaning. It is based on (at the least) understanding the grammar of the language, recognizing and understanding the source's intent (sarcastic, joking, serious), understanding the implications of the situation (including the physical environment, the relationship shared with the other person, and the climate of the encounter), and sharing assumptions about the world and how it operates (what is and is not realistic).

Remembering

Most tests of listening to some extent test how much we remember of what we heard and understood. **Remembering** is the storing of information for later retrieval. If a person gives you directions to a particular place and you understand them but forget the directions before you can write them down, then your listening was not as useful as it might have been.

There are two types of memory—short-term memory (STM) and long-term memory (LTM). Short-term memory is what allows us to remember a telephone number long enough to dial it but not well enough to recall it even five minutes later. Short-term memory is said to be able to handle about five items of information at one time. You can recognize this limitation by trying to remember several names when you are introduced to a large group at a social gathering.

Verbal material stored in STM appears to be encoded by the *sound* of the material rather than the *sight*. For example, if we see the letter *Q* but later mistakenly recall that letter, we are more likely to remember it as a *U* (which *sounds* similar to *Q*) than as an *O* (which looks more like a *Q*). Thus, the information coding and retrieval mechanism of the brain appears to be in part based on the sound of a word, probably as a result of the way we learn the names for things.

Long-term memory stores those items of information that we usually think of as being "committed" to memory (e.g., our hometown, our parents' first names). Basically the difference between STM and LTM is the amount of *repetition* and *rehearsing* that occurs with an individual item of information, and the ease with which the item fits into already stored information. Active listening is a technique for rehearsing material in the STM. It helps you remember the material longer. Thus, active listening is much like programmed learning, which assumes that learning is most effective when learners periodically test themselves on how much they are remembering, then review what they have learned.

Research summarized by Barker (1971) indicates that immediately after we hear something we remember only half. Eight hours later we remember only 35 percent, and two months later we remember 25 percent. Obviously, this assumes we were paying attention in the first place, and that the message was brief and relatively uncomplicated. The "bottom line" with respect to listening is the *residual message*, the kernel the listener remembers.

In this section we have looked at the four interrelated elements that constitute learning. They were (1) hearing; (2) attention; (3) understanding, or auditing; and (4) remembering. In the next section we will discuss different types of listening.

TYPES OF LISTENING

If you were to list some of the typical reasons why you listen to others, what would they be? Probably any list would include at least four types of listening. These four are not mutually exclusive or exhaustive but merely representative.

Pleasurable Listening

The first type of listening would be **pleasurable listening.** Children often wonder how adults can just talk to each other for hours at social gatherings.

As we grow out of childhood, we become more oriented toward talking as a means of socializing and less oriented toward acting (e.g., playing games) as a means of socializing. Obviously, some types of listening experiences must be pleasurable or enjoyable. Pleasurable listening might also include movies, plays, television, music, and many other forms of entertainment. Although we may benefit intellectually or professionally from this type of listening, these gains are by-products and are not the main reason for engaging in pleasurable listening.

Discriminative Listening

A second type of listening is **discriminative listening.** This is a more serious type of listening and is primarily used for understanding and remembering (as discussed in the previous section). Discriminative listening would include most of the serious listening situations in which we find ourselves—in the classroom, listening on the job, listening to instructions, and many others. As a general rule of thumb, the more important the situation (e.g., listening to directions on how to react in an emergency situation), the more important it is to be able to employ this type of listening.

Critical Listening

The third type of listening is **critical listening.** Critical listening is usually needed when we suspect that we may be listening to a biased source of information. For example, if we were to ask a physician to tell us her opinion of Medicare, we would expect that her own feelings would make it hard for her to give a totally objective answer. Critical listening is also associated with being able to detect propaganda devices employed by a communicator. During World War II a number of federal agencies, including the Institute for Propaganda Analysis, identified several specific devices that are still sometimes used as a means of presenting information in a biased or distorted manner. As we examine a few of these devices we will see that they are often used in everyday interpersonal communication situations as well as in more formal mass communication contexts. However, some of the same devices are also *legitimate* forms of presenting information. Thus, the technique itself may not be inherently bad; it is the way in which it is used or misused that determines its value and creates the challenge for the critical listener. With this in mind, let us examine several techniques that may be used to help present ideas. We will also indicate how these techniques may be misused.

The means of developing a point are often called *methods of support* or *materials of support.* There are at least four specific methods of support, including (1) analogy, (2) example, (3) statistics, and (4) testimony or quotation.

Analogy

An **analogy** may be the most concise and graphic way to get a complex idea or a point across. In a discussion of the increasing arrests of young people on drug charges, one student commented: "Relaxing the law would indeed reduce the number of arrests, but it would be like loosening your tie to relieve sweating. It is only a temporary measure that does nothing to eliminate the problem causing the arrests." As it stands, this analogy effectively conveyed the student's position. Suppose, however, that she had gone on to argue that laws, like ties and other articles of clothing, are unnatural constraints that should be discarded. She would then have been on very shaky ground.

An analogy draws parallels between two things or situations, but as we have observed, it is a partial comparison and at some point it breaks down. If the objects of comparison are dissimilar enough to invalidate the attempt to juxtapose them, the analogy is a poor one. In listening critically we must first determine the appropriateness of the speaker's analogy to the subject at hand and then the limits of its use. For example, in one debate a speaker compared a government policy to putting a new muffler on a defective car. "It only makes the car sound better," he commented. "It doesn't solve the problem." His opponent, responding to what he felt was a poor analogy, commented, "Without the new muffler, the car's occupants would be asphyxiated in a matter of minutes. So the new policy is needed immediately."

The test for the critical listener is to determine how accurate or reasonable the comparison is. Analogies are metaphorical ways of explaining ideas, and at some point the analogy eventually breaks down. In other words, the situations usually involve some differences that are important enough to invalidate the comparison being made. It is important to note, however, that analogies may be a very useful and legitimate method to bring about understanding of an idea.

Listeners often recall the examples or analogies used by the speaker and miss the point the speaker intends to illustrate. In analyzing all materials of support, it is critical first to identify the speaker's point and then to evaluate the method of support used to prove it. Remember that materials of support do not in themselves constitute an argument.

Example

The second method of supporting an idea is using an **example.** We have used examples throughout this book to illustrate many of the concepts we are trying to convey. Examples may be very brief specific instances, or they may be quite extended. Examples usually make meaning much clearer for the listener. However, examples, like analogies, can be misused. The critical listener will try to determine if the example being used is actually representative of the point that the communicator is trying to make. In a propaganda device called the **hasty generalization,** one or two examples are cited to prove a point. When using this propaganda device, the speaker *jumps to a conclusion on the basis of very limited evidence.* It is the receiver who must decide, first, whether an example is appropriate to a speaker's point and, second, whether it is being used in lieu of an argument. Consider this example from a student discussion: "My grandparents have lots of money so I don't think old people need Medicare benefits." Most of us tend to generalize from our own personal experiences (or lifelong sets of examples). However, those experiences are often misleading. Examples can be used or abused; the critical listener must make subjective judgments to detect the difference.

Statistics

Statistics are numerical methods of describing events or ideas. Statistics can be rather difficult for listeners to understand, but when used in conjunction with other methods of support, they can help to clarify points considerably. In a discussion of teenage marriages, a person may use an example of a couple who had an unsuccessful marriage, then go on to cite that the divorce rate for couples who marry in their teens is *double* that of older married couples, and that even the divorce rate of older couples is fairly high. Here statistics are used to show that the conclusion drawn from the example is in fact valid and not a hasty generalization.

Statistics can also be abused, however. Advertisements are often misleading when they state, "Skyhighs now relieve pain twice as fast." The assumption is that they act twice as fast as some competitor's product. But perhaps they only relieve pain twice as fast as they did two years ago and indeed take effect no faster than any of the competing products. We don't know. We would have to ask, "Twice as fast as what?" What are the terms of the comparison? Is this product being compared with itself or something else? This use of statistics, like the propaganda devices of card stacking or half truths, is misleading in that it presents a biased or distorted view of the truth.

Another propaganda device that makes use of statistics is the **bandwagon appeal.** One student survey of college cheating showed that certain percentages of students cheat on exams. Using statistics from this survey, a speaker could claim that cheating is acceptable since other people do it too. Statistics, then, can be used properly or improperly depending on the user and the situation. This is illustrated by the old adage "Statistics don't lie, but liars may use statistics."

The critical listener must attempt to determine if the speaker clearly reveals and defines what unit of measure is being used in the statistics and what is being compared (e.g., is a product being compared to itself or to its competitor?).

Testimony or Quotations

The fourth method of supporting an idea is through the use of **testimony or quotations.** Ideas often are more acceptable to listeners if they think the ideas have been accepted by others, especially if those others are either prestigious or expert. For example, in arguing the effects of marijuana, a speaker might use quotations from medical authorities to show that her point or position is supported by expert opinion. Lawyers in the courtroom frequently use this technique to establish the probable validity of their cases. Consider, for example, this courtroom comment:

> Ladies and gentlemen of the jury, the coroner's report showed that the time of death was between midnight and six A.M. on the night of May sixteenth. We have established that my client was nowhere near the scene of the crime on the night of the sixteenth. Therefore, my client could not have committed the murder.

In this case, the coroner's expert testimony helps prove the innocence of the client.

In many informal conversations we cite trusted or respected others who support a given point as a means of making our point more believable. However, testimony and quotations, like other methods of support, can be misused. Often people who are expert in one field have strong *opinions* in fields where they have little or no expertise. The critical listener may catch this and realize that the testimonials used are not valid. Rev. Jerry Falwell's opinions on religion, for example, would probably be acceptable as expert authority; his opinions on apartheid, however, would not have the same validity.

The propaganda device of **plain folks** represents another misuse of testimony. Middle-aged professors who dress like their students in an attempt to identify with their listeners often look ridiculous. Politicians who try to over-identify with their constituents (by milking cows or wearing ten-gallon hats) may be using the plain folks approach.

Probably the most crucial point to remember about critical listening is that you must first listen and be able to identify the point the speaker is trying to make, *then* listen for and evaluate the method of support the speaker uses to prove that point. So often in conversations listeners will remember the example a speaker uses and miss the point that the example was supposed to illustrate.

Empathic Listening

The final type of listening is **empathic listening.** As the term suggests, the listener tries to demonstrate empathy for the speaker. All of us like to feel that a person is being sympathetic during times of difficulty. In fact, in some cities "Dial a Friend" or "warm lines" have been established for just such a purpose. Stephen Covey, in his best-selling book *The 7 Habits of Highly Effective People* (1990), offers the following advice:

> "Seek first to understand" involves a very deep shift in paradigm. We typically seek first to be understood. Most people do not listen with the intent to understand; they listen with the intent to reply. . . . When I say

empathic listening, I mean listening with intent to understand. I mean seeking first to understand, to really understand. (pp. 239–240)

Empathic listening can also be described as listening "between the lines." When we listen between the lines we heighten our awareness and interpersonal sensitivity to the entire message a person may be trying to communicate.

A good definition of this approach to listening is illustrated by the following point of view. "Empathy is perception and communication by resonance, by identification, by experiencing in ourselves some reflection of the emotional tone that is being experienced by the other person. . . . Empathy continues throughout life as the basic mode of significant communication between adults" (Pearce and Newton, 1963, p. 52).

"Empathy" comes from the word *Einfühlung* used by German psychologists; it literally means "feeling into." One friend who was having a problem with his girlfriend talked for over an hour without our saying much more than that we knew how he felt and we sincerely hoped he could work things out. By the end of the hour he had seen a way to resolve the difficulty and left saying, "Thanks so much for helping me figure this thing out!" We really *had* been concerned, and we really *had* listened, but we hadn't offered any suggestions on how to solve the problem. Yet our friend needed someone to talk to, and this opportunity to share his problem with a concerned listener helped

Does the man appear to be an empathic listener? What does his nonverbal communication say?

him gain a new attitude toward the situation. Empathic listening serves as a reward or encouragement to the speaker. It communicates your caring and acceptance and reaffirms the person's sense of worth. This style of listening seems to be most important in terms of strengthening or improving a positive interpersonal relationship between the parties involved.

Empathic listening is often an important part of any client-counselor relationship. One such relationship exists between the patient and the psychotherapist. Theodore Reik (1948), a psychoanalyst, coined the phrase "listening with the third ear" to symbolize this type of listening. Actually, it refers to being as sensitive to visual cues as to vocal cues, but it represents another way of thinking about this style of listening. He describes listening with the third ear in this manner:

> The analyst hears not only what is in the words; he hears also what the words do not say. . . . In psychoanalysis . . . what is spoken is not the most important thing. It appears to us more important to recognize what speech conceals and what silence reveals. (p. 125)

One college student joined two friends and asked them what they were doing on Saturday night. They replied that they were going to the basketball game. Then the topic of conversation shifted for several minutes. Just as they were about to go their separate ways, one of the young men said, "Say, Tom, would you like to go to the game with us on Saturday?" Tom replied, "Oh wow, that sounds like it would be a good time. Yeah, I'd like to go." He admitted later that he wanted to go all along but didn't want to come right out and ask for fear of intruding on their plans. Luckily, the other student was "listening with the third ear" and realized that Tom would enjoy being included in the group.

One difficulty with trying to practice *empathic listening* is that it often requires the opposite frame of mind from that required for *critical listening*. Empathic listening implies a willingness not to judge, evaluate, or criticize but rather to be an accepting, permissive, and understanding listener. Thus, what might be the proper way to improve listening in one context may be the very opposite of what is required to be a good listener in another context. The difficult task for the listener is to determine which skills are most important in which situations.

Two psychologists from Harvard University offer some excellent guidelines on how to use empathic listening (or what they refer to as the "reflective response"):

> At the most general level, we can describe reflective responses by several simple characteristics:
>
> ♦ A greater emphasis on listening than on talking.
>
> ♦ Responding to that which is personal rather than abstract.

- Following the other in his exploration rather than leading him into areas we think he should be exploring.

- Clarifying what the other person has said about his own thoughts and feelings rather than asking questions or telling him what we believe he should be thinking, seeing, or feeling.

- Responding to the feelings implicit in what the other has said rather than the assumptions or "content" that he has talked about.

- Trying to get into the other person's inner frame of reference rather than listening and responding from our own frame of reference.

- Responding with empathic understanding and acceptance rather than with disconcern, distanced objectivity, or overidentification (i.e., internalizing his problem so that is also becomes our own).

Although these brief generalizations may appear to suggest that reflection requires passive and generally inactive behavior on the part of the person who is trying to help or understand, quite the opposite is true. The reflective technique requires very careful and focused listening. It also requires a high degree of selectivity in choosing what to respond to in what the person has said. (Athos and Gabarro, 1978, p. 417) (see also Pearce, 1991.)

HOW TO IMPROVE LISTENING

Most of the experts agree that the first step to becoming a better listener is to develop an awareness of the problem. We have tried to accomplish that objective thus far in the chapter. The second step to improvement is to develop the desire or motivation to behave differently. The third step is to change, or activate new behaviors.

Listen Effectively

Andre (1991) cites an example of ineffective listening when she writes:

Since time is a precious commodity, executives learn to give visitors the impression of having plenty of time to listen to them when, in reality, they are counting the minutes. . . .

It requires either a high degree of concentration which allows for the submergence of matters that normally would be uppermost in the mind, or a skillful display of polite attention in which nods, facial expressions, and assorted vocalizations succeed in giving the impression the listener's thoughts are where they are not. . . . Either tactic, however, was almost invariably accompanied by the recurrent sense of distancing, of being oddly apart from others. (pp. 140–141)

Ineffective listening may take any of the forms described below:

Hearing problems is the general term that covers any of the myriad problems that can decrease or eliminate the range of sounds that can be heard. This is especially important when you consider that hearing is the first step in the listening process. Without adequate hearing, there can be no listening whatsoever.

Overload is the problem associated with hearing too much, having to attend to too many stimuli. The result can be stress, withdrawal, or not being able to focus attention.

Rapid thought goes along with the section on "use your spare time." The problem is that the time is "wasted" as the listener allows his mind to wander.

Noise is the general term used to describe anything that interferes with the communication process. With respect to listening, we can identify noise connected with the physical environment, the channel, and the psychological environment (the matters demanding attention that are on the listener's mind).

Inappropriate approaches to listening is the general category for a host of inappropriate listening behaviors. The most inappropriate is "ambush listening." This is listening for the little piece of information that can be used as the basis for an attack on the speaker. "Insensitive listening" is accepting the speaker's words at face value and not taking into account all the things that affect meaning. "Dan Akroyd listening" is listening only for the facts. "Touchy-feely listening" is listening only for the emotions. "Pseudolistening" is pretending to listen (which many of us were taught—to be polite and act as if we are paying attention even if we aren't).

Ashenbrenner and Snalling (1988) have identified some additional barriers to effective listening:

Judgment: The tendency to evaluate what we hear—often before we have heard it completely.

Preoccupation: Our own concerns become more important than listening to another. We believe that what we are thinking is more important than what the other is saying.

Pseudolistening: We pretend to listen. All our body language says we are attentive, but our thoughts wander elsewhere.

Semantics: Meanings unique to a particular field create misunderstandings when applied outside of its relevance. People are also hesitant to ask another to repeat or clarify.

Excessive talking: We prefer to talk rather than listen to another. We listen for pauses, so we can interject, believing that what we have to say is more important.

Fear: Sometimes we tune out because we are afraid of what the other will say. (pp. 40–41)

Pay Attention

Before we can react appropriately to what a person says, we must pay attention to it. Unfortunately, most people tend to think they are better at this than they really are. William Keefe (1972) writes:

> Not all in this situation see themselves for what they are. Many believe themselves to be good listeners. But they cannot back up their laudatory self-analysis. The Opinion Research Corporation of Princeton, New Jersey, carried out a survey in four large companies. The findings showed that 77 percent of the supervisors interviewed felt themselves to be good listeners. Other data (from their subordinates) gave them the lie. (p. 14)

Earlier in this chapter we stated that the threshold for listening could be improved (lowered to detect more stimuli) by changes in a person's motivation. Thus, a determined effort to pay attention has been found to improve a person's listening considerably.

In addition, those who are otherwise good communicators may not be good listeners. Brilhart (1965) showed that there is no necessary correlation between skill as a communicator and skill as a listener. In fact, several of her findings suggested that good communicators were relatively poor listeners (i.e., there were negative correlations). Thus, if you feel yourself to be a relatively effective speaker, you are even more likely to need listening improvement.

Perhaps you are wondering if it is even possible to improve a person's listening ability. Numerous studies indicate that dramatic improvements are possible even with minimal training (Keller, 1960).

Listen for Main Points or Ideas

A second way to improve your listening is to maintain your motivation to pay attention by listening for the specific main ideas in a message. Earlier in this chapter we discussed the role that *attention* plays in listening. Numerous experimental studies indicate that simply paying attention is one of the most important ways of improving your listening.

Keller describes the techniques this way:

Anticipatory set is defined as the ability to say to oneself as he listens, "I imagine that what the speaker is trying to say is. . . ." This anticipation and comparing of expectation with outcome may cause the listener to pay attention in order to see if he is right. (Keller, 1960, p. 30)

Use Your Spare Time

One of the reasons that paying attention seems to be such a problem for listeners is that the human brain can process information much faster than a person can talk. Research has been conducted in the area of time-compressed speech in which a tape-recorded message is electronically speeded up without changing the pitch level (unless pitch is controlled, the recording begins to sound like a chipmunk as the speed is increased). Depending on the message's complexity, organization, and such, we can understand information relatively well, even up to a rate of 400 to 500 words per minute. The average speaking rate, however, is only 125 to 150 words per minute (Goss, 1982). As a consequence, our minds are seldom fully occupied while listening, and we have a tendency to daydream.

Several listening experts have suggested that this "spare time" that we have (while our mind is working faster than the speaker's rate of speech) may be used to do some extra thinking about what the speaker is trying to say. This may be a bit tricky and seems more suitable for an audience member or group member than for a participant in a two-person conversation.

Ralph Nichols (1957), the nation's foremost authority on listening, suggests that you first anticipate the speaker's next point. From the context of his or her past remarks, you may be able to predict the next point in advance (sometimes you may be surprised). Second, mentally rehearse or review the points that the speaker has already covered. As we stated earlier, this rehearsal is the key factor in transferring information from short-term memory (STM) to long-term memory (LTM). Third, use the tests of critical thinking discussed earlier in this chapter. Listen for the validity and quality of the analogies, examples, statistics, and testimonials the speaker uses. Fourth, listen "between the lines" for what the speaker doesn't say but may be communicating non-verbally through tone of voice or even with visual cues. As we pointed out in Chapter 4, these cues may carry as much or more meaning than the verbal messages. The spare time that is available to the listener can be used for daydreaming and faulty listening, or it can be used more profitably to improve understanding and retention of a speaker's message.

More recently, Nisbet (1988) offers several practical tips for better listening:

1. Be patient—Avoid temptation to rush the speaker. Also, since rate of speaking is 120 words per minute and listening is three to four times faster, it is important not to project the speaker's meaning before he or she has finished.

2. Take time—If one doesn't have time to listen, it is better to state this, rather than half-listen or rush the speaker.

3. Be attentive—Keep one's mind on the subject and speaker. Offer feedback and be active in listening.

4. Be prepared to learn—Don't listen with set ideas or with an unwillingness to change. Be open to other options.

5. Don't overreact to the message—Keep the barriers down. Listen to the full message and meaning of the speaker.

6. Don't overreact to the messenger—Focus on the message content if the speaker is bothering you.

7. Don't pretend—Don't go through the motions of pseudolistening.

8. Don't be preoccupied—Put competing thoughts out of your mind and focus on the speaker and the message.

SUMMARY

In this chapter we have attempted to answer the question, Why listen? by showing how professional and social success may be affected by listening. We discussed the different phases of listening, including hearing, attention, understanding, and remembering. We discussed the different types of listening—pleasurable, discriminative, critical, and empathic—and pointed out that these may call for quite different behaviors. Finally, we suggested that most of us could benefit by improving our listening behaviors, and we suggested ways in which this might be accomplished. They included paying closer attention, listening for main points, and using the spare time between thought rate and speech rate. As a final word on listening, it would be worthwhile for us to keep in mind this ancient proverb: "It is significant that we have two ears but only one mouth, so that we might listen twice as much as we speak."

REVIEW QUESTIONS

1. Which of the four modes of communicating do we use most, and which do we use least?

2. What are some of the variables that influence a person's arousal level? How does this knowledge relate to listening?

3. Give examples of pleasurable, discriminative, critical, and empathic listening.

4. Develop an essay on any topic and use one of each of the following

methods of support to amplify your point: (a) analogy, (b) example, (c) statistics, and (d) quotation or testimony.

5. Describe some of the ways the methods of support may become devices of propaganda.

6. Describe and differentiate between the situations in which critical listening and empathic listening may be more appropriate. Use illustrations from your experiences to support your point of view.

7. How may "anticipatory set" be used to improve listening?

8. Discuss the four techniques of using the spare time between your thought speed and a communicator's speaking speed. After trying these techniques, evaluate their usefulness.

EXERCISES

1. Form the class into a circle of about twenty people (more than one circle if necessary). Have the first person give his or her name and mention something he or she likes. Then have the second person tell about himself or herself and the first person. Then have the third tell about himself or herself and the first two. For example, the third person says: I'm Sally and I like strawberries and he's Jack and he likes guitar; and she's Pam and she likes backpacking. Keep this up until you have gone around the entire circle.

2. Make a tape recording of yourself either in an informal conversation or in a formal speech situation. Play the tape and write an analysis of the factors that make your speech hard to listen to. Then make a list of suggestions on how you might improve your speaking.

3. Write a description (i.e., a case study) of an experience in which a breakdown in listening played an important part. Then write an analysis of how the problem might be avoided or the situation improved in the future.

4. As you listen to a speech given in your class, try to outline it, including (1) the thesis idea, (2) the main points, and (3) the types of supporting materials used (identify and evaluate them). Then compare your outline to that of the speaker.

5. Practice listening to very difficult or unfamiliar information, applying the suggestions in this chapter (i.e., paying attention, listening for the main points, using the "spare time," developing empathic listening).

6. Write a paragraph of factual information. Have one person read it to the class after three students have left the room. Call one student in and read

the paragraph again, then have this student try to repeat it from memory to another who left, who in turn will repeat it to the third. Tape-record this if possible. Analyze the way the original message gets changed.

7. Analyze a television commercial, a political speech, or an informal conversation for the use and misuse of materials supporting the person's ideas (i.e., analogy, example, statistics, and testimony). Write an evaluation of their effectiveness.

8. Have a two-person conversation (dyadic encounter) with someone you choose from your class. Try to find out more about each other than the superficialities of hometown, major subjects, and such. Then (if you agree to beforehand) have each person write a short description of the other person in each dyad, and reproduce a copy of each description for each member of the class. This will motivate you to listen carefully to each other and will help class members to get to know more about each other.

9. In a group discussion, either in class or elsewhere, try to test your listening by restating or paraphrasing a point that has been stated but that you are not sure you understand. You may also try to summarize the main points that have been brought out in the discussion, both to help orient you and the other group members to what the group has already accomplished and to see how well you have been listening to the progress of the discussion.

10. In a discriminative listening situation, try (really try) as often as possible to apply the suggestions offered in this chapter. After a reasonable length of time (e.g., a month), evaluate whether or not this has improved your listening ability.

Suggested Readings

Acuff, Frank L. *How To Negotiate Anything with Anyone Anywhere Around the World.* New York: AMACOM, 1993.

Although this book is primarily about negotiation, there are portions relevant to the topic of listening.

Goss, Blaine. *Processing Information.* Belmont, CA: Wadsworth, 1982.

An excellent technical text that covers listening in an information processing context. Recommended for those interested in the more rigorous material available on listening.

Murphy, Kevin J. *Effective Listening.* Salem, NH: ELI Press, 1992.

This book is a good, practical handbook on how to improve your listening. It is filled with self-tests. It also emphasizes applications to professional settings.

Stewart, John, and **Carol Logan.** *Together: Communicating Interpersonally.* 4th ed. New York: McGraw-Hill, 1993.

This excellent book has a wonderful chapter on listening (Chapter 6) that is well worth the time spent reading it.

Tannen, Deborah. *You Just Don't Understand: Women and Men in Conversation.* New York: Ballantine, 1991.

This best-selling book is a must for all to read in order to improve communication between the sexes!

Wolvin, Andrew, and **C. G. Coakley.** *Listening.* 3rd ed. Dubuque, IA: Brown, 1988.

One of the most complete books available on this subject.

CHAPTER SIX

Relationships in Process

After reading this chapter, you should be able to:

1 Discuss the influence of proximity on attraction.

2 Describe the relationship between similarity and attraction, and identify three variables that qualify predictions about similarity and attraction.

3 Differentiate between the setting and the climate of a relationship, and discuss two critical measures of climate.

4 Discuss the concept of time as a defining characteristic of relationships.

5 Explain a range of relationships that can be characterized by varying levels of trust and information sharing, and discuss recent research on motives for deception.

6 Describe the dimensions of affection and control and how they influence relationship stability.

7 Outline both the building and declining stages of a human relationship as described by Knapp, and discuss various strategies for maintaining relationships.

8 Discuss the defining characteristics of family and the distinctive nature of family communication.

9 Identify three stages in family development and discuss recent research findings about sibling relationships.

10 Explain three different categories of conflict behavior, and discuss two approaches to conflict resolution.

*I*n the movie *When Harry Met Sally,* Billy Crystal and Meg Ryan play two college students who meet for the first time to drive from the University of Chicago to New York. After a long ride and a series of conversations filled with innuendo, flirtation, and bickering, Harry and Sally arrive in the big city all too happy to go their separate ways. Occasionally, they meet by chance—we see them at five-year intervals—exchanging the briefest of confidences.

It's only after Harry's divorce and the breakup of Sally's latest romance that the two become friends, offering support and advice on each other's romantic relationships. He even fixes her up with one of his closest friends—with no dazzling effects. Harry and Sally seem to be experts in each other's faults; "Miss Hospital Corners," he chides at one point. Then one night she calls him in tears because her former boyfriend has just gotten married. The Platonic friendship turns into a romance. What holds the viewer's interest is the pair's uneasy progress from casual acquaintances to friends to lovers—and the question of whether two such apparently dissimilar people can remain together.

In a sense, the movie is emblematic of many of our concerns, for this chapter is about the processes that create human relationships, maintain their stability, and sometimes result in their change, decline, or deterioration. It's about friends, about lovers, and it's also about family. We begin here by examining the major variables of human attraction and several of the characteristics that define all our relationships.

BASES OF HUMAN ATTRACTION

Lauren can have lunch with you in the school cafeteria, but Stephanie can't. You'd love to go to the movies with Michael, but *not* with Dennis. You express your preferences when choosing friends, school leaders, roommates, dates—and eventually a marriage partner.

Even when forced to communicate with people you yourself have not chosen—classmates, fellow employees, and so on—you prefer some people to others. As we examine the major bases of human **attraction,** or *liking,* we shall be looking at many kinds of relationships. The principles discussed here have a bearing on marriage, friendship, family, small-group, and work relationships, for all of these can be seen within a single framework. You should be thinking, then, of the entire web of human relationships as you read about attraction.

Proximity

The most obvious determinant of attraction is **proximity,** or *geographic closeness.* Other things being equal, the more closely two people are located geographically, the more likely they are to be attracted to one another.

The effects of proximity are seen in a number of ways. If you are not

During the freshman year, many long-term friendships develop among students who live in the same dorm.

within a reasonable distance of another person, your chances of meeting and becoming friends are quite slim. How many friends do you have who live more than 3,000 miles away from you? Probably very few. In support of the notion that proximity fosters attraction, several researchers have found that you are far more likely to marry a person who is geographically close to your home or school than someone living or studying far away.

Once you get to know people, proximity also affects whether your relationships will continue. A great number of friendships and courtships are damaged by the effects of physical separation. Perhaps the old saying "Out of sight, out of mind" has some validity simply because of the effort it takes to sustain relationships across many miles. Relationships that do continue despite this obstacle are maintained by the intensity of the rewards derived from them.

Much smaller distances also influence attraction as seen in a classic study of residents in housing projects: Neighbors chose to socialize most with neighbors from the apartment next door and least with those at the opposite end of the floor. And yet the greatest distance between apartments was only eighty-three feet (Festinger et al., 1950).

According to Berscheid (1985), "The association between close physical proximity and attraction is one of the best documented" (p. 445). Why should a few feet make any difference in how friendships are formed, and why, in general, should proximity tend to foster attraction? One theory is that *if we know we are going to be in very close proximity to someone*—living next door or working side by side over a long period of time—*we tend to minimize or even overlook that person's less desirable traits.* It has also been proposed that proximity tends to intensify liking because *opportunities for communication clearly increase as a function of proximity.* For example, in a large company, people who work on the same floor are more likely to share coffee breaks and gossip, go out to lunch together, or even meet after work. And the more two people see of each other, the more likely they are to spend leisure time together, exchange confidences, and offer support in difficult times. Zajonc (1968) found that the more often a subject saw photographs of a particular face, the more he or she liked it. Zajonc's experiments suggest that *familiarity in and of itself may increase liking.*

But when people in proximity are of equal status and start off without negative attitudes toward one another, we cannot predict which people will become friends. Given physical proximity, we still favor some people and reject others. In short, proximity is often a precondition of liking, but there are other bases for attraction.

Similarity

Despite the romantic notion that opposites attract, there is little evidence to bear this out. And a look at the personals columns of many newspapers and magazines will show you how important **similarity** is perceived to be: People want to meet others who share many of their interests, whether it be in sports, music, or travel, and they often seek someone of the same religion, race, and social background.

In a study of mate selection, Buss (1985) found substantial evidence for **assortive mating**—that is, *mating based on similarities.* For example, husbands and wives are usually similar in age (the correlation is 0.8), education, and ethnic background, as well as race and religion and socioeconomic status (p. 47). These six variables show the strongest correlations. As for psychological characteristics, the greatest similarities are in attitudes, opinions, and worldviews. And there are numerous other similarities between husbands and wives: Their verbal abilities correlate highly, and spouses show strong correlations in the degree of their quarrelsomeness, ingenuousness, and extroversion (p. 49).

Buss predicts that as our society becomes more mobile and equality of opportunity increases, our opportunities to find a similar mate will also increase. What's puzzling, however—and there seems no easy answer for this—is that the correlation between spouses with regard to personality traits *decreases* the longer the two are married.

The force of similarity as a basis for attraction is seen not just in mate selection but in all types of human relationships and thus in many forms of communication. According to one theory, within certain limits the more similar the communicators are, the more effective their communication will be. One limiting condition, say Rogers and Shoemaker (1971), is that if the similarities between people are so pervasive that they have the same attitudes and beliefs about every subject, there is no need for communication. For example, the conversation might be deadly at a party in which every person was in agreement about every subject from movies to politics. But similarity clearly prevails. After all, the goal of attitude influence is to change the other person's attitude so that it more closely resembles your own.

Observation, research, and theory all bear out the statement that we like people who appear to be similar to us. Over a hundred years ago Disraeli remarked, "An agreeable person is a person who agrees with me." A more contemporary writer put it this way: "We tend to like people who have the same beliefs and attitudes we have, and when we like people we want them to have the same attitudes we have" (Heider, 1983). In addition, personality, style of dressing, socioeconomic level, religion, age, status, and so forth will affect our feelings toward others. We tend to attract and be attracted to people who are like us, and conversely, we tend to dislike and be disliked by those who differ from us.

If this is the case, then given adequate knowledge of people's attitudes, interests, values, and backgrounds, it should be possible to predict which members of a group will become friends. A classic study of the acquaintance process (Newcomb, 1961) confirms this prediction. The subjects were male students, all strangers to each other, who transferred to the University of Michigan and were allowed to live rent free in a dormitory on campus for one semester. On a long-term basis, those who remained friends after college had shown many similarities in their test results.

But let us focus for a moment on the dynamics of attitude similarity and attraction. Suppose two people who have never met before are to have a discussion on capital punishment and that each is told the other person will be very compatible in terms of personality traits. Or imagine that each is told the other will be incompatible. Brewer (1968), found a high correlation between perceived similarity in attitudes and attraction. Following their discussions the pairs of subjects who expected to be attracted to one another tended to be more similar in their attitude toward capital punishment than discussion partners who expected to be incompatible. In other words, as we communicate with someone we think is similar to us, we are likely to become more similar to that person in our attitudes toward a given issue. In addition, the more we *perceive* that person to be similar to us in attitude, the more we tend to be attracted.

In a more recent study of nonverbal behaviors in friend and stranger dyads, Burgoon and Hale (1988) found that friends were perceived "as more attractive and credible and as expressing more favorable relationship messages than strangers. . . . In particular, friends were seen as more physically and socially attractive, as more competent, and as communicating more intimacy, similarity, and involvement" (pp. 73, 75).

Here and elsewhere when we describe findings about similarity and attraction, we are speaking of *perceived* similarity. As was emphasized in Chapters 1 and 2, human perception is a selective process and not always an accurate one; often we are influenced by how we expect people to look or think or behave. For example, we expect our friends to agree with us on a wide range of topics, and we probably exaggerate the extent of this agreement. No doubt we also tend to overemphasize our differences with those we dislike.

Writing about close relationships, Hatfield and Rapson (1992) stress that "people must have some ideas as to what *their* own attitudes, temperaments and behaviors are if their first impressions are to be affected by perceived and actual similarity/dissimilarity" (p. 211). "We would think," they point out, "that the longer a [close] relationship goes on, the more critically important similarities/dissimilarities come to be. . . . Once people get too close for too long (when couples marry, when parents and children are forced to squeeze together in cramped quarters, when he retires and begins to spend all his time at home) the dissimilarities may begin to rub" (p. 211).

And a recent review interprets research on similarity this way:

> The *realization* of shared reality is more important than similarity itself. Equally, it is not similarity of attitudes, and all the rest, that is important . . . , but KNOWING that you are deeply similar in the meaning you attach to things that counts. Several old and new studies show the importance of assumed similarity in relationships, . . . the fact that couples *think* they are more similar than they are, and that understanding often goes with presumed rather than actual similarity. (Duck and Barnes, 1992, p. 206)

Situations

We qualified our statement about the effect of proximity on attraction with the phrase "other things being equal," and we must temper statements about similarity and attraction in the same way. For things rarely are equal. As we saw in Chapter 2, there are variations in the behaviors and personal characteristics of others—physical attractiveness, for example—that influence liking.

Several situations also qualify what can reasonably be predicted about your attraction to others.

Perceived Reciprocity of Liking

First, your attraction to others can depend on whether **perceived reciprocity of liking** exists—whether *you feel that the people you like also like you*. Certainly, we have all experienced situations in which our liking for a person is intensified by our feeling that he or she likes us too. When we like someone and our feeling is not reciprocated, we tend to lose interest in that person. This common-sense prediction is supported by research findings (Blake and Tesser, 1970).

Finding out that another person likes you is rewarding because it increases your own self-esteem. Suppose, for example, that you are asked to serve on a prestigious committee by one of its members. Once you are on the committee, new elections are held, and the person who endorsed you is nominated for chairman. It is very likely, especially if the committee members are people you don't know, that you may want to vote for the person who picked you—not so much because you owe a favor as because you feel you like that person.

The explanation for such reciprocity is twofold: First, people who like you increase your sense of self-worth; and, second, their "liking" behavior is a compliment, and you return the compliment with reciprocal liking.

Changes in Self-Esteem

A second situation that may influence your choice of people is a **change in your level of self-esteem.** Thus if you have to drop a few courses because they are too difficult and find yourself taking a program that is far less demanding, you may drift away from the few friends you have that are "brains" and spend more time instead with people taking a schedule parallel to your own.

Or consider this example. Sam and Suzy have gone together for almost six months when suddenly she drops him. Because he obviously is not good enough for her, Sam finds his self-esteem at an all-time low. Then along comes Valerie. Sam has never considered her as attractive or intelligent as Suzy, but she seems to be interested in him. Sam strikes up a romance on the rebound.

The rebound phenomenon illustrates what can happen to attraction as a result of a change in the level of one's self-esteem. Studies suggest that when self-esteem has recently been lowered, our need for affiliation increases, and we become more accepting of affection from others. It's then that people we might have considered unappealing may seem more desirable as companions.

Anxiety

Anxiety affects our need to interact or affiliate with others. Schachter (1959) found that high-anxiety conditions (painful electric shock) produce a much more intense desire for affiliation than low-anxiety conditions. And though "misery loves company," it isn't just any company: Anxious subjects prefer to be with others who are anxious too (pp. 17–19).

Anxiety-producing situations can increase your need to be with others and also change your criteria for choosing companions. Imagine yourself stuck on a stalled railroad train for three or four hours or waiting for hours in a hospital to visit a loved one in the intensive-care ward. Apparently, the need to be comforted when sharing unpleasant experiences supersedes other needs for associating with people. Boot camps and fraternity-pledging programs have long operated on this principle. People who share relatively unpleasant experiences often become more cohesive as a group.

Isolation

Isolation from the rewards of others also influences your choice of receivers. Although brief isolation can sometimes be peaceful and pleasant, prolonged isolation is almost always unpleasant. Hence in prisons one of the severest forms of punishment is solitary confinement. And think of the numerous cartoons in which a man shipwrecked on a desert island inhabited only by lovely native women eagerly greets a fellow countryman as "someone to talk to."

Each of these circumstances illustrates that social isolation tends to be less pleasant than interaction with others. Some researchers have found that as we are deprived of the rewards possible from human interaction, we become more receptive to those rewards. Thus another influence on our choice of receivers is the degree to which we have been isolated from contact with others. As we are deprived of social reinforcement, our strong need to interact with other human beings tends to override our standards for acceptable friends.

Some theorists believe that in addition to the many variables we have been discussing, some *differences* between people can also be a basis for attraction—particularly if the people involved have needs that are complementary.

Complementary Needs

There are, of course, relationships in which attraction seems to be based not on similarity but on complementarity. And many of these relationships seem mutually satisfying. Perhaps you can think of a couple who, despite great differences in personality, seem very compatible.

The **theory of complementary needs** seems to contradict some of the findings about similarity that we have been discussing. According to this view, *in selecting marriage partners and even friends, we are attracted to people who are most likely to satisfy our needs* (Winch, 1958). Maximum gratification of needs occurs when two people have complementary rather than similar needs. For example, a woman with a strong need to be protective and a man with a strong need to be dependent might be very compatible. One friend might have a strong need to dominate a relationship, while the other is comfortable only in a submissive role. A restrained, low-keyed spouse might be the perfect foil for the extrovert who dominates every party with funny stories and general clowning. Remember that we are speaking about complementary needs, not complementary attitudes, interests, or values. For example, two people might differ in the intensity of their needs for protection or dominance and still have similarities.

Research has not substantiated this theory (Berscheid, 1985); yet the principle of complementarity has an intuitive appeal. We can all think of instances in which it seems valid: the perfectionist married to the easygoing person who has no difficulty in compromising; business partners, one doing all the wheeling and dealing, the other doing the paperwork. Even in instances where we look at two people and ask, "How did those two ever get together? They're like night and day," it's instructive to think about what each person gets out of the relationship.

One interesting speculation is that some human relationships may be based primarily on similarity, others primarily on complementarity. Perhaps similarity and complementarity both contribute to the rewards of interaction (Thibaut and Kelley, 1985). It is also possible that agreement on values is critical in a short-term relationship and that complementary needs become significant only in long-term relationships (Kerckhoff and Davis, 1962). As we go on to describe some essential characteristics of human relationships, you will read more about the effects of time.

DEFINING CHARACTERISTICS OF RELATIONSHIPS

In an article titled "A Female Best Friend," a married man wrote about a woman, not his wife, who was his best friend:

> I often tell her things I haven't told Janet [his wife] or tell her things before I tell Janet. I am closer to her than I am to any of my male friends. Our relationship is not unusual, I've discovered. In a two-year survey of nearly 2,000 men and women for a book on male relational behavior, I learned that one out of every three men knows a woman, other than his wife, with whom he feels he can "talk about anything." She is usually his mother, sister, a work associate, or, as in my case, a friend. (McGill, 1985, p. 52)

Michael McGill, the author, explained that with his friend Sharon he could be "totally revealing without risk" because she could listen to him without losing objectivity. If, for example, he wanted to take the summer off, she would ask what he expected to do with the free time rather than ask how he would be able to pay his bills (a question far more likely to be asked by his wife).

Trust and understanding, sharing of information, and several other factors clearly play a part in this relationship. In the pages that follow, we shall be discussing five of the basic perspectives from which many kinds of relationships, however different they seem, may be described.

Context

The context of every relationship has two aspects: the setting and the social-psychological environment in which communication takes places and relationships develop.

Setting has an important connection with the principle of similarity: We form relationships with people with whom we share a certain **setting,** or *physical environment,* probably because the shared setting is indicative of similarities. Work relationships, relationships with neighbors, relationships with those who participate in the same sport or are members of the same religion, each take place within a given physical environment, and we are unlikely to have a relationship outside that setting. For example, your supervisor at the office is unlikely to visit you at home. Similarly, your parents, children, or friends are unlikely to come to your office.

Although setting may be significant for some relationships, **climate,** or *social-psychological context,* is important for all of them. Among the most critical measures of climate are confirmation and supportiveness.

Confirmation and Disconfirmation

In studying human communication, we distinguish between *message content* and the *relationship between communicators.* It seems obvious that every message has content, whether the information is correct or incorrect, valid or invalid, or even indeterminable. But every message also defines how it is to be interpreted, and consequently something about the relationship between the people involved. (A mother who cautions her exuberant son by saying, "Please don't run around when we're in a department store," defines her relationship with her child quite differently from the mother who says "Be sure to run around a lot here so that I get good and angry.") Even the most casual message exists on this second level: "Every courtesy term between persons, every inflection of voice denoting respect or contempt, condescension or dependency, is a statement about the relationship between the two persons" (Ruesch and Bateson, 1968, p. 213).*

Thus, as we communicate, we expect more than a simple exchange of verbal and nonverbal information. Each person conveys messages that tell how he or she perceives the other and their relationship, and each expects to receive similar responses. Perhaps the most satisfying interpersonal response we can hope to receive is total **confirmation,** or as Sieburg and Larson define it, *"any behavior that causes another person to value himself more"* (1971, p. 1; italics added). Buber writes: "In human society, at all its levels, persons confirm one another in a practical way, to some extent or other, in their personal qualities and capacities, and a society may be termed human in the measure to which its members confirm one another" (1957, p. 101).

We can illustrate this through a series of brief exchanges between husband and wife. Suppose Kathy comes home after work and says to her husband, "Brian—guess what? I was promoted to divisional manager of the overseas branch today. Isn't that great?" "That's wonderful, Kathy," replies Brian. "You've been working so hard. You really deserve this." Here Brian responds to Kathy and agrees with the content of her statement, thus confirming her very existence as a person. Yet what if he says, "Well, it sounds like it's going to be a pressure job to me. And I hope this isn't going to interfere with our life at home." Brian responds, but rejects the central content of Kathy's statement (that the promotion is a positive thing) and by implication Kathy herself. His statement acknowledges that she received a promotion, but is disconfirming as to its value (for both of them). A third response is possible. Suppose

---

* For an extensive discussion of content and relationship levels of communication, see Watzlawick and associates, (1967), pp. 51–54.

Brian ignores Kathy's statement altogether and asks, "What's for dinner to-night?" This remark probably would have the same impact as a fourth possibility: complete silence. Both are totally **disconfirming behaviors,** *behaviors that cause people to value themselves less;* they reject both the speaker and what the speaker has to say (Sieburg and Larson, 1971).

Psychotherapeutic literature tells us that disconfirmation is one of the most damaging interpersonal responses: "While rejection amounts to the message 'you are wrong,' disconfirmation says in effect 'you do not exist'" (Watzlawick et al., 1967, p. 86). The practical question becomes: What kinds of responses are most confirming or disconfirming? We find part of the answer in the Sieburg and Larson study whose definitions we have already noted. Members of the International Communication Association were asked to describe the behaviors of the persons with whom they most enjoyed and least enjoyed communicating. As we look at the results of this survey, two distinct response styles emerge.

If we list the responses considered most **confirming,** describing them briefly in order of rank, first comes *direct acknowledgment.* The other person acknowledges what you have said and gives you a direct verbal response ("Yes. I see where you're coming from.") Next is the expression of *positive feeling.* He or she conveys positive feeling about what you have just said ("That's a very good idea."). Then comes the *clarifying response.* Here the other person tries to get you to clarify the content of your message ("Could you expand on that a bit?"). A person who gives an *agreeing response* reinforces or affirms what you have already said. The *supportive response* offers comfort, under-standing, or reassurance ("I know just how you feel.").

It seems that the response people find most **disconfirming** is the *tangential response.* Here the other person acknowledges your previous comment but quickly shifts the direction of the conversation ("Did he cover a lot in class today?" "Not much. Does this skirt look too long?"). Next in unpopularity comes the *impersonal response:* Here the other person uses intellectualized speech and avoids the first person ("One often finds oneself getting angry" instead of "I'm getting angry."). An *impervious response* disregards you completely, offering neither verbal nor nonverbal recognition. When the other person gives an *irrelevant response,* he or she changes the subject as would be the case with a tangential response, but this time makes no attempt to relate that response to your previous comment ("I had a lousy day. I'm really ready to quit." "I wonder why Ann hasn't called. Do you think she forgot?"). An *interrupting response* cuts you off before you have made your point. A person makes an *incoherent response* if he or she consistently speaks in sentences that are rambling, disorganized, or incomplete. The *incongruous response* gives you conflicting verbal and nonverbal messages ("Of course you are the one who should decide. It's up to you," said in an exasperated tone of voice).

These lists of behaviors are by no means exhaustive. Nevertheless, they highlight the differences between a confirming response style, which generally acknowledges, supports, and accepts other human beings, and a disconfirming response style, which denies and undermines their personal sense of worth.

The research of Sieburg and Larson no longer stands alone. A review of studies conducted at the University of Denver suggests that "confirmation/ disconfirmation may be the most pervasive and important aspect of interpersonal communication" (Cissna, 1976, p. 1). Certainly, this is a dimension of human relationships with potential for influencing a range of communication outcomes. For example, a recent study finds that perceived confirming behavior contributes to greater rapport between college roommates (Hawken et al., 1991). This is especially important during the first semester of the freshman year—a time when many students have not yet formed other close relationships (p. 306).

Yet to counsel that all our responses to others be totally confirming would be unrealistic. There are times when we want to or must reject the communication of others, at least at the content level. Even in taking issue with others, however, we can keep in mind the importance of maintaining a confirming response style. Supportiveness and defensiveness are two other important measures of climate.

Supportiveness and Defensiveness

How do we break down a person's defensiveness? Not, as you might think, by attacking his or her system of defenses. In encounter groups, for example, an attempt is made to create a psychological atmosphere that is supportive rather than threatening, an atmosphere in which differences of all sorts—in attitude, dress, behavior, life-style—are tolerated. Harrison (1970) explains why the creation of a new environment is necessary:

> The destruction of defenses does not serve learning; instead, it increases the anxiety of the person that he will lose the more or less effective conceptual systems he has with which to understand and relate to the world, and he drops back to an even more desperate and perhaps unrealistic defense than the one destroyed. (p. 85)

The application to all face-to-face communication is clear. Abruptly stripping people of all defenses only increases their distance from others. We can be supportive in all our interpersonal relationships if we know more about the behaviors that reduce or arouse defensiveness.

In his highly influential article on interpersonal trust, Gibb (1961) contrasted two atmospheres that could be established through communication. He called them **supportive** and **defensive climates,** and he described them in terms of six sets of categories (see Table 6.1).

At first glance categories 1 and 4 in the defensive climate seem contradictory: Evaluative, or judgmental, behavior arouses defensiveness, but so does complete neutrality. We can reconcile this apparent contradiction if we recall that complete neutrality is disconfirming because it communicates a lack of concern. Gibb points out that attempts to reassure a troubled person by saying that he or she is overanxious or should not feel bad may be interpreted as a lack of acceptance. It can be highly supportive, however, to show empathy

TABLE 6.1

Defensive Climate	Problem Created	Supportive Climate
Evaluation	Feeling judged increases our defensiveness.	Description
Control	We resist someone trying to control us.	Problem orientation
Strategy	If we perceive a strategy or underlying motive, we become defensive.	Spontaneity
Neutrality	If the speaker appears to lack concern for us, we become defensive.	Empathy
Superiority	A person who acts superior arouses our defensive feelings.	Equality
Certainty	Those who are "know-it-alls" arouse our defensiveness.	Provisionalism

Source: From Jack R. Gibb, "Defensive Communications," *Journal of Communication* 11 (1961): 141–148. Reprinted by permission of The International Communication Association.

with the person's emotions without trying to change him or her. Pearce and Newton, who consider it "the basic mode of significant communication between adults," refer to **empathy** as *"perception and communication by resonance, by identification, by experiencing in ourselves some reflection of the emotional tone that is being experienced by the other person"* (1963, p. 52). (See the discussion of empathic listening in Chapter 5.)

From his survey Gibb concluded that when trust increases, efficiency and accuracy in communication also increase. To this we might add that while a supportive climate is important even in short-term relationships, in more permanent relationships (in marriage or on the job, for example) it has even greater possibilities for influencing all five communication outcomes. As we suggested in Chapter 1, the better the relationship between people, the more likely it is that the other outcomes of effective communication will also occur.

Although there have been many studies of defensive and supportive communication climates, relatively little research exists concerning what defensiveness actually feels like. Gordon (1988) gives us core descriptions of feeling defensive and feeling understood.

Respondents were asked, "What goes on within you when you are experiencing defensiveness? What goes on in your body, in your mind, in your emotions when you are reacting defensively to someone else? . . . What happens, verbally and nonverbally, inside and outside yourself?" (p. 55). The core description of defensiveness included feeling tense, discomforted, "sped-up," gripped by the situation, mentally confused, wanting to move against the other person, and estranged.

On the other hand, an essential description of feeling understood included feeling awakened, empowered (e.g., "I feel strong inside . . . a sense of being exceptionally strong or energetic"), comforted, and moving toward others. In other terms, explains Gordon, "there is a heightening of sensory awareness, self-concept, well-being, and interpersonal solidarity" (p. 61). The feeling of being understood, then, is expansive, whereas defensiveness is experienced as a contraction or turning in upon oneself.

The differences between supportive and defensive climates are vividly seen in classroom interaction. One study shows that perceived professor sexism only seems to affect perceptions of climate in classes taught by male professors: Those perceived as sexist were viewed as less friendly and cooperative—and more defensive. This was how students responded regardless of whether they liked or disliked the class itself (Rosenfeld and Jarrard, 1985). For the most part, college classes, whether liked or disliked, represent relatively defensive and disconfirming climates. This is probably due to the nature of the classroom, with its tests, papers, and other forms of evaluation.

In addition to climate, time is another dimension that helps to characterize relationships.

Time

Time is required for all the qualities of a relationship, regardless of its nature, in order to develop and evolve (Chelune et al., 1984). In general, our knowledge of another person usually must be acquired slowly; interdependence also develops over time, and so do trust and commitment.

Time also affects the *intensity* of human relationships. Marathon encounter groups tacitly acknowledge this principle. The participants are brought together for an extended period—usually six to twenty-four hours. As they learn to express themselves more openly, the interaction reaches a high level of intensity. If the group were to meet only one hour a week for six to twenty-four weeks, such intensity would be difficult to achieve. In terms of our model, it is as though one were pulling the ends of the spring in Figure 1.1 (Chapter 1) farther and farther apart. In other words, a human relationship is not constant; its intensity is affected by the amount of time that passes between encounters.

Communication style tends to change with the passage of time. When two people first meet, they usually try to be as explicit as possible. Even if the two share several interests, one does not assume knowledge of what the other is thinking or trying to say. This kind of insight develops only after long acquaintance. Sometimes two people get to know each other so well that each anticipates what the other is trying to say—they even finish each other's sentences, so to speak. We frequently see this relationship in very close friends or in married couples; to use the terminology of the Russian psychologist Vygotsky, their speech becomes "abbreviated" (1962, p. 141).

One very telling aspect of our relationships is the concept of *investment:* Notice how often the word "spent" is used in talking about time. In a measure designed to assess levels of investment, Lund (1985) included questions about how much time was spent with the other person rather than in doing things or seeing other people, and about the total length of time of the involvement. Her interest as a researcher was in predicting the continuity of personal relationships. No one can predict, of course, that time "invested" offers total security or constancy in a relationship—hence, the bitter complaint "I gave him the best years of my life" has no cogent answer.

While time spent is a way of characterizing relationships, it is meaningful only when integrated with such dimensions as the *quality* of the time and the *desire to spend it*. Desire to spend time and the amount of time two people spend do not always mesh. For example, you may find yourself in a relationship where you and the other person want to be together almost constantly, yet circumstances make it impossible. On the other hand, a man and woman who have been married for many years may spend most of their free time with each other yet have little desire to do so. Or the wife may feel she always wants to spend her weekends with her husband, and the husband may have less desire to be with her; perhaps he'd rather go sailing some weekends even though she doesn't like sailing. Spending more time together is not always the solution. Many counselors and therapists advise that the quality of the time two people spend together—and the degree to which they express their mutual regard—can be more significant than the amount of time spent.

Information Sharing

Not all relationships foster the sharing of information—for example, some are quite guarded with little exchange on either side, others far more open with an ongoing series of exchanges. How much information sharing there is in a relationship can be described in terms of two dimensions: breadth and depth.

Breadth refers to *the variety of topics communicated*. For example, from conversations with your lab partner you may know that he is from California, that he's the oldest of four children and has a sister at your school, that he's active in a political student organization, yet you may still feel you know little about him. There are many relationships in which the range of subjects you talk about is broad, yet discussion remains superficial.

What is lacking is **depth,** *the intimacy of what is communicated.* For example, you can tell someone about the work you do and thus add to the range of information she has about you, but your dissatisfaction with your job or your search for a new one is far more personal and revealing. Such information intensifies the depth of your relationship. Altman and Taylor (1983), who propose this distinction between breadth and depth, are concerned with interpersonal relationships in which both dimensions increase, yet their schema can characterize any relationships—those with our parents, friends, neighbors, or even our employers.

Whether or not we increase the breadth and depth of our communications—that is, whether we continue to talk superficially or begin the process of self-disclosure—depends on certain aspects of the relationship. Petronio and her colleagues (1984) found that in disclosing information, women assign more importance than men do to whether the other person is "discreet, trustworthy, sincere, liked, respected, a good listener, warm, and open." Women also feel more strongly than men that the person disclosing information "be accepted, be willing to disclose, be honest, frank, and not feel anxious, or be provoked into giving information" (p. 271).

Note that the difference between males and females is one of degree, not kind: All the issues mentioned above are important to both sexes, but apparently more so to women.

Trust

Mrs. Ross, whenever I paint a house, I expect to be paid half at the beginning of the job. That's the way I work. I thought I'd mention this to your husband.

Do you want to know what Samantha said about you?

Of course I'll call you next week. I do care about you. It's just that I've had a lot of extra work in the last couple of months. I'm not seeing someone else.

Whatever you say here goes no further than this office.

Each of these statements has something to do with the level of trust between two people. **Trust,** *the belief or feeling that no harm will come from the other in the relationship,* is linked with such concepts as fairness, integrity, and truthfulness. According to Hinde (1981), "the increased vulnerability which rises with intimacy is tolerable only if accompanied by a belief that the partner will not exploit it" (p. 14). The betrayal of trust is one of the most important reasons for a "low point" in an intimate relationship (McAdams, 1984). Some people are so devastated by betrayals of this kind that their loss of trust carries over into later relationships.

Trust is another necessary element of all relationships, not just intimate ones. When you hire a house painter, seek help from a doctor, see your academic advisor, or make a new friend, a certain level of trust must exist.

Trust and Predictability

Millar and Rogers (1987) emphasize the link between trust and predictability: "Conceptually . . . trust involves the predictability and obligatory nature of limitations on future choices; it concerns the individual's attempts to seek and develop dependable sources of rewards" (p. 122). We have to be able to predict the degree to which others will behave reliably, competently, or properly so that we may regulate our own behavior. "Functionally, these predictions produce a sense of certainty about future actions and outcomes that permits decisions and commitments to be made" (p. 122).

Frivolous as it sounds, trust has often been studied by looking at how people behave when they play games. For example, Tubbs examined how third parties were influenced by watching competitive or cooperative game strategies. His results showed that the observation of cooperative (trust-producing) strategies prompted cooperative choices from viewers and that of competitive (distrusting) strategies produced competitive choices (Tubbs, 1971). The study illustrates a frequently found phenomenon—that a given type of behavior by one person tends to elicit a similar response from the other.

Other findings from the observation experiment suggest that there may be a significant difference between trust in an interpersonal relationship and trust in other communication contexts. In this study, trust-inducing behavior was perceived as evidence of good character, but competitive, defense-inducing behavior was seen as evidence of expertness. This is validated outside the laboratory. For example, a young woman who brags about herself and is highly competitive may threaten others so much that they run down her character, but her behavior may still increase their respect for her abilities. We shall see in Chapter 10, however, that in public communication the receiver's willingness to trust the source will depend on the receiver's perception of both character and expertness.

There is evidence that in playing some games, people tend to compete even when it is to their advantage to cooperate. The procedure in certain games is to prevent two players from communicating. When communication between players is permitted, we see a significant increase in the number of cooperative choices (Deutsch, 1960; Deutsch and Krauss, 1960). It seems then that, other things being equal, communication in and of itself sometimes raises the level of trust between people.

Motives for Deception

Are there situations in which deception is perceived as the "normal" or necessary communication alternative? Research by Lippard (1988) with adolescents and young adults identified five primary motives for deception: resources, affiliation, self-protection, conflict avoidance, and protection of others.

Resources, the first category, involved deception to acquire or protect material resources—personal property, money, and so on. When the motive was *affiliation,* deception was used to decrease or increase interaction with another person. Deception *to protect oneself* involved avoiding self-disclosure or enhancing or protecting one's social image. *Conflict avoidance,* which accounted for almost 30 percent of all deception motivation, took many forms: showing acceptance and willingness to do something felt to be undesirable, to prevent criticism or punishment, and deception that maintained the appearance of fidelity to a relationship. The last category, *protection of others,* involved deception to avoid hurting the feelings of another person or to prevent the other person from worrying about the welfare of the subject (p. 95).

One of the most interesting of Lippard's findings is the correlation between power, frequency of interaction, and deception. For example, those most often deceived were the subjects' parents—in other words, those who had the most control over their lives. This finding reinforces earlier research that deception "is frequently a power-balancing strategy" (p. 99). Note that almost 22 percent of all the deceptive actions involved loyalty to friends. And here women were reported to be more likely than men to lie in order to protect another person's feelings, a finding that supports stereotypical perceptions concerning the behavior of women.

The subjects in this study were all young, of an age at which the shaping and preservation of one's self-identity seems to be a central task. Thus, further research must be done before it can be established that at other life stages— middle age, for example—the frequency of deception behaviors changes. Lippard shrewdly points out that "the easy resort to deception as a manipulative strategy does not truly change the power balance; rather, it reinforces the role relationship which creates the imbalance" (p. 102).

The final way in which we will characterize relationships is with respect to affection and control.

Affection and Control

Original work by Leary (1957), well supported by more recent research, proposes that relationships can be described in terms of two primary dimensions: affection and control. **Affection,** the *love/hate aspect of the relationship,* ranges from tender, cooperative, loving behaviors to those that are sarcastic, hostile, and aggressive. **Control,** a second and independent dimension, *also has two poles: dominance/submission.* At one extreme are behaviors we would characterize as competitive, exploitive, and domineering; at the other, we find those that are docile, dependent, and self-effacing. Of course there are many intermediate behaviors: You can be trusting without being overly dependent on someone else's judgment; you can act assertively without being overbearing.

Along the affection dimension, a given behavior, whether loving or hostile, tends to prompt behavior from the other person that is *similar.* So if Beth can't stand Carol and repeatedly acts hostile, it's more than likely Carol will come to respond in the same way to Beth. Conversely, friendly, cooperative behavior from Beth will tend to promote the same response from Carol.

The dominance/submission aspect of human relationships works differently. The control dimension, instead of eliciting similar behavior, tends to promote behavior that is *complementary.* For example, Jack's anxious, docile behavior may provoke his business partner, Don, into acting dogmatic and manipulative. Denise, a real go-getter with wonderful managerial skills, may marry someone who admires and respects these abilities and is relieved to let her take charge of most domestic and financial concerns. Whereas in the area of affection, stability occurs when two people are similar, in terms of control, the most stable relationship occurs when the two are *opposites.*

Without some agreement over the control aspects of a relationship, these have to be constantly renegotiated. Thus, two highly dominant people can find themselves locked in an ongoing power struggle, even over the most minor issues (who decides on what hotel to stay at, who actually signs a legal form, who accepts an invitation). On the other hand, if two people both feel uncomfortable making decisions, each will try over and over again to get the other to assume responsibility. Wilmot (1979) gives an excellent example in describing a man and woman about to go out on a first date:

> When the man arrives, he says, "What would you like to do tonight?" and the young lady replies, "Oh, I don't know, what would you like to do?" He says, "Anything that you want to do is fine with me," and she counters with, "I just don't have a preference—you decide." His final offer is, "I like to please the girl. You decide where we should go." Paradoxically, "trying not to control" is an attempt to limit the other— getting him or her to take responsibility. (p. 104)

As we said, affection and control are two independent dimensions, and relationships vary along both. No one should make the mistake of simply equating love with submission or dominance with hostility. A submissive wife may be very hostile toward her husband, although that hostility seems suppressed. By the same token, a husband who is extremely dominant may also be attentive and affectionate. Each of our actions will reflect "some degree of dominance/submission and some degree of love/hate," for affection and control are essential aspects of all our relationships (Wilmot, 1979, p. 109).

Many other characteristics have been proposed for studying relationships. The five we have discussed—context, time, information sharing, trust, and affection and control—seem to us among the most essential. Clearly, no single characteristic suffices to describe the complexity of human relationships.

LIFE CYCLE OF A RELATIONSHIP

Potentially, every new person you meet may become that one lifelong friend whose relationship you treasure. Although the odds are against it with most acquaintances, there is always that possibility.

Knapp (1984; Knapp and Vangelisti, 1992) has written a thorough analysis of the stages of building, experiencing, and ending relationships, and of the kind of communication that characterizes each stage. These stages are seen as building to a peak and then declining—in his terms, "coming together" and "coming apart."

The outline that follows pertains to relationships geared toward intimacy and permanence. Although most of our relationships are not of this kind, the projected stages still offer a useful framework for understanding relationships in general. Knapp assumes the stages are sequential, that one follows the other with little opportunity for skipping around. We should note, however, that movement can be forward or backward, and many relationships stop at a given stage—for example, experimenting, intensifying, or bonding—and do not go further.

At each stage in a relationship, communication plays a different role. During the early stages, it is aimed at learning about the other person so that decisions concerning the relationship can be made—whether to form a relationship, what subjects are open for discussion, how close or intimate the relationship should be. After this phase, communication is used to maintain, develop, and enhance the relationship as well as to negotiate differences that will increase the satisfaction derived from it. During the final stages, communication helps the partners terminate their relationship by providing a means for saving face, resolving feelings, and (ideally) parting on a positive basis (Rosenfeld and Kendrick, 1984).

Coming Together

Ten stages in all are proposed, and the first five—"coming together"—describe the slow growth of interpersonal relationships.

Initiating refers to the very first attempts we make at conversation with a new person. In Chapter 1 we referred to this as phatic communication. "Hi," "How's it going?" "Think it will rain today?" During this scanning process, communication is generally cautious and conventional: The goals are to make contact and express interest. Much of what we said about perception and first impressions in Chapter 2 relates to this stage of communication.

Experimenting is the phase in which we try sample conversational topics in an attempt to gain some knowledge of the other person. Usually we are asking a lot of questions and exchanging a lot of small stalk. "What's your major?" "What kind of music do you like?" "Where are you from?" Experimenting is a way of learning about similarities and differences *safely*. In this stage we're continually looking for ways of building on some area of common interest. It is much easier to talk to a person once you find the two of you have something in common. And it's more fun. Any commitments at this stage are generally very limited. Usually the relationship is still casual and relaxed: "Like it or not, most of our relationships probably don't progress very far beyond this stage" (Knapp and Vangelisti, 1992, p. 37).

Intensifying marks the beginning of intimacy, sharing personal information, and the beginning of greater informality. This stage is illustrated by the many changes in communication behaviors, both verbal and nonverbal, that take place when acquaintances become close friends. It is always fun to watch couples on campus and try to determine how intense their relationship is just by watching them sit at a table having a cup of coffee. Physical closeness, hand holding, and greater eye contact are just a few of the various indicators that a relationship is intensifying. A greater degree of openness about oneself ("My parents are divorced"; "I'm not a very good student") is another. (We will have a great deal to say about self-disclosure in Chapter 7.)

Integrating takes place when two people begin to consider themselves a couple. Often this attitude is mirrored in the way others begin to treat them. At this time, the two people actively cultivate all the interests, attitudes, and qualities that seem to make them unique as a couple. They may also do this in a symbolic way, identifying a song as "our song," or even exchanging rings. As the two begin to value more and more of the same things, they intensify some aspects of their personalities and minimize others.

Bonding is a more formal or ritualistic stage. It may take the form of engagement or marriage, but even "going steady" is a form of bonding. Through bonding, the couple gain social or institutional support for their relationship. In doing so, they agree to accept a set of rules, or norms, governing their relationship. But bonding itself may change this relationship because it is now "more difficult to break out of. . . . The contract becomes, either explicitly or implicitly, a frequent topic of conversation" (p. 40).

Coming Apart

> The first thing that upset me was that she didn't like my dog, and this bothered me. But we continued to see each other. Then I discovered that she had been married before. I started to wonder about how compatible we were, but we still continued as a couple. Then her former boyfriend started calling her up, which upset me because she didn't tell him about us. We argued a lot and things were tense between us then. I finally decided that I'd had it and wanted out. (Quoted in Baxter, 1984, p. 35)

Relationships may stabilize at any of the building stages preceding bonding, the most intimate stage, but even relationships that reach the closest phase may begin to deteriorate, like the one described above. The termination of a relationship is not simply the reverse of what has been referred to as "coming together." People just don't "drift apart" or "separate"; only when both want to terminate the relationship is the process one of reversal, marked by decreasing contact, intimacy, and so on.

Otherwise, there are several variables that will determine how a relationship ends. Baxter (1982; 1984) argues that how a relationship breaks up depends on who wants to end it (both people? only one?), whether problems came on suddenly, whether the partners confront each other directly, whether their discussions are long or short, whether the two parties want to "save" the relationship, and whether their goal is to change the relationship or to end it. When intimacy is low, one or both parties usually withdraw; when the level of intimacy is high, justifications for terminating seem necessary.

The next five stages in Knapp's analysis describe the increasing deterioration that can occur in relationships that have been at the bonding stage.

Differentiating occurs when two people decide that perhaps their relationship may be too confining. Now they begin to focus on their differences rather than their similarities. They want to "do their own thing," "have a little breathing room"; in other words, they begin to emphasize their individuality. The most obvious change in communication is the increase in the number of fights.

Circumscribing refers to a stage in which couples begin to reduce the frequency and intimacy of their communication. Certain hot topics like money and sex tend to be avoided, since they are too likely to produce more quarreling. Greater formality returns, as if the two people didn't know each other very well. "Is it okay with you if I go for a walk now?" "I don't care. Do whatever you want to."

Stagnating reflects the increasing deterioration of a relationship that the participants are trying to hold together. It might be for religious or financial reasons, or for the sake of children involved, or because of other factors no longer having to do with attraction to the other person. Verbal and nonverbal messages become more and more like those conveyed between strangers. The relationship itself is no longer discussed.

Avoiding is a coping tactic to minimize the pain of experiencing a totally deteriorated relationship. Physical separation often takes place, but we all know couples who live in the same house yet lead completely separate lives. Avoiding often takes place between neighbors or coworkers after a major argument. The participants still must remain physically close, but they manage to keep contact to a minimum.

Terminating is the final stage in any relationship. Knapp, who applies his theory to the briefest of encounters as well as to long-standing relationships, proposes that termination may occur after only a brief conversation or after a lifetime of intimacy. Generally, the longer and more meaningful the relationship, the more painful and drawn out its termination. Messages of distance and dissociation are often exchanged at this time, and usually these summarize and clarify what is happening between the two people—for example, "I don't ever want to see you again!" or "I'll always respect you, but I don't love you any more" (p. 44).

Although the ten stages seem to deal primarily with male-female relationships, many of the concepts and principles apply to same-sex relationships (Peplau, 1981). The names of these stages may be new to you, but we are sure that much of the representative dialogue in Table 6.2 will be familiar.

MAINTAINING RELATIONSHIPS

If you love me, you won't do anything without me.

If you love me, you'll do what I say.

TABLE 6.2

An Overview of Interaction States

Stage	Representative Dialogue
	COMING TOGETHER
Initiating	"Hi, how ya doin'?" "Fine. You?"
Experimenting	"Oh, so you like to ski . . . so do I." "You do? Great. Where do you go?"
Intensifying	"I . . . think I love you." "I love you too."
Integrating	"I feel so much a part of you." "Yeah, we are like one person. What happens to you happens to me."
Bonding	"I want to be with you always." "Let's get married."
	COMING APART
Differentiating	"I just don't like big social gatherings." "Sometimes I don't understand you. This is one area where I'm certainly not like you at all."
Circumscribing	"Did you have a good time on your trip?" "What time will dinner be ready?"
Stagnating	"What's there to talk about?" "Right. I know what you're going to say and you know what I'm going to say."
Avoiding	"I'm so busy, I just don't know when I'll be able to see you." "If I'm not around when you try, you'll understand."
Terminating	"I'm leaving you . . . and don't bother trying to contact me." "Don't worry."

Source: Mark L. Knapp, *Interpersonal Communication and Human Relationships* (Newton, MA: Allyn & Bacon, 1984), p. 33.

If you love me, you'll give me what I want.

If you love me, you'll know what I want before I ask. (Satir, 1988, p. 152)

Two people may establish what they think will be an unending friendship or make a formal commitment through marriage, yet soon discover the pleasure that they felt when the initial bond was made is slipping away. It can be puzzling, even painful, to learn that some kind of effort is needed to keep a relationship going. If a close friend is easily insulted, keeping up the friendship may seem just too difficult to you. If your parents never fought, fighting with your spouse may seem to you a sign that your marriage is in danger. Often we have the idea that if we have to "work at" a relationship, it wasn't meant to be.

Today there is high interest in the study of **relationship maintenance,** or, in simpler language, *how people maintain close and satisfying relationships.* Cast in Knapp's terms, the question is how, once past the "coming together" phases, we can sustain a relationship, keep it from "coming apart"? To use an analogy from automobile maintenance, how do we keep it running?

Theorists and researchers have identified many behaviors or strategies people use that are important in maintaining close relationships. For example, Knapp and Vangelisti include disclosures or openness, verbal and nonverbal expressions of commitment and intimacy, constructive conflict, and—most surprisingly—lying (1992).

We've already spoken of trust and information sharing. Certainly in a close long-term relationship we come to expect an atmosphere of openness and trust in which two people will share a significant amount of personal information—thoughts, feelings, even responses to the relationship itself. There may be more self-disclosures early on, but when things are not going smoothly, your willingness to disclose your feelings is often a means to reestablish intimacy and renew your commitment. Studies of marriage—and much research on relationship maintenance is based on married couples—confirm this:

> Willingness to disclose one's feelings is very sharply related to successful marriage, and conversely, there is much more likely to be disruption in a marriage where there is little mutual sharing of feelings. (Duck, 1991, pp. 128–129)

In a recent study of **openness,** VanLear (1991) found that in relationships that are going well, people continually match their cycles of openness. This evidence of a periodic ebb and flow "between openness and closedness, revelation and restraint" is true for both new acquaintanceships and for intact friendships and romantic relationships (p. 356). VanLear's studies show that acquaintances "match the amplitude of their cycles to fit those of their partners," synchronizing the timing of cycles. In friendships and romantic relationships, partners actually perceive their own cycles of openness and those of the other person as being timed. This mutuality seems to be linked with satisfaction. If a relationship begins to deteriorate and satisfaction decreases, these cycles show increasing fluctuations.

We mentioned in discussing information sharing that women tend to be more self-disclosing than men. According to one study, when husbands believe their marriage is "going well," they see no need to speak about their relationship (Acitele, 1987). These and other findings lend some support to Tannen's observation that women tend to favor "relationship talk" and that for most women talk plays an essential role in maintaining intimacy (1990, p. 86).

Though people tend to talk less about their commitment to each other after the intensifying stage of their relationship, threatened relationships often require verbal statements that reestablish commitment:

> In troubled relationships, the "I love you" phrase may not be enough to convince one's partner he or she is loved. It has become an empty phrase because there have not been enough follow-up behaviors that specifically testify to the declaration of love. . . . *Intensity* has a lot to do with the perceived strength of the commitment talk. This may involve rapt attention and focus achieved through mutual gazes and close proximity; voice volume ("He just kept yelling 'I love Linda' as we walked down the street. It was embarrassing, but it meant a lot to me"); or absolute statements ("I'll *always* love you," or "I'll *never* leave you."). (Knapp and Vangelisti, 1992, p. 267)

As we saw in Chapter 3, when two people are intimate, they often develop a private language. Intimacy can be conveyed through personal idioms—from the pet names people give each other to private ways of talking about sex. In a recent study of intimate play, a less serious aspect of personal relationships, Baxter (1992) includes private verbal codes, physical play, role playing, teasing, gossiping games. "Private verbal code play (i.e., playful idiomatic expression) appears to be a particularly strong indicator of intimacy" (p. 359). In many studies play is not only used as a measure of intimacy but is considered to promote it. Considered a 'low risk' or safe communication strategy," it enables people to moderate conflict and tensions.

Recent studies tell us that conflict is not always destructive, not always a sign of difficulties. Indeed, "far from being the destructive force that most of us would predict, conflict can actually help maintain or even develop a relationship if it is managed right." For example, when two people resolve their conflicts about relationship roles—"the 'who' does 'what' issues"—it will tend to enhance their relationship (Duck, 1991, pp. 127–128). We will have a great deal more to say about conflict at the end of this chapter.

Work by Canary and Stafford (1992) identifies five maintenance strategies (many associated with ways to manage conversations) that have proved most successful in long-term relationships: positivity, openness, assurances, networks, and sharing tasks:

> *Positivity:* Being cooperative, cheerful, optimistic, not criticizing, being patient and forgiving, trying to build the other person's self-esteem (through compliments and other means)
>
> *Openness:* Encouraging the other person's disclosure of thoughts and feelings, stating one's feelings about the relationship, discussing the quality of the relationship as well as past relationship decisions, and what one needs and wants from it

Assurances: Stressing commitment to the other person, implying the relationship has a future, showing love and fidelity

Networks: Spending time with common friends; showing willingness to be with other person's friends or family, including them in activities

Tasks: Sharing duties and tasks jointly including household responsibilities ("Doing my fair share of the work we have to do") (Canary and Stafford, 1992, adapted from pp. 262–263)

In reading about relationship maintenance, keep in mind that the concepts we speak of here are referred to and examined in many parts of this book. For example, we discussed openness and trust earlier in this chapter and will look at other aspects of intimacy and commitment in Chapter 7. It should also be clear that at times researchers define the same variable by somewhat different terminology and that there is no magic list of behaviors: each relationship has to be negotiated and maintained on its own terms.

FAMILY COMMUNICATION

Clearly, the relationships that matter most to us are those in our family: the family represents a very special constellation of relationships.

When we speak of family communication, what do we mean by the term "family"? The legal definition of a family is "a group of people related by blood, marriage or adoption," yet in a national survey of 1,200 randomly selected adults, only 22 percent found it satisfactory. Almost 75 percent preferred "a group of people who love and care for each other" (Seligmann, 1990, p. 38).

One broad and useful definition of **family** is *"networks of people who share their lives over long periods of time; who are bound by ties of marriage, blood, or commitment, legal or otherwise; who consider themselves as family; and who share future expectations of connected relationship"* (Galvin and Brommel, 1991, p. 3).

In traditional families that have existed over many generations, members usually are aware of and interested in the family's unique history. For example, in the memoir *A Romantic Education,* Patricia Hampl writes about her origins:

My mother's "people," as family was referred to, had arrived a full generation or two before my father's. Both of her parents were American-born, even a great grandparent or two. Not "lace curtain," but still, "natives." A great grandfather had owned—or operated—a hotel in Galena, Illinois, a great-aunt had been born in a covered wagon on the way to worthless land in Oregon which sent the whole crew back again in the wagon, pioneers twice over, forward and backward. "Pioneering" was their mythology. They were Irish, Catholic, Midwestern to the marrow. . . . (1992, p. 43)

The Family As a System

Current theorists view the family as a system, emphasizing family relationships rather than individual members. Looking at the family in this way, as a whole rather than the sum of its individual members, shifts attention to patterns of relationships and cycles of behavior rather than causes and effects: "Every member influences the others but is in turn influenced by them" (Bochner and Eisenberg, 1987, p. 542).

In her innovative work with families, therapist Virginia Satir distinguishes between closed and open family systems:

The main difference between them is the nature of their reactions to change, both from the inside and from the outside. In a closed system the parts are rigidly connected or disconnected altogether. In either case, information does not flow between parts or from outside in or inside out. When parts are disconnected, they often appear as if they are operating: Information leaks in and out but without any direction. There are no boundaries.

An open system is one in which the parts interconnect, are responsive and sensitive to one another, and allow information to flow between the internal and external environments. (1988, pp. 131–132)

For Satir, disturbed families are closed systems; nurturing families are open systems. In a closed system, communication is "indirect, unclear, unspecific, incongruent, growth-impeding": rules are covert and out-of-date, with people changing their needs to conform to the rules. In an open system communication is "direct, specific, congruent, growth-producing": rules are open and up-to-date, changing "when need arises" (pp. 134–135).

Communication Rules

Anna Karenina, Tolstoy's much loved nineteenth-century novel, begins, "Happy families are all alike, but each unhappy family is unhappy in its own way." This may not be quite the case. Today theorists emphasize the uniqueness of all families, happy or unhappy; they regard each as distinct, with its own history, values, and behavioral norms.

Just as families have their own sets of values and expectations for their members, they have their own expectations about communication. There seem to be acceptable times to speak about certain topics, issues that are never raised, certain family members who should be approached or not approached, and so on. In other words, each family has a virtual handbook of understood communication rules.

In your family, for example, dinner conversations may be reserved for current things, news, movies. Serious problems and possible changes may be discussed late at night—and only with one parent. Your brother's low grades may be something the family never speaks about openly. Complaints about illness may be given exaggerated attention—or ignored. There may be a family member from whom much information is kept (a grandmother, for example). If you need money, you may always go to your mother, never your father. Or you may have a rule that you never interrupt your father when he is speaking, even if he is telling you something you already know. Communication rules are unique to each family, and over time these rules sometimes have to be revised.

Cohesion and Adaptation

Of the many variables theorists use to describe families, two of the most important are cohesion and adaptation to change. Both these dimensions influence and are influenced by communication (Bochner and Eisenberg, 1987; Galvin and Brommel, 1991).

Cohesion refers to how closely connected or bonded family members are. At the high end of the spectrum are families "so closely bonded and overinvolved that individuals experience little autonomy or fulfillment of personal needs and goals" (Galvin and Brommel, 1991, p. 20). Such families have few boundaries. Family members are all implicated in each other's lives, and there is little privacy: Everyone knows everyone else's business. They share everything, and the level of emotional or physical intimacy tends to be very high.

In families with very low levels of cohesion, on the other hand, family members are so physically and emotionally separated, so uninvolved, that there often seems little connection between them. Few activities are shared, family functions have a low priority, and each person may seem to be on a separate schedule. Writing about how modern technology has eroded contemporary life, one psychologist describes this pattern when he speaks about "the microwave relationship" in family life, with the home becoming "less a nesting place than a pit stop" (Gergen, 1991, p. 66).

Cohesion is sometimes more wished for than actual. In John Cheever's short story "Goodbye, My Brother," four adult children and their families meet at their childhood summer home for a vacation. The narrator, one of the older brothers, begins:

> We are a family that has always been very close in spirit. Our father was drowned in a sailing accident when we were young and our mother has always stressed the fact that our familial relationships have a kind of permanence that we will never meet again. (Cheever, 1978, p. 3)

Yet the narrator is preoccupied by Lawrence, his youngest brother, and resents his repeated criticisms and withdrawals ("goodbyes") from the rest of the family. The story ends with a confrontation on the beach in which the narrator strikes his brother on the head, giving him a bloody wound. Lawrence and his wife leave early the next morning.

Another important dimension by which families are described is **adaptation to change:** Although earlier theorists looked on the family as a system that remains in balance and essentially constant, it has become clear that "family systems not only remain the same, they also change, sometimes suddenly" (Bochner and Eisenberg, 1987, p. 543). The family may be affected by developmental changes that occur in younger children; and later changes that take place with children growing older and leaving home, marrying and introducing new spouses into the family. In the course of time, families also face crises such as divorce, economic reversals, significant illness, or deaths. There seem to be no families exempt from such stresses.

At the high end of the adaptability spectrum are families adapting themselves to any and every change in a way that becomes chaotic. Families who are extremely low in adaptability are described as rigid; they cannot accommodate themselves to change and live by inflexible rules. (Satir [1988] writes that in a closed system rules are inhuman [p. 134].) Most families fall somewhere in between these extremes and at times vary in their adaptability to change.

Although all families undergo stress, researchers propose that it's how the family deals with stress that determines its health. In healthy families, according to one analysis of research findings, family members don't take oppositional attitudes; they don't blame each other. Nor are they preoccupied with themselves; they don't "overanalyze." They tend to emphasize wit and to enjoy themselves. And the family boundaries tend to be conventional. In general, therapists "view adaptability as more critical to the functioning of the family than cohesion" (Bochner and Eisenberg, 1987, p. 556).

Stages in Family Development

Certainly, the nuclear family has undergone drastic changes. For example, the divorce rate has doubled (now at 50 percent) since 1965. Sixty percent of second marriages also fail. One-third of all the children born in the 1980s will live in a stepfamily, and one-fourth of all the children in America are being raised by a single parent. Over one-fifth of the children born today are born to unwed mothers. "An astonishing two-thirds of all mothers are in the labor force, roughly double the rate in 1955, and more than half of all mothers of infants are in the work force" (Footlick, 1990, p. 16).

Yet for all its shortcomings, the family is still one of the most important sources of gratification in our lives: "Challenging those who believe the American family is in decline, a recent Gallup Poll shows family ties still bind across the nation, despite distance, divorce, and changes in lifestyle (Chadwick and Heaton, 1992, p. 170). Among college students, forming new families also seems to be highly valued.

Much of the research on family communication has been reported by Pearson (1989). She identifies the following three stages in the development of the family (pp. 201–227).

Families with Preschool Children

In this stage, birth to age six, children are in their peak years for language learning. We saw in Chapter 3 that the major part of language acquisition comes from the family—particularly from interaction between the child and the primary caretaker, usually the mother. Children begin by using single words. Between eighteen and twenty-four months, two-word phrases appear. By age two they have developed a vocabulary of about three hundred words. By age three it is about one thousand words, and from four to five years old, they add about fifty words a month!

Families with School-Age Children

Children experience increasingly greater independence through each year of maturation. Family communication, while still the dominant force, begins to share influence to an increasing degree with communication from outside. Two dimensions of parent-child communication become important: acceptance-rejection and control-autonomy.

All of us need to feel accepted; however, the degree of acceptance we need will vary with the amount we received from our parents. It is thought that the more accepting our parents, the less we feel need for acceptance as we grow older. In other words, we have developed a feeling of self-worth. Furthermore, if we are raised in a family in which parents exhibit strict control, we tend to feel a higher need for control in later life.

Families with Adolescent Children

This stage tends to be characterized by increased conflict due to the increasing independence of the children. Issues of autonomy and control are very keen during these years. Adolescent children increasingly move away from family communication and toward communication with peers. Due to the intense physiological and psychological changes adolescents experience, certain topics become the focal point of communication. Acceptable topics might range from classes, grades, jobs, sports, future plans, to family news. Taboo topics include sex, parties, alcohol, drugs, and boyfriends and girlfriends. Suffice it to say that the adolescent years are probably the most trying times with regard to family communication. If parents and children can successfully weather the storms, smoother sailing tends to follow.

The enduring effects of our early relationships with our parents have been the subject of much study. Now there is new evidence that other early family relationships—those with our brothers and sisters—influence us throughout our lives and may affect our own marital relationships (Klagsbrun, 1992; Rosenthal, 1992). For example, sibling rivalry can persist long into adulthood. One psychiatrist speaks of how "a woman with an unresolved sibling rivalry from childhood might resent a husband's children from a former marriage." In this case, her conflict about having her husband to herself is "displaced to a new situation a generation later" (C9).

As we age, our relationships with siblings can again take on special importance. For example, work at Purdue University suggests that women who have a close relationship with a sister experience less depression in later life. And Klagsbrun reports, on the basis of her survey, that "women were more likely to feel close to their sisters than men to their brothers and that siblings were more likely to be close as adults if they were within five years of each other in age" (C9). In Chapter 7 we will take a closer look at current research findings about sibling relationships.

APPROACHES TO CONFLICT

A friend of ours recalls how her three-year-old son, seeing his parents in a heated argument, stepped between them, held his arms straight out, and said, "Now just a moment, you two." Although many of us go out of our way to avoid conflict and might characterize ideal relationships as free of argument, by the time we become adults we've usually been at least witness to a great many conflicts, both minor and intense. Few young people reach adulthood without some conflict with their parents, siblings, or peers.

Theorists tend to regard conflict as a natural part of human relationships, one that is not necessarily destructive, although as we'll see in Chapter 13, there are some cultures in which it is traditional for conflict to go unexpressed. For Hocker and Wilmot (1991), conflict is "a natural process inherent in the nature of all important relationships and amenable to constructive regulation through communication" (p. 6). **Conflict,** as they define it, is *an expressed struggle between at least two interdependent parties who perceive incompatible goals, scarce rewards, and interference from the other party in achieving their goals* (p. 12).

Let's look for a moment at the five elements of their definition: expressed struggle—both parties have made their disagreement apparent; perceived incompatible goals ("If we go to that party you want to go to, I can't finish my work this weekend and the meeting is first thing on Monday."); perceived scarce rewards with both parties inclined to perceive insufficient power or self-esteem ("Why do you have to make all the decisions about the house?" "Give me a little credit, will you? Don't you have any confidence in my taste?"); interference—each sees the other as an obstacle to some need or desire ("You never care about what I want."); and interdependence. Note that without some degree of interdependence there would be no conflict: both people would do exactly as they pleased. A young husband and wife may

Most theorists consider conflict a natural part of human relationships— and sometimes a source of positive change.

disagree vehemently on how to discipline their children or whether to move to another city if one gets a promising job offer, but it is their interdependence that keeps them in the relationship.

Conflict Behaviors

There have been numerous attempts by theorists to schematize patterns of response to conflict (for example, Bach and Deutsch, 1985; Sillars et al., 1982; Hocker and Wilmot, 1991). To some extent, these overlap, with different terms sometimes used to describe the same behavior. Sillars et al. (1982) and Hocker and Wilmot (1991) have proposed three categories of conflict behaviors—avoidance, competitive (or distributive) tactics, and collaborative (or integrative) tactics—which are summarized below.

Avoiding

Winston Churchill once remarked that he and his wife had decided at the beginning of their marriage that if they were going to remain married, they should never have breakfast together. Avoidance behaviors include a wide spectrum of evasive strategies intended to head off a confrontation. These range from simple denial to pessimistic or ambivalent statements. For example, in **simple denial,** unelaborated statements are made denying that there is a conflict ("Who's fighting? I'm not angry at all"). **Underresponsiveness** is a "failure to acknowledge or deny the presence of a conflict following a statement or inquiry about the conflict by the partner" (Sillars et al., 1982, p. 85) ("I still don't think that you've fixed the car. What if it stalls again on the highway?" "You'll manage."). In addition to **shifting and avoiding topics**, other tactics you probably recognize include semantic focus, abstractness, joking, ambivalence, and pessimism. **Semantic focus** is an especially interesting dodge; the person trying to avoid conflict focuses on what is being said, then makes statements about what words mean or how to characterize the ongoing conflict and this discussion of words—"semantics," if you will—soon comes to replace the original conflict issue. Often, as we suggested in Chapter 2 and in the discussion of confirmation, the issue is about relationships, not about content. In addition to ambivalent comments concerning the conflict, pessimistic remarks tend to downplay or undermine discussing causes of conflict ("Let's not rehash everything. We've been through this over and over."). **Postponement**, although it is sometimes a strategy for avoidance, can work well, but only if both parties will work out a discussion time that is not too far in the future (Hocker and Wilmot, 1991, p. 106). Planning to have an argument two weeks after the incident that sparked the disagreement is unlikely to accomplish anything.

Competing

In contrast to these strategies of avoidance, competitive tactics are used for the purpose of gaining the upper hand. The assumption here is adversarial: One person must win and the other must lose. Sillars's schema includes several competitive tactics, many of which are satirized in Figure 6.1. These include faulting (direct personal criticism—"You look like a mess"), rejection, hostile questioning ("How can you stand to live like that?"), hostile joking ("If your friends jumped off a cliff, would you jump too?"), presumptive attribution, avoiding responsibility, and prescription.

Presumptive attribution refers to making statements that attribute to the other person feelings, thoughts, or motives that he or she does not acknowledge ("you're just saying that because you know it makes me angry." "You'd like to see me make a fool out of myself." "So you think I can't stand up to my boss.")

One of the most competitive, and forceful of the strategies is **prescription**, which can take many forms. The confrontive person makes requests, demands, threatens, or argues for a given behavior change in the other person that presumably would resolve the conflict. ("Get the job done by tomorrow or I'm not paying." "Clean up your room or you're grounded for the weekend." "If you leave this apartment now, don't come back.") Threats are among the most frequent responses people use during conflict, and there are times when they can generate change, but only if the person being threatened believes— and cares—that the threat will truly be carried out (Hocker and Wilmot, 1991, pp. 110–112). For example, the "tough love" program for working with juvenile delinquents is based, in part, on this premise.

Collaborating

"Collaborating" may not be a part of your vocabulary. People who always think of conflict as a contest of wills find it especially difficult to think about resolving conflict so that all parties come away with some measure of satis-

FIGURE 6.1   "Life in Hell," by Matt Groening   (Copyright © 1988 *Childhood is Hell* by Matt Groening. All rights reserved. Reprinted by permission of Pantheon Books, a division of Random House, NY.)

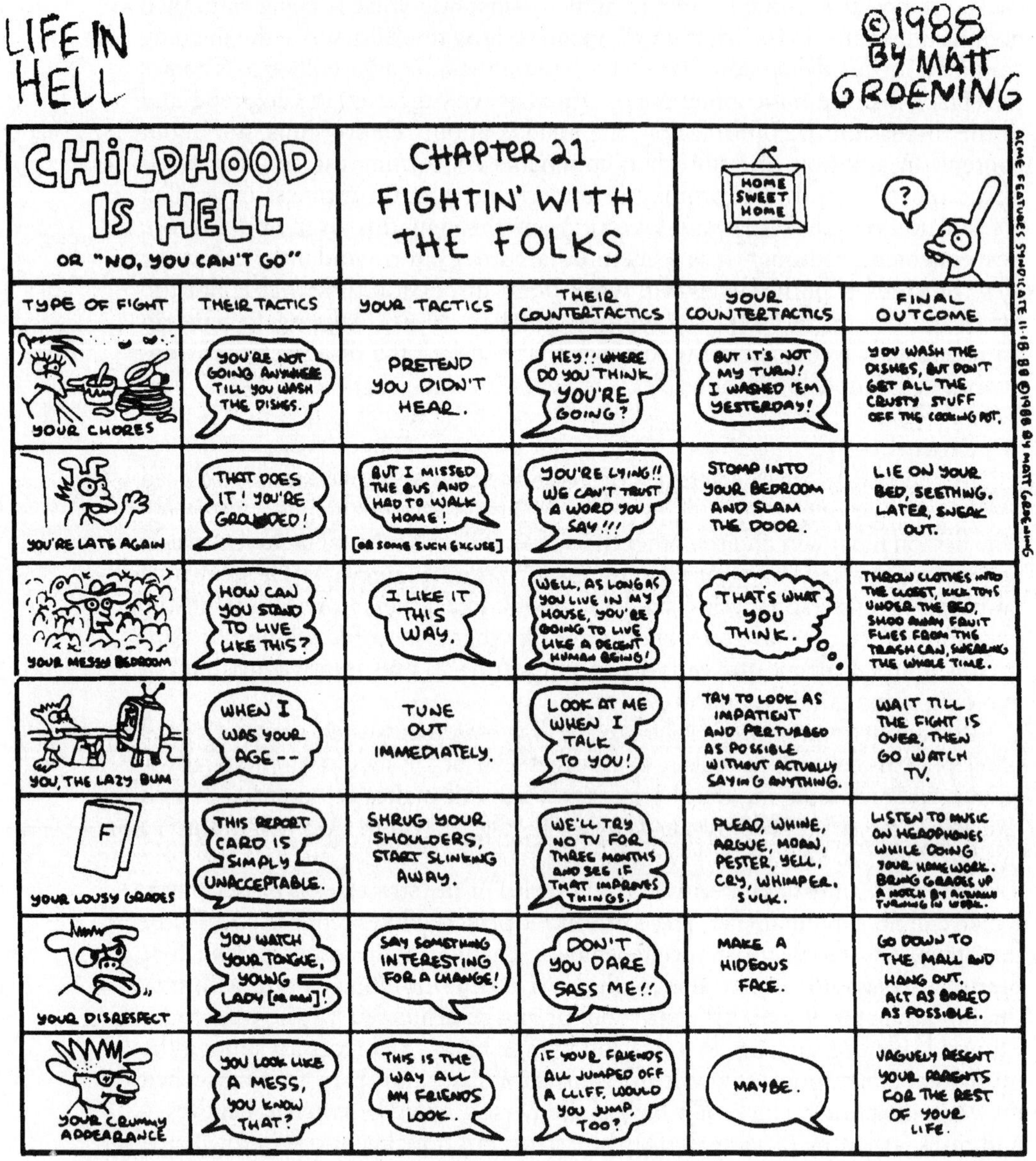

faction. Sillars et al. (1982) provide a summary of collaborative tactics, which we list for you below, giving an example of each.

Description is just that, not blaming or making other evaluations—simply describing (not "You never want to go out," but "I'm feeling depressed because we go out so infrequently."). **Qualification** involves limiting the subject at issue ("Let's not get into why we don't have enough money. Can we figure out how we can manage what we have right now to make it less stressful for both of us?"). By **disclosing your own thoughts and feelings** and **soliciting disclosures** from the other person, you are trying to establish a supportive climate in which conflict may be resolved ("When you talk about dating other men, I get anxious. Are you trying to say that you want to stop seeing me?"). **Negative inquiries** also help to elicit disclosures and greater openness from the other person ("Honey, if there's some way in which I've hurt your feelings, I'd really like to know about it.").

Two important ways in which we can be confirming and still move toward resolution are by showing **empathy** or support ("It's rough right now. We seem to be at each other's throats all the time, and I suppose you're feeling as down about it as I am.") and by **emphasizing commonalities** ("Well, we may not agree on how to cut the budget, but can't we come up with something to save our department from being eliminated?"). Other behaviors that may implement conflict resolution are **accepting responsibility** ("We've both been at fault. I know I was getting more and more hostile, and I just had to get it off my chest.") and **initiating problem solving** ("What would be best for the kids? Let's work this out now.").

Some Principles of Conflict Resolution

According to Hocker and Wilmot (1991), incompatible goals figure in every interpersonal conflict: Once two people clarify their goals and acknowledge that they can't get everything they want, they can work on creating collaborative goals. Their emphasis is on constructive problem solving.

Principled Negotiation

As an outgrowth of their work on negotiation and mediation, Fisher and associates (1991) have described a method of resolving conflict called "principled negotiation," which can be applied to all kinds of disputes—lovers' quarrels or arguments between roommates, colleagues, neighbors, diplomats, even landlords and tenants. Here are the four principles they propose:

First, separate the people from the problem. Because negotiators are human first, it is necessary to deal directly with the people in a dispute so that the relationship and the problem are separated. In addition to trying to perceive other people accurately, both sides should "make emotions explicit and acknowledge them as legitimate." In small-group negotiation, for example, "It does not hurt to say, 'You know, the people on our side feel we have been mistreated and are very upset. We're afraid an agreement will not be kept, even if one is reached. Rational or not, this is our concern. . . . Do the people on your side feel the same way?'" (p. 30). The basic approach is to face the problem, not the people—and preferably to face it side by side, defining what is at issue as a *mutual* problem.

Second, focus on interests, not positions. Fisher and associates advise talking about interests rather than positions—in effect, putting the problem before the answer rather than digging in your heels by taking an inflexible stand:

> When negotiators bargain over positions, they tend to lock themselves into those positions. The more you clarify your position and defend it, the more committed you become to it. . . . Your ego becomes identified with your position. You now have a new interest in "saving face." (pp. 4–5)

By acknowledging that the interests of *both* parties are part of the problem, you avoid putting relationship and substance in conflict. "One useful rule . . . is give positive support to the human beings on the other side equal in strength to the vigor with which you emphasize the problem" (p. 55).

Third, invent options for mutual gain. Among the major obstacles to finding workable alternatives are: making premature judgments, searching for a single answer to the dispute, and thinking that "solving his problem is his problem." Try generating a number of options first, deciding among them later. Because two people often want different things (for example, prestige rather than results or immediate changes rather than long-term changes), their differing interests may actually dovetail.

Fourth and last, insist on objective criteria. As you would expect, criteria vary with situation. Equal treatment, precedent, tradition, moral standards, costs, market value, scientific judgment, or what a court would decide are just a few of the many criteria that might be developed and negotiated, depending on what is at issue. "Try to reach a result based on standards independent of will" (p. 13).

Throughout the process of principled negotiating, many of the collaborative behaviors described in the preceding section would come into play.

Family Conflicts

Pearson (1989) offers some guidelines for resolving conflicts that are specific to family life. Notice how many of these, like Fisher and his associates, stress the interests of *all* parties as well as sharp and concrete focus on delimited issues: (1) Every family member has the right to a hearing in which needs, feelings, attitudes, and goals are openly stated; (2) family members must respond through active listening, empathy, and respect (see Chapter 5 on active listening); (3) each member of the family must be allowed a complete hearing and is obliged to give "honest information"; (4) the nature of the conflict should not be extended: family members should keep it focused on the issue being discussed; (5) emphasize concrete behaviors that can be changed, not abstract ideas about personality traits, roles, and the like; (6) keep the focus on similarities and common ground rather than on differences; and (7) "conflict resolution is more effective if planning has occurred"— for example, some couples or families find it more productive to choose conflict strategies that have worked for them in the past: thus they acknowledge the probability that some conflict will occur over time and agree, whether tacitly or explicitly, on a method of dealing with it (pp. 314–317).

There is no blanket set of rules for conflict resolution, however. One couple might always discuss their differences after taking a long walk together. Another couple might need a cooling-off period instead of tackling what is at issue right away (pp. 316–317). And in many families the right to a hearing or the prospect of planning conflict resolution would be out of the question.

Conflict resolution strategies vary with the needs of different kinds of families and of course with other communication contexts. (In Chapter 10, for example, you will find a conflict grid proposed for analyzing small-group conflicts.) Conflict norms also vary from one culture to another, as we will see in Chapter 13, and bring with them other problems in intercultural communication.

Ambiguity and Disorder

Despite the repeated emphasis on constructive conflict resolution through communication skills, some theorists acknowledge that not all conflicts are amenable to resolution. Sillars and Weisberg (1987) have discussed some of the variables that a "skills approach" often fails to take into account. "Conflict," they point out, "simply cannot be fully appreciated from a highly rational view of human behavior. Sometimes people lose control over conflict—not because they are naive, but because the process itself has disorderly and irrational elements" (p. 148).

Ambiguity, disorder, and confusion are part and parcel of many conflicts. What starts out as a simple argument over "nothing" can heat up and can quickly become chaotic:

> Private arguments do not necessarily conform to public standards of reasonableness, consistency, or relevance in argumentation because a dyad defines its own sense of "correct" or "appropriate" argument. . . .
> In fact, a striking feature of intense interpersonal conflict is the disintegration of conventional patterns of conversation. (Sillars and Weisberg, 1987, p. 149)

In the midst of a vehement argument, conversation may become increasingly emotional and volatile. It may not even be relevant. One person—or both—may suddenly bring up all sorts of past resentments (the popular term for this behavior is "gunnysacking") which intensify and confuse the initial conflict. After a time, two people may even lose the sense of what they started out arguing about.

Perhaps you've been involved in this kind of conflict yourself. One factor that contributes to the disorder and ambiguity is confusion about the source of the conflict. We don't always know why we are angry, and we don't always know why other people respond, or "overreact," the way they do. Tempers escalate, and we're off.

Relationship conflicts can be bitter and chaotic: "A vague sense of dissatisfaction over core relationships may have a rippling effect, creating conflict over many peripheral issues" (p. 151). For example, a couple's argument about when to leave a party may also reflect a struggle over which person has the decision-making power.

Often conflict is also disorganized because it is embedded in daily activities. Many interpersonal conflicts carry a strong element of surprise: They seem to surface out of nowhere and to have no boundaries. For example, conflict can come up just as two people are leaving their house for work, then break off, unresolved, only to recur several days later—perhaps at another inopportune moment. Many interpersonal conflicts resist scheduling and are experienced as outside our control (p. 157).

Conflicts in which all concerned have a clear perception and understanding of their goals and focus on a single delimited issue are more suited to a skills approach, but serious conflicts about relationships are extremely difficult to disentangle.

SUMMARY

This chapter was concerned with relationship processes, and its first focus of attention was the bases of human attraction. Other things being equal, we found, the closer two people are geographically, the more likely they are to be attracted to each other. Although proximity is usually a precondition of attraction, however, people tend to attract and be attracted to those they perceive as similar to themselves. Conversely, they tend to dislike and be disliked by those perceived as different. Several variables qualify generalizations about the similarity thesis—including perceived reciprocity of liking, changes in self-esteem, anxiety, and isolation.

We then turned to five defining characteristics of all relationships. We stressed the importance of social-psychological environment and spoke of what makes for confirming/supportive climates. Time, information sharing, and trust were also examined as were two primary dimensions of all relationships: affection and control.

The next part of our chapter introduced a theory about the life cycle of relationships. We also considered recent findings about behaviors and strategies people use to maintain satisfying relationships.

In discussing family communication, we looked at the family as a system, communication rules, the variables of cohesion and adaptability to change, as well as at stages of family development.

Our final section on conflict examined avoidance, competitive, and collaborative behaviors. Two approaches to conflict resolution were discussed, as were the inherent difficulties in resolving some intense relational conflicts.

REVIEW QUESTIONS

1. What are two ways in which proximity influences interpersonal relationships?

2. How is similarity related to attraction?

3. Describe four variables that qualify generalizations about attitude similarity.

4. Explain the difference between climate and setting.

5. What are the major differences between confirming and disconfirming response styles? Give some examples.

6. How do supportive and defensive climates of communication differ?

7. In what ways can we define relationships in terms of time?

8. What is the essential difference between depth and breadth of information sharing in any relationship?

9. What is the relationship between trust, accuracy, and effectiveness in human relationships?

10. Explain how the dominance/submission (control) dimension of a relationship functions. Give an example.

11. How does the love/hostility (affection) dimension of human relationships function?

12. Identify the building and declining stages of human relationships as defined by Knapp.

13. Specify at least three variables that determine how a relationship will terminate.

14. Discuss at least three strategies that have proven effective for relationship maintenance.

15. Explain at least three defining characteristics of families and what makes family communication distinctive.

16. Discuss two major variables in family communication.

17. List and briefly explain three stages in family development, and summarize recent research about siblings.

18. What are the three categories of conflict behavior? Give examples of each of them.

19. Identify two approaches to conflict resolution and summarize the principles of each.

20. What are some of the difficulties that arise in resolving intense relational conflicts?

EXERCISES

1. Have some friends rate a number of topics on a scale such as the one shown here. Then create two paragraphs, one agreeing with the general attitude of the class on each issue—legalizing the use of drugs, for exam-

ple—and one disagreeing. Put a byline on each of the two paragraphs, using fictitious names. Then have your friends indicate the extent of their attraction to the authors. See whether they prefer the person whom they perceive as holding an attitude similar to their own. This would validate the theory that perceived attitude similarity yields attraction.

Strongly agree	Agree	Neither agree nor disagree	Disagree	Strongly disagree
5	4	3	2	1

2. Create a composite description of the kinds of people you are attracted to. What does this composite tell you about yourself?

3. Describe a situation in which you entered into a relationship on the rebound. Analyze the positive and negative aspects of that relationship. If you were to encounter a similar situation, what, if anything, would you do differently?

4. The next time you observe a disagreement between two people, try to determine whether they are disagreeing on the content level, the relationship level, or both. Relate your observations to two other disagreements that you have experienced, and analyze those disagreements in the same way.

5. Write a paragraph describing someone you trust very much. Then write a description of someone you do not trust. Finally, elaborate on the behaviors that you want to develop and to avoid in building a trusting relationship with someone in the future.

6. Observe five communication events that illustrate five different outcomes of communication (see Chapter 1). Analyze the events in terms of the following questions:
   a. What were the relative frequencies of confirming and disconfirming response styles for each communication event? Does there appear to be any relationship between the type of communication outcome and the predominant response style? If so, why do you think this is the case, and what implications does this have for your own communication behavior?
   b. In which communication events were trust and information sharing most apparent? Why do you think this was so?

SUGGESTED READINGS

Bach, George R., and **Peter Wyden.** *The Intimate Enemy: How to Fight Fair in Love and Marriage.* New York: Avon, 1981.

This book discusses constructive ways to resolve conflicts between the sexes. Numerous people have found it a useful guide to problem-solving communication in romantic relationships.

Bach, George R., and **Ronald M. Deutsch.** *Stop! You're Driving Me Crazy.* New York: Berkeley, 1985.

A popular analysis of conflict, discussing many "crazy-making" strategies and what to do about them.

Duck, Steve. *Understanding Relationships.* New York: Guilford Press, 1991.

A synthesis of recent research and a readable, practical discussion of interpersonal relationships by an authority on the subject.

Fisher, Roger, William Ury, and **Bruce Patton.** *Getting to Yes: Negotiating Agreement without Giving In.* 2d ed. New York: Penguin, 1991.

The authors present a contemporary view of negotiating and show how you can negotiate ethically. They explain the findings of "The Harvard Negotiating Project" as well as how to use them.

Galvin, Kathleen M., and **Bernard J. Brommel.** *Family Communication: Cohesion and Change.* 3rd ed. New York: Harper Collins, 1991.

This is a comprehensive text on communication within functional families. The authors make use of many first-person narratives to illustrate issues and concepts.

Hocker, Joyce L., and **William W. Wilmot.** *Interpersonal Conflict.* 3rd ed. Dubuque, IA: Brown & Benchmark, 1991.

An excellent book on the subject of conflict management.

Knapp, Mark L., and **Anita L. Vangelisti.** *Interpersonal Communication and Human Relationships.* 2d ed. Newton, MA: Allyn & Bacon, 1992.

The authors analyze communication patterns in developing and declining relationships as well as the strategies and behaviors people use to maintain satisfying relationships.

Lerner, Harriet G. *The Dance of Anger.* NY: Harper Collins, 1989.

A popular but useful discussion of how anger, if used properly, can bring about positive change in relationships.

Satir, Virginia. *The New Peoplemaking.* Mountain View, CA: Science and Behavior Books, 1988.

A lively and invaluable discussion of family communication by a pioneer in the field of family therapy. Excellent examples and illustrations and many practical insights.

Vaughn, Diane. *Uncoupling.* New York: Random House, 1990.

A look at how and why personal relationships deteriorate. The author gives us numerous case histories and examples.

When Harry Met Sally

This film takes a lighthearted look at the evolution of a friendship into a romantic relationship.

PART II
CONTEXTS

CHAPTER SEVEN

*T*wo-Person Communication

CHAPTER OBJECTIVES

After reading this chapter, you should be able to:

1 Discuss the two-person context as a social system, explaining the concepts of norms, roles, and disruptive power.

2 Discuss increasing changes in the doctor-patient relationship and research findings about relational communication specific to it.

3 Identify four ways to assess the quality of a two-person relationship.

4 Discuss the concept of the Johari window, give several reasons for self-disclosure and reluctance to disclose. Explain when self-disclosure is appropriate.

5 Identify five qualities that describe intimacy in an interpersonal relationship.

6 Discuss affiliation and commitment in two-person communication, and summarize research findings concerning sibling relationships.

7 State the relationship between need for affiliation and need for dominance.

8 Distinguish between relationship structures that are complementary, symmetrical, and parallel.

9 Explain how status affects interpersonal communication and distinguish between dominance and power.

10 Discuss several principles of assertive behavior and explain DESC Scripting as well as two other techniques of assertiveness training.

Nancy sees her doctor in the morning, meets her friend Annette for lunch, works on a project with a colleague, buys a pair of shoes, takes a cab, and returns home for dinner with her husband. Each of her actions involves a dyadic relationship.

The **two-person context,** or *dyad,* represents the *smallest unit of human interaction* and in many ways serves as a microcosm of all larger groups. As defined in Chapter 1, it encompasses the full range of human relationships—from the most brief and casual, so often colored by first impressions, to the most intense and long lasting.

Many studies have emphasized similarity-dissimilarity, rational decision making, and conscious analysis of two-person relationships. Keep in mind, however, that not all relationships are headed toward intimacy (Delia, 1980). In fact, intimate relationships are the fewest in number. Delia proposes a new and very useful perspective for studying relationships, which we outline below.

First, you often form a relationship not as something pursued for its own sake—not because you desire one—but as an outgrowth of some joint task or activity. For example, you may need a lab partner in your physics course, or you may have to collaborate with someone on a project at work.

Second, the demands of the situation (here we include social activities, contexts, and institutions) often organize your inferences and perceptions, establish your expectations of the relationship, and shape the way it evolves. For example, in buying a pair of shoes, you don't usually evaluate the salesclerk's personal traits. "Whether the salesclerk is witty, warm and loving is irrelevant to . . . buying shoes" (p. 98).

And third, Delia reminds us that "many stable and enduring relationships are limited to a specific context or range of contexts and do not imply increasing intimacy" (p. 99). Thus two men may meet for tennis every Sunday yet never see each other in any other social situations. Two partners in a law firm may get on well, even go out to lunch every week during working hours, yet never socialize after business hours.

Finally, although the degree of satisfaction you get from a relationship and the way in which it develops will be based on your implicit judgments about the other person, "these judgments vary with the context and the trajectory of the relation" (p. 100). For example, it may be very important to Bruce that his lawyer is painstaking and rigorous, but he may well value different qualities in a girlfriend. To put it simply: Some qualities and judgments will be important in some relationships, while other very different qualities and judgments will be important for others.

Delia's four principles provide us with a framework within which all relationships operate. In the following discussion of social setting, we take a closer look at the variables of their operation: norms and roles. As you will see, norms and roles apply to all kinds of two-person relationships, regardless of their degree of intimacy.

THE SOCIAL SETTING

No two people, no matter how intense their relationship, live totally untouched by the rules and expectations of society. As their relationship evolves, they also develop a kind of society in miniature, a two-person social system with some of its own rules and expectations, its own rewards and punishments.

Norms

As suggested in Chapter 4, **norms** are *rules, whether implicit or explicit, about behavior,* rules from which we develop certain expectations about how people will act. We have norms for sex, eating, visiting, grading exams, tipping, childrearing—in fact, for every aspect of human life. Even two people meeting for the first time follow norms as to appropriate communication behaviors: "There are rules for taking and terminating a turn at talking; there are norms synchronizing the process of eyeing the speaker and being eyed by him; there is an etiquette for initiating an encounter and bringing it to an end" (Goffman, 1972).

Norms exist on a number of social levels and are often transferred from one relationship to another—not always with the same measure of success. Some are shared by almost all members of a given culture, others are specific to families, ethnic groups, communities, or regions of a country. In certain parts of California, for example, the nude after-dinner soak in a Jacuzzi might be taken for granted—but probably not at a dinner party that included visitors from the Midwest or the Northeast.

When you and I first meet, each of us already has a great many expectations (however misguided) about how the other will behave. As we get to know one another, we may also establish some norms of our own. When dating, for example, a couple decides what are acceptable or unacceptable behaviors concerning a number of things, such as places to go, topics of conversation, love making, and so on.

Occasionally, the norms in an intimate relationship are made unusually explicit. For example, since the 1970s there has been a growing tendency among couples to formalize such norms in a personal marriage contract. Such a contract can cover any number of issues. Consider the following list (adapted from Hunt, 1976, pp. 99–100):

1. What last name should the wife use?

2. Should there be children?

3. What last name will the children have?

4. Should birth control be used?

5. Is there a religious commitment?

6. How will the children be raised?

7. Will the wife work?

8. What will be the relationship of each spouse to the other's relatives?

9. How will earning money and housework be divided?

10. Who will control family finances?

11. Where and how will the couple live?

12. What will be the attitude toward sexual fidelity?

Initially, a contract may minimize power struggles and conflicts. It is essential to realize, however, that normative agreements may have to be changed as the people who made them change. And some contracts actually specify conditions for negotiating new terms or renewing the old ones.

Although we have no research yet on whether living with such a contract influences the way a couple communicates, Knapp and Vangelisti believe that "the existence of the contract probably does influence the way participants talk to each other" (1992, p. 270). They point out, for example, that

> sometimes couples feel that the contract signifies ownership. Either explicitly or implicitly, messages may be based upon the fact that the other person "belongs to me"—"You're my wife and you'll do as I tell you." (p. 269)

In general, certain relationships seem to establish more norms than others. One team of researchers reports that the frequency with which norms are established is linked to the **disruptive power** each person has over the other—that is, *the power one person has to keep the other from doing what he or she wants to do* (Murdoch and Rosen, 1970). In some relationships, one person has much more disruptive power than the other. When both have high disruptive power, they tend to establish a greater number of normative agreements—perhaps because both know that "overuse of their power can be self-defeating" (Murdoch and Rosen, 1970, p. 273). When disagreements between two people are common, normative agreements often reduce the level and frequency of conflict. If Dan always prefers boating and Cynthia always wants to go camping, they can decide to alternate these activities. If Cynthia has greater disruptive power than Dan, they may end up going camping most of the time. Either arrangement is a normative agreement (see also Ilich, 1980).

Norms then are guidelines that limit and direct behavior. We accept them because they allow us to establish standard operating procedures—ground rules, if you will—that make the behavior of others more predictable and decrease the need for communicating about that behavior. If a married couple reaches an agreement about where to spend Christmas and Easter holidays each year or about who handles the finances, there is no need to renegotiate these decisions repeatedly. Thibaut and Kelley (1985) put it well when they write that effective norms "can reduce the costs of interaction and eliminate the less rewarding activities from a relationship. They can act to improve the outcome attained by members of a dyad and to increase their interdependence." As they also point out, a conformity agreement tends to become rewarding in and of itself.

Not all normative agreements are rewarding. Some are inappropriate for a given relationship. Some restrict communication in an unhealthy way. Others are too rigid. For example, if a normative agreement exists between father and son that the son will never question the father's judgments or decisions, the son may forfeit his own good judgment simply because it conflicts with his father's opinion. Ellis (1984) believes that our attempts to live by norms that we are virtually unaware we have assumed, standards inappropriate for our own well-being, cause a great deal of psychological damage. He bases his rational-emotive school of psychotherapy on the premise that norms can best serve us if we know that they exist and can periodically evaluate their appropriateness.

Roles

Doctor-patient, child-parent, student-teacher, lover-lover, friend-friend, husband-wife, player-coach, employee-supervisor, grandparent-grandchild. These are just a sampling of the many sets of roles possible within a two-person relationship. The term "role" is unsettling. Actors play roles, and you might be wondering what roles have to do with human communication—especially two-person communication—in which, ideally, communication is based on mutual trust, not game-playing. Roles relate to the norms we've just been talking about. In any given culture, some norms apply to all members and others apply to only some members. A **role** is simply a *set of norms that applies to a specific subclass within the society.*

Think of Nancy, the young woman described at the beginning of this chapter, as a patient, a friend, a colleague, and a customer as well as a wife. Like Nancy, each of us assumes multiple roles. Yet, in assuming them, we do not become automatons, nor do we necessarily sacrifice our individuality.

Expected versus Enacted Roles

There are numerous situations in which a person's expected and enacted roles are quite different. A parent is expected to minister to the needs of the child, to provide financial support, and so on. But the enacted role of parent may in fact be quite different. So may the role of the child. In a memoir about her Australian childhood, Jill Ker Conway, a former president of Smith College, has written of an eight-year drought and its emotional and physical toll on her parents. The family lived on an isolated sheep farm and during violent dust storms Conway's father would sometimes awaken screaming from night-mares of his experiences in the trenches during World War I:

> It was usually I who woke him from his nightmares. My mother was hard to awaken. She had, in her stoic way, endured over the years two bad cases of ear infection, treated only with our available remedies, hot packs and aspirin. One ear was totally deaf as a result of a ruptured eardrum, and her hearing in the other ear was much reduced. Now her deafness led to a striking reversal of roles, as I, the child in the family, would waken and attempt to soothe a frantic adult. (1990, p. 59)

Even when such an obvious reversal of roles does not take place, people interpret their roles differently. For example, one man might view the role of father as a stern disciplinarian, another as a completely permissive companion, another as a firm but loving teacher.

Granted, we "enact" roles. We shall not say, however, that we are actors in a completely theatrical sense: Somes roles are more central to us than others. Thus the intensity with which a person takes on various roles differs: Some will be enacted casually, with little or no involvement, and others with great commitment. When we enact a role with any measure of intensity, we communicate from within that role—that is, we take a certain stance. We also internalize certain expectations about how we should respond and how other people should respond to us. ("How dare you talk to your mother that way?" asks the outraged mother.) Most communication takes place within the boundaries of these expectations.

Of course, we are more comfortable in some roles than in others. Usually the roles we don't enjoy playing are those that create conflict. Role conflict, and the misunderstandings to which it gives rise, illustrate the interdependence of role, self-concept, and communication. Let's look at two types of role conflict, both of which tend to create problems in communication.

Interrole Conflict

A person is likely to experience **interrole conflict** when *occupying two (or more) roles that entail contradictory expectations about a given behavior.* Suppose that while proctoring an exam, Lisa sees her friend cheating during the test. As a proctor, she feels obliged to report the cheating. As a friend, she may feel that loyalty demands she overlook what she has just seen. The options in this case seem clear. The demands of each role are known. They conflict, and one must be chosen over the other.

But consider a more delicate situation. Early in the fall semester Don and Louise met in the student union and started dating. He was a French instructor, and she was taking third-year French with the department chairman. Halfway through the school year, the chairman had to be hospitalized. It was decided that Don would teach the second term of third-year French. When it came time to award the French prize, Don found himself in an uncomfortable situation. Louise, he believed, was the best student in the class; yet he felt that his objectivity as a judge had been compromised. His conflicting roles as instructor and boyfriend made him extremely uneasy, and he ended up giving the French award to the second-best student in the class.

Intrarole Conflict

An **intrarole conflict** presents other kinds of problems; it involves *contradictory expectations concerning a single role.* For example, Kathy and Maxine, two friends who are close and very supportive of each other, often discuss personal problems. Suppose Kathy believes that Maxine is making a big mistake in initiating a divorce, that Maxine herself is contributing to the problem and that she very much needs psychological help. As a friend, Kathy usually sees herself as a listener, someone who does not interfere but allows the other person to clarify her feelings. She also values being truthful, but fears being intrusive or meddling. She is not at all certain how she should respond. Questions such as these about appropriate behaviors and boundaries in friendship have to do with intrarole conflict.

To make our discussion of norms and roles more concrete, we will focus on one form of two-person communication that is limited to the rather specific setting of clinical medicine.

Doctor and Patient

The doctor-patient relationship is unique and has traditionally been governed by many norms concerning power, status, and competence. Moreover, the doctor-patient relationship often involves disclosures on the part of both: It's assumed that the doctor will be open with the patient concerning the nature of any illness, the prognosis, fees, and so on, and that the patient will communicate openly with the doctor. Today, for example, it's routine for a doctor to ask a new patient if he or she takes drugs. For doctors to treat patients effectively, they must gain patient trust and cooperation. It is for this reason that doctors are training medical students to increase their understanding of nonverbal communication and develop better listening skills (Goleman, 1991; Belkin, 1992).

The roles of doctor and patient seem to be in transition, and certainly the doctor-patient relationship has never been more embattled. Many reasons have been proposed: the soaring costs of medical services and health insurance; the AIDS crisis; the increasing specialization of doctors; the rising costs of malpractice insurance, which are increasingly passed down to patients; the attempt of many large companies to cut back on insurance coverage for employees.

The decline in public trust and satisfaction is dramatically reflected in the growing number of malpractice suits. A recently reported Harris poll indicates that patients are switching doctors in response to "doctor-patient communication concerns." Here are some of the reasons patients gave for making a change:

Doctor didn't spend enough time with patient: 51 percent
Doctor wasn't friendly: 42 percent
Doctor didn't answer questions honestly and completely: 40 percent
Doctor wasn't knowledgeable and competent: 37 percent
Doctor didn't explain problems understandably: 30 percent
Doctor didn't treat patient with respect: 27 percent
Doctor wasn't always available when needed: 27 percent (Nazario, 1992, B1)

The dissatisfaction appears to be mutual. For their part, doctors must deal with escalating fees for malpractice insurance; review by insurance carriers, governmental agencies, and other administrators; wary and distrustful patients; and unrealistic patient expectations of medical "miracles." There are even predictions that telemedicine, "the delivery of health-care information over communications links," the use of computers for diagnostic decision, and other innovations will radically undercut the doctor's role (Williams, 1989, p. 299).

Paradoxically, one of the major reasons cited for dissatisfaction is linked with the proliferation of new medical technologies. Medical advances have significantly increased life expectancy, made it possible to transplant vital organs, and introduced many sophisticated and highly effective diagnostic techniques, yet patients complain about expensive and unnecessary tests, their dehumanizing aspects, as well as the limited amount of time doctors are willing to spend with them.

Dr. David Rogers, professor of medicine at Cornell University Medical College, has described some implications of the new technologies for both doctor and patient:

Residents may know by virtue of technology what is physically wrong with a patient, but they consequently tend to miss the personal interactions I use with patients to try to make them feel more comfortable and less fearful. Why do I sit on the side of the bed of some patients? How is my listening different from theirs? Why do I respond to patient's questions, worries, hopes or fears in the particular way I do? . . . [Residents forget] how often the doctor himself must become part of the treatment, and that in so doing the doctor can often improve patient outcomes. (Rogers, 1989, R38)

Dr. Rogers expresses a legitimate concern about the future of the doctor-patient relationship, and there is some recent research on how the relational communication of doctors is perceived (Street and Wiemann, 1988). A study by Burgoon and associates (1987) confirms the importance of relational communication in improving doctor-patient relationships and, to a lesser degree, in gaining patient compliance. Burgoon reports that doctors' messages that "convey openness, interest, willingness to listen, involvement, warmth, similarity, equality, and some formality" (p. 321) are linked with maximum patient satisfaction. This is true of cognitive satisfaction ("believing that one is well informed by the physician about the illness, prescribed medications and prognosis"), affective satisfaction (feelings of trust, acceptance, liking), and satisfaction with how the doctor conducts the examination. Receptivity is the strongest predictor of patient satisfaction throughout. There are other findings of particular interest in studying interpersonal communication of this type. For example, a patient's affective satisfaction including disclosure "increases as a physician is perceived to express *less* dominance, more similarity, more immediacy, as well as more receptivity." On the other hand, feeling well informed by one's doctor is maximized when the doctor shows "receptivity, involvement, relaxation, *and* formality." In the section that follows, we will be looking more closely at several of these variables as well as others that affect the quality of all two-person relationships.

ASSESSING THE QUALITY OF A TWO-PERSON RELATIONSHIP

Because most, if not all, of our **qualitatively high relationships** involve only two people, quality is a crucial issue in this setting. In distinguishing interpersonal—that is, high-quality—from noninterpersonal—that is, low-quality—relationships, Miller and Steinberg (1975) were the first to introduce several important concepts.

First, in qualitatively high relationships, *information about the other person is primarily psychological rather than cultural and sociological.* Most cultural and sociological information is easy to come by. It includes the other person's sex, age, occupation, group memberships—in other words, information accessible to most people, even without knowing the other. But for me to have psychological information about you—to know what your likes and dislikes are, or your goals, or perhaps your fears—the two of us must engage in a relationship.

A second characteristic of high-quality relationships is that *rules for that relationship are developed by the two people involved* rather than being rules set by tradition. For example, our relationship may be such that although it's usually expected that a visitor calls before coming to someone's apartment, you may come to mine whenever you like—and without calling. You may open the refrigerator and help yourself. You may phone me even in the middle of the night. And you may always use my car. Remember, each interpersonal relationship establishes different rules, but they are individual rather than traditional rules.

Third, the *roles* in a high-quality relationship *are defined primarily by personal characteristics rather than by situation.* For example, Ellen may always take care of bills, correspondence, and arranging for house repairs because Cliff, her husband, hates doing these things. In turn, he may do the weekly shopping and all the vacuuming because they agree that he is more efficient at both.

And fourth, *the emphasis* in a high-quality relationship *is on individual choices* rather than group choices. We shall see the importance of individual choices *and* psychological information—that is, knowledge of personal attitudes and beliefs, highly individualized behavior, and so on—as we discuss self-disclosure, one of several variables affecting relationship quality.

Remember that the concept of quality applies to all two-person relationships, not just intimate ones. Thus many of the variables to be examined here also have an impact on more casual relationships (power, for example, can be as much a factor in your work relationships as it is in your marriage). The first variable we shall consider is self-disclosure.

Self-Disclosure

Self-disclosure is *making known information about oneself.* We disclose a great deal about ourselves through our facial expression, posture, clothing, tone of voice, and countless other nonverbal cues, though much of that behavior is unintentional. But "self-disclosure" as we use the term here is intentional. Not only is it an integral part of two-person communication; it occurs more often in this context than in any other kind of communication.

Self-disclosure is an attempt to let authenticity enter our social relationships, and we now know that it is related both to mental health and self-concept development: "I have known people," writes Jourard, one of the foremost researchers on self-disclosure, "who would rather die than become known. . . . When I say that self-disclosure is a symptom of personality health, what I mean really is that a person who displays many of the other characteristics that betoken healthy personality . . . *will also display the ability to make himself fully known to at least one other significant human being"* (1964, p. 24).

A variety of studies link self-disclosure with intimacy and marital satisfaction (Waring and Chelune, 1983; Chelune et al., 1984). In fact, self-disclosure is the distinguishing feature between couples in therapy and those who are not: between couples in therapy, self-disclosure is not synchronized (Chelune et al., 1985).

The Johari Window

One of the most innovative models for conceptualizing levels of awareness and self-disclosure in human communication is the **Johari window** (Luft, 1969). ("Johari" derives from the first names of the two psychologists who developed it, Joseph Luft and Harry Ingham.) Essentially, the model offers a way of looking at the interdependence of intrapersonal and interpersonal affairs. The illustration in Figure 7.1 represents you as you relate to other human beings by four quadrants—in effect, four panes of a single window. The size of each quadrant or pane is determined by awareness, by yourself and by others, of your behavior, feelings, and motivations—and the degree to which this information is shared. Unlike most windowpanes, those of the Johari window sometimes change in size.

Each of you may be described by a Johari window. Quadrant 1, the **open quadrant,** will reflect your general openness to the world, your willingness to be known. It comprises *all aspects of yourself known to you and to others.* This quadrant is the basis for most two-person communication.

By contrast, quadrant 2, the **blind quadrant,** consists of *all the things about yourself that other people perceive but that are not accessible to you.* Perhaps you tend to monopolize conversation unwittingly, or you think of yourself as quite a wit but your friends find your humor heavy-handed. Then again you might feel quite confident and yet have several nervous mannerisms that others are aware of but you are not. The blind quadrant could contain any of the unintentional communicative stimuli mentioned in Chapter 1.

In quadrant 3, the **hidden quadrant,** you are the one who exercises discretion. This quadrant is made up of *all the things you prefer not to disclose to someone else,* whether they concern yourself or other people: your salary, your parents' divorce, your feelings about your roommate's closest friends, your overdue bills, and so on. In short, this quadrant represents your attempts to limit input or information concerning yourself.

The last pane, quadrant 4, is the **unknown quadrant.** The blind quadrant is unknown to you though known to others. The hidden quadrant is unknown to others but known to you. Quadrant 4 is completely unknown. It represents everything about yourself that has never been explored, either by you or by other people—all your untapped resources, all your potential for personal growth. You can only infer that it exists or confirm its existence in retrospect.

Configurations of the Johari window depend upon one's interaction style. Thus Dan, who is unwilling to let business colleagues or even friends learn much about him, will have a very small open area (quadrant 1) and therefore a large hidden area (quadrant 3). His brother Ted, who is very willing to disclose information but cannot receive feedback, will have a large open area (quadrant 1) and a large blind area (quadrant 2). Numerous configurations are possible.

The four quadrants of the Johari window are interdependent: a change in one quadrant will affect others. As you disclose something from the hidden quadrant, for example, you make it part of the open quadrant; you enlarge it and reduce the size of the hidden quadrant. Should friends tell you about your nervous mannerisms, this information becomes part of the open quadrant, with a corresponding shrinkage of the blind quadrant. Such change is not always desirable. Sometimes, for example, telling a person that he or she seems nervous only makes him or her more ill at ease. Because inappropriate disclosure of a feeling or perception about another can be damaging, your friends will need to use some discretion in the feedback they give you about quadrant 2.

Basically, however, Luft proposes that it is rewarding and satisfying to enlarge the open quadrant—that is, not only to learn more about yourself and

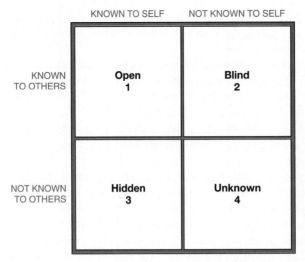

KNOWN TO SELF   NOT KNOWN TO SELF

KNOWN TO OTHERS

Open
1

Blind
2

NOT KNOWN TO OTHERS

Hidden
3

Unknown
4

FIGURE 7.1   The Johari Window

(*Source:* Joseph Luft, *Of Human Interaction,* Palo Alto, CA: National Books Press, 1969. Copyright © 1969 by National Books Press. By permission of National Books Press.)

thus gain insight but to reveal information about yourself so that others will know you better too. He also believes that greater knowledge of self in relation to others will result in greater self-esteem and self-acceptance. If you can learn more about yourself and others, you can change the shape of your own Johari window. An improved window might look something like the one in Figure 7.2.

Trust and Reciprocity

Although at times strangers make startling self-disclosures in face-to-face encounters, these usually have few consequences. Suppose a woman sitting next to you on a transatlantic flight tells you about her concern for her teenage daughter, who is living with a man twice her age. In a sense, that's an easier thing for her to tell to you, a total stranger, than to her next-door neighbors. Often when we make our supposed disclosures to strangers, we have very little to lose. And many of these so-called disclosures have to do with past events ("I was adopted," "I was in analysis for five years," and so on), rather than with present events and feelings about those events.

Authentic self-disclosure—whether between acquaintances, coworkers, friends, or lovers—is not one-sided: it tends to be reciprocal. It is an exchange process that can and often does prompt greater disclosure from the other person and often results in more positive feelings between the two. The work of Jourard (1979) and others confirms this sequence of behavior: *When one person discloses something about himself or herself to another, he or she tends to elicit a reciprocal level of openness in the second person.* Jourard calls the pattern the **dyadic effect.** Many studies support Jourard's principle: "One person's intimate disclosure encourages intimate disclosure by the listener,

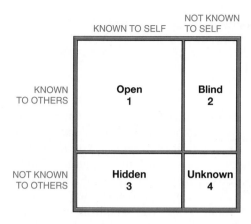

FIGURE 7.2 An Improved Johari Window

and superficial disclosure encourages superficial disclosure in return" (Derlega et al., 1987, p. 174).

Reciprocal self-disclosure tends to be gradual. And it seems to take place only after the two people have reached a basic level of trust (Wheeless and Grotz, 1976) or solidarity (Wheeless, 1976). Thus we expect that early in a relationship disclosures will be less intimate and that as mutual trust is established, they will become more revealing. Knapp and Vangelisti (1992) observe that in the intensifying stage of a relationship, there are often a great number of self-disclosures.

In long-term relationships the content of these disclosures tends to stabilize. For example, several studies of marital satisfaction show an interesting pattern of high self-disclosure among happily married couples—but only of positive information. In a recent novel about a couple getting a divorce, the wife's many negative comments about her present feelings toward her husband prompt him to ask that she stop telling him how she feels. "If I knew any more," he tells her, "I'd be paralyzed."

"Nobody wants to discover that a valued way of life is ending," writes Vaughn (1987, p. 42), who studied separated and divorced couples. She reports a clear pattern that emerges regardless of the type of couple involved—"married or living together, straight or gay, young or old." According to her survey, there is usually one partner (the "initiator") who wants to break out of the relationship and a remaining partner who wishes to maintain it and may be oblivious to the problem, even though the relationship is deteriorating. For a long period, however, the initiator tends to avoid conflict. Rather than complaining, for example, an initiator may become sullen and angry and show far less intimacy—all in an effort to demonstrate unhappiness. Vaughn reports several reasons that initiators avoid confrontation; these include uncertainty about being able to terminate the relationship, fear of hurting the partner, self-protection from arguing, and not wanting to give up the partner completely. Thus, close relationships sometimes generate secrecy rather than openness, hiding problems until it becomes too late to solve them. Vanlear (1987) found increasing private-personal disclosure between dyads "until they reached a zenith (usually toward the end of the relationship), which was followed by a sharp decline" (p. 314).

To Disclose or Not Disclose

You choose to be open with another person for many different reasons. It may be because something very good has happened to you (a new job) or is troubling you (a financial problem or an imminent divorce). You may wish to clarify experiences for yourself (discussing a recent family argument might be almost therapeutic), or you may be trying to get the other person to reciprocate by also talking. And there are times when you use *selective* self-disclosure to create an impression of yourself that you would like the other person to have—for example, at a party Jon may let Trish know that he's unhappily married because he finds himself attracted to Trish.

People often use self-disclosure to maintain or develop relationships—by keeping the other person up to date on his or her life, to control and manipulate the other person, or to enhance the relationship by letting the other person know something that will increase the intimacy, depth, and breadth of their relationship (Rosenfeld and Kendrick, 1984; Derlega and Grzelak, in Chelune et al., 1979). So we have some mixed motives for disclosure, and on occasion disclosing can be manipulative.

Indeed, self-disclosure can be risky, and when we avoid disclosing, one of the primary reasons may be that we fear projecting a negative image. (The society in which we live requires perfection, yet if I reveal myself, you'll know that I'm far from perfect.) Other reasons include fear that information may later be used against us, losing control over the other person or the situation, not wanting to seem like an exhibitionist, and not wanting to commit oneself publicly to something. Sometimes fear of rejection keeps us from disclosing essential aspects of ourselves, but this very withholding makes it impossible for us to be known (Rosenfeld, 1979).

One summary of research on self-disclosure finds: (1) "people believe in high self-disclosures to others they like, . . . (2) people tend to overestimate their self-disclosures, . . . (3) . . . self-disclosure does not cause liking, . . . (4) liking inhibits self-disclosure" (Haslett, 1987, pp. 205–206).

When Is Self-Disclosure Appropriate?

Self-disclosure is often an attempt to let authenticity enter our social relationships. At times it is an attempt to emphasize how we enact our roles rather than how others expect us to enact them. It may even be an attempt to step out of a role entirely. When does it work? When does it improve human relationships?

One recent study finds that *appropriate* self-disclosure contributes significantly to greater rapport between roommates (Hawken, et al. 1991). If you disclose too much, these researchers suggest, you may cause your roommate to withdraw "and to be too withdrawn doesn't allow for the type of exchange

Gender studies show a consistent pattern of higher self-disclosure among females.

of personal information needed to develop a close relationship" (1991, p. 305).

Luft (1969) describes several characteristics of appropriate self-disclosure, five of the most important being these:

1. It is a function of the ongoing relationship.

2. It occurs reciprocally.

3. It is timed to fit what is happening.

4. It concerns what is going on within and between persons present.

5. It moves by small increments. (pp. 132–133)

By applying these standards to any of your attempts at self-disclosure that didn't come off, you may be able to determine what went wrong.

Intimacy

The quality of a two-person relationship is also measured by the degree of intimacy involved (McAdams, 1989). Our *expectations* about intimacy in a given relationship seem to be very important. For example, a recent study of married couples (Kelley and Burgoon, 1991) suggests that agreement on what each spouse expects in the relationship is crucial to satisfaction and, further, that agreement about the wife's behavior is a major issue:

It appears critical to both men and women that they agree on what level of intimacy the wife is to express in the relationship. It is possible that the wife is the relational barometer in the marriage. (p. 64)

Research by Gudykunst and Hammer (1988) finds "there is more self-disclosure, attraction, attributional confidence . . . in high-intimacy relationships than in low-intimacy relationships" (p. 596). But what does "intimacy" mean to you? In a fascinating field study on the subject, Waring and his associates (1980) posed this question in interviews and found five categories of response: people associated intimacy with sharing thoughts, beliefs, fantasies, interests, goals, and backgrounds. Sexuality was not given as part of the general definition of intimacy. Intimate relationships are not necessarily sexual.

Of the other attempts to study and define intimacy, one of the most promising views **intimacy** as *a relational process "in which we come to know the innermost, subjective aspects of another, and are known in a like manner"* (Chelune et al., in Derlega, 1984; italics added). Beyond this, the authors argue that an intimate relationship is characterized by mutuality, interdependence, trust, commitment, and caring.

Mutuality, where partners engage *"in a joint venture,"* must be present in an intimate relationship. Remember, the emphasis is on *relationship*:

Intimate relationships have at their center a mutual process like finely choreographed dancers in which a balance of movement, of sharing, occurs. (p. 29)

Through **interdependence** "partners learn *in what ways they can depend upon one another for support, resources, understanding, and action,* and they agree upon future dependence" (p. 31). Closely related to **trust** is **commitment,** the extent to which the *two people see their relationship as continuing indefinitely and make efforts to ensure that it will continue.* And **caring,** of course, is *concern for the other's well-being and demonstrated affection for the other.*

Measured by these criteria, intimacy is not characteristic of all marriages, and many intimate relationships exist that are not marriages. It's also clear that intimate relationships can involve same-sex or opposite-sex partners. In fact, several recent studies of intimacy are of older siblings.

A relationship between two siblings is unique in many ways (Klagsbrun, 1992; Gold, 1989*b*). Older siblings share a history of lifetime experiences; they are usually peers and can satisfy many of the needs and desires satisfied by friends. Siblings can also supply what Gold calls " 'blood is thicker than water' loyalty. . . . No combination of these dimensions is found in any other adult dyadic relationship" (1989*b*, p. 1).

Remember that each pair of siblings has a different relationship. In a family of three children, for example, the oldest and middle child may be very close, while the youngest may be more isolated—from one or both of the others. Parents often have idealized expectations that all their children will have inherently similar—and of course positive—relationships. This hoped for democracy of feeling sometimes leads to disappointment on all sides.

On the basis of her research, Gold described **five types of sibling relationships:** *intimate, congenial, loyal, apathetic,* and *hostile.* In intimate relationships there is strong emotional interdependence between siblings expressed through mutual love, protection, concern, understanding, empathy, and durability (1989*a*, p. 42). Interestingly enough, siblings who are hostile are not indifferent; in fact, they devote "as much psychological energy [to] their sibling relationships" as intimate pairs (1989*b*, p. 6).

Research on how pairs of siblings interact in later life finds that in general they show greater closeness or intimacy, that this becomes an important source of satisfaction—even if the two live far apart—and that it contributes to emotional well-being. Even siblings who were not close as children frequently become closer in old age, and age differences that once seemed immense become unimportant.

Gold also found that widowhood increases feelings of closeness—particularly if both siblings have been widowed. Subjects suggested that the lack of emotional intimacy with a spouse "encourage[s] them to seek siblings, especially sisters, as confidantes and sources of emotional support" (1987, p. 207).

One common finding in all sibling research, says Gold, is that "pairs of sisters report the closest and most intimate relationships." Next come brother-sister pairs:

> It is not the sister-sister combination per se that affects the quality of the interactions but rather the presence of a female as one of the dyad members. (1989*a*, p. 207)

Relationships between pairs of brothers are far less likely to be intimate, though the lack of intimacy is often regretted. In one study only 15 percent of brother pairs were noted as intimate with the remaining 85 percent being rated as either hostile or apathetic. Differences in how boys and girls are socialized would seem to account for these data.

These studies offer further evidence that the need for intimacy in interpersonal relationships persists throughout our lives. Hatfield (1984) believes that each of us can develop intimacy skills. She recommends that people be encouraged "to accept themselves as they are" (p. 216), "to recognize their intimates for what they are" (p. 217), and "to also express themselves" (p. 217). Intimacy skills can also be developed by learning to deal with the responses of others—that is, learning not to apologize for your feelings or clam up and withdraw when the other person reacts negatively to what you say. Emphasis on intimacy as a process allows us to see that intimacy can be worked on—it doesn't just happen.

Affiliation and Commitment

Another important variable of relationship quality and a significant predictor of how two people will interact is the strength of their affiliative needs.

The **need for affiliation** may be seen as a continuum from highly affiliative to antisocial behavior. The high affiliater, who prefers being with others to being alone, enjoys and seeks out companionship. We describe such a person as friendly, gregarious, and generally sociable. The person who is low in the need for affiliation probably prefers being alone and has much less desire for companionship. Since this behavior is not very reinforcing to other people, the low affiliater is usually described as unfriendly or unsociable.

Most of us place ourselves somewhere between the two extremes on this continuum. Since two-person communication is potentially the most intimate, those of us with strong needs for affiliation seem to be the most willing to make the commitments required.

And yet many cannot handle that intimacy and the commitment it ultimately demands. This is especially characteristic of the young and is reflected in the current divorce rate. It is still young people who are granted over half the divorces in the United States; those who married youngest claim the highest share.

For many people the absolute commitment to another human being demanded by marriage is frightening or at best constraining. During the last two decades the rapid increase in the number of unmarried couples who are living together has been well-documented not only in the United States but in France, Australia, and many other countries. For many couples, living together is a trial marriage of sorts, a way of getting to know each other well enough to find out whether a marriage would work. Examining this "cohabitation revolution," Bumpass and Sweet (1989) report that cohabitation is a rather "short-lived state," with most couples either marrying or breaking off their relationships within a few years. In fact, between 1975 and 1984, 40 percent of all couples studied either married or stopped living together after a year, and 33 percent lasted only two years. At the end of five years only one out of ten couples was still living together. On the other hand, 60 percent of cohabitation unions ended in marriage.

There seems to be a negative correlation between cohabitation and marital stability with the divorce rate for couples who lived together before marriage significantly higher than for couples who did not: "the proportion separating or divorcing within 10 years is a third higher among those who lived together before marriage than among those who did not (36 vs. 27 percent)" (p. 10). Earlier research supports these findings (Booth and Johnson, 1988).

The lingering question is why this should be so, since living together would presumably allow people more information about each other and more time to resolve possible conflicts. Some experts believe, however, that people who choose cohabitation prior to marriage have "a different set of values, values that carry with (them) an ethic that relationships are breakable if they're not personally satisfying"—in other words, they may be people more likely to terminate a relationship that is not completely satisfying. Sociologist Andrew Cherlin proposes some other reasons—the increasing economic status of women, increased sexual freedom among those who are not married, and "increased emphasis on personal satisfaction in intimate relationships, less emphasis on working together" (cited in Marbella, 1989, E7).

Consider the relationship of a young man and woman in their twenties—let's call them Kathy and David—who have been living together for two years. During this time Kathy's job with a textile manufacturer has become increasingly responsible. Last year she was made director of her division and given a substantial raise. David now feels that he would like to get married, but Kathy insists that she doesn't want to spoil what she has. "David and I appreciate each other, but we don't take each other for granted. I don't feel bound to him. When I have to visit one of our mills in Virginia for a few days, I just take off. I don't feel guilty about leaving Dave alone. If we were married, we wouldn't be free any more. We'd expect more things from each other." They might. On the other hand, what Kathy doesn't realize is that even by "just living together" the two have created expectations and developed certain ground rules for their behavior.

As we saw in Chapter 6, if a relationship reaches the integrating stage, both people must intensify at least some aspects of their personality and minimize others. If a relationship goes on to the bonding stage, that commitment is in some sense formalized. In a romantic relationship, the commitment might be the announcement that the couple is "going steady," or it might be an engagement or a marriage.

Some people consistently avoid such a commitment. One reason may be that a previous commitment proved disappointing or constricting. And there are people who have never made a complete commitment to another human being. One psychologist describes the fear of commitment as characterized by "the Dance-Away Lover":

> The Dance-Away's repeated romantic disillusionments are the consequences of his discomfort with the intimacy and commitment love entails. The Dance-Away Lover is preoccupied with the fear of being trapped. He clings to his independence lest, in her eagerness to possess him, someone succeed in sucking him into a web of obligations and responsibilities. (Goldstine et al., 1977, p. 27)

Even after making a partial commitment, he or she will later maneuver to avoid intimacy by becoming unavailable—forgetting appointments, working late, withdrawing emotionally, or even withholding sexually.

In examining the difference between "love" and "commitment," Lund (1985) included such items on her Commitment Scale as "How likely is your relationship to be permanent?" "How likely is it that you and your partner will be together six months from now?" and "In your opinion, how likely is your partner to continue this relationship?" Commitment, she found, has to do with the *expectation* a relationship will continue; love has more to do with *desire*. Although a high correlation exists between the two, love and commitment are still independent.

We spoke in Chapter 6 of control as a primary dimension of all relationships. It has two poles: dominance/submission. These elements are variables in all two-person relationships, as you will see in the discussion that follows.

Dominance, Status, and Power

Your mother and father have been married for twenty-four years. Who is the dominant partner? Who has the power? The first question is usually easy to answer. The second may be more difficult. Let's examine the issue of dominance first.

Dominance

Like the need for affiliation, the **need for dominance** can be imagined as a continuum: At one end is the person who always wants control over others; at the other end, the person with an extremely submissive style of communication. The vast majority of us fit somewhere in-between.

We know some other things about people with a strong need for dominance. For example, they also tend to have a strong need for achievement. An association also seems to exist between dominance and self-concept. A person with an unfavorable self-concept tends to be submissive rather than dominant. In a dyad one person often defers to the other. This is true not only of friendships and romantic relationships but of work and classroom situations. For example, one of your authors assigned two-person projects to his students. One student, let's call him Gary, complained bitterly that Ron, his partner, made all the decisions and never let him participate in the planning. Yet each time the two were observed at work, Gary accepted all Ron's ideas and directives, making no attempt to express his own point of view. Gary's submissiveness is typical of the person with low self-esteem: unable or afraid to influence others yet resentful of always being the one who is dominated. Oddly enough, the hesitancy itself tends to intensify dominating behavior in others.

When we combine what we know about behaviors associated with the needs for affiliation and dominance (see Table 7.1), we see some of the communication patterns that are possible in a two-person relationship as well as in a larger group. Allowing for the uniqueness of each, we can still make some predictions about how the two people will interact if we know something about the strength of their individual needs for affiliation and dominance. Janet has a high need for dominance but a low need for affiliation, so we expect her to be analytic, to make many judgments, to be resistant, and so on; if Mark has a low need for dominance but a high need for affiliation, we expect him to acquiesce much of the time, to cooperate with Janet, and so on. But if, like Janet, Mark has a high need for dominance, there is likely to be conflict between them, or the two will have to work out some satisfactory agreements regulating their behavior—at least for a time. To put it in other terms, they themselves will have to develop rules for their relationship.

Dominance has been studied in research on relationship structure. Phillips and Wood (1983) define three relationship structures. **Complementary structures** are *based on differences between the partners;* one is dominant and the other submissive. **Symmetrical structures** are *based on similarities,* as when both partners are dominant or both are submissive. On the other hand, **parallel structures** are *based on some combination of complementary and symmetrical interactions:* suppose, for instance, that Brian is dominant and Tina submissive

TABLE 7.1

Some Behaviors Associated with Needs for Dominance and Affiliation

	High Dominance	**Low Dominance**
High Affiliation	Advises	Acquiesces
	Coordinates	Agrees
	Directs	Assists
	Initiates	Cooperates
	Leads	Obliges
Low Affiliation	Analyzes	Concedes
	Criticizes	Evades
	Disapproves	Relinquishes
	Judges	Retreats
	Resists	Withdraws

Source: Adapted from David W. Johnson, *Reaching Out: Interpersonal Effectiveness and Self-Actualization,* 2d ed. © 1981, p. 44. Reprinted by permission of Prentice-Hall, Inc., Englewood Cliffs, NJ.

with respect to finances, their roles reverse with respect to disciplining their two children, and both Brian and Tina are dominant when it comes to deciding on family vacations.

Of the three, the favored relationship structure is the parallel one (Harrington, 1984). This is the most flexible structure and probably most common because it enables us to adapt most easily to the demands of new situations. Although the complementary relationship with the male dominant is seen as "typical," the number of such relationships seems to be declining with the rise of the two-career marriage and the upswing in women's and minority-group rights. It's still the case, however, that the most rejected relationship is one in which the female is dominant. Some things haven't changed that much.

Status

Whether we like to acknowledge it or not, **status,** *the position of an individual in relation to another or others,* has at least some relationship to the issue of establishing control within a two-person relationship. Potter (1978) has written at length about a familiar strategy for achieving higher status in human relationships; he calls it "one-upmanship." No doubt the popularity of his tongue-in-cheek descriptions of how to gain the upper hand stems from their authenticity. In one guise or another, the one-upper is known to all. He or she is always busier than you are, goes to more expensive places, knows more important people, and—most telling of all—is a chronic name dropper.

Potter comes through with one-upmanship techniques for all of us: doctor

How would you rank the status of an athlete for an American child?

and patient, business person, artist, sport enthusiast, wine lover. And he has not forgotten the college student. If you want to be one up before exams have started or after they are over, you might give either of two impressions: that you spend all your time studying or that you never open a book.

Status has marked effects on the form of all communication, no matter how unstructured. If two people are unequal in status, there is a good chance that the one with higher status will control the topics of conversation as well as the length of the discussion. Higher status may even enable that person to avoid a discussion entirely. If a bank president and a teller are conversing, for example, and the teller asks a question that seems too personal, the bank president will probably respond in a way that makes the teller uncomfortable about pursuing the subject. On the other hand, subordinates sometimes "disclose personal problems to their supervisors, but the reverse does not usually happen. . . . Self-disclosures are most often employed between people of equal status" (Hargie et al., 1987, p. 192).

Perceptions of status are immediately reflected in greetings as well as in forms of address. "Hi" may be permissible for some encounters; "Hello" or "Good morning" may be more appropriate for others. The higher-status person is often addressed by title and last name ("Good morning, Dr. Jones"), and the lower-status person by first name or even a briefer version of that name ("Hi, Judy"). One sociologist observes that greetings may also affirm a subordinate's willingness to maintain lower status (Goffman, 1972). American military practice, for instance, requires that the subordinate salute first and hold the salute until it is returned by the person of higher rank. Observe people of different status greeting one another and see whether these behavior patterns are borne out by your own experience.

Status differences between members of a two-person relationship affect content as well as communicative style. In larger social systems those interested in achieving higher status tend to distort what they say to their superiors in order to create the most favorable impression possible. In other words, they create a filter through which only the more pleasant information passes. This phenomenon has been called the **MUM effect**—from *Mum about Undesirable Messages* (Rosen and Tesser, 1970).

No doubt the status filter operates at a number of levels within the federal government. We also expect this filtering process to exist in all sorts of institutions and businesses—hospitals, schools, legal firms, department stores. And some of us can personally attest to the presence of the MUM effect within our own families.

The MUM effect is also present in dyads, even when two people are similar in status. Each tries to communicate so that he or she either maintains an existing status level or achieves a higher one. And though each enters the relationship with a certain status, it may change as a result of interaction.

The MUM effect can be thought of as a form of interference. In a two-person relationship the temptation to distort messages and thus put oneself in a favorable light is especially great for the person in the lower-status position. On the other hand, the higher-status person may be aware of sometimes receiving distorted messages. Of course, there is less message distortion when people communicate within an atmosphere that encourages feedback.

Power

Identifying one person in a dyad as the more dominant doesn't always explain who wields the power. **Power** and dominance, as Wilmot (1979) reminds us, are not synonymous:

> One of the more exciting trends in the study of communication is viewing interpersonal power in relational terms. You do not *have* power—it is given to you by the others with whom you transact. (p. 105)

Wilmot is saying that power has to be granted by one person to the other. If I do not accept your authority, you cannot dominate me. In other words, power has much to do with how we perceive ourselves. For example, one of our students wrote of her conversation with a local librarian, who asked why she was checking out fifteen books on broadcasting:

> I told her that I was doing a term paper for one of my college classes. "You go to school?" she asked, "I don't know how you find the time with children and a husband."
>
> "It's not easy," I replied, "but I make it work. It is a dream come true for me. I hope to go on to law school," I said, glowing with satisfaction. "Boy-oh-boy, how lucky you are that your husband lets you," she replied. "It wouldn't matter," I told her. "I'd do it anyway." People tell me all the time that I am lucky to have a supportive husband. It is not luck. That is the only kind of husband I would have. (Locklair, 1992, p. 4)

Among married couples, especially when both spouses are working, one of the major subjects of power struggles is money—whose it is, how it will be spent. As one marital expert explains,

> Nothing has as much symbolic meaning as money. It's a measure of self-worth and identity. . . .
> It's a force of power and control, with the person who makes more money having greater power and control. Finally, money is a symbol of love—of what one partner can do for the other. (Cited in Associated Press, 1992, p. B4)

A recent *Esquire* survey of married couples asked respondents what issue they fight about most. Money headed the list, and the other responses were equally interesting:

Money	41 percent
Household chores	31 percent
Relatives	25 percent
Sex	18 percent
Friends	11 percent
Vacations	5 percent
Religion	5 percent
Kids	4 percent

Writing of the feelings and problems that characterize various life stages, one psychiatrist observes that married couples in their late twenties and thirties "tend to feel *too* dependent on each other. Each of us in this era of our life comes to recognize that, in some pervasive and inchoate way, we have given our loved one's opinion, glances or moods *too much power* to affect and determine us" (Gould, 1978, p. 199; italic in original). Gould goes on to give examples in which each spouse feels personal happiness is totally controlled by the other. In an intimate relationship, this is particularly true during a time of stress or great change. For example, a long, difficult stint in graduate school or a job change might very well increase the need for emotional support and thus the emotional dependence on the loved one.

We've been looking at several variables affecting the quality of interpersonal relationships. Power and dominance, which were among the last discussed, are directly related to assertiveness—and so are the kinds of role conflicts we took up earlier. This relationship should become clear as we turn to the final section of our chapter on assertiveness training.

ASSERTIVENESS TRAINING

One specialist in assertiveness training for women distinguishes between aggressive behavior, in which you stand up for your rights in a way that violates the rights of the other party, and assertive behavior, in which you stand up for your legitimate rights in a way that does not violate the rights of the other party. In these terms, **assertiveness** is "*a direct, honest, and appropriate expression of one's feelings, opinions, and beliefs*" (Jakubowski-Spector, 1973, p. 2; italics added).

Today **assertiveness-training** workshops and classes of every description are readily available. Some are daylong workshops; some are groups that meet for one hour each week for a ten- or twenty-session course. Although many programs are designed with women in mind, there are some classes for men, too.

Some Principles of Assertiveness

To someone unaccustomed to being assertive, learning to become so can feel strange and uncomfortable. There is a world of difference, however, between being assertive and offensive. Berko and associates (1985) identify these principles of assertiveness as important:

1. "You cannot change other people's behavior; you can only change your reaction to it" (p. 212)—you can't, for example, stop your uncle from asking very personal questions, but you can say you don't want to discuss the matter.

2. "People are not mind readers" (p. 214). If you don't ask for what you want—whether it be a promotion, a loan, or greater freedom and more privacy—others will not know.

3. "Remember that habit is no reason for doing anything" (p. 214). Just because your older brother is always the one who gets to use the car on weekends is no reason that this pattern should continue.

4. "You cannot make others happy" (p. 214). Others have responsibility for their own feelings; you can't "make" anyone feel anything.

5. "In any relationship you will incur some disapproval" (p. 214). So accept it.

6. "Don't be victimized" (p. 214).

7. "Worrying about something will not change it" (p. 215).

8. "Adopt the attitude that you will do the best you can—and if someone doesn't like it, that's their problem, not yours" (p. 215).

9. "Remember that assertion does not mean aggression" (p. 215).

10. "When you decide to be assertive, be aware of the consequences" (p. 216)—for example, don't tell the boss you'll quit if you don't get a raise, unless you are ready to quit if the answer is no.

Techniques of Assertiveness Training

Counselors use a wide range of techniques, some self-styled, some very closely following the techniques of behavior modification or behavior therapy. The aims are to extinguish unassertive behaviors and patterns of response and to develop and reinforce more assertive ones, often by teaching new communication skills that involve persuasion and confrontation. Assertiveness training is also concerned with correcting nonverbal behaviors that undercut what we think of as assertive statements. For example, a person who is being interviewed for a job might be speaking about her qualifications but avoiding eye contact with the interviewer or speaking in a voice that is almost inaudible.

Some counselors advise clients to tape-record conversations with people with whom they are likely to have assertiveness problems and then analyze their own responses. Often, clients are asked to participate in exercises with others that involve confrontation. Some confrontation exercises take place within the class or workshop. Others are to be enacted at home or in other settings outside the group meeting. It took Joanne, a graduate student in history, several weeks to work up to this declaration to her husband: "When you asked me to type your master's essay, you said you'd try to help with the house so I wouldn't fall behind in my classes. But you've seen me stay up late night after night and haven't offered to do any of the chores. Finals are coming up soon. Now that your paper is typed, I really need some help from you."

Among the most popular techniques for teaching assertiveness skills is **behavioral rehearsal,** *"a special kind of roleplaying experience in which the individual practices or rehearses those specific assertive responses which are to become part of her behavioral repertoire"* (Jakubowski-Spector, 1973, p. 12; italics added). Together counselor and participant choose some situation in which the latter has had difficulties in being assertive. For example, a young woman in her early twenties who felt that her mother was treating her like a child chose to role-play a recent argument. In that conversation the mother had reminded her daughter of a dentist appointment the following day, and then went on to also remind her to tell the dentist about a chipped tooth, and—adding insult to injury—mentioned that there was free parking in the back of the dentist's office. During the first role play the counselor plays the mother and the young woman plays herself. A discussion of her responses follows with some suggestions for more effective behaviors on her part. Participant and counselor then reverse roles with the counselor showing the participant other, more assertive ways to respond to the situation. For example, instead of the participant's, "Ma, I know that. Listen, I can take care of myself," the counselor's comment is:

> Ma, I think it's time that I told you how I feel. I know that you're just trying to be helpful but, to tell you the truth, when you tell me what to do—like you just did—I feel as though I'm two years old and I find myself resenting it. I would like you to stop treating me that way. (Jakubowski-Spector, 1973, p. 14)

In the next discussion the participant reacts to how she has seen the counselor handle the situation; she is encouraged to use the more appropriate assertive response and to select some modeled behaviors that she herself would like to repeat in the next round of role play. In the discussion that follows and in succeeding role plays her effective responses are encouraged and given positive reinforcement by the leader, who is careful to give positive feedback before any criticisms. Slowly, the new, more assertive behavior pattern is shaped and perfected.

Another assertiveness technique being taught involves learning **DESC Scripting** (Bower and Bower, 1980). **D** stands for "describe": You describe the troubling behavior as concretely as possible; **E** is for "express": you say what you think and feel about what you have just described; **S** is for "specify": you tell the other person what you want; and **C** is for "consequences": you make clear to the other person, as concretely as possible, exactly what positive or negative consequences there are for complying or not complying with your requests. Suppose, for example, that Ann and Bob have been seeing one another for almost a year and that whenever they're at a party, Bob finds ways to run her down in front of their friends. Using DESC Scripting, Ann would first describe how he jokes and makes remarks at her expense. She would then express how she feels when this happens (in her case, a combination of humiliation and anger). To specify what she wants, she'd explain that she wants Bob to treat her consistently, to be as thoughtful and accepting as he is when they're alone instead of using her at parties as a kind of foil or "straight man" for his public image. And finally, Ann would have to spell out the consequences of Bob's continuing that behavior. She might say, for example, that the next time it happened, she'd get up and leave the party; or that she'd end the relationship. But most important, she'd have to be ready to follow through on what she says. If she sits through another party at which she's the object of Bob's ridicule, DESC Scripting is simply a useless exercise.

Suppose, however, that one of these assertiveness techniques is learned and applied consistently. Can training of a relatively short duration extinguish habits—in this case, ways of communicating—that have been reinforced over long periods of time? And can these newer, more assertive patterns be maintained once you leave the class or the workshop or once you stop thinking about the four stages of DESC Scripting?

The effectiveness of such training seems to depend to a great degree on the relative strength of its rewards and how these stack up against the rewards for nonassertive communication. One very important reward for all nonassertive behavior is avoiding conflict, anxiety, and disapproval. It can be upsetting to stand up to your parents, to insist that you deserve a raise when you get a promotion, to repeat that you will not pay for damaged merchandise and that you must speak with the store manager. On the other hand, the increased self-esteem and the satisfaction of individual needs that are often the results of a more assertive communication style are powerful reinforcers. But different things are reinforcing for different people. It is likely that for some the avoidance of conflict will be such a strong reward that it will far outweigh the many gains to be made through more assertive behavior. As always, a reinforcer has to be defined in terms of the individual. Moreover, a reward must also be defined in terms of a given culture. A distinctly assertive communication style would not be acceptable in all countries or, for that matter, in all minority cultures.

SUMMARY

The dyad is in many ways a microcosm of all larger groups and thus encompasses many kinds of relationships from the most casual to the most intimate and long lasting. Our first major topic was the social setting within which two-person communication must be viewed. Members of a dyad are strongly influenced by the norms they have already adopted, and they also establish some normative agreements of their own as they interact. In addition, the roles they enact affect how they will respond to each other; we examined some consequences of conflicts within and between roles. The changing, sometimes troubled nature of the doctor-patient relationship was given special attention.

Because quality is so frequently an issue in assessing two-person relationships, we looked at several measures of high quality. We first discussed the importance of self-disclosure, its relationship to trust, and the reasons people choose to self-disclose or to avoid disclosures. Intimacy was seen as a process—one that has to be developed and maintained. Affiliative need and willingness to make commitments were also seen as important variables, as were dominance, status, and power. Cohabitation and marital stability were also discussed.

In examining assertiveness, we identified several principles that might reasonably guide behavior. Three techniques for teaching assertiveness skills were discussed including DESC Scripting.

REVIEW QUESTIONS

1. How are disruptive power and norms related to two-person communication?

2. Explain the distinction between expected and enacted roles.

3. Distinguish between intrarole and interrole conflict and give an example of each.

4. Explain why the doctor-patient relationship has changed, and discuss some recent findings on communication between doctor and patient.

5. What are four means by which we can assess the quality of an interpersonal relationship?

6. What are the four levels of awareness and disclosure exemplified by the Johari window?

7. State four reasons for self-disclosure and four for its avoidance.

8. Identify five characteristics of appropriate self-disclosure.

9. What are the five qualities that characterize intimacy in interpersonal communication?

10. Discuss the research findings on intimacy in later-life relationships of siblings.

11. Explain how affiliation and commitment affect interpersonal relationships.

12. How are need for affiliation and need for dominance related?

13. Explain how complementary, symmetrical, and parallel relationship structures differ.

14. What are two ways in which status affects two-person communication?

15. What is the difference between dominance and power in an interpersonal relationship?

16. Identify at least five principles of assertiveness.

17. How does DESC Scripting work? Explain two other techniques used to teach more assertive behavior.

EXERCISES

1. Select one of the role-playing situations listed in the appendix. Determine what norms appear to operate in the specific role-playing situation selected. How might these norms be adhered to and violated in terms of the expected and enacted roles of the interviewer and respondent?

2. Write a short paper in which you analyze some communication difficulties that might arise for a college student as a result of role conflicts.

3. In a small group—five people or so—have each person attempt to increase his or her awareness of self and others by telling each of the others one positive and one negative impression he or she has formed about that person. If there is time, have a free discussion in which group members go into greater depth, asking for and giving further impressions.

4. Create two or three different role-playing situations similar to those listed in the appendix. Select members of the class to role-play the situations in which the players have different dominance and affiliation needs. How do

differences in these needs affect the communication patterns in the interview?

5. After observing a conversation between two people, try to determine what specific messages (nonverbal as well as verbal) reveal the dominance or submissiveness of each communicator. Make the same observations with respect to affiliative or antisocial behaviors. Do the characteristic roles shift from time to time?

6. Role play the following exercises and try to use assertive (not aggressive) behaviors.
   SCENE 1
   Bank Customer: You have been a customer of this bank for over twenty years. You request an installment loan on a new car and are refused.
   Bank Employee: A long-time customer of the bank wants an installment loan to purchase a car. Current bank policy does not provide for installment loans on automobiles because the interest rates aren't profitable to the bank.
   SCENE 2
   Bank Employee: A customer wants to cash a $10,000 check against uncollected funds (a check from another state). The bank policy requires a ten-day waiting period.
   Bank Customer: You just came in from another state and you go to the bank to cash a $10,000 check drawn on an out-of-state bank. It is important that you have the cash on that day for the closing on the house you are purchasing. Because the check is drawn on an out-of-state bank, the teller refuses to give you the cash.

SUGGESTED READINGS

Duck, Steve. *Understanding Relationships.* New York: Guilford Press, 1991.

A synthesis of recent research and a readable, practical discussion of interpersonal relationships by an authority on the subject.

Howards End

Based on E.M. Forster's novel, this film is the story of two English families and how their lives become intertwined. A dramatic portrait of an extraordinary range of relationships—between siblings, spouses, lovers, and friends.

Klagsbrun, Francine. *Mixed Feelings: Love, Hate, Rivalry and Reconciliation Among Brothers and Sisters.* New York: Bantam, 1992.

A close look at the bonds and rivalries between siblings and their effects in later life. The author includes a great many examples drawn from her interviews.

Luft, Joseph. *Of Human Interaction.* Palo Alto, CA: National Press, 1969.

This book elaborates on the rationale behind the Johari window model as well as its application. It also explains more fully the value of self-disclosure. A classic treatment of the subject.

McAdams, Dan P. *Intimacy: The Need to Be Close.* New York: Doubleday, 1989.

The author develops his own theory about intimacy, illustrating it with many extended examples.

Mizer, Jean. "Cipher in the Snow." *Today's Education,* November 1964.

This is the story of a boy who was overlooked by everyone and one day dropped dead in the snow.

Wilmot, William. *Dyadic Communication.* 3rd ed. Reading, MA: Addison-Wesley, 1987.

The third edition of an outstanding and lucidly written text on two-person communication. The author makes use of theories and research from a number of disciplines.

CHAPTER EIGHT

*I*nterviewing

CHAPTER OBJECTIVES

After reading this chapter, you should be able to:

1 Distinguish between five types of interview questions and give an example of each.

2 Identify five types of improper questions the interviewer should avoid.

3 Describe the funnel sequence as it is used in the body of an interview.

4 Describe two main advantages of the nondirective interview technique.

5 Distinguish between five types of responses to interviewers' comments in a counseling interview.

6 Identify six characteristics of successful appraisal interviews.

7 Identify five suggestions for interviewers in a selection interview.

8 Identify five suggestions for interviewees in a selection interview.

*I*n the 1992 presidential election Ross Perot announced his candidacy while being interviewed on *Larry King Live*. Similarly, Bill Clinton and George Bush appeared on several television programs to be interviewed. In 1992, the televised interview rose to new heights as an important political weapon.

Interviews are popular not only in politics but in the entire entertainment industry. Witness the success of such talk shows as Donahue, Oprah, Geraldo, Sally-Jesse Raphael, Arsenio Hall, Jay Leno, and David Letterman.

If you associate interviews only with job hunting, your definition of the term is too narrow. The interview encompasses many of the elements of all two-person communication. When you consult a doctor, canvass door to door for a political candidate, or ask a stranger for detailed instructions on how to get to a particular place, you are in some sense involved in an interview, or a "conversation with a purpose," which we think is a good definition (Bingham and Moore, 1924, p. 3).

Another good definition is: "a process of dyadic, relational communication with a predetermined and serious purpose designed to interchange behavior and involving the asking and answering of questions" (Stewart and Cash, 1988, p. 3). However, even this definition is somewhat limited, since it limits interviews to those with a *serious* purpose. The interview has also become a popular form of entertainment on a variety of television news and public interest shows and documentaries.

Interviews serve a number of functions, as can be seen from Table 8.1. The interviewer may gather or convey information, influence people's attitudes, and at times influence their behavior. An appraisal interview, for example, often exercises a major influence on an employee's morale. The interview is also a valuable research tool. It allows the interviewer to gather more complete information than could be obtained in a questionnaire or a telephone conversation and to make full use of nonverbal as well as verbal cues. It also enables the interviewer to interpret or explain questions more easily, thus increasing the likelihood of getting answers from the respondent.

Regardless of the type of interview you are expecting, Freund (1992) offers some great practical advice when he writes:

The game plan I recommend . . . contains four steps . . .

+ What do I want?
+ Where do I start?
+ When do I move?
+ How do I close?

Stated affirmatively, these four steps will help you—on significant issues such as [money]—to:

TABLE 8.1

Ten Interview Objectives

Objective	Description	Example
Getting information	Interviewer gathers facts, opinions, or attitudes from respondent.	Census taker collects data.
Giving information	Interviewer presents facts, opinions, or attitudes to respondent, often as a form of instruction.	Doctor explains to patient how to maintain a balanced diet.
Persuading	Interviewer attempts to influence respondent's attitude and ultimately his or her behavior.	Student tries to convince an instructor to give a make-up exam.
Problem solving	Interviewer and respondent attempt to identify causes of a problem and together seek a possible solution.	Parent and teacher discuss child's reading difficulties.
Counseling	Respondent seeks advice from interviewer on a matter of personal concern. (closely related to problem-solving interview).	Client requests legal advice from an attorney.
Job seeking or hiring	Interviewer and respondent exchange information on which to base an employment decision.	Campus recruiter meets with senior students.
Receiving complaints	Interviewer tries to minimize the respondent's dissatisfaction.	Store manager speaks with customer about defective merchandise.
Reviewing performance	Interviewer offers feedback on respondent's performance and helps establish specific goals to be met by next appraisal interview.	Editor-in-chief of newspaper gives periodic evaluation of each of the editors.
Correcting or reprimanding	Interviewer and respondent, usually in the roles of superior and subordinate, meet to discuss respondent's need to improve performance (ordinarily most effective when handled informally and with a helpful rather than critical tone).	Maintenance supervisor of airline discusses with mechanic areas in which technical competence must be improved.
Measuring stress	Interviewer determines how respondent acts under pressure.	Personnel director of large corporation selects a top executive.
	Interviewer gathers information from a respondent who does not wish to divulge it.	Army officer questions a military prisoner.

- Assess your realistic expectations;

- determine an appropriate starting point;

- devise a constructive concession pattern;

- arrange the ultimate compromise. (p. 92)

STANDARDIZED AND UNSTANDARDIZED INTERVIEWS

Whatever his or her objectives, the interviewer may use one of two approaches: standardized or unstandardized. The **standardized interview** consists of *a set of prepared questions from which the interviewer is not allowed to deviate.* The interviewer poses the questions precisely as they are worded on the form. He or she does not even have the option of changing their order. The standardized interview has one distinct advantage: uniform responses over a large number of interviewers and respondents. An inexperienced interviewer may still be able to conduct a fairly successful interview. As a rule, more skill is required as the interview becomes less structured.

The **unstandardized interview** *allows the interviewer as well as the respondent considerable latitude.* The interviewer may deviate from any of the prepared questions. He or she may follow up a prepared question with one of his or her own to obtain a more complete or appropriate answer. He or she may drop a question that seems unsuitable or one that might put the respondent on the defensive. If he or she suddenly discovers an interesting subject that had not been anticipated, the interviewer has the freedom to pursue this line of questioning as far as is desired. In short, the unstandardized interview gives the interviewer considerable flexibility and potential for discovery.

As we have described them, the standardized and unstandardized interviews are extremes. In fact, some standardized interviews allow some departure from the prepared questions; some unstandardized interviews do not permit the interviewer unlimited freedom. No matter how the interview is structured, however, some feedback must flow between interviewer and respondent. In the discussion that follows, let us assume that the interviewer is conducting an unstandardized interview in which he or she can make maximum use of feedback from the respondent by departing where necessary from the list of questions.

Both parties in an interview can sometimes be pretty suspicious of each other. One author cites an extreme example of the statesman Talleyrand, "who upon learning that the Russian ambassador had committed suicide, is reported to have mused, 'I wonder what he is up to?' " (Ramundo, 1992, p. 11).

TYPES OF INTERVIEW QUESTIONS

Interviewing is essentially dialogue, dialogue in which one party, the interviewer, guides the direction of the conversation by means of a series of questions. A skillful interviewer knows a great deal about the art of questioning. He or she responds to the answers received by modifying subsequent responses—particularly the kinds of questions that are being asked. We can illustrate by first looking at several categories of questions.

Open versus Closed Questions

The **open question** resembles an essay question on a test; it *places no restrictions on the length of the respondent's answer*. It also allows the respondent more latitude in interpreting the subject to be discussed. Examples of open questions would be, "Would you please summarize your work experience?" and "What are your feelings about your marriage?" The interviewer may want to use open questions early in the interview to get the respondent to relax and reveal more personal information.

The advantages of the open question are: It may reveal what the interviewee thinks is important; it may reveal an interviewee's lack of information or understanding in an area; it may bring out an interviewee's feelings on an issue, possible prejudices, and stereotypes; and it provides the interviewer with a good example of the interviewee's communication skills. The disadvantages of an open question are that it takes a great deal of time and may limit the progress of the interview, and it reduces the number of topics that can be covered (Weaver, 1985).

The **closed question** is more specific and *usually requires a shorter, more direct answer*. Contrast the following with the two open questions just given: "How many years of work experience have you had in this field?" and "What aspect of your marriage seems to trouble you most?" Closed questions may restrict the respondent still further by requiring a simple yes-or-no answer. "Would you like to work for a small corporation?" or "Do you feel you have a happy marriage?"

As you can see from these examples (and those in Table 8.2), the open questions are often more appropriate at the early part of the interview; the closed questions can be used to focus the conversation more as you go. This approach to interviewing is known as the *funnel sequence* and is illustrated in Figure 8.1.

The closed question has the following advantages: More questions can be asked in more areas and in less time than with open questions; the interviewer can guide and regulate the interview with a great deal of control; and closed questions are often easier and less threatening for the interviewee and so tend to put the interviewee at ease. The disadvantages of a closed question include: It provides little or no information "surrounding" the issue raised in the

TABLE 8.2

Open versus Closed Question

Interviewer	Open Question	Closed Question
Prospective employer	What do you think about money?	What starting salary were you thinking of?
Boss	What do you think about our new policy?	Do you like our new plan?
Teacher	How is your term paper coming?	Do you need help?
Doctor	How have you been feeling?	Is your back hurting again?
High school counselor	Have you thought about going to college?	Can you afford $10,000 a year tuition?

question, and it may close off areas that would be potentially valuable for the interviewer in his or her effort to arrive at a decision concerning the interviewee.

Primary versus Probing Questions

Primary questions *introduce a new topic in the interview.* All the examples of open and closed questions that were presented earlier are examples of primary questions. A very different type of question is called a **probe** or **secondary question.** This is *a follow-up to a primary question and is intended to elicit elaboration* from the interviewee. Such remarks as, "I see. Can you tell me more?" or "Why don't you go on?" tend to bring about further comment on a previous statement. Short pauses may elicit the same reaction, allowing the respondent to express thoughts more completely. Other examples of probes or follow-up questions are:

Go on.	How do you mean?
Tell me more.	Could you elaborate?
Yes?	Would you fill me in some more on that?
Uh huh?	Do you have any other reasons?
Why?	Because of what?
Why not?	Silence

The probing question has the advantage that it can significantly increase the amount of information gained from the interviewees. It allows them to elaborate as much as they are willing to. The biggest disadvantage is that it can put the other person on the defensive. For example, "Why not?" may imply criticism. In addition, the other person may begin to resent being probed

FIGURE 8.1   Funnel Sequence

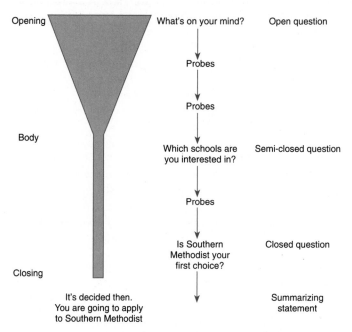

(*Source:* Adapted from Moffatt, *Selection Interviewing for Managers,* New York, Harper & Row, 1979, p. 83.)

further than anticipated. This could result in an actual loss of information if the person decides to terminate or distort responses.

Leading versus Neutral Questions

Neutral questions are those which *do not explicitly or implicitly suggest the desired answer*. **Leading questions** *are the opposite*. Obviously, the interviewer can obtain more accurate information by employing the neutral questions.

Stewart and Cash (1988) offer the following examples:

The varying degrees of direction and the distinction between neutral and leading questions are illustrated in the following questions.

Leading Questions	*Neutral Questions*
1. You like close detail work, don't you?	1. Do you like close detail work?
2. You're going with us, aren't you?	2. Are you going with us?

Leading Questions	*Neutral Questions*
3. Do you oppose the union like most workers I've talked to?	3. What are your attitudes toward the union?
4. Wouldn't you rather have a Buick?	4. How does this Buick compare to other cars in this price range?
5. How do you feel about these asinine government rules?	5. How do you feel about these government rules?
6. When was the last time you got drunk?	6. Tell me about your drinking habits.
7. Have you stopped cheating on your exams?	7. Did you cheat on your last exam?
8. Would you classify yourself as a conservative or a radical?	8. Would you classify yourself as a reactionary, conservative, moderate, liberal, radical, or other?
9. Don't you think tax reform is unfair to farmers?	9. How do you feel about tax reform? (pp. 67–68)

The Loaded Question

A more volatile and often annoying type of leading question is the **loaded question,** which *stacks the deck by implying the desired answer*. This form of

It is possible to analyze the interview techniques you see every day, such as people being interviewed on local or national news programs.

the closed question is sometimes used to back the respondent into a corner. In effect, the interviewer poses and answers his or her own questions: to a left-wing militant, "Isn't it true that violence can only make matters worse?"; to the secretary of defense at a press conference, "Hasn't your new policy been tried in the past with no success?" Such questions are emotionally charged, and they immediately put the respondent on his or her guard. Undeniably, loaded questions are sometimes used to advantage, especially in the news media. Thus a report can ask a politician questions that are on the lips of many voters, forcing him or her to meet the issues head on. Nonetheless, if we are interested in getting information, the loaded question is a doubtful technique. A better way, for example, to question the secretary of defense might be, "Would you explain the advantages and disadvantages of your new policy?"

The loaded question has no advantages unless the goal is to see if the interviewee can handle a threatening, hostile situation. The disadvantages are rather easy to surmise: The interviewee loses whatever trust may have existed, may become "unraveled," and may feel negatively toward the interviewer and the organization she or he represents.

SUSPECT QUESTIONS AND HOW TO HANDLE THEM

Title VII of the Civil Rights Act of 1964 prohibits employment discrimination on the basis of race, color, sex, marital status, religion, or national origin. The first Civil Rights Act prohibiting discrimination was passed in 1866 (all persons were given the same rights as "white citizens"), and the latest was in 1974, the Vietnam Era Veterans Readjustment Act, which promoted the employment of Vietnam era veterans. In addition, the 1964 Civil Rights Act was amended in 1978 to specifically cover pregnant women, and the Age Discrimination Act of 1967 was amended in 1978 to protect workers age forty to seventy from employment discrimination.

In general, questions that are lawful relate specifically to the job, attitudes about work, health if relevant to the particular work, past employment, educational background, and capabilities. Just about everything else, whether seemingly irrelevant (e.g., hobbies) or not, could be considered discriminatory.

Specifically, the Equal Employment Opportunity Commission (EEOC) has set up the following subjects as the source of discriminatory questions: change of name, maiden or former name, previous foreign address, birthplace of self or family, religion, complexion or skin color, citizenship or national origin, foreign military service, name and address of *relative* to be notified (*person* is okay), arrest or conviction record, or height (unless related to the job).

Single people, for example, cannot be asked if they live with their parents, get along with them, or plan marriage. Engaged people cannot be asked if they plan to marry, what the occupation of the future spouse is, or plans for work after marriage. Married people cannot be asked if they own a home, have debts, the spouse's occupation, possibility of relocating, (for women) what the husband thinks of your working, what the extra money will be used for, plans for a family, or ages of children. Plans are not in themselves unlawful, but they cannot be used for unlawful screening purposes.

When an individual is asked an illegal discriminatory or suspect question, there are several alternatives one can follow:

1. Of course, if the interviewee thinks the question harmless and does not care about the fact that it could be used as an unlawful screening device, she or he may simply go ahead and answer it.

2. The interviewee can inform the interviewer that the question is a personal one and she or he would be happy to answer any questions related to qualifications necessary for the job.

3. The interviewee can ask what the thrust of the question is in relation to the job, what the interviewer wants to know.

4. The interviewee can indicate that the question is not relevant, and go on to answer it (e.g., "That question has no bearing on my qualifications for the position, but I'll answer it anyway").

5. The interviewee can refuse to answer the question on the grounds that it is not related to qualifications for the job.

6. The interviewee can ignore the question and respond with an indication that she or he is willing to answer relevant questions.

7. Of course, the interviewee can stop the interviewer by expressing the belief that the question is discriminatory and (if desired) that she or he will file a complaint with the EEOC!

There are several problems in responding to suspect questions, most of which center around the belief that *no* responses or a hostile response to the question will decrease the odds of obtaining the job, and obtaining the job may be more important than the problem created by the suspect question. However, if the interviewer asks questions other than those related to qualifications for the job, and the ultimate effect is an underrepresentation of minorities and other protected groups in that employer's work force, then the company could be vulnerable to a Title VII lawsuit. Remember that the interviewer may not realize that he or she is asking improper questions, either through a lack of familiarity with the guidelines or because he or she spontaneously asks questions without thinking about their discriminatory impact (Wilson and Goodall, 1991).

TYPES OF INADEQUATE RESPONSES

Regardless of the kinds of questions chosen, the interviewer is never completely sure of obtaining the number and quality of answers he or she would like to have. Interviewing is a dynamic process, not a programmed event. It cannot move forward without the participation of the respondent. Thus another aspect of interviewing skill involves handling **inadequate responses.** Let us look at five that the interviewer can anticipate and try to avoid.

No Answer

First, suppose that the respondent gives no answer—that is, either refuses to answer (the familiar "No comment" or "I'd rather not say") or says nothing at all. A sufficient number of such responses will bring the interview to a dead end. The interviewer might follow up such a response with a second, related question. If necessary, the line of inquiry might be dropped altogether.

Partial Answer

Imagine instead that the respondent gives a partial answer. The interviewer might then restate the part of the question that has not been answered. If the respondent gives a good many partial answers, the interviewer should review the questions asked. Perhaps some could be subdivided and posed individually. In general, it is best to avoid asking more than one question at a time.

Irrelevant Answer

Reacting appropriately to an irrelevant answer is more complex because there are two reasons the respondent may have gone off on a tangent: He or she may not have understood the question completely or may be making a conscious effort to avoid answering it. Politicians, it seems, frequently evade questions by offering irrelevant answers.

Inaccurate Answer

Often a respondent who does not wish to disclose information will offer an inaccurate answer, especially if revealing the truth would be embarrassing. Unfortunately, an inaccurate answer is often difficult for the interviewer to detect, especially in an initial interview. Of course, the accuracy of the information the interviewer receives is determined in part by the respondent's motivation. A person who feels threatened by an interview is more inclined to provide data within what he or she perceives to be the interviewer's expectations. And as we saw in discussing the MUM effect, people sometimes respond inaccurately in an attempt to maintain their status level or achieve a higher one. It has been found, for example, that people (particularly those with high incomes) overestimate the number of plane trips they have made but play down any automobile loans they have taken out (Lansing and Blood, 1964).

Whether they are intentional or not, inaccurate responses are damaging not only to the interviewer but to the respondent. If he or she will be seeing the interviewer again—as is probable after an appraisal, or counseling interview—it is likely that some of these distortions will be revealed at a later date. If the interviewer finds that over a series of meetings the respondent has been giving inaccurate answers, he or she should consider possible reasons for this behavior. The interviewer has much to gain from establishing great rapport with the respondent, putting the individual at ease so that he or she feels it will not be personally damaging to tell the truth.

Ororverbalized Answer

The respondent who gives an ororverbalized answer tells the interviewer much more than he or she wants to know. Sometimes lengthy answers contain a great deal of irrelevant information. A high percentage of ororverbalized responses will severely limit the number of topics that an interviewer can cover in the time allotted. He or she should try as tactfully as possible to guide the respondent back to the heart of the question, and to do this the interviewer may wish to increase the number of closed questions.

Response Sets

As if these difficulties were not enough to contend with, it now seems that there are people who have a response set to agree (yea-sayers) or to disagree (nay-sayers). Couch and Keniston (1960), two psychologists who have analyzed response tendencies as a personality variable, describe yea-sayers as impulsive people who respond easily to stimuli. Nay-sayers, on the other hand, inhibit and suppress their impulses and tend to reject emotional stimuli. The language in which statements are cast also affects response bias. Yea-sayers are particularly attracted to statements that are enthusiastic and colloquial in tone. On the rare occasions when nay-sayers do agree, they are inclined to go along with statements that seem guarded, qualified, or cautious. Further research findings will be needed, however, before the interviewer can attempt to offset bias by the way he or she constructs questions.

INTERVIEW STRUCTURE

In addition to developing skill in the art of questioning, the interviewer is sometimes responsible for giving the meeting structure. Much of what we have said thus far can be applied to relatively unstructured communication as well as to interviews. But in most cases an interview should have an apparent structure—an opening, a body, and a closing—and the interviewer will have specific responsibilities during each part.

Opening of the Interview

In beginning an interview, an interviewer has three basic responsibilities. The first is to introduce the objectives of the interview to the respondent. Although these usually seem obvious to the interviewer, a brief statement of purpose is reassuring to the other party: An employee who is called in for a routine appraisal, for example, may perceive it as a reprimand interview unless the purpose is made clear. A second task for the interviewer is to establish rapport with the respondent, to get him or her to feel that the interviewer can be trusted and that the meeting does not present a threatening situation. The interviewer's third and most important responsibility is motivating the respondent to answer questions. Sometimes the respondent's interest seems ensured. For example, a person applying for a job will probably do his or her utmost to answer questions. But what if you are conducting some research interviews? Typically, respondents consider door-to-door canvassing a nuisance, and they may be reluctant to talk. An interviewer should never assume that a potential respondent is just waiting to be interviewed. Instead he or she should act as though the person is busy and try to show briefly why it is important that the person give a few moments of his or her time.

Wilson and Goodall (1991) identify three related goals of the opening part of the interview:

1. To make the interviewee feel welcomed and relaxed

2. To provide the interviewee with a sense of purpose

3. To preview some of the major topics to be covered (p. 53)

Body of the Interview

The body of the interview constitutes the major portion of time spent with the respondent, and it should be carefully planned for best results. If at all possible, it should be free from interruptions, phone calls, and other distractions so that both parties remain as relaxed as possible. We have seen that a number of different types of questions can be used in an interview. Each has advantages and disadvantages; the student of interviewing should at least be familiar with them. In addition, the sequence of questions used is important.

The first step in interview planning is to determine the topics to be covered. What, for example, is the typical content of the employment interview? One analysis of twenty employment interviews lists the topics shown in Table 8.3 as the most frequently discussed.

After selecting the topics, the interviewer then determines the actual sequence of questions. At this point the **funnel sequence** is often useful: *The interviewer begins with broad questions and gradually makes them more*

TABLE 8.3

Themes of Twenty Employment Interviews

Theme	Percentage*
Information about the company	100
General organizational orientation	90
Specific job area	60
Promotion policies	
Information about the candidate	80
Job expectations	75
Academic background	75
Prepared for the interviews	70
Scholastic record	70
Military status	60
Work experience	60
Geographical preference	50
Interviewing for other jobs	
Information about the interviewer	25
Job	25
Background	10
Where he or she lives	

*Refers to the percentage of observed interviews in which this theme occurred.
Source: Adapted from Cal Downs, "A Content Analysis of Twenty Interviews," *Personnel Administration and Public Review* (September 1971):25.

specific (Kahn and Cannell, 1968). Here is a funnel sequence that was used in a discussion of population control:

1. What are your views about increasing population growth in the United States?

2. What are your feelings about controlling our population growth?

3. Do you think legalized abortion should be used to help control population in the United States?

4. Should there be restrictions on abortions?

5. What restrictions should there be?

Because each question in the sequence is more specific than the preceding one, the interviewer can reconstruct a more complete picture of the respondent's attitudes and at the same time evaluate specific answers in relation to the general issue. The funnel sequence may be used for any number of individual topics within the body of the interview.

The funnel sequence is just one of several ways of organizing the exchange. In their discussion of the research interview, Kahn and Cannell (1968) offer some advice about selecting the sequence of topics that might well apply to almost any type of interview:

> The sequence of topics themselves should be planned to make the total interview experience as meaningful as possible, to give it a beginning, a middle, and an end. More specifically, the early questions should serve to engage the respondent's interest without threatening or taxing him before he is really committed to the transaction, and to exemplify and teach him the kind of task the interview represents. The most demanding of questions might well be placed later in the interview, when respondent commitment can be presumed to have peaked—and fatigue has not yet set in. Sometimes the riskiest of questions may be put very late in the interview, so that if they trigger a refusal to continue, relatively little information is lost. This procedure seems prudent, but it risks also the possibility of an unpleasant leavetaking. (p. 578)

Conclusion

The possibility of an unpleasant or at least an unsatisfying conclusion points to the importance of skillfully terminating the interview. All too often interviews end abruptly because of a lack of time, and both parties are left feeling the need for closure, or resolution.

Almost any interview profits from a summary of the ground covered. It can range from a brief statement to a review of all the major points discussed. Then, if some action is to be taken as a result of the interview (hiring a person, for example), the nature of the next contact should be agreed on. If each person thinks the other will initiate the contact, both may wait too long before following up. More than one job has been lost this way. Finally, a written summary may be sent to the respondent. In appraisal interviews this procedure is especially helpful: Both parties then have a written record of the agreed-upon objectives for the employee's future job responsibilities. The summary will also serve as a record of the employee's progress.

NONDIRECTIVE INTERVIEW TECHNIQUE

We have seen various ways in which the interviewer can conduct an interview or reinforce the interview structure. The **nondirective interview technique,** however, demands skill of a different order. In this approach, which is often used in counseling or problem solving, the interviewer tries to *restate the essence of the respondent's answers without making value judgments about them or offering advice.* The aim is to encourage interviewees to elaborate on previous statements in greater depth and thus gain insight into the situation so that they can help solve their own problem. It reflects the joke "How many psychiatrists does it take to change a light bulb? Only one, but the light bulb has to *really want* to be changed."

In the nondirective interview, you convey to the person that you are listening and empathizing with the situation. Banville (1978) illustrates the technique with an example of a problem statement that you might hear from a typical college friend and some samples of common responses:

A. "I can't figure out what's wrong, but lately I've had a tough time getting up during the week. On Saturday and Sunday when I could sleep later, I'm up at the crack of dawn!"

   1. "If I were you, I'd try getting to bed a little earlier during the week and stay up later on Friday and Saturday nights." (Advice-giving.)

   2. "The reason you do that is because you're not happy with your job." (Interpretation.)

   3. "Didn't you realize when you enrolled in those classes that they would be too heavy a load for you? Why did you take eighteen units in the first place?" (Cross-examination.)

   4. "Oh, yeah, I know, I think that's a pretty common thing. It's nothing to be concerned about." (Reassurance.)

5. "It sounds like your everyday responsibilities are getting you down." (Paraphrasing.) (pp. 172–173)

How would you respond to a friend who came to you with this problem? Banville offers five types of responses. The last response—paraphrasing—is the one to use in nondirective interviews.

Advice Giving, Interpretation, Cross-Examination, Reassurance, and Paraphrasing

Advice giving is highly judgmental and implies the person can't find a solution to the problem. If, for example, you respond by saying, "If you had picked decent classes, you wouldn't have such a hard time getting up during the week," you are making a judgment, which often brings out defensiveness in the speaker.

Suppose, instead, you gave your **interpretation:** "You're just feeling that way because you are worried about final exams." Here you are trying to get to the cause of the problem—but you often run the risk of being seriously in error.

Cross-examination is sometimes used in an attempt to learn more about the situation. Often the well-intentioned interviewer tries to proceed in logical fashion, eliciting yes-or-no answers, with such questions as, "Did the problem start this semester?" "Would you say you have been happy this term?" "So, you hate your eight o'clock class, huh?" These questions hardly convey a sense of helpfulness to the person.

When you offer **reassurance,** you try to "smooth things over" by telling the person something like, "Oh, I think everybody has that happen to them," or "I think things always work out for the best." Such responses can sometimes help, but often the person feels as if he or she still has a problem. No real insight is gained and no solution is found.

Paraphrasing is the preferred method for responding to a person who is expressing his or her feelings about a problem situation. When you paraphrase, your intent is to keep the focus of attention on *that person's* feelings, ideas, and insights rather than your own. Paraphrasing is also called reflecting, and statements rather than questions are often used. For example, you might say, "It sounds like this is bothering you." It shows you are reacting to the person's feelings as well as hearing the content of his or her message. This technique also acts like a probe in that it encourages the person to elaborate and gain further understanding about the situation. Finally, it shows that you are accepting rather than judging the person's feelings, and this leads to further self-disclosure and trust (Cahn and Tubbs, 1983).

Interviewer Empathy

Interviewer empathy is an important ingredient in the nondirective interview technique. McComb and Jablin (1984) studied employment interviews to determine the perceived empathy of interviewers. From their review of literature, the authors conclude that verbal behaviors associated with empathy include appropriate silence, probing questions, verbal encouragers, restatements, and questions calling for clarification. They found that interviewers who interrupted interviewees were perceived by the interviewee as nonempathic, unless it was an interrupting *question*. Also, the longer it took for an interviewer to respond, the greater the probability he or she would be perceived as nonempathic. Probing questions and questions calling for clarification were associated with perceptions of interviewer empathy. Interestingly, however, whether or not the interviewer was perceived as empathic or actually engaged in empathic behaviors, there were no differences with respect to the interviewee being called back for a second interview. The empathic behaviors may have made the interview experience more enjoyable and created more positive feelings (certainly important) but had no consequences for the important outcome of being called back for another interview.

HELPFUL HINTS

Several authors have compiled some helpful hints for achieving greater success in interviewing. Murnighan (1992) offers an excellent tip based on practical experience. He writes,

> One of my mentors gave me some terrific advice: He told me that the most important thing in an interview was to make sure they liked me. Certainly I needed to show that I knew what I was talking about. But the most important thing was personal—I should try to make sure that they liked me. I don't think he was saying that I should hide my true personality so that I could get this job—at least I hope not. Instead, he was telling me to be pleasant, smile a little here and there—in general, to be someone that they would like to have as a colleague. (p. 27)

Sussman and Krivonos (1979) offer the following suggestions:

> Regardless of the specific purpose of the interview (employment, appraisal, reprimanding, or firing) there are general guidelines we can offer which should improve your performance, the performance of the interviewee, and the general climate of the interviewing session.

1. Plan the interview carefully.

2. Establish a climate of comfort and rapport with the person you are interviewing.

3. Conduct the interview in a comfortable environment.

4. Keep distractions in the situation at a minimum.

5. Be prepared to listen.

6. Try to be as objective as possible.

7. Keep the purpose of your interview in mind.

8. Frame your questions so that you get adequate responses from the person you are interviewing.

9. Decide whether open or closed questions will give you the information you want.

10. Avoid directed (leading or loaded) questions, unless they serve your specific purpose.

11. Choose language that the interviewee understands, but do not "talk down" to him or her. Be clear but not condescending.

12. Provide some kind of a summary of what was decided, discussed, and/or considered in the interview.

13. Provide the interviewee with a statement of what future action is expected from him or her based on the interview and what is expected from you based on the interview. (p. 130)

Latham and Wexley (1981) summarize the findings on what characteristics are likely to make a *performance appraisal* interview successful:

1. High levels of subordinate participation in the performance appraisal result in employees' being satisfied with both the appraisal process and the supervisor who conducted it. The importance of this statement is that subordinate participation in the appraisal interview appears to increase acceptance of the supervisor's observations.

2. Employee acceptance of the appraisal and satisfaction with the supervisor increases to the extent that the supervisor is supportive of the employee.

3. The setting of specific goals to be achieved by the subordinate results in up to twice as much improvement in performance than does a discussion of general goals.

4. Discussing problems that may be hampering the subordinate's current job performance and working toward solutions has an immediate effect on productivity.

5. The number of criticisms in an appraisal interview correlates positively with the number of defensive reactions shown by the employee. Those areas of job performance that are most criticized are least likely to show an improvement. There appears to be a chain reaction between criticisms made by the supervisor and defensive reactions shown by the subordinate with little or no change in the subordinate's behavior.

6. The more subordinates are allowed to voice opinions during the appraisal, the more satisfied they will feel with the appraisal. (pp. 150–151)

SUMMARY

The interview is defined as "conversation with a purpose." It is more structured than dyad communication and may involve more than two people. Interview objectives, various types of questions and responses, and ways of structuring the interview were discussed. The nondirective interview technique was explained, and the chapter concluded with some practical hints for successful interviewing.

REVIEW QUESTIONS

1. What are five different types of interview questions? Give an example of each.

2. What are five types of questions the interviewer should not ask of job applicants?

3. What is the funnel sequence?

4. Name three steps that might be used in terminating an interview.

5. Describe two main advantages of the nondirective interview technique.

6. What are five types of responses in a counseling interview? Give an example of each.

7. Identify six specific hints for success in an appraisal interview.

8. Identify five specific hints for success in a selection interview.

9. Identify five specific hints for interviewers for success in a selection interview.

EXERCISES

1. Select one of the role-playing situations listed in the appendix. Determine what norms appear to operate in the specific role-playing situation se-

lected. How might these norms be adhered to and violated in terms of the expected and enacted roles of the interviewer and respondent?

2. Videotape an interview conducted by your classmates. Play back the interview and have the class evaluate it in terms of the suggested procedures for conducting the beginning, body, and end of an interview.

3. Role play the part of respondent to a classmate, providing inadequate responses to develop his or her ability to probe for better answers. Then switch roles and take the test yourself.

4. Role play the following examples, attempting to use the nondirective interview technique.

SITUATION 1

Manager: Paul, one of the supervisors in the computer services department has asked to see you about what he says is really "a problem." You are not really sure what the problem is, but you have heard that he is having personnel problems in his department. In thinking through the approach you might take with Paul, what things should you consider?

Employee: You are one of the supervisors in the computer services department. You have arranged to meet with your manager about a personnel problem concerning one of your employees. The problem is that this employee is competent in the job that he performs and you really depend on him to get things done. However, he makes life miserable for everyone. He has a very negative approach towards the other employees and communicates a very "superior" attitude. Just the other day you asked him to consult with one of the other employees before making a program revision. He did this, but the other employee was so upset with his approach that she came to you about the problem. This is really a dilemma for you because on one hand this employee does the job well, but on the other hand he causes real conflict in the department.

You really want the manager to solve the problem for you. So, you continually ask him, "What would you do?" "I need some advice." If the manager begins to use an approach that gets you to "solve your own problem," then begin to think what *you* can do.

SITUATION 2

Supervisor: It has come time for you to appraise Bill, one of your employees. Bill is the product of a misused appraisal system. Because of inflated past appraisals, he's received a couple of promotions he probably didn't deserve, judging by his present performance. He does an average job, but at his level and pay you expect a lot more from him. Bill joined your group about a year ago on a lateral transfer when another group was reducing head count. Initially you had high hopes for him based on those performance appraisals, but he hasn't lived up to your expectations. He usually gets his work done, but sometimes misses deadlines. He never seems to be around when you need him in a hurry, and you're not sure you can count on him when the chips are down. As a result you usually end up giving the tight-deadline jobs to Ron or June.

Bill's problem is that he loves to talk, especially if there's a good rumor to be spread. He seems to know the "right" people and delights in talking about "inside information" and "political power plays." This may have been a factor in his past promotions. This not only takes him away from his job and chews up his time, but it wastes your time and other people's. You've talked to him several times about this, but somehow the message never seems to get through. In your annual appraisal of Bill you rate him as just meeting standard. Since he has been rated so high in the past, you know that he will be upset. In getting ready for your appraisal discussion, what approach would be best?

Employee: You are Bill and your supervisor has just arranged a time for you to discuss your performance appraisal. You have always received good appraisals and you really don't expect that much different this time. When your supervisor tells you that he has rated you as "just meeting standard," you get very upset. You indicate that you have always received good appraisals in the past. In fact, the last five years you have received two promotions.

You are a "talker" and you try to dominate the interview with your reactions. Hold on to your negative attitude until the supervisor does some things to make you "cool down." When he does this, begin to respond objectively.

SUGGESTED READINGS

Bell, Arthur H. *The Complete Manager's Guide to Interviewing.* Homewood, IL: Dow Jones-Irwin, 1989.

This interviewing guide contains the latest legal restrictions and guidelines for interview questions, verbal and nonverbal techniques for interviewing, active listening, and the best environment. Effective interviewing is structured into eight easy-to-follow stages. The entire interview process is provided to enable the interviewer to make the best selection possible.

Bolles, Charles. *What Color Is Your Parachute?* City: Ten Speed Press, published annually.

This book is an invaluable source for seeking a job.

Stewart, Charles J., and **William B. Cash.** *Interviewing: Principles and Practices.* 6th ed. Dubuque, IA: William C. Brown, 1991.

This has excellent and comprehensive coverage of interviewing. In addition to covering the basics, it has entire chapters on special types of interviews. It includes surveying, information gathering, employment performance appraisal and disciplining, counseling, and the persuasive interview.

Wilson, Gerald L., and H. Lloyd Goodall, Jr. *Interviewing in Context.* New York: McGraw-Hill, 1991.

This paperback is quite thorough and offers many practical tips. It has a unique section entitled, "Troubleshooting the Interview," which lists dozens of questions the reader may have about interviewing and the pages in the book that answer each question.

CHAPTER NINE

Small-Group Communication

CHAPTER OBJECTIVES

After reading this chapter, you should be able to:

1 Describe two theories that have been used to explain compliance with social pressure.

2 Describe the problem of "groupthink."

3 Describe the four phases of a typical group's development.

4 Describe the relationship between group size, member satisfaction, and group performance.

5 Distinguish between task and consideration functions in leadership.

6 Identify six common difficulties that small groups encounter in developing ideas and solving problems.

7 Discuss the four levels of conflict.

8 Explain the importance of differentiating between an idea opponent and a personal opponent.

9 Describe four ways in which a group can arrive at a decision.

Although group communication skills have been valued for many years, recently there has been a dramatic increase in the emphasis placed on this type of expertise. One professional association reported in 1992 that Harvard, Syracuse, UCLA, the University of Illinois, the University of Michigan, BYU, SMU, and the University of Tennessee are just a few of the many universities that have increased their requirements for students to take group communication courses to improve their teamwork and communication skills (AACSB, 1992). One of the reasons is that more and more careers require teamwork and group committee work. One author stated:

> It's been estimated that across the country 11 million meetings are held daily. Since most meetings are more than mere two-person tete-a-tetes, that means that on any given day at least 33 million Americans, and probably many, many more, are attending a meeting.
>
> According to a survey done by the Cincinnati-based Burke Marketing Research company, the average executive spends 16 1/2 hours a week at meetings. The executives surveyed consider one-third of the gatherings they attend to be unnecessary. (Ludmer-Gliebe, 1989, p. F1)

Many contemporary organizations believe that participation is the best way to improve productivity and satisfaction. They want employees involved in problem solving and decision making. They realize that employees can contribute information and new ideas and in turn become more committed to their implementation. Tjosvold (1988) argues that

> this participatory approach to management leadership is based implicitly on the assumption that conflict can be useful, and that conflicts may be discussed productively. If employees do not feel free to discuss their opposing ideas, then they may conclude that participation is a meaningless shell that does not deserve their commitment. (p. 62)

Actually, most of us spend at least some of our time as members of problem-solving groups. A student council, a parent-teacher committee on sex education in the public schools, a commission investigating the causes of prison riots, a fund-raising committee for a political party, and a tenants' association organized to fight rent increases have much in common. Despite the diverse issues that concern them, each group consists of several human beings with different ideas, skills, and levels of interest. Each group has a problem to solve and must determine the best way to go about solving it— ideally by making use of the resources of all its members.

This chapter is about the kind of communication that takes place in small groups, particularly in **problem-solving,** or *task-oriented,* groups. We shall focus first on the ways in which such groups typically function and second on the ways individual members can improve their effectiveness in them. In doing so, we begin to extend the communication model outlined in Chapter 1 and developed in Chapters 7 and 8. The dyad is sometimes referred to as a "two-person group," and often two people will engage in problem solving. But in discussing the small group, particularly the problem-solving group, we shall follow the definition offered in Chapter 1: namely, that a small group is a collection of individuals who influence one another, derive some satisfaction from maintaining membership in the group, interact for some purpose, assume specialized roles, are dependent on one another, and communicate face to face (Tubbs, 1992). A small group will meet some but not necessarily all six criteria.

TYPES OF SMALL GROUPS

Small-group experience is by no means confined to problem solving. Each of us is simultaneously a member of many small groups. The first and most informal are **primary groups,** *the basic social units to which we belong.* Our first primary group is our family. Our childhood friends constitute another.

A social identity forms once a person realizes he or she belongs to a group. Social identity is

> that part of an individual's self-concept which derives from his [or her] knowledge of his [or her] membership in a social group (or groups) together with the value and emotional significance attached to that membership.

Some groups have strong norms that control behavior.

> One of the major cognitive tools individuals use to define themselves vis-a-vis the world in which they live is social categorization, "the ordering of social environment in terms of groupings of persons in a manner which makes sense to the individual." (Gudykunst and Hammer, 1988, p. 571)

In the company of adult friends, neighbors, and others with whom we socialize—fraternity or sorority groups, classmates, teammates, even street gangs—we continue and *extend our primary-group relationships* to **casual** or **social groups.** While these relationships may be relatively short-lived, their influence on later thinking and behavior is often considerable. Newcomb (1963) found that the attitudes and values of college students were influenced significantly by the friends and acquaintances they made while at college. To a lesser degree, these changes were still present thirty years after graduation. Occasionally, members of primary or social groups solve problems together, but much of their communication is spontaneous and informal.

As members of **learning** or **education groups,** we *come together* in an attempt *to teach or learn something about a given subject.* Quarterback clubs meet to learn more about football. Film groups get together to share their interpretations of movies. Seminars and courses involving group interaction also constitute learning groups. Brilhart and Galones (1992) refer to such groups as "enlightenment groups," in which members may attempt to solve problems but have no authority to implement their decisions.

Sooner or later, most of us will belong to **work groups,** which *have specific goals to achieve,* often within the context of a job. Membership may be required by virtue of employment in an organization rather than because of individual interest in the group. Group members may have little in common other than that their jobs require them to interact. That they receive payment for their individual contributions adds a unique dimension to this type of group. And whereas a member of a social or a learning group might remain relatively inactive, the consequences of not participating in a work group can be more severe (reprimands, ostracism, or even loss of employment).

The most highly publicized use of work groups to solve company problems has been the quality circle. Quality circles originated in Japan as an attempt to improve product quality, save money, and allow workers to utilize their talents more fully. Mohr and Mohr (1983, p. 233) report that 6,300 companies in the United States have quality circles, including half of the *Fortune 500* companies. One factory worker was quoted as saying he liked quality circles for this reason: "When the company hired me, I came with a brain . . . at no extra charge."

The most recent innovation in work groups is the **self-directed work team (SDWT).** This is defined by Fisher (1993) as "a group of employees who have day-to-day responsibility for managing themselves and the work they do with a minimum of direct supervision. Members . . . typically handle job assignments, plan and schedule work, make production and/or service related decisions, and take action on problems" (p. 15).

Increasingly, modern organizations are striving to use their employees more effectively. Wellins and associates (1991) identify three reasons why SDWTs seem to work so well:

1. Those closest to the work know best how to perform and improve their jobs.

2. Most employees want to feel that they "own" their jobs and are making meaningful contributions to the effectiveness of their organizations.

3. Teams provide possibilities for empowerment that are not available to individual employees. (p. xvi)

Using SDWTs allows employees to have a much greater level of empowerment and increases productivity (and lowers product costs). Wall and associates (1992) report that Mrs. Field's Cookies, Levi Strauss, AT&T, General Electric, IBM, and Xerox are just a few of the many companies that are utilizing this very creative new form of leadership (p. 12).

At one time or another some of us will also belong to **therapeutic groups,** whose members *come together to learn about themselves and to improve their interpersonal relationships.* Unlike learning groups, which focus on mastering a given subject, therapeutic groups are consciously concerned with process—with the small-group experience itself. Therapeutic groups usually take one of two forms: the psychotherapeutic group or the encounter group. The first usually meets over a longer period of time than the second and is largely conducted in conjunction with individual therapy. The encounter group may vary in length from a minilab that lasts two to three hours to a marathon that lasts several days. Depending on its focus, the group may be a personal growth lab, a group dynamics lab, a couples lab, or an organizational development session. It may be a group with one or more leaders, or it may be a leaderless, or self-analytic, group that uses taped instructions for each of its meetings.

Homans (1950, p. 1) has described membership in small groups as "the first and most immediate social experience of mankind." More specifically, he defines a group as "a number of persons who communicate with one another often over a span of time and who are few enough so that each person is able to communicate with all the others, not at secondhand, through other people, but face-to-face." As you read this chapter, you might give some thought to this definition.

GROUP DYNAMICS

While we are all familiar with the problems and pleasures associated with family roles, in the business world, we discover other aspects of group membership. One of the major complaints about committees and other problem-solving small groups is that they take up too much time and seldom accomplish as much as they should. To make better use of the time spent in small groups, we have to know something about how people ordinarily behave in them.

Remember when you first came to college? There were a lot of situations in which you didn't know exactly how you were supposed to act. In situations which are unfamiliar we all look to others for cues on what is the appropriate thing to do. In these situations we are especially vulnerable to social influence. In the movie *Big,* Tom Hanks goes to a cocktail party in a light blue tuxedo, and everybody laughs at him for not dressing appropriately. All of us have been in situations like that.

Conformity Pressure

A great deal of research has been done on conformity pressure and the effect it has on our behaviors. The original work was conducted in which people had to estimate how much a point of light appeared to move in a dark room. Since the light does not move at all, the optical illusion regarding the amount of movement is highly sensitive to social influence. The researchers found that individual estimates of autokinetic movement vary a great deal. To one person it might seem that the light has moved two inches; to another the distance might seem to be six inches. Yet Sherif (1967) found that a person who first views this phenomenon when he or she is isolated from others and observes it several times under these conditions will develop a standard of his or her own so that all his or her subsequent estimates of distance fall within this range. On the other hand, when a person witnesses the autokinetic effect for the first time as a member of a group, the group establishes a norm; if that person is then exposed again to the autokinetic effect, he or she will make estimates in terms of the group norm. Moreover, a person who has made initial judgments in isolation and then overhears others estimate the distance will correct his or her own estimate so that it tends to converge with that of the others.

A more recent case of group conformity pressure was illustrated in the 1992 movie *A Few Good Men,* starring Jack Nicholson, Demi Moore, and Tom Cruise. In this film, the marines in a military unit would discipline a member of their unit who was out of line with the group's norms. This practice was referred to as a "Code Red" and usually consisted of some type of physical punishment. In this particular case it resulted in an accidental death. The entire movie illustrates several group dynamics concepts discussed in this chapter.

One of the criticisms of conformity research has been that subjects rarely get to argue their point of view against the majority opinion. Yet even in studies that allow dissenting members to present their arguments, considerable conformity behavior still occurs (Grove, 1965). These studies distinguish between **private acceptance** of a judgment or opinion and **public compliance**— that is, *between whether people change their thinking as a result of hearing* *opinions different from their own or whether they say they agree with the group when in fact they disagree.*

Private acceptance is more likely to occur when (1) the individual greatly values membership in the group, (2) opinion is unanimously against him or her, (3) the issue in question is ambiguous to begin with, or (4) the group is under pressure to achieve an important goal (Cartwright and Zander, 1968). Public compliance usually stems from the desire to avoid the unpleasantness of conflict. After maintaining a dissenting opinion for a long time, a person may be made so uncomfortable by social pressures that as a peace-keeping gesture, he or she gives the impression of going along with the rest of the group. A number of studies have shown that the person who conforms readily tends to be (1) more submissive or dependent, (2) high in the need for social approval and low in the need to be outstanding, (3) more often female than male, and (4) lacking in self-confidence (Hare, 1962).

Social Influence

We have looked at conformity behavior in terms of the individual member. Now let us examine the behavior of the group. We know that the group tends to exert most pressure to conform on newcomers, who have not yet earned the right to deviate from group norms. Fraternities and sororities often deal out harsh criticism when rushees and pledges dress or act differently from other members of the group. Yet a great many of the same deviations are tolerated when they exist in fraternity members who are upperclassmen.

Groups with a high level of cohesiveness tend to exert strong conformity pressures. It seems that the more closely knit the group, the more the members resist allowing anyone to become a member who does not share their values. Members with the greatest prestige tend to be "super representatives" of the attributes that are highly valued by the group. The typical football team captain is usually one of the best athletes on the team. Similarly, the gang leader is often one of the gang's toughest members. In each case the person who best represents the qualities esteemed by the group has the most prestige.

How does the cohesive group behave when one of its members takes a stand quite different from that of the rest? Schachter (1951) found that initially the deviant gets most of the group's attention. Each member will probably say or do something to persuade the lone dissenter to come around to the position held by the rest of the group. These efforts may go on for some time. Eventually, the deviant either gives in—there is no way of knowing, of course, whether this is simply public compliance—or is ignored or rejected.

An explanation of what makes most of us yield to social pressure is offered by Festinger's **social comparison theory**. Festinger (1954) believes that *all human beings have a need to evaluate their own opinions and abilities and that when they cannot do so by objective nonsocial means, they compare them with those of other people.* How do you tell, for example, whether you are a good driver? Clearly, by comparing your performance with that of other drivers. Similarly, you find out whether you are liberal in your political views by comparing them with those of others. In other words, in the absence of objective criteria, you rely on the opinions of others to determine the validity of your own.

In the Schachter experiment a discrepancy existed between the opinions of one group member and the rest of the group. Social comparison theory predicts that in such a situation group members will act to reduce the discrepancy and that the person with the discrepant opinion will tend to change his or her position so that it is closer to that of other group members. We saw this to be the case not only in the Schachter experiment but in some of the studies of the autokinetic effect, where individual judgments tend to converge with group norms. However these phenomena are explained, the tendency to conform seems clear. In the following section we shall examine conformity as it affects group decisions.

The Quality of Group Problem Solving

In studying group dynamics, a reasonable question to ask is how groups compare with individuals in problem solving. Will the number of people in the group affect the quality of the decision? Will people meeting together generate a greater number of novel ideas than they would working in isolation? In short, how does the presence of others influence the way we think?

Acceptance of Risk

It has been established that members of groups tend to conform. As yet, however, nothing has been said about the direction of that conformity. When we call someone a "conformist," we usually think of him or her as somewhat conservative. Conformists don't rock the boat. They don't create dissension. They go along with group norms. They probably go along with group decisions. It would seem that because they conform, they take few risks, and from this we might guess that the decisions of the group would also tend to be conservative or at least cautious.

Suppose you are on your way to a meeting in which your group will advise Mr. A, an electrical engineer, about the pros and cons of a certain career choice. Should he remain in the large electronics corporation for which he works, where he is assured a high level of security and moderate financial rewards, or should he accept an offer from a small, recently founded company that will offer him a higher starting salary and share in the firm's ownership but whose future is highly uncertain? What odds will you give—one in ten, three in ten, and so on—that the new company turns out to be financially sound and thus that Mr. A will do better joining it than remaining where he is? Whatever the odds you choose, chances are that if a group discussion follows, it will significantly increase your estimate of Mr. A's chances for success.

The **risky shift phenomenon** is the name given this *tendency of people to increase their willingness to take risks as a result of group discussions.* It is by no means confined to decisions about careers. Here, for example, are summaries of a few of the experimental problems that have demonstrated a shift toward risk after group communication:

> A man with a severe heart ailment must seriously curtail his customary way of life if he does not undergo a delicate medical operation which might cure him completely or might prove fatal.

> A captain of a college football team, in the final seconds of a game with the college's traditional rival, may choose a play that is almost certain to produce a tie score, or a more risky play that would lead to sure victory if successful, sure defeat if not.

> An engaged couple must decide, in the face of recent arguments suggesting some sharp differences of opinion, whether or not to get married. Discussions with a marriage counselor indicate that a happy marriage, while possible, would not be ensured. (Wallach et al., 1962, p. 77)

Several explanations of the risky shift phenomenon have been proposed; we shall consider three of them in brief fashion. The first is that within a group no member feels totally responsible for the decision. This might explain the actions of lynch mobs: A person who might never dare commit a murder alone suddenly helps carry out a lynching. The second possibility is that those who argue in favor of risky positions are more persuasive than those who are conservative and that they therefore influence others in favor of riskier decisions. The first two hypotheses have little experimental support. A third and more likely possibility is that Western culture tends to value risk taking over conservative behavior. The result, as Wheeler (1970) puts it, is that

> just as an individual practices his tennis game because there is a cultural value placed on being slightly better than other people, he changes his risk level in the direction valued by the culture so that he can feel he is slightly "better" than his peers. This does not mean that the individual automatically changes his risk level but that he reinterprets elements in the situation and focuses on arguments favoring risk. (p. 106)

As you find yourself participating in task-oriented groups, it is important to realize that the group decision is likely to be riskier than the average of the positions taken by individual group members before their interaction.

Groupthink

We discussed the concept of norms in Chapter 7. Suffice it to say that in the small group, social influence is even more powerful than it is in the dyad. Moreover, as we know from the principles of balance theory, the judgments of other people affect our attitudes, beliefs, and values as well as our perceptions.

Norms need not be negative in their effect. Sometimes it's possible to establish constructive norms that will improve group functioning. In describing the top decision-making group at AT&T, John de Butts, chairman of the board, had this to say:

> We don't avoid arguments. We all agree in advance not to agree with anything unless we truly believe in it. (Kleinfeld, 1979, p. 100)

This constructive norm at AT&T is designed to avoid the "groupthink" problem that often occurs when subordinates in large organizations are afraid to disagree with the boss.

In general, "groupthink" refers to a problem-solving process in which ideas accepted by the group are not really examined, and opposing ideas are suppressed. Janis (1982) lists eight main symptoms of groupthink: (1) Members share the illusion of invulnerability, providing the impetus to take extraordinary risks while failing to see early signs of danger; (2) warnings and other negative feedback are rationalized away; (3) members believe they are moral and thus can ignore the ethical implications of what they do; (4) leaders of other groups are considered evil and, therefore, not people with whom negotiations are reasonable; (5) members who stray from the group's beliefs are pressured to conform; (6) members avoid speaking out when not in favor of the group's actions, thus self-censure replaces group censure; (7) members share the illusion that agreement is unanimous; and (8) members screen the group, and especially the leader, from adverse information. With groupthink in operation, the group considers few alternatives, fails to scrutinize accepted ideas, fails to gather all the necessary information, fails to consider all the sides of an issue, and fails to consider alternative plans in the event the plan selected is rejected by others or does not work.

Level of Creativity

Another issue concerning the kinds of solutions groups reach has to do with creativity. Consider this problem. The Lang Advertising Agency has five writers on its staff. It is bidding for the Hudson's Bay Scotch account and must submit a sales presentation and advertising program to the prospective client. Should all five writers work independently and submit their own programs to the advertising director, or should the five be brought together to tackle the problem? Which procedure will generate a greater number of original ideas?

In essence we are asking whether **brainstorming** is an effective problem-solving technique. This approach, first introduced in the advertising firm of Batten, Barton, Durstine & Osborn in 1939, was designed to offset tendencies of group members to be inhibited by pressures to conform. Brainstorming had several rules. There was to be no criticism of ideas. "Freewheeling" was encouraged: The more way out the idea, the better. Quantity was desired: The greater the number of ideas, the better. Taking off on other people's ideas—either by improving one or by showing how two different ideas could be combined—was also encouraged (Osborn, 1957). Raudsepp (1980) cites his own research at Princeton University which indicates that by using this technique, individuals are able to increase their creative performance by 40 to 300 percent (p. 10).

There is evidence that when the group is a cohesive one and when members have had previous training in brainstorming techniques, the results can be highly successful (Cohen et al., 1960). It has been suggested that the effectiveness of brainstorming will depend on several variables, including the relationships between group members, the nature of the problem to be solved, and the type of leadership the group has (Kelley and Thibaut, 1969).

Tubbs (1992) offers the following lists of idea killers, which often serve to reduce group creativity as well as productivity:

- That's ridiculous.
- We tried that before.
- That will never work.
- That's crazy.
- It's too radical a change.
- We're too small for it.
- It's not practical.
- Let's get back to reality.
- You can't teach an old dog new tricks.
- We'll be the laughingstock.
- You're absolutely wrong.
- You don't know what you're talking about.
- It's impossible.
- There's no way it can be done.

On the other hand, "igniter phrases" such as those listed below often promote creativity and group productivity by establishing a psychological climate in the group which encourages creative thinking:

- I agree.
- That's good!
- I made a mistake. I'm sorry.
- That's a great idea.

- I'm glad you brought that up.

- You're on the right track.

- I know it will work.

- We're going to try something different today.

- I never thought of that.

- We can do a lot with that idea.

- Real good, anyone else?

- I like that!

- That would be worth a try.

- Why don't we assume it would work and go from there. (pp. 238–239)

Additional research by Comadena (1984) found that "individuals who were high producers of ideas perceived the brainstorming task as more attractive, were low in communication apprehension and possessed higher ambiguity tolerance than those individuals low in ideational productivity" (p. 261). The author concludes from his findings that the best brainstormers are those interested in the brainstorming topic and not afraid to communicate their ideas. This indicates that although brainstorming may achieve its best effects by reducing the problems associated with criticism and the question of "quality," individual predispositions to communicate still play a major role in the outcome.

The Role of a Group Member

Nine psychotherapists have formed a group to help block the passage of mental health legislation that they consider repressive. Ostensibly, the group's members are equal in status. No leader has been appointed. In this context each of the therapists has the same role—that of group member. Because of your interest in small-group communication and your friendship with one of the therapists, you are allowed to attend the meeting as an observer.

After attending a few meetings, you begin to notice that Bob knows a lot about existing mental health laws. He also makes a number of suggestions for actions the group might take: contacting legislators, raising funds for a series of broadcasts on the issue, distributing handbills about the implications of the new law. Matt, another member of the group, has few ideas of his own and tends to go along with any concrete proposals for group action. "I'm for that. Why not try it?" he often says. Frank, on the other hand, has more ideas than he knows what to do with. He proposes solutions, one after another—some sound, others extreme. Initially, he is very enthusiastic, but he never seems to carry through any of his suggestions. To the chagrin of most of the group, Kay usually punches holes in other people's arguments. "It will never work," she chides. "What do we use for money? People aren't going to contribute. They don't understand the issue."

Here are four people in the role of group member. Each interprets it somewhat differently. You think you see some individual patterns of inter-action emerging, but to be accurate, you need a method of describing various behaviors.

One of the more important accomplishments of small-group research has been the development of several such systems. The most widely known is **interaction process analysis (IPA),** developed at Harvard University by Robert Bales (1970). The twelve categories of IPA are virtually self-explanatory (see Figure 9.1), and they offer a valuable framework from which to view the functions and patterns of communication. Each interaction is assigned to one of the categories, and when the scoring has been completed, certain behavior patterns become apparent.

In the group we have been discussing, Bob's statements would tend to fall in categories 4 (gives suggestion) and 6 (gives information), Matt's in 3 (agrees), Frank's in 4 (gives suggestion), and Kay's in 10 (disagrees). The responses of other members of the group may be more diversified so that no single category or set of categories predominates, but over an extended period we could probably identify the characteristic behaviors of each member. In

FIGURE 9.1   Categories for Interaction Process Analysis

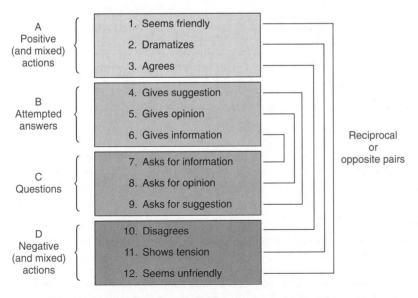

(*Source:* Robert Freed Bales, *Personality and Interpersonal Behavior,* New York: Holt, Rinehart and Winston, 1970. Copyright © 1970 by Holt, Rinehart and Winston, Inc.)

any case Bales's method of classifying human interaction gives us a systematic way to analyze group communication. By means of these categories, we can classify each communicative act regardless of its content.

As you look at the list in Figure 9.1, you might ask yourself which categories describe your own actions in small groups. There is a good chance that you will find yourself performing only a limited number of these behaviors. For example, one friend of ours summed up his participation in groups by saying, "I often like to play the devil's advocate and give people a bit of a hard time." If his statement is accurate, we would expect that most of his interactions (like those of Kay in the group we described) would fall in category 10 of the IPA. There are groups that need at least one critical member, someone willing to challenge others, but the last thing in the world some groups need is another devil's advocate. In general, it seems foolish to assume that any behavior or set of behaviors is appropriate in all situations; there is much to be said for developing some degree of role flexibility.

Tubbs (1992) has adapted the classification of rules that originated with Benne and Sheats (1948).

Group Task Roles

These behaviors are directed toward accomplishing the group's objective through the facilitation of problem solving:

- *Initiating-contributing:* Proposing new ideas or a changed way of regarding the group goal. This may include a new goal or a new definition of the problem. It may involve suggesting a solution or some way of handling a difficulty the group has encountered. It may also include a new procedure for the group to better organize its efforts.

- *Information seeking:* Asking for clarification, for authoritative information and facts relevant to the problem under discussion.

- *Opinion seeking:* Seeking information related not so much to factual data as to the values underlying the suggestions being considered.

- *Information giving:* Offering facts or generalizations based on experience or authoritative sources.

- *Opinion giving:* Stating beliefs or opinions relevant to a suggestion made. The emphasis is on the proposal of what ought to become the group's values rather than on factors or information.

- *Elaborating:* Expanding on suggestions with examples or restatements, offering a rationale for previously made suggestions, and trying to determine the results if a suggestion were adopted by the group.

- *Coordinating:* Indicating the relationships among various ideas and suggestions, attempting to combine ideas and suggestions, or trying to coordinate the activities of group members.

- *Orienting:* Indicating the position of the group by summarizing progress made and deviations from agreed-upon directions or goals or by raising questions about the direction the group is taking.

- *Evaluating:* Comparing the group's accomplishments to some criterion or standard of group functioning. This may include questioning the practicality, logic, or procedure of a suggestion.

- *Energizing:* Stimulating the group to action or decision, attempting to increase the level or quality of activity.

- *Assisting on procedure:* Helping or facilitating group movement by doing things for the group—for example, performing routine tasks such as distributing materials, rearranging the seating, or running a tape recorder.

- *Recording:* Writing down suggestions, recording group decisions, or recording the outcomes of the discussion. This provides tangible results of the group's effort.

Group-Building and Maintenance Roles

The roles in this category help the interpersonal functioning of the group. They help alter the way of working; they strengthen, regulate, and perpetuate the group. This is analogous to preventive maintenance done to keep a mechanical device such as a car in better working order:

- *Encouraging:* Praising, showing interest in, agreeing with, and accepting the contributions of others; showing warmth toward other group members, listening attentively and seriously to the ideas of others, showing tolerance for ideas different from one's own, conveying the feeling that one feels the contributions of others are important.

- *Harmonizing:* Mediating the differences among the other members, attempting to reconcile disagreements, relieving tension in moments of conflict through the use of humor.

- *Compromising:* Operating from within a conflict situation, one may offer a compromise by yielding status, by admitting a mistake, by disciplining oneself for the sake of group harmony, or by coming halfway toward another position.

- *Gatekeeping and expediting:* Attempting to keep communication channels open by encouraging the participation of some or by curbing the participation of others.

- *Setting standards or ideals:* Expressing standards for the group and/

or evaluating the quality of group processes (as opposed to evaluating the content of discussion).

* *Observing:* Keeping a record of various aspects of group process and feeding this information, along with interpretations, into the group's evaluation of its procedures. This contribution is best received when the person has been requested by the group to perform this function. The observer should avoid expressing judgments of approval or disapproval in reporting observations.

* *Following:* Going along with the group, passively accepting the ideas of others, serving as an audience in group discussion.

Individual Roles

These behaviors are designed more to satisfy an individual's needs than to contribute to the needs of the group. These are sometimes referred to as self-centered roles:

* *Aggressing:* Deflating the status of others, disapproving of the ideas or values of others, attacking the group or the problem it is attempting to solve, joking maliciously, resenting the contributions of others and/ or trying to take credit for them.

* *Blocking:* Resisting, disagreeing, and opposing beyond reason; bringing up dead issues after they have been rejected or bypassed by the group.

* *Recognition seeking:* Calling attention to oneself through boasting, reporting on personal achievements, acting in inappropriate ways, fighting to keep from being placed in an inferior position.

* *Self-confessing:* Using the group as an opportunity to express personal, non-group-related feelings, insights, ideologies.

* *Acting the playboy:* Showing a lack of involvement in the group's task. Displaying nonchalance, cynicism, horseplay, and other kinds of "goofing-off" behaviors.

* *Dominating:* Trying to assert authority or superiority by manipulating others in the group. This may take the form of flattery, asserting a superior status or right to attention, giving directions authoritatively, and/or interrupting others.

* *Help seeking:* Attempting to get sympathy from other group members through expressions of insecurity, personal inadequacy, or self-criticism beyond reason.

♦ *Special-interest pleading:* Speaking on behalf of some group such as "the oppressed," "labor," "business," usually cloaking one's own prejudices or biases in the stereotype that best fits one's momentary need.

Cohesiveness

Probably one of the most important by-products of group interaction is the emotional commitment that may evolve from having worked on a problem with others. In a classic study conducted during World War II, it was found that women who participated in group discussions on how best to cook unpopular cuts of meat (and thus leave favored cuts for the troops overseas) were much more likely to try out new recipes than were women who simply listened to a speech intended to persuade them to do so (Cartwright and Zander, 1968).

This kind of emotional commitment seems to increase as attraction to the group increases. **Cohesiveness** has been defined as *"the total field of forces acting on members to remain in the group"* (Schachter, 1951, p. 191). It may also be considered in terms of the loyalty and high morale of group members. Think of groups you have either been in or observed that were closely knit. Two groups that are not necessarily problem-solving groups but that illustrate high levels of cohesion are the Kennedy clan and Michael Jackson's family. Cohesiveness, which connotes pride of membership, often intensifies as a group becomes more successful. We are all familiar with the popular chant of crowds at sporting events, "We're number 1, we're number 1."

In general, cohesive groups have interested and committed members who enjoy each other's company. The group is not always highly productive, but its members do tend to help each other with problems, to adapt well to crisis situations, and to ask questions openly. We referred earlier to the conformity demands made by a cohesive group on its members. It is true, however, that they may sometimes feel free to disagree more openly than members of less cohesive groups.

In discussing emotional reactions to groups, it is only fair to acknowledge that things do not always turn out so positively. Working with others can also be frustrating, boring, and unsettling. The point is that the socioemotional dimension of group interaction constitutes a very real and powerful part of group behavior. Many people think that feelings have no place in a problem-solving group. On the contrary, feelings are very much involved in group behavior and should be studied as vigorously as its logical and rational aspects.

Research by Drescher and associates (1985) indicate that several factors influence group cohesiveness. From their review, the authors conclude that factors that encourage cohesion include self-disclosure, giving feedback, pregroup training, and member personality compatibility. Consequences of cohesion include communication level and conformity, both of which increase with cohesion; also, cohesion seems to be pleasing in and of itself. The main thrust of the article is that cohesion is a multidimensional construct that may be measured (1) at the level of the member or the group, (2) as both a cause and effect of other group variables (it appears to relate to many aspects of group process), (3) as a category of nonverbal behavior (e.g., attendance, duration of a group hug), verbal behavior (e.g., quantity of agreement), content of talk (e.g., intimate versus nonintimate topics), and self-ratings of hard-to-observe constructs (e.g., thoughts and emotions), and (4) as a point in time or (more logically) as a development process with increments.

Phases of Group Development

It has been said that, like a human being, each group has a life cycle: It has a birth, childhood, and maturity, and ultimately it ceases to exist. A number of theories have been proposed about what growth typically occurs in a group, and these are based on the study of either problem-solving or therapeutic groups (especially encounter groups). It is important to understand the phases of group development because this understanding provides a framework upon which group growth may be measured, provides a basis for making predictions about the group's progress, and allows a leader to plan interventions aimed at affecting the group's growth. Understanding allows for the best predictions, and the best predictions allow for the best responses to the group. For example, avoiding group conflict is not a good response since conflict is a normal part of group development.

Theorists seem to agree that growth and development in the group are the result of both the needs of the individual members and the social forces created within the group itself. Typically, these forces interact in a predictable way, with the group going through several stages or phases. Some theorists identify four phases, others three, and there are other differences in interpretation as well. For example, some theorists believe that the various phases occur even if a group meets only once (Tuckman, 1965; Fisher, 1970). Others hold that the phases occur over the life history of a group that meets repeatedly (Bennis and Shepard, 1956; Thelen and Dickerman, 1949). And still a third faction contends that all the group phases occur in each meeting and continue to recur throughout the group's life history (Schutz, 1958; Bales and Strodbeck, 1951). This third theory seems the most likely and the most valuable in providing insight into group development. Keeping these different viewpoints in mind, let us look at the four-phase model of group development as it is represented in the literature.

Phase 1: Forming really begins prior to the first meeting, when members begin the process of separating themselves from attachments that could interfere with the group, and attempt to learn about the group and/or other members. Forming lasts anywhere from one day to several weeks as members attempt to learn about the group members and the task that needs to be accomplished. Interaction is cautious, characterized by ambiguous language and a great deal of agreement (which is easy with ambiguous statements). Minimal work is accomplished, and the phase doesn't end until the norms are relatively clear. Questions uppermost in members' minds are "What is this group about?" "Do I fit in?" "Do I want to be in or out?"

Phase 1 is also a period in which group members break the ice and begin to establish a common base for functioning. This stage is sometimes referred to as a period of "orientation," "inclusion," or "group formation." Initially, people may ask questions about one another, tell where they are from, and generally make small talk. It seems that early in the life of a group, members are interested in building a working relationship that is psychologically comfortable. Even members of the most ambitious problem-solving groups usually spend some time socializing.

Phase 2: Storming is a normal and expected response to the orientation phase: While the orientation or forming phase built group solidarity, storming or conflict is the assertion of individuality (re: response to feelings of being "swallowed up" by the group). The agreement and ambiguity of the first phase give way to clear, unambiguous, and direct language, and agreement now is on specific issues, albeit agreement is low. During this phase the group loses part of its group identity, confusion over goals may increase, and minimal work is accomplished (still!). Storming usually revolves around two issues (regardless of the *specific* content, these two issues are usually the bottom line, the *real* issues): How close/how far should we be from each other emotionally, and is the leader a fool or "all wise"? Control and affection are the issues (see Chapter 6).

This period of dissent and controversy is ripe for communication failures: The more emotionally charged the discussion, the more prone group members are to jump to conclusions, lose their tempers, or interpret the comments of others as threats or criticisms. One student description clearly tracks the movement from Phase 1 to Phase 2:

> We talked about personal interests until some common ground was established, then we found we could talk about the assignment more freely. But after talking about non-subject things, it was hard to keep the line of talk on the problems at hand. Some wanted to get the assignment accomplished while two guys in the group continually swayed the conversation to things that were easier to talk about, but had nothing to do with the subject (Howard has a big thing for John Deere farm machinery). At first we were constantly trying not to hurt anyone's feelings, so we let the conversation drift. We didn't question or reject each other's ideas, and I feel we often settled for less than we should have. The longer we were in the group together, the more we got to know each other and the more times we voiced our real opinions. That's when the tempers started to flare!

Phase 3: Norming is marked by several levels of "balance" in response to the storming phase: Individuality and groupness balance, group goals and individual goals balance, closeness is balanced, and the role of the leader and the leader's authority are defined. Note that "balance" does not mean "resolved" since the balance is a delicate one easily upset.

In Phase 3, group cohesion begins to emerge, and the group starts functioning more smoothly as a unit. Here is Fisher's (1974) description of Phase 3:

> Social conflict and dissent dissipate during the third phase. Members express fewer unfavorable opinions toward decision proposals. The coalition of individuals who had opposed those proposals which eventually achieve consensus also weakens in the third phase. (p. 142)

Phase 4: Performing is the *period of consensus and maximum productivity.* Dissent is very much out of place at this time, so that few negative or unfavorable comments are expressed. Group spirit is high, and a great deal of mutual back patting takes place. Group members joke and laugh and reinforce each other for having contributed to the group's success.

In an early article Thelen and Dickerman (1949) did a good job of summarizing the group phases:

> Beginning with individual needs for finding security and activity in a social environment, we proceed first to emotional involvement of the individuals with each other, and second to the development of a group as a rather limited universe of interaction among individuals and as the source of individual security. We then find that security of position in the group loses its significance except that as the group attempts to solve problems it structures its activities in such a way that each individual can play a role which may be described as successful or not in terms of whether the group successfully solved the problem it had set itself. (p. 316)

The tail end of Phase 4 is signaled by several member behaviors: Lateness increases, absence increases, daydreaming and other signs of withdrawal increase, and the overall level of involvement in the group decreases. There is a great deal of anxiety associated with ending the group, and members respond differently to this anxiety—all the way from those who refuse to admit the group is ending and run around collecting phone numbers and addresses and planning the party, to those who talk about how terrible the group experience was and are glad it's over. Just as the preorientation stage required potential group members to begin to *invest* themselves in the group, the final stage requires members to *divest* themselves of the group.

While the four phases are different, they are not mutually exclusive: Overlap in behaviors is apparent; however, predominant behaviors are recognizable and may be used to judge the phase the group is in. "Usual" problems associated with each phase are forcing the group to jump into the problem during forming, avoiding conflict or storming during the second phase, norming or ignoring social aspects of group life during the third phase, not allowing members to respond as they *feel* (e.g., taking disparaging remarks seriously), or to talk out their feelings, and not providing methods for postgroup feedback during the last phase.

Due to the difficulty in identifying discrete phases, Cissna (1984) has argued that there is reasonable doubt that these phases even exist as identifiable entities. However, Table 9.1 shows the consistency of research identifying similar group phases.

Of course, not every group will develop precisely along the lines described above. Nevertheless, an awareness of the recurring themes in group development should enable us to improve our perception and understanding of group dynamics.

GROUP STRUCTURE

The distinction between group structure and group dynamics is somewhat arbitrary, for the way a group is constituted has considerable influence on how it functions. In our discussion of structure, we shall be concerned with three communication variables: group size, networks, and leadership.

Group Size

Think back to the groups you have belonged to that ranged in size from three to fifteen members. As the group got larger, what did you notice about the quality of the communication? How did you feel about your part in the discussions? How satisfied were you with them? It has been known for a number of years that as group size increases, the satisfaction of each member decreases. In larger groups a few people account for almost all the talking; the rest do very little. If you remember larger groups as boring and slow-moving, you probably were among the more silent members. We have seen a

TABLE 9.1

Summary of Literature on Group Phases				
	Phase 1	**Phase 2**	**Phase 3**	**Phase 4**
Thelen and Dickerman (1949)	Forming	Conflict	Harmony	Productivity
Bennis and Shepard (1956; 1961)	Dependence	Interdependence	Focused work	Productivity
Tuckman (1965)	Forming	Storming	Norming	Performing
Fisher (1970; 1974)	Orientation	Conflict	Emergence	Reinforcement
Bales and Strodbeck (1951)	Orientation	Evaluation		Control
Schutz (1958)	Inclusion	Control		Affection

number of student groups fail to develop into effective decision-making bodies because a great many people spent most of their time listening to a few long, complicated speeches made by a handful of members.

Group size affects performance as well as satisfaction. For example, larger groups tend to take more time to reach decisions, particularly if unanimity is required. We also know that as group size increases, a number of subgroups may form, and that these factions tend to polarize and to distract members from the problems at hand.

You can get some idea of the subgroups that may develop by looking at the potential communication relationships within groups of various sizes. Bostrom (1970) showed that in a dyad, for example, only two relationships are possible—A to B or B to A; but in a triad, or three-person group, there are nine possibilities:

1. A to B	4. B to C	7. A to B and C
2. A to C	5. C to B	8. B to A and C
3. B to A	6. C to A	9. C to A and B

The table following shows how rapidly complexity increases as groups gain in size. Bostrom calculated all the communication relationships possible within groups of three to eight people (pp. 257–258). Small wonder that to most people, belonging to a large group is less satisfying than belonging to a small one.

Number in Group	Interactions Possible
2	2
3	9
4	28
5	75
6	186
7	441
8	1,056

For our purposes the most practical question we can ask is: What size group seems best for problem solving? In a tongue-in-cheek discussion of government cabinets, the world's most powerful committees, Parkinson (1964) reasons that ideally a cabinet should consist of five members. Nevertheless, membership usually increases to seven or nine and then from ten toward twenty. In addition to the obvious difficulty of assembling all these people at one time, writes Parkinson,

> there is a far greater chance of members proving to be elderly, tiresome, inaudible, and deaf. Relatively few were chosen from any idea that they are or could be or have been useful. A majority perhaps were brought in merely to conciliate some outside group. The tendency is therefore to

report what happens to the group they represent. All secrecy is lost and, worst of all, members begin to prepare their speeches. They address the meeting and tell their friends afterward about what they imagine they have said. . . . Internal parties form and seek to gain strength by further recruitment. (p. 54)

As membership expands beyond twenty, the whole quality of the committee changes so that "the five members who matter will have taken to meeting beforehand" (p. 55).

While not to be taken literally, Parkinson's amusing description of the life cycle of the committee has essential validity. Although it is true that a greater variety of ideas tend to be expressed in large groups, such groups have several limitations we have already mentioned. Generally, the optimum size for a problem-solving group is five to seven members. This figure seems to have the greatest number of advantages.

Communication Networks

In *Further Up the Organization* Robert Townsend (1985), the man who revitalized Avis Rent a Car and has headed numerous other business enterprises, has some provocative things to say about how management should be organized. One of his proposals is that all positions with "assistant to" in the title be abolished. In making his point, Townsend presents three charts; these are reproduced in Figure 9.2. Unlike the regular assistant, who is given authority to make decisions, the assistant-to "moves back and forth between the boss and his people with oral or written messages on real or apparent problems—overlapping and duplicating efforts and make-working." Further on in his book, the author makes this observation about structure:

In the best organizations people see themselves working in a circle as if around one table. One of the positions is designated chief executive officer, because somebody has to make all those tactical decisions that enable an organization to keep working. In this circular organization, leadership passes from one to another depending on the particular task being attacked—without any hang-ups. (p. 134)

Townsend is talking about **communication networks,** *patterns of human interaction.* As you read on, try to decide for yourself whether his recommendations have merit. You might reserve your judgment, however, until after you have read the section on leadership.

In Figure 9.3 we see several frequently used communication networks: the Wheel, Chain, Y, Circle, and All-Channel networks. Note that in this illustration each is a five-person group. In the Wheel, one person—who usually becomes the leader—is the focus of comments from each member of the group. As the central person in the network, he or she is free to communicate with

FIGURE 9.2   Three Types of Management Organization

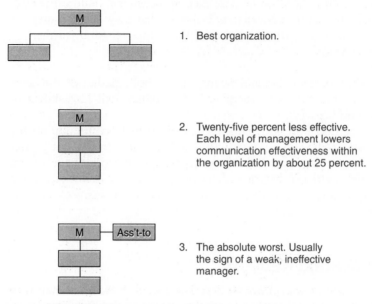

1. Best organization.

2. Twenty-five percent less effective. Each level of management lowers communication effectiveness within the organization by about 25 percent.

3. The absolute worst. Usually the sign of a weak, ineffective manager.

(*Source:* Robert Townsend, *Further Up the Organization,* New York: Knopf, 1985. Copyright © 1970, 1984 by Robert Townsend.)

the other four, but they can communicate only with him or her. In the Chain network three people can communicate with those on either side of them, but the other two with only one other member of the group. The Y network resembles the Chain: three of the five people can communicate with only one person. Unlike these systems, which are centralized and tend to have leaders, the Circle and All-Channel patterns are decentralized and sometimes leader-

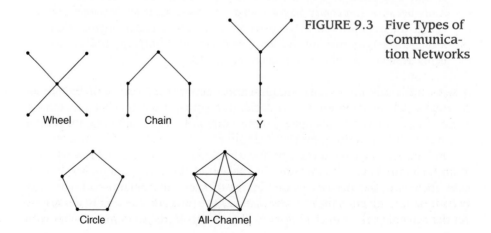

FIGURE 9.3   Five Types of Communication Networks

Wheel   Chain   Y

Circle   All-Channel

less. In the Circle each person may communicate with two others, those on either side of him. In the All-Channel network, sometimes called "Concom," all communication lines are open; each member is able to communicate with all the other members.

In studying small-group communications, we want to know how the type of network used affects group performance in problem solving and how given patterns affect interpersonal relationships within the group. Much of the research on networks is based on an experiment by Leavitt (1951) in which five subjects were each given different information essential to the solution of a problem in symbol identification. By using various networks (the Y, Wheel, Chain, and Circle), Leavitt manipulated the freedom with which information could be transmitted from one subject to another, and he then compared the results. The Wheel, the most centralized of the four networks, produced the best organized and fastest performance; the Circle group, the least centralized, was the most disorganized and unstable, and proved slowest in solving the problem. The biggest drawback of the Circle network, as another researcher has observed, is that it tends to generate a large number of errors as members try to communicate information around it (Bavelas, 1950).

Numerous studies of networks have been patterned after the Leavitt experiment, but the results are not easy to summarize. It is sometimes argued, for example, that certain networks are inherently more effective because of their structure, but Guetzkow and Simon (1955) believe that there are other factors to be considered. A particular network may handicap a group not in its ability to solve a problem but in its ability to organize itself so that it can solve the problem. This is an interesting hypothesis, especially in the light of Leavitt's original finding that Y, Wheel, and Chain groups were able to organize themselves so that each eventually established one procedure it used over and over, whereas members of Circle networks did not. Guetzkow and Simon believe that once a group has established a procedure for working together, it can perform efficiently regardless of its type of network.

The nature of the problem to be solved also affects performance. Groups with centralized networks are better at identifying colors, symbols, and numbers, and solving other simple problems. Decentralized networks have the edge over centralized ones when dealing with problems that are more complex—arithmetic, word arrangement, sentence construction, and discussion problems (Shaw, 1964).

Because most of the communication we are concerned with relates not to symbol identification and the like but to more complex issues, decentralized networks will usually be most desirable. For example, the Wheel, though efficient in its use of time, tends to lower the cohesiveness of a group, reduce its inventiveness, and make it too dependent on its leader (Guetzkow and Simon, 1955). Another advantage of decentralized networks is that they tend to provide the most satisfaction for individual members. The All-Channel network seems desirable for a number of reasons. Although initially it tends to be more inefficient and time-consuming, it maximizes the opportunities for corrective feedback, which ultimately should result in greater accuracy. Furthermore, freedom to speak to anyone else in the group creates high morale. These findings are important to keep in mind in the event that group discussions you participate in are characterized by inaccuracy or low morale.

Leadership

For many years people believed that leaders are born, not made, and a search was conducted to determine the traits of the "born leader." The quest has been largely unsuccessful. We do know that usually a leader is more self-confident and more intelligent than other members of his or her group. Some studies suggest that the leader is better adjusted and more sensitive to the opinions of other group members. Nevertheless, these traits are by no means reliable predictors of leadership. No single set of traits seems important in all situations. The successful commander of an air force squadron is not necessarily effective in an administrative post at the Pentagon. The outstanding teacher is not always a worthwhile dean or department chair.

Recent studies have led us to view leadership not as a quality but as a series of functions that groups must have performed. The leader then becomes the person who successfully performs a number of these functions, and sometimes leadership will pass from one person to another or be divided among group members. Thus far two major leadership activities have been identified: task functions and consideration functions. Neither set is in itself sufficient to satisfy all the group's needs.

Task functions are *activities that help the group achieve its goals*. In terms of the IPA categories in Figure 9.1, the activities might include giving and asking other members for suggestions, opinions, and information (categories 4 through 9). Other task functions might be orienting the group on how best to proceed, clarifying the remarks of others, and summarizing group process.

Consideration functions have to do with morale. They include *any activities that improve the emotional climate or increase the satisfaction of individual members*: showing agreement, support, or encouragement; gatekeeping (that is, allowing members who might otherwise be ignored to speak); and so on.

It is often difficult for one person to perform task and consideration functions simultaneously (Gaddy et al., 1987). Suppose that an emergency meeting of a school board is called to prevent a walkout of the teachers and that two board members monopolize the discussion in an unconstructive way. Someone will have to steer the conversation back to the problem at hand, which requires immediate action, and in doing so he or she may bruise a few egos. It takes considerable skill for the person who has done the offending to also conciliate the offended. For this reason the group often develops two or more leaders: a task leader, whose primary concern is that the job be done and the group perform well, and a social leader, whose first interest is in maintaining the group's high morale. Nevertheless, the most valuable leaders are those able to perform both task and consideration functions successfully.

Support for the concept that leaders are made, not born, comes from the Leavitt (1951) study of communication networks. Whereas in decentralized networks there was found to be little agreement among members as to the identity of the group's leader, in centralized networks such as the Wheel, Chain, and Y, people who occupied central positions and were thus able to channel communication were considered leaders. (Leadership and popularity are by no means synonymous, however.)

One way of successfully handling group consideration functions is with humor. Smith and Powell (1988) studied its use by group leaders. They conclude,

> This study examined the effects of humor used by a group leader in terms of the target of the humor. The results indicate that the leader who used self-disparaging humor was perceived as more effective at relieving tension and encouraging member participation, and appeared more willing to share opinions. The leader who used superior-targeted humor received lower ratings on helpfulness to group communication and willingness to share opinions. The leader who used subordinate-targeted humor received lower ratings on social attractiveness and as a tension reliever and summarizer of members' input. In some instances, the leader who used no humor received higher ratings. (p. 279)

Earlier research has found that humor facilitated group cohesiveness, gave insight into group dynamics, reduced tension, and enhanced group enjoyment.

Although we have stressed leadership functions rather than traits, there are specific behaviors often characteristic of leaders. If we compare those who get weeded out with those who emerge as leaders, we see some clear-cut differences. The first tend to be quiet, uninformed or unskilled, inflexible, and bossy or dictatorial; they also spend a great deal of time socializing. In contrast, emergent leaders tend to speak up, to have good ideas and state them clearly, to care about the group, and to make sacrifices and build cohesiveness (Bormann, 1976). In sum, leadership functions include a number of behaviors that can be learned.

In conclusion, we remember the thoughts on leadership of E. M. Estes, former president of General Motors:

> Leadership is the courage to admit mistakes, the vision to welcome change, the enthusiasm to motivate others, and the confidence to stay out of step when everyone else is marching to the wrong tune.

CORRELATES OF EFFECTIVE GROUPS

Anyone who has participated in problem-solving group discussions knows that they can be time-consuming, boring, and sometimes infuriating. Furthermore, the decisions groups make may be of poor quality and may be ignored by those who must carry them out. Yet even totally ineffective committees are not that easily disbanded. There are countless situations in which we cannot make decisions on our own; we must work within a group. As we have already seen, group structure—the size of a group, for example—can influence the effectiveness of problem-solving communication. In this section we shall be looking at some other correlates of small-group effectiveness.

It would be nice if we could automatically improve our communication behaviors by reading about what makes small groups successful. Unfortunately, improvement is not so easily attained. It does come, however, with participation. In summarizing several studies, McGrath and Altman (1966) comment, "The adage 'Practice makes perfect' seems to be fairly well substantiated by small group research. The more task training and experience groups and group members have, the better they perform as individuals and as groups" (p. 58).

The process by which improvement takes place is probably that of social learning. Behaviors that are productive tend to be reinforced by other members of the group, and those that are unproductive tend to be extinguished because they go unrewarded. Granted that no amount of reading can replace the experience of being part of a group, there are still some lessons we can learn from reading about communication. We can learn what the behaviors are that make for successful groups and then try to practice them when we do participate. In some situations we may be able to do no more than improve our own performance within the group. In other cases we may be able to design as well as engage in more effective group activities.

Idea Development and Problem Solving

For several years communication scholars have tried to identify ways of becoming a better small-group participant. For example, Gouran and his associates (1978) found three communication behaviors that were seen by members of small groups as particularly helpful or effective in solving problems. They were (1) introducing relevant issues or ideas, (2) amplifying or expanding on ideas, and (3) documenting assertions. For example, instead of saying all members of Sigma Phi Delta fraternity are goof-offs, it would be better to state that "according to the Office of the Dean of Students, Sigma Phi Delta fraternity has the lowest grade point average of all the fraternities on campus." Two helpful *procedural* behaviors were singled out: (1) maintaining a goal orientation rather than getting sidetracked and (2) pursuing issues systematically rather than in a disorganized fashion (p. 62). With these findings in mind, let's look at some of the communication behaviors to avoid in small groups.

If you were to interview members of several different kinds of small groups about the difficulties they encounter in developing ideas and solving problems, you would find at least six recurring complaints: (1) Group objectives are not clearly stated or agreed upon, (2) group members do not come up with enough ideas, (3) the group does not carry through discussion of each issue until it is resolved, (4) members rarely help one another, (5) conflict between members becomes so intense that it is counterproductive, and (6) conclusions are not reached or agreed upon.

Standard Agenda

In an attempt to correct some of these shortcomings, many groups try to follow an agenda or schedule that will help them make better use of their time and resources. One of the most widely known group agendas is that adopted from a problem-solving sequence of questions developed several decades ago by John Dewey. This approach has often been called the "Standard Agenda" because, as you can see below, the questions are broad enough to be applied to just about any problem.

1. What are the limits and specific nature of the problem?

2. What are the causes and consequences of the problem?

3. What things must an acceptable solution to the problem accomplish?

4. What solutions are available to us?

5. What is the best solution?

Ideal Solution Form

Although groups have been aided by the Standard Agenda for years, experimental evidence shows that two other problem-solving sequences—the Ideal Solution Form and the Single Question Form—result in greater accuracy (Larson, 1969). Like the Standard Agenda, both these instruments involve a series of questions intended to stimulate the thought of group members and to keep them from reaching an impasse. In the Ideal Solution Form, notice the realistic emphasis on approximating ideal goals:

1. Are we all agreed on the nature of the problem?

2. What would be the ideal solution from the point of view of all parties involved in the problem?

3. What conditions within the problem could be changed so that the ideal solution might be achieved?

4. Of the solutions available to us, which one best approximates the ideal solution? (p. 453)

Single Question Form

The Single Question Form has a slightly different emphasis. By constantly referring the group back to a single objective, it attempts to concentrate the group's energies on the problem and keep members from going off on a series of tangents:

1. What is the single question, the answer to which is all the group needs to know to accomplish its purpose?

2. What subquestions must be answered before we can answer the single question we have formulated?

3. Do we have sufficient information to answer confidently the subquestions? (If yes, answer them. If not, continue below.)

4. What are the most reasonable answers to the subquestions?

5. Assuming that our answers to the subquestions are correct, what is the best solution to the problem? (p. 453)

Nominal Group Technique

The use of discussion methods is one way to increase the effectiveness of a group. One method commonly used in business and industry is the *nominal group technique* (NGT).

The NGT method has six phases. First there is silent, independent generation of ideas, written down on paper. The second round is a round-robin listing of ideas on a large newsprint page so everyone can see. The third step is a discussion or clarification of points but without critique. In the fourth step, everyone individually rates the ideas. The fifth step is a clarification of the vote, and the sixth is a final ranking of ideas.

This method circumvents some of the problems of groupthink, such as the focus effect and the illusion of anonymity.

When compared to unstructured groups, NGT provided better decisions (Jarobe, 1988).

No matter which problem-solving technique is used, effective groups have some elements in common. In a fascinating study comparing effective to ineffective groups, Hirokawa (1983) found:

> The "successful" groups make an attempt to analyze the problem *before* attempting to search for a viable solution to the problem, while the "unsuccessful" groups immediately begin working on a solution to the problem before attempting to analyze it and understand it. (p. 304; italics added)

This research supports the problem-solving sequence advocated in all three of the approaches discussed above.

Resolution of Conflict

One value of the four-phase model of group development discussed earlier is that it enables us to see that regardless of whether a group follows an agenda or a schedule, conflict will be a legitimate part of the small-group experience. Should we avoid conflict or meet it head on? Some group members try to avoid it at all costs; others seem to thrive on it. Somewhere between these extremes is a realistic attitude toward conflict, one that will result in maximum gain for all parties concerned. Smith and Berg (1987) define group conflict as "the clash of oppositional forces including ideas, resources, interests, wishes or drives" (p. 634).

If several approaches to conflict, along with their outcomes, are plotted on a grid, our alternatives become clear. In the model of conflict resolution in Figure 9.4, these outcomes are related to the task and consideration functions that each group must have performed. The horizontal axis, "Concern for production of results," measures task functions; the vertical axis, "Concern for people," measures consideration functions.

The 1,1 position on the grid is the laissez-faire approach. It represents complete neutrality. The person with this attitude avoids pushing for the resolution of any issue that might introduce dissension; yet he or she shows

FIGURE 9.4   The Conflict Grid

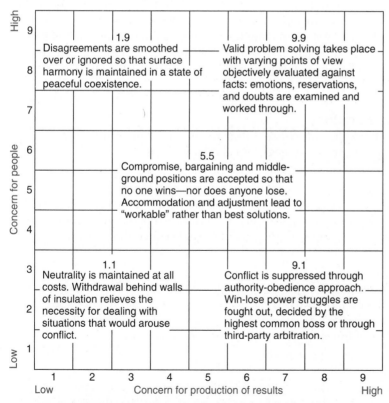

(*Source:* Robert Blake and Jane Mouton, "The Fifth Achievement," *Journal of Applied Behavioral Science* 6, 1970, 418. Herbert M. Johnson, Publisher.)

no regard for other members of the group. The 1,9 position is person-oriented. Its goal is surface harmony, accomplished by subordinating task to consideration needs. The person who takes this position strives for the appearance of good feeling by suppressing conflicts wherever possible. The 5,5 position represents the desire for compromise. Although it seems effective, this midway point leaves conflict unresolved; no one loses, but no one gains either. The hard-nosed or exclusively task-oriented approach is represented by the 9,1 position. This attitude is typified by such remarks as "Let's get the ball rolling and the job done." But the job often remains undone because of the lack of concern for group feelings.

Each of these positions has disadvantages when compared with the 9,9 approach. Here the point of view is that we must allow conflicts to be expressed openly while working vigorously at the tasks confronting the group. This means keeping the conflict directed at the problem before the group rather than at the personalities of dissenting members. Comments such as "Anyone who thinks that must be crazy" are taboo. In this view task and consideration needs are both met. Conflict is not suppressed, but it is not allowed to disrupt the progress of the group or to undercut morale.

On a grid, things look simpler than they are. Perhaps the biggest stumbling block in conflict-resolving communication in our society is the high value we place on "winning." We often cling tenaciously to our position or even move to a more extreme one just to avoid giving the other person the satisfaction of having "won." In a small group the win-or-lose mentality can only be destructive.

Levels of Conflict

Phillips (1988) has identified a four-tiered model of conflict that is useful in identifying the various stages of escalating conflict:

Level I: Differences
At this level the goal is to resolve the conflict. There is a free exchange of undistorted information. The emotional tone is one of anticipation and confidence in the ability of the parties to resolve their differences.

Level II: Dispute
At level II the goal has shifted to losing as little as possible. The exchange of information has now become guarded. The parties often prepare calculated as opposed to spontaneous messages. The emotional tone becomes that of forced politeness and anxious impatience.

Level III: Contention
The goal is no longer to find a mutually acceptable level of gain or loss. It is to win. The parties exchange information not for the purpose of resolving the problem but to prove something. The emotional tone is stressful. Exchanges are heated because the parties fear losing. At the

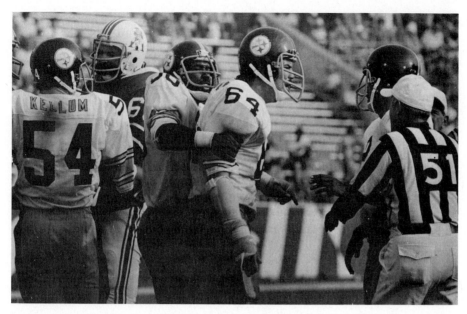

Have you ever experienced conflict in a group situation?

latter stages, parties are frustrated and exhibit anger toward opponents and sometimes their partners.

Level IV: Limited Warfare
The goal is now to diminish the opponent's power so that the opponent is no longer a threat. Both parties begin actively to seek out political allies. Whatever facts were originally at issue are completely obscured. The fight has taken on a life of its own. The emotional tone is hurt, anger, and disgust.

Level V: All Out War
The objective is to eliminate the other party. Cost is no longer a concern. Victory is paramount. Both parties avoid each other at all costs. The emotional tone is total disdain. (Phillips, 1988, pp. 66–71)

Idea Opponents and Personal Opponents

One of the most common mistakes in small-group communication is to confuse *personal opponents* with *idea opponents*. Research on effective problem solving clearly shows that groups can be superior to individuals in solving problems because more ideas are produced and they come from several different vantage points. Also, each person's ideas tend to generate ideas from others. Furthermore, the ideas can often be improved or refined through group discussion. This is the phenomenon of *idea opposition;* good ideas are improved upon by being tested and opposed by others. For example:

> *Bob:* I suggest we clean up this problem by developing a basic form for all students to fill out. It'll save them time at registration each term. Why not use the C180 form and modify it?
>
> *Sally:* I like the concept, Bob, but I think the D series form would be even more streamlined. And it eliminates some of the sexist wording on the C forms.
>
> *Bob:* You know, I think you're right. The D series would be perfect!

Idea opposition, then, is a basic requirement for problem solving. On the other hand, the research on social influence and conformity shows that one very normal human tendency is to dislike others who disagree with us. So we sometimes become defensive and turn *idea opponents,* who could be helpful and constructive, into *personal opponents,* who are likely to become destructive to the group and to us personally. In the discussion below, Bob falls victim to this common tendency:

> *Bob:* I suggest we clean up this problem by developing a basic form for all students to fill out. It'll save them time at registration each term. Why not use the C180 form and modify it?
>
> *Sally:* I like the concept, Bob, but I think the D series form would be even more streamlined. And it eliminates some of the sexist wording on the C forms.
>
> *Bob:* You know, Sally, you have a one-track mind. You see sexism in everything. You would get a hell of a lot further in your career if you would get that chip off your shoulder.

Bob has just turned Sally from an idea opponent into a personal opponent. Even if he's right about Sally overdoing her feminism, this is probably not the right time or place to comment on it.

There are effective behaviors for resolving conflict. First, we should try to agree on a definition of what actually constitutes the problem. Sometimes people swept away in an argument do not realize that they may not even be arguing about the same point. Second, we should explore possible areas of agreement. Two parties rarely disagree completely on a given issue, and their goals may not be mutually exclusive. Next, we can determine what specific changes each faction must make to resolve the issue satisfactorily. Most conflicts are resolved by some modifications in the original preferences of both sides. And fourth, we must not resort to personal attacks but must keep the conflict directed at the issue.

Patterns of Decision Making

Decisions can be avoided, demanded, or agreed on. Assuming that decisions will actually be made, let us briefly examine four rather different ways of carrying out the process.

One writer goes quite far in stating that "achieving concensus is the essential purpose of interpersonal communication" (Phillips, 1966, p. 39). Although this position fails to account for several other important communication goals, we heartily agree that consensus is one of the most desirable outcomes of interaction in small groups. The term can mean a majority opinion, but we use **consensus** to denote *agreement among all members of a group concerning a given decision.* Juries in criminal cases must reach consensus, and those that cannot—hung juries—are ultimately dismissed.

Pace (1988) studies high- versus low-consensus groups. He found the following differences in interaction:

High Consensus
1. Used more than one method of integrating or unifying diverging points of view into one decision

2. Changed integration methods from episode to episode

3. Generated a wide variety of possible solutions to the problem

4. Generated solutions to the problem in the early stages of discussion

5. Terminated episodes by voicing agreement for an idea or claim

Low Consensus
1. Rarely used more than one method of integration within a single episode

2. Repeated one type of integration method from episode to episode

3. Generated a limited number of possible solutions to the problem

4. Generated solutions to the problem in the later stages of discussion

5. Terminated episodes by changing topics or by introducing claims which went unacknowledged or undeveloped (p. 200)

Few groups are as concerned as they should be about trying to reach consensus on decisions. We tend to forget that the people who help make a decision are often those who are also expected to carry it out. And given a choice, most people who disagree will resist enacting it. Therefore, problem-solving groups should try to reach consensus to ensure maximum satisfaction and commitment to the decision by all members.

The **majority vote** represents *the wishes of at least 51 percent of a group's members.* Although it is not nearly as satisfying as consensus, it does allow some group harmony in decision making. After as much deliberation on the problem as time permits, there may still be a substantial split in opinion. The majority vote allows the group to proceed despite this. The major limitation of the majority vote is that the dissenting members may be numerous and may be bitterly opposed to the decision. If so, they may be expected to resist carrying it out. When feasible the majority vote can be used to establish whether a group is near consensus. If a split still exists and time allows, deliberation should continue. If continued discussion does not prove fruitful, the majority vote may be used to reach the decision.

A still less desirable method of arriving at a decision is **handclasping,** or **pairing.** This term applies when various *minority members within a group form a coalition to help each other achieve mutually advantageous goals.* Their decision may not represent common sentiment in the group, but they overpower the majority by dint of their collective numbers. This pattern seems characteristic of political life. It is a common practice for legislators to vote for each other's bills in order to compel support for their own. In the short run, coalitions may be quite successful, but ultimately they can have disastrous effects on group morale. Furthermore, members of coalitions sometimes forget that these bargains exact obligations.

Most groups have at some time been the victims of **railroading,** which occurs when *one or a few group members force their will on the group.* This technique is used most frequently by a leader or particularly influential member, and, of course, it is the one most likely to produce resentment and resistance.

Since reaching consensus is the most desirable method of decision making within the small group, it is instructive to turn to a few of the research findings on the subject. Gouran (1969) compared the conversation of groups who were able to reach consensus with that of groups who were not. He found that the discussion in the first groups had a greater proportion of "orientation statements," statements explicitly directing the group toward the achievement of its goal or helping it resolve conflict. A follow-up study reported that orientation statements contained fewer self-referent words and phrases—"I," "me," "my," "I think," and so on—and that highly opinionated statements, which were characteristic of groups that had difficulty reaching consensus, contained more self-referent words (Kline, 1970).

Findings about orientation statements bear out our commonsense expectations, but we cannot follow our hunches. We might predict, for example, that if group members expressed their ideas clearly and briefly (in one or two minutes), they would facilitate the group's progress. It has been found, however, that clarity and length of statements are not significantly related to the group's ability to reach consensus. These data need to be substantiated by further research.

Testing the Group's Effectiveness

It is to be hoped that in the near future we shall have more experimental findings pinpointing the communication behaviors that help discussion groups achieve their goals. For the time being, however, we have to agree with Mortensen (1970), who comments that "far more is known about the dynamics of groups than about the distinctive communicative properties, functions, and outcomes in groups" (p. 309), and with Gouran (1973), who states:

> Although it is relatively easy to specify a list of outcomes on which research in group communication can concentrate, the task of identifying

communication behaviors potentially related to those outcomes is considerably more complex. The problem is that there are simply so many individual variables which could be associated in some meaningful way with consensus, effectiveness of decisions, satisfaction, and cohesiveness. (p. 25)

For these reasons most of us learn about what goes on in groups from our firsthand experience as members. Sometimes, however, this knowledge can be increased through special exercises. One frequently used technique is called the "fishbowl discussion." Two groups form concentric circles. The inner group carries on a discussion; the outer comments on what it has observed. The two groups then switch positions and repeat the procedure. Each member is allowed to leave the discussion long enough to observe the behavior of the others in the group. He or she may be aided by a list of pointers about what behaviors to be looking for.

SUMMARY

In this chapter we began to extend our model by looking at the dynamics of small-group communication with special emphasis on problem-solving, or task-oriented, groups. We observed the strong influence of social pressure on individual group members, and in discussing the "risky shift phenomenon" and the problem of "groupthink" we examined the direction of conformity behavior. The larger question we raised was how the quality of problem solving is affected when people work together instead of singly. Role behavior, another aspect of group dynamics, was also surveyed. Although role flexibility is desirable, most people interpret the role of group member rather narrowly, performing only a few of the behaviors described by the IPA categories, and few of the group membership functions identified by other researchers.

After touching on some characteristics of cohesive groups and on the phases of group development, we considered three aspects of the structure of a group that affect its functioning: size, communication network, and leadership. Limiting the size of the group to five to seven members seems to ensure maximum performance and satisfaction. Among communication networks the All-Channel pattern offers the greatest opportunity for corrective feedback and high morale, though the centralized systems are more efficient. Two concepts of leadership were discussed, and analysis of leadership functions rather than traits was recommended.

The last question raised was practical: How can the small group be made more effective? First, the use of an agenda makes the most of time and resources. Second, an awareness of various attitudes toward conflict allows group members to resolve conflicts in a way that respects both task and human concerns. A third correlate of small-group effectiveness is an approach to decision making that ensures commitment to the decision by all members of the group.

REVIEW QUESTIONS

1. Discuss two theories that have been used to explain compliance with social pressure. How does each explain this phenomenon?

2. How does groupthink encourage conformity?

3. Identify the four phases of group development and describe briefly the type of communication characteristic of each.

4. What is the relationship between group size, membership satisfaction, and group performance?

5. How do task and consideration functions in leadership differ?

6. What are six common difficulties that small groups encounter in developing ideas and solving problems?

7. Discuss the four levels of conflict.

8. Why is it important to encourage idea opposition and avoid personal opposition?

9. What are four ways of arriving at a decision in a group? What are some relative advantages and disadvantages of each?

EXERCISES

1. Have five people solve the "sinking ship" exercise in the appendix independently. After individual solutions have been reached, ask these people to solve the same problem in a group. Compare the individual solutions with the group solution. In what ways is the risky shift phenomenon illustrated?

2. Observe an actual problem-solving group. Listen carefully for statements that indicate the four phases of group development. Record any statements that represent any of these phases. Notice also whether the group does *not* seem to go through these four phases. Compare your observations with others who have observed different groups. Do most of the observations correspond to the research findings?

3. Conduct an in-depth study of a group of which you are a member. Keep a journal of the group's interaction pattern and activities and write a paper in which you analyze: (a) the communication network(s) of the group, (b) the leadership functions, (c) the group's cohesiveness, (d) members' satisfaction, and (e) methods of conflict resolution.

4. Analyze the most successful group discussion that you have ever participated in. What specific factors were presented that accounted for its success?

SUGGESTED READINGS

Brilhart, John, and **Gloria J. Galanes.** *Effective Group Discussion.* 7th ed. Dubuque, IA: William C. Brown, 1992.

This little book is one of the better texts on the subject. Especially helpful are its practical chapters: "Preparing to Discuss," "Procedures for Effective Decision-Making and Problem Solving," "Leading Discussions," and "Organizing and Leading Learning Discussions."

Fisher, Kimball. *Leading Self-Directing Work Teams: A Guide to Developing New Team Leadership Skills.* New York: McGraw-Hill, 1993.

This book is one of the finest available on this subject. It explains in detail how to use SDWTs in any organization. Since it is written for the practitioner, it is highly readable.

Gardner, John W. *On Leadership.* New York: Free Press, 1990.

This outstanding book is written from the perspective of member of the president's cabinet. It is very worthwhile reading!

Janis, Irving L. *Group Think.* 2d ed. Boston: Houghton Mifflin, 1982.

This classic book identifies the common mistakes groups have made throughout some of history's most infamous fiascos. Analysis includes such debacles as Pearl Harbor, the Vietnam War, Watergate, and others. Important guidelines are included for avoiding groupthink.

Larson, Carl E., and **Frank M. J. LaFasto.** *Teamwork: What Must Go Right/ What Can Go Wrong.* Newbury Park, CA: Sage, 1989.

This book applies communication theory to the context of groups. It is based on some highly innovative research which included interviews with several successful teams from IBM to a Mt. Everest expedition, from a superbowl championship team to a cardiac surgical team, and from an aircraft carrier to a successful Broadway play company. The eight common ingredients for successful teamwork are explored.

Maddux, Robert B. *Team Building: An Exercise In Leadership.* Rev. ed. Los Altos, CA: CRISP Publications, 1992.

This is a very brief handbook with lots of practical tips on leadership and teamwork. It is ideal for students or others who want to improve their team skills.

Tubbs, Stewart L. *A Systems Approach to Small Group Interaction.* 4th ed. New York: Random House, 1992.

This book takes a rather novel "systems approach" in the analysis of communication in the small group. Topics covered in the present chapter are there dealt with in greater detail. Emphasis is on the complex interplay of twenty-four variables that relate to small-group processes.

CHAPTER TEN

Public Communication

CHAPTER OBJECTIVES

After reading this chapter, you should be able to:

1 Define three dimensions of source credibility.

2 Describe four modes of delivery.

3 Outline five popular patterns of message organization.

4 Describe the use of at least two types of supporting materials and state the general research findings regarding the effects of using evidence in persuasive communication.

5 Distinguish between the assimilation effect and the contrast effect, and describe the relevance of each to the problem of how much change a speaker should advocate.

6 Specify under what conditions one-sided and two-sided messages are most effective.

7 State the conditions under which climax- and anticlimax-order messages are most effective.

8 State the general research findings regarding the relative effectiveness of messages containing stated versus implied conclusions.

*P*eggy Noonan, famous speech writer for President Reagan, wrote the following about public communication:

> A speech is part theater and part political declaration; it is a personal communication between a leader and his [or her] people; it is art, and all art is a paradox, being at once a thing of great power and great delicacy.
>
> A speech is poetry: cadence, rhythm, imagery, sweep! A speech reminds us that words, like children, have the power to make dance the dullest beanbag of a heart. (Noonan, 1990, p. 68)

For centuries, public communication has been one of the cornerstones upon which civilizations have been built. Communication as a discipline has grown out of the traditions of the great ancient rhetoricians from Aristotle and Cicero to the modern orators such as Martin Luther King and Bill Clinton. Throughout the ages public communication has served to unite as well as inspire people to action. This chapter is designed to help you improve your public communication abilities.

A DEFINITION

In Chapter I we defined face-to-face communication. We have since examined two contexts in which it occurs: dyads and small groups. Two-person interaction comes closest to an equal exchange between communicators. Theoretically each person is responsible for half of all the verbal and nonverbal messages transmitted; each is both speaker and listener. When we become members of problem-solving or therapeutic groups, the balance shifts and the communication process changes. We speak for shorter periods of time; we listen longer. Yet we still think of ourselves as speakers and listeners, senders and receivers of messages.

In public communication one person is designated the speaker, and the rest are cast in the complementary role of listeners, or audience members. Participants are still face to face and are still sending and receiving communicative stimuli. Anyone who has tried to speak before an audience whose members are reading the paper, sleeping, or doing other things that denote lack of attention knows all too well that audiences do send messages as well as receive them. But the balance of message sending is quite uneven—the speaker initiates most of the verbal messages, and, though audience members often send nonverbal messages (applause, laughter, catcalls, and so on), audiences in general are not usually expected to contribute verbal messages except in a question-and-answer period following the speech. Despite this imbalance, public communication is still face-to-face communication, and we frequently find ourselves participating in it as either speakers or listeners.

In Chapter 1 we outlined three distinctive aspects of the public communication experience (Hart et al., 1975, pp. 23–24). First, it tends to occur in what are usually considered public rather than private places—auditoriums, classrooms, and the like rather than homes, offices, and other private gathering places. Second, public speaking is a "pronounced social occasion" rather than a more informal and unstructured one. It is usually planned in advance. There may be an agenda, and other events may precede and follow the speaker's presentation. And third, public communication involves behavioral norms that are relatively clear-cut.

For all these reasons public communication often demands that the speaker be much more deliberate and organized. In private conversation we tend to value spontaneity and informality, but the same spontaneous, unplanned approach is usually inappropriate to the public speaking situation. The list that follows summarizes ten unique demands of public communication (Hart et al., 1975):

1. *The message must be relevant to the group as a whole*—not merely to one or a few individuals in that group. In public communication, the "common denominator" must be constantly searched for by the speaker.

2. *"Public" language is more restricted,* that is, it is less flexible, uses a more familiar code, is less personal in phrasing, and is filled with fewer connotations than is "private" talk.

3. *Feedback is more restricted,* since it is limited to subtle nonverbal responses in many instances.

4. *There is greater audience diversity* to deal with. In public communication we face the difficulty of entering *many* "perceptual worlds" simultaneously.

5. As the size of the audience increases, there is a greater chance of *misinterpreting feedback,* since there's so much to look for.

6. The speaker must do a more *complete job of speech preparation,* since there is so little direct moment-to-moment feedback to guide his or her remarks.

7. The *problem of adaptation* becomes paramount since one message must suffice for many different people.

8. *Audience analysis is more difficult* and necessarily more inaccurate when many people are interacted with simultaneously.

9. It is sometimes *difficult to focus attention* on the message because of the great number of distractions a public situation can entail.

10. *A greater amount of change* is possible in public communicative settings since the message reaches more people in a given unit of time. (p. 25)

In addressing an audience, a speaker ordinarily has at least one of three purposes: to inform, to entertain, or to persuade listeners. When that purpose is to inform, the speaker is primarily concerned with the outcome of information gain, an aspect of understanding discussed in Chapter 1. Speaking to entertain is directed toward pleasure, a second outcome that we have discussed. When the speaker's intention is to persuade, the desired outcome is attitude influence. The speaker may try to establish an attitude not previously held by the listeners or to reinforce or change one that they already hold. Persuasive speeches may also attempt to elicit some action. The political candidate ultimately wants our vote, not just our agreement on various issues. The saleswoman wants us to purchase the product she is selling, not simply to be aware of its superiority to other products. Nonetheless, attitude change is the intermediate goal to achieve before prompting action.

Informing, entertaining, and persuading are by no means mutually exclusive purposes. In fact, the classification, though traditional, is thought by some to be rather arbitrary. A persuasive speech about this country's diplomatic relations with China may also be informative and entertaining. Comedians like Joan Rivers and Bill Cosby speak primarily to entertain, yet their material frequently includes persuasive social commentary as well. An informative lecture on animal life, delivered in an entertaining and appealing style, may yet persuade audience members of the need for establishing wildlife preserves.

Most of the public communication experiences in which you find yourself either as speaker or listener will involve some persuasion—usually in addition to information gain and perhaps to entertainment. Therefore, this chapter will give more emphasis to public communication that attempts to be persuasive. We begin with a consideration of the speaker apart from his or her message.

THE SPEAKER

How will the speaker be perceived by the audience? On what basis will they form their judgments? In Chapter 2 we examined some principles of person perception and talked about the basis on which we form our first impressions of others. In Chapter 6 we examined some of the bases for our most permanent attraction to other people. We also discussed trust as it affects communication, particularly informal transactions between people. We spoke of trust as facilitating human relationships. We shall speak in this chapter about another aspect of trust—usually referred to as "source credibility"—as it relates to the public communication experience.

Source Credibility

I can say categorically that this investigation indicates that no one on the White House staff, no one in this administration, presently employed, was involved in this very bizarre incident. What really hurts in matters of this sort is not the fact that they occur, because overzealous people in campaigns do things that are wrong. What really hurts is if you try to cover it up. (Richard M. Nixon in an August 29, 1972, press conference, referring to the Watergate break-in)

During the administrations of recent presidents the American public has become painfully aware of the term "credibility gap." In its broadest sense, **credibility** refers to *our willingness to believe what a person says and does.* It is undoubtedly the most important influence on our judgment of a speaker. One writer describes credibility as the attitude a listener holds toward a speaker (McCroskey, 1978). Thus, credibility is in the mind of the listener.

Dimensions of Credibility

Credibility is not a new concept. In the fourth century B.C. Aristotle used the term "ethos" to refer to the personal characteristics of a speaker that influence the audience. A person with high *ethos* was thought to possess a high level of competence, good character, and goodwill toward his or her listeners. Aristotle believed that these qualities helped a speaker gain audience acceptance of his or her message.

Writing from the perspective of twentieth-century social psychology, Hovland and associates (1953) identified two components of *ethos* as expertness and trustworthiness. The two are roughly equivalent to Aristotle's components (if you combine his concepts of good character and goodwill).

During this century considerable research has been conducted on the subject of source credibility. Notice our use of the word "source." Although a speaker is usually perceived as the source of his or her message, this is not always the case. When a United Nations delegate addresses the General Assembly, she may not be considered the source of her message. Similarly, when an executive of a large oil company discusses Middle Eastern affairs, he may be seen not as the originator of his message but simply as a spokesperson for the firm. In most instances, however, the source of the message will be viewed as the speaker.

Credibility is not a constant. Each person's perception of a source varies. Moreover, the credibility of any source varies from topic to topic (for example, Martina Navratilova would be more persuasive talking about tennis than football). Credibility may also vary from one situation to another (for example, a teacher may be a high-credibility source in a classroom but a low-credibility source on the witness stand in a courtroom). Nonetheless, for some time researchers have attempted to determine whether there are in fact elements of credibility that do not vary. The results of a series of such studies are summarized by McCroskey (1966), who finds essentially two dimensions of ethos: authoritativeness and character. **Authoritativeness,** or expertise, refers to the speaker's perceived command of a given subject—*how intelligent, informed, competent, and prestigious we think the speaker is.* **Character,** a vaguer but no less important dimension, refers to the speaker's perceived

Source credibility involves both authoritativeness and character.

intentions and trustworthiness—*how objective, reliable, well motivated, and likeable the speaker seems to be.*

Both elements enter into our judgments of credibility. If a physician who also holds a doctorate in chemistry argues that preservatives in baby food have no adverse effects, most audiences will regard her as a high-credibility source. If it is then disclosed that she is a consultant to one of the largest producers of baby food in this country, her credibility may suffer a sharp decline. While the audience may not question her expertise, it will question her motives as well as her ability to be objective about a position from which she stands to gain. In one study, a convicted criminal produced no attitude change in his audience in arguing for greater personal freedom and less police power, but significant attitude change when he argued for greater police power. By supporting a position that seemed to be against his own interests, he increased his credibility considerably (Walster et al., 1966).

Many writers on public speaking believe that a third dimension of ethos is **dynamism**—that is, *how forceful, active, and intense the speaker seems to be.* It is proposed that other things being equal, the speaker who is self-assured and conveys a message with liveliness and vigor should be perceived as having higher credibility than a more reserved, passive, and slow-moving speaker. On the other hand, if the motivations of the more dynamic speaker are questionable (for example, the convicted criminal arguing for greater freedom and less police power) or the speaker's authoritativeness is in doubt, we would not expect him or her to be perceived as a high-credibility source. And if the presentation is too aggressive and vigorous, receivers may suspect that the motivation is self-interest and may doubt the speaker's capacity to be objective.

> Riggio et al. (1987) state that expressive, articulate, . . . or tactful persons may be more successful in situations involving self-presentation or persuasiveness simply because they are generally perceived as more credible than individuals who lack these basic communication skills. (p. 568)

The importance of dynamism in shaping judgments about credibility seems to vary with the individual receiver. Some audience members are much impressed by a bold, assertive speaker, yet for others dynamism plays little part in perceptions of source credibility. Perhaps this variation explains why in research on credibility, dynamism is a less stable factor than either authoritativeness or character.

Information on sex differences and the effects on credibility are summarized by Pearson (1985). She indicates that men and Anglo-Saxons (perceived to have high status) are considered more effective than women, Mexican-Americans, and blacks (who are perceived to have low status). When sex differences exist (and there is a growing body of research that fails to find differences), male sources are perceived as more competent, and female sources are perceived as higher in trustworthiness.

Hart and associates (1975) offer the following suggestions: To enhance perceptions of *competency,* associate yourself with other high-credibility sources, use self-references to demonstrate familiarity with the topic, use the special vocabulary of the topic, and be well organized. To enhance perceptions of *trustworthiness,* entertain alternate points of view, make sure verbal and nonverbal behaviors are congruent, demonstrate how the listener's benefit is considered, and indicate your similarity with audience members. To enhance perceptions of *dynamism,* control delivery variables (e.g., few nonfluencies), use intense language, and use somewhat opinionated language so as not to appear wishy-washy.

To sum up, **source credibility** refers to *the receiver's perception of the speaker's authoritativeness on a given topic, his or her character, and, to a lesser degree, dynamism.*

Throughout our discussion of credibility let us remember the word "perception." Credibility has to do not with what the speaker *is* but with what the receiver perceives him or her to be. Regardless of demonstrated expertise or good character, no speaker has high credibility for every audience. The vice-president of an airline may be a high-credibility source when addressing employees but not when speaking before the Federal Aviation Administration. In lecturing on the influence of mass communication on voting patterns, a sociologist from the University of Chicago may be a high-credibility source to his students; to his colleagues, however, his credibility may be considerably less.

Because it is linked to perception, a speaker's credibility varies not only from one audience to another but from one point to another during the speech. Time, then, is a variable not only in two-person and small-group communication but in public communication, where the speaker is perceived in terms of his or her extrinsic, intrinsic, and ultimately total credibility.

The scales in Table 10.1 have been developed for measuring a listener's evaluation of any speaker. Scales numbered 1, 2, and 3 measure *authoritativeness*; 4, 5, and 6 measure *character*; and 7, 8, and 9 measure *dynamism*. The closer the rating to the left end of the scale, the higher the perceived credibility.

Extrinsic Credibility

Extrinsic credibility refers to *the credibility a source is thought to have prior to the time he or she delivers the message.* For example, if Jesse Jackson or Gloria Steinem gives a speech on your campus, his or her reputation will undoubtedly influence your evaluation of that speech. Similarly, if the top student in your class gives a speech, your previous impression of him or her affects your attitude toward the message.

Burke (1992) describes his impression of the dynamic appearance of Senator Ted Kennedy upon first seeing him:

> I heard a murmur run through the gathering. Heads turned, my own included, to witness the entrance of Senator Edward Moore Kennedy. He stood a striking six feet two inches tall, a broad-shouldered man with a mop of brown hair, stylishly long. The jaw jutted out like a granite ledge pointed unmistakenly toward the future.
>
> Here before my very eyes, was the unquestioned heir to the Kennedy throne. . . . He exuded charisma, just as his brothers had, and the air in the church seemed to crackle with his presence. (p. 1)

TABLE 10.1

Speaker's Name							
1. Competent	___	___	___	___	___	___	___	Incompetent
2. Experienced	___	___	___	___	___	___	___	Inexperienced
3. Important	___	___	___	___	___	___	___	Unimportant
4. Honest	___	___	___	___	___	___	___	Dishonest
5. Open-minded	___	___	___	___	___	___	___	Closed-minded
6. Kind	___	___	___	___	___	___	___	Cruel
7. Active	___	___	___	___	___	___	___	Passive
8. Fast	___	___	___	___	___	___	___	Slow
9. Emotional	___	___	___	___	___	___	___	Calm

Source: From Lawrence B. Rosenfeld, *Analyzing Human Communication*, 2d ed. (Dubuque, IA: Kendal/Hunt, 1983).

There has been ample research on the influence of extrinsic credibility. The typical study involves the delivery of the same speech (sometimes tape-recorded for greater consistency) to several audiences but with the speaker introduced differently to each. For example, a taped speech (supposedly for a radio program) favoring lenient treatment of juvenile delinquents was presented to three separate groups of high school students, but the speaker was identified to one group as a juvenile court judge, to the second as a neutral member of the studio audience, and to the third as an audience member who had a criminal record and had been a juvenile delinquent himself. As might be expected, the speech that was supposedly delivered by the judge, a high-credibility source, was considered much fairer than the speech delivered by the ex-convict. The judge's speech also resulted in more attitude change than the ex-convict's (Kelman and Hovland, 1953).

A number of studies confirm that speakers with high credibility tend to have more influence on an audience's attitudes than do those with low credibility. One summary of the literature qualifies this statement with the observation that "the perceived-competence aspect adds to persuasive impact more than the trustworthiness aspect does. By competence we mean the perceived expertness, status, intelligence, etc., of the attributed source; by trustworthiness, we refer to his perceived disinterestedness, objectivity, and lack of persuasive intent" (McGuire, in Lindzey and Aronson, 1969, p. 187). But the credibility of the speaker does not seem to have a significant effect on the level of the audience's comprehension (Petrie, 1963). Credibility appears to be a more important consideration when we are persuading an audience than when we are informing them.

Intrinsic Credibility

Extrinsic credibility is only one aspect of credibility. Your total credibility as a speaker consists of how you are perceived by the audience before your speech plus the impressions you make while delivering it. In other words, a speaker comes into a speaking situation with some level of credibility and adds to or detracts from it by what is said. **Intrinsic credibility** is the name often given to this *image that a speaker creates as a direct result of his or her speech.*

Former President Ronald Reagan was referred to as the "Great Communicator." He gave many eloquent speeches, such as when he reassured the country as well as the families of the astronauts who had died in the *Challenger* explosion in January 1986. He said that they had "'slipped the surly bonds of earth' to 'touch the face of God.'" (Reagan, Ronald, 1989, p. 400).

Each of us may be accomplished in some way or make certain claims about our good character or even be a poised and dynamic speaker. By and large, however, we are not perceived as high-credibility sources. Our major opportunities for increasing our credibility come during the actual presentation of our speech.

One way in which you may increase your intrinsic credibility as a speaker is by *establishing a common ground* between you and your audience. This rhetorical technique has been successfully used for centuries. For example, Daniel J. Boorstin, a well-known historian, opened a speech to an audience of Associated Press managing editors with these remarks:

> Gentlemen, it's a great pleasure and privilege to be allowed to take part in your meeting. It is especially a pleasure to come and have such a flattering introduction, the most flattering part of which was to be called a person who wrote like a newspaperman.
>
> The historians, you know, sometimes try to return the compliment by saying that the best newspapermen write like historians but I'm not sure how many of the people present would consider that a compliment.
>
> This afternoon I would like to talk briefly about the problems we share, we historians and newspapermen, and that we all share as Americans. (Boorstin, in Linkugel et al., 1969, p. 204)

Boorstin attempted to show his listeners that he was sympathetic to their point of view and that he and they shared certain things—notably, that they were writers, that they had some of the same problems, and that they were Americans. As you may recall from Chapter 6, balance theory predicts that similarities tend to increase liking and that in general we tend to like those who agree with us on a substantial proportion of salient issues. Thus it is quite possible that a speaker's intrinsic credibility will increase if he or she can convince the audience that a common ground exists between them.

Another influence on the character dimension of credibility is **humor.** Many speakers use humor as a means of ingratiating themselves with the audience. Bill Russell, former player-coach of the Boston Celtics, applied this approach to advantage in an address to members of a small college. He would *like* to say, he remarked, that it was a rare privilege to be in their town and he would like to say that this stop was one of the highlights of his travels. Then Russell paused. The laughter of the audience indicated that they knew this was not true. Russell then went on to say that he *could* honestly say that he was very happy to have the chance to meet and speak with the people in the audience.

Research on the use of humor in speeches indicates that though it may not increase the listeners' understanding or change their attitude toward the speaker's topic, it affects their perception of the person's character. In general, they like a speaker more when he or she uses humor (Gruner, 1970).

In a recent summary of research, Gruner (1985) offers six suggestions for the use of humor in public communication:

1. "A modicum of apt, relevant humor in informative discourse will probably produce a more favorable audience reaction toward the speaker" (p. 142). The effect is on ratings of "character" and not the other dimensions of credibility.

2. "Humor that is self-disparaging may further enhance speaker image" (p. 142). The self-disparaging remarks, however, need to be indirect, more

"witty" than of low humor, and "based on clever word-play, *not* direct exaggeration of one's own personal defects" (p. 143).

3. "Apt, relevant humor in a speech can enhance interest in that speech; this generalization must be qualified and limited, however" (p. 143). The limitation is this: This applies only when other factors that might raise interest (e.g., suspense or an animated delivery) are not present.

4. "Apt, relevant humor seems not to influence the effectiveness of persuasive speeches either negatively or positively" (p. 144).

5. "Humor may or may not make a speech more memorable" (p. 144). There is some mixed evidence, but it seems that humor helps recall a little, especially in the long run (delayed recall).

6. "The use of satire as a persuasive device may have unpredictable results" (p. 144). The problem is that sometimes audience members do not perceive the serious thesis of the satire.

Other variables that have been found to increase a speaker's credibility are effective delivery, apparent sincerity, the use of relevant evidence, and a clear pattern of organization. We shall have more to say about some of these variables further along in this chapter.

Delivery

Another significant influence on how we judge the speaker is delivery. For years two guidelines for effective delivery have been naturalness and poise. A speaker's delivery should not draw attention from the content of the message—as it might, for example, if it were overly dramatic or reflected lack of confidence. Hamlet's advice to a group of actors was similar:

> Speak the speech, I pray you, as I pronounce it to you, trippingly on the tongue: but if you mouth it, as many of your players do, I had as lief the towncrier spoke my lines. Nor do not saw the air too much with your hand, thus; but use all gently: for in the very torrent, tempest, and, as I may say, the whirlwind of passion, you must acquire and beget a temperance that may give it smoothness. (Act 3, Scene 2)

Good delivery involves much more than mere fluency in speaking. It includes the effective use of many of the visual and vocal cues we discussed in Chapter 4: eye contact, hand gestures, posture, and general physical appearance as well as vocal quality, pitch, volume, and rate of speech.

Visual Cues

Direct eye contact with audience members is one of the most important nonverbal cues in public speaking. The speaker who spends too much time looking at note cards or staring at the floor or ceiling or the feet of various listeners fails to make use of an important advantage—the preference for direct eye contact (Cobin, 1962). As we observed in Chapter 4, many people feel that a person who continually averts his or her eyes while speaking is concealing something. Like members of dyads and small groups, members of audiences seem to find eye contact particularly rewarding.

A related aspect of delivery is facial expression. Since facial cues constitute the single most important source of nonverbal communication, audiences generally favor a speaker whose facial expression is somewhat animated and varied over a speaker whose delivery is deadpan or expressionless.

Bodily action can also add to or detract measurably from a speaker's impact on the audience. For example, a relaxed but alert posture helps to communicate poise. Lecterns may be helpful for holding note cards, but at times they seem to inhibit a speaker's gestures and movements. Moving about the room frequently adds variety and interest to a speech. The speaker may take a step forward to emphasize a point, or move from one spot to another in making a transition from one main point in the speech to another. This technique is called *moving on transition*. Of course, a speaker who constantly paces back and forth across the room soon calls attention to these movements and away from what is being said.

Another form of bodily action involves the use of gestures of the head, shoulders, arms, and hands. Burke (1992) describes the characteristics of Senator Ted Kennedy's public speaking style when he writes:

> The right hand jutting forward for emphasis, the speaking style, unfinished sentences punctuated by uhs and ahs, the quick grin, and the nearly perpetual motion. . . . (p. 56)

Vocal Cues

Vocal delivery in the public speaking situation is somewhat similar to that in less formal communication settings. As we saw in Chapter 4, vocal delivery includes four types of cues: (1) volume, (2) rate and fluency, (3) pitch, and (4) quality. Because the receiver is playing a less active role, however, the message sender's vocal delivery becomes more apparent. For example, deficiencies in vocal quality—breathiness, hypernasality, poor articulation, and so on—are likely to be particularly noticeable in public speaking (Malandro and Barker, 1982).

Demands for adequate volume in public speaking are obvious. The speaker must be able to project his or her voice so that it is heard by all the members of the audience.

Both fluency and rate of speech can also have considerable influence on an audience. How many times have you heard a speaker who uses a lot of "ahs," "uhs," and "ums"? This annoying habit, along with the needless repetition of such words and phrases as "like," "well," and "you know," falls into the category of nonfluencies. We have seen in Chapter 4 that nonfluent speakers tend to be irritating and boring to listen to because their rate of speech is slower. Moreover, the image they tend to project is one of passivity and hesitancy. Each of us is nonfluent at times, and this is normal. Research on fluent and nonfluent speakers shows, however, that fluency not only enhances image in the eyes of the audience but also produces more attitude change when the speaker's speech is persuasive (McCroskey and Mehrley, 1969).

The rate of speech can also be too fast. Some speakers talk rapidly to ease anxiety. However, the audience becomes very aware of the speaker's discomfort. Attention to one's breathing will tell the speaker if he or she is talking too fast.

The solution is to become conscious of one's breathing before the speech. Begin to inhale deeply and slowly. Fill the lungs to capacity and hold for a couple of seconds, then release the air slowly and completely. Continue the breathing exercise until normal breathing is under control. The breathing exercises promote inner stability and a sense of calm.

The pitch of the voice as well as the rate of speech can affect how well a speech is received. We observed in Chapter 4 that people expect a voice to be varied in pitch and, in fact, sometimes derive information about emotions from changes in pitch. Although pitch level does not affect the amount of information that can be understood, it will influence the receiver's attitude toward the sender and the content of the message (Eakins, 1969).

Modes of Delivery

Modes of delivery refers to the *amount of preparation and the type of presentation a speaker employs.* There are four modes of delivery commonly used in public communication; each serves a different purpose and has some strengths and weaknesses.

The first mode, **impromptu delivery,** describes the speech presented with little preparation. In essence, the speaker stands before the audience and thinks out loud. This style has one advantage: maximum spontaneity. It suffers, however, from the lack of advance planning. Less formal kinds of communication place a high premium on spontaneity, but public address usually requires a more formal style of delivery. Impromptu speeches are usually assigned to the speaker only a moment or two before the speech is to be delivered. The speech itself may last only a minute, but almost all the elements of a speech are there for analysis (content, organization, use of language, and so on). The inherent difficulties of impromptu speaking were suggested by Mark Twain when he remarked that "it usually takes more than three weeks to prepare a good impromptu speech."

The second and the most formal mode of delivery is **reading from manuscript.** In direct contrast to the impromptu speech, this type of delivery requires complete preparation. For broadcasters, politicians, and other people whose remarks are often quoted, this technique is a valuable one. It allows the speakers to be extremely precise in phrasing a message and to minimize the possibility that it will be misconstrued. The speech is delivered exactly as it has been prepared. For the average person, however, manuscript speaking requires an unnecessarily long preparation time. It has another limitation. It makes the speaker so reliant on reading from manuscript that he or she is unable to look up at the audience, except for very brief periods of time. Thus, the ability to adapt the message to audience feedback is drastically reduced.

Memorized speech is the third mode of delivery. Here the entire speech has been planned beforehand, written in manuscript, and then committed to memory. The speaker is therefore free to look at the audience instead of reading from notes or manuscript. Although memorized speech might sound like the most effective kind of delivery, it has two drawbacks. The first is the problem of robotlike delivery; many of the natural qualities of human communication—vocal inflection, facial expression, gesture, and so on—may be lost. Second, human memory being what it is, the speaker runs the risk of forgetting part of the message. If this happens to you and you have to sit down before you have finished, you are unlikely to forget the experience for a long time.

The fourth mode of delivery is **extemporaneous speaking.** Extemporaneous delivery combines the advantages of careful speech outlining and planning with the spontaneity of impromptu speaking. The person who uses this style speaks from minimal notes (preferably on small cards).

Dickson (1987) recommends the following use of notes: Reduce the speech to a "key-word" outline. For easy visibility:

Doublespace.

Capitalize trigger words or key words.

Use lots of white space between phrases to avoid confusion.

Number pages. (p. 71)

Generally, the speaker rehearses aloud until he or she becomes familiar enough with the speech content. The speech may be worded slightly differently each time it is rehearsed, and the precise wording is sometimes chosen only when the speech is actually delivered. Extemporaneous speaking is a style that allows the speaker to be well prepared and yet flexible enough to respond to audience feedback. For these reasons it seems well suited to the public speaking situations that most of us will encounter. We emphasize, however, that different speaking situations unquestionably require different modes of delivery.

We can be more specific about the role of delivery as a variable in public speaking. When a speaker's message is weak (that is, when he or she uses no evidence to support assertions), good delivery has no significant effect on attitude change. But when good delivery is used in combination with a strong (that is, well-documented) message, a speaker elicits significantly greater attitude change in the audience than one who delivers the same message but has poor delivery (McCroskey and Arnold, cited in McCroskey, 1968, p. 207). This finding is important because it confirms that the various aspects of speech making are interrelated. Delivery alone cannot produce attitude change. Nevertheless, poor delivery distracts from an otherwise effective message, whereas good delivery allows listeners to concentrate on the quality of the message, giving it optimum impact.

The Sleeper Effect

Despite its impact on an audience's receptivity, credibility does not appear to have a sustained influence on persuasion. Earlier we mentioned a study in which a speech favoring a lenient attitude toward juvenile delinquency produced maximum attitude change when presented by a high-credibility source. This influence was greatest immediately after the speech was delivered. Differences resulting from the speaker's credibility tended to diminish over time so that the attitude change produced by the high-credibility source decreased and the message from the low-credibility source gained ground, producing more attitude change. This trend is sometimes called **the sleeper effect.**

The sleeper effect seems to result from the listener's tendency to dissociate the source and the message—presumably because he forgets who the source is. In experiments during which the listener was reminded of the source of the message, the high-credibility source regained his significantly greater influence on attitude change over the low-credibility source (Pratkanis et al., 1988). Apparently the sleeper effect can be overcome if audience members are reminded of the source of the message. President Bush often used this tactic in press conferences when he answered questions by referring to speeches he made in the past.

We have tried to isolate two important aspects of public communication that relate primarily to the speaker: source credibility and delivery. Although over time the influence of the source of the message seems to decline and the impact of the message itself gains ground, the ultimate effectiveness of any speech is determined by its appropriateness to the particular audience. So before considering how best to construct the message, let us turn our attention to the audience.

THE AUDIENCE

If delivering a speech is a new experience for you, the suggestion that you analyze your audience beforehand, or even as you are speaking, may come as something of a shock. When you stand before this group of people, you may view them only as the proverbial sea of faces. Yet some common characteristics have brought them together in the first place. Are they predominantly parents, college students, liberals, Roman Catholics, business people, educators, or anthropologists? Just about any group of listeners who gather in one place will do so for some of the same reasons. By establishing these reasons, you may find a strategy that allows you to appeal to the majority of audience members.

Audience Analysis

According to Clevenger (1966) there are at least two traditional methods by which the speaker may determine how best to adapt a message to a given audience: demographic analysis and purpose-oriented analysis.

Demographic Analysis

In **demographic audience analysis** *the speaker first considers some general characteristics of the audience members*—age, sex, geographic background, occupation, socioeconomic level, education, religion, and so on. These known characteristics suggest inferences about the audience's beliefs, attitudes, and values. Such inferences are then used to gear the message to what seems to be the audience's level and interests. This does not mean that as a speaker you change the thrust of your argument, but rather that you adapt its presentation for maximum impact.

Let us consider for a moment the value to the speaker of knowing before-hand certain relevant data about the members of the audience. Imagine that you are to give a talk on the causes of inflation. It might be extremely valuable to know something about the occupations of audience members. For example, you would expect the values and viewpoints of members of a labor union to be different from those of a group of business executives. In adapting your speech to these two audiences, you would probably choose a less formal language style for the union members than for the executives. You might say that large wage increases "fan the flames of inflation" rather than "perpetuate the inflationary cycle." With the executives you might choose a statistical approach showing percentage inflationary increases; with the union audience, you might talk about the cost of an average market basket from one year to the next.

Having a knowledge of demographic variables also makes it easier for the speaker to establish some *common ground* with audience members. This is often accomplished with an anecdote or a joke or a remark by the speaker indicating some sort of identification with the audience. It is common practice, for example, for a politician who comes from a small town to make some remark about his or her own upbringing when addressing a small-town audience. In his acceptance speech to the Democratic National Convention, former President Jimmy Carter made an appeal to delegates from many different regions of the United States when he remarked: "Now, our party was built out of a sweatshop on the old Lower East Side, the dark mills of New Hampshire, the blazing hearths of Illinois, the coal mines of Pennsylvania, the hardscrabble farmbelt, the Southern coastal plains and the unlimited frontiers of America" (*The New York Times,* July 16, 1976, p. A-10).

As we shall illustrate in discussing message variables, in all public communication the construction of a message is inherently linked to the speaker's analysis of the audience. Consider, for example, *selecting materials of support.* Suppose a speaker knows that she is a low-credibility source for the audience.

She may wish to use more evidence. Initially, at least, the use of good evidence enhances credibility. Also, the kind of evidence the speaker uses will be different for different audiences. For an audience of Hispanics being urged to take adult education courses in English, quotations from Hispanics who have moved out of the barrios and secured high-status jobs because of their bilingual skills will probably be more persuasive than quotations from English teachers who lack any knowledge of Spanish.

The speaker's *choice of language* is another variable that ideally should be influenced by a knowledge of audience characteristics. Given this audience, will the terminology be familiar? Will the connotations of the words as used by the speaker be understood by the entire group? Are the metaphors and analogies appropriate for this audience? These are some of the many considerations for any speaker who has some prior knowledge about the demographic makeup of the audience.

There are numerous other ways in which demographic information about audience members may be used to one's advantage. Suppose, for example, that you plan to deliver a persuasive speech on the prevention of hijacking and that you have information about the *level of education of audience members*; virtually all of them will be college graduates and half will have advanced degrees. In this instance it would be wise to take into account the finding that intelligent or better-educated audiences respond more readily to two-sided rather than one-sided appeals.

Former President Ronald Reagan used the National Republican Convention to deliver this farewell speech to the American people as well as to appeal to the television audience to vote Republican:

> Before we came to Washington, Americans had just suffered the two worst back-to-back years of inflation in 60 years. Those are the facts. And as John Adams said: "Facts are stubborn things."
>
> Interest rates had jumped to over 21 percent—the highest in 120 years—more than doubling the average monthly mortgage payments for working families—our families. When they sat around the kitchen table, it was not to plan summer vacations, it was to plan economic survival.
>
> Facts are stubborn things.
>
> Industrial production was down, and productivity was down for 2 consecutive years.
>
> The average weekly wage plunged 9 percent. The median family income fell 5½ percent.
>
> Facts are stubborn things.
>
> Our friends on the other side had actually passed the single highest tax bill in the 200-year history of the United States. Auto loans, because of their policies, went up to 17 percent—so our great factories began shutting down. Fuel costs jumped through the atmosphere—more than doubling. Then people waited in gas lines as well as unemployment lines.
>
> Facts are stubborn things. (1989, p. 11)

It is important to emphasize that gathering demographic information is only the first step in audience analysis. Very often, the speaker goes on to make *inferences about the beliefs, attitudes, and values of the audience.* Often the speaker is trying to determine in advance what position audience members are likely to have about a given issue before public communication actually takes place. This might well help him or her to decide how much attitude change to attempt in the speech. Once you determine what position audience members are likely to take on a given issue, it is probably wise to construct a persuasive appeal that is within their latitude of acceptance. Otherwise, the appeal will be too discrepant with initial attitudes and will create a "boomerang effect" (see "How Much Change to Attempt," below). The usefulness of the assimilation-contrast theory will depend on how well the speaker analyzes the audience. For example, given information about the average age of audience members, you might try to anticipate how discrepant your position on a particular issue would be from that of your audience. It is generally believed, for instance, that younger audiences tend to be more receptive to change and older audiences more conservative. Therefore, a speech favoring decriminalization of marijuana would probably be seen by a college-age audience as moderate but by their parents or grandparents as radical.

In certain audiences there will be more variability concerning important demographic characteristics. Here the speaker might find it necessary to *appeal to a target audience* within the larger audience, especially if the speaker's aim is persuasion and it is known that there will be a distinct group of opinion leaders within the audience.

Purpose-Oriented Analysis

A second mode of adapting the message to the audience is **purpose-oriented audience analysis.** Instead of analyzing audience characteristics, *the speaker begins by asking himself or herself what information about the audience is most important for the speaker's purposes.* If you are an economist giving an informative speech about devaluation of currencies, you will want to know how much of an economics background the average listener has. Sometimes this information is easy to establish; sometimes you will have to make inferences. In any case, you begin with a general idea of audience level and constantly refer back to it as you prepare your speech. Can you assume that the listener will know what the gold standard is, or will you have to explain the concept in some detail? Will a quote from John Kenneth Galbraith be recognized as evidence from a high-credibility source? Will the audience be familiar with the basic concepts of statistics or probability theory? In contrast to demographic analysis, in which you gather information about the audience before preparing your speech, purpose-oriented analysis will be an ongoing part of your message preparation.

Both these approaches are concerned with audience variability, with adapting a message to a specific audience. One interesting question we might ask in this connection is, are audiences equally persuasible?

Listener Persuasibility

Persuasibility, as the term implies, refers to *a listener's susceptibility to persuasion.* A question that researchers and public speakers have often raised is whether there is a difference between men's and women's openness to persuasion.

Research indicates that women are often more readily swayed than men (Tuthill and Forsyth, 1982). This pattern was not always borne out in studies of children, however, which suggested that willingness to be persuaded might be learned as part of the female sex role. An interesting study of Montgomery and Burgoon (1977) found that **psychological sex** is a better predictor of sex differences in persuasibility than anatomical sex. Feminine females are more persuasible than masculine males, whereas androgynous males and females hardly differ.

As the female sex role in our society continues to undergo redefinition, differences in persuasibility will be less and less predictable. In fact, Rosenfeld and Christie (1974) concluded that it has become "futile to attempt to conclude that one sex is more persuasible than another" (p. 23).

A second question that has been the object of much research concerns the correlation between personality and persuasibility. Is it true, for example, that some people are resistant to changing their minds in all situations whereas others go along with almost everything one says? Early research on this question looked for "those attitudes or personality factors leading to low or high resistance to *a wide variety of persuasive communication on many diverse topics.*" Some people were more persuasible than others, regardless of the subject of the persuasive appeal. Furthermore, these people tended to be more easily persuaded in either direction on a given topic—to be more in favor of, or more opposed to, cancer research, for example (Janis and Field, in Hovland and Janis, 1959).

In another study the same research team tried to identify the personality characteristics linked to persuasibility. It is generally agreed that persuasible people tend to have low self-esteem, a perception that presumably extends to their opinions: Such people value the opinions of others more than their own. By contrast, the person who resists persuasion is described as "likely to be little affected by external standards in other kinds of situations, to have a mature and strong self-image, to value subjective feeling and have a relatively rich inner life, to examine himself and his role in life to an extent that may include marked self-criticism, and to be independent without being rebellious" (Linton and Graham, in Hovland and Janis, 1959, p. 96).

Although there is little the speaker can do to control for such variables as listener persuasibility, it is still of interest to know that some personality differences affect persuasibility. This information might be especially useful in demographic audience analysis. For example, before an all-male audience, a female speaker might attempt a more thoroughgoing persuasive strategy than she would before an all-female audience that was already well disposed toward her argument.

Persuasion theory has a lot to offer us in the way of advice on how best to go about the process of persuading others. The most famous persuasion theory is known as *Monroe's motivated sequence*. It has five steps:

1. *Attention.* First, you gain the attention of your audience. You do this in your introduction. You can show the importance of your topic, make a startling statement, tell a dramatic story, pose a rhetorical question, arouse curiosity, or use visual aids.

2. *Need.* Next, you must show that a problem currently exists. State the need clearly and dramatize it with relevant supporting materials (i.e., definitions, examples, statistics, quotes, or analogies). This arouses their need for a solution.

3. *Satisfaction.* Next, you satisfy the need by providing a solution to the problem. Make sure your plan has enough specifics to show how it satisfies the need.

4. *Visualization.* Next, help the audience visualize the plan by showing its benefits. It is important to use vividness to show how the members of the audience will benefit from adopting your plan.

5. *Action.* Finally, specify what the audience members can do. Give them an address to write to, or a phone number to call, or a place to go. Then use a strong conclusion to stimulate them to act. For excellent examples of this technique, see the sample speeches at the end of this book. (see also Lucas, 1992)

THE MESSAGE

When we feel strongly enough about an issue to get up and speak in front of others, we sometimes confuse intensity with effectiveness. We may speak out passionately on a particular issue, but sometimes we fail to obtain the desired outcome—whether it be information gain, attitude change, or action. Noting this tendency among relatively inexperienced speakers, one public communication expert observed:

> Gone from . . . contemporary discourse are the familiar introduction, body and conclusions; the statement and partition of issues; internal summaries; topical, spatial, chronological, or any other particular kind of order. More typically today . . . college coeds begin to talk with rambling personal experiences, sometimes rather dramatic, and finish about where they started, with a liberal sprinkling of "you knows" in between. (Haiman, in Linkugel et al., 1969, p. 157)

In order to avoid the rambling pattern described above, experts recommend the traditional use of introduction, body, and conclusion to organize a speech.

The **introduction** provides the opportunity to establish a common ground, gain the audience's attention, establish the thesis of the speech, and relate the importance of the topic or speech. A preview of what's coming is also a good idea, as this orients the audience and aids in their listening. By the end of the introduction, audience members should be attentive, familiar with the speaker and with what is to come, and should *want* to hear the speech. The introduction "sets up" the audience for the speaker and his or her speech.

The **body** of the speech presents the information and/or arguments indicated in the introduction. This is the largest part of the speech, possibly as much as 80 percent, unless the audience is hostile, in which case the introduction might be very long. In general, the body of a speech should contain few points (remember from the listening chapter that audiences forget half of what they hear immediately after hearing it, and then lose another half within a few months). The fewer the number of points, the higher the probability the audience members will remember what is said.

The **conclusion** often gets the most attention since members know you are about to end. With this in mind, it comes as no surprise that the conclusion of the speech reviews what was said and finishes the speech with some memorable remarks. The message remembered, the "residual message," is tied significantly to the last words of the speech, so those last words must emphasize for the audience, in a memorable way, exactly what each member might best remember of the speech.

Notice the strong conclusion from General Douglas MacArthur's speech to the cadets at West Point. MacArthur was a national hero after the Korean War and was very old when he spoke. Think how you would feel if you were a cadet and were listening to this:

The shadows are lengthening for me. The twilight is here. My days of old have vanished—tone and tints. They have gone glimmering through the dreams of things that were. Their memory is one of wonderous beauty, watered by tears and coaxed and caressed by the smiles of yesterday. I listen, then, but with thirsty ear, for the witching melody of faint bugles blowing reveille, of far drums beating the long roll.

In my dreams I hear again the crash of guns, the rattle of musketry, the strange, mournful mutter of the battlefield. But in the evening of my memory, I come back to West Point. Always there echoes and re-echoes: duty, honor, country.

Today marks my final roll call with you. But I want you to know that when I cross the river, my last conscious thoughts will be of the corps, and the corps, and the corps.

I bid you farewell. (Safire, 1992, p. 78)

In this portion of the chapter we shall concentrate on ways of preparing and presenting messages that will ensure optimum effectiveness. For centuries students of public communication have discussed the subject of organizing speech material, the use of supporting materials, the speaker's choice of language, as well as several other options available to the speaker in choosing an appropriate strategy for persuasion. Only within the twentieth century, however, have experimental investigations allowed us to put some of these age-old notions to the test.

In studying **message variables,** or *alternative ways of presenting a message,* we shall review over thirty years of research. This period is one of the most fruitful in providing experimental clarification of some long-standing questions. We shall find, however, that some of the answers are more complex than we might have anticipated, that many substantive issues are still unresolved, and that there are some very important elements of speech preparation about which few research data exist. Many practical aspects of speech preparation are illustrated in the annotated speeches in the appendix.

Organization

According to many theorists, virtually all speeches consist of an introduction, a body, and a conclusion. At some point within the speech there may also be a direct statement—a thesis sentence—that crystallizes the speaker's central idea. This theme, whether stated directly or not, will be elaborated in the main and subordinate points of the speaker's presentation. How the speaker chooses to organize and elaborate on speech materials is an issue of some concern, particularly for those with little experience or training in public speaking.

No research points to a single pattern of organization as the most desirable. In assembling speech materials the speaker must find the pattern best suited to his or her particular message and to the particular audience to be addressed. (We have already discussed some aspects of the adaptation of speech materials to one's audience when we discussed audience analysis.) A speaker has many options in organizing materials. In the following pages we shall discuss five of the more popular patterns.

Topical Organization

Among the most popular ways of ordering speech material is a **topical organization.** Here, *the speaker moves from one topic to the next in a way that clearly demonstrates how they are related.* Usually the speaker first prepares an outline in which the main points of the speech are in the form of a traditional outline and in which some concepts are subordinated to others. Making an outline is usually a part of any speech preparation, regardless of its patterns of organization. The following topical outline was prepared by a student for a speech on the human nervous system:

I. The central nervous system consists of the brain and the spinal cord.
- A. The brain has three distinct regions, each with a special function:
  1. Forebrain
  2. Midbrain
  3. Hindbrain
- B. The spinal cord has two distinct functions:
  1. Sensory functions
  2. Motor functions
II. The peripheral nervous system connects the central nervous system to the rest of the body.
- A. Afferent nerves carry neurochemical impulses from the body to the brain
  1. Somatic nerves (from the extremities)
  2. Visceral nerves (from the abdomen and chest)
- B. Efferent nerves carry neurochemical impulses from the brain to the body
  1. Somatic nerves (to the extremities)
  2. Visceral nerves (to the abdomen and chest)

Chronological Organization

Instead of arranging material topically, the speaker might choose a **chronological organization,** which uses time as an organization mechanism. Using this pattern, it is possible *to move from a review of the past into a discussion of contemporary events, and,* if desirable, *conclude with a projection into the future.* Or one can start by *discussing a current situation and trace its origin backward in time.*

Numerous themes—not simply historical ones—lend themselves to a chronological pattern of organization. The speaker might be discussing capital punishment, birth control, foreign affairs, or pornography.

Spatial Organization

A third method of arrangement is **spatial organization.** This pattern uses space or geographical position as an organizing principle. For example, in a speech about our solar system, one student briefly described each planet, beginning with Mercury (the one closest to the sun) and moving in order away from the sun to the planet Pluto. The spatial pattern is more limited as a means of organization, but it is one that is sometimes necessary. It might be well suited, for example, to the discussion of such topics as trade routes, territoriality among animals, and the distribution of bilingual communities within the United States. Moreover, there are times when a speaker makes use of spatial organization in only part of a speech. An instructor using topical organization in a lecture on Russian military history might also use spatial organization to analyze the strategy used during a single battle.

Problem Solution

Another very popular pattern of organization is **problem solution.** We find it in speeches of every kind, particularly in affirmative speeches during debates and in speeches concentrated on persuasion. *The speaker describes what he or she believes to be an existing problem and then offers a plan that will alleviate or resolve it.* For example, in a speech about automation one speaker first introduced a three-part problem: (1) that automation resulted in loss of jobs; (2) that many of those who lost their jobs were not easily retrained for more highly skilled jobs; and (3) that some of those who were capable of taking on such jobs were unable to relocate. Having described this problem in some detail, she proposed a three-part solution: (1) a shorter workweek; (2) the development of new domestic industries; and (3) the creation of new foreign markets for these products.

Causal Organization

Like the problem-solution pattern, **causal organization** has two major divisions. *The speaker argues either from cause to effect or from effect to cause.* For example, a speaker might describe a condition such as alcoholism and the deteriorating effects it has on the human body and then go on to discuss its underlying causes. In this case, the sequence is from effect back to cause. Under other circumstances, the causes of alcoholism (unhappiness, personal failures, and so on) might be discussed first, with the speaker then going on to discuss its effects.

We have described five ways of organizing speech materials; many others are possible. To date, however, there are no acceptable data as to which pattern is most effective. This is a decision that the speaker must make on an individual basis.

Materials of Support

After deciding on the pattern of arrangement that best suits the topic, the speaker is ready to gather various **materials of support**—*forms of evidence* that develop or strengthen each of the points to be made. These materials include examples, statistics, quotations, and analogies.

As aids in gathering supporting materials, the speaker may consult some of the standard reference works, such as *Reader's Guide to Periodical Literature, Education Index, Biography Index,* the *World Almanac,* any set of encyclopedias, *Who's Who, Psychological Abstracts,* and the *Congressional Record.* All these sources will be available in the reference section of most libraries. In most cases, such reference works will lead the speaker to the books, magazines, and journals that will be most helpful.

Examples

The use of examples is so much a part of other, less formal modes of communication that we tend to be unaware that it is frequently a method of support in speech making. By adding examples to a discussion, the speaker can make his or her presentation more concrete. For instance, in a speech given in 1975, Representative Yvonne Burke of California first made a general statement about the acceptance of women in many new fields, including mass communication and politics. She went on to elaborate:

> For example, when the national TV networks aired their usual election night extravaganzas last November, for the first time NBC and CBS had special commentators assigned to report exclusively throughout the evening on the way women were faring at the polls. Leslie Stahl reported for CBS and Barbara Walters for NBC. (Burke, in Braden, 1975, p. 144)

Sometimes the vivid detail available in an example gives the speaker a chance to make a presentation more dramatic. There is, for instance, a world of difference between discussing the effects of an earthquake in terms of damage costs and describing the experience of a single family whose home has been destroyed.

When examples were well chosen and representative of what they are intended to illustrate, they buttress the various points the speaker is trying to develop. How much a receiver can be led to infer for a given example depends upon his or her critical listening skills.

Statistics

Sometimes a speaker can summarize much numerical data through the use of statistics and at the same time increase his or her authoritativeness with reference to the subject being discussed. When Lee Iacocca spoke to the National Association of Manufacturers, he used statistics to dramatize the need for educational success. He said:

> We're turning out high school graduates who will have a hard time even *understanding* the problems, let alone tackling them. Somebody did a study (oh, hell, we're always doing studies). Seventy-five percent of our high school students don't know what *inflation* is . . . 66 percent don't know what *profits* are . . . and 55 percent don't have a clue as to what a government *budget deficit* is. (So the size has no meaning to them.)
>
>   Hell, 60,000 of our graduates last year could barely read their diplomas. (I couldn't read *mine* either, but it was in *Latin*. Theirs were in *English*.) (1989, p. 456)

In addition to clarifying and developing a point, statistics can sometimes present a revealing overview of the topic under consideration. Thus in one talk on job satisfaction, the speaker quoted several dissatisfied workers who had been interviewed concerning their jobs. But then he went on to show his audience a bar graph based upon Gallup polls. The bar graph illustrated that the negative reactions were not at all representative of the work force.

In certain settings—mass and organizational communication, for example—it is common practice for a speaker to use such a visual presentation of statistics. Another popular visual presentation of statistics is the line chart. Statistics may be represented in several other graphic ways, but of course, they are most frequently introduced directly into the body of the speech. In general, statistics seem most appropriate when the speaker can make a particular point more clearly and concisely with them than with elaborate description.

Quotations

The most obvious use of quotation within a speech is for the dramatic, sometimes eloquent qualities that can be conveyed to the audience. The speeches of Margaret Thatcher, Martin Luther King, Jr., John Kennedy, and other public figures are constantly being tapped for their power and command of language. Many phrases and sentences of their speeches have entered the language. Paraphrase would not seem to do them justice. For example, it would be difficult and self-defeating to paraphrase John Kennedy's famous

> Ask not what your country can do for you. Ask what you can do for your country.

Even speakers known for their eloquence and command of language make use of quotation for dramatic effect, particularly in the opening or conclusion of a talk. For example, in "I Have a Dream," a speech that is exemplary for its eloquence and power, Martin Luther King, Jr., concluded by quoting the words of a spiritual:

> When we allow freedom to ring, when we let it ring from every village and every hamlet, from every state and every city, we will be able to speed up that day when all of God's children, black men and white men, Jews and Gentiles, Protestants and Catholics, will be able to join hands and sing in the words of the Old Negro spiritual, "Free at last! Free at last! Thank God almighty, we are free at last!" (King, in Linkugel et al., 1969, p. 294)

Of course, quotations are cited for many reasons other than eloquence. If the quoted source has knowledge or experience greater than that of the speaker, the quotation may be used to add validity to the speaker's argument and, indirectly, to enhance credibility. In our discussions of social influence and conformity (see Chapters 6 and 9), we have seen that attitudes and beliefs become more acceptable to us if we think they have been accepted by others— especially if those others are perceived as being of higher status. It is one thing for a speaker to assert that the government's fiscal policies have failed. It is quite another, however, to quote a Harvard economics professor who says exactly the same thing. To most audiences the expert's opinion is much more credible.

There are numerous other examples. In arguing about the effects of alcohol on the human body, a speaker might support his or her position with quotations from medical authorities. Lawyers in court frequently call on or cite an expert witness to establish the validity of their cases: "Ladies and gentlemen of the jury, the coroner's report showed that the cause of death was a bullet wound indicating the angle of the bullet was downward. We have established that my client is twelve inches *shorter* than the deceased and could not have fired the gun from such an angle. Therefore, my client could not have committed the murder."

Analogies

A speaker who draws an **analogy** makes a *comparison between two things or situations on the basis of their partial similarities.* As a method of support, an analogy can function in several different ways.

First of all, an analogy may be used for clarification. For example, one speaker was discussing the effect of a college degree on a person's earning power throughout his or her career. She compared the college graduate to a stone flung by a slingshot (education). For a short time, she explained, the college student's earning power is impeded, but the college graduate catches up and then shoots past the average wage earner who holds no degree.

An analogy may also be used to dramatize a point. Thus a speaker might compare dumping industrial wastes into the environment to adding a spoonful of dirt to each of our meals. Or he or she might use an analogy to make a point seem less significant. The speaker might argue, for example, that the environment is so vast that pollutants have no more effect than would adding a spoonful of dirt to an ocean.

On many occasions an analogy is the most concise way to get a complex idea or point across. Often the analogy is an extended comparison, as in the following speech. When the *Challenger* astronauts were killed, then President Reagan gave one of his best speeches in which he used an analogy. He said,

> There's a coincidence today. On this day 390 years ago the great explorer Sir Frances Drake died aboard ship off the coast of Panama. In his lifetime the great frontiers were the oceans. And a historian later said, "He lived by the sea, died on it, and was buried in it." Today we can say of the Challenger Crew: Their dedication was, like Drake's, complete.
>
> The crew of the space shuttle Challenger honored us by the manner in which they lived their lives. We shall never forget them, nor the last time we saw them—this morning, as they prepared for their journey, and waved good-bye, and "slipped the surly bonds of earth" to "touch the face of God." (Noonan, 1990, p. 257)

In this case, analogy is used. That is a frequent practice in public speaking, one that was explored more fully when we discussed critical listening.

During the course of a speech a speaker sometimes makes use of many kinds of supporting materials. For example, in arguing that United States foreign aid policy was not meeting its objectives, one student gave *examples* of specific countries that had worsening relations with the United States even though they were receiving a substantial amount of foreign aid. He used *statistics* to show the increasing amount of aid to various countries over the year and the simultaneous rise of communism in some of those countries. He also gave *quotations* from experts on foreign relations who argued that our foreign aid policy was ineffective. Finally, he drew an *analogy* between the United States' giving foreign aid and a person playing the stock market: "When an investment does not pay off," he said, "it is wise to stop investing in a losing cause and reinvest in another, more profitable venture."

The Effectiveness of Evidence

Despite the widespread use of materials of support in all kinds of public communication, there is much to be learned about the effects of evidence in persuasive communication. McCroskey's (1969) summary of experimental research gives us several generalizations about evidence as a message variable. First, a source perceived by the audience as having low or moderate credibility can increase his or her credibility by using good evidence and can also increase the amount of *immediate* attitude change in the audience. (On the other hand, a source who is initially perceived as having high credibility has little to gain from use of evidence in terms of immediate change.) Second, to have an effect on immediate attitude change or on perceived source credibility, the speaker's evidence must be new to members of the audience. And third, using good evidence seems to have *long-term* effects on attitude change whether the speaker was initially perceived as having low, moderate, or high credibility (this is the case regardless of the quality of his or her delivery). McCroskey points out the need for further, more imaginative research on how evidence functions within a persuasive argument. Among the research questions he suggests are (1) which types of evidence (statistics, quotations, and so on) have the greatest effect on attitude change and (2) whether the use of evidence to persuade functions differently in different cultures.

Visual Aids

Without question, visual aids make presentations more vivid and interesting. Visual aids include objects and models, demonstrations, illustrations (i.e., artwork, photos, tables, charts, handouts), as well as audiovisuals (i.e., audiotape, videotape, film, and slide/tape combinations). With the increasing sophistication and availability of computers, presentations are becoming more and more dramatic with computer-generated graphics. Figures 10.1 through 10.3 give a few examples.

The effective use of visual aids includes the following considerations:

1. Prepare the aids well in advance and get used to using them.

2. Keep all aids *simple* (based on the audience analysis, for example, what is "simple" for IBM employees may be difficult for sixth-grade students).

Visual aids need to be vivid and clear to help reinforce the points being made.

3. Be sure the aids can be seen, heard, and so on.

4. When using aids that require special equipment, such as videorecorders, overhead projectors, slide projectors, film projectors, and screens, be sure the equipment is *available, delivered* on time and to the right place, that it *works,* and that *you know how to work it.*

5. Be sure the aids suit the situation with respect to the size of the room and its capabilities (e.g., a room with an echo is problematic, as is a room without the capacity to dim the lights), and audience expectations.

6. Be sure the aid enhances the speech or is an integral part of the speech.

7. Talk to your audience and *not* the visual aid.

The important message here is that a visual aid is *audience and situation specific.* This makes it clear why an audience analysis is necessary.

Language

From the beginning of this book we have stressed the difficulties inherent in trying to create a meaning in the mind of another human being. In two-person and small-group communication, for example, we are concerned that the connotations of the words used be similar for all the people participating in a given transaction. In broader terms, we are concerned with the use of shared, rather than private, meaning. These concerns are multiplied many times over in public communication, where a message is likely to be long and

FIGURE 10.1   Computer Graphics

complex, feedback between sender and receiver is apt to be quite limited, and the number of receivers increases sharply. In the following pages we shall explore some questions of style—some ways in which the clarity, appeal, and persuasiveness of a message are affected by the speaker's use of language.

Vividness

According to Collins and associates (1988) *vividness,* in the context of communication, means concrete and colorful language (p. 1). Compare, for example, the vagueness of "A period of unfavorable weather set in" with the more pointed "It rained every day of a week."

Vigorous writing and speaking are often grounded in specifics. Thus the various methods of support are important not only from a logical but from a stylistic point of view. Sometimes a speaker must discuss a subject that is relatively abstract—for example, the responsibilities of a free press or the three-part division of government—but the presentation becomes more vig-

FIGURE 10.2   **Computer Graphics**

GRAPHICS IMPROVE COMMUNICATION

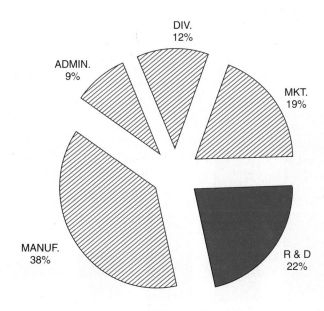

REVENUE DISTRIBUTION

orous, more capable of sustaining audience attention, if it is also somewhat concrete.

Senator George Graham Vest (Missouri) spoke eloquently about even so humble a subject as his dog. Notice how beautifully he paints a verbal picture:

> One absolutely unselfish friend that man can have in this selfish world, the one that never deserts him, the one that never proves ungrateful or treacherous is his dog. . . . He will kiss the hand that has no food to offer: he will lick the wounds and sores that come in encounter with the roughness of the world. . . .
>
> If fortune drives the master forth an outcast in the world, friendless and homeless, the faithful dog asks no higher privilege than that of accompanying him, to guard him against danger, to fight against his enemies. And when the last scene of all comes, and death takes his master in its embrace and his body is laid away in the cold ground, no matter if all other friends pursue their way, there by the graveside will the noble dog be found. His head between his paws, his eyes sad, but open in alert watchfulness, faithful and true even in death. (Safire, 1992, p. 164–165)

FIGURE 10.3   Computer Graphics

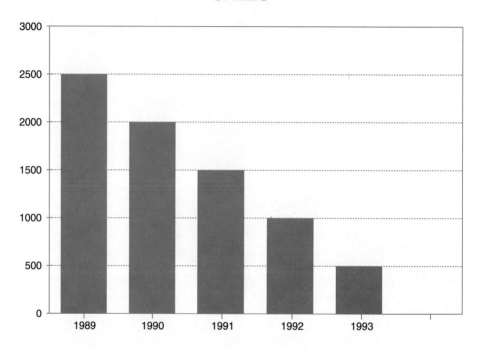

SALES

Metaphor

Since classical times writers have argued that the use of metaphor enhances credibility—presumably by reflecting the speaker's intelligence as well as by entertaining and pleasing the audience. In fact, Aristotle described a command of metaphor as "the mark of genius." **Metaphor** has been defined as "*language that implies a relationship, of which similarity is a significant feature, between two things and so changes our apprehension of either or both*" (Deutsch, 1957, p. 73; italics added). Metaphors differ from analogies, which we have already discussed; in an analogy the comparison is partial ("Education is *like* a slingshot" and "Dumping industrial wastes into the environment is *like* adding a spoonful of dirt to each of your meals"), whereas in a metaphor two different things are said to be equivalent ("Education *is* a slingshot").

President George Bush, in his inaugural speech, used colorful language when he said,

> Some see leadership as high drama and the sound of trumpets call-ing; and sometimes it is that. But I see history as a book with many pages. . . .
> The breeze blows, a page turns, the story unfolds—a small and stately story of unity, diversity, and generosity, shared and written together. (Noonan, 1990, p. 337)

Theorists concerned with persuasion have long wondered whether there is any significant difference between a message that is literal and straightforward in its arguments and one that makes use of metaphor. Suppose, for example, that a speaker argues against government aid to needy students. Would she be better off saying "In education governmental help is not compatible with our national goals," or would the listeners be more inclined to agree with the argument if the speaker used a bold metaphor such as "Governmental help is the kiss of death"?

Before we can make a definitive statement about the relationship between attitude change and the widespread use of metaphoric language, researchers will have to explore other kinds and uses of metaphor.

Intensity

Although metaphor is sometimes considered an aspect of intensity, message intensity is also reflected in a speaker's choice of high- and low-intensity words. In Table 10.2 we see a comparison of high- and low-intensity modifiers and verbs used in a study by McEwen and Greenberg (1970). Their research, which is a comparison of high- and low-intensity messages on the same subject, indicates that audiences regard more highly intense messages as clearer and also more logical. In fact, audiences regard the sources of those messages as more trustworthy, dynamic, and competent. The researchers suggest that high-intensity messages may be more persuasive because they provide "a greater impetus to adopt the message-advocated position" (p. 341). According to an earlier study, however, language that is highly intense or emotional has a boomerang effect if the audience's initial attitude is discrepant with that of the speaker (Bowers, 1963). For example, when speaking in favor of the Equal Rights Amendment, a radical feminist would be less likely to persuade a group of women initially opposed to the bill if her language was highly emotional than she would if she used words of lesser intensity.

TABLE 10.2

High- and Low-Intensity Words		
	High Intensity	**Low Intensity**
Modifiers	positively	perhaps
	greatly	possibly
	most	some
	definitely	slightly
	extremely	somewhat
Verbs	be	seems to be
	causes	may cause
	must	could

In his speech to a national educator's group, Benjamin Alexander (1989) used moderately intense language, as you can see:

> When Dr. Nyangoni called and asked me to speak on the topic, "Reflections on Education and Our Society," she stated, "you will be addressing the largest professional educational association in the world."
>
> Once upon a time . . . I like that expression—so let me say it again. Once upon a time, we passed out homework in our schools . . . and not condoms, and it was not "Teacher Training and Driver Education." It was "Teacher Education and Driver Training." We trained our drivers but we educated our teacher.
>
> We did not have courses like "Physics without mathematics," "Chemistry made easy," and "Mathematics without fractions." Yes, once upon a time—we did not coddle students by passing them when they should have been held back. (p. 563)

McCroskey proposes that language that is highly intense will magnify "the perceived discrepancy of a communicator's message." He goes on to say, "Increasing perceived discrepancy tends to enhance the effectiveness of an initially high-credibility source but reduce even further the effectiveness of an initially low-credibility source" (McCroskey, 1978, p. 203). In other words, a dynamic, emotional presentation by a speaker perceived as a high-credibility source is going to be more effective than the same presentation by a speaker perceived as being low in credibility. Recall the discussion of word power in Chapter 3. It's very likely that when Ossie Davis says in a speech that English is "my goddamn enemy," he is going to be more persuasive than a speaker who is less well known and less highly regarded and who uses comparable language.

Transitions

It is possible to discuss transitions from the standpoint of either organization or style, for a **transition** is *the verbal bridge between two parts of a speech*. Transitions are more easily developed if the points in a speech flow somewhat logically from one to another. In the speech about the planets in our solar system, the transitions were made quite easily. "Beginning with the planet nearest the sun we find Mercury," the speaker began. For the transition to the next point, he said, "Continuing our journey away from the sun we find Venus." He continued, using the analogy of a journey as a vehicle for devising smooth transitions. To avoid repeating himself, he used some variation in each transition. He said, "The third planet we encounter is Earth," Then, "As we leave the blue and green planet, we set out for the red planet, Mars." In this speech, spatial organization made the movement from one point to the next seem logical and easy to follow.

There are any number of ways of smoothly relating two concepts to each other. In discussing leadership, a speaker might move from one part of her speech to another by saying, "Let us turn from the leadership of yesterday to my second concern, the leadership of tomorrow." Effective transitions add more than finishing touches to a speech. They clarify the speaker's train of thought for the listener, they help give the speech unity and coherence, and sometimes they help make the argument seem well reasoned.

Economy of Language

Those long-winded birds. They're all the same. The less they have to say, the longer it takes them to say it. (Harry S. Truman on politicians; quoted in Miller, 1973, p. 177)

Signal-to-noise ratio, *the relationship between the essential and extraneous information contained in any message,* is a measure of interference. A concept that can be applied to all contexts of communication, it seems particularly relevant to any discussion of public speaking. Let us say at the outset that a certain amount of repetition, or redundancy, is necessary in most communication. This is certainly the case in public communication, where members of the audience have little chance to ask a speaker for clarification—at least before the question-and-answer period that may follow. A limited amount of redundancy ensures that the speaker's main points will not be misinterpreted. Nonetheless, there is little need to hammer the point home over and over again. We all know what torture it can be to sit through a public address by a long-winded speaker.

The speaker who is concise has the gift of selection. By omitting what is unnecessary and repetitious, he or she makes every word count. Economy in the use of language is a distinct stylistic advantage. Perhaps that is what one of President Franklin Roosevelt's close associates was driving at when early in Eleanor Roosevelt's public speaking career he gave her this terse bit of advice: "Have something to say, say it, and then sit down."

Humor and Satire

John Kennedy's use of humor was memorable. One of his best known quips was his opening remark to an audience at SHAPE headquarters in Paris in 1961: "I do not think it altogether inappropriate to introduce myself to this audience. I am the man who accompanied Jacqueline Kennedy to Paris and I have enjoyed it." We have already touched on the subject of humor in our discussion of credibility. We saw that although humor affects whether an audience likes a speaker, it may not influence the speaker's perceived expertness. And yet, as they prepare their speeches, there is no doubt that the majority of speakers are scrupulous about including humorous elements. Even if the subject is one of great urgency, there will often be at least some effort to win over the audience with a joke or two. In fact, opening a speech with a joke is a frequent practice and is often recommended in handbooks on public speaking. Reportedly, one of Gerald Ford's speech writers was concerned solely with the writing of humorous material.

Appeals to Fear

You want to persuade your audience that driving without safety belts is dangerous, that smoking can cause cancer, that disarmament will be detrimental to national security. What should your strategy be? Is the audience more likely to be persuaded if you appeal to fear? And if so, what level of fear is optimal?

There have been a number of studies examining the relationship between fear and attitude change. The original research, on dental hygiene, found that the higher the level of fear arousal, the less attitude change took place (Janis and Feshbach, 1953). This is an appealing conclusion; none of us wants to feel vulnerable to persuasive "attacks" based on fear. We like to think, for example, that we are immune to all the television commercials that promote a product by playing on our fear of being unpopular, unattractive, or even offensive to others.

But the question turns out to be more complex. Many researchers report a strong positive correlation between fear arousal and attitude change. For example, under high-fear conditions students urged to get tetanus inoculations showed significantly greater attitude change than those given the same advice under low-fear conditions. High-fear conditions resulted in more behavior change as well: More students did get tetanus shots (Dabbs and Leventhal, 1966).

How do we reconcile these apparently contradictory results? One theory (McGuire, 1968), supported by much recent evidence, suggests that the relationship between fear and attitude change takes the form of an inverted U curve. According to this theory low fear arousal results in little attitude change, presumably because the level is so low that the listener gives the message no special attention. As the level increases to the intermediate range, attitude change also increases. This is the optimal range for persuasive communication. Once the level of fear becomes extremely high, attitude change declines sharply because the listener responds defensively to the message, which interferes with message reception. Suppose, for example, that while lecturing on the harmful effects of smoking, a speaker goes into a painfully detailed description of emphysema and then shows her audience photographs of patients with terminal lung cancer. It is very likely that her listeners will become so anxious that they have to block out the message entirely, so that the speaker's efforts at persuasion then become self-defeating.

We do know that when a source has high credibility, a strong appeal to fear will be more persuasive than a mild appeal to fear (Miller and Hewgill, 1966). For example, if the speaker lecturing on the harmful effects of smoking is a doctor, her strong appeal to fear is likely to induce more attitude change among her listeners than it would if she were a woman with no medical training who had given up smoking.

There are so many other variables influencing persuasion that, given the incomplete state of present-day research, it is still too soon to make definitive statements about how effective appeals to fear will be in public communication.

How Much Change To Attempt

Confrontation is a persuasive style that has come to dominate numerous public communication contexts. The use of this strategy brings up an important question: Assuming that the speaker is interested in maximum persuasion, how much change should he or she argue for?

Let us explain the question by giving an example. Suppose the issue under discussion is whether or not the federal government should provide welfare benefits for the unemployed. Let the continuum in Figure 10.4 represent the range of opinion on this issue, and let us assume that there are 100 possible attitudes. Suppose Greg's preferred position on welfare can be quantified at 65. Surrounding this point on the scale is a range of opinions that Greg also finds acceptable, sometimes referred to as his "latitude of acceptance". Beyond this point is a latitude of noncommitment and, finally, a latitude of rejection, a range of opinions that he finds unacceptable. Imagine that Greg's latitude of acceptance goes from 50 to 75. If the speaker advocates a position within this range—55, for example—the discrepancy between this view and Greg's favored position is relatively small. Researchers have found that, other things being equal, such a moderate discrepancy will tend to shift listener attitude toward the position advocated by the speaker (Hovland et al., 1953). That is, the listener tends to perceive the speaker's position as closer to his or her preferred position than it really is; in fact, the listener tends *to assimilate, or accept, the change in attitude urged by the speaker*. This phenomenon is often referred to as an **assimilation effect**.

In the hope of bringing about maximum attitude change, the speaker may, of course, advocate a position that falls within the listener's latitude of rejec-

FIGURE 10.4   The Assimilation Effect: One Listener's Attitude
toward Welfare

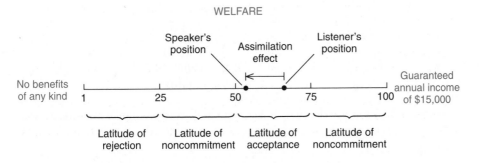

tion. This is the rationale behind confrontation tactics. But the results have often been disappointing. Research has shown that when a message falls within the latitude of rejection, the listener tends to perceive the message as even more discrepant with his or her viewpoint than it actually is and therefore to reject it. Thus, instead of producing greater attitude change, the speaker elicits *a negative reaction on the part of the listener* that has variously been referred to as a **backlash, boomerang effect,** or **contrast effect.**

Bear in mind that the more deeply committed you are to your system of beliefs or to a given position, the narrower your latitude of acceptance will be. Thus, in trying to persuade listeners whose minds are fairly well made up, a speaker should advocate a relatively moderate amount of change to produce the optimum reaction.

One Side or Two Sides?

Suppose that you want to persuade a mixed (male and female) audience to be more sympathetic toward the women's movement. Should you present only your side of the issue, or should you also discuss the case against it?

We now know that if audience members are initially receptive to a message and are unlikely to hear any arguments opposing it, then a one-sided approach will probably be more persuasive than a two-sided approach. In this case your effort would probably be directed toward reinforcing existing attitudes rather than changing values. If, on the other hand, the audience is likely to be skeptical or hostile to the speaker's point of view or will hear later arguments opposing it, a two-sided approach will probably be more effective. You can prepare a two-sided argument by listing the pros and cons of your subject and trying to anticipate the objections of the skeptical listener. If you are speaking on the women's movement, your list might look something like this:

Pros	*Cons*
1. Women are paid less than men for comparable jobs.	1. Women are poorer job risks than men because women often leave work soon after they marry.
2. Women are denied some legal rights of ownership.	2. Women enjoy more legal protection than men do; they also receive alimony in the event of divorce.
3. Women are always assumed to be responsible for child care and housework; these responsibilities should be shared by men.	3. Woman's natural role is in the home, and this is her highest fulfillment.

Once you have made such a list, you will find evidence that refutes or substantiates the arguments against you. As you speak, you present the first points and acknowledge the extent to which the objections are invalid and do not negate your main arguments. You then go on to cite evidence supporting your side of the issue.

Why should a two-sided approach work when the listener is likely to hear opposing arguments later on? Inoculation theory suggests an explanation in the form of a medical analogy. There are two ways in which a doctor can help a patient resist a disease: maintain the patient's state of health by prescribing a balanced diet, adequate rest, and so on, or inoculate the patient with a small amount of disease so that the patient builds up antibodies. Now, imagine that your patient, the audience member, is about to be attacked by a disease—that is, a persuasive message discrepant with your own. When you use a one-sided approach, you offer support: you give arguments in favor of your position and try to make the listener strong enough to ward off attacks. When you use a two-sided approach, you "inoculate" the listener through exposure to a weak form of the disease—the counterargument—so that he or she can refute it and thus build up defenses against future attacks. **Inoculation theory** holds that *inoculation is more effective than support in building up resistance because listeners exposed to a weak version of the counterarguments tend to develop an immunity to later arguments favoring that side.* You might try this tactic to see whether your experience corroborates the predictions of inoculation theory. Remember, though, that an inoculation must be a weak version of the disease.

A final point to be made is that the one-sided approach seems to work better if most of the members of your audience are poorly educated or of low intelligence. Perhaps in this case presenting both sides confuses listeners, leaving them uncertain which side you actually advocate.

Climax Order or Anticlimax Order?

If you had three arguments, one of which was clearly the strongest, would you use it first or save it for last? When you use the **climax order** of presentation, *you save your strongest argument until last;* when you use the **anticlimax order,** *you present your strongest argument first* and then proceed to the weaker arguments. Which order to use poses a serious question when you would like to change group opinion on an important issue.

Research evidence on this question does not clearly favor one approach over the other. Nevertheless, if we take into account the existing attitudes of our listeners, we are able to come up with some answers. If the audience is initially interested in your topic and favorable to your point of view, you can better afford to save your strongest argument for last. Presumably, the audience will be willing to give you the benefit of the doubt. If, on the other hand, your listeners are initially opposed to your point of view, you may be more effective if you use your most persuasive argument first (Karlins and Abelson, 1970).

Two important assumptions underlie the issue of climax versus anticlimax order. The first is that you are able to determine which of your arguments your listeners are likely to perceive as strongest or most persuasive. It is not always possible to know in advance how your audience will react to a given line of reasoning. Even seasoned public speakers have been surprised by audience response to a particular argument or, for that matter, to a casual remark. The second assumption is that you can know in advance whether most of the audience will be for or against your stand on a particular subject. In almost all cases some audience members will favor your position and others will not. Thus you are forced to make your choices about climax or anticlimax strategy on the basis of what you know about the majority of your listeners, knowing full well that these choices will be the wrong ones for the remaining listeners. Any decision you make will win over some listeners and risk alienating others.

Stated or Implied Conclusions?

Have you ever tried to persuade someone by hinting at something? Sometimes it works, but sometimes the other person doesn't get the hint at all. Public speakers have long wondered whether it is more persuasive to state the conclusion of a speech explicitly or to allow listeners to draw their own conclusions from the arguments presented.

One argument in favor of implicit conclusions is that if the speech is already comprehensible on its own, an explicit conclusion is unnecessary. It has also been proposed that listeners with a high level of interest or ego involvement are more likely to be persuaded by an implied than by an expressed deduction, which might offend them if they hold an opposing view.

Despite these considerations, and the fact that one early study (Thistlethwaite et al., 1955) found no difference in attitude acceptance between conclusion drawing and no-conclusion drawing, most studies confirm that you have a better chance of changing audience attitude if you state your conclusion than if you allow listeners to draw their own (Tubbs, 1968). One reason for this seems to be that in making their own summation of your argument, listeners may distort it; they may even find support for their own point of view in the new information you present.

Speak First or Have the Last Say?

Consider the situation in which two speakers, Doreen and Chris, are to debate an issue. Is it to Doreen's advantage to speak first, or would she have maximum impact if she spoke following Chris? In other terms, would learning and remembering the first argument interfere with learning and remembering the second?

According to a classic paper on the issue (Miller and Campbell, 1959), two persuasive communications are retained equally well if presented together and measured immediately. If audience attitudes are measured a week later, however, we expect a **primacy effect**—that is, *the first communication is remembered somewhat better than the second*. If there is a long delay between the two speakers and audience attitudes are measured right after the second speaker's presentation, we expect a **recency effect**—that is, *the second message is remembered somewhat better than the first*. Suppose, however, that there is a delay not only between the two speakers but in the measurement of audience attitude. In this instance, primacy and recency seem to cancel out each other, for neither message has the dominant impact.

A more recent study of the primacy-recency issue finds "the more recent information somewhat more influential shortly after the communications and the earlier information after a longer time lapse" (Luchins and Luchins, 1970, p. 68; McGuire, 1985, p. 273). Over time, however, conflicting communications tend to converge so that aspects of both communications are integrated into a more balanced view. Given these findings, the speaker's message, credibility, and delivery are likely to be more important than whether the speaker is first or last.

It is tempting to apply what is known about message variables to less formal kinds of communication. For example, if you want to persuade your parents to finance a new car for you, you might find yourself speculating about whether to hint or come right out and ask for it—and then whether to use a one-sided or two-sided approach. The research findings we have discussed, however, are based primarily on speaker-audience situations. Although they may indicate some trends in other kinds of communication, the information about message variables is most relevant to person-to-group communication.

SUMMARY

One of the most formal modes of human communication we experience is public, or person-to-group, communication. We have tried to view it here in terms of both the speaker's and the listener's experience, giving special attention to persuasive rather than information communication.

The single most important judgment we made about the speaker, apart from his or her message, concerns credibility. Judgments about source credibility, as we saw, are not constant; they vary not only from audience to audience but from one time to another. In general, the high-credibility source has greater influence than the low-credibility source, but the impact of credibility on persuasion is greatest immediately after the message is received. Delivery is a second important speaker variable. In this chapter we discussed both the visual and vocal aspects of delivery and then went on to evaluate four modes of delivery: impromptu speaking, reading from manuscript, memorized speech, and extemporaneous speaking.

Our next topic was the audience itself, which we viewed from the speaker's vantage point. We described two methods—demographic and purpose-oriented analysis—that a speaker might use to adapt a message to a particular audience. Research findings on how listener persuasibility correlates with sex differences and personality traits were also examined.

Our treatment of the message itself focused on message preparation and structure rather than content. We discussed the organization of speech material, the use of supporting materials, and the speaker's choice of language as well as several other options available to the speaker in choosing an appropriate strategy. Thus we have an opportunity to review research findings on such diverse topics as appeals to humor or fear; the degree of change to attempt in a speech; and the relative effectiveness of one-sided versus two-sided messages, climax-versus anticlimax-order messages, and stated versus implied conclusions.

REVIEW QUESTIONS

1. What are three dimensions of source credibility? What are the differences between extrinsic, intrinsic, and total credibility?

2. What are the visual and vocal cues that contribute to audience judgments about delivery? Name the four modes of delivery, giving some of the advantages and disadvantages of each.

3. Discuss five possible ways of organizing speech materials.

4. Describe two methods of support and the general research finding concerning how a speaker's use of evidence affects his or her efforts to persuade.

5. What is the difference between the assimilation effect and the contrast effect? How do these concepts relate to how much change a speaker should advocate?

6. Under what conditions is a one-sided message most effective? Under what conditions is a two-sided message most effective?

7. Under what conditions is a climax-order message most effective? Under what conditions is an anticlimax-order message most effective?

8. What is the general research finding regarding the effectiveness of messages containing (1) stated conclusions, and (2) implied conclusions?

EXERCISES

1. Select a speech from a newspaper or magazine such as *Vital Speeches.* Analyze the speech by answering the following questions:
   a. What was the purpose of the speech?
   b. What was the most probable state of the speaker's extrinsic and intrin-

sic credibility in terms of the three major dimensions of source credibility? What factors in the message and context of the message led you to your conclusions?

c. What method(s) of organization does the speech illustrate?

d. What forms of support were used? How effective were they?

e. How effective was the speaker's use of language?

f. Was humor or satire used? If so, what seemed to be the speaker's purpose in using it?

g. Were fear appeals used? If so, were they used appropriately (that is, according to research findings)?

h. Was the message one-sided or two-sided? Was it appropriate, given the conditions of the speech?

i. Was a climax or an anticlimax order used? Was it the more appropriate order for the situation in which the message was given?

j. Was the conclusion stated or implied? Was it the more appropriate technique for the situation in which the message was given?

2. If you were asked to present a speech to the audience that heard the speech used in exercise 1, how would you go about analyzing the audience?

3. Making use of what is known about message variables, write a three- to four-minute extemporaneous speech to persuade and present it to your class. Remember to aim for clarity and to make your presentation relevant to your listeners' interests. You may wish to choose a topic from the list that follows these exercises.

4. Give a one-minute impromptu speech on a topic assigned to you by a classmate or by the instructor. Try to determine your purpose and organization in the short time available.

5. Take your identity and membership cards out of your wallet or purse, and conduct an audience analysis on the groups to which you belong. Write a short paper on different approaches that would be appropriate for the different groups.

6. Tape-record one of your speeches, and play it back for self-analysis. What changes would you make if you were to give it again?

7. Here is a list of speech topics and thought starters for use in preparation of speeches.

Water pollution	Mental illness
American Indians	Alcoholism and drug abuse
Latin American relations	Computers
Divorce	Overcrowded airports
Overcrowded universities	The high cost of dying
Farm bankruptcy	Involuntary sterilization
Flood control	The Academy Awards

Personality—what is it?
Muslim beliefs
Causes of earthquakes
Ethnocentrism
Why the Great Lakes tilt
The continental drift theory
Hazards in the home
What makes people buy
Social stratification
Interpreting dreams
The scientific lie detector
Improving your memory
Learning to listen
Wedding customs
Plastic surgery
Trick photography
Sky diving
Taxidermy
Baseball in America
Music
Writing good letters
The importance of friendship
The honor system
The Nobel prize
Buying a car
Women leaders
Revision of the penal system
Prayer in public schools
Prostitution
Public works for the unemployed
The overorganized society
Japanese investment in the United States
Sex education in the schools
Slaughterhouses
The space program
Speech pathology
Suicide
Tornadoes
China
The Strategic Air Command
Air traffic safety
Anarchy
Atheism
Capitalism
Culture

Morality
Prejudice
Slander
Abortion
Birth control
Boxing
Censorship
Cigarette smoking
Conformity
Country music
Cryogenics
Pornographic films
Driver education
Drunk drivers
Cocaine
Euthanasia
The FBI
Firearms regulation
Foreign aid
Forest fires
Fraternities and sororities
Free college education
Grading systems
Hell's Angels
The John Birch Society
The Ku Klux Klan
Lecture classes
The metric system
Communism
Football for the spectator
Nuclear testing
Living together
Dieting fads
The communication gap
South Africa
Television evangelists
Urban blight
Rationalizing
Abstract art
Misleading advertising
Animal research
The armed forces
Demographic changes
Siamese twins
The laser beam

Empathy   Medical practices
Illiteracy   Herpes
Libel
AIDS

SUGGESTED READINGS

Hasling, John. *The Audience, The Message, The Speaker.* 5th ed. New York: McGraw-Hill, 1993.

This little paperback is an excellent "how-to" book about public communication.

Kaplan, Burton. *The Managers Complete Guide to Speech Writing.* New York: Free Press, 1988.

This book contains principles of strategic speech writing necessary for business presentations. The author's goal is to provide speakers with fundamental skills for all types of speeches. The skill-oriented approach is promised to be successful for all—from the beginner to the professional.

Lucas, Stephen E. *The Art of Public Speaking.* 4th ed. New York: McGraw-Hill, 1992.

This book is well written and looks at the topic from a skills perspective.

Safire, William. *Lend Me Your Ears: Great Speeches In History.* New York: Norton, 1992.

This books contains nearly 1,000 pages of some of the greatest speeches of all time. It includes speeches by Art Buchwald, George Bush, Demosthenes, Barbara Jordan, Abraham Lincoln, Malcolm X, Martin Luther King, Jr., John Kennedy, Jeane Kirkpatrick, Margaret Chase Smith, Elizabeth Cady Stanton, Margaret Thatcher, Sojourner Truth, and Boris Yeltsin along with dozens of others. This is a great source of quotes as well as a rich sourcebook.

Tedford, Thomas. *Public Speaking in a Free Society.* New York: McGraw-Hill, 1991.

This is a book on public communication which emphasizes the free-speech and ethical aspects of public communication. It is quite comprehensive.

CHAPTER ELEVEN

Organizational Communication

CHAPTER OBJECTIVES

After reading this chapter, you should be able to:

1 Explain three functions communication performs in organizations.

2 Define and illustrate supportive supervisory communication.

3 List five ways in which people adapt to information overload.

4 Explain the law of diminishing returns as it relates to downward communication.

5 Identify the five types of power.

6 List five functions of upward communication.

7 Describe the differentiation-integration problem in organizations as its relates to horizontal communication.

8 Explain the formula that expresses the important variables in the development of rumors.

9 Describe the three types of message distortion that occur during rumor transmission.

*W*hat do you think these five situations have in common?

1. A plant manager sits down with one of her subordinates to conduct an annual job-performance-appraisal interview.

2. A hospital administration committee meets to decide how to implement a 10 percent budget cut for the next year.

3. A personnel manager gives a presentation to salaried employees summarizing their new hospitalization benefits.

4. The president of a university meets with a group of students who are complaining about an increase in their tuition fees.

5. A major oil company advertises on television to show the positive impact the company has had on a local community.

By now you have probably figured out that all five of these situations involve **organizational communication.** More correctly, they involve *human communication that occurs within the context of organizations*—for it is people who do the communicating, not organizations. These examples show the wide range of events that can be called "organizational communication." They also illustrate the overlap between organizational communication and the other communication contexts (two-person, small-group, public, and mass communication). Any and all of these four types of communication can be associated with organizations.

We spend a good part of our lives as members of organizations. Although we tend to think first of business organizations, this also includes schools, churches, military institutions, and even clubs. This chapter focuses on communicating in these organizations, especially communicating on the job.

ORGANIZATIONS: A DEFINITION

An organization has been defined as "a collection, or system, of individuals who commonly, through a hierarchy of ranks and division of labor, seek to achieve a predetermined goal" (Rogers and Rogers, in Hanneman and McEwen, 1975, p. 218). Let us look more closely at three essential characteristics of organizations that relate to this definition (see Figure 11.1).

Early in the industrial revolution, it was found that *organizations could produce more by allowing individuals to specialize* through a **division of labor** than by making each person produce an entire product—as artisans had been doing for centuries. In one classic example, a factory produced pins at a rate of twenty pins per person per day using traditional methods. After dividing the labor into eighteen different specific operations, it was able to produce 4,800 pins (of comparable quality) per person per day.

Eventually, specialized functions require individual supervision. This re-

FIGURE 11.1 A Simplified Organization Chart of a Manufacturing Plant

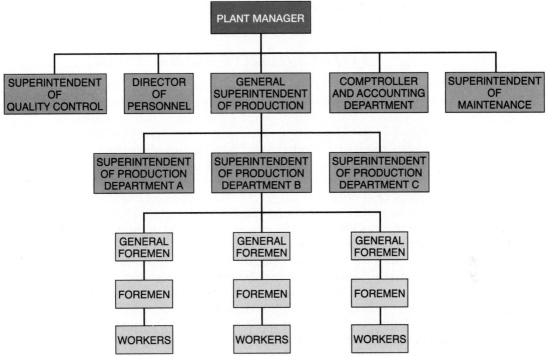

quirement has necessitated the concept of **span of control** in organizations— that is, *a limit on the authority of the individual supervisor.* Span of control is often determined by the number of people who can effectively be managed by one supervisor. As more workers are added to the organization, more supervisors are needed, and more upper-level managers are in turn required to oversee their activities. Thus more and more levels are added to the vertical dimension of the organization, and a hierarchy, or **pyramid of control,** is established.

The pyramid of control is often used to depict which people formally report to which others in an organization. When orders are sent down (or up) through this formal system, the process is referred to as using the "chain of command," or the formal communication system in an organization. People in the organization may also communicate informally—that is, outside the channels indicated on the organization chart. This is called the "informal system" and is directly related to the sections in this chapter on horizontal communication and informal communication. Both types of communication help the organization to move toward achieving its goals.

The defining characteristics of organizational communication are the structural factors in the organization that require members to act in certain expected roles. For example, a college professor is expected to behave in certain ways while in the classroom. At a social event, however, he or she may seem a very different person since the same role expectations do not apply in this particular setting.

TOTAL QUALITY MANAGEMENT

One of the problems created by classical organizational structures is the overspecialization of people. For example, people in a hospital may be in patient care or pharmacy, or accounts payable and have very little knowledge of what those in the other departments are doing. If you have ever had to wait in an emergency room of a hospital, you know the incredible delays and inefficiencies that are created by this high degree of specialization.

As business organizations have felt the need to become more competitive in a global economy, there has been a rapidly growing need for what is referred to as *total quality management* (TQM). In short, *TQM* refers to the need to serve customers better. People are becoming tired of poor quality and service and are flocking to companies that provide higher quality. We are all familiar with Ford Motor Company's slogan "Quality is Job One."

Ironically, Japanese firms are best known for having developed very high quality products. Yet, the Japanese learned these practices from the guru of quality W. Edwards Deming, an American who introduced these concepts in Japan during the 1950s. Part of Deming's idea is to treat other departments within an organization as "internal customers." So, to go back to the hospital example, the patient care department can be totally effective only if they have efficient, high-quality service from pharmacy, radiology, admitting, and so on.

Although these concepts may seem obvious, most organizations do not do a very good job of implementing them. For example, how long do you have to stand in line when registering for classes at your school? Some universities have also begun to use TQM practices to improve service to their customers (i.e., by implementing phone or computer registration). Hendrickson and Psarouthakis (1992) argue that by serving customers better, organizations can compete far more effectively. Rothschild (1992) cites the example of the Disney corporation, which was losing a great deal of money after the death of Walt Disney. But, by introducing the concepts of strong customer service (e.g, Disneyland and Disney World) and by providing high-quality entertainment (e.g., films like *Beauty and the Beast, Little Mermaid,* and *Aladdin*), the company has turned its profit picture completely around. In fact, its chief executive officer, Michael Eisner, made over $40 million in one recent year.

Not only is the nature of many jobs changing but the type of employees in those jobs is changing also. Lambert (1992) cites data from the Bureau of Labor Statistics which show that these changes are dramatically influencing organizational communication. Historically, organizations have been overwhelmingly male and white. Even as recently as 1985, white males composed

47 percent of the work force and white females 36 percent. However, by the year 2000 it is projected that this will change and that the following groups will constitute entrants into the American work force:

White women	34.9 percent
White men	32.1 percent
Black men and women	12.8 percent
Hispanic men and women	14.6 percent
Asian and other men and women	5.7 percent

(Lambert, 1992, p. 15)

Given such startling changes in demographics, it will become increasingly necessary to learn to communicate within a context of cultural diversity. And the study of human communication in organizations is more relevant today than ever before.

Cetron and Davies (1991) have also predicted numerous other changes in organizations. For example, persons aged twenty-nine to fifty-nine will account for two-thirds of all those in the work force. Furthermore, almost all growth of the labor force over the decade from 1990 to 2000 will be in this age group. They also predict that union membership will continue to decline nationally. It reached 17.5 percent in 1986. According to the United Auto Workers, it will fall to 12 percent by 1995 and to less than 10 percent by the year 2000. This changing of the work force will be another factor for new college graduates entering the work force to contend with.

IMPORTANCE OF COMMUNICATION

Chester Barnard once wrote that "the first executive function is to develop and maintain a system of communication" (1938, p. 82). Barnard's statement has proved prophetic. Some years ago, in a survey of the presidents of one hundred of the largest corporations in the United States, it was found that 96 percent believed there was a "definite relationship" between communication and employee productivity (Lull et al., 1955). More recently, these findings were reaffirmed (Zelko and Dance, 1965):

> When managers and other responsible persons in business organization are asked how much of the work day is spent in communicating, the replies range from about 85 to 99 percent, with most saying that it is above 90 percent. (p. 21)

Recent surveys conducted by the University of Michigan (1990), Pennsylvania State University, and Wake Forest University (1991) have documented the importance of communication skills to organizational success. For example, in the Penn State survey of corporate executives, the most mentioned qualities looked for in recent graduates were:

1. Oral and written communication skills (83.5 percent of responses)

2. Leadership skills (79.7 percent)

3. Analytical skills (75.3 percent)

4. Ability to work in teams (71.4 percent)

5. Ability to manage rapid change (65.9 percent)

6. A sense of social, professional and ethical responsibility (64.3 percent)

7. Financial management (46.7 percent) (Pennsylvania State University, 1992)

Schein (1978) studied the stages of people's careers in organizations and underscored the importance of communication abilities at every one of those stages. To be successful, he found, we must remain able to change with changing demands:

> We need ideas, perspective, and emotional support from others. . . . One of the most important skills to be developed in learning how to cope more effectively is how to establish more meaningful relationships with other people. This . . . is a prime skill needed for people whose careers will be spent within organizational contexts. . . . *Interpersonal competence is increasingly coming to be a critical skill not only in dealing with self and family development problems, but for career advancement as well.* (p. 77; italics added)

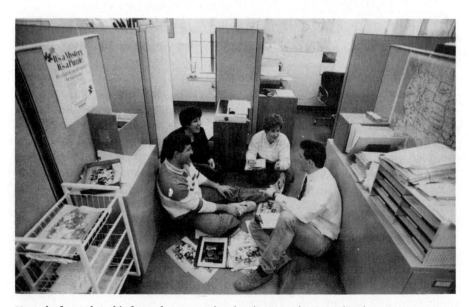

How do formal and informal communication interact in organizations?

Schein points out that after finishing college, young people in new jobs often face a rude awakening. They feel that with their up-to-date knowledge and training, they should be making a major contribution. As they enter this new world of work, however, they find that developing interpersonal skills is of overriding importance. Their frustration is expressed in the following excerpts:

> All the problems I encounter boil down to communication and human relations. (Initiate in a consumer goods company)

> I thought I could sell people with logic and was amazed at the hidden agendas people have, irrational objections; really bright people will come up with stupid excuses. . . . (Initiate in an aerospace company) (p. 99)

Research confirms the importance of communication skills at all levels of employment, from the initiate all the way up to the president. Jennings (1971) studied the common patterns of those who are promoted fastest. Jennings describes their communication style in the following way:

> Executives tend to use a feather-light touch with their subordinates and peers. The heavy hand of the lower positioned manager is frowned upon at high corporate levels. The terms "style" and "panache" are often used to mean the ability to say and do almost anything without antagonizing others. People tend to work better when they do not have to work at saving face. To be mobility-bright also means to present oneself in a manner becoming to the dignity and stature of the superiors above. It means to behave as though the executive were at a higher level than his present one. (p. 69)

One of the most wide-sweeping changes in organizational communication is the increase in teamwork. For example, in 1991 Boeing announced that its new Boeing 777 jetliner was going to be built by teams. The company set up more than 200 "design-build teams. These teams were comprised of employees from engineering, quality control, finance, and manufacturing. Each one concentrates on a specific part of the aircraft. Even suppliers and potential customers are sometimes included in team meetings" (Wall, 1992, p. 110).

Another facet of this change is the increase in employee **empowerment**. Empowerment is giving workers more latitude to make decisions and to implement them. Fisher (1993) defines empowerment as:

$$\text{Empowerment} = f(A \times R \times I\,A)$$

where A = authority
$\quad\;\; R$ = resources
$\quad\;\; I$ = information
$\quad\;\; A$ = accountability

In other words, in order to be able to make decisions, workers need to be given not only the authority but sufficient training and budget, as well as critical information. Then, they must be held accountable for their decisions (p. 14).

Conrad (1985) identifies three functions communication performs in organizations. They are:

The command function: Communication allows members of the organization to "issue, receive, interpret, and act on *commands*" (p. 7). The two types of communication that make up this function are directions and feedback, and the goal is the successful influence of other members of the organization. The outcome of the command function is coordination among the many interdependent members of the organization.

The relational function: Communication allows members of the organization "to create and maintain productive business and personal *relationships* with other members of the organization" (pp. 7–8). Relationships on the job affect job performance in many ways, for example, job satisfaction, the flow of communication both down and up the organizational hierarchy, and the degree to which commands are followed. The importance of good interpersonal skills is highlighted on the job when you consider that many of the necessary relationships are not chosen but forced by organizational circumstances, making the relationships less stable, more prone to conflict, less committed, and so on.

The ambiguity-management function: Choices in an organizational setting are often made in highly ambiguous circumstances, for example, multiple motivations exist since choices affect coworkers and the organization, as well as oneself, the organization's objectives may not be clear, and the context within which the choice needs to be made may be unclear. Communication is the means for coping with and reducing the ambiguity inherent in the organization: Members talk with each other in an effort to structure the environment and make sense of new situations, which entails gaining and sharing information.

In the next section we see the critical role that the supervisor plays in the organization's success or failure.

Supervisory Communication

If we know that communication is important to organizational success, then it becomes important to specify which types of communication are *most* important to the organization. Using such terms as "communication satisfaction" (Downs et al., 1974) and "communication climate" (Dennis et al., 1974; Dennis, 1975), a number of researchers have attempted to do just this. Employees are asked to answer a number of questions about various aspects of communication in their own organizations. Their answers are then statistically analyzed through factor analysis, a method that helps researchers identify the communication factors that are seen as most important by those studied. Dennis (1975) identified five factors considered by members of organizations to be of prime importance in communicating. These factors, and some questions used to measure them, are as follows:

1. **Superior to subordinate communication:** As measured by such questions as, To what extent does:

   - Your superior make you feel free to talk to him or her?

   - Your superior listen to you when you tell him or her about things that are bothering you?

   - Your superior encourage you to let him or her know when things are going wrong on the job?

2. **Downward communication:** As measured by such questions as:

   - Do people in top management say what they mean and mean what they say?

   - Is top management providing you with the kinds of information you really want and need?

   - Are you satisfied with explanations you get from top management about why things are done as they are?

3. **Superiors' perceptions of communication with subordinates:** As measured by such questions as:

   - Do you believe your subordinates are frank and candid with you?

   - Do you believe your colleagues (coworkers) are really frank and candid with you?

   - Do you believe that your subordinates think that *you* understand *their* problems?

4. **Upward communication:** As measured by such questions as:

   - Do your opinions make a difference in the day-to-day decisions that affect your job?

   - Do you believe your views have any real influence in your organization?

   - Does your superior let you participate in the planning of your own work?

5. **Reliability of information:** As measured by such questions as:

   ♦ Do you think that information received from your subordinates is reliable?

   ♦ Do you think that information received from your colleagues (or co-workers) is reliable?

Clearly, **supervisory communication** is considered the most important factor influencing an employee's communication satisfaction. The effective supervisor is described as supportive. Or, as Likert puts it: "In all interactions . . . each member [of the organization] will view the experience as supportive and one which builds and maintains his sense of personal worth and importance" (1961, p. 103). In Chapter 6 we learned that people particularly need confirmation and support from their superiors. The boss who tries "tough talk" on employees seems to create negative side effects such as increased grievances, absenteeism, employee turnover, and even sabotage. Naturally, this leads to decreased productivity and product quality in the organization.

Iacocca (1984), once president of Ford Motor Company, describes in his number 1 best-seller how Henry Ford II executed what has become one of the most publicized firings in corporate history:

> As I took my seat at the table, Henry hemmed and hawed. He had never fired anyone, and he didn't know how to begin. "There comes a time when I have to do things my way," he finally said. "I've decided to reorganize the company. This is one of those things that you hate to do, but you have to do it anyway. It's been a nice association"—I looked at him in disbelief—"but I think you should leave. It's best for the company."
>
> At no point during our entire forty-five minute meeting did he ever use the word "fired."
>
> "What's this all about?" I asked.
>
> But Henry couldn't give me a reason. "It's personal," he said, "and I can't tell you any more. It's just one of those things."
>
> But I persisted. I wanted to force him to give me a reason because I knew he didn't have a good one. Finally, he just shrugged his shoulders and said: "Well, sometimes you just don't like somebody."
>
> "Your timing stinks," I said. "We've just made a billion eight for the second year in a row. That's three and a half billion in the past two years. But mark my words, Henry. You may never see a billion eight again. And you know why? Because you don't know how . . . we made it in the first place!" (pp. 127–128)

Obviously, Lee Iacocca would not classify Henry Ford II as a very supportive boss. The supportive boss is described as one who listens, cares, and is receptive to feedback (both positive and negative).

More recently these findings were confirmed by Petelle and associates (1988), who write:

> Supervisors and subordinates maintain a set of communication expectations (anticipated communicative behaviors) for themselves and for others. For example, asking relevant questions, discussing one's intentions openly, being honest, are communicative behaviors that a supervisor or subordinate may expect of self or of others. (p. 299)

Krone (1992) found that subordinates who believed that their supervisors were on their side had higher job satisfaction. Also the subordinates who felt that their boss was not on their side were more likely to go behind the boss's back and to resort to politics to get their ideas accepted (p. 13). Similarly, Roach (1991) studied leadership among department chairs in a university. He found that the use of threats, punishment, and emphasis on position power are detrimental to faculty job satisfaction. Conversely, he found that when positive communication approaches were used, job satisfaction and supervisory ratings were higher (p. 87).

To summarize, effective supervisory communication means applying many of the concepts discussed throughout this book. It means that supervisors are more likely to be effective if they can establish a relationship with employees that includes mutual trust and supportiveness. And their success in establishing such a relationship will be determined by the verbal and nonverbal cues they give.

In the remaining sections of this chapter we shall examine four other factors Dennis (1975) found under the traditional categories for analyzing organization communication: (1) downward communication, (2) upward communication, (3) horizontal communication, and (4) informal communication.

Downward Communication

After supervisory communication, the second most important factor in determining communication climate in the organization is **downward communication.** Such communication *is initiated by the organization's upper management and then filters downward through the "chain of command."*

Swift (1973) describes a problem in downward communication that often faces managers:

> Let's suppose that everyone at X Corporation, from the janitor on up to the chairman of the board, is using the office copiers for personal matters; income tax forms, church programs, children's term papers, and God knows what else are being duplicated by the gross. This minor piracy costs the company a pretty penny, both directly and in employee time, and the general manager—let's call him Sam Edwards—decides the time has come to lower the boom. (p. 59)

If you were Sam Edwards, how would you communicate to your subordinates about this problem? First you might consider some communication alternatives. Our model in Chapter 1 referred to these as "channels." Some typical channels of downward communication are

Interorganization memos	Letters sent home
Department meetings	Posters
Face-to-face conversations with subordinates	Telephone calls
Company newspaper	Speech to all employees
Bulletin boards	Videotape recordings
Fax	Electronic mail
Voice mail	

Any of these, alone or in combination, could be employed to get the message about photocopying to your employees. However, as the chart in Figure 11.2 shows, people are so busy that they are often hard to contact.

Sam Edwards of the X Corporation is an experienced manager, and he also knows that if he overloads his people with too much information they will begin to make more errors. Given the costs and the potential benefits involved, Edwards decides to write a memo about the abuse of photocopying privileges. In doing so, he avoids bogging down his supervisors with more time-consuming forms of communication, such as meetings.

Miller (1964) and Hawes (1971) have identified seven ways in which people adapt to information overload. They are (1) *omission* (failing to handle all the information), (2) *error* (ignoring or failing to correct errors when made), (3) *queuing* (letting things pile up), (4) *filtering* (dealing with input in categories ranked according to a priority system), (5) *approximation* (lowering standards of precision), (6) *multiple channels* (delegation of information processing to others), and (7) *escape* (refusal to handle the input at all).

Effectiveness of Downward Communication

Research on the effectiveness of different forms of downward communication has shown that using a combination of channels tends to get the best results. In a classic study, Dahle (1954) found that channels were ranked in the following order of effectiveness (from most to least effective);

1. Combined oral and written	4. Bulletin board
2. Oral only	5. Grapevine
3. Written only	

(See also Yates and Orlikowski, 1992.) In other words, in terms of actually getting the information through to employees accurately, a combination of written and oral channels gets the best results. Sending the same message through more than one channel creates *redundancy,* and redundancy seems to be helpful not only in getting messages through but in ensuring that they will be remembered. For example, a busy executive may get a memo reminding

FIGURE 11.2

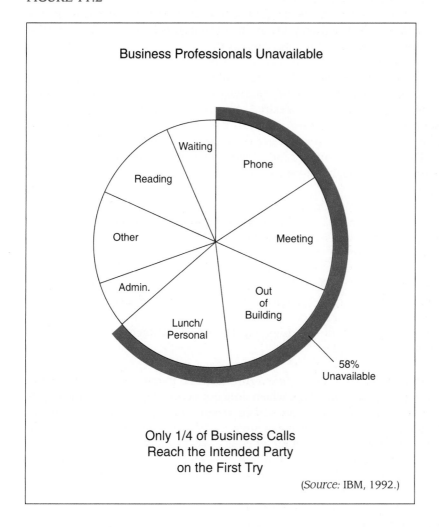

Business Professionals Unavailable

Only 1/4 of Business Calls
Reach the Intended Party
on the First Try

(*Source:* IBM, 1992.)

her of an executive committee meeting that day at one o'clock. By lunch hour, however, her busy activity schedule has caused the meeting to slip her mind. At lunch, the chairperson of the executive committee says, "Don't forget the meeting at one this afternoon." The woman replies, "Thanks for reminding me, it almost slipped my mind. It's been one of those days."

One of the paradoxes of communicating in organizations is that busy people seem to require more reminders (that is, more message redundancy) to act on the downward communication they receive. On the other hand, as the number of memos, meetings, phone calls, and so on increases, each person becomes that much busier, since it requires time to attend to each of these messages. Therefore, an important consideration in organization communication is the so-called **law of diminishing returns,** which states that *more is* *better, up to a point.* For example, a more open flow of communication is good up to a point, after which the receiver may become overloaded. A supervisor of our acquaintance believed very firmly in communicating fully with subordinates. The net result of her good intentions was that employees in the department had to check their mailboxes about every two hours to keep up with the continual barrage of memos. Naturally, this volume of communication kept employees from being as productive as they might otherwise have been. This relationship between communication frequency and desired effect is illustrated in Figure 11.3.

Another characteristic of downward communication is lack of accuracy; in other words, "people often don't get the message straight." Conboy (1976) cites a study that polled one hundred industrial managers to determine what percentage of a message got through to lower organizational levels. The results are somewhat surprising:

Board of directors	100 percent of communication content
Vice presidents	67 percent
General supervisors	56 percent
Plant managers	40 percent
Foremen	30 percent
Workers	20 percent (Conboy, 1976, p. 27)

This message distortion in downward communication is beautifully illustrated in the following example:

Colonel communicates to Major: At 9 o'clock tomorrow there will be an eclipse of the sun, something which does not occur every day. Get the men to fall out in the company street in their fatigues so that they will see this rare phenomenon, and I will then explain it to them. Now in the case of rain, we will not be able to see anything, of course, so then take the men to the gym.

   Major passes message to Captain: By order of the Colonel tomorrow at 9 o'clock there will be an eclipse of the sun. If it rains, you will not be

FIGURE 11.3

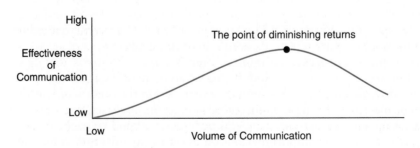

able to see it from the company street, so, then, in fatigues, the eclipse of the sun will take place in the gym, something which does not occur every day.

The Captain then said to the Lieutenant: By order of the Colonel in fatigues tomorrow, at 9 o'clock in the morning the inauguration of the eclipse of the sun will take place in the gym. The Colonel will give the order if it should rain, something which does occur every day.

The Lieutenant then told the Sergeant: Tomorrow at 9, the Colonel in fatigues will eclipse the sun in the gym, as it occurs every day if it's a nice day. If it rains, then this occurs in the company street.

The Sergeant then instructed the Corporal: Tomorrow at 9, the eclipse of the colonel in fatigues will take place because of the sun. If it rains in the gym, something which does not take place every day, you will fall out in the company street.

☐ *Finally, one Private said to another Private:* Tomorrow, if it rains, it looks as if the sun will eclipse the Colonel in the gym. It's a shame that this does not occur every day. (Zima, unpublished)

More will be said about message distortion later in this chapter in the section on informal communication.

McCormack (1984) cites a real-life example of distortion in downward communication:

In the early 1970s one of Arnold Palmer's endorsees was Lincoln Mercury, and I told Gar Laux, then the general manager of Lincoln Mercury, that if he was interested we could arrange to use a couple of Lincolns as the photographic backdrop in a forthcoming series of Arnold's print ads for his apparel licensee, Robert Bruce.

Gar was delighted by this opportunity for "free" advertising and said, "just let us know when and where you want the cars and we'll make sure they get there."

Several weeks later, the head of our apparel division received a call from a lower-echelon Lincoln Mercury executive who wanted to know where the cars should be sent and what colors they should be. "Bermuda, three weeks from today," our executives told him, but as to color, which really didn't matter, he said, "I don't know. Whatever you have. What about a navy or a maroon?"

Several days before the shoot, our apparel executive received a call from a different employee at Lincoln Mercury who this time wanted to know precisely where in Bermuda the cars should be shipped. "We've had to charter a plane," he said, "because our Bermuda dealer doesn't have a blue or a maroon car. In fact," he added, "there's only one of each on the Eastern seaboard, and the plane first has to fly to Boston to pick up the maroon car and then to Washington to get the navy blue." (p. 176)

It seems obvious that as organizations increase in size, the frequency of these kinds of snafus* increases.

Power

Power often comes into play in organizational relationships. It is especially relevant, but not limited, to downward communication. When we think of powerful people, we think of Donald Trump or Lee Iacocca or Sandra Day O'Conner. The classic typology of power was originally written by French and Raven (1962). They identified five types of power: three types of power that are available to a supervisor based on his or her position in the organization and two types of personal power.

Legitimate power is the authority a person has by virtue of her or his position. For example, a boss can hire, give orders, authorize paychecks, and require things to be done.

Reward power is the ability to use rewards to influence other people. Allowing a person to take time off and giving pay increases or bonuses or awards are a few examples.

Coercive power is the ability to influence individuals by withholding rewards such as pay increases, promotions, business travel, or a desirable office as well as the use of punishment such as reprimands, suspensions, and ultimate termination.

Expert power, a type of personal power, is the ability to influence another based on one's knowledge, experience, or judgment which the other person needs. Dr. Henry Kissinger has often been consulted by United States presidents because of his considerable expertise even when he does not hold any position in their administrations.

Referent power, another type of personal power, is the ability to influence someone because of his or her desire to identify with the power source. The so-called yes-man is someone who will do what is asked in order to please the boss. The follower who takes this behavior to the extreme is called a *sycophant*.

Pfeffer (1981) has identified several practical power strategies and tactics, which are discussed below: the selective use of objective criteria, forming coalitions, and cooptation.

All organizations make decisions according to certain criteria. Sometimes the **selective use of objective criteria** can influence decisions. For example, members of Congress may agree to reduce the budget deficit by a certain percentage but will usually fight savagely to keep a military base from being closed in their districts in order to save jobs. In this way they are able to use

---

* Situation normal, all fouled up.

their power to selectively apply the budget cuts only to districts other than their own.

The **forming of coalitions** represents another power strategy. In union there is strength. If you want to increase your power, you can team up with someone of equal or greater power. Coalitions can be other units within an organization, an outside expert who has great credibility, or other outside constituencies. Fraternities and sororities have practiced this for decades by forming Greek Councils. Children will attempt to influence their parents by citing what is being allowed in other families. And companies will hire expert witnesses to help win product liability suits.

The tactic of **cooptation** involves an attempt to change the attitude of powerful individuals by bringing them into partnership. It is a special form of coalition formation. For example, student leaders who are protesting some university policy may be invited into membership on the task force to correct the problem. Often students are invited to sit on committees in order to win their support. Similarly, complaining employees may be placed in charge of solving the problem they are concerned about. This is a special example of participative decision making, the only difference being that the individuals tend to start out antagonistic rather than neutral. Pfeffer (1981) states that the reason that cooptation is so often effective is that it increases

> identification and commitment to the organization, gives the representatives a stake and legitimate position in the organization, and motivates them to be interested in the organization's survival and success. (p. 167)

A special case of organizational power is that of those who control the "purse strings." Financial people always seem to have disproportionate power in organizations. Halberstam (1986), in his best-selling book *The Reckoning*, chronicling the auto industry, cites the problems at Ford Motor Company following the era of the "whiz kids" led by Robert McNamara, who later became secretary of defense and head of the World Bank. The whiz kids were MBA graduates of America's finest business schools who applied financial methods to the benefit and the detriment of the company:

> The coming of McNamara to the Ford Motor Company, his protégé Lee Iacocca once said, was one of the best things that ever happened to the company, and his leaving it, Iacocca added, was also one of the best things that ever happened. (p. 207)

Keller (1989) describes General Motors by writing,

> The company has always been run by two distinct types. The first is the real power, the finance people. It is from their ranks that the chairmen [of the Board of Directors] have been selected. . . . The second type is the product engineers. They are the real "car guys." . . . The finance staff is the circulatory system of the company, recruited from the best schools

and compensated on a salary scale that is more lucrative than the rest of the corporation." . . . At General Motors, the finance staff is supreme; it exerts far too much influence over the company. . . . [It results in] the tyranny of the number crunchers. (pp. 23, 27)

Whether you agree with these authors or not, it certainly seems true that financial people wield a great deal of power in organizations. So if you are interested in power, there's a tip.

Upward Communication

The third and fourth most important factors in organizational communication, as studied by Dennis, seem to be involved primarily with **upward communication**—*the process whereby the ideas, feelings, and perceptions of lower-level employees are communicated to those at higher levels in the organization.* When employees are not told *why* they must do things and are not shown the results of their efforts, they tend to become frustrated and disillusioned about their work. One worker told us that he had worked for company X for thirty years and for all he knew he had never done anything right because he only got feedback when he did something wrong.

Research has shown that upward communication can serve at least five important functions:

1. It provides management with needed information for decision making.

2. It helps employees relieve the pressures and frustrations of the work situation.

3. It enhances employees' sense of participation in the enterprise.

4. It serves as a measure of the effectiveness of downward communication.

5. As a bonus, it suggests more rewarding uses of downward communication for the future. (Scholz, 1962, p. 61)

Ironically, although its importance is obvious, upward communication is not always encouraged by management. One reason for this may be that the messages superiors hear from subordinates are not always pleasant or flattering. In one rather extreme case, a foundry manager was reportedly so unreceptive to bad news that his environmental engineers were afraid to tell him the extent to which their foundry was dumping pollutants into a neighboring river. Eventually, the foundry had legal problems with another factory located downstream. The problems could probably have been averted if the manager had been more responsive to the ideas and feelings of his subordinates.

The facetious employee performance appraisal form in Table 11.1 gives examples of the type of information subordinates might want to communicate to their bosses from time to time.

TABLE 11.1

Guide to Employee Performance Appraisal

Performance Factors	Performance Degrees				
	Far Exceeds Job Requirements	Exceeds Job Requirements	Meets Job Requirements	Needs Some Improvements	Does Not Meet Minimum Requirements
Quality	Leaps tall buildings with a single bound	Must take running start to leap over tall buildings	Can only leap over an average building with no spires	Crashes into buildings when attempting to jump over them	Cannot recognize buildings at all, much less jump
Timeliness	Is faster than a speeding bullet	Is as fast as a speeding bullet	Not quite as fast as a speeding bullet	Would you believe a small bullet?	Wounds self with bullets when attempting to shoot
Initiative	Is stronger than a locomotive	Is stronger than a bull elephant	Is stronger than a bull	Shoots the bull	Smells like a bull
Adaptability	Walks on water consistently	Walks on water in emergencies	Washes with water	Drinks water	Passes water in emergencies
Communication	Talks with God	Talks with the angels	Talks to himself	Argues with himself	Loses those arguments

Some bosses might laugh with their employees, others might not think it funny at all. The employer who can see the good-natured humor in some of the entries may be said to have a higher degree of **upward receptivity** or *willingness to receive messages from subordinates.* Upward receptivity is most often associated with the so-called open-door policy in business. If a manager has his or her door open, this signals a willingness to communicate with employees. Unfortunately, an open door does not always signify an open mind. It has been pointed out that the best open-door policy is really one in which a superior opens the door of the subordinate's office to initiate communication. Such action indicates even greater willingness on the superior's part to meet employees halfway in opening the communication channels.

Indeed, initiative on the part of the employer would seem to be one of the best ways to "open the door" to communication within the organization. A number of studies have shown, for example, that most subordinates feel reluctant to communicate information to superiors. That reluctance can be increased (or decreased) by a number of circumstances. In conferences between college students and their professors, students rated professors as more receptive, more trustworthy, and better qualified if they did not sit with a desk between themselves and the students (Widgery and Stackpole, 1972). And, as might be expected, nervousness on the part of the students increased their sensitivity to such variables during the conference. So even such nonverbal factors as closed doors and imposing desks can serve as additional barriers to upward communication.

In another example of nonverbal upward communication, one person wrote to John Molloy, who writes a column on "dressing for success," asking whether a man should wear an earring in a corporate setting. Molloy (1989) entitled his response, "Earring will snag on corporate ladder." He answered, "The only way a young executive wearing an earring can move up in most companies is to be a woman" (p. 3C). So upward communication can be intentional or unintentional, verbal or nonverbal.

A special type of upward communication is **ingratiation**. This is defined by Liden and Mitchell (1988) as *"an attempt by individuals to increase their attractiveness in the eyes of others"* (p. 572). The authors identify three main forms of ingratiation. The first is flattery. Those who are attempting to "get in good" with others above them will often flatter or compliment the other person (often falsely). The second is self-disclosures and advice requests. Ingratiators may reveal personal information or may request the advice of a superior to gain favor. Third is attitude similarity and sincerity. The ingratiator will attempt to stress any similarities between himself or herself and the target person. However, research has shown that any of the ingratiating behaviors mentioned will be effective only if the target person perceives them as sincere (pp. 580–581).

Upward communication is less likely to occur if there are *psychological barriers* between superior and subordinate. Summarizing the literature on this point, Gemmill (1970) states three major psychological barriers that affect upward communication:

1. If a subordinate believes that disclosure of his feelings, opinions, or difficulties may lead a superior to block or hinder the attainment of a personal goal, he will conceal or distort them.

2. The more a superior rewards disclosure of feelings, opinions, and difficulties by subordinates, the more likely they will be to disclose them.

3. The more a superior discloses his own feelings, opinions, and difficulties to subordinates and his superior, the more likely subordinates will be to disclose theirs. (pp. 107–110)

These findings seem to confirm what we have learned about downward communication—that is, that the supervisor who is seen as supportive is preferred. If we feel that we can be ourselves with a superior, that he or she will not use our mistakes against us, we are much more likely to communicate openly. And as a result, the superior is likely to have a better "feel" for the workings of his or her operation. In addition, Gordon and Infante (1991) found that employees strongly valued the freedom to speak their mind to superiors. When that freedom of speech is reduced, their commitment to the organization is markedly reduced (p. 151).

Even when upward communication is effective, however, bosses still have a hard time picturing the organizational realities at levels below them. The reasons for this difficulty are summarized by Reich (1970):

> Top executives know what they are told. In effect, they are "briefed" by others, and the briefing is both limiting and highly selective. The executive is far too busy to find out very much for himself; he must accept the information he gets, and this sets absolute limits to his horizons. Yet the briefing may be three steps removed from the facts, and thus be interpretation built upon interpretation—nearer fiction than fact by the time it reaches the man at the top. The man at the top turns out to be a broker, a decider between limited alternatives. (p. 54)

As we have observed, organizational communication style differs according to the levels of the sender hierarchy. Rice (1987) writes:

> Managers spend most of their time communicating (75–80 percent), about 60 percent of which is oral (phone, face-to-face, or in meetings). Higher-level managers spend more time communicating with subordi-

What are the advantages and disadvantages of employee involvement in organizations?

nates than do lower-level managers; senior managers initiate more downward communication than upward communication; those at lower levels engage in more peer communication; only a small amount of managerial time is actually spent making decisions; managers communicate more in situations of greater innovation and uncertainty; and written communication is less likely to capture the attention of managers because of their fragmented, interrupted schedules. (p. 68)

Harold Geneen, former chairman of the board of International Telephone and Telegraph Corporation, writes in his book *Managing* (1984) how he encouraged upward communication in his multi-billion-dollar conglomerate:

> Our basic and primary policy then became a system in which any staff man could go anywhere in the company and ask any kind of questions and get any kind of answers he could and he could report his findings straight to my office. The only proviso was that he had to inform the manager involved exactly what he was doing before he sent his report upstairs. He did not need his superior's permission to send the report, but he could not act behind the man's back . . .
>
> One of our basic policies at ITT, which grew out of our experience, . . . was: *No surprises!*
>
> Ninety-nine percent of all surprises in business are negative. No matter how adept we were as a management team, mistakes would be made, the unexpected would happen, problems would arise. But the earlier we discovered and dealt with the unexpected problem, the easier it would be to solve. . . .
>
> I wanted no cover-ups, no surprises. (pp. 84, 94)

Keeping these factors in mind, one might conclude that an organization must have effective upward communication if it is to survive.

Horizontal Communication

The survival of a modern organization often depends on the degree to which it specializes. Anyone who has visited a busy hospital, for example, will readily notice the high degree of specialization or differentiation that exists in such an organization. Medical services constitute only one part of the hospital organization. Other units that are vital to its operation include maintenance departments and administrative services such as accounting and personnel.

Coordination or integration of all these diverse units is required to keep the organization running efficiently. It is not unusual in a large university, for example, to find two or more departments teaching similar concepts and even using the same textbooks without knowing it because of a lack of coordination between units. This phenomenon is known as a "differentiation-integration problem" (Lawrence and Lorsch, 1969). It illustrates the intense need for effective **horizontal communication** in organizations—that is, *"the exchanges between and among agencies and personnel on the same level of the organization chart"* (Conboy, 1976, p. 29; italics added).

Horizontal communication frequently suffers in organizations because of employee loyalty to a given department. Groups within the organization compete for power and resources, and new employees are taught to be loyal to their department and not to trust or help those outside it. This situation is intensified in organizations that reward people and groups on a competitive basis. Naturally, if there are four promotions to be awarded among ten departments, rivalries will develop.

In such situations, each department may consider itself to be at the top of the organization. In a manufacturing plant, for example, production departments consider themselves to be the "kingfish" of the organization and regard accountants as "paper shufflers," engineers as "eggheads," and personnel specialists as "the last to know and the first to go." Obviously, members of the other departments would hardly agree.

In summarizing the literature, Goldhaber (1990) has identified four functions of horizontal communication in an organization:

1. *Task coordination:* The department heads may meet monthly to discuss how each department is contributing to the system's goals. Another example of coordination is the frequent use of team-teaching or team-writing found in university communities.

2. *Problem solving:* The members of a department may assemble to discuss how they will handle a threatened budget cut; they may employ brainstorming techniques.

3. *Information sharing:* The members of one department may meet with members of another department to give them some new data. One department at a university recently rewrote its entire curriculum. In order to inform other departments about these major revisions (which affected most segments of the university), the faculty held several meetings with representatives of the other departments to explain the new curriculum.

4. *Conflict resolution:* Members of one department may meet to discuss a conflict inherent in the department or between departments. (p. 121)

Ineffective horizontal communication has been cited as one important factor in the space shuttle *Challenger* accident in January 1986. Since horizontal communication *can* help an organization function more effectively and may even be necessary to avoid tragic accidents, how do we bring it about?

The Linking-Pin Function

A solution offered by Likert (1967) is the **linking-pin function**, which is illustrated in Figure 11.4.

FIGURE 11.4   The Linking-Pin Function (indicated by arrows)

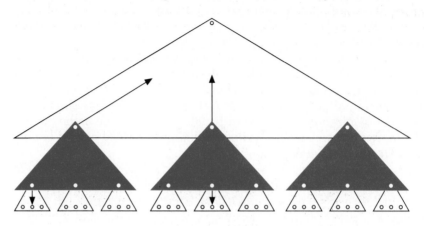

The type of structure shown in Figure 11.4 uses committees made up of people with overlapping—or linking—group memberships in the organization to help coordinate efforts upward, downward, and across the system. Unfortunately, if groups in the organization are rewarded on a competitive basis, overlapping group structure fails to function as intended because of the low levels of trust that exist between group members (see Chapter 3 for a discussion of trust and self-disclosure).

Reducing Barriers

Some steps can be taken to reduce the barriers to horizontal communication. Schein (1970) describes four procedures or guidelines that have proved successful in some cases:

1. Relatively greater emphasis given to *total organizational effectiveness* and the role of departments in contributing to it; departments measured and rewarded on the basis of their *contribution* to the total effort rather than their individual effectiveness.

2. *High interaction* and *frequent communication* stimulated between groups to work on problems of intergroup coordination and help; organizational *rewards given partly on the basis of help* which groups give to each other.

3. Frequent *rotation of members* among groups or departments to stimulate high degree of mutual understanding and empathy for one another's problems.

4. *Avoidance of any win-lose situation;* groups never put into the position of competing for some organizational reward; emphasis always placed on pooling resources to maximize organizational effectiveness; rewards shared equally with all the groups or departments. (p. 102)

A number of *organizational development* (OD) strategies include one form or another of team-building activities, which are designed to implement Schein's four guidelines. Keep in mind, however, that these are only guidelines and may not apply in every situation.

Informal Communication

Last but not least we shall examine the informal channels of communication used in organizations. Such channels are often labeled "rumor mills" and "the grapevine." The term "grapevine" is said to have originated during the Civil War. According to Smith, "In those days, intelligence telegraph lines were strung loosely from tree to tree in the manner of a grapevine, and the message was often garbled; thus, any rumor was said to be from the 'grapevine'" (Smith et al., in Budd and Ruben, 1972, p. 273).

Rosnow (1988) defines a rumor as "a proposition for belief . . . disseminated without official verification" (p. 14). Researchers theorize that rumors help relieve emotional tensions and generally arise under ambiguous circumstances.

It has long been known that ineffective or inadequate downward communication creates an information vacuum in an organization. This vacuum usually is filled by rumors, which are often educated guesses. For example, company X, an organization with over 10,000 employees in its home headquarters in the East, began construction of a new plant on the West Coast. Immediately, a rumor started circulating among the employees that the entire company was going to move its operation west in retaliation for severe union-management problems that had recently developed. When management failed to communicate its intentions to stay in its present location in the East, great fear and unrest developed among the employees. In this case, the rumor was untrue; nevertheless, management felt that the employees' fears about their jobs might help "tame down" union activity. So they deliberately allowed the company's plans to remain ambiguous.

German and Rath (1987) stress the importance of the office "grapevine," writing that "many students tend to equate oral communication with formal public address. . . . But our research indicates that much, if not most, oral communication takes place in largely informal circumstances" (p. 340). They go on to say that one manager stated that when he really needed information, he had his greatest success around the water cooler (or the copying machine).

Variables in Rumor Development

Rosnow (1988) further proposed that rumors are a function of the *ambiguity* of the situation multiplied by the *importance* of the issue. Obviously, the loss of over 10,000 jobs in a city of about 70,000 people is a matter of critical importance. However, rumor transmission is slowed down by a person's *critical sense* that the rumor might not seem valid. These three variables (importance, ambiguity, and critical sense) can be expressed in the following equation:

$$R = i \times a \times \frac{1}{c}$$

According to this equation, rumor R is directly encouraged by importance i and ambiguity a but inversely related to one's critical sense c. In the case of company X, for example, many employees felt that it would probably be too costly to abandon all the company's facilities and technical equipment in the East and start operations all over again in the West; these people did not believe the rumor that was circulating among the other employees and thus did nothing to help spread it.

Types of Message Change

Rumors undergo three types of message change as they pass from one person to another. These changes are (1) leveling, (2) sharpening, and (3) assimilation. **Leveling** is the *process whereby some details are omitted.* Not all the details of a message are interesting to relate, so people tend to get to the point as soon as possible, leaving out what they consider the extraneous details. **Sharpening** is the *exaggeration of certain parts of the rumor.* Suppose, for example, Professor Smith was told to leave Dean Jones's office after a heated exchange of words. When the incident was described by Jones's secretary, Professor Smith had been "thrown out" of the dean's office. And by the third transmission there had been a "fight in the dean's office." As you can see, the story gets more interesting (and less accurate) with each telling. **Assimilation,** a more complicated change, refers to *the way people distort messages to accord with their own view of things.* In a classic study by Allport and Postman (1947), a picture was shown to subjects who were to describe the picture to a second person, who would then tell a third, and so on. The picture showed the interior of a subway car with a roughly dressed white man holding a razor in his hand and talking to a well-dressed black. In the retelling of the story, the razor was moved from the white man's hand to that of the black. Obviously, this detail fit in more closely with racial stereotypes held by the subjects in the experiment.

Speed and Accuracy

Using a method called *Episodic Communication Channels in Organizations (ECCO) Analysis* in which subjects identify persons from whom they have heard a rumor and pinpoint when they heard it, Davis (1953*a*; 1953*b*) and others have described several additional characteristics of grapevine communication. The grapevine, they point out, is one of the fastest methods of communicating in an organization. The grapevine is also often quite accurate. (Davis [1972] found between 80 and 90 percent accuracy in the case of noncontroversial rumors.) And the grapevine may carry a lot of information. For example, think about the information you get from friends on which courses (and professors) to take and which to stay away from. Finally, the grapevine is not considered reliable by most people in an organization—mainly because of the three types of message distortions described above. Tubbs and associates (1973) surveyed six hundred randomly selected automotive employees to identify which sources of information were (1) most frequently used, (2) most preferred, and (3) most reliable. The alternative channels that were used in the study are listed below:

Information rack
Department meetings
Formal presentation by plant
  management
Movie or slide presentations
Letters sent home
Suggestion plan
Daily newspaper
TV
Radio
Grapevine
Foreman or supervisor (word of
  mouth)
Personnel department (word of
  mouth)

Corporate central office memos
Public affairs newsletters
Union publications
Management bulletin board
Notice with paycheck
Union representative (committee
  person)
Coworker in same department
Coworker in other department
Division or plant publications
  (newsletter, newspaper, mag-
  azine, or handout)
Posters
Other ways

Results of the study indicate that the grapevine ranked as the second most frequently used channel of organizational communication (the most-used channel was the employee's immediate supervisor). As a source of information, however, the grapevine was ranked *next to last* on both reliability and desirability. So the grapevine is considered by employees to be an important, but not always preferred, channel of communication within an organization.

SUMMARY

In this chapter we have discussed human communication that occurs in the context of organizations. We have seen that this context involves more people and is more complex than public communication.

Initially, we discussed three defining characteristics of organizations. Division of labor, or the process of organizing work so that employees produce only part of a product, was shown to increase overall efficiency. "Span of control" was defined as the range of people under the authority of one supervisor. The pyramid of control, or hierarchy of supervision, in an organization was depicted on a chart indicating formal channels of communication. We also mentioned that the informal communication networks are in addition to those shown on the organization chart.

Second, we discussed the growing importance of communication in a postindustrial society. Evidence indicates that quality of communication in organizations relates to overall performance goals. This has been found to be true in such widely divergent organizations as engineering firms, hospitals, manufacturing plants, and universities.

In downward communication a basic problem is how to communicate enough information to employees without "overloading them." In this respect, a combination of written and oral messages seems to be more effective than either written or oral messages alone. More message distortion seems to occur at lower levels in the organization, and superior to subordinate communication has been shown to be the single most important component in successful organizational communication. The most desired type of supervisory communication style is the supportive style.

Upward communication, or communication from subordinate to superior, has proved valuable to upper management in maintaining an accurate picture of day-to-day organizational operations. As we have seen, however, there are numerous nonverbal as well as psychological barriers to effective upward communication. Again, a supportive or receptive supervisory style is more likely to promote upward communication.

Horizontal communication was defined as the method that helps to coordinate all the diverse functions of an organization. We saw here the paradox between the need for specialization of functions on one hand and the need for coordination of these functions on the other.

In the last section we examined the role of informal communication in organizations. Research has shown that transmission of rumors in an organization is influenced by the importance and ambiguity of the situation as well as by the critical sense of the people involved. Leveling, sharpening, and assimilation were shown as three forms of message distortion that commonly occur in the transmission of rumors. Finally, we found that grapevine communication is a frequently used but not necessarily preferred source of information in organizations.

REVIEW QUESTIONS

1. What are three functions communication performs in organizations?

2. What is the general research finding regarding the type of supervisory style that is preferred by employees?

3. What are five ways in which people adapt to information overload?

4. Explain the law of diminishing returns as it relates to downward communication.

5. Discuss and illustrate the five types of power.

6. What are five functions of upward communication?

7. What are two barriers to upward communication?

8. Explain the differentiation-integration problem in organizations.

9. How does this relate to horizontal communication?

10. Explain the formula $R = i \times a \times (1/c)$ as it relates to rumors.

11. Identify the three types of message distortion that occur during rumor transmission.

EXERCISES

1. Have the class break up into groups of five or six, and discuss the following. If you were Sam Edwards and were faced with the problem of employees using the photocopier for personal business (see pp. 361–362), how would you try to solve it? Have each discussion group decide on a specific plan of attack for solving this problem. Then have the groups share their solutions with the entire class. What organizational communication issues are involved in this case problem? What other issues are indirectly related to this problem?

2. Divide the class into small groups and have each group discuss the following case problem. After each group has shared its reactions with the other groups, discuss the principles from this chapter that are illustrated by the case.

   In the men's sportswear department of Samson's Department Store two men and four women are regularly employed as sales personnel. In addition to salary, they receive a bonus determined by how much their daily volume of sales exceeds a quota. Mr. Wilcox, the buyer, is head of the department, but during his frequent absences his assistant buyer, Mr. Jones, is in charge. In addition to six regulars, during the summer the department employs several extra salespersons. These are college students on vacation, who have been given some training by the store's personnel department. They are eager beavers and often outsell the regulars. They also work for a salary plus bonus.

   During Mr. Wilcox's absence on a buying trip, the regulars complained to Mr. Jones that the extras were making it difficult for them to make their quotas, that they mixed up the stock and generally were a nuisance. Mr. Jones, a close friend of one of the regulars, ordered the extras to take care of the stock and to sell only when customers were waiting. On his return, Mr. Wilcox countermanded this order; he told the extras to get in there and sell or look for other jobs. A competitive spirit, he said, was good for the department. The regulars are now more resentful than ever; customers are beginning to notice the bad feelings, and some of them have taken their trade elsewhere.

Which one of the following comments on this situation seems to you most sound?

a. Mr. Wilcox should return to the position taken earlier by his assistant—that is, instruct the extras to work on stock and handle customers only when no regular is free.

b. In addition to telling the extras to sell at top capacity, Mr. Wilcox should call the regulars in, take a firm stand with them, and advise them to increase their sales or look elsewhere for work.

c. Mr. Wilcox is right: A competitive spirit is good for the department. Beyond making this point clear, he should continue to maintain a hands-off policy and let the situation work itself out.

d. Mr. Wilcox should pay the extras a straight hourly wage.

e. Mr. Wilcox should investigate the activities of all employees and also check into the company's compensation plan.

3. Have five people leave the classroom. Then bring them back into the room one at a time. Start a rumor by giving the first person a short description of an event. Be sure the story has at least a few details such as time, location, names, number of people involved, and so on. Or show a picture of an event and ask the person to describe what is going on in the picture. Then have each person in turn give his or her version of the story (or picture) to the next person who comes back into the room. Have the rest of the class try to keep track of the leveling, sharpening, and assimilation that occur as the story is told and retold.

4. Discuss the following case and determine answers to the two questions that follow:

A clinical psychologist at a university feels that his interviews with a client should be recorded on tape and that the benefits to be derived from such recordings would be impaired if the client knew in advance that the recording was to be made. The psychologist sometimes uses these recordings in his classroom to illustrate his lectures, always without the knowledge of the client, though the client's name is not revealed to the class.

What should be the university's policy in this matter? How should the policy be communicated? What considerations are there in trying to communicate this policy?

5. Suppose you are a manager of an office and you hear that the head of your account department (who is married) is believed by many to be having an affair with a married woman in the personnel department. You (Mr. Wilson) call him (Mr. Townsend) into your office to discuss this matter. Have two people in the class role play this conversation. How would you change the conversation if you were taking into account what we discussed about rumors in this chapter?

SUGGESTED READINGS

Goldhaber, Gerald M. _Organizational Communication._ 5th ed. Dubuque, IA: William C. Brown, 1990.

Certainly one of the best, if not _the best,_ book available on this subject. It is comprehensive, accurate, and very well written. Must reading for anyone wanting to know more about this subject.

Jablin, Frederic M., Linda L. Putnam, Karlene H. Roberts, and **Lyman W. Porter,** eds. _Handbook of Organizational Communication: An Interdisciplinary Perspective._ Newbury Park, CA: Sage, 1987.

This is one of the most comprehensive books available on this subject. The book consists of numerous essays written by some of the most highly respected scholars in the field. It is quite advanced and is recommended for the serious student.

Lau, James B., and **A. B. (Rami) Shani.** _Behavior in Organizations: An Experiential Approach._ 5th ed. Homewood, IL: Irwin, 1992.

This book is a very popular text with dozens of communication-related experiential exercises that are easily used by student leadership groups. It is a very useful resource book.

O'Hair, Dan, and **Gustav Friedrich.** _Strategic Communication: In Business and the Professions._ Boston: Houghton-Mifflin, 1992.

This rather unique book examines a wide variety of topics all related to organizational communication. In addition, one of your authors went to graduate school with Dr. Friedrich many years ago.

Roger and Me.

This 1991 film won an academy award for best documentary. It is a scathing albeit tongue-in-cheek look at General Motors through the eyes of an underground journalist. It offers rich material for class discussion regarding organizational communication, especially with the outside media.

Smeltzer, Larry, John Waltman, and **Donald Leonard.** _Managerial Communication: A Strategic Approach._ 2d ed. Needham Heights, MA: Ginn Press, 1991.

This comprehensive text covers many aspects of organizational communication. It also includes several excellent chapters on written communication and the strategies behind each message.

CHAPTER TWELVE

Mass Communication

CHAPTER OBJECTIVES

After reading this chapter, you should be able to:

1 Explain how mass communication, because it is mediated, differs from personal encounters; and identify four characteristics of mass communication.

2 Explain the concept of the gatekeeper and describe several variables influencing gatekeeper choice.

3 State two theories concerning the flow of messages from the mass media to individual receivers.

4 Explain the concept of the active audience and its connection with selective attention.

5 Discuss the research findings on media uses and gratifications.

6 Discuss the extent to which the mass media disseminate information and influence attitudes.

7 Describe the influence mass communication has on social learning, particularly in children, and sum up the issue of media violence.

8 Discuss the implications of the new communication technologies, including their relationship to the mass media and effects on interpersonal communication.

What a computer message can accomplish within an office, CNN achieves around the clock, around the globe: it gives everyone the same information, the same basis for discussion, at the same moment. That change in communication has in turn affected journalism, intelligence gathering, economics, diplomacy and even, in the minds of some scholars, the very concept of what it is to be a nation.

HENRY, 1992, p. 24

*N*ot everyone agrees that satellite-fed news gathering is going to require a new kind of journalism. It seems clear, however, that mass communication as we know it—through television, films, radio, newspapers, magazines, and books—is undergoing enormous changes. To establish how such diverse experiences can all be encompassed by the term "mass communication" is the first task of this chapter.

A FIRST DEFINITION

Mediated Encounters

As suggested in Chapter 1, every aspect of mass communication is **mediated,** and mediated encounters are different from personal encounters (Avery and McCain, 1982). First, the *sensory input potential for receivers is more limited.* Second, *receivers* of a mediated message *have little or no control over its sources*—that is, feedback is extremely limited. And finally, *the sources* of mediated messages *are known either in a limited way or* not known at all, *only imagined.*

In Woody Allen's film *The Purple Rose of Cairo,* Mia Farrow plays a young woman who escapes her lackluster husband and depressing job by constantly going to the movies. One night the young handsome hero of a movie she is watching steps off the screen and addresses her directly, asking why she has seen the movie so many times. A romance develops between Farrow and the celluloid hero, and for a time she loses her point of reference as her fantasies become real. What Woody Allen plays with here is the failure to distinguish between mediated and personal encounters—the media experience (film) becoming more real than the interpersonal.

As we amplify our definition of mass communication, keep in mind Wright's (1986) point that mass communication is not defined in terms of technological achievements:

It is not the technical apparatus of the mass media that distinguish mass communication. . . . Rather, it is a special kind of social communication involving distinctive characteristics of the audience, the communication experience, and the communicator. (p. 7)

According to Wright, in **mass communication** *the audience is relatively large, heterogeneous, and anonymous to the source.* The *experience is public, rapid, and fleeting.* The *source works* through a *complex organization* rather than in isolation, and *the message may represent the efforts of many different people* (pp. 5–8).

The Audience

Consider again the first element in Wright's definition: the audience. Perhaps most significant for our purpose is its size. News of the Gulf War was watched by millions on network television, and CNN's coverage was virtually continuous. Similarly, the riots in Los Angeles following the Rodney King

Mass communication can, for a time, bind together audiences of immense size and diversity.

verdict—as well as a videotape of King's beating by police—were viewed by a vast audience, who also turned to other media: radio, newspapers, and magazines. Although in person-to-group and organizational settings, face-to-face interaction is often possible, in mass communication, the size of the audience makes it impossible for the mass communicator and audience members to interact face to face. In addition to being a diversified group, the receivers in mass communication are, for the most part, unknown to the source. This is not to say that members of a mass communication audience are isolated from other human beings. It is possible—in fact, very likely—for us to experience mass communication as members of dyads, small groups, or organizations. Husband and wife may be out seeing a movie. Half the dorm may be watching the Olympics on television. The day after a show opens, the entire cast of a theatrical production may be reading the newspaper reviews in the director's apartment.

The Communication Experience

As for the second element, the communication experience itself, it is intended for rapid consumption by great numbers of people. Moreover, it is characterized as public rather than private because the messages are not addressed to particular individuals. Think of a public official addressing a very large audience of farmers in a public hall. Although the speaker may not know any of the farmers personally, he or she is aware of the audience as a group and is directing what is said to those people. If the same problems were to be discussed on a radio broadcast, that message would be received by a highly diversified group of people who were, for the most part, unknown to the speaker. This is one of the important ways in which mass communication and the public, or person-to-group, communication described in Chapter 10 differ.

The Source of Communication

The third element in this definition of mass communication, the source of the communication, is not working in isolation but rather from within a complex organization. This means that there may be considerable expense involved because of the division of labor that is part and parcel of such organizations. There are two points to be made here. First, the message itself represents the efforts of many different individuals, which we shall understand more clearly when we discuss the concept of the gatekeeper. Second, these people represent a complex organization which, in this country, is usually concerned with making a profit.

As we said in Chapter 1, mass communication events sometimes require the efforts of hundreds of people, months of preparation, and millions of dollars. Individual salaries can be spectacular. (Consider, for example, the $14 million salary CBS offered David Letterman to leave NBC.)

Profits in mass communication are often equally spectacular—a fact that has prompted an increasing number of corporate takeovers. During the 1980s, book publishing, long considered a "gentleman's occupation" with little hope of great financial gain, became both profitable and competitive with the proliferation of paperback books, the sale of book-club rights, and, more recently, the sale of film rights for best-selling novels—Tom Clancy's *The Hunt for Red October,* Marguerite Duras's *The Lover,* and Scott Turow's *Presumed Innocent,* to name just a few. In fact, the success of Turow, a practicing lawyer, has prompted a number of other lawyers to try their hand at writing courtroom thrillers. Advances to several well-known fiction writers have reached dizzying figures. According to *The Wall Street Journal,* Stephen King was promised over $30 million for his next four books, "sight unseen."

We have said that in this country the mass media are usually concerned with making a profit, and a good part of that profit will depend upon advertising. Although there are countries in which the mass media are independent of such concerns, in the United States advertising dominates mass communication. And certainly awareness of the extent to which advertising maintains the mass media should affect the source credibility mass communicators have for their audiences. There are many ethical considerations as well. For example, one estimate is that by age sixteen the average viewer will have seen over 600,000 commercials, yet recent studies show that children have difficulty in telling the difference between programs and commercials (Kunkel and Roberts, 1991). There is no doubt that possible conflicts between the profit-making functions of the mass media as businesses and their responsibilities to the public can also affect the free flow of information.

In this chapter our first concern will be with how mass communication is related to other modes of human communication. As we have seen, mass communication is not face-to-face communication. It is mediated, and this immediately sets it apart from the other communication contexts we have been discussing. We have considered several defining elements of mass communication: the audience, the communication experience, and the communicator. If we are to evaluate mass communication within the framework of other communication contexts, we must add still another element to Wright's definition: the limited feedback possible in mass communication.

Delayed Feedback

Feedback is given in mass communication. There should be no confusion about this. It is true, for example, that television viewers can write or telephone a network concerning a given program and that enough letters, calls, or responses to a rating survey will affect the future of that program. But usually those viewers will not be face to face with the television producer or, for that matter, with the executive in charge of programming, and the feedback will not be as immediate or complete as it would be on a face-to-face basis. And since mass communication usually involves a chain or network of individuals, the feedback intended for one person in the chain is likely to reach a different member of the chain. Moreover, it is sometimes impossible for the source in mass communication to respond to and make public all the feedback that is received. For example, the *Seattle Times* receives approximately 7,000 letters to the editor each year; *The New York Times,* roughly 40,000. A large metropolitan paper such as the *Times* can print only about 5 percent (Dominick, 1993, p. 487). Letters to the editor vary a great deal in content: They express praise or disagreement, offer observations from personal experience, comment on "shameless" editorials, or correct points of information. Today, of course, audience members need not wait for their letters to arrive; they can fax their disapproval.

So despite the striking differences that seem to set off mass communication from other kinds of human communication, there is also a degree of overlap between different modes. As we discuss the mass communication process, we shall also see some ways in which mass and face-to-face communication perform complementary functions.

THE PROCESS OF MASS COMMUNICATION

The Gatekeeper

Essential to an understanding of the workings of mass communication is the concept of the **gatekeeper.** A gatekeeper is *a person who, by selecting, changing, and rejecting messages, can influence the flow of information to a receiver or group of receivers.* Although the concept of the gatekeeper might be applied to other contexts of communication—think, for example, of our discussion in Chapter 11 about how rumors are created—it is particularly relevant to mass communication.

Imagine yourself for a moment as the wire editor of a metropolitan newspaper. You are looking at a computer screen. It is your job to go through all the news items provided by the various wire services to which your paper subscribes. On an average day there might be some 3,000 items, out of which only 200 will be selected. As you go over all this copy on the screen, you have to ask yourself questions: "Did we run anything in yesterday's paper that was like it?" "Will this copy be of broad enough interest for our readers?" "Are other papers covering it?" "Is there room for this story today?" "What are the chances that there will be more important stories later in the day?" "Will we make the deadline if we wait?"

These are some of the considerations that determine which items are discarded and which are selected and edited. Gatekeeping is a necessary aspect of mass communication, and gatekeepers exist in all the mass media. For example, a researcher for a television documentary can include only a limited amount of information in a half-hour program; a film editor might have to reduce fifteen minutes of footage to a two-minute segment for a particular scene; the reader in a publishing house might select five out of a hundred manuscripts to be reviewed by house editors.

Moreover, in mass communication we find a network or *chain* of gate-keepers. The following is a simplified example of the gatekeeping process: The senior editor of a monthly art magazine gets an idea for an article and discusses the idea with the editor-in-chief, who approves it. The senior editor then assigns it to a free-lance writer and specifies the length of the article and the number of color transparencies needed for the illustrations. The writer decides which aspects of the story to include and adapts the coverage to the needs of the magazine, then selects appropriate color transparencies from several sources.

Once the article is written, it goes back to the senior editor, who reads it, suggests how much editing it needs, and then assigns the work to an assistant editor. The author of the article then reviews the changes and answers any editorial queries. The managing editor checks the color transparencies, selects half, and turns them over to the art director. The copy is set electronically, and the layout and photographs are handled by a member of the art department. Before the article appears in the magazine, it is reviewed and approved by the managing editor and the editor-in-chief.

This is a much simplified version of the chain of gatekeepers involved in even the publication of a single, uncontroversial magazine article. Imagine, if you can, the number of gatekeepers who may be involved in the publication of the entire magazine. Gatekeeping in mass communication involves a selection process that has analogies with the selection process going on in all other contexts of communication—from two-person to organizational.

Although there are often multiple gatekeepers, critical decisions in the mass media are sometimes made by a single person. For example, Bob Furnad was in charge of the CNN control room during the William Kennedy Smith trial. Just as the accuser was called to the stand by the prosecutor, Furnad suddenly heard that former hostage Terry Anderson was to make his first public appearance at 3:30 that afternoon:

> What should Furnad do: continue to cover the long-awaited testimony of the accuser in the most publicized rape trial in history or cut away to Terry Anderson's press conference. . . .
>
> The decision is made quietly, almost imperceptibly: no matter what is happening at the trial, CNN will cut away to Anderson. Their best hope is that his appearance will coincide with the trial's recess, due to come at 3:30. (Zoglin, 1992, p. 31)

The gatekeeper's choices concerning what information to select and reject are influenced by many variables. Bittner (1985) identifies the following:

The first, is **economics:** Most mass media in this country are profit making, or concerned with how their money is raised and spent. Thus, advertisers, sponsors, and contributors may have a major impact on news selection and editorials. For example, some radio stations even give listeners an opportunity to respond on the air to editorials with which they disagree.

Second, such **legal restrictions** as libel laws will affect news selection and presentation. Federal Communications Commission regulations also have an impact, particularly on the issue of who will be allowed to own and operate a broadcasting facility. And local regulations are influential: for instance, local regulation of X-rated movies on cable television (the Supreme Court held that local governments can regulate what appears on cable).

Deadlines affect depth as well as the time available to determine the accuracy of news selected. And deadlines also affect *what* will be broadcast: When only a brief amount of time is available, the gatekeeper makes choices concerning relative importance. When the gatekeeper must choose between two stories of equal worth, it's the one that has a video story that usually is selected (p. 378).

The gatekeeper's **ethics,** both personal and professional, also influence the news that will be selected. It's an ethical judgment that determines how much back-bending will take place to be "fair" to a sponsor or a cause endorsed by that sponsor. Personal ethics—and the extent of the gatekeeper's awareness of his or her own beliefs—will influence whether the gatekeeper's likes and dislikes, attitudes, and interests play a part in news selection. For example, it's possible that a financial columnist could affect a company's stock with a story and allow friends to have inside information before the story is printed.

A fifth factor is **competition** among media: In a market with several available sources, such competition is likely to raise the overall level of professionalism, thus ensuring a more objective presentation of information. On the other hand, a town with only one newspaper usually gets one point of view—that of the paper's editor.

Sixth, **news value,** *the intensity of an item in comparison with all others available,* and **news hole,** *the amount of space or time it takes to present the story,* need to be balanced. Besides balancing these two, gatekeepers must weigh the claims of local interest against those of national interest. For example, how much time should be given to a new statewide campaign to conserve water when the president has just made a major foreign policy announcement?

Another of the important factors that affects what gatekeepers select or reject is the **reaction to feedback,** although that feedback is delayed. If a political cartoon offends an ethnic group, for example, and that group has representatives who write irate letters or insist on a public apology, a magazine editor might deliberate a long time before including another cartoon of that kind. Reactions to two television dramas on teenage suicide resulted in a public controversy over whether such programs were more damaging than helpful. Here again is an instance in which the gatekeeper must weigh media goals against public opinion.

The gatekeeper function can also involve complex questions concerning federal control of broadcast licensing, the general freedom of the media to present information, censorship, and the responsibilities of the mass media to the public. Everette Dennis of Columbia University's Gannett Center for Media Studies has compared the ubiquitous nature of the mass media to "a kind of central nervous system for the nation and, perhaps, the world" (1988, p. 349), noting the "sheer, raw power" of the media and their virtual monopoly on many kinds of information. He points out that because the media make choices concerning which issues, events, or people are more important than others, they establish an agenda of sorts. If they do not tell us what to think, they "do tell us what to think about as they narrow and refine the focus of public discussion" (p. 350).

There have been many disagreements concerning the role and responsibilities of those in the media. Dennis describes an incident following a ceremony honoring educators at the White House rose garden:

> President Reagan passed by Sam Donaldson of ABC News who asked whether the Bork nomination would be withdrawn. Even before the President responded (his answer: "Over my dead body!"), some of the teachers yelled, "Shut up!" Amid hissing and booing, there was an angry exchange between the teachers and the reporters present. "You've ruined the ceremony," said one of the teachers. One added, "We're disappointed with you, Mr. Donaldson!" While another said, "We teach our students that all rights have responsibilities." Donaldson angrily shouted back at the teachers, saying he was disappointed they didn't understand freedom of the press and the role of the White House press corps. (Dennis, 1988, p. 350)

In arguing for "responsible communication" in the media, Redding (1988) emphasized that "responsible" does not necessarily mean "safe" or "compliant." "Silence itself can be irresponsible," and irresponsible communication sometimes involves a lack of verbal messages.

Other kinds of silence are also possible. The Gulf War presented a particularly critical incident for journalists in many ways (Zelizer, 1992). During wartime, one ethical dilemma for the press has usually been "'how to communicate events fairly and accurately, without revealing confidential military information'" (p. 68). Yet several critics maintain that editors and members of the press were too accepting about the government's pool system: In recent years the Pentagon has restricted news gathering through a press pool, with only a few journalists witnessing action and then reporting back to other correspondents. MacArthur (1992) and others have argued that government figures about Iraqi troop strength were exaggerated as were accounts of the success and importance of "smart bombs" and that, in effect, the news media were reduced to "a state of subservience" by being limited to pool coverage.

The Gulf War also established the ascendancy of CNN's satellite-fed news over network news for wartime reporting—with the networks and newspapers often looking to CNN's coverage. By remaining in Baghdad to continue reporting behind enemy lines, Peter Arnett of CNN became the object of public criticism:

> When Arnett reported that the allies had bombed a plant producing infant formula and not biological weapons as the U.S. insisted, and public fears intensified that his dispatches were being used for propaganda purposes, journalists spoke out in his behalf. (Zelizer, 1992, p. 74)

To many reporters, Arnett became "the first war correspondent of the global village" (p. 75).

It is clear that technological development will make ethical issues about the mass media even more complex. We will discuss ethical questions about mass communication in Chapter 14.

Message Flow

Hypodermic Needle Model

In early studies of mass communication, it was generally believed that the flow of information from source to receiver was always direct and immediate. According to this view, often referred to as the **hypodermic needle model,** *each audience member receives messages directly from the source of a given medium.* The implication is that if the "injection" is powerful enough, it will "take"—that is, it will influence the receiver in some way. A further implication of such a theory is that the mass media can have an almost magical, and sometimes a potentially dangerous, effect on audiences (especially if the media are used to mount massive propaganda campaigns).

For example, when Ross Perot ran for president in 1992, he tried to maintain strict control over the flow of messages he wished to deliver to the American people. He initiated his campaign with early appearances on *Larry King Live* and participated in the presidential debates, but he kept his appearances on panel shows and other interviewing formats to a minimum. Instead, he was able to finance a series of half-hour television programs of his own making in which he spoke directly to the people and was not subject to questioning from the press and various political analysts.

Opinion Leaders

The first study to change the direction of thinking about message flow in mass communication was an analysis done in 1948 of how and why people had decided whom they would vote for during the 1940 presidential campaign. The researchers were interested in the general impact of mass media on voting behavior and especially on the people who changed their voting intention during the course of the campaign. Their findings are particularly surprising to proponents of the hypodermic needle model of mass communication. One important finding was that broad coverage of the campaign by the mass media simply reinforced the initial preferences of the voters. Even more significant is the finding that for people who did change their minds about how they would vote, the major source of influence was **personal influence**—*the influence of other people.* In other words, even in mass communication contexts, the receiver had to be viewed within a larger social setting (Lazarsfeld et al., 1968).

Given our discussions of attitude influence and similarity (Chapter 6) and social influence in a small-group setting (Chapter 9), it should not be surprising to learn that we are influenced by members of the many groups we belong to—family members, fellow workers, club members, church members, and so on. The findings of Lazarsfeld and others take this a step further, suggesting that within the groups to which we belong, certain people have a particularly strong influence. These people have been called **opinion leaders**—*"individuals who, through day-to-day personal contacts, influence others in matters of decision and opinion formation"* (Wright, 1986). And the decisions concern all kinds of matters, not just voting—for example, what type of car to buy, the most fashionable way to dress, the best school to attend, and so on.

Opinion leaders can come from any social, economic, or occupational level. Within different levels of society, there are different opinion leaders. They all tend to be better informed and to be heavy users of the various mass media. They read more newspapers and magazines; they watch the coverage of political and social issues by the broadcast media. And in addition to receiving greater exposure to the mass media, they tend to be influenced by them. This influence, in turn, is passed on to others in face-to-face communication.

It was this discovery that generated a **two-step flow model** of mass communication. According to this theory, on many occasions *information is passed from the various mass media to certain opinion leaders and from these leaders to other people within the population.* Further studies suggests that it is often more accurate to think in terms of **multiple,** or **n-step, flow model,** since opinion leaders may also be consulting with others whom *they* consider opinion leaders.

In studying mass communication in relationship to other communication contexts, the concept of opinion leadership is crucial, for it makes clear the complementary roles of mass and face-to-face communication.

> Opinion leaders are not a group set apart, and . . . opinion leadership is not a trait which some people have and others do not. . . . Opinion leadership is an integral part of the give-and-take of everyday personal relationships. . . . An opinion leader can best be thought of as a group member playing a key communications role. (Katz and Lazarsfeld, 1964)

The Active Audience

Along with such concepts as multiple-step flow and opinion leadership has come a new concept of the receivers of mass communication. Implicit in the hypodermic needle model is the concept of a passive audience, a group of rather compliant people who, given a potent enough message, receive and absorb whatever was intended by the mass media. Such an audience could be manipulated into buying whatever product was given the most advertising nationwide or voting for the candidate who had the most exposure on radio and television. It is an audience made up of people who do not interact with other human beings or accept group norms, people who are not, in fact, seen as living within a social context. But today the receivers of mass communication are increasingly thought of as an **active** or **obstinate audience.** You have already seen some reference to this concept in Chapter 5, in our discussion of critical listening. Schramm and Roberts (1971) characterize this newer view of the mass communication audience well:

> an intensely active audience, seeking what it wants, rejecting far more content than it accepts, interacting both with the members of the groups it belongs to and with the media content it receives, and often testing the mass media message by talking it over with other persons or comparing it with other media content. (p. 191)

In what ways is an audience active? Perhaps the most obvious way is in the selection of the mass communication to which it will be exposed. You control what you listen to, watch, and read. You buy the newspaper of your choice. You go to the movies you like. You choose from among many television programs, and if you find yourself watching something you don't like, you can turn it off. If you own a VCR, you rent videotapes of what you want to see or tape programs yourself. In many ways, we can control this aspect of communication more readily than we can control face-to-face communication. It is much easier, for example, to turn off the television set if we dislike a program or even to walk out of a theater in the middle of a bad film than it is to conclude face-to-face communication so abruptly. Increasingly widespread use of the VCR has had an impact not only on family interaction but on the mass media; today it offers a significant challenge to research in mass communication (Morgan and Shanahan, 1991).

Selective Exposure

To put it another way, the person who watches a particular television program to the end or finishes reading a particular newspaper editorial tends to agree with the attitudes and opinions being presented. These are examples of a phenomenon known as **selective exposure,** *the tendency to choose communication that will confirm your own opinions, attitudes, or values.* This is a broad concept, and we have already seen in Chapter 6 how it can work on a one-to-one basis. We tend to like and seek out those whose beliefs, attitudes, and values are similar to our own, and to dislike and avoid people we perceive as different from us in these respects. Selective exposure is equally present in mass communication, where, for example, the vast majority of people who read the *Nation* are liberals and most of the people who read the *National Review* are conservatives.

Selective Attention

In addition to the selective nature of our exposure to the mass media, our perception itself is selective. As we examined perception in Chapter 2, we spoke about **selective attention,** *in which the receiver processes certain of the available stimuli while filtering out others.* This screening process takes place in mass communication just as it does in other contexts of human communication. It takes place whether we are watching a situation comedy, a political debate, or a sports event.

A case in point is the study of a football game that took place between Princeton and Dartmouth. It turned out to be a rough contest: Princeton's star player suffered a broken nose and later in the game a Dartmouth player broke his leg. Films of the game were shown to students from both schools involved. To almost all the Princeton students the game was "rough and dirty," with Dartmouth making over twice the number of infractions made by Princeton. Dartmouth students felt that both sides were to blame and that charges against Dartmouth were unfounded. In concluding their study, the authors wrote, "There is no such thing as a 'game' existing 'out there' in its own right which people merely 'observe.' The 'game' exists for a person and is experienced by him only insofar as certain happenings have significance in terms of his purpose" (Hastorf and Cantril, 1954, p. 133).

Concepts such as selective attention are well illustrated by examples from the political arena. In the televised Bush-Dukakis debates, Bush supporters tended to see him as the "winner," and Dukakis supporters for the most part saw him as the "winner." Responses to the debates between Clinton, Bush, and Perot were similar. As we assess the various outcomes of mass communication, we shall see other ways in which beliefs, attitudes, and values of the receiver influence his or her perceptions.

In discussing selective attention, we use the word "receiver" rather than "audience member" to emphasize once again the continuity between the receiving function in face-to-face communication and the receiving function in mass communication. Message reception is an active process: it is behavior. Listening to the radio is behavior, watching television is behavior, and so is reading a best-seller or a newspaper. When engaged in any of these activities, individual receivers are selecting and processing information.

At the other end of the communication cycle we have seen a parallel selection process at work in the gatekeeping function. We have also seen that the flow of information from the mass communicator to the individual receivers sometimes involves opinion leaders and therefore face-to-face communication, so that at times there is a multiple-step flow rather than a direct flow of information. Similarly, the flow of feedback from the individual receiver to the mass communicator can also involve several steps. For example, parents concerned about the violence present in children's television programs may take group action through an organization such as Action for Children's Television, which in turn gives feedback not only to various television stations but to governmental agencies that regulate the broadcast media.

Another way of looking at the selectivity of receivers of mass communication is to examine how and when they use particular mass media as well as the basis for their choices.

Media Uses and Gratifications

The relationship between personal and mediated communication continues to be an important area of research. Those who study the interface between mass and interpersonal communication stress that the media to which we attend are an integral part of our interpersonal world. One comparison of how various media and interpersonal communication sources are used finds that "media and interpersonal sources serve similar functions. . . . They are both used by people 'to connect (or sometimes disconnect) themselves. . . . with different kinds of others (self, family, friends, nation, etc.)'" (Rubin et al., 1988, p. 607). Moreover, Rubin and Rubin (1985) argue that mass media use is goal directed—that is, people make choices about what media they will use for particular reasons.

Others go so far as to argue that "generation" as a signifier of human time relationships is not as accurate as groups based on media relationships (Gumpert and Cathcart, 1985). They propose that we distinguish between precomputer and postcomputer generations and that the difference in generations has less to do with age than with computer literacy and its effect on how the world is viewed. In these terms, computer-literate people have a different view of "public" and "private" information than those not as literate.

Given this position, two questions may be asked: First, what are the reasons we choose one medium over another? Second, which media can serve as alternatives for each other?

On the basis of their findings, Lichtenstein and Rosenfeld (1984) argue that our perceptions of each medium are culture-bound: We are taught, socialized, to view each medium in a particular way and to understand which media may serve as alternatives for others. When our object is to learn about the world, we choose newspapers and magazines—not recorded music or films. When our object is to learn about ourselves and our immediate environment, we turn to friends. Although books and magazines are regarded as possible alternatives, films, commercial TV, radio, and recorded music are not even considered sources of information. When we want to be entertained, many media may be selected, including commercial television, friends, recorded music, films, and radio; in this instance, newspapers and public TV are not regarded as alternatives. On the other hand, if the motivation is to kill time, choices seem to be commercial television, magazines, and radio (and not friends or public television).

Lichtenstein and Rosenfeld conclude that the decision to make use of mass communication channels is a two-part process: First, we are taught what motivations each medium can gratify; then, based on that information we all share, each of us makes individual choices (p. 409). Though the choices are personal decisions, our perceptions of what different media offer are relatively consistent: We tend to have a stable image of the perceived gratifications of each medium—film, books, newspapers, and so on. And that image is independent of whether we use the medium ourselves or whether we evaluate it for ourselves or for people in general (p. 410). Choices are not determined solely by this shared information, however.

Research on television viewing shows several demographic patterns: Females are more likely to use television for companionship; "younger people watch television to pass time, the middle-aged watch to pass time and seek information, and elders watch to seek information." But when older people live in larger households, they are less likely to seek companionship by turning to television; older people who interact with others a great deal use television to relax, to be entertained, and to find topics of conversation (Rubin et al., 1988, p. 609).

According to Snow, the mass media function as a social form and may be "the most important institution in contemporary American society," enabling us to manage many types of social affairs and influencing how we experience even mundane aspects of our lives (1987, p. 228). Snow believes that we use media to establish and maintain routinized behavior as well as to help maintain particular rhythm and tempo moods: "To the extent that people schedule their daily use of media, interaction with media takes on a rhythm and tempo of its own" (p. 229). They may read the paper at a set time each morning, always listen for the weather report at a particular time and on a particular radio station, and follow certain television programs each day of the week with unwavering constancy—*Prime Time Live* on Thursday, *Dallas* on Friday, *Saturday Night Live* on Saturday, and the like. Thus for some the day's activities are ordered around their interactions with the media, and such disruptions as undelivered newspapers and preempted programs become disturbing, not necessarily because of the loss of media content but because of the loss of a sense of order, or stability.

Some of us also use mass media to facilitate nonmedia activities. In these circumstances, the mood created by the internal rhythm and tempo of the medium becomes extremely important. We may read mysteries when we go on vacation, listen to music while studying, and listen to talk shows while driving late at night. Snow speculates that "as interaction with mass media increases, media becomes a major resource in the development of appropriate rhythms and tempos within individuals and throughout society" (p. 231).

At this point in our chapter we turn to an examination of some of the effects and outcomes of mass communication. This discussion will have a dual purpose. We hope first to illustrate more concretely the concepts we have been talking about and second to evaluate some of the various effects and outcomes of mass communication, particularly as they relate to less formal communication contexts.

Some Effects and Outcomes

Most closely related to the concept of message flow is the study of how the mass media disseminate information.

The Diffusion of Information

Through the mass media we learn about innovations, discoveries, accidents, assassinations, revolutions, and natural disasters. How soon after these events we hear about them, and what the sources of our information were are questions that preoccupy those interested in the **diffusion of information**—that is, _how quickly news or information travels and the communication channels through which it spreads to a community of receivers._ When considered in terms of a major news story, diffusion has been described as the process by which "the facts of a story filter into the stream of community life—diffuse through it, so to speak—color it, change its complexion, reach and affect in some way nearly every person in it" (Deutschmann and Danielson, 1960, p. 345).

Dominick (1993) identifies three stages in the diffusion of news: _newsbreak, dissemination,_ and _saturation:_

> **Newsbreak** . . . consists of the time it takes for reporters to transmit the essential facts of a story back to a media organization, which in turn publishes or broadcasts the news. . . . The **dissemination stage** . . . consists of the period during which the news is spreading through the audience and during which the facts are becoming known to the members of some community or society. The last stage, called **saturation,** occurs when most of the population has heard the story and it can no longer be classified as breaking news. . . . We will define saturation as occurring when approximately 90 percent of the population has heard the news. (p. 530)

"Diffusion" refers to the spread of all kinds of information or news—not just information that generates shock or excitement. Thus news of a flu immunization program is usually diffused to the public through several media. This is also true of news of an imminent hurricane or the strike of a citywide transportation system. One recent effort to reach a very wide audience is the cocaine-prevention campaign of the National Institute on Drug Abuse. Through televised messages, the institute stressed the dangers of crack for nonusers and specified that there is help available for addicts.

When the space shuttle _Challenger_ exploded during launching in early 1986, killing all on board, the diffusion of information was virtually instantaneous. The launching itself was being televised, so millions actually saw the explosion. And there were many more viewers, including schoolchildren, because Christa McAuliffe, chosen as the first teacher to participate in a space mission, was one of the *Challenger* crew. A National Science Foundation survey found that after learning of the explosion, 57 percent of the population immediately turned on their televisions and that by the end of that day 95 percent had watched some coverage of the disaster (Wright et al., 1989).

The most thoroughgoing examination of news diffusion focused on another unanticipated news event of major proportions: the assassination of President John F. Kennedy on November 22, 1963. By 1 P.M. Central Standard Time, a half-hour after he had been shot, Kennedy was pronounced dead, and by then 68 percent of the adult population in the United States had heard of the assassination. By 2 P.M. the figure was up to 92 percent, and it had reached 99.8 percent by 6 P.M. (Sheatsley and Feldman, in Greenberg and Parker, 1965, pp. 152–153). Just as significant as the thoroughness and rapidity of the flow of information in this case is the means by which people received their information. The primary source was other people: 49 percent of the population learned about it from face-to-face exchanges or telephone calls. Radio and television accounted for another 47 percent, with the remaining 4 percent attributed to other sources such as newspapers. But this situation is unique, for Kennedy's assassination was an extraordinary event. The diffusion of news was rapid, and it was complete. One researcher writes, "The murder of President Kennedy concentrated all channels of communication—both mass media and person to person—on a single incident at the same time" (Greenberg, in Greenberg and Parker, 1965, p. 89). In other words, there was a single focus of all the channels of communication.

This is certainly not the case for the diffusion of all public information. In most instances, 90 percent of those who are aware of a given news event first learn about it through the mass media. Radio and television predominate as the first sources of such information, with newspapers usually being the first source for less significant events.

There is some evidence that the way in which information will be disseminated depends on the importance of that information. According to this view, if a news event is of almost crisis proportions, "interpersonal channels of communication are as important as mass media in disseminating initial information" (Greenberg, 1964, p. 495). Person-to-person communication will also have a major role in disseminating information about lesser known events. For news events that are at intermediate levels of importance, however, the mass media will be the most pervasive first source of information.

It is important, as Wright (1986) and others have emphasized, to think of the roles of face-to-face and mass communication as complementary rather than mutually exclusive. At times an encounter with a friend who tells you about a recent news event (the hijacking of a plane, for example) prompts you to turn to one of the mass media for further information. Or something you learned from the mass media prompts a discussion with someone who then adds to your knowledge of the event by mentioning details that were not part of the magazine article you read or the televised news summary you heard. And then there are times when we experience mass communication in the company of others (family members, friends, coworkers, for example), so that there is a constant interplay between what is being conveyed through the mass media and the awareness of personal responses to those communicative stimuli.

We have been speaking essentially about message flow and the spread of information through a community of receivers. But as we know from our discussion of persuasion in Chapter 10, some message senders have as their primary intention not information gain but attitude influence, and even messages intended primarily to inform often make persuasive appeals. Thus once a message has been received, it remains to evaluate the persuasive impact of that message, and this is the subject of our next discussion.

Attitude Influence

Roughly 70 million out of the 107 million adults in the United States either watched or listened to the first of four debates between John Kennedy and Richard Nixon in 1960. Moreover, many who did not see or hear the debates through the broadcast media soon read about them in the newspapers. Within twenty-four hours, "67 percent of all newspaper readers (. . . virtually the entire adult population) read about the first debate . . . and about half talked about each of the debates within the same time period" (Katz and Feldman, in Kraus, 1962, p. 192).

The Kennedy-Nixon debates have been the focus of intense study, and the consensus of opinion is that exposure to the debates through the mass media had little effect on changing initial voting intentions. As many studies have noted, when viewers were asked about who had "won," Kennedy supporters tended to see Kennedy as the winner of the debates, while Nixon supporters, for the most part, saw Nixon as the winner. We noted more recent examples of this phenomenon in other presidential debates.

However, according to Stephen Wayne (1992), author of several studies on presidential elections, debates can sometimes influence attitudes when the voters are independent or less partisan in their initial beliefs. For these voters,

> the debates can increase interest and can clarify, color, or even change perceptions. Before debating, Kennedy was thought by many to be less knowledgeable and less experienced than Nixon; Carter was seen as an enigma, fuzzier than Ford; Reagan was perceived to be more doctrinaire and less informed than his first Democratic opponent, President Carter. These debates enabled . . . candidates to overcome these negative perceptions. In the end the debates proved to be important to the success of their candidacies. (p. 229)

One particularly interesting issue Wayne addresses is which candidate benefits more from the debate format—the incumbent or the challenger:

The experiences of Kennedy in 1960, Carter in 1976, and Reagan in 1980 suggest why debates tend to help challengers more than incumbents. Being less well-known, challengers have more questions raised about them, their competence, and their capacity to be president. The debates provide them with an opportunity to satisfy some of these doubts in a believable setting and on a comparative basis. By appearing to be at least the equal of their opponents, the challenger's image as a potential candidate is enhanced. (p. 229)

Like the great numbers of people who watched the aftermath of the Kennedy assassination on television, many of the people watching the presidential debates are involved in a group experience. So even here, where there seems to be a complete absorption in mass communication, there is probably a considerable amount of face-to-face communication taking place, with viewers commenting to each other about the way the debaters look and speak, and the effectiveness of the points they make. It is likely, too, that many of the small groups who watch the debates are made up of people who share a great many attitudes, beliefs, and values.

There is another point to be made from studies of debates. As a result of watching the debates, some people learn more about the issues, so that there is some information gain, but they also form impressions of the candidates through the debaters' nonverbal cues. During the second presidential debate in 1992, newspapers were quick to pick up on a moment when President Bush looked at his watch while one of the other candidates was speaking. This was variously interpreted in the press; some read the gesture as discomfort, others as boredom. From facial expression, tone of voice, posture, hand movements, and so on, viewers also tend to form stronger personality impressions of the candidates. But as is true in other communication contexts, increased understanding does not *ensure* persuasion or attitude influence. Indeed, people who viewed the debates between Kennedy and Nixon changed their voting intentions "*less* than non-viewers" (Katz and Feldman, in Kraus, 1962, p. 209).

It seems, then, that exposure to other points of view through the mass media often serves simply to strengthen or reinforce the receiver's initial attitudes and opinions. Many studies of voting behavior (and mass media advertising) confirm this tendency.

Despite what representatives of television and other media think of as their formative role in shaping public opinion—particularly on political issues—there is a great deal of selection taking place on the part of the receivers of mass communication. Note the comparative source credibility of the various mass media for different groups of people. According to a comprehensive survey of research, "while television is usually nominated by the public as its prime source of information . . . political information is . . . more closely related to newspaper reading." In addition, political advertising seems to have only very minor effects on voting decisions—and these are largely on late deciders "and may influence voters against as well as for the advertised candidate" (McGuire, 1985, p. 278).

There is growing evidence, however, that some mass media programs concerned with health promotion and safety can produce changes not only in awareness but in attitudes and subsequent behavior. For example, a survey of media campaigns designed to raise public consciousness about the dangers of smoking and to help smokers quit found that mass media campaigns, including national ones, were effective and that the most effective were mass media self-help clinics (Flay, 1987). Such programs tracked groups or individuals on television as they tried to quit smoking. In addition to following the programs, participants often used written self-help materials, which they requested by calling a hotline.

Another highly promising use of mass media is demonstrated by the Harvard Alcohol Project, which designed a national campaign to reduce drunken driving by increasing public awareness of the need to select a "designated driver" before social events (Carter, 1989, D11). In 1989 over forty episodes of television series including *The Cosby Show, Family Ties,* and *Cheers* carried messages about drunken driving. These were not public service spots inserted as commercials; mention of the problem and the proposed solution was embedded within the program's storyline. Thus a small scene in *Hunter* included a waitress who after bringing drinks to a table, commented: "Who gets the soda water? You? Well, I guess somebody has to drive."

Jay Weinstein, director of communications at the Harvard School of Public Health, which organized the Harvard project, believes inserting messages into individual programs is more persuasive than using public service announcements because audience members involve themselves in the dramatic development of programs with a storyline. "They identify with the characters. And if a character has a commitment to a message, it's far more effective than a talking head lecturing you" (D11).

Social Learning through Role Models

In learning new behaviors, it is not always necessary for us to perform behaviors and be reinforced; we also learn new responses simply by observing them in others. This process is known as **modeling,** or **imitation.** Modeling goes on throughout one's lifetime but is especially important during the formative years of childhood. Today movies, books, and radio and television programs set before children a truly bewildering number of models for behavior. It is in part through such sources that children acquire information about the world and develop conceptions about their future roles. Through the mass media, children build up some ideas about various occupations and the status and material gain accorded people on the basis of their jobs. For example, seven out of every ten television dramas seen on prime time are about science and technology, so that each week the average viewer sees one or two scientists and eleven doctors. The mass media make available a number of other role models. In this section, we shall look at some ways in which the female role is presented and defined by some of the mass media.

On an average day you don't have to sit before your television set very long before you see an overwrought woman complaining that her husband's shirt has a ring around the collar or her dishes aren't sparkling or her kitchen floor doesn't shine the way her neighbor's does. The viewer's general impression is that women exist in a predominantly domestic setting and their concerns center largely around their homes, husbands, and children. In the 1960s a content analysis of the occupational roles portrayed on television programs reported that the viewer was given an unrealistic representation of the lives of both males and females (De Fleur, 1964). For the most part, it was the men on view who held the lucrative and more interesting jobs, and beyond that the proportion of working men to working women was in no way an accurate reflection of the status quo. In general, content analyses from the 1950s through the 1970s agree that male characters outnumber female characters by three to one; in action-adventure shows there is a five to one ratio (U.S. Department of Health and Human Services, 1982, p. 54).

How far has television come from that image? Although the number of women entering the work force has steadily increased, we find the sexes still stereotyped by occupation (Liebert and Sprafkin, 1988). A survey of television commercials found that women were portrayed in eighteen different occupations, whereas the number of occupations for men was forty-three. Moreover, 56 percent of all the women in these commercials were depicted as housewives, and 75 percent of the ads featuring women were for kitchen or bathroom products (Dominick and Rauch, 1972). Between 64 and 70 percent of the women characters portrayed on television do not hold jobs, and over 90 percent of the prestigious jobs represented are held by male characters. What's more, women are overrepresented as victims, with heroic roles usually being assigned to men (U.S. Department of Health and Human Services, 1982, p. 54).

Since the late 1970s there have been some improvements. Women have, to a minor extent, held jobs that were difficult or daring. Such depictions include a woman lawyer on *Hill Street Blues;* two women police officers on *Cagney and Lacey;* and women reporters on *Mary* and *Murphy Brown.* But a broad survey of gender roles on television indicates that women characters whose work is glamorous and dangerous tend to be "single, sophisticated, and often divorced. . . . Some observers say . . . that these new roles are not really so different from past roles because the women still usually depend on men, they are more emotional than men, and there is more concern for their safety" (U.S. Department of Health and Human Services, 1982, pp. 54–55).

Women have long held a place in American movies, and there have been some serious, even profound film characterizations of women. Nonetheless, many of the most important films of the early 1970s—often referred to as "buddy movies"—focused on two male characters in some sort of high or low adventure. In fact, several film critics have remarked that the most popular film couple of the 1970s was Paul Newman and Robert Redford. Although in Hollywood movies women have stereotypically been portrayed as sex objects, vamps, nurturant mothers, and "airheads," there seem to be some recent changes including a growing number of female producers and directors. And we are now seeing a number of films in which women are cast in a dominant or heroic role—Meryl Streep in *Silkwood,* Linda Hunter in *Terminator 2,* Demi Moore in *A Few Good Men.* And in *Thelma and Louise,* sometimes described as a perverse buddy movie, Susan Sarandon and Geena Davis play two women involved in shooting a man after he makes sexual advances and then flee rather than surrender to authorities. A very uncharacteristic portrayal of women, this film made sparks fly. People either loved it or hated it.

A study of female roles in women's magazine fiction from 1940 to 1970 reveals four different ways in which women are portrayed: "single and looking for a husband, housewife-mother, spinster, and widowed or divorced—and soon to remarry" (Franzwa, 1974, p. 137). In each instance, the woman is defined by the presence or absence of a man in her life. Work almost always plays a secondary role in the lives of these heroines, and when it does take on a greater importance for a female character, her relationships with men deteriorate—a punishment, it would seem, for her interest in a career. With such models, it is not surprising that many women link high personal achievement with social rejection and loss of femininity. Of course, little girls do not see many adult films or read magazine fiction, but until recently few female characters on children's programs received positive outcomes for achievements that were not of a domestic order.

But the mass media also move (some more slowly than others) with the currents of social change. Many traditional women's magazines have articles about women who choose not to marry or women who manage households yet maintain careers; and newer magazines such as *Working Woman* and *Working Mother* reflect the needs of women in the nineties.

Gatekeepers

Probably more significant than such changes in media content will be a change in the makeup of the gatekeepers of mass communication. In television reporting, for example, we now see more female and minority newscasters. Similarly, members of various ethnic and racial minorities are beginning to surface in less stereotyped roles on entertainment programs, but infrequently (Gates, 1989). Still, FCC figures show that though over the past five years there have been increasing job opportunities in broadcasting for both women and minorities, it's still true that women and minorities are far more likely to have lower-paying clerical jobs (Robb, 1991). In the past few years there has also been a considerable decline in minority ownership of broadcast properties (Sheridan, 1991). In a 1990 study of women and minorities as network television newsmakers and correspondents, the news items and people they covered, researchers Ziegler and White found that during the last twenty-five years there has been little advance in how minorities and women are presented.

Although there seems to be few studies of minority employment in the mass media, there is some research on the employment of women. Researchers have compared men and women in television broadcasting in terms of types of jobs, status, salaries—even their story assignments. For example, in Fung's 1988 survey of network television journalists only a third were female. "A total of 39% of network news producers were female, but only 18% of correspondents and 15% of bureau chiefs," and out of 29 news vice presidents there were only 6 women (cited in Smith et al., 1989, p. 228). Fung also suggested that male TV anchors are hired on the basis of their experience as journalists whereas selection of female TV anchors tends to be based on "cosmetic appeal."

The authors find no systematic discrimination in terms of salary but note that as increasing numbers of women entered journalism (and public relations) in the 1980s, salaries in both fields declined. There is no easy answer for this or for the Smith survey report that "only 10% of news directors were women" (p. 244). For news directors the median was about fourteen years of experience, and it is possible that the percentage of female news directors will increase as more women are in the field over a longer period of time. Although the study finds little "tangible sexism" that could be the basis for legal action, it suggests that sexist attitudes toward women in the mass media still exist (Smith, 1989). The critical issue is whether the nineties will show an increased proportion of women and minorities in the top levels of management.

Social Learning and Media Violence

The average television set—not so lovingly called the "electronic babysitter"—is on more than seven hours each day and since the 1950s has significantly altered family life (Liebert and Sprafkin, 1988, p. 7). Indeed, there are now television sets in 98 percent of all American homes. It hardly seems surprising, then, that today children are exposed to television virtually from birth. Even the average six-month-old can be found positioned before a television for almost an hour and a half each day. The average child's viewing time increases and peaks right before he or she is about to start elementary school at about two and a half hours, "though after that viewing time seems to diminish somewhat, there is a steady increase in viewing from age eight into early adolescence, with viewing averaging almost four hours per day" (p. 5).

From the middle school years onward we see an increase in the use of print media, and during adolescence a definite increase in the use of radio. For the first ten years of our lives, however, television is the dominant mass medium to which American children are exposed. It is not surprising, therefore, that much of the attention given to possible effects of media violence on children should center on television.

A child psychiatrist at the University of Washington calculates that by the time the average American child graduates from high school, he or she has seen 18,000 murders on television. An earlier survey of television programming reported that during the early evening, a time when it is estimated that

26.7 million children were watching television, there were violent incidents shown approximately once every 16.3 minutes. When the movie *Jaws 2* appeared on television one evening in 1986, it was watched by 1,840,000 children between ages six and eleven.

Since the early 1970s there has been more violence on weekend programs for children than on prime time television, and for many years controversy over the effects of televised violence was intense. Many researchers argued that viewing violence on television teaches children to be more aggressive, and some identified media violence as a cause of juvenile delinquency. Others countered that watching televised violence has no effects or that it has cathartic value for viewers, working as a kind of escape valve for violent emotion. Today there is no evidence that viewing violence has any cathartic effects.

On the contrary, we now have an extensive body of research on media violence, and since 1969 the government itself has initiated large-scale investigations of the problem (Surgeon General's Advisory Committee, 1972; Liebert and Sprafkin, 1988). In 1982, the National Institute of Mental Health completed a two-volume report, *Television and Behavior,* that explored a broad spectrum of issues and summarized the massive research of earlier studies. Concerning violence and aggression, the report concluded:

> Violence on television does lead to aggressive behavior by children and teenagers who watch the programs. Not all children become aggressive, of course, but the correlations between violence and aggression are positive. (U.S. Department of Health and Human Services, National Institute of Mental Health, 1982, p. 6)

According to the report, children who watch television may learn to accept violent behavior as normal. And in their face-to-face encounters children imitate the aggressive models they see on television. This relationship between televised violence and aggressive behavior exists in both boys and girls and extends from preschoolers to older adolescents.

The effects of watching televised violence can be even more subtle and pervasive. There is evidence that as viewers we also learn to be victims and identify with victims. The 1982 report observes that "many heavy viewers may exhibit fear and apprehension, while other heavy viewers may be influenced toward aggressive behavior" (p. 90).

One recent study (Cantor and Hoffman, 1991) examines *why* children enjoy watching frightening films and programs and confirms what other researchers have suggested—that suspense is an important element that intensifies enjoyment. We are all familiar with ways in which suspense is created within films and television programs: Events can be foreshadowed not only verbally, through dialogue, but through music and visual symbols and effects. In rating endings, children found somewhat greater enjoyment when the film ended with characters escaping harm. Nevertheless, children enjoyed watching a frightening film regardless of whether it was resolved by the ending. And enjoyment of "scary films" increases with the age of the child.

In another study (Cantor and Omdahl, 1991) researchers report, not surprisingly, that children who watched television dramatizations of life-threatening events—for example, a house fire or a drowning—showed greater fear and intense negative emotions. After even a brief exposure to threatening scenes, children rated similar incidents more likely to occur, they rated the effects as more severe, and they worried more about potential risk and harm to themselves. Their liking of an activity related to a threatening event also declined (for example, choosing swimming after seeing a drowning incident). Researchers suggest that children exposed to such programming in the mass media may suffer more long-lasting effects, perceiving greater risk and feeling more vulnerable.

Ours is by any standards a violent age, and we cannot single out the mass media as the source of all our social ills. We must remember, too, that mass communication is in essence a human creation and that some of its most important effects are indirect and cumulative.

IMPLICATIONS OF THE NEW COMMUNICATION TECHNOLOGIES

Imagine being asked to come up with a list of the newest communication technologies and their innovations—a formidable task. By now we're familiar with cellular telephones, computers, electronic mail, satellites, videotex, and facsimile machines. Electronic document interchange, or data traffic, is revolutionizing business communications by transferring information from one computer to another over telephone lines. And some experts predict that the use of fiber-optic cables in the home will herald a new information age with the promise of interactive television.

These and other technological changes are increasing the **speed** of communication at an exponential rate. You can fax your résumé to a prospective employer so that it is received the same day you see an ad. International meetings can be set up and documents exchanged at a previously unimagined pace. The tempo of many transactions accomplished via the media is accelerating.

In addition to the greater speed with which messages are transmitted, we see major changes in the **volume** of information transmitted, stored, and retrieved. For example, the greater ease with which type is set electronically as well as the advent of desktop publishing have dramatically increased the number of books, newsletters, and magazines that are available to us.

Williams (1989) explains that the new technologies can be thought of as **"media extensions"**—that while the media function "as extensions of our basic senses and communication modes, . . . the new media are not usually systems in themselves. Instead they extend existing systems" (1989, p. 122).

Although use of the **personal computer** has lagged far behind business and institutional computer use, changes in computer technology make it likely that home use will become far more frequent. Today computers are being designed that you can hold in the palm of your hand. Pen computers that read handwriting are being perfected. A pocket computer that combines computer and telephone technology will allow you "to send and receive messages around the world—not, just the name and number snatches available on today's pages, but full documents and, eventually, with voice messages and pictures" (Schwartz, 1992, pp. 45–47). In addition to a variety of databases, electronic books of all kinds are now available to computer users. Thus far the greatest interest has been in reference books: One publisher estimates that since 1990, people have bought almost 400,000 electronic encyclopedias (Rogers, 1992, p. 66).

By means of the **fax,** or **facsimile,** we can transmit images not only of written documents but visual materials such as graphs, maps, and photographs. Essential equipment for every office, fax machines have become affordable for the home as well. Thus they enable telecommuting, allowing people to work from their home and send and receive messages almost instantaneously. You can now find faxing facilities not only in local stores but in hotels as well as air terminals and other public places, and one-way faxing during commercial air travel seems likely before very long.

According to one estimate, each year in the United States approximately a billion messages are exchanged through **electronic mail.** Although a great part of these messages represent business communication, theorists from several disciplines are now beginning to consider the social implications of elec-

What would you see as the advantages and disadvantages of participating in a video training session?

tronic mail. For example, bulletin-board services in large cities ensure that, as one psychologist puts it, "there is almost always someone 'out there' to talk to":

> Most large cities offer bulletin-board services, which allow individuals to place an announcement of their interests on a file open to all users of the system. In this way computer conversations develop, and fanciful sub-cultures spring to life, sharing interests—at any time of day or night. . . . Many local bulletin boards are also connected to national routing services that transmit messages overnight and free of charge from one bulletin board to another across the country. . . . Many participants speak of the warm and accepting relations that develop within these contexts—much like the corner bar, where there are always old buddies and new friends. (Gergen, 1991, pp. 58–59)

The technology on speech-recognition systems is developing rapidly and will soon be more common not only in banks and telephones but in the home for computers and VCRs. And the hope is that one day the technology will include language translation. A recent first step in that direction is the development of an overseas computer telephone that translates messages from one language to another—the result of the collaboration of Carnegie Mellon University in Pittsburgh, Japan's Advanced Telecommunications Research Institute, and Germany's Siemens company and Karlsruhe University. The first demonstration was in early 1993.

Table 12.1 illustrates how many of the new technologies are linked with

TABLE 12.1

New Technologies in Traditional Levels of Communication

Level	Traditional Form	Technology Application
Interpersonal	Face to face, mail, telephone	Video telephone, personal computer linkage, electronic mail, voicegrams
Small group	Face to face	Telephone conference, teleconference, computer conference
Organizational	Face to face, memo, intercom, telephone, meetings	Telephone conference, electronic mail, computer-aided management, information system, facsimile
Public	Newspapers, magazines, books, television, radio, films	Videotape, video disk; cable TV; direct satellite TV; videotex, teletext; digital information systems

Adapted from Frederick Williams, *The New Communications*, 2d ed., p. 133. Used by permission of Wadsworth Publishing. Belmont, CA, © 1989.

traditional levels of communication. We've already mentioned the use of tel-emedicine in Chapter 7. Business is increasingly using teleconferencing, and there are hopes that one day this will be as productive for medical practice. For example, through interactive television and other technologies, specialists hundreds of miles away can examine and diagnose patients in small hospitals or clinics in rural areas, often saving them the costs of travel to large cities and unnecessary hospitalization. In education the potential of cable and closed-circuit television are being tapped, and there are innovative educational exchange programs—aided by satellite and computer. For example, a program in the New York area enables students from selected high schools to corre-spond via electronic mail with Russian high school students on a weekly basis. And in the future, through electronic or voice mail, conferences between parents and teachers will probably be far more frequent.

The Convergence of Computing and Telecommunications

Telecommunications applies technology "to extend the distance over which humans or their intermediaries, such as computers can communicate," writes Williams. In public use it refers to "the telephone, telegraph, or data networks as point-to-point communication, or radio and television as broad-cast communication" (1991, p. 4).

Among the most striking results of technological advances is the **conver-gence of telecommunications and computing into a single system**—sometimes known as *the intelligent network*. This network is regarded not only as a technology but as an "information resource."

In the past, our views of mass communication assumed distinctions be-tween the various media, print, film, broadcasting, and so on. For example, videotex is an electronic information technology that transmits and retrieves data, including graphic information: It makes possible interactive communi-cation between large computer databases and users of office or home video monitors linked to cable-television or telephone lines. Yet videotex is "prob-ably losing its distinct identity. In the home, it is merging with home comput-ers. In the office, it is merging with conventional office automation systems" (Forester, 1987, p. 130). In a lighter vein, one newspaper noted that Absolut Vodka ran what the company thought was the first "talking ad" in one of the print media—courtesy of a microchip—only to find that another company had introduced a comparable talking ad the week before.

How will the intelligent network affect our lives at home? One vision of the future household includes wireless fax and personal computer links; dial-up educational and television services; improved online banking and home shopping; integrated emergency alarm systems for fire, police, and medical assistance; customized electronic newspapers in videotex or fax format; as well as other services needed to work from one's home. In addition, Williams explains, "the coming portability should allow these services to be easily shifted to anywhere you wish to call 'home,' including on the road or at the office" (1991, pp. 98–99).

What we are seeing now, in many aspects of our lives, is a blurring of distinctions between the media and a considerable degree of overlap in functions. Garnham outlines a few of the questions that have thrown communications policy decisions into confusion:

> Is videotex print publishing or broadcasting? Should cable be a common carrier like the switched telecommunications network or should it be regulated like broadcasting? Should the telephone company itself be allowed to control the provision of both text and TV services as well as voice and data overbroadband networks? (1985, p. 66)

Effects on Interpersonal Communication

How will these new technologies affect interpersonal communication? It seems fair to say that for at least a segment of our population a number of face-to-face transactions would be mediated by computers and interactive television. This does not necessarily mean that there will be less interpersonal communication, however.

Applications of technological advances (customized television feeds, for example) could also intensify the **selectivity** of the mass communication audience. Conversely, technology has also enabled the mass media to become far more selective. For example, in book publishing books can now be printed as needed, with certain sections added or dropped, according to the demands of a given readership.

Certain technological innovations seem well suited to enhance rather than limit communication. In organizational communication, for example, video-conferencing may come to be used by many companies on a routine basis. Some experts propose that telecommunications can be used as a "major new force for organizational design and redesign" (Keen, 1987, p. 593). According to Keen, business telecommunications will "inherently involve . . . organizational, as well as technical change" (p. 594). And as we've already seen, there are already educational applications of technology, many of which encourage rather than impede communication.

Technological Literacy

Earlier in this chapter we referred to the view that the gap between generations may have less to do with age than with computer literacy. Perhaps we will have to extend that statement to technological literacy in general. There is growing concern that technology is creating a gap between those who can use, afford, and understand it and those who cannot.

The application of fiber-optics is a case in point. Many communication experts believe that the introduction of fiber-optic cables into private residences—now in its experimental stages—will be the beginning of a new information age. According to their predictions, fiber-optic cables will "vastly increase the amount of audio, video, and computer data that can flow in and out of the home" (Markoff, 1989, sec. 3, p. 1).

One specialist predicts that through interactive education via video and computer links it will be possible for fiber-optics networks to raise the level of education in rural areas and revitalize many small towns (p. 15).

Yet some experts fear that because fiber-optics networks are so costly, they will result in "an information technology elite" dividing the rich from the poor and possibly separating urban from rural areas—as, for example, when a fiberoptic cable is laid between two cities but bypasses a smaller community (p. 15). Thus the larger concern for fiber-optics and many other technologies is whether they will bring people together or divide them.

Prospects for a Global Human Community

Of necessity, the new communication technologies have vastly increased the amount of intercultural communication. People of different cultures have more information about each other and are more accessible than ever before. They are also more interdependent. But the race for breakthroughs in technology—superconductors, for example—has also made for more competition, particularly on a national level.

The hope that technological advances would contribute to a global human community has been voiced by communication theorists for many years. Buck (1988) has argued that "the mass media allow for the first time spontaneous emotional communication on a global level" and that "media, by their very presence, may be creating the emotional basis for a global community" (pp. 351–352). The long-term effects of the new technologies have yet to be seen.

In putting the "new" information technology in perspective, however, it is important to emphasize that this "revolution" is not without historical precedents and that, over time, human beings have adapted to many new and unfamiliar technological innovations all the way from the printing press to the telephone and television—each of which seemed at the time to disrupt, even threaten, "'normal' human life" (Finnegan, 1989, p. 111). Of itself, technology does not eliminate the active role of the audience:

> If computers are introduced into an organization, for example, whether in local government . . . or an office, . . . their effects on efficiency, on their users, and on the overall power structure vary, depending crucially not so much on technical specifications as on social and political factors: how they are introduced and who has access to and control of them. (p. 117)

No absolute consequences result from technology, Finnegan explains, whether they be from writing, print, or computer networks:

> The challenge of the most recent developments in information technology, by which not just textual but numerical, graphic, pictorial, and auditory information can be represented, recorded, and disseminated, could also be used to widen our view of what can be processed and transmitted through the communication process. The *potential* is there—but it does not dictate to us. (p. 123)

SUMMARY

In this chapter we saw that mass communication, by its very nature, is mediated. Following Wright, we defined the audience in mass communication as relatively large, heterogeneous, and anonymous to the source. The experience itself was characterized as public, rapid, and fleeting, and the source was seen as working through a complex organization. It was also pointed out that the feedback in mass communication was limited and not as complete as it is in face-to-face communication.

We also discussed the mass communication process in terms of the gate-keeper concept and influences on gatekeeper choice, the various theories about how messages flow from source to receiver, and the concept of the active audience. We saw that the flow of information from the mass communicator to individual receivers sometimes involved opinion leaders, with mass and face-to-face communication playing complementary roles.

The next section of this chapter was an assessment of some of the effects and outcomes of mass communication. Although the mass media are often extremely effective in disseminating information, we saw that information gain by no means ensures attitude influence. Often, exposure to several points of view through the mass media simply reinforces the receiver's initial attitudes, particularly with respect to voting intentions. We also looked at some of the many role models presented by the media, and employment of women and minorities as gatekeepers, and at the effects of media violence on antisocial behavior.

In a final section of our chapter we explored some of the implications of the new communications technologies. Despite their increases in the speed and volume of communication, the new media were seen primarily as extensions of existing media. The convergence of computing and telecommunications as well as some effects on interpersonal communication were discussed. We also looked at the problem of technological literacy. In closing, we tried to make clear that so-called revolutions in technology have historical precedents and that the possibility of a global human community will depend on the human application of technology rather than on technology itself.

REVIEW QUESTIONS

1. Identify three aspects of mass communication that are mediated.

2. What are four distinguishing characteristics of mass communication?

3. Discuss the concept of the gatekeeper. Give one example of how gate-keeping in mass communication differs from gatekeeping in face-to-face communication.

4. What are six factors that may influence the information a gatekeeper chooses to select or reject?

5. Discuss two different theories about how messages flow from the mass media to individual receivers.

6. What is meant by the concept of the active audience?

7. What are some of the research findings on media uses and gratifications?

8. What is the general research finding concerning the relationship between a news event's importance and the channels through which it is disseminated?

9. How effective are the mass media in influencing the receiver's attitudes? Support your answer with an example.

10. How does mass communication affect the social learning process in children? Support your answer with an example.

11. What is the consensus of opinion among social scientists about whether viewing media violence influences our behavior in face-to-face encounters?

12. Explain the relationship between the new technologies and the mass media as traditionally conceived.

13. What are two of the effects of the growing convergence of computing and telecommunications?

14. What are some of the ways in which the new technologies might affect interpersonal communication?

15. Discuss technological literacy and its possible effects on communication.

16. Discuss the "newness" of the new communication technologies and speculate upon their possible effects in bringing about a global human community.

EXERCISES

1. Follow an event of major significance as covered by a weekly news magazine, a metropolitan newspaper, and a local newspaper. Relate your

findings to what you have read about the gatekeeping function of the mass media.

2. Watch a controversial television program (preferably a panel discussion or a talk show) in the company of at least five other people and observe the quality of their interaction and their comments about the program. Do the responses of the receivers reinforce each other? Is there an opinion leader in the group?

3. Compare the coverage of an event of moderate importance as presented by three different media: newspaper, television, and radio. Which was the most comprehensive? Which seemed most objective and which most partisan? Illustrate each of your answers with examples.

4. Select four children's programs at random from the daily television programming offered during after-school hours. Watch each of the programs and then discuss the presentation of sex and occupational roles as well as the degree of violence, if any, that you observed. Compare your own observations with the discussion of role models and media violence in the last section of this chapter.

5. Do a content analysis of the news as presented by three different networks for the same evening. Discuss what each network chose to emphasize and further discuss the worldview implied by each of the three choices.

SUGGESTED READINGS

Atwan, Robert, Barry Orton, and **William Vesterman,** eds. *American Mass Media: Industries and Issues.* 3rd ed. New York: Random House, 1986.

In this collection of classic and lively contemporary readings, the editors have two concerns. The first is to give an overview of the various industries that have developed and still maintain the primary channels of mass communication; the second is to examine the major social, cultural, and political issues that influence and are influenced by such industries.

Creedon, Pamela J., ed. *Women in Mass Communication: Challenging Gender Values.* Newbury Park, CA: Sage, 1989.

A diverse collection of essays that includes individual essays on women in journalism, radio, television, advertising, and public relations.

Dominick, Joseph R. *The Dynamics of Mass Communication.* 4th ed. New York: McGraw-Hill, 1993.

This is a comprehensive overview of the various mass media, with special emphasis on social effects, economics (bottom-line concerns of today's industries), global communication, and new technologies.

Gergen, Kenneth J. *The Saturated Self: Dilemmas of Identity in Contemporary Life.* New York: Basic Books, 1991.

A thought-provoking argument about the effects of new communication technologies upon self-concept and interpersonal relationships.

Liebert, Robert M., and **Joyce Sprafkin.** *The Early Window: Effects of Television on Children and Youth.* 3rd ed. New York: Pergamon Press, 1988.

The authors view television as the young child's "early window" on the world. They assess all the theory and research concerning children's attitudes, behaviors, and development, weighing the negative as well as the prosocial effects of television watching for children.

MacArthur, John. *Second Front: Censorship and Propaganda in the Gulf War.* New York: Hill and Wang, 1992.

A fascinating study of government censorship of the press during the Gulf War, the government's previous relationship with the media, and the responses of the press corps. The author includes many interviews.

McLuhan, Marshall. *Understanding Media: The Extension of Man.* New York: New American Library, 1973.

Professor McLuhan expands upon his controversial premise that "the medium is the message." In other words, what is being communicated by a given medium is, according to McLuhan, determined by the form of the medium rather than by its content. A fast-moving and provocative statement that draws on examples as various as *MAD* magazine and the "murder by television" by Lee Harvey Oswald.

McLuhan, Marshall, and **Bruce R. Powers.** *The Global Village: Transformations in World Life and Media in the 21st Century.* New York: Oxford University Press, 1992.

A vision of life in the twenty-first century in which users of technology must deal with two different ways of perceiving the world.

Rogers, Everett M., and **Francis Balle,** eds. *The Media Revolution in America and Western Europe.* Paris-Stanford Series, vol. 11. Norwood, NJ: Ablex, 1985.

This fine collection of essays by leading American and European scholars represents a step toward internationalizing the findings of mass communication. For advanced students.

Wayne, Stephen J. *The Road to the White House, 1992: The Politics of Presidential Elections.* New York: St. Martin's, 1992.

The author summarizes "the state of the art and science of presidential electoral politics." Chapter 7, "Image Building and the Media," will be of special interest.

Zelizer, Barbie. "CNN, the Gulf War, and Journalistic Practice." *Journal of Communication* 42 (1992): 66–82.

This article looks at how the Gulf War served as a critical incident, leading journalists to reexamine and evaluate their professional practice and the boundaries of their authority.

CHAPTER THIRTEEN

*I*ntercultural Communication

CHAPTER OBJECTIVES

After reading this chapter, you should be able to:

1 Discuss how cultural groups differ from other groups with shared characteristics, and define "intercultural communication."

2 State three broad communication principles that have important implications for intercultural communication.

3 Identify and explain at least three ways in which language can interfere with communication between cultures.

4 Explain how nonverbal messages, including those that express emotion, vary from culture to culture and can be misinterpreted.

5 Describe how cultural roles and norms, including norms about conflict, affect intercultural communication.

6 Discuss the effects of differences in beliefs and values on people from different cultures.

7 Explain the concept of ethnocentrism and discuss two reasons for stereotyping of groups.

8 Describe some of the personal, political and social effects of intercultural communication.

9 Identify seven principles that would promote community building.

*T*he 1965 revision of U.S. immigration policies is changing the character of some of our major cities. For example, during the last two decades over a million immigrants have come to New York City, most of them from the West Indies, Latin America, and Asia (Foner, 1987, p. 1). Today the other new leading immigrant city is Los Angeles, and other cities receiving large numbers of immigrants include Chicago, Houston, Miami, and San Francisco (p. 4). In *The Middleman and Other Stories* (1988), Bharati Mukherjee portrays some of these new immigrants "trying on their new American selves, shouldering into their new country." She is writing, she explains, of "the eagerness and enthusiasm and confidence with which the new immigrants chase the American dream. But sometimes they get the American codes wrong, by being too aggressive, for example" (quoted in Healy, 1988, p. 22).

When members of different cultures communicate, getting the codes wrong is a common experience. Throughout this book we have discussed cultural differences in connection with many aspects of communication. As we have seen, intercultural communication can occur in any of the contexts we have discussed in the past few chapters, from intimate two-person communication to formal organizational and mass communication. Whenever intercultural communication occurs, the differences in the participants' frames of reference make the task of communication more complicated and more difficult, especially since participants may not be aware of all aspects of each others' cultures. In fact, one reason intercultural communication has fascinated scholars in the past few years is that it reveals aspects of our own communication behavior that we might not otherwise notice as distinct, such as our attitude toward time.

From another perspective, adjustment to a foreign culture often includes experiences of *culture shock:* "feelings of helplessness, withdrawal, paranoia, irritability, and a desire for a home" (Koester, 1984, p. 251). To compound the problem, readjustment to one's home culture after an experience in another culture produces a shock of its own: *reverse culture shock*. This may result from changes in attitudes, ways of interacting, and the like. In fact, those of us who are most adaptable to the foreign culture will probably experience the greatest *unanticipated* reentry shock (Koester, 1984).

Over 20 million people from outside the United States visit each year, and during 1991 to 1992, the number of foreign students attending colleges and universities in the United States was 419,585. The five leading countries from which these students came were China, Japan, Taiwan, India, and the Republic of South Korea (Zikopoulos, 1992). As the amount of intercultural communication we engage in increases, it becomes more important for each of us to understand some of its problems and implications.

A DEFINITION OF CULTURE

In Chapter 1 we defined **intercultural communication** as *communication between members of different cultures (whether defined in terms of racial, ethnic,* *or socioeconomic differences).* As this definition suggests, the divisions between cultural groups are not established or absolute; we may choose one or more of a variety of characteristics to identify a group of people as having a common culture. We may, for instance, speak of natives of California, Nebraska, and New Hampshire as being from different regional cultures (West Coast, Midwest, and New England); we may identify each of them as a member of an urban or rural culture, or as a member of a Jewish or Irish culture; we may speak of them all as members of a broader Western culture. Although scholars disagree as to which of these designations may properly be said to be a cultural group, to a certain extent all of them are.

Culture is *a way of life developed and shared by a group of people and passed down from generation to generation.* It is made up of many complex elements, including religious and political systems, customs, and language as well as tools, clothing, buildings, and works of art. The way you dress, your relationships with your parents and friends, what you expect of a marriage and of a job, the food you eat, the language you speak are all profoundly affected by your culture. This does not mean that you think, believe, and act exactly as everyone else in your cultural group. Not all members of a culture share all its elements. Moreover, a culture will change and evolve over time. Still, a common set of characteristics is shared by the group at large and can be traced, even through great changes, over many generations.

Culture As Learned

A popular cartoon that appeared during a period when many Americans were adopting Vietnamese War orphans depicted a woman announcing to her husband that the daughter they had adopted as a Vietnamese infant had spoken her first words that day. "English or Vietnamese?" he asked. Language, like culture, is so much a part of us that we tend to think of it as genetically transmitted, like the more physiological characteristics of race and nationality. As we attempt to communicate with people from other cultures and reconcile our differences, it is important that we remember culture is *learned.*

Because culture is learned, not innate, an infant born in Vietnam of Vietnamese parents but brought to the United States and raised as an American will be culturally an American. Because culture is learned, it also changes as people come into contact with one another or as their experiences change their needs. *The Covenant,* a novel by James Michener, describes how various cultural groups in South Africa changed as they came in contact with one another. Influenced by the demands of the new world and by their contact with the tribes who were there before them, the early Dutch settlers and their descendants became a separate cultural group, distinct in their way of living and speaking, from the Dutch in the homeland they had left behind them.

Some of the reasons people have so many problems communicating across cultural boundaries is suggested in this definition of culture:

A culture is a complex of values polarized by an image containing a vision of its own excellence. Such a "tyrannizing image" takes diverse forms in various cultures such as "rugged individualism" in America, an individual's "harmony with nature" in Japan, and "collective obedience" in China. A culture's tyrannizing image provides its members with a guide to appropriate behavior and posits a super-sensible world of meaning and values from which even its most humble members can borrow to give a sense of dignity and coherence to their lives. (Cushman and Cahn, 1985, p. 119)

In a sense, then, it is the culture that provides a coherent framework for organizing our activity and allowing us to predict the behavior of others. People from other cultures who enter our own way may be threatening because they challenge our system of beliefs. In the same way, we ourselves may become threatening to others as we enter a foreign culture and challenge the cultural foundations of their beliefs.

Distinctions among Cultures

Differences between two cultural groups range from the slight to the very dramatic. The culture of the Yanomami people, a Stone Age tribe in Brazil, has little in common with the highly industrialized cultures of Japan or the United States. Many Americans, with their heritage of sympathy for union organization and antipathy toward big business, are amazed at such Japanese work customs as employees' beginning the day by singing a company song and the expectation that employees will stay with one company for life.

In recent years many Europeans and Americans have been shocked by the continuing Islamic death threat against novelist Salman Rushdie because of his novel *Satanic Verses*. The book outraged followers of Islam, who considered it blasphemous. Rushdie, a British subject, has lived in hiding since 1989.

Radical differences among cultures usually occur when there has been little exchange between them or, in some cases, with other cultures in general. What distinguishes one cultural group from another, however, is not always so evident. A New Yorker and a Californian will have cultural differences and similarities. Both may celebrate Thanksgiving and the Fourth of July with much the same sense of tradition associated with those holidays. On a day-to-day basis, however, they are likely to eat somewhat different foods, although probably with the same kind of utensils. They are likely to speak the same language but with different accents and a few different words or phrases. Both will speak more or less the same language as people who have always lived in England and Ontario, and they may even share many of the same values, but cultural differences are likely to become more evident as the Americans, Canadians, and British communicate with one another. Similarly, differences among cultures do not occur abruptly at regional or national borders but gradually, over a range (Samovar and Porter, 1991*a*).

MEANS OF INTERCULTURAL COMMUNICATION

Because of the technological innovations of the last two decades, writes Gergen, "contemporary life is a swirling sea of social relationships" (1991, p. 61). In that sea we must place the growing number of intercultural relationships. A dramatic increase in intercultural communication has come about primarily through high-tech developments in both aviation and electronic communication networks.

Consider first the extraordinary rise in our use of air transportation. Once an experience for the privileged few, international air travel is now routine and accessible to millions. We vacation in foreign capitals, we attend professional conferences and trade fairs, we fly to business meetings. Students in high school as well as college participate in study-abroad programs. Members of the scientific community attend international conferences on medical and

New technology is creating many opportunities for intercultural communication—for example, this "spacebridge" class with simultaneous translation between Tufts University and the University of Moscow.

environmental issues. Tourist groups from Europe and Asia are a common sight in large American cities.

We have come to take for granted the use of telephone, radio, newspaper, books, wireless services, and network television. Now satellite technology has brought the immediacy of political events into our homes—whether it be in the unprecedented coverage of the Gulf War by CNN or in the televised images of Bosnia's suffering people. As we saw in Chapter 12, the expansion of a vast electronic communications network has linked peoples of the world many times over. And the technologies of computers, electronic mail, teleconferencing, and fax, we are told, are only the beginning.

OBSTACLES TO INTERCULTURAL COMMUNICATION

Although modern means of travel and communication have brought us into contact with virtually the whole world, the technical capacity to transmit and receive messages is not, in itself, enough to allow people who have vastly different cultures to communicate with one another. Dramatic improvements in the technological means of communication have in many instances outstripped our abilities to communicate effectively with people who have different languages, different beliefs and values, and different expectations of relationships. Repeatedly, interaction between people of different cultures has created far more misunderstanding than understanding.

Of the many principles used by theorists to describe the communication process, several clearly apply to intercultural exchanges. The first is *a shared code system,* which of course will have *two aspects—verbal and nonverbal.* Sarbaugh (1979) argues that without such a shared system, communication will be impossible. There will be degrees of difference, but the *less* a code system is shared, the *less* communication is possible.

In his work anthropologist Edward Hall makes the distinction between high- and low-context cultures (1976). We can think of them along a continuum as, for example, in Figure 13.1. High- and low-context cultures have several important differences in the way information is coded. Members of **high-context cultures** are more skilled in reading nonverbal behaviors "and in reading the environment"; and they assume that other people will also be able to do so. Thus they speak less than members of low-context cultures; and in general their communication tends to be indirect and less explicit. **Low-context cultures** on the other hand, stress direct and explicit communication: "verbal messages are extremely important . . . and the information to be shared is coded in the verbal message" (Samovar and Porter, 1991*b*, pp. 234–235; Gudykunst and Kim, 1992, pp. 44–45).

Among members of high-context cultures are the Chinese, Korean, and Japanese. Notice our own position in Figure 13.1—within the low-context end of the spectrum, yet not at the very bottom. In comparing Americans with

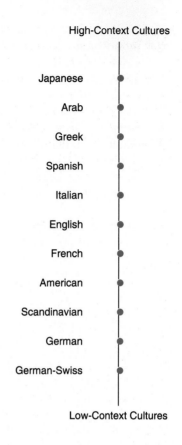

FIGURE 13.1   Sampling of Cultures
Arranged along the High-
Context/Low-Context
Dimension   (*Source:* Larry A.
Samovar and Richard E. Porter,
Communication Between Cultures,
Belmont, CA: Wadsworth, 1991, p.
235.)

Malays and Japanese, Althen offers a clear example of the high-context/low-
context dimension:

> Americans focus on the words people use to convey their ideas, infor-
> mation and feelings. They are generally quite unskilled in "reading" other
> people's non-verbal messages. "Oh, you Americans!" said an exasperated
> Japanese woman who was being pressed to express some details about
> an unpleasant situation, "You have to say everything!" (Althen, 1992,
> p. 416)

Second, different *beliefs and behaviors* between communicators establish
the basis for different assumptions from which to respond. In fact, our own
beliefs and behaviors influence our perceptions of what other people do. Thus
two people of different cultures can easily attribute different meanings to the
same behavior. If this happens, the two behave differently with neither being
able to predict the other's response. Yet as we saw in Chapter 7, predictions
are an integral part of being able to communicate effectively. Writing of his

trip to East Africa, American essayist Edward Hoagland described how Gabriel, who was from the Sudan, served him a drink:

> Gabriel explained that it was his duty as a host to make me want to share with him whatever he had. I suggested that it was foolish for us to argue about the nature of hospitality in our two countries. . . . This sufficed for a while, but because I was not drinking my share of the sherry he became agitated again that I was not participating in the ritual of being his guest. I didn't know whether the way he knitted his forehead was from a host's unease, from empathy with my discomfort with . . . [my] headache, or from real twinges of a kind of pain of his own. (1979, p. 213)

A third principle discussed by Sarbaugh that has important implications for intercultural communication is the *level of knowing and accepting the beliefs and behaviors of others*. Notice that there are two components: knowledge and acceptance. It isn't so much the catalogue of differences—that is, the knowledge of such differences—that creates a problem. It's also the level of your acceptance. For example, writing about a tribe of African hunters called the Ik, anthropologist Colin Turnbull tried to come to terms with his own feelings of repulsion. The Ik, he knew, were uprooted hunters and the violent way they now lived—stealing each other's food, killing, and so on—could be explained by the fact that their entire society had been uprooted. Turnbull *knew* a great deal about the beliefs and behaviors of the Ik, but he could not *accept* the people of that culture. As an anthropologist, however, he still brings to his perceptions a certain objectivity—simply in declaring his responses.

The degree to which we judge a culture by our own cultural values and refuse to consider other cultural norms will determine how likely it is that effective communication takes place. At one extreme, we have participants in a transaction who both know and accept the beliefs and behaviors of others; at the other, we have those who neither know nor accept. And in this instance the probability of a breakdown in communication is extremely high (Sarbaugh, 1979).

Adopting a shared code system, acknowledging differences in beliefs and behaviors, and learning to be tolerant of the beliefs and behaviors of others all contribute to effective communication.

American anthropologist Mary Catherine Bateson tells of visiting her husband's family in Beirut on her honeymoon and being frustrated because, although she spoke to them in Armenian, her in-laws kept responding in English:

> Then, on the fourth or fifth day of our visit, his mother set out to make *chee kufta,* a dish in which finely ground lamb is kneaded at length with bulgur wheat, parsley, and onions until the raw meat simply disappears into the wheat. It's one of those dishes, shaped by their mother's hands, that sons go home to eat. Greatly daring, I went into the kitchen and

took over the kneading. After that day, my in-laws began to answer me in Armenian, the handling of the meat and grain and the sharing of what I had prepared having transformed me into a different person. . . . (1990, p. 126)

Verbal Messages

The European Community's translation service in Brussels recently held an exhibition of signs that had been translated into English with some hilarious results including "Please leave your values at the front desk" (from a Paris hotel) and "Our wines leave you nothing to hope for" (this from a Swiss restaurant) (Goldsmith, 1992, B1). On a personal level, learning a foreign language improperly, even if just a few words are involved, can create immediate difficulties. For example, a Japanese businessman who was transferred to the United States explained his frustration in trying to find affordable housing; he kept asking about renting a "mansion," the word he had been taught instead of "apartment."

Language differences can go much deeper than simple translation ambiguities, however. Have you ever asked someone to translate a word from another language to you, only to have him say "Well, it doesn't translate into English exactly, but it means something like . . ."? As we saw in our discussion of the Whorf hypothesis in Chapter 3, languages differ more than strict word-for-word translations often indicate because the people who speak the languages have different needs.

Even when we can manage to translate from one language to another with literal accuracy, the deeper meanings are often lost because they are rooted in the culture of the language. Consider the following description of how the failure to understand the deeper meanings of words may interfere with communication between people who do not share a culture:

There may be no better example to illustrate cultural mistranslation than the word *Red.* To Westerners "the Reds" conjures up images of blood, fire, fierceness, e.g., *red with anger, . . . seeing red,* but the Russian translation *krasnyi* has a different aura. For example, to a Russian

krasnyi = beautiful
pryekrasnyi = exquisite
krasnaya ryiba = fine fish (e.g., salmon)
krasnoye zoloto = pure gold ("red" gold)
krasna devitza = beautiful girl

Rather than *Red,* a far, far better symbolic translation of this word into English is *Golden,* as in a *Golden opportunity, . . . The Golden Age,* etc.

No doubt a Russian might translate this word back into Russian to mean "the color of money!" . . .

I was once highly embarrassed when using our common term *Red Indian* (American Indian, in British usage) to an American audience, some of whom took it to refer to an Indian communist. Colors are no more translatable than words. (Cherry, 1971, pp. 16–17)

Literal translations from one language to another often create misunderstandings because they do not account for culture-based linguistic styles. The elaborate style used in Arabic with its rhetoric of exaggeration, compliment, and multiple extended metaphors is puzzling to those unfamiliar with it. Even a yes-or-no answer can be misconstrued:

An Arab feels compelled to overassert in almost all types of communication because others expect him to. If an Arab says exactly what he means without the expected assertion, other Arabs may still think that he means the opposite. For example, a simple "No" by a guest to a host's request to eat or drink more will not suffice. To convey the meaning that he is actually full, the guest must keep repeating "No" several times coupling it with an oath such as "By God" or "I swear to God." (cited in Gudykunst and Ting-Toomey, 1992, p. 227)

You can also get an inkling from this of how an Arab might interpret a single succinct "No" from someone speaking in English.

A grasp of the subtleties in language style is particularly important in matters of diplomacy. For example, Sir Hamilton Gibb of Oxford University suggests that "the medium in which the aesthetic feeling of the Arabs is mainly . . . expressed is that of word and language—the most seductive, it may be, and certainly the most unstable and even dangerous of all the arts" (cited in Kaplan, 1992, p. 41). In general, many career diplomats feel that our embassies need more foreign service officers proficient in foreign languages—particularly Arabic (p. 61).

When two cultures vary widely in their perceptions of how language functions in communication—and certainly this is true of high- and low-context cultures—there may even be differences in how the very act of *asking* a question is evaluated. For example, the person asking a question may think it necessary and innocuous; the person being asked may be offended and even avoid telling the truth. In Japanese business transactions, for example,

one avoids the direct question unless the questioner is absolutely certain that the answer will not embarrass the Japanese businessman in any way whatsoever. In Japan for one to admit being unable to perform a given operation or measure up to a given standard means a bitter loss of face. Given a foreigner so stupid, ignorant, or insensitive to ask an embarrassing question, the Japanese is likely to choose what appears to him the lesser of two evils. (Hall and Whyte, in Mortensen, 1979)

Nonverbal Messages

Kurt Vonnegut, in his novel *Jailbird,* describes a woman attempting to interview a refugee of undetermined national origin. She tries a number of languages, looking for one they might have in common, and as she changes from one language to another, she changes her gestures as well.

Nonverbal communication systems vary from culture to culture just as verbal systems do, but we often overlook the symbolic nature of nonverbal systems. Many American travelers abroad have been embarrassed when they discovered that the two-fingered gesture they use to mean "Give me two" is assigned a different, obscene meaning in many countries. They have also been mistaken when they assumed that a nod always means yes. In some countries, a nod means "no"; in others a nod, or yes, simply indicates that a person understood the question. In this country, the gesture for "okay" is made by forming a circle with the thumb and forefinger while the other fingers are held up. But in France this gesture means "you're worthless," and in Greece it's a vulgar sexual invitation (Ekman et al., 1984).

Confusion in nonverbal indicators may be much more complex. In Chapter 4 we considered some of the different ways that cultures regard such nonverbal factors as the use of time and space. As we discussed then, we rely on nonverbal cues to give us information about the meaning we are to assign to a verbal message. Because we often interpret these nonverbal cues unconsciously, the message received is often very different from the one the speaker intended.

As we noted in Chapter 4, vocal cues such as volume are used differently in different cultures. In the Arab countries, men are expected to speak loudly to indicate strength and sincerity, at a volume that Americans consider "aggressive, objectionable, and obnoxious." A Saudi Arab may also lower his voice to indicate respect to a superior. In an exchange between an American and an Arab, the confusion of signals is likely to be disastrous. If the Arab speaks softly to indicate respect, the American is likely to raise his voice, because in *his* culture, one asks another person to speak more loudly by raising one's own voice. The Arab, thinking the American is suggesting that he is not being respectful enough, will lower his voice even more. The American responds by raising his voice again, and the cycle continues until the American is shouting and the Arab is no longer audible. "They are not likely to part with much respect for one another" (Hall and Whyte, in Mortensen, 1979, pp. 408–409).

The expression of emotion is also regulated by culture. For example, a gesture that Americans often misunderstand is the Japanese smile, cultivated for use as a social duty in order to appear happy and refrain from burdening friends with one's unhappiness. There are several cross-cultural studies of attitudes toward the display of emotion. For example, one study of people in England, Italy, Japan, and Hong Kong (Argyle et al., 1986) found that the Italians and the English allow more expressions of distress and anger than the Japanese. In fact, another study found that Japanese children are slower than North American children to identify anger—probably because "Japanese are socialized from an early age to avoid the expression of emotions like anger" (Gudykunst and Ting-Toomey, 1988*a*, p. 386). Moreover, it seems that in some cultures the display of emotions is limited to emotions that are "positive" and do not disturb group harmony (p. 396).

One aspect of a shared code system that contributes to the smooth flow of conversation and ultimately to understanding is **synchrony,** *the sharing of rhythms* (Gudykunst and Kim, 1992; Douglis, 1987). When people speak, they develop a rhythm, a dancelike beat that emphasizes and organizes meaning during conversation—a phenomenon to be observed between family members, friends, and lovers—even business associates. It is during a beat or stress that a speaker will often reveal important information or introduce a new topic into the conversation. It seems that timing in conversation can be affected even by a few microseconds and speakers who stay in sync not only have better understanding but a better relationship.

This rhythmic pattern is also seen in the nonverbal behavior that accompanies conversation: Speaking patterns are accented by nonverbal gestures and movements that follow the beat. But when two people are from different cultures or linguistic backgrounds, even their expectations for speech rhythms and nonverbal behaviors may be vastly different. Consciousness about synchrony also seems to vary from culture to culture. Hall has found people from Northern Europe and North America less aware of such rhythms than people from Asia, Latin America, and Africa:

> The fact that synchronized rhythmic movements are based on the "hidden dimensions" of nonverbal behavior might explain why people in African and Latin American cultures (as high-context nonverbal cultures) are more in tune and display more sensitivity toward the synchronization process than people in low-context verbal cultures, such as those in Northern Europe and the United States. (Gudykunst and Ting-Toomey, 1992, p. 281)

Relationships: Norms and Roles

Cultures also vary in the contexts in which verbal and nonverbal systems are used. When we think of making friends with a foreign student or of working with people abroad in business situations, it is important to remember that personal and working relationships are not the same and do not develop the same way in every culture. People in different cultures expect different behaviors from one another in a relationship. One culture's friendly gesture might be considered aggressive or impertinent in another culture, for example, while a gesture of respect or deference might be interpreted as inappropriate reticence or as defiance, depending on the cultural context.

Norms
Norms, as we discussed in Chapter 7, are *established rules of what is accepted and appropriate behavior.* Although we often use these rules as if

they are absolute or instinctive standards, they are actually culturally developed and transmitted. If you grew up in the United States, for instance, you were probably taught to "speak up" clearly and to look at a person who is speaking to you, and that mumbling and looking away when someone addresses you is disrespectful. These norms would seem natural and logical to you, but not all cultural groups interpret these behaviors as good manners. We have already seen that people in some cultures drop their voices as an indication of respect and deference. White American police officers patrolling Hispanic neighborhoods have often misinterpreted a similar gesture: Hispanic children are taught to lower their eyes, as a gesture of respect, when a person in authority addresses them. The police, who had been brought up with opposite norms, interpreted the gesture as sullen and resentful, and reacted accordingly.

"A smile is the same in any language," is a saying that was popular a few years ago and that still shows up occasionally. In fact, though, a smile and related attempts to be friendly are interpreted in cultural contexts. An American student's smile of greeting to a non-Western student might be interpreted as superficial, sexually suggestive, or even rude; the American student, in turn, is likely to interpret the other's failure to return the smile as unfriendly or even hostile (Samovar and Porter, 1991*a*, pp. 346–347).

Understanding **conflict norms** becomes particularly important when a disagreement seems to be brewing between two people from different cultures. Sillars and Weisberg (1987) identify at least two important variables that distinguish how members of a given culture view interpersonal and family conflicts: (1) expressivity, and (2) privacy and individuality.

Even in this country there is considerable cultural variation in the amount of emphasis placed on **expressive communication** about conflict. Studies have shown that "North American and Black American males may regard deep personal feelings as too personal to express openly"; that Jews frequently value discussion and analysis so highly that by "mainstream" standards they may seem argumentative; that Irish families in family therapy dealt with conflicts through allusion, sarcasm, and innuendo rather than engage in verbal confrontations. In each instance we see a set of assumptions about what constitutes conflict and how it should be negotiated or resolved—or perhaps ignored.

One reason we cannot apply the expressive norms of mainstream America to other groups is that so many cultures place far less value on individual self-disclosures. Talking about feelings and being open about one's dissatisfactions—even with a member of your family, for example—is not always considered appropriate behavior, and many of the suggestions for resolving conflict mentioned in Chapter 6 would be difficult to apply to intercultural contexts. In fact, in many cultures keeping problems to oneself is strongly favored, and a stoic attitude often develops. For example, in working-class families, problems are frequently regarded as "lying outside the family and within the realm of natural economic, social, and biological conditions that are futile for the family to address. Thus [family members] may adopt a passive problem-solving style that emphasizes family cohesion over active problem solving" (p. 159).

The direct expression of conflict is also considered inappropriate in cultures that deemphasize explicit verbal coding of information and pay more attention to subtle cues and indirect messages. In such cultures, discretion and indirectness are the norms for dealing with conflict, and they of course are upheld and understood by members. This is true, as we have seen, of the Chinese and Japanese (Chapter 6). So while we might perceive the indirect treatment of conflict as cowardly, members of another type of culture might view our more confrontational approach as lacking in taste (Gudykunst and Ting-Toomey, 1988*b*, p. 160).

Cultural norms about **privacy and individuality** are equally variable. In the two-person and familial relationships of mainstream America, a great deal of autonomy is expected—especially among the middle class. Thus during a conflict, advice from friends and others outside the immediate family may be looked upon as an infringement of privacy. They are certainly not expected to intervene. In extended families, however, there is a more public aspect of relationships: "Because extended networks promote communal and traditional norms, there are more definite guidelines for resolving conflicts" (p. 161). There are even times when conflicts are settled not through personal communication but through the intervention of a third party. In Japan this is sometimes the case.

According to Sillars and Weisberg's survey of research, emphasis on co-operation, affiliation, and dependence is stressed by such groups as Africans, Native Americans, Asians, West Indians, Japanese, Mexicans, Mormons, and Catholics. Their norms dictate that some conflicts will be minimized or even solved indirectly for the good of the group. For example, in the tribal meetings of Native Americans or native Alaskans, it is expected that the individual will put group goals before personal ones and reach consensus (pp. 160–162). Sometimes the mainstream American ideal of agreeing to disagree becomes "an impractical and even undesirable goal" (p. 162).

Roles

Roles, as we discussed in Chapter 7, are *sets of norms that apply to specific groups of people in a society.* Roles, too, vary markedly among cultures. Differences in the respective roles of men and women may represent some of the most apparent cultural differences in human relationships: how unmarried couples should behave and whether they should be chaperoned, how men and women should behave toward each other in business situations, what a husband's and wife's responsibilities are to one another and to their respective families.

Researchers from several disciplines acknowledge that dual-culture marriage is different from a marriage in which both partners share a common culture. For example, there are cultural differences in decision-making power and self-disclosure patterns, and there is general agreement that there is less use of self-disclosure among northern Europeans than among people from Mediterranean cultures. "Perhaps," writes Rohrlich, "what is lacking is a set of Johari windows . . . which graphically depict the amount of open, blind, hidden and unknown areas of disclosure representative of cultures" (1988, p. 41). The author stresses that to marry someone from another culture is, in effect, marrying that culture. When one spouse fails to communicate interest or assumes that the other is not attached to his or her culture, there may be serious problems. In this view, an awareness of cultural differences must precede the development of appreciation and sensitivity: "The cultural difference is what makes the fabric of the marriage more varied, interesting, and richer" (p. 42).

Many other roles are dictated culturally. For example, the director of a conversant program (a program in which foreign students learning English were matched with native-speaking American students for informal practice in the language) at a major U.S. university routinely cautioned American women students not to meet their male Algerian conversants alone in their homes because their (the Americans') intentions would be misconstrued.

Many international students who come to this country for graduate study support themselves with jobs as teaching assistants. In interviews with graduate students (TAs) from England, Thailand, Japan, and China, Ross and Krider (1992) found how different their expectations are about the roles of teacher and student and about procedures in the classroom. For example, the assistants were not prepared for the degree of verbal interaction between student and teacher that takes place in the American classroom. Although all thought this to be positive, some felt challenged. One teaching student said:

> I felt that sometimes with their comments, I was being made fun of and not taken seriously. . . . I always felt like they were trying to test my knowledge base with all their questions. (p. 284)

Accustomed to far greater formality in the university, assistants were also surprised to see students eating and drinking during class though some seem to have grown accustomed to the practice.

Beliefs and Values

Even if you've never traveled outside of the United States, you have heard stories about how American politicians and presidents have inadvertently insulted Polish or Latin American audiences when trying to speak to their audiences in the unfamiliar languages. Movies and television shows provide a glimpse of many ways of life, including the roles and norms of Hawaiian-American, Asian, Native American, and numerous other cultures. Although the portrayals are not always accurate, they help to give us a sense of some cultural differences.

It is much more difficult to comprehend and accept the values of another culture when they differ from our own. More than any other aspect of the culture taught us from birth, our values seem to be universal absolutes. Values determine what we think is right, good, important, beautiful; we find it difficult to accept that what is right or good is as relative to culture as the word for "book" or "stove," or as the way our food is prepared or our clothes are made. It may be difficult for a Westerner to adjust to the combinations or seasonings of an unfamiliar Middle Eastern or Asian cuisine. It is even more difficult to accept that some cultures eat plants or animals that we do not classify as food, and still more difficult to understand why, in the face of mass starvation in India, cattle wander the streets unrestrained, protected by religious taboos. People of other cultures, meanwhile, may be appalled at Americans' willingness to eat meat, or at the casualness with which we often have meals "on the run," without ceremony.

Nonetheless, living in another country over a long period of time sometimes leads to changes in value systems—particularly when people do not remain insulated within their own cultural group. In a recent study DiMartino (1991) examined the effect of culture on moral values—specifically, through the interpretation of moral and conventional dilemmas. Her subjects, Sicilian-American men and women, had all come to the United States as young adults. She found that the women relied more on reasoning and used more moral than conventional adjectives in their interpretations whereas Sicilian-American men seemed to "retain the thinking patterns acquired as children in Sicily" (p. 318). DiMartino explains that while the men seemed to have stayed within a "cultural cocoon," spending all their leisure and work time with other Sicilian Americans, their wives—because of their involvement with children and community—negotiated two different social systems and thus had to develop other values and moral standards (p. 318). In fact, these women often complained "that their husbands were too conservative and too tied to the 'old' ways" (p. 318).

Other recent cross-cultural research suggests that sometimes our system of beliefs and values can improve our ability to adapt to living in another country. A study of Tibetan refugees who resettled in India shows that they have been extremely successful in adjusting to their new environment and have made many economic and social gains. Mahmoudi (1992) found that Tibetan views and institutions concerning religion, government, economics, and education were critical to their adjustment. Most important, it seems, was the sense of community engendered by Tibetan religious beliefs:

> Mahayana Buddhism provides the Tibetans not only with a design for living but also with a rather positive, industrious, pragmatic, and balanced view of life. . . .
>
> [For the Tibetans] actions promote life affirmation based on the good deeds performed by the individual and the community. The Tibetan Buddhism worldview promotes a "can do" attitude with a healthy dose of cheerfulness. (p. 23)

Mahmoudi believes that Tibetans can provide a model for other international refugee populations.

BARRIERS TO INTERCULTURAL UNDERSTANDING

We cannot learn another language by simply memorizing its vocabulary and grammatical structures. A language is a complex system, intricately related to culture, and it cannot be mastered by simple substitutions. Nor can we master a culture by memorizing a list of symbols, norms, and values, even if it were possible to memorize all of them. The meaning of "red" and "gold," the proper amount of time to devote to a business transaction, the appropriate way to behave toward a person in authority—these are not isolated factors; they are all part of the intricate pattern of a culture (Hall, 1959, pp. 99–105). Learning aspects of a given culture, therefore, will not allow you to understand that culture in the same way you understand your own.

The book *Blue Collar Worker,* by John Coleman (1974), illustrates some of the difficulties of understanding another culture. Coleman, a university president, spent some months working at a number of menial jobs, including collecting garbage, digging ditches, and working in a restaurant kitchen. Although the jobs and his contact with the people he worked with (none of whom knew he was a university president) taught him a great deal about the way of life of an unskilled worker, his understanding was ultimately very limited. He lived on his wages from his blue-collar jobs, but his salaries from the university and from the companies on whose boards he served supported his family, paid his children's tuitions, and met his insurance payments; as a result, he had no firsthand experience of living on an unskilled worker's pay. He learned how a garbage collector is supposed to act and how his supervisors, coworkers, and the people whose garbage he collected behaved toward him, but the roles he played ultimately had little effect on his self-concept because when his leave from the university ran out, he would go back to his job as university president. In many ways, Coleman was never "really" a blue-collar worker.

If you have spent summers in an unskilled job in a restaurant or factory, you may have noticed that the summer-employed college students and the more regular, full-time employees tend to form separate groups at lunchtime and after work. Although both groups of people hold similar jobs at the same place, they generally feel they have little in common. If you are returning to school after some years of working in or outside your home, you may feel quite isolated from the younger students around you, at least at first. You probably feel that you have very different ways of life outside of class, different roles in your families, different ways of spending your leisure time, and different expectations of your education. Not all these differences are necessarily cultural, but in both cases, the groups of people are divided by more than a collection of differences; their entire ways of life are different.

The more diverse two cultures are, the wider the division between their people, and the less they can come to really understand one another. Coleman's blue-collar coworkers shared, in most cases, Coleman's language, many of his social and political values, and the same national heritage, yet Coleman could never understand what it was to be a blue-collar worker. The division between cultural groups who have less contact with one another is likely to be greater and even more difficult to reconcile. As much as a native United States citizen of non-Asian heritage may study Korean culture, for example, he or she can never really understand what it is to be brought up in that culture.

Ethnocentrism

We are not aware of the many aspects of our culture that distinguish it from others; in fact, many of the aspects of communication and culture discussed in this book came to be recognized not through the direct study of communication but through the study of other cultures. Culture, as Hall (1976) describes it, "can be understood only by painstaking or detailed analysis." As a result, a person tends to regard his or her own culture "as though it were innate. He is forced into the position of thinking and feeling that anyone whose behavior is not predictable or is peculiar in any way is slightly out of his mind, improperly brought up, irresponsible, psychopathic, politically motivated to a point beyond all reason, or just plain inferior" (p. 38).

The tendency to judge the values, customs, behaviors, or other aspects of another culture *"using our own group and our own customs as the standards for all judgments"* is **ethnocentrism.** Because culture is unconscious, it may be inevitable that we regard "our own groups, our own country, our own culture as the best, as the most moral" (Samovar and Porter, 1991a). Psychologist Roger Brown (1986) puts it another way: "It is not just the seeming universality of ethnocentrism that makes us think it ineradicable but rather that it has been traced to its source in individual psychology, and the source is the individual effort to achieve and maintain positive self-esteem. That is an urge so deeply human that we can hardly imagine its absence" (p. 534).

An Australian-born historian recalls her visit to England after graduating from the University of Sydney and writes of weekend visits with her English hosts:

> They could not have been kinder, but I resented their air of superiority toward Australians. . . . I came to wait for the ultimate compliment which could be counted on by Sunday breakfast. I knew the confidential smile and the inclination of the head would be followed by "You know, my dear, one would hardly know you were not English." I couldn't control the irritation produced by such accolades, and would usually begin by telling preposterous stories about life in the outback to emphasize how different I was. (Conway, 1990, p. 206)

In a recent study of intercultural anxiety, Stephan and Stephan (1992) looked at a group of American college students who had been in Morocco on a four-day visit. One finding was that students who tested high in ethnocentrism tended to have a higher level of anxiety. The researchers used these six statements to measure ethnocentrism, asking students to rate each response on a ten-point scale from strongly disagree to strongly agree:

1. Americans have been very generous in teaching other people how to do things in more efficient ways.

2. English should be accepted as the international language of communication.

3. Primitive people have unsophisticated social and political systems.

4. The fact that America was able to put a man on the moon is evidence of America's technological superiority.

5. Minority groups within a country should conform to the customs and values of the majority.

6. In many countries people do not place a high value on human life—to them, life is cheap. (Adapted from p. 93)

It seems that, to some degree, every group teaches its members to be ethnocentric.

Hall (1976) believes that ethnocentrism complicates intercultural communication even when both parties in the interaction attempt to keep open minds:

> Theoretically, there should be no problem when people of different cultures meet. Things begin, most frequently, not only with friendship and good will on both sides, but there is an intellectual understanding that each party has a different set of beliefs, customs, mores, values, or what-have-you. The trouble begins when people start working together, even on a superficial basis. Frequently, even after years of close association, neither can make the other's system work! . . . Without knowing it, they experience the other person as an uncontrollable and unpredictable part of themselves. (p. 210)

Stereotyping

As discussed in Chapter 2, we tend to impose stereotypes on groups of people, which limits our communication with those groups. It is almost impossible for us *not* to stereotype a group of people with whom we have no personal contact; furthermore, without personal contact, it is almost impossible for us to dispel the stereotypes we acquire about the group. We saw in

Chapter 2 that stereotypes are inadequate because they are generalizations based on limited experience. Certainly, the sources of our information about people of different cultures are often inaccurate. For example, Driessen (1992) writes about the stereotyping of people from Mediterranean cultures:

> The stereotype of the excessively gesticulating Spaniard linked to his spontaneous, emotional, quick-tempered and high-spirited disposition . . . persists in the images of Spain created by the tourist industry but also surfaces in recent ethnographies. (p. 242)

Gumpert and Cathcart (1984) identify our main source of information about foreigners as television. According to their finding, the stereotyped images from the media even influence our face-to-face interaction with people of other cultures. Along with French and Japanese teams, the two researchers conducted a cross-cultural study of television stereotyping of American, French, and Japanese people.

Recently, content analyses (Dominick, 1993) show that Arab men tend to be presented on television by one of three negative stereotypes:

> (1) terrorists (although only a miniscule amount of real Arabs fit this category, it is prevalent in the media); (2) oil sheik (not too many fit in here either); and Bedouin desert nomad (only 5 percent of Arabs in real life are Bedouin). (p. 515)

Theorists emphasize that in addition to creating expectations about how people will behave, stereotypes often set in motion self-fulfilling prophecies because we act on information we believe to be true (Hamilton et al., 1992). This is especially the case in intercultural communication, where our information about others tends to be so limited.

EFFECTS OF INTERCULTURAL COMMUNICATION

Effects on the Individual

Although intercultural communication increasingly affects the world we live in, most scholars agree that the obstacles to intercultural communication and understanding will probably always mean that little of that communication will occur at a personal level. Travel is easier and more feasible economically than it was for our parents and grandparents, for example, but few people travel extensively enough to have much personal acquaintance with people of other cultures.

Even within our own country we tend to stay within our own groups and subgroups. Today the needs and desires of people of many groups to affirm and preserve their cultures are reflected in demands for more bilingual education, multicultural programs and curriculums, and textbooks that better represent all cultural contributions to our literature and history. Among the swelling immigrant population in this country's largest cities we find ethnic groups clustering in their own neighborhoods. New York, for example, has its Russian, Korean, and Indian sections, as in "Little Bombay," a densely packed area with row on row of stores stocking Indian spices, saris, videos, newspapers—every imaginable evidence of this thriving culture.

For anyone who reads books and newspapers, who watches television and is concerned with international events, the world has grown larger. The mass media have brought us images of Chinese students demonstrating in Tiananmen Square, the events leading up to the dismantling of the Soviet Union, and a starving Somalian population. We can no longer escape knowledge of world hunger or turn away from the impact of international events.

Although it is often assumed that international understanding increases as a result of cultural and educational exchanges over an extended period of time, scholars believe that this hoped-for goal must be demonstrated empirically. Thus there have been several studies of student exchange programs. For example, Rohrlich and Martin (1991) studied the adjustment of U.S. college students to studying abroad as well as their readjustment to returning home; they found women to be more satisfied than men upon returning, perhaps because their life-style at home was more independent than when living with a host family (pp. 178–179). Another investigation (Carlson and Widaman, 1988) compared 450 students from the University of California who spent their junior year studying at a European university (Sweden, Spain, France, the Federal Republic of Germany, Italy, and the United Kingdom were the countries involved) with students who remained on campus during the junior year. At the end of the school year, the study-abroad group had higher levels of cross-cultural interest, international political concern, and cultural cosmopolitanism. And when compared with students who remained at home, students who studied abroad also reported significantly more positive and more critical attitudes toward their own country (p. 14)—a finding consistent with earlier research. So relatively long-term study abroad may contribute to more favorable attitudes and increased international understanding, but there is still much to be learned about how such attitudes develop.

Social and Political Effects

We are no longer limited to being members of our own small community; we are citizens of the world as well, affected by political, economic, and social changes.

Communications, banking, and manufacturing have become increasingly international. Companies that deal in many commodities usually have offices, factories, and distributors in several countries or all over the world. As a result, the economies of the world's nations have become more and more intertwined, and the goods available in the nations that trade freely are drawn from the world at large. American companies have built plants and oil wells and in doing so created jobs in other countries. Similarly, companies from many parts of the world have created jobs for people in the United States. There have been multinational manufacturing efforts, and consortiums involving goods and services of every kind. Airbus Industrie, for example, is a consortium made up of the English, the French, the Germans, the Spanish, and the Dutch. Now, that joint venture may be extended to include the United States—and perhaps other international partners: In 1993 Boeing and Airbus agreed to explore the possibility of building an 800 passenger "superjumbo" airliner.

Not all the implications of an international economy are positive, however. When Iraq invaded Kuwait in 1990, for instance, there was much concern that the world's oil would be restricted and increasingly subject to Iraq's political actions. Economic problems in many areas of the world have resulted in repeated incidents of racial and ethnic conflict. Following several years of

No amount of information we read about intercultural communication can substitute for face-to-face encounters with people of other cultures and backgrounds.

recession and widespread unemployment, U.S. attitudes toward Japan have become extremely negative with Japan bashing characterized by one writer as "the national sport" (Krauthammer, 1992), and in the last few years a number of books have been published that many critics feel demonize the Japanese.

Yet our interdependence is clear. The United Nations, one of the most famous international organizations, is far more than a forum for political debate. Like many other international agencies, it deals actively with "the mechanics of living," such as the needs for food, health care, and education in many countries. International organizations also work on behalf of international refugees who, according to U.N. statistics, number between 15 and 20 million. Some international organizations provide such services as literacy training, education in such areas as modern agricultural methods, and help in organizing the local craft production into profitable cottage industries that market their goods beyond the immediate community. These services help to increase productivity and raise standards of living.

Cultural Effects

From the earliest times, cultures have been affected by contact with one another. Traders and the Mongol invasions once brought gunpowder, macaroni, and other Asian goods from Asia to Europe; later, immigrants brought these and other goods and customs to the United States. The Norman invasion of England in the eleventh century permanently affected the English language, not only from contact with the French language but because French became the language of the aristocracy and English the language of the peasants. European explorers brought horses to Native Americans, Native Americans taught early settlers how to grow corn and tobacco, and those settlers and their descendants drove the Native Americans westward. These are only a few examples of how trade, war, conquest, and migration have affected cultures throughout history.

As intercultural communication becomes more common and widespread, the effects of cultural contact are more pronounced and rapid. These are evident in the increased availability of goods that once would have been available, if at all, only to the very rich: tea from India, coffee from Brazil, woolen cloth from Britain, wine from France and Italy. It is also apparent in the spread of Western technology, health care methods, and Hilton Hotels in the "underdeveloped" nations, and the spread of Japanese industry and business methods in the United States.

Most people would not question the value of some aspects of cultural exchange, such as the introduction of sanitation methods that curb epidemics, or agricultural methods that save thousands from starvation. But many, including a number of scholars of culture, question the value of other aspects of cultural exchange. They ask whether certain so-called Stone Age and aboriginal communities that have been isolated for hundreds of years truly benefit from sudden contact with the outside world—whether, for example, exposure to war as well as sources of illness and pollution might outweigh what we consider the "advances" of civilization. The possibilities raise many ethical questions.

Intercultural exchange leads to **cultural homogenization,** *the tendency for cultures in contact with one another to become increasingly similar to one another.* Cultural homogenization implies that some aspects of one culture will dominate and eliminate the corresponding aspects of the other. The "standard American" voices we hear on television, for instance, are responsible for a standard American dialect and the disparagement of nonstandard dialects spoken by people who live in specific regions of the country. As a result of mass communication and travel, columnist Ellen Goodman notes, "We dress alike, we eat alike, and I guess we are destined to sound alike" (1981).

But even if we are familiar with foods from all over the world and blue jeans are as popular in Russia as in the United States, emphasis today is increasingly on our diversity. It is *differences* that have become the issue in conflicts not only between racial and ethnic groups in our own country but in those of other countries. Robert Jay Lifton, a psychiatrist who has written on the holocaust, believes that our discomfort at seeing televised images of human suffering can be a catalyst for change by evoking empathy and compassion:

> The evidence is there, on the screens, and in millions of human minds. Televised images can change the world.
>
> As survivors by proxy, can our witness be transformed into life-enhancing action—in Bosnia in this case, but also in other areas of death and suffering such as the famine in Somalia? (1992, p. 24)

Given enough understanding of regional as well as national cultures, it is possible to preserve individual differences of many kinds and allow members of various subcultures or groups to coexist and flourish. Indeed, Gudykunst and Kim maintain that "cultural and ethnic diversity are necessary for community to exist" (1992, p. 255); and they propose seven principles for building community, principles for which each of us must be responsible:

1. *Be committed.* We must be committed to the principle of building community in our lives, as well as to the individuals with whom we are trying to develop community.

2. *Be mindful.* Think about what we do and say. Focus on the process, not the outcome.

3. *Be unconditionally accepting.* Accept others as they are; do not try to change or control them. . . . Value diversity and do not judge others based only on their diversity.

4. *Be concerned for both ourselves and others.* Avoid polarized communication and engage in dialogue whenever possible. Consult others on issues that affect them and be open to their ideas.

5. *Be understanding.* Recognize how culture and ethnicity affect the way we think and behave. Search for commonalities. . . . Balance emotion, anxiety, and fear with reason.

6. *Be ethical.* Engage in behavior that is not a means to an end but behavior that is morally right in and of itself.

7. *Be peaceful.* Do not be violent or deceitful, breach valid promises, or be secretive. Strive for harmony. (Adapted from pp. 267–268)

SUMMARY

In this chapter, we discussed intercultural communication, which has become increasingly prevalent in the last few decades. We defined "culture" as the way of life developed and shared by a people and passed down from generation to generation. Because cultures vary along a range, the differences between two cultures may be slight or very dramatic. Even when two cultural groups are very similar, however, the differences between them are likely to become more evident in intercultural communication.

Intercultural communication has increased rapidly because of technological advances that have made long-distance communication more feasible and more available to the general public. Despite the advances in the means of sending and receiving messages, however, there are still many obstacles to intercultural communication. Differences in cultural factors such as language, nonverbal communication systems, relational roles and norms (particularly conflict norms), and beliefs and values that are deeply rooted in the whole cultural system often lead to intercultural misunderstanding.

Because we are not aware of the aspects of our own cultures in ourselves, the barriers to intercultural communication are complex and formidable. Ethnocentrism and stereotyping both limit our ability to deal with people beyond our own communities.

REVIEW QUESTIONS

1. Explain the difference between culture shock and reverse culture shock.

2. How do cultural groups differ from other groups that have shared characteristics?

3. Why is it important for effective intercultural communication to understand that culture is learned, rather than innate?

4. Why do cultures vary along a range, rather than being clearly distinct from one another?

5. What are the two major reasons that intercultural communication has increased in the last decades?

6. State three communication principles with significant implications for intercultural communication.

7. Identify at least three aspects of culture.

8. Explain the major difference between high-context and low-context cultures.

9. Explain at least three ways in which language is an obstacle to intercultural communication.

10. Describe at least three aspects of nonverbal communication that vary from culture to culture.

11. How can cultural roles and norms affect communication between cultures?

12. What are two variables that influence how members of a culture view conflict. Give an example of each.

13. Explain how differences in beliefs and values can prove to be obstacles in intercultural communication.

14. What is ethnocentrism? Why does it interfere with intercultural communication? Give an example.

15. Give two reasons for the stereotyping of cultural groups.

16. Identify several personal, political, and social effects of intercultural communication.

17. What is meant by "cultural homogenization"?

18. Explain the need for community building and state seven principles that have been proposed.

EXERCISES

1. Make a list of some of the cultural groups in your own region or state, including the group (or groups) that founded your community. To what extent have these groups been in contact with one another? To what extent

have they remained distinct from one another? List some ways in which these cultural groups have affected your own culture, such as your traditions, religious beliefs, and language.

2. Find three current articles about a cultural group, such as a group in Japan or Saudi Arabia, that has recently come into extended business or diplomatic contact with the United States. List at least five ways in which that culture, or that of the United States, has been affected by this contact.

3. List at least eight cultures, both inside and outside the United States, with which you communicate in some way (through personal contact, your work or business communication, or mass media). With which of these groups is your communication personal? With which is it institutional? In at least one case in which your contact with the other culture is primarily institutional, describe some ways in which your understanding of the people in that group is limited by your communication with them.

4. Think of a group of people that you feel have specific, shared, cultural characteristics, for example, Californians, southerners, New Yorkers, blacks, whites, Amish, Japanese, Russians, Chinese. Describe the people as a group, and list the characteristics that you think distinguish that group from others. To what extent is your description a stereotype? What is the source of your information about the group? Can you think of some reasons why your stereotype might be inaccurate? Can you think of some ways in which it might affect your communication with individual members of that group?

5. Listen to a national newscaster report the news on television. Do you think that such newscasters' use of language has affected the way you speak? Do you think their use of language affects what you consider to be good English? Why?

SUGGESTED READINGS

Baldwin, James. "Stranger in the Village." In *The Price of the Ticket.* By James Baldwin. New York: St. Martin's, 1985.

This is a moving essay on the experience of a black American who comes to live in an isolated European village.

Barnlund, Dean C. *Communicative Styles of Japanese and Americans: Images and Realities.* Belmont, CA: Wadsworth, 1989.

A comparative study that is thorough and clear-sighted. The author examines many stereotypical notions about the Japanese and the Americans.

Carroll, Raymonde. *Cultural Misunderstandings.* Translated by Carol Volk. Chicago: University of Chicago Press, 1988.

The author, who is French, has written a fascinating analysis of many of the cultural differences between the French and the Americans that generate so much misunderstanding on both sides.

Cushman, Donald P., and **Dudley D. Cahn, Jr.** *Communication in Interpersonal Relationships.* Albany, NY: SUNY Press, 1985.

An excellent book for the advanced student. There are good summaries of intercultural material in Chapter 8, "Cultural Communication and Interpersonal Relationships," and Chapter 9, "Cross-cultural Communication and Interpersonal Relationships."

Foner, Nancy, ed. *New Immigrants in New York.* New York: Columbia University Press, 1987.

This collection of essays by scholars from several disciplines examines the influence of New York City on its new immigrants as well as their influence on city life.

Gudykunst, William B., and **Young Yun Kim.** *Communicating with Strangers: An Approach to Intercultural Communication.* 2d ed. New York: McGraw-Hill, 1992.

The authors approach this excellent introduction to intercultural communication by providing students with a solid grounding in theoretical issues. Building community through diversity is the subject of the final chapter.

Gudykunst, William B., and **Young Yun Kim,** eds. *Readings on Communicating with Strangers: An Approach to Intercultural Communication.* New York: McGraw-Hill, 1992.

These readings have been selected to illustrate concepts across cultures or ethnic groups. The editors have an interdisciplinary focus which makes the book an invaluable resource.

Hall, Edward T. *Beyond Culture.* Garden City, NY: Doubleday, 1976.

The author of this book, an anthropologist, is an important researcher in cultural aspects and differences and in their affects on intercultural communication in business and diplomacy.

Hall, Edward T. *The Silent Language.* New York: Doubleday, Anchor, 1973.

This is one of the earliest books on nonverbal communication and its relationship to culture. The author describes a number of aspects of culture, such as the use of time and space, and discusses their implications for intercultural communication.

Kaplan, Robert. "Tales from the Bazaar." *The Atlantic,* 270 (August 1992): 37–61.

A fascinating report on Arabists, U.S. diplomats in the Middle East, and the long-term effects of their immersion in Arab culture.

Samovar, Larry A., and **Richard E. Porter,** eds. *Intercultural Communication: A Reader.* 6th ed. Belmont, CA: Wadsworth, 1991.

An outstanding collection of readings. Coverage is comprehensive and timely.

PART III

ETHICS

*E*thics and Communication

After reading this chapter, you should be able to:

1 Define ethics.

2 Discuss Aristotle's concept of the golden mean, and give two examples of it.

3 Compare and contrast the ethical views of Kant and the utilitarians.

4 Discuss the concept of the veil of ignorance and its relationship to a theory of justice.

5 Identify the excuses people give in defending lies and discuss three ethical issues concerned with lying. Give examples from at least three communication contexts.

6 Discuss three issues concerning the disclosure of information. Give four examples of contexts in which they might occur.

7 Explain the difference between whistleblowing and leaking information, and discuss the ethical issues raised by each.

*I*n the melee of charges and countercharges during the 1992 presidential campaign, no candidate was exempt. Often the subject seemed to be ethics, not politics. Questions about Bill Clinton's character were repeatedly raised by his opponents—one accusation had to do with his reported infidelity, another with attempts to avoid military service during the Vietnam War. George Bush's statement that he was "out of the loop" and had no knowledge of the illegal arms-for-hostages trade with Iran was challenged several times; and opponents questioned his ethics in bringing personal attacks on Clinton into the debates. Ross Perot had several different explanations of why his period of naval service had been cut short and why, in mid-campaign, he had pulled out of the presidential race. In an article titled "Lies, Lies, Lies," one columnist addressed the question of whether anyone was telling the truth (Gray, 1992).

This chapter examines some of the thorny issues related to ethics in communication, or "communicating with integrity." The study of communication has always reflected an interest in ethics. As we saw in Chapter 10, three hundred years before the birth of Christ, Aristotle discussed the importance of appeals to *ethos,* personal characteristics such as honesty and credibility, in communication.

Ethics has been defined as *the study of the general nature of morals and of the specific moral choices to be made by a person.* Notice the word "choice." Ethics involves communication choices so that, by examining and becoming more aware of our own values, we become more responsible for the consequences of our actions.

All of us have probably been on the receiving end of unethical behavior. Yet we seem to be more sensitive on the receiving end than when we behave in ways others consider unethical. Sometimes we feel we are simply being assertive, while others feel they are being "used." Bowie argues that what this issue involves is "a fundamental moral principle, the principle of respect for [other] persons" (1985, p. 167).

As we shall see in this chapter, trying to impose our own ethical values on others often leads to conflict. For example:

> We may find . . . that our concern for others' welfare conflicts with the value that we place on individual freedom, and we may face a dilemma when others resent our efforts to help them. (Lyons, 1984, p. 16)

How to reconcile the claims of personal freedom with those of moral responsibility has been debated over the centuries.

Giving thought beforehand to the basis of our ethical choices enables us to think through rather than rationalize our decisions:

> If ethical principles are to be a guide to future behavior rather than a rationalization of acts already performed, it's important for us to stake out our moral turf before we are thrust into a specific situation. . . . The

motivation to act ethically can be self-imposed, socially mandated, or divinely inspired. But regardless of the impetus, we need to have a way to determine the difference between right and wrong, good and bad, virtue and vice. (Griffin, 1991, p. 355)

In this chapter we begin by looking at some of the major ethical principles proposed by Western thinkers and then examine several issues that arise in many different communication contexts.

PRINCIPLES

The Golden Mean

Aristotle is thought of by many scholars as the founder of the communication discipline. A Greek biologist—and a tutor to Alexander the Great—he believed that ethics had to do with inner character rather than just overt behaviors.

Perhaps no concept in philosophy has been more widely cited than Aristotle's **golden mean.** According to Aristotle, morality is to be found in moderation. Aristotle views moral virtues as choices or modes of choice. He considers each virtue as the mean, the middle path between two extremes—excess and deficiency. We can see this most clearly with the virtue of temperance, the mean between eating and drinking too little or too much. Similarly, courage would be the mean between the extremes of fear (deficiency) and overconfidence (excess). Truthfulness would be the mean between false modesty and boastfulness; justice would be the mean between distributing too few goods (or punishments) and too many (Aristotle, 1947, pp. 333–337).

Some have interpreted Aristotle as saying that good is that which is desirable for its own sake—in other words, it is an end in itself. Since Aristotle was a biologist, he might have been interested in modern studies showing that people who report having committed fewer acts which they consider immoral also report significantly lower levels of stress; there are also findings that those who volunteer to help others actually live longer (Schuller, 1991, p. 97).

Though Aristotle is emphasizing what is within the range of human possibility, it is important not to misinterpret the principle of the golden mean. To advocate moderation is not to say that all behaviors are acceptable: "There is no mean for adultery, murder, theft. . . . Not every action nor every passion admits of a mean" (1947, p. 341). Similarly, Aristotle condemns lying while saying that "truth is noble and full of praise."

The aim of ethics for Aristotle is the happiness of the individual while the aim of politics involves the welfare of the entire community. Although Aristotle believed personal ethics were subordinate to politics, this did not create a conflict of loyalties:

This principle does not entail that the individual must sacrifice his interests to those of the community, except under unusual conditions such as war, because he assumed that the needs of both normally coincide. (Abelson, 1967, p. 85)

Our own interests, Aristotle would say, are usually in harmony with those of our society.

The Categorical Imperative

Suppose that every time you made a decision about ethics and acted on it your decision became a universal law. This is the guiding principle proposed by the eighteenth-century German philosopher Immanuel Kant:

Act only according to that maxim by which you can at the same time will that it should become a universal law. (1959, p. 39)

Kant's principle is known as **the categorical imperative**—that is, a command or obligation to act (an "imperative") that is absolute ("categorical")—one with no exceptions or conditions.

A categorical imperative makes certain behaviors unacceptable under any circumstances. For example, to Kant telling the truth is a sacred duty. There are no circumstances under which it would be acceptable for us to lie because, says Kant, we always harm someone by telling a lie and if we don't harm a particular person, still we do harm to humankind by undermining the nature of law. Take an extreme case—one that Kant himself considered: Would you tell a lie to prevent a murder? Kant argues that telling a lie even to prevent a murder would not be justified.

For Kant morality is measured by our *intentions to obey universal laws of morality* rather than by the consequences or outcomes of our actions—even if they will spare another's feelings or protect that person's welfare.

Many consider Kant's most significant contribution to ethical theory to be his requirement of "universal obedience to a rule of action":

It expresses more precisely and unambiguously the "golden rule" to be found in all the great religions, and it has been incorporated, in one form or another, in most modern systems of ethical theory. (Abelson, 1967, p. 95)

We find Kant's emphasis on universals in many religious systems and writings including the Ten Commandments of the Old Testament and Saint Augustine's prohibition that all lies are sins:

To use speech, then, for the purpose of deception, and not for its appointed end, is a sin. Nor are we to suppose that there is any lie that is not a sin, because it is sometimes possible, by telling a lie, to do service to another. (Augustine, 1961)

Utilitarianism

In sharp contrast to Kant, British philosophers Jeremy Bentham and John Stuart Mill place primary value not on our moral intentions but on the *outcomes* or *consequences* of our actions.

Bentham proposed a "hedonistic calculus," in which the amount of pleasure an action creates is weighed against the amount of pain it causes. Mill refers to the foundation of utilitarianism as the Greatest Happiness Principle:

Actions are right in proportion as they tend to promote happiness, wrong [insofar] as they tend to produce the reverse of happiness. (Mill, 1968, p. 249)

Happiness is the greatest good, and for Mill "happiness" refers to "pleasure and the absence of pain," unhappiness, to pain and the lack of pleasure. Mill extends the notion of happiness to include not simply pleasure but quality so that pleasure is defined more broadly and includes intellectual pleasure and other values.

Mill's later formulation of utilitarianism in the nineteenth century is the best known:

Seek the greatest happiness for the greatest number.

Utilitarianism grew out of concern for political and social reforms—hence its emphasis on what will benefit the greatest number of people—and was responsible for English legislative reforms during the nineteenth century (Abelson, 1967, p. 96). According to this view, the claims and welfare of individuals or smaller groups have to be subordinated to the claims of the greatest number of people.

Justice and the Veil of Ignorance

The contemporary American philosopher John Rawls argues for a principle of justice rather than utility. In *A Theory of Justice* (1971), a book on political and social philosophy, he suggests a fair procedure by which we can agree on common ethical principles: To free ourselves of bias and self-interest because of our social position, education, and so on—what are sometimes called "accidents of birth"—Rawls proposes that we should all be placed behind a **veil of ignorance**:

> First of all, no one knows his place in society, his class position or social status; nor does he know his fortune in the distribution of natural assets and abilities, his intelligence and strength, and the like. Nor, again, does anyone know his conception of the good, the particulars of his rational plan of life, or even the special features of the psychology such as his aversion to risk or liability to optimism or pessimism. More than this, I assume that the parties do not know the particular circumstances of their own society. (p. 137)

Because we do not know our situations in society or our natural assets, argues Rawls, "no one is in a position to tailor principles to his advantage" (p. 139). We don't know which principles would be in our own interest. This also eliminates the possibility of groups banding together to form a coalition, for they do not know how to favor themselves. Once all these factors are corrected for, we make an ethical decision in which there will be unanimity of choice—fairness: No single person, group, or generation will be favored. [Rawls believes "the notion of the veil of ignorance is . . . implicit in Kant's ethics" (p. 140).]

Imagine the world as redesigned by Rawls:

> The participants may be male or female, 10 years old or 90, a Russian or a Pole, rookie or veteran, black or white, advertising executive or sales representative for a weekly. As we negotiate social agreements in the situation of imagined equality behind the veil of ignorance, . . . we inevitably seek to protect the weaker party and to minimize risks. In case I emerge from the veil as a beginning reporter rather than a big-time publisher, I will opt for fair treatment for the former. The most vulnerable party receives priority in these cases and the result, Rawls would contend, is a just resolution. (Christians et al., 1991, p. 18)

Rawls proposes then that a principle of justice or fairness must include protection of those whose position in the society is weakest—whether due to age, illness, status, or income—and that what is moral is what is fair for all.

Ethical principles from many other cultures and other times could, of course, be represented here. Our hope is that those we have looked at will serve as a springboard for discussion and reflection as you consider some of the issues involved in making ethical choices about communication.

ISSUES

Lying

Perhaps one of the most obvious breaches of ethics is lying. Distorting the truth is so common that one survey found that 75 percent of those polled believed that there is less honesty in government than there was a decade ago (Gray, 1992, p. 32).

In her study of lying, philosopher Sissela Bok defines a lie as *"an intentionally deceptive message in the form of a statement"* (1989a, p. 15; italics added); she emphasizes a person's *intention* to deceive or mislead through verbal communication. Paul Ekman, whose research on deception in nonverbal communication we looked at in Chapter 4, also links lying with the liar's *intention* either to conceal by "leaving out true information" or to falsify, "presenting false information as if it were true" (1985, p. 41).

There is less agreement on how to regard ambiguous or equivocal communication. We've already spoken of euphemisms and unintentionally equivocal language in Chapter 3. Bavelas and her colleagues (1990) define "equivocation" as "avoidance," "communication that is not straightforward: it appears ambiguous, contradictory, tangential, obscure, or even evasive" (p. 28). They argue that the person who equivocates "is not the cause of equivocation. Rather [it] is the result of the individual's communicative situation" (p. 54). In our discussion the assumption will be that we can and do make choices about ethical and unethical behaviors.

In the movie *Glengarry Glen Ross,* which is based on the Pulitzer Prize winning play by David Mamet, several real estate salesmen try to hustle and swindle customers into buying large land deals. At one point in the film, a customer is having second thoughts and wants his large check back. The salesman played by Al Pacino says that it has not been cashed by the home office yet, and the customer has nothing to worry about, whereupon another salesman comes into the office and says that he has in fact sent the check in. Later Al Pacino virtually explodes over the incident, telling the other salesman that he is never supposed to open his mouth in front of a customer until he knows what he has already been told. In other words, any lie is all right as long as it gets the sale.

Although this film portrays an absolute nadir in business ethics, situations in which we encounter lying are not always so sharply drawn. People have even cited moral reasons for lying. Thus a perennial question in ethics is whether there are circumstances when telling a lie is acceptable. Bok finds that, in giving excuses to defend their lying, people appeal to four principles: They say they were lying to avoid harm, to produce some benefits, for the sake of fairness, or even for the sake of truth (usually a truth known to them but not to others) (p. 76).

To some degree, Bok's analysis overlaps with the results of Lippard's study of deception (1988) in which people gave five reasons for lying: to protect or acquire material resources (for example, money, an apartment, or a job); to decrease or increase their affiliation with others; to protect themselves either by avoiding self-disclosure or enhancing or protecting their self-image; to avoid conflict; to protect other people. (For more detail, see Chapter 3.)

Let's consider a lie that is told to avoid harm by protecting someone else's feelings. As we noted in Chapter 6, Knapp and Vangelisti (1992) include lying among the behaviors and strategies people use to maintain close relationships:

> For most couples, the real issue is whether a lie will have a damaging effect on the relationship and whether the motivation for lying is well intentioned. (p. 237)

They then propose three questions in thinking about the lie: "(1) Will this lie help both of us? If the lie is solely for the benefit of one partner, it is more likely to be viewed negatively and incur more relationship damage. . . . (2) Is the lie consistent with the rules of fairness in the relationship? . . . (3) Does your partner (the lied to) believe you have his or her best interests at heart—both generally and in this specific situation?" (p. 237).

Imagine yourself as the person lied to in this relationship, and consider your own views. Would you want to know if someone you loved was unfaithful to you, or would you prefer to be spared the pain? A related issue here is whether a lie such as this which seems to protect actually does. Granted, it avoids conflict, one of the reasons people frequently give for lying; but what does it protect—the relationship itself, the person lied to, the liar? Is it in your best interest to remain in the same relationship to the other person, or might you be better off finding out "the worst," trying to hammer out the difficulties, and having the option of ending the relationship?

Consider a more structured two-person relationship. Suppose you are a doctor who discovers that your elderly patient is suffering from a terminal illness and has only a few months to live. Your patient is terrified of even the slightest illness. Do you tell him the truth about his condition?

We know that Kant's categorical imperative would prohibit lying under any circumstances. Aristotle's golden mean might suggest some middle ground between assuring the patient he is fine and telling him everything about his condition including the amount of time he has to live. On the other hand, a utilitarian might argue that the patient would be happiest *not* knowing—happiness here being defined as pleasure, or the absence of pain. We also know that it's on such grounds that the family of a patient often asks a doctor not to tell him the truth: A utilitarian might think of this decision as producing the greatest happiness for the greatest number. A principle of justice is more difficult to apply, unless we agree on what constitutes "protection." If everyone must be treated equally, the doctor's decision will be the same for *all* patients.

In a recent article on medical ethics, several doctors affirmed their obligation to tell the truth, unless patients had made clear that if they were dying they did not want to be told. Patients, it was suggested, should state early on the level of information they are comfortable with. This position is a subject of debate even among doctors.

Issues about lying arise in virtually every communication context. For example, during a job interview suppose you say you have far more computer experience than you do because you think that will ensure getting hired. If you then go home and learn what you need before you get the job, would you say this is a "white lie," one that harms no one else? Many people seem to have a repertoire of lies they identify as harmless: "What a perfect gift."

"Mr. Thomas is out for the day." "I have to work late tonight." "I'd love to stay, but I have so much work to do this evening." Do you think white lies are harmless?

In public and mass communication, lying is sometimes defended for the sake of producing benefits, even for the sake of truth. The ethical dimension of public communication raises many questions, especially about communication from government sources, where so much depends upon public trust. There have been times when governmental decisions about deception were later justified as being in the interest of national security. For example, as more information about the Iran-contra scandal unfolded, it became clear that there had been many denials from government officials at the same time that incriminating documents were being shredded. In public communication, as in other communication contexts, we can see how initial lying, whatever its motivation, often leads to an intricate web of lies.

Let's consider arguments in mass communication about lying for the sake of some greater truth. For example, suppose a reporter is writing about the welfare system, and, to gain access to inside information, he misrepresents himself: Under an assumed name he applies for welfare by posing as a homeless person. Suppose also that his intention is to write an article that will not only sell newspapers but may institute possible reforms. Is his lying justified— and if so, on what grounds?

We might return again to the ethical principles looked at earlier. It seems difficult here to follow the golden mean. Given the extremes of identifying oneself as a reporter or posing as a welfare applicant, perhaps a middle path could be taken if the reporter requested interviews with administrators (noting too if they declined to give information) and also interviewed many applicants to the system.

Kant's universal rule suggests that our reporter's deception is just plain wrong; regardless of his motive, the means cannot justify the end. In contrast, utilitarians might argue that the negative consequence of lying (the pain it might cause to the few deceived) would be far outweighed by the number of others who would benefit so that the ends justify the means. (The assumption here of course is that we can be sure of the consequences of our actions.) A theory of justice requiring fairness for all might argue against unfairness to those being lied to.

Issues about the media's obligation to its audience are well framed in the following questions:

> Does the press have a legitimate advocacy function, or does it best serve democratic life as an intermediary, a conduit of information and varying opinions? In a similar vein, should the press mirror events or provide a map that leads its audience to a destination? The kind of responsibility for justice that a particular medium is seen to possess often depends on how we answer these intermediate questions about the press's proper role and function. (Christians et al., 1991, p. 114)

Photos from NBC's *Dateline* program on safety in which a GM pickup truck is struck broadside. Notice the puffs of smoke under the truck in the top photo, produced by remote-controlled ignitors to ensure the truck would burst into flames upon impact.

Consider the case of NBC and GM. In November of 1992 *Dateline NBC* had an investigative report on the safety of certain models of GM pickup trucks. The television program was considering a possible flaw in the design of the gas tanks: These are outside the steel frame and built into either side of the vehicle. The question was whether this made GM's trucks likely to explode upon impact during a side-collision, and there were lawsuits against GM pending at the time. NBC aired a dramatic video—a crash test in which a GM truck bursts into flames after being struck from the side by another vehicle. Later GM charged that NBC had rigged the test by installing remote-controlled toy rockets under the truck to be sure it would explode. After GM filed a lawsuit against the network for "dishonest sensationalism" and an independent investigation was completed, NBC issued an apology. In March of 1993, Michael Gartner, head of NBC News, resigned; three *Dateline* producers were dismissed; and a *Dateline* reporter was transferred to a Miami station.

Misrepresentations in the mass media have enormous ramifications because of the size of the audience and the frequently high credibility of the source. Members of a mass communication audience must also be able to distinguish between fact and public relations information. Carole Gorney, a professor of journalism at Lehigh University, observes:

> Public relations consultants should be held accountable for participating in litigation journalism. The practice counters the groups' codes of ethical standards requiring consultants to avoid corrupting the channels of communication and the processes of government. (Gorney, 1993, A15)

To avoid such problems, sources should be clearly acknowledged and conflicts of interest made explicit.

Misrepresentation in public communication also violates public trust and results in a loss of credibility. For example, in 1988 Senator Joseph Biden gave a speech in which he used parts of a talk by British Labor Party leader Neil Kinnock without crediting him. After being accused of plagiarism, Biden, then a candidate for President, was forced to withdraw from the presidential race and no doubt ruined his chances of a future bid.

Such issues are not as remote as they might seem. In high school and college, students are warned against plagiarizing, whether it be in submitting the paper of another student or using work from books or articles without acknowledgment or quotation. Charges of plagiarism can have serious and long-term effects on a student's academic record.

Secrets, Disclosures, and Privacy

Issues about disclosures and secrecy naturally dovetail with those about lying. Many philosophers and theologians have debated the ethics of lying. But what about the ethics of disclosing information known to us—particularly the secrets of other people. What are our obligations? Do we have to protect others? Do we always have to make known what we know? And how should we protect ourselves when our welfare seems to depend upon exposing others?

Take a case in which disclosing what you know about someone's behavior will probably result in disciplinary action. Ann is a college freshman. She and three other freshmen live in a two-bedroom suite that has its own bathroom. Ann and Kim share a bedroom, and so do their suite-mates, Karen and Liz. In this dormitory students are allowed to sign in guests who can then sleep overnight. The problem begins when Kim starts signing in guests who stay several days at a time, take drugs in the room, and camp out in the bathroom. The other three roommates become very ill at ease. They never know who might turn up in the suite or exactly what will happen. More significant— they don't know what is the right thing to do about it.

If you were one of these three students, what would you do? Consider some of your alternatives. You start by ignoring the parade of visitors, but suppose it only gets worse; and you find you can't study in the room or even feel comfortable when you go to sleep. Do you decide on a moderate course of action and make a firm request that Kim tell her friends to leave? If that fails, what are some of your options—calling your parents, talking to the dean, going to the RA in your dorm? For these students, the next step seemed to be going to the RA, the resident for their floor in the large dormitory. Even then, they felt a conflict—Kim's behavior was endangering their welfare, yet appealing to a higher authority felt like turning someone in, "ratting" on them.

Here's an instance in which a conflict can arise not about whether to lie but whether to tell the truth. In a sense, this is an issue about loyalties—about getting a fellow student in trouble even though you feel that what she is doing is wrong. (This is what makes the honor system so difficult to enforce.) By disclosing information about someone else you know that you will affect her welfare. Her parents might find out. She might be expelled. Perhaps Ann also fears that she might be harmed when Kim's friends learn what has happened.

Issues concerning disclosure of information occur in many different communication contexts. For example, imagine yourself as a reporter for the school newspaper. As part of your job, you interview a university official, and she gives you some controversial information on the promise that you will not reveal her as the source: grades of several athletes have been altered to raise their academic average. Later a heated debate is stirred up by your article, and the dean of students demands to know the source of your information. Of course, the dean also controls the budget for your paper, and though he does not threaten to take money away, there is always that possibility. What would you do? What are your loyalties to the newspaper, the source, and the dean?

Complex questions concerning disclosure and the right to privacy have been raised in the case of Anne Sexton, an American poet who wrote freely of her own sexual fantasies, her preoccupation with death, and her emotional breakdowns. In 1974, at the age of forty-five, Sexton committed suicide. There has been considerable interest in her personal life, due in part to the number of self-disclosures and autobiographical material in her own work. In 1991 Diane Wood Middlebrook published a biography of Sexton. Her book made use of material that had never before been used in the biography of a major American figure: Over three hundred audiotapes of therapeutic sessions with the subject's psychiatrist. Although the tapes were used with the consent of Sexton's daughter, Sexton herself left no instructions as to whether this was allowable (Stanley, 1991).

The book created an intense controversy, and several ethical questions emerged. The first is what many psychiatrists saw as a dramatic violation of medical ethics by Sexton's psychiatrist, Dr. Martin Orne. Sessions between doctor and patient are strictly confidential. Several prominent psychiatrists spoke of Orne's betrayal of both his patient and profession.

The judgment of Sexton's daughter in allowing the tapes to be used was also criticized, and the chairman of the ethics committee of the American Psychiatric Association asserted:

> A patient's right to confidentiality survives death. . . . Our view is that only the patient can give that release. What the family wants does not matter a whit. (cited in Stanley, 1991, A1–C13)

How to weigh the biographer's needs for information against the subject's right to privacy is another troubling issue. While there certainly have been other biographers who discussed their subjects with psychiatrists, direct access to the doctor's records or transcripts has been rare. One often cited instance is a biography of Winston Churchill by Lord Moran, his personal physician, which describes how severely Churchill had been impaired by a stroke—the facts of which had been kept from the British people (C13).

The *right to privacy,* so often discussed as an ethical issue, becomes particularly complex in connection with all the mass media—not merely in connection with books. In April of 1992, after being told that *USA Today* was about to publish an article saying that he had AIDS, former tennis star Arthur Ashe disclosed his condition. Ashe quickly called a news conference in New York. He acknowledged that he had contracted the HIV virus through a blood transfusion during heart surgery and would have preferred, he said, not to have made his condition known to the public because he wanted to protect the privacy of his family. As it turned out, several journalists who also had this information had elected not to publish it. One editorial in *U.S. News & World Report* (Ruby, 1992) argued that there is a difference between the *right* to publish and the *obligation* to publish.

Journalists are repeatedly faced with balancing concerns with what is often called "the public's right to know" with concerns about an individual's right to privacy. Is it, for example, the public's right to know that a person is a homosexual? Is it the public's right to know the name of a rape victim in a much publicized trial?

Several ethical questions involving the mass media were raised by the

Rather than have a news magazine disclose he had contracted AIDS, tennis great Arthur Ashe reluctantly called his own news conference to announce his condition.

1991 trial of William Kennedy Smith. Smith, a member of the prominent Kennedy family, was accused of raping a twenty-nine-year-old woman in Palm Beach, Florida. Journalistic practice of major news organizations has been to protect the privacy of rape victims by not using their names without their consent, and at first the networks and other media withheld the woman's name and blocked out her face. But after *NBC Nightly News* identified the woman, a few news organizations, including *The New York Times,* published her name. Despite its longstanding practice of protecting the identity of alleged rape victims, the *Times* also published a profile on the woman noting that she was often seen at Palm Beach bars and that she was unmarried but had a child. These actions set off furious debate among journalists about the right to privacy and the need to provide information to the public. *The New York Times* came in for particular criticism. Many of its own editors and reporters expressed outrage about a profile questioning the accuser's character; one of their objections was the lack of a comparable profile on William Kennedy Smith (Glaberson, 1991). Smith, a medical student, was acquitted by the jury.

Questions about the public's right to know are especially common in political reporting. Regarding invasion of privacy issues, Christians and others (1991) point out:

The law that conscientiously seeks to protect individual privacy excludes public officials. [Chief Justice] Brandeis himself believed strongly in keeping the national business open. Sunlight for him was a great disinfectant. While condemning intrusion in personal matters, he insisted on the exposure of all secrets bearing on public concern. In general, the courts have upheld that political personalities cease to be purely private persons. . . . (p. 138)

Since the press has tremendous latitude in deciding what is newsworthy and has sometimes catered to tastes for gossip and sensationalism, these writers advocate "additional determinants . . . to distinguish gossip and voyeurism from information necessary to the democratic-decision making process" (p. 138)

Whistleblowing

As members of groups, we enact certain roles and adopt specific behavioral norms. Many of these are implicit, unstated, but nonetheless they are expectations about our behavior as a group member. Each professional organization also has its principles and standards of behavior that all members promise to uphold. In **whistleblowing,** *a member of a group makes a charge about the violation of ethical standards or norms within that group itself.* A journalist writes about how another journalist has misled a criminal into giving self-incriminating information. A doctor on the staff of a large hospital accuses the chief surgeon of malpractice. An employee of a savings-and-loan association tells the president that officials in the organization are getting interest-free loans and other privileges.

Bok identifies three elements that make whistleblowing particularly charged: dissent, breach of loyalty, and accusation (1989*b*, pp. 214–215).

First, it is a form of *dissent* because "it makes public a disagreement with an authority or majority view" but also has "the narrower aim of casting light on negligence or abuse, of alerting the public to a risk and of assigning responsibility for that risk."

Second, the message itself is viewed "as a *breach of loyalty* because it comes from within. The whistleblower, though he is neither coach nor referee, blows the whistle on his own team."

The third element, *accusation,* "singles out specific groups or persons as responsible"—and furthermore, the accusation is about "a present or an imminent threat" (pp. 214–215).

In recent years whistleblowing has become extremely common in many organizations. In one case involving the sale of aircraft engines to an Israeli general, a GE employee accused the company of diverting approximately $40 million in U.S. military aid. In a lawsuit, a former GE employee accused the company of attempting to fix the price of industrial diamonds and of dismissing him when he reported the charges to a senior vice-president.

Although motives remain a question in whistleblowing cases—a whistleblower may be awarded a significant sum from monies reclaimed by the government—it is true that whistleblowers have often been ignored, transferred, demoted, or fired. Recently one writer observed that "the number of such suits suggests that something is wrong with Corporate America's internal ethics system" and proposed that organizations adopt this policy:

1. Aggressively publicize a reporting policy that encourages employees to bring forward valid complaints of wrongdoing.

2. Defuse fear by directing complaints to someone outside the whistleblower's chain of command.

3. An independent group, either in or out of the company, should investigate it.

4. Show employees that complaints are taken seriously by publicizing the outcome of investigations whenever possible. (Driscoll, 1992, p. 36)

Whistleblowing occurs not only in government and business organizations but in many other kinds of groups. For example, in 1986, Margot O'Toole, a young post-doctoral fellow at M.I.T., testified that an important scientific paper on immunology by Thereza Imanish-Kari; David Baltimore, a Nobel laureate in biology; and others contained some results that were fraudulent. Dr. O'Toole, who had worked as a research assistant to Dr. Imanish-Kari, maintained that certain experiments reported in the paper had not been carried out and that some other results cited had been falsified. Her allegations set off what became one of the most controversial long-term investigations of misconduct in scientific research.

As a consequence of her whistleblowing, Dr. O'Toole lost her job and was ostracized, unable to find work within the scientific community for four years. In 1991, however, her charges were upheld by a government panel: Dr. Baltimore, who though not directly accused of fraud had repeatedly defended the paper, resigned as head of Rockefeller University and issued an apology to Dr. O'Toole for strong criticism of her behavior.

Here issues of whistleblowing were further complicated by the status, reputation, and credibility of the people involved.

Leaks

Another way of communicating information is through a **leak**—*previously unknown information is made known to others, but its source, unlike that of whistleblowing, remains anonymous*, at least to the general public. For example, information might be leaked to the press by someone who may be a familiar source but whose identity is concealed. Of course, leaking information protects the source and often evades the responsibility of confirming the truth about the information that is given.

Although most of us may not be in a position to "leak" information in the strict sense of the term, gossip and rumor are common communication behaviors that raise ethical questions. (The subject of rumors was discussed in more detail in Chapter 11.) In formal contexts, leaks often have immediate and widespread repercussions. For example, a leak about the head of a large company can not only damage reputations but have drastic affects on a company's stock, thus affecting thousands of shareholders as well company employees.

In 1993, James D. Robinson III, chief executive officer of American Express for fifteen years, resigned after what one writer described as a boardroom "coup" (Burrough, 1993). The struggle between Robinson and some of his board of directors stemmed from growing disenchantment with his leadership and ethical practices, including a smear campaign against Swiss financier Edmond Safra which resulted in a public apology and an $8 million settlement. Robinson's attempt to save face before stepping down after mounting pressure to resign was foiled when information was leaked to Safra; then to *The Wall Street Journal* and *Fortune,* which issued a press release in December of 1992 (p. 223). The struggle went on until January 1993, when American Express announced Robinson was quitting.

When government information is leaked, sources are often accused of being motivated by partisanship, which is almost impossible to verify. Such questions, while justifiable, can sometimes be used to divert attention from the charges themselves.

In 1992, Peter Fleming, a special Senate counsel, investigated the leak of Anita Hill's previously confidential allegations of sexual harassment by Clarence Thomas. At the time of the disclosure, Thomas had been nominated for Supreme Court Justice, and the leaked information resulted in lengthy testimony by Hill, Thomas, and others during Judge Thomas's confirmation hearings. The journalist who broke the story of the allegations on October 6, 1991, Timothy Phelps of *Newsday,* was called to appear before the Senate counsel. Asked to disclose his source of information, Phelps refused. In his opening statement he said:

> I respectfully decline to answer the special independent counsel's questions here today because they are posed for the explicit reason of seeking the identity of my sources.
>
> I do so not only in an assertion of my right under the First Amendment, but also of those of my readers and of the American people. They have a need and a right to know that serious allegations had been made against a nominee to the Supreme Court. (cited in Barringer, 1992, p. 20)

Phelps's argument that the First Amendment guarantees freedom of the press and protects the right of confidentiality for its sources has a long history among journalists. In 1976, for example, Daniel Schorr, a CBS reporter, released a secret report by Congress on CIA activities; when subpoenaed by the House Ethics Committee, he refused to identify his source on similar grounds. Arguments about the ethics of leaking information by the mass media are especially difficult to resolve; often they involve balancing claims for actions done for the public good against the very damaging loss of credibility and reputation for those people who are singled out.

Clampitt (1991) argues that "leaks are tantamount to anonymous whistle blowing . . . [and] using a leak is particularly dubious in nature and should be undertaken in the rarest of circumstances" (p. 271). In comparing whistle-blowing and information leaks, Bok weighs the consequences of each:

> In fairness to those criticized, openly accepted responsibility for blowing the whistle should . . . be preferred to the secret denunciation or the leaked rumor—the more so, the more derogatory and accusatory the information. What is openly stated can be more easily checked, its source's motives challenged, and the underlying information examined. Those under attack may otherwise be hard put to it to defend themselves against nameless adversaries. Often they do not even know they are threatened until it is too late to respond. (1989b, p. 215)

As you think about the ethical issues we have been discussing, keep in mind that intercultural communication often increases their complexity. For example, we sometimes have no knowledge about another culture's ethical values. Differences between how low- and high-context cultures value language will also influence what must be made explicit and what is tacitly understood. Rhetorical frames of reference may be very different: What is regarded as a lie in one culture may be understood by members of another as an exaggeration for the sake of politeness. The social norms of another culture may collide with our own: For example, if it is expected that a representative of a foreign company in Saudi Arabia will offer the ruling sheik a great sum of money for his birthday, he may regard this practice not as *baksheesh* but as bribery. And as we saw in Chapter 13, norms about disclosures and privacy also vary considerably. A harmless disclosure in one culture may constitute a betrayal in another.

Opotow (1992) writes of a further complexity, the possibility of moral exclusion—that is, perceiving individuals or groups as being *"outside the boundary in which moral values, rules, and considerations of fairness apply"* (p. 422). As new communication technologies emerge and intercultural communication continues to increase, the need for an ethical base that is morally inclusive becomes an issue that will affect us all.

SUMMARY

In this chapter we explored ethical decision-making in communication. To establish a baseline for discussion, we considered some representative ethical principles that have been proposed by Western thinkers. We examined Aristotle's concept of the golden mean, a middle path between two extremes. In

Kant's categorical imperative we saw human actions judged as ethical by their intent rather than their outcomes. In the utilitarian view, on the other hand, greatest value was placed on the outcomes or consequences of our actions, with moral choice being governed by the greatest good for the greatest number of people. And in Rawls's philosophy of justice the guiding principle was fairness for everyone in the society, including the most vulnerable.

We then turned to several fundamental issues in ethics. We discussed lying as well as the reasons often given to defend lying—for example, lying to avoid harm or to protect another person. Next we examined questions about the ethics of secrecy, disclosures, and rights of privacy, both in public and personal life. Finally, we looked at the complex issues of whistleblowing, in which a group member makes an accusation about violation of ethical standards within the group itself, and of leaking information, in which the source of information remains anonymous.

As we have tried to show, difficult ethical questions surface not just in organizational, public, and mass communication but in the most informal and intimate contexts. Ethics are not lofty principles for other people; we are all involved in making moral choices—often on a daily basis.

REVIEW QUESTIONS

1. Give your definition of "ethics."

2. What is Aristotle's concept of the golden mean, and what is its implication for ethical choices? Give two examples.

3. Explain Kant's principle of the categorical imperative.

4. Discuss the basic ethical principle of the utilitarians.

5. Compare and contrast the views of Kant and the utilitarians on making decisions about ethics.

6. What is the concept of the veil of ignorance, and how does it relate to Rawls's theory of justice?

7. What are the four principles people often appeal to in defending lies?

8. Identify three ethical issues concerned with lying, and include examples from at least three communication contexts in your discussion.

9. Summarize three ethical issues related to the disclosure of information. Describe four contexts in which they might arise.

10. Identify three elements that are present in whistleblowing, and give two examples of it.

11. What is the difference between whistleblowing and leaking information?

12. What ethical issues are raised by whistleblowing and leaks?

EXERCISES

1. Describe three different situations, involving (1) your friend, (2) your parents, (3) your employer, in which you had to make a difficult decision about ethics. In each case, discuss the basis and motives for your decision; then evaluate whether your decisions were consistent from an ethical standpoint. If not, why not?

2. At a small party, your friend reads aloud a very personal letter, identifies who wrote it, and then asks the entire group what they think of it. No one at the party knows the letter writer. Discuss the ethics of this behavior and of possible responses from people at the party.

3. Reread the discussion in this chapter concerning the dispute over the Anne Sexton biography. Have several members of the class role-play the situation described, each presenting the ethical issues involved from one point of view: the psychiatrist who permitted tapes of Sexton's therapy sessions to be used; the head of the American Psychiatric Association; Sexton's biographer; Sexton's daughter, who granted permission; or the book's publisher. Include one person who represents and speaks for Anne Sexton herself. Then have the class discuss the validity of each position.

4. Identify a story currently in the news that is controversial and involves an ethical issue discussed in this chapter. Compare and contrast coverage of the incident by two major newspapers, a tabloid, two television stations, and a weekly news magazine. In each case, how is the information represented? What kind of language is used to describe the people involved? Is the treatment of all parties objective or partisan?

SUGGESTED READINGS

Bok, Sissela. _Lying: Moral Choice in Public and Private Life._ New York: Vintage, 1989.

An important book by a contemporary philosopher. The author examines lying in terms of ethical theory and illuminates her discussion with examples from many different contexts.

Christians, Clifford, G., Kim B. Rotzoll, and **Mark Fackler.** _Media Ethics._ 3rd ed. New York: Longman, 1991.

This is an excellent and comprehensive treatment of media ethics with detailed case studies on each issue discussed.

Gudykunst, William, and **Young Yun Kim.** _Communicating with Strangers: An Approach to Intercultural Communication._ New York: McGraw-Hill, 1992.

Chapter 14 of this text offers some guidelines for resolving conflict and building a sense of community between people with different ethical norms.

Ibsen, Henrik. *An Enemy of the People.* In Henrik Ibsen, *Selected Plays.* New York: Modern Library, Random House.

A complex and provocative play about the effects of whistleblowing, written by a great Norwegian playwright of the nineteenth century.

MacIntyre, Alasdair. *A Short History of Ethics.* New York: Macmillan.

This is a history of moral philosophy from the time of the early Greeks to the twentieth century.

Appendix and Supplementary Exercises

Anyone who has ever taught a course in speech communication realizes that there is often a major gap between the theory and the application of that theory. This appendix includes some supplementary exercises which may be used to help bridge the above-mentioned gap. For maximum benefit, however, the behaviors stimulated by these exercises should be discussed to show their relationship to the conceptual material presented in this text and to class lectures. It is important to keep in mind that the exercises are a *means* of increasing student learning and are not an end in themselves.

Two-Person Role-Play Exercises

1. STUDENT-PROFESSOR CONFERENCE

Jane: You are a college sophomore in Dr. Patterson's speech communication class. You are dissatisfied with a grade for one of your class projects and are trying to persuade Dr. Patterson to give you a higher grade.

Dr. Patterson: You have had ten students come to your office to complain about their low grades. Jane has been an uninterested student all semester long. Now she enters your office.

2. PARENT-SON EPISODE

Parent: You have been looking for a lost article of your son's clothing and you find some pornographic pictures in one of the drawers of his dresser.

Seventeen-Year-Old Son: You have just been out with some friends and you find your parent in your room.

473

3. EMPLOYER-APPLICANT INTERVIEW

Employer: You are looking for a man or woman to hire as a summer salesperson in your department store. You are primarily looking for someone who can relate to your college customers.

Applicant: You are a twenty-year-old college student who desperately needs a summer job to help finance your way through school. You have had no sales experience but are popular and personable.

4. EMPLOYER-EMPLOYEE INTERVIEW

Employer: You have noticed that the work of one of your employees has been substandard lately. He has worked for you as a used-car salesman for the past five years and has been a better-than-average salesman. You have just received a call from his wife that he has been drinking somewhat lately and that she suspects him of having spent several nights with another woman. She is completely against any drinking, and she gets upset when he drinks even one beer or mixed drink. You call him in for a discussion.

Employee: You have been disappointed about your level of pay lately and you would like to be considered for a promotion as a used-car sales manager. You have been moonlighting at a second job lately to buy your wife a special birthday gift.

5. COUNSELOR-STUDENT INTERVIEW

Student: You are a college student who has become involved in drug use to an extent that you feel it is becoming a problem. You go to the university counseling center to get some help.

Counselor: You are employed by the university counseling center to give help to students who seem to have problems of various kinds. You are eager to help in any way you can. A student has just entered your office.

6. SALESMAN-CUSTOMER INTERVIEW SITUATION

Problem: You as a salesman sold two cars to two brothers. You assured them that the cars would be delivered in approximately five to six weeks. Under normal operating conditions, this would have been a true statement, one which you could very easily fulfill. However, just before both cars are scheduled for production, the company goes on strike. As the salesman, it is your duty to assure both brothers that:

1. The strike won't last too long.
2. They will get their cars as soon as the strike is over.
3. You are doing all you can to get their cars here as soon as possible.

The problem is further intensified after the strike ends. Delivery is already three weeks late, but to make matters worse, the car was shipped, but it has in some way gotten lost while en route and no one seems to have any idea where it is.

Situation: The two brothers are calling every day to ask about their cars. Each time they call, they tell you they are getting less and less interested in the cars. In fact, toward the end they are both talking about canceling their orders. They both think that in some way you have pulled a fast deal on them. It is your job to make them understand (1) the reason the cars are delayed and (2) that the cars will be along shortly.

7. EMPLOYER-EMPLOYEE INTERVIEW SITUATION

Place: The dealer's office.

People: The dealer and the service manager.

Occasion: The service manager, who has been with the dealership five years, has apparently been neglecting his job recently. Unapplied mechanics time has been rising, the shop is being left much dirtier than usual. In general, it appears that the service manager is not minding his business as he should. He has been a good service manager in the past, and the dealer doesn't know what has happened to change the situation. The purpose of the interview is to enable the dealer to find the cause of the problem and determine what can be done to alleviate it.

Group Role-Play Exercises

The Sinking Ship

You are one of seven people who are the only survivors of a passenger ship that was hit in the South Pacific by an old World War II mine. You are now trapped in the bottom of the ship's hold, with only a small air lock to let you return to the surface. It takes approximately three minutes to operate the air lock to allow one person to escape.

The hold is steadily filling with water, and judging by the list of the ship, you have at the most fifteen minutes before the ship sinks quickly to the bottom of the 37,000-foot-deep Mariana trench.

Your problem is one of survival. You are to determine as quickly as possible the most equitable way of deciding who will be saved in the fifteen minutes' time. Remember that it takes three minutes to save each person, so the maximum number that can be saved is five.

As each person is "saved," he or she will separate from the group and sit in a chair. Both the amount of time taken by each person in the air lock and the remaining time left for the victims will be watched closely.

To impress the disaster victims with the seriousness of their situation, it is necessary to emphasize that those who are left in the hold will suffer a most hideous death— death by drowning.

Ability-Grouping Meeting

The participating group members (group A) are to assume they represent the English teachers in a senior high school. The principal of the school has asked them to meet by themselves to formulate their recommendations pertaining to ability grouping in their classes for next year. ("Ability grouping" for this situation means the use of standardized test results as a basis of placement of students in class sections.) Two years ago the students were placed in classes on the following basis: above average ability, average ability, and below average ability. The following year students were not placed in classes on the basis of ability but were randomly placed into class sections. The principal is aware of some dissatisfaction with the grouping of students in English classes; thus, he or she is asking for the recommendation of the teachers involved.

Procedure. The participation group (group A) will meet in the center of the room for a period of twenty minutes to discuss the situation presented above. They realize that they must reach a decision before they meet with the principal. The rest of the members (group B) will observe group A's activity during their meeting. Following this twenty-minute period, group B will meet in the center of the room to discuss what they observed from group A's activity. (They will meet for approximately twenty minutes.) Group A will observe group B's evaluation. At the end of this period group A and group B will combine for a general reaction and/or summary of the two group meetings.

Case Problems

A clinical psychologist at a university feels that interviews with a client should be recorded on tape and that the benefits to be derived from such recordings would be impaired if the client knew in advance that the recording was to be made. The psychologist sometimes uses these recordings in the classroom to illustrate lectures, always without the knowledge of the client, though the client's name is not revealed to the class.

Question: Should the psychologist use these tape recordings as class demonstrations without the permission of the client?

Jan Dorn is an attractive twenty-year-old college student majoring in art. She is a student in Dr. Thompson's small-group communication class. Jan and her husband, Jim, rent a home on the same block where Dr. Thompson lives. Jim and Dr. Thompson have met and become friends as well as neighbors. Jim is currently serving six months' duty in the army. With comfortable financial support from her parents, Jan is able to continue her education.

The first day of class Jan appears without her wedding ring, and in her self-introduction she does not reveal the fact that she is married. As the term progresses, Dr. Thompson learns that Jan has had a number of male members of the class spend the night at her house. On Easter Sunday Jan and Jim (home on leave) unexpectedly visit Dr. Thompson and his wife at their home.

Question: How should Dr. Thompson react in this situation?

Two years ago Sandy (now twenty) became engaged to Thad against the wishes of her parents and the rest of her family. None of them liked him, especially Sandy's mother. However, since the engagement was what Sandy wanted, they all went along with it. Her parents never said she couldn't get married, and they were willing to pay for the wedding. After two years, Thad called Sandy and broke the engagement. Her whole family was angry and thought that Sandy had seen the light as well. She acted as if she had; in fact, she went out with some other boys and seemed to have a good time. Unknown to her family, though, she still loved Thad and, despite what he had done, still wanted to marry him. A few months later Thad met Sandy where she worked. She hadn't seen him for four weeks. Unexpectedly, they eloped. Her family had no idea he had come into town and didn't know what had happened until after the fact.

Question:　How can this couple improve their relationship with her family?

The problem lies with my communication. I don't say much in class or give much feedback. Whenever I am part of a group, whether in a class or in the fraternity, I don't feel a strong attraction toward the group. I am always putting myself in the background to observe. I feel firmly convinced that any communication on my part will not help the situation and that, by participating in the group, I will lose some of my concentration on the conversation. I very rarely feel any rewards from being in a group. I can associate with a group and understand their beliefs and feelings, but I can't really become a part of it. If forced to participate or be a part of the group, I generally do a poor job and don't get much out of it. I don't like conforming with rules or goals that other people have set. There are many things that I don't wish to share with others.

Question:　How might this person overcome this difficulty?

My difficulty in communication isn't unusual in today's society. It is the communication gap between the young and old generations. That difficulty of communication happened between me and my parents, mainly my father.

Compared with other families, we have more difficulties than usual because of his Japanese and my Latin traditions.

When I was twelve years old, I left my farm home in Brazil and went to attend high school; until then I had just a Japanese education due to the influence of my family and the Japanese colony I lived in. So, at twelve I started a completely new life far from home. I don't know if it is the peculiarity of this age, but I had no trouble in accepting changes—after one year I was completely absorbed by the Latin customs and education (that's why I don't act like a Japanese but like a Brazilian). Since then there has been a conflict between my father and me which is both a generation gap and a culture gap.

Question:　How might this person and the father improve their relationship?

A waitress is serving water to a customer in a crowded airport coffee shop at 7:30 A.M. The cashier, a woman about fifty years old, calls over to the waitress (she looks about eighteen years old) and says: "Don't let one person take a table for four. Use a table for two. You're taking up four spaces for one person. Don't ever do it again!" The waitress says nothing but goes away from the scene.

The customer, a man in a three-piece suit, responds to the cashier (who is seated off to his right and behind him), "When you get a nonsmoking section, I'll go to a different spot." The cashier responds, "You'll have a long wait, because we're not getting any nonsmoking section." The man continues to talk out loud to no one in particular—so that the cashier and others can hear. "I can't stand sitting with smoke blowing in my face." Later, he pays his bill without looking at the cashier or saying anything to her. She hands him his change without saying anything to him.

Question:　How might this situation have been handled differently?

Organizational Communication Case Problems

You are the manager of a manufacturing plant that employs about 5,000 people. Due to increasing material costs and absenteeism, as well as decreasing efficiency, one of your products has become about 8 percent more expensive than a local competitor's product. Your major purchaser has threatened to buy from your competitor unless you can bring your price back in line with the competition. If you lose this account, five hundred people will have to be laid off. You must find a way to cut costs and save those five hundred jobs. What do you do? How should you go about communicating this problem, and to whom?

Jim Wells, Superintendent

You are the superintendent of a department employing about seventy-five men and women and six supervisors. You like your job and the supervisors and employees who work for you. You feel that they cooperate with you in most ways.

This morning you notice that one of your supervisors, Bill Jackson, has not yet arrived. Since Bill is very conscientious and was working on a rush job, you wonder what happened. Bill is thoroughly dependable, although he is a bit dogmatic. If something delays him, he always tries to call you. You are about to call his home when one of Bill's men, Joe Blake, comes in. Joe is a good-natured kid just out of high school, but this time he is obviously angry. He says he is not going to work for Bill and will quit unless you give him another supervisor. Evidently Bill had come in, started to work, and lost his temper when Joe didn't do something right.

Bill very rarely loses his temper, so you wonder if something else is wrong. You do not want to get him into another argument, or to criticize him. Instead you are going to try to get him to talk about what is bothering him.

You talk with Joe for several minutes, and after he tells you his side of the story, he says he feels better and is ready to go back to work for Bill. You have just called Bill and asked him to drop around when he has a chance. Bill said he would come right over and is walking toward your office right now.

Bill Jackson, Supervisor

You have just come back to work after a series of the most humiliating and irritating experiences you have ever had. Last night your next-door neighbor had a wild drunken party at his house that kept you awake most of the night. When you called him at 3:00 A.M. and told him to be less noisy, he was abusive and insulting. Things quieted down, and you finally got to sleep but you overslept. Since you are working at a rush job at the company, you skipped breakfast to hurry to work. As you were leaving your house, you noticed that someone had driven a car across your lawn and torn out several feet of your new hedge. You were certain that your neighbor or one of the drunks at his party had done it. When you went to his house, he not only denied it but he also threatened to knock your teeth out, and you knew he was big enough to do it.

When you arrived at work an hour late, you discovered that Joe Blake, a young high school recruit, had made a mistake that delayed you several hours, or at least it would have if you hadn't caught it. Naturally, you gave him a good going-over for his carelessness. You noticed that he went to see your supervisor, Jim Wells. You don't like that kind of attitude in a young squirt and decide that, if he has gone in there squawking, you'll make him wish he'd never been born.

You have had all you can stand and the big boss better not get tough with you because he'll have one hell of a time getting the job done without you. Your boss, Jim Wells, had that kid in his office for quite a while before he phoned for you to come in. Gabbing when there's work to be done—that's certainly a lousy way to run things. You are on your way to Jim's office now and have no intention of wasting time on a long discussion.

Calendar Memorial Hospital

Calendar Memorial Hospital is a 750-bed general hospital located in a large industrialized city of the Midwest. The hospital employs approximately 3,000 people.

You have been employed at Calendar Memorial Hospital for five years. You were hired as an administrative assistant; two years later you were promoted to the position of assistant administrator of general services and very recently to assistant administrator of professional service.

You are looking forward to your new assignment because it is consistent with your career goals and ambitions. If you can effectively improve the existing professional service, you are sure of consideration for the number 1 position when the present administrator retires in approximately four years. Even if you are not selected for this post at Calendar, you are confident that you could become administrator at a similar institution if you so desire. However, everything hinges on the successful completion of your new assignment.

On your recommendation the hospital has decided to combine the individual departments of physical therapy and rehabilitation therapy into a single unit. This decision was made in response to several factors. First, patient volume has increased 17 percent in physical therapy and 23 percent in rehabilitation therapy over the past two years. Future patient volume projections indicate increased activity in these areas. Second, since both areas deal with like patients, they have similar problems, use similar items, and can be more efficiently operated under one budget. Third, the two areas are located adjacent to each other, and combining staff members under one management is a logical step. Fourth, the administration wants to ensure an efficient work flow from one area to the other, and finally, administration wants to maximize the amount of employee substitution within these two areas. (The department of physical therapy employs ten therapists, six physical therapy assistants, four porters, and one scheduling clerk. The department of rehabilitation employs five therapists, three therapy assistants, three porters, and one scheduling clerk.)

Up to this time the two units have been managed by two separate department heads. Unfortunately, in spite of the common goals these two areas share, they are antagonistic toward each other—blaming each other for scheduling problems, patient mix-ups, uneven work flows, and so on.

You are asked to recommend one person as department head for both units. This individual will report to you, but your recent promotion will force you to spend the majority of your time and attention on other professional services. You are fully aware that the wrong individual in this position could create some serious problems in both areas. Therefore, you want to select the best possible candidate because it will not only affect the departments involved but will also contribute to your future effectiveness. After considerable deliberation, you have decided to recommend either Mary (the department head of rehabilitation therapy) or Tom (the department head of physical therapy) for the new position.

Mary: Mary, age twenty-six, came to the hospital three years ago, immediately after completing her occupational therapy program at a nearby university. While somewhat inexperienced as a department head, she had demonstrated managerial ability and leadership potential. She was the first occupational therapist hired when the hospital introduced an OT program, and she was very instrumental in developing the program to its present size and capacity. She has a definite flair for developing strong interpersonal relationships with her employees and patients, and her patients are always well attended to in spite of an ever-growing work load. Her employees are willing to assist each other with assignments, and the department has adopted the philosophy, "When one person works, we all work; when the work is done then we all can relax." There have been times, however, when you felt Mary could be more formal with her subordinates. For example, minor infractions of the rules are sometimes allowed to go "unnoticed," and Mary frequently spends a disproportionate amount of time with the work schedule attempting to accommodate everyone's special requests for "time off."

Tom: Tom, age forty-seven, is a registered physical therapist with twenty-three years' experience. Fifteen of these years have been at Calendar Hospital; first as a therapist, then as an assistant chief, and finally for the past nine years as department head. He has always been a dedicated, competent, and effective employee. Managerially speaking, he is considerably more authoritative than Mary, and his closer supervision has led to an unparalleled patient incident and employee safety record. Very rarely is there a problem in either of these two areas. He insists that his staff deliver the best care and treatment to patients, and he tolerates no nonsense or "goofing off" from any of his subordinates. He is 100 percent honest and forthright with his people and lets them "know where they stand" at all times. His frankness, however, is frequently misinterpreted as insensitivity and has led to a departmental turnover rate (either by transfer or resignation) that is 8 percent higher than that of any other area of the hospital. The employees who remain in his unit proudly attest to the fact that "when we do things, we do them right."

Questions: 1. Which of the two candidates will you recommend and why?
2. What factors weighed most heavily in your decision?
3. How will you notify Tom and Mary of your decision?

Meet in groups of five to decide the answer to the above questions.

Campustown State Hospital

The Campustown State Hospital is located in Campustown, Pennsylvania, and is part of the state university. Its objectives are threefold:

1. To provide the best possible patient care

2. To be recognized as an understanding medical research center

3. To have a medical and nursing school of the highest caliber

Most of the buildings are approximately twenty years old, and some need refurnishing. The library is somewhat limited, as are the laboratory and classroom facilities. Even so, the hospital has a good reputation.

The director of the hospital usually decides on how funds will be spent after he consults the individual members of his senior advisory board. They are:

Associate Director, Patient Care
Assistant Director, Research
Assistant Director, Teaching

Each is well recognized in his or her field.

Meet as a group with four people playing the following roles. Try to reach consensus on how to divide the $50,000 grant.

Director: You have a group of nationally known doctors on your staff, and you are proud of your hospital. One of your major problems is trying to maintain some balance between your three objectives: (1) patient care, (2) research, and (3) teaching. This is especially difficult when money must be allocated. You usually call on your senior advisory board members individually and listen to their requests. Then you decide how the money should be allocated. The last grant you received, $10,000, went to the research group for laboratory equipment. No matter how you decide, one group or another feels hurt because each thinks its function is most important and its needs greatest.

You have just received a new grant of $50,000 with no strings attached as to how the money will be spent. It was stated that, if in the opinion of the donors the money was spent wisely, there was a possibility of a similar grant in subsequent years. In view of the hard feelings resulting from your past decisions, you have decided to use a group decision, and you have called the senior advisory board together.

Associate Director, Patient Care: The primary purpose of any hospital is to render the best possible patient care. Expense should be no concern, but unfortunately it is to the staff and patients alike. Consequently any opportunity to improve the service rendered should be grasped. The last time a grant ($10,000) was received, it went to the research group. This should be your turn.

There are a number of worthwhile projects that should be undertaken.

1. The south wing of the hospital is hot in the summer and cold in the winter. The estimated cost of installing adequate heating and cooling is $45,000. This would include a central system plus storm windows and screens, awnings, and the like.

2. New machines that remove old wax, clean, and wax the asphalt tile floors are now available. These could not only do a better job but also replace some of the hard-to-get custodians (janitors). The cost of each machine is $1,000, and three are needed.

3. The patient records are now kept in a number of different locations and should be centralized. One of the present store-rooms (1B) could be converted and new files installed for a cost of $10,000.

4. There is only one x-ray machine, and it has periodic breakdowns. A new one would cost $25,000, and the old one could serve as a standby.

You have heard a rumor that a grant has been made, and you just received a call from the director. He said he wanted to talk to you and the other members of the senior advisory board. This is a surprise because he usually talks to each of you individually when money is involved.

Assistant Director, Research: Like General Electric, you believe "Research is our most important product." Without it patient care couldn't be improved, and the young doctors wouldn't have anything new to learn. You have established quite a name for yourself and your fellow researchers by going out and getting grants for research. The hospital staff hasn't been as much help as they should be. They could at least provide you with adequate space. Actually you'd like a research center like the one at Mayo's; it cost $250,000. You've been offered a job there, but you'd be just a little frog in a big pond rather than running the show as you do here. Last time money was available, you got $10,000 for equipment, but that's just a small part of what you really need.

You and your group are on the brink of a breakthrough on heart disease, and every penny you can get you'll pour into that effort. The foundations have been generous, but it takes so long to get the money that you can't wait.

One of the things that has always been a thorn in your side is the lack of funds available for you and your group either to take trips to scientific conventions or to host a symposium here. For someone of your renown this is an insult. For $10,000 a year you could gain $50,000 worth of ideas and experience (and get personal recognition). You'd like to offer a $1,000 award each year for the outstanding researcher on your staff. This would be a real incentive to get and keep good researchers.

The director has called you to his office for a meeting of the senior advisory board.

Assistant Director, Teaching: You are basically more of an educator than a doctor and find your position in a hospital operated in conjunction with a university ideal. As part of the university, the hospital's primary function is to train doctors, nurses, technicians, and others so that medical science can help the country or world live better and longer.

Applications to your medical school have not increased, and applications for your internships and residencies have actually declined. A number of the latter are being filled by foreign doctors, which is good in one way, but they aren't well prepared. As you see it, this situation is a result of a number of things. One is the desire of many students to train at more glamorous hospitals. Others want to go where more specialized fields are better developed. Many of the problems could be remedied if you had money to spend for the following improvements:

1. Increased pay for residents and interns. With $15,000 a year the pay could be increased to attract better men and women. Another $10,000 should be spent to improve their living quarters in the hospital.

2. Expanded library facilities. New books and journal subscriptions are needed; better storage and improved cataloging are necessary. This would cost $10,000.

3. More classrooms. There is a wasted storage room (1B) that could be converted into a classroom for $15,000. This would be a big help.

4. Lack of new ideas. A system of visiting professors or guest lecturers should be instituted so that the professors and students could have personal contact with some of the big names. This program could cost from $10,000 to $25,000 depending on its scope.

The director has called a meeting of the senior advisory board, and you suspect it is to discuss allocation of funds. The last grant went entirely to the research group, and you feel that you have a right to any new money that is available.

The Vacation

At Boston State University, the state was unable to provide any raises for state employees for the fiscal year 1985.

One morning in December of the following year, Steve Thomas, associate dean of the College of Business, heard an advertisement on the radio for special air fares from Boston to New York, New Jersey, and so on for $98 round trip. The air fares were to last until January 20, 1986. Coincidentally, President Jennings had distributed a memo giving all employees of the university two paid days off during the Christmas holiday season. (These employees would normally work while the university was between semesters.) He said in the memo that this was his way of saying thanks and that the time off was not to be charged against their vacation days and that this was to help make up for the lack of a raise the previous year.

Steve asked his boss, Ted, the dean, if they could offer a trip and the two days off to their two secretaries as a bonus out of nonappropriated funds. The two secretaries work on management development programs which brings in almost $100,000 a year. Ted said yes, providing they spent only $400 per person and that they actually had some professional meetings with another university while they were on the trip to gather information which would have a direct application to the jobs they had at Boston State. Steve then told both secretaries Maggie and Jennie, who thought this was a great idea to partially make up for the lack of a raise from the previous year.

The Christmas season came and went, and neither secretary was able to fit the vacation into her schedule. Jennie asked Steve if there was a time limit on the offer since the special air fares had been extended indefinitely due to fare wars between the airlines and since a new air carrier was starting up service in the Boston area. Steve said that his intention was to give a bonus and that the main thing was to take advantage of the low air fares. In other words, there was no time limit on the offer.

In March Jennie asked Steve if she could use her trip in May to go to Washington, D.C., with her boyfriend of several years on a business trip. The air fare was $98, and she was asking for two days off. Steve signed the approval and took it to Ted for his signature. Ted said that he had thought the offer was a "use-or-lose" one which had expired January 20. Steve said that he had thought that, since the cheap air fares had been extended, the offer to the secretaries was still in effect. Ted said that he specifically remembered that this offer was good only for the holiday season when the faculty were away from the university and the work load was quite low.

When Jennie was told of this, she tore up the travel request and felt worse than if Steve had never even made the original offer. In spite of her disappointment, she continued to work in a highly professional manner, not letting her feelings affect her performance.

Question: How would you have handled this situation if you had been Steve or Ted?

The San Francisco Bank

Andy Hanna is a senior loan officer at the San Francisco Bank, a large commercial bank with an annual loan volume of over $200 million. Andy is one of twenty loan officers in the bank's credit department. He services accounts totaling over $10 million in outstanding loans. He has degrees in business and law and over ten years of banking experience.

One evening in January, Andy was required to attend a board meeting of one of his commercial accounts. The meeting started promptly at 7:00 P.M. and was scheduled to end at 9:30. The company was located in a different city, thus requiring a three-hour drive before the meeting. The meeting lasted until 11:30, and Andy was required to remain throughout. Andy decided to save the bank the expense of a hotel and breakfast and drove home to San Francisco, arriving at 3:00 A.M.

The next morning, Andy slept in and came to work at 10:00 A.M., whereupon John Jackson, Andy's supervisor, came up to the desk and said, "Where were you this morning?" (Normal starting time at the bank is 7:45 A.M.) Andy responded, "I was home in bed." He went on to explain the events of the night before. John told Andy that the bank's president, Peter Prince, had made his customary walk through the bank at 7:50, and he noticed Andy's absence and furthermore noticed that Andy's name was not on the travel log sheet. He inquired about Andy's whereabouts. Mr. Jackson was embarrassed to admit that he did not know where Andy was either.

The outcome was that Mr. Jackson told Andy that he was expected to be at his desk at 7:45 regardless of job responsibilities requiring late-evening meetings. Andy then complained that he thought this was unreasonable since he felt his only alternatives had been:

1. To call Jackson at home at 11:30 P.M. after the meeting had ended or at 3:00 A.M. when he got back to San Francisco to tell him that he would be late getting to work the next day.

2. To set the alarm at 7:45 A.M. and call the bank to tell them he would be late.

3. To spend the night in a hotel and get to work about 1:00 P.M. the next day.

4. To do as Jackson asked and get about three hours' sleep.

Mr. Jackson said, "I don't care. You either get in here on time at 7:45 or get a hotel room and call in first thing in the morning explaining where you are and why." After a long, heated discussion, Andy stopped trying to convince Mr. Jackson. However, from then on when Andy and the other loan officers were required to travel in the evening, they made a practice of staying overnight in a hotel room and coming in to work at 1:00 P.M. the next day. This practice cost the bank an average of $100.00 (including breakfast) for each trip; Mr. Jackson was satisfied with this resolution.

Questions: 1. What do you think about the events in this case?
2. Do you agree with the way this issue was resolved?
3. What would you do differently if you had been (a) Mr. Jackson or (b) Andy?
4. What characteristics about Andy are significant to the way this issue might be handled?

Microcomputers, Inc. (A) (Bill Simpson)

Bill Simpson, director of training for Microcomputers, Inc., was on the telephone talking long-distance with one of his consultant-trainers about an upcoming program. Bill heard a loud knock on his door, which was open at the time. He turned around to see a person dressed in jeans and a work shirt standing in his doorway. Bill felt annoyed, since it was clear that he was busily engaged at the time. He felt his pulse quicken as he continued his conversation on the phone. In the back of his mind he was planning to tell the rude person at the door not to interrupt people's telephone conversations like that. He gestured to the person that he couldn't talk right now. Within three to four minutes Bill was off the phone, and he turned his attention to the person standing in the doorway.

You are Bill. Conduct a conversation with the person in your office doorway. His name is Al Bemus. You have been with the company only two months, and you have never met this person before.

Microcomputers, Inc. (A) (Al Bemus)

You are Al Bemus, a maintenance worker for Microcomputers, Inc. You have been with the company for ten years and do your job well. You are a high school graduate with some resentment toward the "college kids" who predominate in the company. Most of them are electrical engineers who are very smart technically but who are difficult to relate to. They also seem to think they are better than you.

You have a work order signed by Bill Simpson, the director of training, to take some tables out of the company's main training and conference room. These tables have been there for five weeks. Your crew is in the process of taking the tables out of the room, and you have gone to Bill Simpson's office to have him sign the work sheet showing that the tables were removed according to the request. You get to Simpson's office and see him on the phone. This annoys you, since you are already behind schedule and this is another unnecessary delay. You knock on the door once to attract his attention, since he is turned so that he can't see you. After several minutes, he gets off the phone and turns around.

Conduct a conversation with Simpson regarding this work order.

Microcomputers, Inc. (B) (Bill Simpson)

After a short conversation with the person in your doorway, you find that it is a maintenance man named Al Bemus, whom you have not met previously. Al has a work order signed with your name on it (but it is not your signature). It is a request to have six tables set up in your main training and conference room. The work order called for the tables to be left in the room for five weeks. The five weeks are over today. Al tells you that the tables are being taken out of the room at this very moment. You have an ongoing training session which meets twice a week for twelve weeks in that room. The new tables for that room have not arrived. Your class is scheduled to meet tomorrow. If the present tables are taken out of the room, you will be in a difficult situation, since the class cannot continue without them and there is no other room like this one available.

This problem arose when your secretary signed the work order for you (which is all right with you normally). However, in this case, since the new tables haven't arrived, you need to keep these tables for at least another month until the new ones come in.

Talk to this maintenance man and try to convince him to let you have the tables for another month.

Microcomputers, Inc. (B) (Al Bemus)

Now you find after some conversation with Simpson that the work order requesting the tables to be first set up and then removed five weeks later is somewhat outdated. He still needs the tables to remain for a while longer. As he tries to convince you to leave them, be either cooperative or stubborn, depending on how he treated you in the first part of this exercise. If you feel that he was not treating you as you like to be treated, give him a hard time. Tell him you can't do what he is asking you to do. If he was effective in communicating with you in the first part of this exercise, and if you like the approach he is taking now, then give him what he wants.

Disclosure Game*

The immediate object of Hatha Yoga is to master the various *asanas*. Each of these is a specific position which one's body assumes. A novice begins to assume one of these positions and finds that his or her muscles "protest." The means by which one fully enters an *asana* is to enter it up to one's limit and then to press gently at this limit. There can be no forcing, no cheating. The novice enters a position no further than has been "earned."

One can view authentic dialogue as a kind of interpersonal *asana*. The ultimate in dialogue is unpremeditated, uncontrived, spontaneous disclosure in response to the disclosure of the other. The following is an exercise aimed at helping a person discover his or her limits in ongoing dialogue. The first person discloses himself or herself on the first topic until both partners are satisfied there is no more to be said. Then, the other person does likewise. Then, on to the next *asana,* or topic. The rule is complete honesty, respect for one's own limits (as they are experienced in the form of embarrassment, anxiety, and so forth). As soon as this point is reached, the person declares he or she is at a limit. The partners can then discuss reasons for the reserve, and the person may overcome it.

---

* Found in Sidney M. Jourard. *Self-Disclosure: An Experimental Analysis of the Transparent Self* (New York: Wiley, 1971), p. 173–178 (slightly adapted). Copyright © 1971 by John Wiley & Sons, Inc. Reprinted by permission of John Wiley & Sons, Inc.

PART 1: DISCLOSURE

1. My hobbies, interests, and favorite leisure pursuits

2. What I like and dislike about my body—appearance, health, and so forth

3. My work—satisfactions, frustrations

4. My financial situation: income, savings, debts, investments, and so forth

5. Aspects of my parents I like and dislike; family problems encountered in growing up

6. Religious views, philosophy of life, what gives meaning to my life

7. My love life, past and present

8. Problems in my marriage or in my dealings with the opposite sex at present

9. What I like and dislike about my partner on the basis of this encounter

PART 2: PHYSICAL CONTACT

The same rules of respect for one's own limits, and one's partner's, apply.

1. Massage the head and neck of the partner

2. Massage the shoulders of the partner

3. Give a back rub

4. Rub the stomach of the partner

5. Massage the partner's feet

Sample Speeches

MINGLED BLOOD

RALPH ZIMMERMANN*

"Mingled Blood" won first place in the men's division of the 1955 Interstate Oratorical Contest. Later that year, Mr. Zimmermann graduated from Wisconsin State College at Eau Claire; in the fall, he entered law school at the University of Wisconsin in Madison; and the following spring, in March 1956, he died, a victim of hemophilia, the blood disease he describes so eloquently in this speech. That year's edition of *Winning Orations* of the Interstate Oratorical Association made the inclusion of "Mingled Blood" especially poignant, for it was dedicated to his memory. The speech was also printed and distributed by The National Hemophilia Foundation of New York City.

In this speech Zimmermann relies upon compelling personal narrative, which he

---

* Both the introduction and this excerpt are from Wil A. Linkugel, R. R. Allen, and Richard Johannesen. *Contemporary American Speeches,* 2d ed. (Belmont, CA.: Wadsworth, 1969), pp. 199–203. The introduction is reprinted by permission. The speech is reprinted by permission from *Winning Orations, 1956* (Evanston, IL: The Interstate Oratorical Association, 1956).

occasionally supports with scientific and historical data. In this way, he seeks to make the problems created by hemophilia real, painful, and tragic. Which portions of the speech do you find especially effective? Do you feel that Zimmermann's descriptions are so realistic at times that they might be too painful to a listener? Does the speaker's ethos derived from personal affliction mitigate this problem?

Zimmermann's conclusion is worth special attention. It brings the speech to an emotional climax and simultaneously creates admiration and respect for the speaker as a hemophiliac. Note those aspects of the conclusion that you think are instrumental in bringing the speech to such a moving end.

Startling statement gains attention and establishes personal credibility.

1. I am a hemophiliac. To many of you, the word signifies little or nothing. A few may pause a moment and then remember that it has something to do with bleeding. Probably none of you can appreciate the gigantic impact of what those words mean to me.

Definition adds clarification and quotes an authoritative source.

2. What is this thing called hemophilia? Webster defines it as "a tendency, usually hereditary, to profuse bleeding even from slight wounds." Dr. Armand J. Quick, Professor of Biochemistry at Marquette University and recognized world authority on this topic, defines it as "a prothrombin consumption time of 8 to 13 seconds." Normal time is 15 seconds. Now do you know what hemophilia is?

The question adds a personal touch to a clinical definition.

3. It is by no means a 20th century phenomenon. Ancient writings reveal the Jewish rabbis, upon the death of first born sons from bleeding after circumcision, allowed the parents to dispense with this ceremony for any more sons. Family laws of ancient Egypt did not permit a woman to bear any more children if the first born should die of severe bleeding from a minor wound. How odd it seems to link the pyramids of the 4th dynasty with prothrombin consumption of 1955.

Historical information.

4. Hemophilia has had significant influence on the pages of history. Victoria, the queen of an empire on which the sun never set, was a transmitter of this dread ailment. Through her daughter, Alice, it was passed to the Russian royal family and Czerevitch Alexis, heir apparent to the throne of Nicholas II. Alexis, the hemophilic heir apparent, was so crippled by his ailment that the Bolshevik revolters had to carry him bodily to the cellar to execute him. And through Victoria's daughter, Beatrice, it was carried to the sons of the Spanish monarch, Alfonso XIII. While this good queen ruled her empire with an iron hand and unknowingly transmitted this mysterious affliction, my forebears, peasants of southern Germany, worked their field, gave birth to their children, and buried their dead sons. Hemophilia shows no respect for class lines. It cares not whether your blood be red or blue.

Adds a bit of "news" and human interest.

Technical terms are mixed with metaphors for greater impact.

5. For hemophilia is a hereditary disease. It afflicts only males, but paradoxically is transmitted only by females. The sons of a victim are not hemophiliacs, and do not pass it on. However, all of the daughters are transmitters. Of the transmitter daughter's children, half of the girls may be transmit-

ters like their mother, and half of the sons may be hemophiliacs. Thus the net spreads out and on. Theoretically, it follows strict Mendelian principles. But because it is a recessive characteristic, it may lie dormant for generation after generation. As far back as my ancestral line can be traced, there is no evidence of hemophilia until my older brother Herbert and me. The same is true of 50 percent of America's bleeders.

Back to the personal side of the story.
Points to the irony and tragedy.

6. And there are many of us. Medical authorities estimate that there are some 20,000–40,000 hemophiliacs of all types in the United States. Clinically we divide into three groups: classic hemophilia AHG, and two other less common types of hemophilia, PTC and PTA. I am a classic hemophiliac—the real McCoy.

Use of statistics for perspective.

7. What does it really mean to be a hemophiliac? The first indication comes in early childhood when a small scratch may bleed for hours. By the time the hemophiliac reaches school age, he begins to suffer from internal bleeding into muscles, joints, the stomach, the kidneys. This latter type is far more serious, for external wounds can usually be stopped in minutes with topical thromboplastin or a pressure bandage. But internal bleeding can be checked only by changes in the blood by means of transfusion or plasma injections. If internal bleeding into the muscle or joint goes unchecked repeatedly, muscle contraction and bone deformity inevitably result. My crooked left arm, the built-up heel on my right shoe, and the full length brace on my left leg offer mute but undeniable testimony to that fact. Vocal evidence you hear; weak tongue muscles are likely to produce defective L and R sounds.

Specific and graphic examples add powerful emotional appeal.

Relates to listener's value of physical health.

8. Childhood and early adolescence are the danger periods of a hemophiliac's life. As recently as November, 1950, *The Science Digest* reported that 85 percent of all hemophiliacs die during that period. While the figure is exaggerated, it tends to indicate this salient point: if society can keep a hemophiliac alive until after adolescence, society has saved a member. During those years, society is given a responsibility it too often refuses to accept.

Citing other sources of authority.

9. You might ask—but what can I do? What do you expect of me? The answer lies in the title of this oration: mingled blood. For all that boy needs is blood, blood, and more blood. Blood for transfusions, blood for fresh frozen plasma, blood for serum fractions. Not Red Cross Bank Blood, for stored blood loses its clot-producing factors. But fresh blood directly from you to him in a matter of hours. Your blood, dark and thick, rich with all the complex protein fractions that make for coagulation—mingled with the thin, weak, and deficient liquid that flows in his veins. Blood directly from you to the medical researcher for transformation into fresh frozen plasma or antihemophilic globulin. During those years, his

Specifically indicating what action the listener can take.

Personalizing the appeal.

very life is flowing in your veins. No synthetic substitute has been found—only fresh blood and its derivatives.

Childhood stories evoke memories within each of us.

10. Because medical science had not advanced far enough, and fresh blood not given often enough, my memories of childhood and adolescence are memories of pain and heartbreak. I remember missing school for weeks and months at a stretch—of being very proud because I attended school once for four whole weeks without missing a single day. I remember the three long years when I couldn't even walk because

Vivid language.

repeated hemorrhages had twisted my ankles and knees to pretzel-like forms. I remember being pulled to school in a wagon while other boys rode their bikes, and being pushed to my table. I remember sitting in the dark empty classroom by myself during recess while the others went out in the sun to run and play. And I remember the first terrible day at the big high school when I came on crutches and built-up shoes carrying my books in a sack around my neck.

Making clear the main idea. Using high-intensity words.

11. But what I remember most of all is the pain. Medical authorities agree that a hemophilic joint hemorrhage is one of the most excruciating pains known to mankind. To concentrate a large amount of blood into a small compact area causes a pressure that words can never hope to describe. And how well I remember the endless pounding, squeezing pain. When you seemingly drown in your own perspiration, when your teeth ache from incessant clenching, when your tongue floats in your mouth and bombs explode back of your eye-

Extensive use of metaphors for emphasis.

balls; when darkness and light fuse into one hue of gray; when day becomes night and night becomes day—time stands still—and all that matters is that ugly pain. The scars of pain are not easily erased.

Change of pace.

12. Once a hemophiliac successfully passes through the dangerous period, his need for blood steadily decreases and his health improves. The nightmare of youth is gradually hidden behind a protective curtain of objectivity that is seldom raised. In contrast to my childhood days, I can look back on more than three years of college with joy and a sense of achievement. I've had some good breaks. I've been in debate and forensics for four years and had a variety of satisfying

Shows positive outlook and "normalcy."

experiences. I've been lucky in politics. My constituents, the student body at our college, elected me President of Student Government. Like so many other American youths, I've worked my way through college as a clerk in a hardware store. On warm weekends, while not a Ben Hogan at golf, I have shot an 82. And back home, a girl wears my wedding band.

13. For today, except for periodic transfusions, my life is as normal as anyone else's, and my aims and ambitions are the same as anyone else's. But now, a different type of social relationship needs to be found. Because a hemophiliac is so totally dependent on society during his early years and be-

Shows the character side of his credibility.

cause his very existence is sometimes then precarious, society now tends to lag in recognizing the change. It sometimes fails to realize that this hemophiliac's life is no longer in serious question and that now his right to aspire to any new height should not be frowned on by a society still vividly remembering the past. Now, he seeks neither pity nor privilege. He wishes to be regarded not as a hemophiliac but rather a human being to be evaluated like any human being.

Emotional appeal adds a sense of urgency.

14. I cannot change that part of my life which is past. I cannot change my hemophilia. Therefore, I must ask you to help those hemophiliacs that need help. For I remember too well my older brother Herbert, so shattered in adolescence by hemophilia, that his tombstone reads like a blessing: "May 10, 1927—April 6, 1950, Thy Will Be Done." And I ask you to help hemophiliacs because one day my grandson may need your blood. But I also must ask you to recognize a hemophiliac for what he is today; to realize that past is prologue, that weakness sometimes begets strength; that man sometimes conquers. And so I pray:

Quotation for all to learn from.

15. "God give me the courage to accept the things that I cannot change; the power to change the things which I can; and the wisdom always to know the difference between the two."

THE STRANGLER

CHARLES SCHALLIOL*

In March 1967, as a freshman at Indiana University, Charles Schalliol won first place with this speech in the men's division of the intercollegiate Indiana Oratorical Association contest at Hanover College.

As a pattern for advocating a policy to cope with the urban air pollution situation, Schalliol uses a clear-cut presentation of the nature and scope of the problem, the contributing causes, and a combination of solutions. It would be useful to evaluate this speech by applying the criteria for evaluation listed in Chapter 10, *Public Communication*. However, because Mr. Schalliol analyzes the causes of the problem in some detail, two additional questions are useful. Are the causes he presents the real ones? Does his solution eliminate or alleviate *each* of the causes?

In exploring all phases of the problem and its solutions, he relies heavily on statistics and expert testimony for evidence. As part of your analysis of the speech, apply the appropriate . . . criteria for soundness to the testimony and statistics.

Note also the imagery used in the introductory illustration; it vividly depicts the problem on which he wishes to focus. Another stylistic feature is the use of metaphors for air pollution—strangler, murderer, crippler, and thief. Each of these metaphors is related to a particular facet of the problem.

* Both the introduction and this excerpt are from Wil A. Linkugel, R. R. Allen, and Richard Johannesen. *Contemporary American Speeches*, 2d ed. (Belmont, CA: Wadsworth, 1969), pp. 246–250. The introduction is reprinted by permission. The speech is reprinted by permission from *Winning Orations, 1967* (Detroit: The Interstate Oratorical Association, 1967), pp. 54–57.

An analogy and attention getter. Surprising date.

1. The strangler struck in Donora, Pennsylvania, in October of 1948. A thick fog billowed through the streets enveloping everything in thick sheets of dirty moisture and a greasy black coating. As Tuesday faded into Saturday, the fumes from the big steel mills shrouded the outlines of the landscape. One could barely see across the narrow streets. Traffic stopped. Men lost their way returning from the mills. Walking through the streets, even for a few moments, caused eyes to water and burn. The thick fumes grabbed at the throat and created a choking sensation. The air acquired a sickening bittersweet smell, nearly a taste. *Death* was in the air.

Language vivid-ness.

Use of example.

2. Before the clouds of fog lifted from Donora, twenty had died, and 6,000 or half of the population, were bedridden. Donora was the site of America's first major air pollution disaster.

Use of statistics arouses concern for the problem.

3. The concern of public health officials is no longer for small towns like Donora. What happened there in 1948 is now happening in New York City, Los Angeles, and Washington. If New York is struck in the same proportions as was Donora, 12,000 will die, and 4,000,000 will be driven to their beds.

Analogy to a criminal.

4. Air pollution is a common criminal! But it's uncommon in the magnitude and the scope of its crimes. In Donora, air pollution filled the role of "The Strangler," but it also terrorizes in other roles as well.

5. The increasing size of the metropolitan areas is compounding the problems local authorities must face. Since 1940, our population has grown by 50,000,000, the use of energy has quadrupled, disposable income has increased 60%; yet our air supply remains the same. In such a setting air pollution is a murderer. According to Edward Parkhurst, a noted health authority, death rates are "consistently higher in the central cities of 50,000 and over than in places under 10,000 and in rural areas in non-metropolitan districts." The Census Bureau further establishes that life expectancy is three years greater in the rural states than in the urban states.

Citing an author-ity and using a quotation.

6. The 1964 National Conference on Air Pollution concluded, "The evidence that air pollution contributes to the pathogenesis of chronic respiratory disease is overwhelming." Chronic bronchitis, chronic constrictive ventilatory disease, pulmonary emphysema, bronchial asthma, lung cancer, and the common cold are all associated with air pollution.

Technical terms add to perceived credibility of the speaker.

7. During one period of extremely high air pollution in N.Y.C., in 1954, records showed 200 deaths above normal levels. These cases of shortened life expectancy, sickness, and death are largely due to air pollution. Air pollution is seldom a cause in itself, but it substantially compounds other health problems. In short, air pollution, as the murderer and the strangler, is turning our huge population centers into death traps.

8. While its crimes against health are the most pressing reasons

*Extending the
analogy.*

we have for the abatement of air pollution, atmospheric pollution plays other roles as a community irritant. These are far more noticeable to the vast majority of urban dwellers. The most readily observed form of atmospheric pollution is manifested in the dark sullen clouds continually hovering over our large metropolitan regions. These clouds of sulphur fumes are an eyesore, cause skin irritation, continual coughing, and most important, form a traffic hazard both for motorists and airlines. During periods of peak air contamination, Los Angeles traffic is slowed by as much as 15 miles per hour.

9. In testimony before the Committee on Public Works of the United States Senate, New Jersey Turnpike officials validated 22 reports of accidents occurring because of poor visibility largely due to air pollutants from burning refuse, garbage and industrial concentrations.

*Logical appeals
and references to
supporting mate-
rial from experts.*

10. In testimony before the same Senate committee, Newark Airport officials reported that as early as 1946 the number of hours in which visibility was cut to six miles or less by smoke alone, or in combination with other factors, totaled 4,359 hours that year—nearly 50% of the total hours during the year. On some occasions air pollutants alone were even sufficient to ground planes at Idlewild Airport. In reviewing accident cases for 1962, the Civil Aeronautics Board listed six cases in which obstruction of view due to air pollution was the primary cause. On this basis, since 1960, 50 aeronautical accidents may well have been due to atmospheric pollution. Thus, air pollution fulfills another role on the criminal roster—that of crippler, maimer and indiscriminate killer in automotive and air accidents.

11. Last, and of equal importance, air pollution is one of America's worst thieves. In addition to the property damage due to accidents, air pollution is directly responsible for the loss of approximately $65 per capita per year in property damage. According to a staff report to the Senate Committee on Public Works in 1964, sulphur dioxide, hydrogen sulfide, and ozone are all common pollutants in cities which cause damage to metal, rubber, leather, and electrical components.

*This extended
analogy also
gives continuity
to the speech.*

12. Thus, air pollution is perpetrating crimes against man in nearly every form of enterprise he undertakes. It operates as a strangler, murderer, crippler, and even a thief.

13. As Dr. Luther L. Terry, Surgeon General of the United States, underscored the problem: "We are so sophisticated scientifically that men can breathe in the airless void beyond the earth's atmosphere. And yet, we are so primitive that the quality of the air we breathe on the surface of the earth continues to deteriorate."

*Analysis of causes
of the problem.*

14. What is the cause of such massive air contamination? Charles Rothman, Environmental Loss Prevention Engineering Consultant, states that the estimated 133 million tons of pollu-

tants poured into the United States atmosphere every year stem from five major sources: Transportation, manufacturing, electric power generation, space heating, and the burning of refuse.

15. Industry was once considered the major polluting influence of our atmosphere. This is no longer the case. The automobile has become overwhelmingly the most serious problem we face in air pollution control. As the Senate Subcommittee on Air and Water Pollution expresses it, "automotive exhaust is cited as responsible for some 50% of the national air pollution problem." And the problem of automotive fumes shows every sign of becoming more acute. While America currently has 86 million motor vehicles on its streets and highways, the Public Health Service estimates that we will have more than 120 million internal combustion machines on our highways by 1980.

More expert testimony.

16. In the words of Louis J. Battan, air pollution expert and meteorologist, "The automobile is becoming one of modern society's chief social diseases. More people must be moved with less smoke, or the greater quantities of smoke will surely lead to fewer people."

17. While automotive problems are the most severe, it would be a grave error to underestimate the importance of the other sources of pollution. Industrial problems are still crucial in many ways. The sulfurous compounds spewing from concentrated industrial complexes result in property deterioration, pungent city odors, and eye irritation.

18. Even without the presence of automotive petroleum refuse, these manufacturing problems in combination with refuse burning and improper home heating systems can alone create genuine air pollution problems in our great cities.

19. Athelstan Spilhaus of the University of Minnesota's Institute of Technology aptly sums up our air pollution problem in thirteen words: "We don't consume anything, we simply convert every product we touch into waste!" Unfortunately for America, this is substantially true. We do fill our atmosphere

Intense language for concreteness.

with almost every conceivable form of waste, turning our sky into a veritable aerial sewer. However, this process is not in any way inevitable. With the sophisticated scientific technology we possess today, a technical solution either has been or soon can be found for our air pollution maladies. There is no reason why this criminal should continue to terrorize our lives.

20. However, there is no patented sure-fire solution. In fact, many of the corrective measures advocated by today's finest scientific minds are no more than tentative theories, but at least they are a basis from which we can begin to attack the problems causing our tainted air. As in the case of Los Angeles County, which has substantially cut air pollution, we

can take the best action currently available. To procrastinate longer will only aggravate the situation.

Example of solutions to the problem (the organizing pattern is problem-solution).

21. California, the nation's leader in air pollution control, is now taking steps to alleviate the automotive problem, by requiring auto makers to equip all new motor vehicles sold in the state with after-burners which drastically reduce the quantity of pollutants emitted from exhausts. However, even this step adopted on a nationwide scale would not eliminate the problem. By the year 2000, pollutants from internal combustion engines would still have reached critical levels.

22. Thus, after-burners should be employed nationwide, but we must also realize that this is only a temporary measure, and we should begin to work toward a more tractable solution. Two long term alternatives which Howard R. Lewis, United States Health Consultant, proposes are: One, continue and expand research on electric automobiles for metropolitan usage; and two, begin developing and expanding public transportation systems. Dr. Lewis holds that electric cars and improved public transportation would make gasoline powered autos unnecessary in large urban areas.

23. Dr. Charles Rothman, Environmental Engineering Consultant for the United States Government, also observed that while industrial pollution continues to contaminate our air, most of the devices necessary for adequate control were invented and feasible years ago. The difficulty lies in getting industry to mete its social commitment. Tax legislation now known as Senate Bill 1670, calling for fast 36 month write-offs on air pollution equipment, is a giant step toward stimulating increased abatement. It is even possible to turn atmospheric emission control into profit. The petroleum industry, according to a November 1966 issue of *Newsweek,* will market some $40 million dollars worth of sulphur in 1967 that would otherwise have been pumped into the air.

Personalizing the appeal.

References to the opening example adds continuity.

Adds a sense of urgency.

24. In spite of any action the government and industry take, a large part of the responsibility must rest with the public. If public sentiment ignores the existence of air pollution as criminal, little will be done. We must alert Americans to the consequences inaction will cause, and to the fact that every major American city is a potential Donora—no one is free from America's greatest criminal. If we ignore air pollution it will loom ever larger. In the words of Professor Morris B. Jacobs, former director of the Department of Air Pollution Control, "It is now time to end this plague. Time to look beyond narrow vested interests, to awake from slumbering too long—and save ourselves. We had better act now. It will soon be too late."

References

Chapter 1   The Process of
Human Communication

Acuff, Frank L. *How to Negotiate Anything With Anyone Anywhere Around the World* (New York: American Management Association, 1993).

Avery, Robert K., and Thomas A. McCain. "Interpersonal and Mediated Encounters: A Reorientation to the Mass Communication Process," in Gary Gumpert and Robert Cathcart, eds., *Inter/Media: Interpersonal Communication in a Media World,* 2d ed. (New York: Oxford University Press, 1982), pp. 29–40.

Barnlund, Dean C. "Toward a Meaning-Centered Philosophy of Communication," *Journal of Communication* 11 (1962), 198–202.

Beebe, Steven A., and John T. Masterson. *Communicating in Small Groups: Principles and Practices,* 2d ed. (Glenview, IL: Scott, Foresman, 1986).

Begley, Sharon, and Fiona Gleizes. "My Granddad, Neanderthal?" *Newsweek* (October 16, 1989), 70–71.

Bochner, Arthur P. "The Functions of Human Communication in Interpersonal Bonding," in Carroll C. Arnold and John Waite Bowers, eds., *Handbook of Rhetorical and Communication Theory* (Boston: Allyn and Bacon, 1984), pp. 544–621.

Conner, Daryl. *Managing At The Speed of Change* (New York: Random House, 1993).

Dance, Frank E. X. "Toward a Theory of Human Communication," in Frank E. X. Dance, ed., *Human Communication Theory: Original Essays* (New York: Holt, Rinehart and Winston, 1967), pp. 288–309.

———. "The Concept of Communication," *Journal of Communication* 20 (1970), 201–210.

———. "A Speech Theory of Human Communication," in Frank E. X. Dance, ed., *Human Communication Theory* (New York: Harper & Row, 1982), pp. 120–146.

DiPaolo, Mary. "Cellular Phones Ring in a Revolution." *Ann Arbor News* (February 5, 1989), E1.

Fisher, Kimball. *Leading Self-Directed Work Teams.* (New York: McGraw-Hill, 1993).

Fisher, Roger, and William Ury. *Getting to Yes: Negotiating Agreement without Giving In* (Boston: Houghton Mifflin, 1981).

Freud, Sigmund. *The Psychopathology of Everyday Life,* in A. A. Brill, ed. and trans., *The Basic Writings of Sigmund Freud* (New York: Modern Library, 1938).

Gardner, R. A., and B. T. Gardner. "Teaching Sign Language to a Chimpanzee," *Science* 165 (1969), 664–672.

Garrett, Wilbur E., ed. *National Geographic* 176 (October 1989), 560.

Goldhaber, Gerald M. *Organizational Communication,* 5th ed. (Dubuque, IA: Brown, 1990).

Goyer, Robert S. "Communication, Communicative Process, Meaning: Toward a Unified Theory," *Journal of Communication* 20 (1970), 4–16.

Griffin, Em. *A First Look at Communication Theory* (New York: McGraw-Hill, 1991).

Gudykunst, William B., and Young Yun Kim. *Communicating with Strangers,* 2d ed. (New York: McGraw-Hill, 1992).

Haney, William V. *Communication and Interpersonal Relations,* 6th ed. (Homewood, IL: Irwin, 1992).

Hart, Roderick P., Gustav W. Friedrich, and William D. Brooks. *Public Communication* (New York: Harper & Row, 1975).

Haslett, Beth. "Acquiring Conversational Competence," *Western Journal of Speech Communication* 48 (1984), 107–124.

Imai, Masaaki. *Kaizen: The Key to Japan's Competitive Success* (New York: McGraw-Hill, 1986).

Kageyama, Yuri. "Farmer Beeps Until The Cows Come Home," *Ann Arbor News* (July 11, 1992), A3.

King, Albert S. "Revitalizing Management: Education Survey Design Relevance in Business Schools." *Mid-American Journal of Business* (Spring 1987), 34–39.

Knapp, Mark. *Interpersonal Communication and Human Relationships* (Boston: Allyn and Bacon, 1984).

Laitner, Bill. "Baby Talk Takes a Prenatal Twist," *Detroit Free Press* (November 6, 1987), 2B.

Lewis, Peter H. "As Cries of 'Fax it' Abound, It Pays to Assess Your Own Need for Speed," *Ann Arbor News* (January 11, 1989), B3.

Littlejohn, Stephen W. *Theories of Human Communication,* 2d ed. (Belmont, CA: Wadsworth, 1983).

Lucas, Stephen. *The Art of Public Speaking,* 4th ed. (New York: McGraw-Hill, 1992).

Luft, Joseph. *Of Human Interaction* (Palo Alto, CA: National Press, 1957).

Moll, Richard W. "Getting into College: An Admissions Man Says It Isn't So Hard," *The New York Times,* January 7, 1979, Educ. p. 5.

Morse, Melvin, and Paul Perry. *Closer to the Light* (New York: Villard Books, 1990).

Muchmore, John, and Kathleen Galvin. "A Report of the Task Force on Career Competencies in Oral Communication Skills for Community College Students Seeking Immediate Entry into the Work Force," *Communication Education* 32 (1983), 207–220.

Pace, R. Wayne. *Organizational Communication Foundations for Human Resource Development* (Englewood Cliffs, NJ: Prentice-Hall, 1983).

Popcorn, Faith. *The Popcorn Report* (New York: Doubleday, 1991).

Premack, D. "The Education of S*A*R*A*H," *Psychology Today* 4 (1970), 55–58.

Putnam, L. "The Search for Modern Humans," *National Geographic* 174 (October 1988), 439–477.

Rosenberg, Morris. *Conceiving the Self* (New York: Basic Books, 1979).

Samovar, Larry A., and Richard E. Porter. *Intercultural Communication: A Reader* (Belmont, CA: Wadsworth, 1972).

Schein, Edgar H. *Career Dynamics: Matching Individual and Organizational Needs* (Reading, MA: Addison-Wesley, 1978).

Southwestern Bell Telephone. *Annual Report* (1988).

Stewart, John, ed. *Bridges, Not Walls,* 4th ed. (Reading, MA: Addison-Wesley, 1986).

Tubbs, Stewart L. *A Systems Approach to Small Group Interaction,* 4th ed. (New York: McGraw-Hill, 1992).

Wall, Bob, Robert S. Solum, and Mark Sobol. *The Visionary Leader.* (Rocklin, CA: Prima Publishing, 1992).

Weiner, Norbert. *The Human Use of Human Beings: Cybernetics and Society* (New York: Avon, 1967).

Willing, Richard. "Clinton's Style May Short-Circuit Watchdog Role," *The Detroit News* (November 29, 1992), B1, B5.

Chapter 2   Person Perception

Adelmann, Pamela. "Possibly Yours," *Psychology Today* 22 (April 1988), 8, 10.

Asch, S. E. "Forming Impressions of Personality," *Journal of Abnormal and Social Psychology* 41 (1946), 258–290.

Asch, Solomon E., and M. Zukier. "Thinking about Persons," *Journal of Personality and Social Psychology* 46 (1984), 1230–1240.

Bandura, Albert. "Reflections on Nonability Determinants of Competence," in Robert J. Sternberg and John Kolligian, Jr., eds., *Competence Considered* (New Haven: Yale University Press, 1990).

Barge, J. Kevin, David W. Schlueter, and Alex Pritchard. "The Effects of Nonverbal Communication and Gender on Impression Formation in Opening Statements," *Southern Communication Journal* 54 (1989), 330–349.

Berscheid, Ellen. "Interpersonal Attraction," in Gardner Lindzey and Elliot Aronson, eds., *Handbook of Social Psychology,* Vol. II, 3rd ed. (New York: Random House, 1985), pp. 413–484.

Berscheid, Ellen, and Elaine Walster. "Physical Attractiveness," in L. Berkowitz, *Advances in Experimental Social Psychology,* Vol. VII (Orlando, FL: Academic Press, 1974), pp. 158–215.

Bonaguro, E., and J. C. Pearson. "The Relationship between Communicator Style, Argumentativeness, and Gender," paper presented at the annual convention of the Speech Communication Association Convention, Chicago, November 1986.

Brown, Roger. *Social Psychology,* 2d ed. (New York: Free Press, 1986).

Bruner, Jerome. *Actual Minds, Possible Worlds* (Cambridge, MA: Harvard University Press, 1986).

Cheek, Jonathan, and Bronwen Cheek. *Conquering Shyness* (New York: Dell, 1990).

Clark, Ruth Anne, and Jesse G. Delia. "Cognitive Complexity, Social Perspective-Taking and Functional Persuasive Skills in Second- to Ninth-Grade Children," *Human Communication Research* 3 (1977), 128–134.

Deloria, Vine. *We Talk, You Listen* (New York: Macmillan, 1970).

Duck, Steve. *Understanding Relationships* (New York: Guilford, 1991).

Dullea, Georgia. "On Corporate Ladder, Beauty Can Hurt," *The New York Times,* June 3, 1985, C13.

Erwin, P. C., and A. Calev. "Beauty: More Than Skin Deep?" *Journal of Social and Personal Relationships* 1 (1984), 359–361.

Floyd, J. *Listening: A Practical Approach* (Glenview, IL: Scott, Foresman, 1985).

Gagnard, Alice. "A Sociocultural Close-Up: Body Image in Advertising," in Pamela J. Creedon, ed., *Women in Mass Communication* (Newbury Park, CA: Sage, 1989), pp. 261–262.

Gilligan, Carol. *In a Different Voice: Psychological Theory and Women's Development* (Cambridge, MA: Harvard University Press, 1982).

Gilligan, Carol, Janie Victoria Ward, and Jill McLean Taylor, eds. *Mapping the Moral Domain* (Cambridge: Harvard University Press, 1989).

Gudykunst, William, and Stella Ting-Toomey. *Culture and Interpersonal Communication* (Newbury Park, CA: Sage, 1988).

Heilman, Madeline, and Melanie H. Stopeck. "Attractiveness and Corporate Success: Different Causal Attributions for Males and Females," *Journal of Applied Psychology* 70 (1985), 379–387.

Hewitt, Jay, and Karen German. "Attire and Attractiveness," *Perceptual and Motor Skills* 64 (1987), 558.

Hiller, D., and W. Philliber. "Predicting Marital and Career Success among Dual-Working Couples," *Journal of Marriage and Family* 44 (1982), 53–62.

Hirschfeld, Al. *Hirschfeld: Art & Recollections from Eight Decades* (New York: Scribner's, 1991).

Hosman, L. A., and J. W. Wright. "The Effects of Hedges and Hesitation on Impression Formation in a Simulated Courtroom Context," *Western Journal of Speech Communication* 51 (1987), 173–188.

James, William. *Principles of Psychology,* Vol. I (New York: Dover, 1950).

Janos, Paul. "The Self-Perceptions of Uncommonly Bright Children," in Robert J. Sternberg and John Kolligian, Jr., eds., *Competence Considered* (New Haven: Yale University Press, 1990).

Jones, Melinda. "Stereotyping Hispanics and Whites: Perceived Differences in Social Roles as a Determinant of Ethnic Stereotypes," *Journal of Social Psychology* 131 (1991), 469–475.

Jones, Warren H., Jonathan Cheek, and Stephen R. Briggs. *Shyness: Perspectives on Research and Treatment* (New York: Plenum, 1986).

Kagan, Jerome. *Unstable Ideas: Temperament, Cognition, and Self* (Cambridge: Harvard University Press, 1989).

Kaplan, M. F. "Measurement and Generality of Response Dispositions in Person Perception," *Journal of Personality* (1976).

Kelley, Harold H. "The Warm-Cold Variable in First Impressions of Persons," *Journal of Personality* 18 (1950), 431–439.

Kleinke, Chris L. *Meeting and Understanding People* (New York: Freeman, 1986).

Knapp, Mark L., and Anita L. Vangelisti. *Interpersonal Communication and Human Relationships,* 2d ed. (Newton, MA: Allyn & Bacon, 1992).

Kutner, Lawrence. "Parent & Child," *The New York Times* (Jaunary 2, 1992), C12.

LaFrance, M., and C. Mayo. "A Review of Nonverbal Behaviors of Women and Men," *Western Journal of Speech Communication* 43 (1979), 76–95.

Lazier-Smith, Linda. "Advertising: Women's Place and Image," in Pamela J. Creedon, ed., *Women in Mass Communication* (Newbury Park, CA: Sage, 1989), pp. 247–260.

Liebert, Robert M., and Joyce Sprafkin. *The Early Window: Effects of Television on Children and Youth,* 3rd ed. (New York: Pergamon Press, 1988).

Luchins, A. S. "Primacy-Recency in Impression Formation," in Carl I. Hovland et al., eds., *The Order of Presentation in Persuasion,* Vol. I (New Haven, CT: Yale University Press, 1957), pp. 33–61.

McCroskey, James C., and John A. Daley, eds. *Personality and Interpersonal Communication* (Beverly Hills, CA: Sage, 1987).

McCroskey, J. C., and V. P. Richmond. "Power in the Classroom I: Teacher and Student Perceptions," *Communication Education* 32 (1983), 175–184.

Malpass, Roy, and Jerome Kravitz. "Recognition for Faces of Own and Other Race," *Journal of Personality and Social Psychology* 13 (1969), 330–334.

May, Brett A. "The Interaction Between Ratings of Self, Peer's Perceptions, and Reflexive Self-Ratings," *Journal of Social Psychology* 131 (1991), 483–493.

Nurmi, Jari-Erik. "The Effect of Other's Influence, Effort, and Ability Attributions on Emotions in Achievement and Affiliative Situations," *Journal of Social Psychology* 131 (1991), 703–715.

Onyekwere, Evelyn O., Rebecca B. Rubin, and Dominic A. Infante. "Interpersonal Perception and Communication Satisfaction as a Function of Argumentativeness and Ego-Involvement," *Communication Quarterly* 39 (1991), 35–47.

Pearson, Judy Cornelia, Lynn H. Turner, and William Todd-Mancillas. *Gender & Communication,* 2d ed. (Dubuque, IA: William C. Brown, 1991).

Ritter, Jean M., and Judith H. Langlois. "The Role of Physical Attractiveness in the Observation of Child-Adult Interactions," *Developmental Psychology* 24 (1988), 254–263.

Rosenthal, R., and B. M. DePaulo. "Expectancies, Discrepancies, and Courtesies in Nonverbal Communication," *Western Journal of Speech Communication* 43 (1979), 76–95.

Ross, Michael, and Garth J. O. Fletcher. "Attribution and Social Perception," in Gardner Lindzey and Elliot Aronson, eds., *Handbook of Social Psychology,* Vol. II, 3rd ed. (New York: Random House, 1985), pp. 73–122.

Schaffer, Carrie, and Sidney Blatt. "Interpersonal Relationships and the Experience of Perceived Efficacy," in Robert J. Sternberg and John Kolligian, Jr., eds., *Competence Considered* (New Haven: Yale University Press, 1990), pp. 229–245.

Secord, P. F. "Facial Features and Inference Processes in Interpersonal Perception," in Renato Tagiuri and Luigi Petrullo, eds., *Person Perception and Interpersonal Behavior* (Palo Alto, CA: Stanford University Press, 1958).

Segall, M. H., D. T. Campbell, and M. J. Herskovits. "Cultural Differences in the Perception of Geometric Illusions," in D. R. Price-Williams, ed., *Cross-Cultural Studies* (Baltimore: Penguin, 1969), pp. 95–101.

Staley, Constance Courtney, and Jerry L. Cohen. "Communicator Style and Social Style: Similarities and Differences between the Sexes," *Communication Quarterly* 36 (1988), 192–202.

Sternberg, Robert J., and John Kolligian, Jr., eds. *Competence Considered* (New Haven: Yale University Press, 1990).

Storms, Michael D. "Videotape and the Attribution Process: Reversing Actor's and Observer's Point of View," *Journal of Personality and Social Psychology* 27 (1973), 165–175.

Trenholm, S., and T. Rose. "The Complaint Communicator: Teacher Perceptions of Appropriate Classroom Behavior," *Western Journal of Speech Communication* 45 (1981), 13–26.

Tubbs. Stewart L. "Interpersonal Trust, Conformity, and Credibility," paper delivered at the annual convention of the Speech Association of America, New York, December 1969.

Veenendall, Tom, and Rita Braito. "Androgeny in Spouse Interaction," in Lea P. Stewart and Stella Ting-Toomey, eds., *Communication, Gender, and Sex-Roles in Diverse Interaction Contexts* (Norwood, NJ: Ablex, 1987), pp. 31–48.

Veenman, S. "Perceived Problems of Beginning Teachers," *Review of Educational Research* 54 (1984), 143–178.

Watzlawick, Paul, Janet Helmick Beavin, and Don D. Jackson. *Pragmatics of Human Communication* (New York: Norton, 1967).

Weir, John. "Gay-Bashing, Villainy and the Oscars," *The New York Times* (March 29, 1992), 17, 22–23.

Wilson, Paul. "Perceptual Distortion of Height as a Function of Ascribed Academic Status," *Journal of Social Psychology* 74 (1968), 97–102.

Wolf, Naomi. *The Beauty Myth* (New York: Anchor/Doubleday, 1991).

Zimbardo, P. "Psychological Power and Pathology of Imprisonment," unpublished manuscript, Stanford University, Palo Alto, CA, 1971.

———. *Shyness* (Reading, MA: Addison-Wesley, 1990).

Chapter 3 The Verbal Message

Althen, Gary. "The Americans Have to Say Everything," *Communication Quarterly* 40 (1992), 413–421.

Becker, Carl. "Reasons for the Lack of Argumentation and Debate in the Far East," in Larry A. Samovar and Richard Porter, eds., *Intercultural Communication: A Reader,* 6th ed. (Belmont, CA: Wadsworth, 1991), pp. 234–243.

Bell, Robert A., Nancy L. Buerkel-Rothfuss, and Kevin E. Gore. "Did You Bring the Yarmulke for the Cabbage Patch Kid?" *Human Communication Research* 14 (1987), 47–67.

Berryman, C. L., and L. R. Wilcox. "Attitudes toward Male and Female Speech: Experiments on the Effects of Sex-Typed Language," *Western Journal of Speech Communication* 44 (1980), 50–59.

Blumenthal, Michael. "The Eloquence Gap," *New Republic* (November 14, 1988), 18–19.

Bostrom, Robert, John R. Basehart, and Charles Rossiter. "The Effects of Three Types of Profane Language in Persuasive Messages," *Journal of Communication* 23 (1973), 461–475.

Bradac, J. J. "The Language of Lovers, Flovers, and Friends: Communicating in Social and Personal Relationships," *Journal of Language and Social Relationships* 2 (1983), 141–162.

Bradac, J. J., M. R. Hemphill, and C. H. Tardy. "Language Style on Trial: The Effects of 'Powerful' and 'Powerless' Speech upon Judgments of Victims and Villains," *Western Journal of Speech Communication* 45 (1981), 327–341.

Bradac, J. J., and A. Mulac. "A Molecular View of Powerful and Powerless Speech Styles," *Communication Monographs* 51 (1984), 307–319.

Brown, Roger. *Words and Things: An Introduction to Language* (New York: Free Press, 1958).

Brown, Roger, and Eric Lenneberg. "A Study in Language and Cognition," *Journal of Abnormal and Social Psychology* 49 (1954), 454–462.

Bruner, Jerome. *Actual Minds, Possible Worlds* (Cambridge, MA: Harvard University Press, 1986).

Burgoon, M., J. P. Dillard, and N. E. Doran. "Friendly or Unfriendly Persuasion: The Effects of Violations of Expectations by Males and Females," *Human Communication Research* 10 (1983), 283–294.

Cameron, Deborah, ed. *The Feminist Critique of Language* (London: Routledge, 1990).

Carmody, Deirdre. "College Recruiters and Counselors Share Some Tips from the Trenches," *The New York Times* (October 11, 1989), B6.

Carroll, Raymonde. *Cultural Misunderstandings,* trans. by Carol Volk (Chicago: University of Chicago Press, 1988).

Crane, Loren, Richard Dieker, and Charles Brown. "The Physiological Response to the Communication Modes: Reading, Listening, Writing, Speaking, and Evaluating," *Journal of Communication* 20 (1970), 231–240.

Daly, John A., Anita L. Vangelisti, and Suzanne M. Daughton. "The Nature and Correlates of Conversational Sensitivity," *Human Communication Research* 14 (1987), 167–212.

Davis, Hayley. "What Makes Bad Language Bad?" *Language & Communication* 9, no. 2/3 (1989), 1–9.

Elliott, Norman. "Communicative Development from Birth," *Western Journal of Speech Communication* 48 (Spring 1984), 184–196.

Galvin, Kathleen M., and Bernard J. Brommel. *Family Communication: Cohesion and Change* (New York: HarperCollins, 1991).

Gonzalez, David. "What's the Problem with 'Hispanic'? Just Ask a 'Latino'," *The New York Times* (November 15, 1992).

Griffin, Em. *A First Look at Communication Theory* (New York: McGraw-Hill, 1991).

Goldman, Ari. "Clerics Advised on AIDS Preaching," *The New York Times* (November 28, 1989), B3.

Haney, William V. *Communication and Organizational Behavior,* 4th ed. (Homewood, IL: Irwin, 1973).

Haslett, B. J. *Communication: Strategic Action in Context* (Hillsdale, NJ: Erlbaum, 1987).

Haslett, Beth. "Acquiring Conversational Competence," *Western Journal of Speech Communication* 48 (Spring 1984), 107–124.

Hayakawa, S. I. *Language in Thought and Action,* 4th ed. (Orlando, FL: Harcourt Brace Jovanovich, 1978).

Heilbrun, A. B. "Measurement of Masculine and Feminine Sex-Role Identities as Independent Dimensions," *Journal of Consulting and Clinical Psychology* 44 (1976), 183–190.

Kellerman, Kathy, Rodney Reynolds, and Josephine Bao-sun. "Strategies of Conversational Retreat: When Parting Is Not Sweet Sorrow," *Communication Monographs* 58 (1991), 362–383.

Kirkwood, William G. "Truthfulness as a Standard for Speech in Ancient India," *Southern Communication Journal* 54 (1989), 213–234.

Krauss, Robert M. "The Interpersonal Regulation of Behavior," in Dwain N. Walcher, ed., *Early Childhood: The Development of Self-Regulatory Mechanisms* (Orlando, FL: Academic Press, 1971), pp. 187–208.

Laing, R. D. *Self and Others,* 2d ed. (New York: Penguin, 1972).

Legum, Colin. "The End of Cloud-Cuckoo-Land," *New York Times Magazine* (March 28, 1976), 18–19+.

Liska, J., E. W. Mechling, and S. Stathas. "Differences in Subjects' Perceptions and Believability between Users of Deferential and Nondeferential Language," *Communication Quarterly* 29 (1981), 40–48.

Mabry, Edward. "A Multivariate Investigation of Profane Language," *Central States Speech Journal* 26 (1975), 39–44.

Martin, J. N., and R. T. Craig. "Selected Linguistic Sex Differences during Initial Social Interaction of Same-Sex and Mixed Sex Dyads," *Western Journal of Speech Communication* 47 (1983), 16–28.

Miller, C., and K. Swift. *Words and Women* (Garden City, NY: Anchor, 1976).

Motley, Michael. "Mindfulness in Solving Communicator's Dilemmas," *Communication Monographs* 59 (1992), 306–314.

Osgood, Charles E. "Probing Subjective Culture Part 1. Crosslinguistic Tool-Making," *Journal of Communication,* 24 (1974a), 21–35.

———. "Probing Subjective Culture Part 2. Crosscultural Tool-Using," *Journal of Communication* 24 (1974b), 82–100.

Osgood, Charles, George Suci, and Percy Tannenbaum. *The Measurement of Meaning* (Urbana: University of Illinois Press, 1957), chaps. 1–4.

Palmer, Mark T. "Controlling Conversations: Turns, Topics and Interpersonal Control," *Communication Monographs* 56 (March 1989), 1–18.

Pearson, Judy Cornelia, Lynn H. Turner, and William Todd-Mancillas. *Gender & Communication,* 2d ed. (Dubuque, IA: William C. Brown, 1991).

Piaget, Jean. *The Language and Thought of the Child.* 3rd ed. (Atlantic Highlands, NJ: Humanities, 1962).

Quina, Kathryn, Joseph A. Wingard, and Henry G. Bates. "Language Style and Gender Stereotypes in Person Perception," *Psychology of Women Quarterly* 11 (1987), 111–122.

Quindlen, Anna. "The Skirt Standard," *The New York Times* (December 6, 1992), Sec. 4, p. 19.

Rossiter, Charles, and Robert Bostrom. "Profanity, 'Justification,' and Source Credibility," paper delivered at the annual conference of the National Society for the Study of Communication, Cleveland, 1968.

Safire, William. *On Language* (New York: Quadrangle, 1980).

———. *Language Maven Strikes Again* (New York: Doubleday, 1990).

Samovar, Larry A., and Richard Porter, eds. *Intercultural Communication: A Reader,* 6th ed. (Belmont, CA: Wadsworth, 1991).

Scotton, Carol M. "Self-Enhancing Codeswitching as Interactional Power," *Language & Communication* 8, no. 3/4 (1988), 199–212.

Shimanoff, S. D. "The Role of Gender in Linguistic References to Emotive States," *Communication* 8 (1988), 199–212.

Shorris, Earl. *Latinos: A Biography of the People* (New York: Norton, 1992).

Sillars, Alan L., and Judith Weisberg. "Conflict as a Social Skill," in Michael E. Roloff and Gerald R. Miller, eds., *Interpersonal Processes: New Directions in Communication Research* (Newbury Park, CA: Sage, 1987), pp. 140–171.

Sontag, Susan. *AIDS and Its Metaphors* (New York: Farrar, Straus and Giroux, 1989).

Stevens, William K. "Stronger Urban Accents in Northeast Are Called Signs of Evolving Language," *The New York Times,* July 21, 1985, A36.

Tan, Amy. "Mother Tongue," in *The Best American Essays 1991,* Joyce Carol Oates, ed. (New York: Ticknor & Fields, 1991).

Tannen, Deborah. *You Just Don't Understand: Women and Men in Conversation* (New York: Ballantine Books, 1990).

Whorf, Benjamin Lee. *Language, Thought, and Reality,* ed. by John B. Carroll (Cambridge, MA: MIT Press, 1956).

Wittig, Monique. "The Mark of Gender," in Nancy Miller, ed., *The Poetics of Gender* (New York: Columbia University Press, 1986), pp. 63–73.

Chapter 4   The Nonverbal Message

Agins, Teri. "Breaking Out of the Gray Flannel Suit," *The Wall Street Journal* (March 23, 1992), B8.

Albas, Cheryl. "Proxemic Behavior: A Study of Extrusion," *Journal of Social Psychology* 131 (1991), 697–702.

Anderson, P. A. "Nonverbal Communication in the Small Group," in R. S. Cathcart and L. A. Samovar, eds., *Small Group Communication,* 4th ed. (Dubuque, IA: Brown, 1984).

Anderson, P. A., and K. K. Sull. "Out of Touch, Out of Reach: Tactile Predispositions as Predictors of Interpersonal Distance," *Western Journal of Speech Communication* 49 (1985), 57–72.

Anderson, Virgil A. *Training the Speaking Voice,* 3rd ed. (New York: Oxford University Press, 1977).

Argyle, Michael. *The Psychology of Interpersonal Behavior,* rev. ed. (Baltimore: Penguin, 1985).

Barringer, Felicity. "Psychologists Try to Explain Why Thomas and Hill Offer Opposing Views," *The New York Times* (October 14, 1991), A18.

Barnlund, Dean C. *Interpersonal Communication: Survey and Studies* (Boston: Houghton Mifflin, 1968).

Bateson, Gregory, et al. "Toward a Theory of Schizophrenia," *Behavioral Science* 1 (1956), 251–264.

Birdwhistell, Ray L. *Introduction to Kinesics* (Louisville, KY: University of Louisville Press, 1952).

———. *Kinesics in Context* (Philadelphia: University of Pennsylvania Press, 1970).

Blubaugh, Jon. "Effects of Positive and Negative Audience Feedback on Selected Variables of Speech Behavior," *Speech Monographs* 36 (1969), 131–137.

Bowler, Ned. "A Fundamental Frequency Analysis of Harsh Vocal Quality," *Speech Monographs* 31 (1964), 128–134.

Bremmer, Jan, and Herman Roodenburg, eds. *A Cultural History of Gesture* (Ithaca, NY: Cornell University Press, 1992).

Buck, R. *The Communication of Emotion* (New York: Guilford, 1984).

Buck, Ross. "Communication with Machines," *American Behavioral Scientist* 31 (1988), 341–354.

Buller, David B., Krystyna D. Strzyzewski, and Frank G. Hunsaker. "Interpersonal Deception: II. The Inferiority of Conversational Participants as Deception Detectors," *Communication Monographs* 58 (1991a), 25–38.

Buller, David B., Krystyna D. Strzyzewski, and Jamie Comstock. "Interpersonal Deception: I. Deceivers' Reactions to Receivers' Suspicions and Probing," *Communication Monographs* 58 (1991b), 1–23.

Burgoon, Judee K., and Jerold L. Hale. "Nonverbal Expectancy Violations: Model Elaboration and Application to Immediacy Behaviors," *Communication Monographs* 55 (March 1988), 58–79.

Cody, M. J., P. J. Marston, and M. Foster. "Paralinguistic and Verbal Leakage of Deception as a Function of Attempted Control and Timing of Questions," in R. Bostrom, ed., *Communication Yearbook* 8 (Beverly Hills, CA: Sage, 1984).

Condon, John. "So Near the United States: Notes on Communication between Mexicans and North Americans," in Larry A. Samovar and Richard E. Porter, eds., *Intercultural Communication: A Reader,* 6th ed. (Belmont, CA: Wadsworth, 1991), pp. 106–112.

Corbin, Martin. "Response to Eye Contact," *Quarterly Journal of Speech* 48 (1962), 415–418.

Costanza, Mark. "Training Students to Decode Verbal and Nonverbal Cues: Effects on Confidence and Performance," *Journal of Educational Psychology* 84 (1992), 308–313.

Darwin, Charles. *Evolution and Natural Selection,* ed. by Bert James Loewenberg (Boston: Beacon, 1959).

Davitz, Joel R., and Lois Jean Davitz. "The Communication of Feeling by Content-Free Speech," *Journal of Communication* 9 (1959*a*), 6–13.

———. "Correlates of Accuracy in the Communication of Feelings," *Journal of Communication* 9 (1959*b*), 110–117.

———. "Nonverbal Vocal Communication of Feeling," *Journal of Communication* 11 (1961), 81–86.

Diehl, Charles F., Richard C. White, and Paul H. Satz. "Pitch Change and Comprehension," *Speech Monographs* 28 (1961), 65–68.

Dolgin, K. M., and J. Sabini. "Experimental Manipulation of a Human Nonverbal Display: The Tongue Show Affects an Observer's Willingness to Interact." *Animal Behavior* 30 (1982), 935–936.

Durrell, Lawrence. *Bitter Lemons* (London: Faber, 1957).

Eakins, Barbara J. "The Relationship of Intonation to Attitude Change, Retention, and Attitude toward Source," paper delivered at the annual convention of the Speech Association of America, New York, December 1969.

Eisenson, John, and Mardel Ogilvie. *Speech Correction in the Schools,* 4th ed. (New York: Macmillan, 1977).

Ekman, Paul. "Communication through Nonverbal Behavior," Progress Report, Langley Porter Institute, San Francisco, 1965*a*.

———. "Differential Communication of Affect by Head and Body Cues," *Journal of Personality and Social Psychology* 2 (1965*b*), 726–735.

Ekman, Paul, and Wallace V. Friesen. "Constants across Cultures in the Face and Emotion," *Journal of Personality and Social Psychology* 17 (1971), 124–129.

Ekman, Paul, and Wallace V. Friesen. *Unmasking the Face: A Guide to Recognizing Emotions from Facial Cues,* 2d ed. (Palo Alto, CA: Consulting Psychologists Press, 1984).

Ekman, P., W. V. Friesen, and J. Bear. "The International Language of Gestures," *Psychology Today* 18 (May 1984), 64–69.

Ekman, Paul, and Maureen Sullivan. "Who Can Catch a Liar?" *American Psychologist* 46 (1991), 913–920.

Faludi, Susan. "Speak for Yourself," *The New York Times Magazine* (January 26, 1992), 10, 26.

Forgas, Joseph P. "The Role of Physical Attractiveness in the Interpretation of Facial Cues," *Personality and Social Psychology Bulletin* 13 (1987), 478–489.

Freedman, Daniel G. "The Survival Value of Beards," *Psychology Today* 3 (October 1969), 36–39.

Freyre, Gilberto. *New World in the Tropics* (Westport, CT: Greenwood Press, 1980).

Gaddy, C. D., et al. *Applied Science for Plant Managers* (Columbia, MD: G. P. Courseware, 1987).

Goldhaber, Gerald M. "Gay Talk: Communication Behavior of Male Homosexuals," paper presented at the annual convention of the Speech Communication Association, Chicago, December 1974.

Goleman, Daniel. "Sensing Silent Cues Emerges as Key Skill," *The New York Times* (October 10, 1989), C1, 8.

Greene, J. O., H. D. O'Hair, M. J. Cody, and C. Yen. "Planning and Control of Behavior during Deception," *Human Communication Research* 11 (1985), 335–364.

Gudykunst, William B., and Young Yun Kim. *Communicating with Strangers*. 2d ed. (New York: McGraw-Hill, 1992a).

Gudykunst, William B., and Young Yun Kim. *Readings on Communicating with Strangers* (New York: McGraw-Hill, 1992b).

Gurvitch, Georges. *The Spectrum of Social Time*. Trans. by Myrtle Korenbaum (Dordrecht, Netherlands: Reidel, 1964).

Hall, Edward T. *The Silent Language* (New York: Fawcett, 1959).

———. *The Hidden Dimension* (Garden City, NY: Doubleday, 1966).

———. *The Dance of Life* (Garden City, NY: Doubleday/Anchor, 1984).

Hall, Edward T., and William Foote Whyte. "Intercultural Communication: A Guide to Men of Action," in Alfred G. Smith, ed., *Communication and Culture: Readings in the Codes of Human Interaction* (New York: Holt, Rinehart and Winston, 1966), pp. 567–576.

Hargie, Owen, Christine Saunders, and David Dickson. *Social Skills in Interpersonal Communication* (Cambridge, MA: Brookline Books, 1987).

Harms, L. S. "Listener Judgments of Status Cues in Speech," *Quarterly Journal of Speech* 47 (1961), 164–168.

Harrison, Randall. "Nonverbal Communication: Explorations into Time, Space, Action, and Object," in Jim Campbell and Hal Hepler, eds., *Dimensions in Communication* (Belmont, CA: Wadsworth, 1965), pp. 158–174.

Hegstrom, T. G. "Message Impact: What Percentage Is Nonverbal?" *Western Journal of Speech Communication* 43 (1979), 134–142.

Heslin, R., and T. Alper. "Touch: The Bonding Gesture," in M. Wiemann and R. P. Harrison, eds., *Nonverbal Interaction* (Beverly Hills, CA: Sage, 1983).

Hess E. H. "Attitude and Pupil Size," *Scientific American* 212 (April 1965), 46–54.

———. *The Tell-Tale Eye* (New York: Van Nostrand Reinhold, 1975).

Jones, Nigel, Judith Kearins, and John Watson. "The Human Tongue Show and Observer's Willingness to Interact." *Psychological Reports* 60 (1987), 759–764.

Jones, S. E., and E. Yarbrough. "A Naturalistic Study of the Meanings of Touch," *Communication Monographs* 52 (1985), 19–56.

Kinzel, August. "Towards an Understanding of Violence," *Attitude* 1 (1969).

Kleinke, C. R. "Compliance to Requests Made by Gazing and Touching: Experiments in Field Settings," *Journal of Experimental Social Psychology* 13 (1977), 218–223.

————. *Meeting and Understanding People* (New York: Freeman, 1986).

Knapp, Mark L., and Hall, Judy. *Nonverbal Communication in Human Interaction,* 3rd ed. (New York: Harcourt Brace Jovanovich, 1992).

Knapp, M. L., and M. E. Comadena. "Telling It Like It Isn't: A Review of Theory and Research on Deceptive Communication," *Human Communication Research 5* (1979), 270–285.

Konner, Melvin. "The Enigmatic Smile," *Psychology Today* 21 (March 1987), 42–46.

La Barre, Weston. "The Language of Emotions and Gestures," in Warren Bennis et al., eds., *Interpersonal Dynamics,* 2d ed. (Homewood, IL: Dorsey, 1968), pp. 197–205.

Laing, R. D. *Self and Others,* 2d rev. ed. (New York: Pantheon, 1969).

Lefkowitz, Monroe, Robert R. Blake, and Jane Srygley Mouton. "Status Factors in Pedestrian Violation of Traffic Signals," *Journal of Abnormal and Social Psychology* 51 (1955), 704–706.

Leo, J. "Reprogramming the Patient," *Time* (December 19, 1983), 79.

Libby, William L., and Donna Yaklevich. "Personality Determinants of Eye Contact and Direction of Gaze Aversion," *Journal of Personality and Social Psychology* 27 (1973), 197–206.

"Losing an Accent, Gaining—What?" *The New York Times* (January 9, 1979), C12.

"The Love That Won't Shut Up," *Time* (September 29, 1975), 6.

Madonik, Barbara. "I Hear What You Say, but What Are You Telling Me?" *Canadian Manager* 15 (Spring 1990): 18–20.

Mehrabian, Albert. "Orientation Behaviors and Nonverbal Attitude Communication," *Journal of Communication* 17 (1967), 324–332.

————. "Communication without Words," *Psychology Today* 2 (1968), 53–56.

————. *Nonverbal Communication* (Chicago: Aldine, 1972).

————. *Public Places and Private Spaces* (New York: Basic Books, 1976).

Mehrabian, Albert, and Martin Williams. "Nonverbal Concomitants of Perceived and Intended Persuasiveness," *Journal of Personality and Social Psychology* 13 (1969), 37–58.

Montagu, M. F. A. *Touch: The Human Significance of the Skin* (New York: Columbia University Press, 1971).

Morris, Desmond, Peter Collett, Peter Marsh, and Marie O'Shaughnessy. *Gestures* (New York: Stein and Day, 1979).

Motley, Michael T., and Carl T. Camden. "Facial Expression of Emotion: A Comparison of Posed Expressions versus Spontaneous Expressions in an Interpersonal Communication Setting," *Western Journal of Speech Communication* 53 (Winter 1988), 1–2.

Nowicki, Stephen, Jr., and Marshall P. Duke. "A Measure of Nonverbal Social Processing Ability in Children," paper presented at the American Psychological Society, June 1989.

Pearson, Judy Cornelia, Lynn H. Turner, and Wm. Todd-Mancillas. *Gender & Communication,* 2d ed. (Dubuque, IA: William C. Brown, 1991).

Ray, George B., Eileen Berlin Ray, and Christopher J. Zahn. "Speech Behavior and Social Evaluation: An Examination of Medical Messages," *Communication Quarterly* 39 (1991), 119–128.

Reece, Michael, and Robert N. Whitman. "Expressive Movements, Warmth, and Verbal Reinforcement," *Journal of Abnormal and Social Psychology* 64 (1962), 234–236.

Rosenfeld, Howard M. "Effect of Approval-Seeking Induction in Interpersonal Proximity," *Psychological Reports* 17 (1965), 120–122.

Rosenfeld, Lawrence B., and Timothy G. Plax. "Clothing as Communication," *Journal of Communication* 27 (1977), 24–31.

Rule, Sheila. "Nothing Prepares You for Apartheid," *The New York Times Magazine* (May 4, 1986), 34 + .

Rybczynski, Witold. *Looking Around: A Journey Through Architecture* (New York: Viking Penguin, 1992).

Samovar, Larry A., and Richard E. Porter. *Communication between Cultures* (Belmont, CA: Wadsworth, 1991).

Scheflen, Albert E. "Quasi-Courtship Behavior in Psychotherapy," *Psychiatry* 28 (1965), 245–257.

Smith, W. J., J. Chase, and A. N. Leiblich. "Tongue Showing: A Facial Display of Humans and Other Primate Species," *Semiotica* 11 (1974), 201–246.

Snyder, M. "The Many Me's of the Self-Monitor," *Psychology Today* 14 (March 1980), 33–40, 92.

Sommer, Robert. *Personal Space: The Behavioral Basis of Design* (Englewood Cliffs, NJ: Prentice-Hall, 1969).

Soskin, William F., and Paul E. Kauffman. "Judgment of Emotion in Word-Free Voice Samples," *Journal of Communication* 11 (1961), 73–81.

Starkweather, John A. "Content-Free Speech as a Source of Information about the Speaker," *Journal of Abnormal and Social Psychology* 52 (1956), 394–402.

———. "Vocal Communication of Personality and Human Feelings," *Journal of Communication* 11 (1961), 63–72.

Steinzor, B. "The Spatial Factor in Face-to-Face Discussion Groups," *Journal of Abnormal and Social Psychology* 45 (1950), 552–555.

Stewart, J., and G. D'Angelo. *Together: Communicating Interpersonally,* 2d ed. (New York: Random House, 1980).

Sypher, Howard E., Beverly Davenport Sypher, and John W. Haas. "Getting Emotional: Affect in Interpersonal Communication," *American Behavioral Scientist* 31 (1988), 372–383.

Trager, George L. "Paralanguage: A First Approximation," *Studies in Linguistics* 13 (1958), 1–12.

Van Riper, Charles. *Speech Correction,* 4th ed. (Englewood Cliffs, NJ: Prentice-Hall, 1984).

Weick, Karl E. "Systematic Observational Methods," in Gardner Lindzey and Elliot Aronson, eds., *The Handbook of Social Psychology,* 2d ed., Vol. II. *Research Methods* (Reading, MA: Addison-Wesley, 1968).

Weitz, Shirley, ed. *Nonverbal Communication: Readings with Commentary,* 2d ed. (New York: Oxford University Press, 1979).

Williams, Frederick, and John Tolch. "Communication by Facial Expression," *Journal of Communication* 15 (1965), 17–21.

Willis, F. N., and H. K. Hamm. "The Use of Interpersonal Touch in Securing Compliances," *Journal of Nonverbal Behavior* 5 (1980), 49–55.

Winstead, Barbara A., Valerian J. Derlega, et al. "Friendship, Social Interaction, and Coping with Stress," *Communication Research* 19 (1992), 193–211.

Wolfe, Tom. *The Right Stuff* (New York: Bantam Books, 1980).

Zuckerman, M., B. M. DePaulo, and R. Rosenthal. "Verbal and Nonverbal Communication of Deception," in L. Berkowitz, ed., *Advances in Experimental Social Psychology,* Vol. 14 (Orlando, FL: Academic Press, 1981).

Chapter 5   Listening

Acuff, Frank L. *How To Negotiate Anything with Anyone Anywhere Around the World* (New York: AMACOM, 1993).

Andre, Rae. *Positive Solitude* (New York: HarperCollins, 1991).

Aronoff, Craig E., Otis W. Baskin, Robert W. Hays, and Harold E. Davis. *Getting Your Message Across* (St. Paul, MN: West, 1981).

Ashenbrenner, Gary L., and Robert D. Snalling. "Communicate with Power," *Business Credit* 90 (1988), 39–42.

Athos, Anthony G., and John J. Gabarro. *Interpersonal Behavior: Communication and Understanding in Relationships* (Englewood Cliffs, NJ: Prentice-Hall, 1978).

Barker, Larry. *Listening Behavior* (Englewood Cliffs, NJ: Prentice-Hall, 1971), p. 17.

Barker, L., R. Edwards, C. Gaines, K. Gladney, and F. Holley. "An Investigation of Proportional Time Spent in Various Communication Activities by College Students," *Journal of Applied Communication Research* 8 (1981), 101–109.

Bostrom, Robert. "Patterns of Communicative Interaction in Small Groups," *Speech Monographs* 3 (1970), 257–263.

Bostrom, Robert N., and Enid S. Waldhart. "Memory Models and the Measurement of Listening," *Communication Education* 37 (1988), 1–13.

Brilhart, Barbara. "The Relationship between Some Aspects of Communicative Speaking and Communicative Listening," *Journal of Communication* 15 (1965), 35–46.

Broadbent, Donald. *Perception and Communication* (Elmsford, NY: Pergamon, 1958).

Brooks, William D. *Speech Communication,* 4th ed. (Dubuque, IA: Brown, 1981).

Corey, S. "The Teachers Out-Talk the Pupils," in Samuel Duker, ed. *Listening: Readings* (New York: Scarecrow Press, 1966), p. 88.

Covey, Stephen. *The 7 Habits of Highly Effective People* (New York: Simon & Schuster, 1990).

Crane, Loren, Richard Dieker, and Charles Brown. "The Physiological Response to the Communication Modes: Reading, Listening, Writing, Speaking, and Evaluating," *Journal of Communication* 20 (1970), 231–240.

Fisher, Helen. "The Four Year Itch," *USA Weekend* (October 23–25, 1992), 4–7.

Floyd, J. J. *Listening: A Practical Approach* (Glenview, IL: Scott, Foresman, 1985).

Girard, Joe. *How To Sell Anything to Anybody* (New York: Warner, 1977).

Goss, Blain. *Processing Information* (Belmont, CA: Wadsworth, 1982).

Hargie, Owen, Christine Saunders, and David Dickson. *Social Skills in Interpersonal Communication.* (Cambridge, MA: Brookline Books, 1987).

Hunt, Gary, and Louis Cusella. "A Field Study of Listening Needs in Organizations," *Communication Education* 32 (1983), 393–401.

Keefe, William. *Listen, Management* (New York: McGraw-Hill, 1971).

Keller, P. "Major Findings in Listening in the Past Ten Years," *Journal of Communication* 10 (1960), 29–30.

Kelly, Charles M. "Emphatic Listening," in Robert S. Cathcart and Larry A. Samovar, eds., *Small Group Communication: A Reader,* 2d ed. (Dubuque, IA: Brown, 1974).

Kern, E. "The Brain: Part II: The Neuron," *Life* (October 22, 1971).

McCormack, Mark H. *What They Don't Teach You at Harvard Business School: Notes from a Street Smart Executive* (New York: Bantam, 1984).

Moray, Neville. *Listening and Attention* (Baltimore: Penguin, 1969).

Murphy, Kevin J. *Effective Listening* (Salem, NH: 1992).

Nichols, Ralph. "Listening Is a 10-Part Skill," *Nation's Business* 45 (1957), 56–60.

Nisbet, Michael A. "Listen—Who Said It Was Easy," *Canadian Banker* 95 (1988), 38–41.

Parkin, Alan J., Anne Wood, and Frances K. Aldrich. "Repetition and Active Listening: The Effects of Spacing Self-Assessment Questions," *British Journal of Psychology* 79 (1988), 77–86.

Pearce, C. Glenn. "Learning How to Listen Empathically," *Supervisory Management,* 36: 11.

Pearce, L., and S. Newton. *The Conditions of Human Growth* (New York: Citadel Press, 1963), p. 52.

Peters, Thomas J., and Robert H. Waterman. *In Search of Excellence: Lessons from America's Best Run Companies* (New York: Harper & Row, 1982).

Rankin, Paul. "The Measurement of the Ability to Understand Spoken Language," unpublished Ph.D. dissertation, University of Michigan, 1926, p. 43.

Reik, Theodore. *Listening with the Third Ear* (New York: Grove Press, 1948), p. 125.

Roethlisberger, Fritz. *Management and Morale* (Cambridge, MA: Harvard University Press, 1955), p. 95.

Rogers, Carl. *On Becoming a Person* (Boston: Houghton Mifflin, 1961).

Steil, Lyman, Larry L. Barker, and Kittie W. Watson. *Effective Listening: Key to Your Success* (Reading, MA: Addison-Wesley, 1983).

Stettner, Morey. "Salespeople Who Listen," *Management Review* 77 (1988), 44–45.

Stewart, John. *Together: Communicating Interpersonally,* 4th ed. (New York: McGraw-Hill, 1993).

Tannen, Deborah. *You Just Don't Understand: Women and Men in Conversation* (New York: Ballantine Books, 1991).

Wolvin, Andrew. "Meeting the Communication Needs of the Adult Learner," *Communication Education* 33 (1984), 267–271.

Chapter 6   Relationships in Process

Acitele, L. K. "When Spouses Talk to Each Other about Their Relationship," *Journal of Social and Personal Relationships* 5 (1987), 185–199.

Altman, I., and D. Taylor. *Social Penetration: The Development of Interpersonal Relationships* (New York: Irvington, 1983).

Anderson, Norman H. "Likeableness Ratings of 555 Personality-Trait Words," *Journal of Personality and Social Psychology* 9 (1968), 354–362.

Bach, George R., and Ronald M. Deutsch. *Stop! You're Driving Me Crazy* (New York: Berkley Publishing, 1985).

Barnlund, Dean C. *Interpersonal Communication: Survey and Studies* (Boston: Houghton Mifflin, 1968).

Baxter, Leslie A. "Forms and Functions of Intimate Play in Interpersonal Relationships," *Human Communication Research* 18 (1992), 336–363.

Baxter, Leslie. "Strategies for Ending Relationships: Two Studies," *Western Journal of Speech Communication* 46 (1982), 223–241.

———. "Trajectories of Relationship Disengagement," *Journal of Social and Personal Relationships* 1 (1984), 223–241.

Berscheid, Ellen. "Interpersonal Attraction," in Gardner Lindzey and Elliot Aronson, eds., *Handbook of Social Psychology,* Vol. II, 3rd ed. (New York: Random House, 1985), pp. 413–484.

Blake, Brian F., and Abraham Tesser. "Interpersonal Attraction as a Function of the Other's Reward Value to the Person," *Journal of Social Psychology* 82 (1970), 67–74.

Bochner, Arthur P., and Eric M. Eisenberg. "Family Process: System Perspectives," in Charles R. Berger and Steve H. Chaffee, eds., *Handbook of Communication Science* (Newbury Park, CA: Sage, 1987), pp. 540–563.

Brewer, Robert E. "Attitude Change, Interpersonal Attraction, and Communication in a Dyadic Situation," *Journal of Social Psychology* 75 (1968), 127–134.

Buber, Martin, "Distance and Relation," *Psychiatry* 20 (1957).

Burgoon, Judee K., and Jerold L. Hale. "Nonverbal Expectancy Violations: Model Elaboration and Application to Immediacy Behaviors," *Communication Monographs* 55 (March 1988), 58–79.

Buss, D. M. "Human Mate Selection." *American Scientist* 73 (January–February 1985), 47–51.

Canary, Daniel J., and Laura Stafford. "Relational Maintenance Strategies and Equity in Marriage," *Communication Monographs* 59 (1992), 243–267.

Chadwick, Bruce A., and Tim B. Heaton. *Statistical Handbook on the American Family* (Phoenix, AZ: Oryx Press, 1992).

Cheever, John. "Goodbye, My Brother," in *The Stories of John Cheever* (New York: Knopf, 1978), pp. 3–21.

Chelune, G. J., J. T. Robison, and M. J. Kommor. "A Cognitive Interaction Model of Intimate Relationships," in V. J. Derlega, ed., *Communication, Intimacy, and Close Relationships* (Orlando, FL: Academic Press, 1984).

Cissna, Kenneth N. "Interpersonal Confirmation: A Review of Current Theory and Research," paper delivered at the Central States Speech Association Convention, Chicago, April 1976.

Deutsch, Morton. "The Effect of Motivational Orientation upon Trust and Suspicion," *Human Relations* 13 (1960), 123–137.

Deutsch, Morton, and Robert M. Krauss. "The Effect of Threat on Interpersonal Bargaining," *Journal of Abnormal and Social Psychology* 61 (1960), 181–189.

Duck, Steve. *Understanding Relationships* (New York: Guilford Press, 1991).

Duck, Steve, and Melanie K. Barnes. "Disagreeing About Agreement," *Communication Monographs* 59 (1992), 199–209.

Festinger, Leon, Stanley Schachter, and Kurt Back. *Social Pressures in Informal Groups* (New York: Harper & Row, 1950).

Fisher, Roger, William Ury, and Bruce Patton. *Getting to Yes: Negotiating Agreement without Giving In,* 2d ed. (New York: Penguin, 1991).

Footlick, Jerrold K. "What Happened to the Family," *Newsweek* (Fall/Winter 1990), 14–20.

Galvin, Kathleen M., and Bernard J. Brommel. *Family Communication: Cohesion and Change* (New York: HarperCollins, 1991).

Gergen, Kenneth. *The Saturated Self* (New York: Basic Books, 1991).

Gibb, Jack R. "Defensive Communication," *Journal of Communication* 11 (1961), 141–148.

Gordon, Ronald D. "The Difference between Feeling Defensive and Feeling Understood," *The Journal of Business Communication* 25 (Winter 1988), 53–64.

Hamachek, D. E. *Encounters with Others: Interpersonal Relationships and You* (New York: Holt, Rinehart and Winston, 1982).

Hampl, Patricia. *A Romantic Education,* 2d ed. (Boston: Houghton Mifflin, 1992).

Harrison, Roger. "Defenses and the Need to Know," in Robert Golembiewski and Arthur Blumberg, eds., *Sensitivity Training and the Laboratory Approach* (Itasca, IL: Peacock, 1970), pp. 80–90.

Hatfield, Elaine, and Richard L. Rapson. "Similarity and Attraction in Close Relationships," *Communication Monographs* 59 (1992), 209–212.

Hawken, Leila, Robert L. Duran, and Lynne Kelly. "The Relationship of Interpersonal Communication Variables to Academic Success and Persistence in College," *Communication Quarterly* 39 (1991), 297–308.

Heider, Fritz. *The Psychology of Interpersonal Relations* (Hillsdale, NJ. Lawrence Erlbaum Assoc., 1983).

Hinde, R. A. "The Bases of a Science of Interpersonal Relationships," in S. Duck and R. Gilmore, eds., *Personal Relationships,* Vol. I (Orlando, FL: Academic Press, 1981).

Hocker, Joyce L., and William W. Wilmot. *Interpersonal Conflict,* 3d ed. (Dubuque, IA: Brown, 1991).

Kerckhoff, A. C., and K. E. Davis. "Value Consensus and Need Complementarity," *American Sociological Review* 7 (1962), 295–303.

Klagsbrun, Francine. *Mixed Feelings: Love, Hate, Rivalry, and Reconciliation Among Brothers and Sisters* (New York: Bantam, 1992).

Knapp, Mark. *Interpersonal Communication and Human Relationships* (Boston: Allyn and Bacon, 1984).

Knapp, Mark L., and Anita L. Vangelisti. *Interpersonal Communication and Human Relationships,* 2d ed. (Newton, MA: Allyn & Bacon, 1992).

Leary, Timothy. *Interpersonal Diagnosis of Personality* (New York: Ronald Press, 1957).

Lippard, Paula V. "'Ask Me No Questions, I'll Tell You No Lies': Situational Exigencies for Interpersonal Communication," *Western Journal of Speech Communication* 52 (Winter 1988), 91–103.

Lloyd, Sally A. "Conflict in Premarital Relationships: Differential Perceptions of Males and Females," *Family Relations* 36 (1987), 290–294.

Lund, M. "The Development of Investment and Commitment Scales for Predicting Continuity of Personal Relationships," *Journal of Social and Personal Relationships* 2 (1985), 3–23.

McAdams, D. P. "Human Motives and Personal Relationships," in V. J. Derlega, ed., *Communication, Intimacy, and Close Relationships* (Orlando, FL: Academic Press, 1984).

McGill, Michael. "A Female Best Friend," *The New York Times Magazine* (March 24, 1985), 52.

Mellinger, Glen D. "Interpersonal Trust as a Factor in Communication," *Journal of Abnormal and Social Psychology* 52 (1956), 304–309.

Millar, Frank, and L. Edna Rogers. "Relational Dimensions of Interpersonal Dynamics," in Michael E. Roloff and Gerald R. Miller, eds., *Interpersonal Processes: New Directions in Communication Research* (Beverly Hills, CA: Sage, 1987), pp. 117–139.

Miller, A. "Role of Physical Attractiveness in Impression Formation," *Psychonomic Science,* 19 (1970), 241–243.

Newcomb, Theodore M. *The Acquaintance Process* (New York: Holt, Rinehart and Winston, 1961).

Pearce, L., and S. Newton. *The Conditions of Human Growth* (New York: Citadel, 1963).

Pearson, Judy C. *Communication in the Family* (New York: Harper & Row, 1989).

Peplau, Letitia Anne. "What Homosexuals Want," *Psychology Today* 15 (1981), 28–38.

Petronio, S., J. Martin, and R. Littlefield. "Prerequisite Conditions for Self-Disclosing: A Gender Issue," *Communication Monographs* 51 (1984), 268–273.

Rogers, Everett M., and Floyd Shoemaker. *Communication of Innovations* (New York: Free Press, 1971).

Rosenfeld, Lawrence B., and M. J. Jarrard. "The Effects of Perceived Sexism in Female and Male College Professors on Students' Descriptions of Classroom Climate," *Communication Education* 34 (1985), 205–213.

Rosenfeld, Lawrence B., and W. L. Kendrick. "Choosing to Be Open: Subjective Reasons for Self-Disclosing," *Western Journal of Speech Communication* 48 (1984), 326–343.

Rosenthal, Elizabeth. "Troubled Marriage? Sibling Relations May Be at Fault," *The New York Times,* (August 18, 1992), C1, C9.

Ruesch, Jurgen, and Gregory Bateson. *Communication: The Social Matrix of Psychiatry* (New York: Norton, 1968).

Satir, Virginia. *The New Peoplemaking* (Mountain View, CA: Science and Behavior Books, 1988).

Schachter, Stanley. *The Psychology of Affiliation* (Palo Alto, CA: Stanford University Press, 1959).

Seligman, Jean. "Variations on a Theme," *Newsweek* (Winter/Spring 1990), 38–46.

Sieberg, Evelyn, and Carl Larson. "Dimensions of Interpersonal Response," paper delivered at the annual conference of the International Communication Association, Phoenix, April 1971.

Sillars, Alan L., Stephen F. Coletti, Doug Parry, and Mark A. Rogers. "Coding Verbal Conflict Tactics," *Human Communication Research* 9, no. 1 (Fall 1982), 83–95.

Sillars, Alan L., and Judith Weisberg. "Conflict as a Social Skill," in Michael E. Roloff and Gerald R. Miller, eds., *Interpersonal Processes: New Directions in Communication Research* (Newbury Park, CA: Sage, 1987), pp. 140–171.

Tannen, Deborah. *You Just Don't Understand: Women and Men in Conversation* (New York: Ballantine Books, 1990).

Thibaut, John W., and Harold Kelley. *The Social Psychology of Groups* (New Brunswick, NJ: Transaction Books, 1985).

Tubbs, Stewart L. "Two Person Game Behavior, Conformity-Inducing Messages and Interpersonal Trust," *Journal of Communication* 21 (1971), 326–341.

VanLear, C. Arthur. "Testing a Cyclical Model of Communicative Openness in Relationship Development: Two Longitudinal Studies," *Communication Monographs* 58 (1991), 337–361.

Vygotsky, Lev Semenovich. *Thought and Language,* ed. and trans. by Eugenia Hanfmann and Gertrude Vakar (Cambridge, MA: MIT Press, 1962).

Walster, Elaine. "The Effect of Self-Esteem on Romantic Liking," *Journal of Experimental Social Psychology* 1 (1965), 184–197.

Walster, Elaine, and Leon Festinger. "The Effectiveness of 'Overheard' Persuasive Communications," *Journal of Abnormal and Social Psychology* 65 (1962), 395–402.

Watzlawick, Paul, Janet Helmick Beavin, and Don D. Jackson. *Pragmatics of Human Communication* (New York: Norton, 1967).

Wilmot, William W. *Dyadic Communication,* 2d ed. (Reading, MA: Addison-Wesley, 1979).

Winch, Robert F. *Mate Selection: A Study of Complementary Needs* (New York: Harper & Row, 1958).

Zajonc, Robert B. "Attitudinal Effects of Mere Exposure," *Journal of Personality and Social Psychology* 9 (1968), 1–29.

Chapter 7   Two-Person Communication

Associated Press. "Money Often Causes Marital Problems, Experts Say," *The Ann Arbor News* (August 12, 1992), B4.

Belkin, Lisa. "In Lessons on Empathy, Doctors Become Patients," *The New York Times* (June 4, 1991), A1, B5.

Berko, R. M., A. D. Wolvin, and D. R. Wolvin. *Communicating: A Social and Career Focus,* 3rd ed. (Boston: Houghton Mifflin, 1985).

Booth, Alan, and David Johnson. "Premarital Cohabitation and Marital Success," *Journal of Family Issues* 9 (1988), 255–272.

Bower, S., and G. Bower. *Asserting Yourself,* 2d ed. (Reading, MA: Addison-Wesley, 1980).

Bumpass, Larry, and James Sweet. "National Estimates of Cohabitation: Cohort Levels and Union Stability." NSFH Working Paper No. 2 (June 1989), revision of paper presented at the 1988 meeting of the Population Association of America.

Burgoon, Judee K., et al. "Relational Communication, Satisfaction, Compliance-Gaining Strategies, and Compliance in Communication between Physicians and Patients," *Communication Monographs* 54 (1987), 307–324.

Chelune, G. J., et al. "Self-Disclosure and Its Relationship to Marital Intimacy," *Journal of Clinical Psychology* 40 (1984), 216–219.

Chelune, G. J., J. T. Robison, and M. J. Kommor. In V. J. Derlega, ed., *Communication, Intimacy, and Close Relationships* (Orlando, FL: Academic Press, 1984).

Chelune, G. J., L. B. Rosenfeld, and E. M. Waring. "Self-Disclosure in Distressed and Nondistressed Couples," *American Journal of Family Therapy* 13 (1985), 24–32.

Conway, Jill Ker. *The Road from Coorain* (New York: Vintage, 1990).

Delia, J. G. "Some Tentative Thoughts concerning the Study of Interpersonal Relationships and Their Development," *Western Journal of Speech Communication* 44 (1980), 97–103.

Derlega, V. J., and J. Grzelak. "Appropriateness of Self-Disclosure," in G. J. Chelune, ed., *Self-Disclosure* (San Francisco: Jossey-Bass, 1979).

Derlega, Valerian J., Barbara A. Winstead, Paul T. P. Wong, and Michael Greenspan. "Self-Disclosure and Relationship Development: An Attributional Analysis," in Michael E. Roloff and Gerald R. Miller, eds., *Interpersonal*

Processes: New Directions in Communications Research (Beverly Hills, CA: Sage, 1987), pp. 172–187.

Duck, Steve. *Understanding Relationships* (New York: Guilford Press, 1991).

Ellis, Albert. *Reason and Emotion in Psychotherapy* (New York: Citadel, 1984).

Goffman, Erving. *Relations in Public: Microstudies of the Public Order* (New York: Harper & Row, 1972).

Gold, Deborah T. "Siblings in Old Age: Something Special," *Canadian Journal on Aging* 6 (1987), 199–215.

———. "Men and Their Siblings," paper presented at the 42nd Annual Scientific Meeting of the Gerontological Society of America, Minneapolis, November 1989*a*.

———. "Sibling Relationships in Old Age: A Typology," *International Journal of Aging and Human Development* 28 (1989*b*), 37–51.

Goldstine, Daniel, et al. *The Dance-Away Lover and Other Roles We Play in Love, Sex, and Marriage* (New York: Morrow, 1977).

Goleman, Daniel. "All Too Often, The Doctor Isn't Listening," *The New York Times* (November 13, 1991), C1, C5.

Gould, Roger L. *Transformations: Growth and Change in Adult Life* (New York: Simon and Schuster, 1978).

Gudykunst, William B., and Mitchell Hammer. "Factors Influencing Uncertainty Reduction in Interethnic Relationships," *Human Communication Research* 14 (1988), 569–601.

Hargie, Owen, Christine Saunders, and David Dickson. *Social Skills in Interpersonal Communication* (Cambridge, MA: Brookline Books, 1987), pp. 187–208.

Harrington, M. R. "The Relationship between Psychological Sex-Type and Perceptions of Individuals in Complementary, Symmetrical, and Parallel Relationships," unpublished dissertation, University of North Carolina, 1984.

Haslett, B. J. *Communication: Strategic Action in Context* (Hillsdale, NJ: Erlbaum, 1987), pp. 196–224.

Hatfield, Elaine. "The Dangers of Intimacy," in V. J. Derlega, ed., *Communication, Intimacy, and Close Relationships* (Orlando, FL: Academic Press, 1984).

Hawken, Leila, Robert L. Duran, and Lynne Kelly. "The Relationship of Interpersonal Communication Variables to Academic Success and Persistence in College," *Communication Quarterly* 39 (1991), 297–308.

Hunt, Bernice Kohn. *Marriage* (New York: Holt, Rinehart and Winston, 1976).

Ilich, John. *Power Negotiating: Strategies for Winning in Life and Business* (Reading, MA: Addison-Wesley, 1980).

Jakubowski-Spector, Patricia. *An Introduction to Assertive Training Procedures for Women* (Washington, DC: American Personnel and Guidance Association, 1973).

Jourard, Sidney M. *The Transparent Self: Self-Disclosure and Well Being* (Princeton, NJ: Van Nostrand, 1964).

———. *Self-Disclosure: An Experimental Analysis of the Transparent Self* (Melbourne, FL: Kreiger, 1979).

Kelley, Douglas L., and Judee K. Burgoon. "Understanding Marital Satisfaction and Couple Type as Functions of Relational Expectations," *Human Communication Research* 18 (1991), 40–69.

Klagsbrun, Francine. *Mixed Feelings: Love, Hate, Rivalry, and Reconciliation Among Brothers and Sisters* (New York: Bantam, 1992).

Knapp, Mark L., and Anita L. Vangelisti. *Interpersonal Communication and Human Relationships,* 2d ed. (Newton, MA: Allyn & Bacon, 1992).

Locklair, Jeanne. "Why Can't a Woman Be More Like a Man?" (1992), unpublished paper.

Luft, Joseph. *Of Human Interaction* (Palo Alto, CA: National Press, 1969).

Lund, M. "The Development of Investment and Commitment Scales for Predicting Continuity of Personal Relationships," *Journal of Social and Personal Relationships* 2 (1985), 3–23.

Marbella, Jean. "Living Together before Tying Knot No Longer Guarantees Marriage Will Work," *The Ann Arbor News* (June 22, 1989), E7.

McAdams, Dan P. *Intimacy: The Need to Be Close* (New York: Doubleday, 1989).

Miller, G. R., and M. Steinberg. *Between People* (Chicago: Science Research Assoc., 1975).

Murdoch, Peter, and Dean Rosen. "Norm Formation in an Independent Dyad," *Sociometry* 33 (1970), 264–275.

Nazario, Sonia L. "Medical Science Seeks a Cure for Doctors Suffering from Boorish Bedside Manner," *The Wall Street Journal* (March 17, 1992), B1, B6.

Phillips, G. M., and J. T. Wood. *Communication and Human Relationships* (New York: Macmillan, 1983).

Potter, Stephen. *The Complete Upmanship* (New York: New American Library, 1978).

Rogers, David E. "Out of Touch," *Technology Reports, Wall Street Journal* (November 13, 1989), R38.

Rosen, Sidney, and Abraham Tesser. "On Reluctance To Communicate Undesirable Information: The MUM Effect," *Sociometry* 33 (1970), 253–263.

Rosenfeld, L. B. "Self-Disclosure and Avoidance," *Communication Monograph* (1979), 63–74.

Rosenfeld, L. B., and W. L. Kendrick. "Choosing To Be Open: Subjective Reasons for Self-Disclosing," *Western Journal of Speech Communication* 48 (1984), 326–343.

Street, Richard L., Jr., and John M. Weimann. "Differences in How Physicians and Patients Perceive Physicians' Relational Communication," *The Southern Speech Commnication Journal* 53 (1988), 420–440.

Tannen, Deborah. *You Just Don't Understand* (New York: Ballantine Books, 1990).

Thibaut, John W., and Harold H. Kelley. *The Social Psychology of Groups* (New Brunswick, NJ: Transaction Books, 1985).

Turow, Joseph. *Playing Doctor: Television, Storytelling, and Medical Power* (New York: Oxford University Press, 1989).

Vanlear, C. Arthur, Jr. "The Formation of Social Relationships: A Longitudinal Study of Social Penetration," *Human Communication Research* 13 (1987), 299–322.

Vaughn, Diane. "The Long Goodbye," *Psychology Today* 21 (1987), 37–42.

Waring, E. M., and G. J. Chelune. "Marital Intimacy and Self-Disclosure," *Journal of Clinical Psychology* 39 (1983), 183–190.

Waring, E. M., et al. "Concepts of Intimacy in the General Public," *Journal of Nervous and Mental Disease* 168 (1980), 471–474.

Wheeless, Lawrence R. "Self-Disclosure and Interpersonal Solidarity: Measurement, Validation, and Relationships," *Human Communication Research* 3 (1976), 47–61.

Wheeless, Lawrence R., and Janis Grotz. "The Measurement of Trust and Its Relationship to Self-Disclosure," *Human Communication Research* 2 (1976), 338–346.

Williams, Frederick. *The New Communications,* 2d ed. (Belmont, CA: Wadsworth, 1989).

Wilmot, William W. *Dyadic Communication,* 2d ed. (Reading, MA: Addison-Wesley, 1979).

Chapter 8   Interviewing

Banville, Thomas G. *How To Listen—How To Be Heard* (Chicago: Nelson-Hall, 1978).

Bingham, Walter V., and Bruce V. Moore. *How To Interview* (New York: Harper, 1924).

Cahn, Dudley D., and Stewart L. Tubbs. "Management as Communication: Performance Evaluation and Employee Self-Worth," *Communication* 12 (1983), 46–54.

Downs, Cal W., G. Paul Smeyak, and Ernest Martin. *Professional Interviewing* (New York: Harper & Row, 1980).

Freund, James C. *Smart Negotiating* (New York: Simon & Schuster, 1992).

Girard, Joe. *How To Sell Anything to Anybody* (New York: Warner, 1977).

Hanna, M. S., and G. L. Wilson. *Communicating in Business and Professional Settings* (New York: Random House, 1984).

Kahn, Robert L., and Charles F. Cannell. *The Dynamics of Interviewing: Theory, Technique and Cases,* 2d ed. (New York: Wiley, 1968).

Lansing, J. B., and D. M. Blood. *The Changing Travel Market,* Monograph 38 (Ann Arbor, MI: Survey Research Center, 1964).

Latham, Gray P., and Kenneth N. Wexley. *Increasing Productivity through Performance Appraisal* (Reading MA: Addison-Wesley, 1981).

McComb, K. B., and Fred Jablin. "Verbal Correlates of Interviewer Empathic Listening and Employment Interview Outcomes," *Communication Monographs* 51 (1984), 353–371.

Moffatt, Thomas L. *Selection Interviewing for Managers* (New York: Harper & Row, 1979).

Murnighan, J. Keith. *Bargaining Games* (New York: William Morrow and Company, 1992).

Ramundo, Bernard A. *Effective Negotiation* (New York: Quorum Books, 1992).

Stewart, Charles J., and William B. Cash. *Interviewing: Principles and Practices,* 5th ed. (Dubuque, IA: Brown, 1988).

Sussman, Lyle, and Paul D. Krivonos. *Communication for Supervisors and Managers* (Sherman Oaks, CA: Alfred, 1979).

Weaver, Richard L. *Understanding Business Communication* (Englewood Cliffs, NJ: Prentice-Hall, 1985).

Wilson, Gerald L., and H. Lloyd Goodall, Jr. *Interviewing in Context* (New York: McGraw-Hill, 1991).

Chapter 9   Small-Group Communication

AACSB, "Responses To Customers Drives Curriculum Changes," *American Assembly of Collegiate Schools of Business Newsline* 22 (Summer 1992), 1–3.

Bales, Robert. *Personality and Interpersonal Behavior.* (New York: Holt, Rinehart and Winston, 1970).

Bales, Robert, and Fred Strodbeck. "Phases in Group Problem Solving," *Journal of Abnormal and Social Psychology* 46 (1951), 485–495.

Bavelas, Alex. "Communication Patterns in Task-Oriented Groups," *Journal of the Acoustical Society of America* 22 (1950), 725–730.

Benne, Kenneth D., and Paul Sheats. "Functional Roles of Group Members," *Journal of Social Issues* (1948), 41–49.

Bennis, Warren G., and Herbert A. Shepard. "A Theory of Group Development," *Human Relations* 9 (1956), 415–457.

———. "Group Observation," in Warren Bennis, Kenneth Benne, and Robert Chin, eds., *The Planning of Change* (New York: Holt, Rinehart and Winston, 1961), pp. 743–756.

Bormann, Ernest. *Discussion and Group Methods,* 2d ed. (New York: McGraw-Hill, 1976).

Bostrom, Robert. "Patterns of Communicative Interaction in Small Groups," *Speech Monographs* 37 (1970), 257–263.

Brilhart, John, and Gloria Galanes. *Effective Group Discussion,* 6th ed. (Dubuque, IA: Brown, 1992).

Cameron, N. *The Psychology of Behavior Disorders* (Boston: Houghton Mifflin, 1947).

Cartwright, Dorwin, and Alvin Zander. *Group Dynamics,* 3rd ed. (New York: Harper & Row, 1968), pp. 139–151.

Cissna, Kenneth. "Phases in Group Development: The Negative Evidence," *Small Group Behavior* 15 (1984), 3–32.

Cohen, David, John W. Whitmore, and Wilmer H. Funk. "Effect of Group Cohesiveness and Training upon Creative Thinking," *Journal of Applied Psychology* 44 (1960), 319–322.

Comadena, M. E. "Brainstorming Groups: Ambiguity Tolerance, Communication Apprehension, Task Attraction, and Individual Productivity," *Small Group Behavior* 15 (1984), 251–264.

Drescher, S., G. Burlingame, and A. Fuhriman. "Cohesion: An Odyssey in Empirical Understanding," *Small Group Behavior* 16 (1985), 3–30.

Festinger, Leon. "A Theory of Social Comparison Processes," *Human Relations* 7 (1954), 117–140.

Fisher, B. Aubrey. "Decision Emergence: Phases in Group Decision Making," *Speech Monographs* 37 (1970), 53–66.

———. *Small Group Decision Making: Communication and the Group Process* (New York: McGraw-Hill, 1974).

Fisher, Kimball. *Leading Self-Directed Work Teams: A Guide To Developing New Team Leadership Skills* (New York: McGraw-Hill, 1993).

Gaddy, C. D., et al. *Applied Behavioral Science for Plant Managers* (Columbia, MD: Corneswane, 1987).

Geneen, Harold, with Alvin Moscow. *Managing* (Garden City, NY: Doubleday, 1984).

Gouran, Dennis. "Variables Related to Consensus in Group Discussions of Questions of Policy," *Speech Monographs* 36 (1969), 387–391.

———. "Group Communication: Perspectives and Priorities for Future Research," *Quarterly Journal of Speech* 59 (1973), 22–29.

Gouran, Dennis S., Candace Brown, and David R. Henry. "Behavioral Correlates of Quality in Decision-Making Discussions," *Communication Monographs* 45 (1978), 51–63.

Grove, Theodore. "Attitude Convergence in Small Groups," *Journal of Communication* 15 (1965), 226–238.

Grubb, Henry Jefferson. "Social Cohesion as Determined by the Levels and Types of Involvement," *Social Behavior and Personality* 150 (1987), 87–89.

Gudykunst, William, and Mitchell R. Hammer. "The Influence of Social Identity and Intimacy of Interethnic Relationships on Uncertainty Reduction Processes," *Human Communication Research* 14 (1988), 569–607.

Guetzkow, Harold, and Herbert A. Simon. "The Impact of Certain Communication Nets upon Organization and Performance in Task-Oriented Groups," *Management Science* 1 (1955), 233–250.

Hare, A. Paul. *Handbook of Small Group Research* (New York: Free Press, 1962).

Hirokawa, Randy Y. "Group Communication and Problem-Solving Effectiveness: An Investigation of Group Phases," *Human Communication Research* 9 (1983), 291–305.

Homans, George C. *The Human Group* (San Diego, CA: Harcourt Brace Jovanovich, 1950).

Huse, Edgar, and Thomas G. Cummings. *Organization Development and Change,* 3rd ed. (St. Paul, MN: West, 1985).

Janis, Irving L. *Group Think,* 2d ed. (Boston: Houghton Mifflin, 1982).

Jarobe, Susan P. "A Comparison of Input-Output, Process-Output, and Input-Process-Output Models of Small Group Problem-Solving Effectiveness, *Communication Monographs* 55 (1988), 121–142.

Kelley, Harold H., and John W. Thibaut. "Group Problem Solving," In Gardner

Lindzey and Elliot Aronson, eds., *The Handbook of Social Psychology*, 2d ed., Vol. IV. *Group Psychology and Phenomena of Interaction* (Reading, MA: Addison-Wesley, 1969), pp. 1–101.

Kleinfeld, J. "Top Level Committees at AT&T." *Flint Journal* (January 12, 1979), 100.

Kline, John. "Indices of Orienting and Opinionated Statements in Problem-Solving Discussion," *Speech Monographs* 37 (1970), 282–286.

Larson, Carl. "Forms of Analysis and Small Group Problem Solving," *Speech Monographs* 36 (1969). 452–455.

Leavitt, Harold J. "Some Effects of Certain Communication Patterns on Group Performance," *J. of Abnormal and Social Psych.* 46 (1951), 38–50.

Ludmer-Gliebe, Susan. "We Gather Together . . . Constantly," *Ann Arbor News* (January 15, 1989), F1–F2.

McCroskey, James C. An *Introduction to Rhetorical Communication* (Englewood Cliffs, NJ: Prentice-Hall, 1968), p. 207.

McGrath, Joseph, and Irwin Altman. *Small Group Research* (New York: Holt, Rinehart and Winston, 1966).

Mohr, William L, and Harriet Mohr. *Quality Circles: Changing Images of People at Work* (Reading, MA: Addison-Wesley, 1983).

Mortensen, C. David. "The Status of Small Group Research," *Quarterly Journal of Speech* 56 (1970), 304–309.

Newcomb, Theodore M. *Personality and Social Change* (New York: Dryden, 1943).

———. "An Approach to the Study of Communicative Acts," *Psychological Review* 60 (1953), 393–404.

———. "Persistence and Regression of Changed Attitudes: Long Range Studies," *Journal of Social Issues* 19 (1963), 3–14.

Osborn, Alex F. *Applied Imagination* (New York: Scribner, 1957).

Pace, Roger C. "Communication Patterns in High and Low Consensus Discussion: A Descriptive Analysis," *The Southern Speech Communication Journal* 53 (1988), 184–202.

Parkinson, Cyril Northcote. *Parkinson's Law* (New York: Ballantine, 1964).

Phillips, Gerald. *Communication and the Small Group* (Indianapolis: Bobbs-Merrill, 1966).

Phillips, Ronald C. "Manage Differences before They Destroy Your Business," *Training and Development Journal* (September 1988), 66–71.

Raudsepp, Eugene. *More Creative Growth Games* (New York: Perigee, 1980).

Schachter, Stanley. "Deviation, Rejection and Communication," *Journal of Abnormal and Social Psychology* 46 (1951), 190–208.

Scheidel, Thomas, and Laura Crowell. "Idea Development in Small Discussion Groups," *Quarterly Journal of Speech* 50 (1964), 140–145.

Schein, Edgar H. "The Chinese Indoctrination Program for Prisoners of War," *Psychiatry* 19 (1956), 159–160.

Schutz, William. *FIRO: A Three-Dimensional Theory of Interpersonal Behavior* (New York: Holt, Rinehart and Winston, 1958).

Shaw, Marvin E. "Communication Networks," in Leonard Berkowitz, ed., *Advances in Experimental Social Psychology,* Vol. I (Orlando, FL: Academic Press, 1964), pp. 111–147.

——. *Group Dynamics: The Psychology of Small Group Behavior,* 3rd ed. (New York: McGraw-Hill, 1981).

Sherif, Muzafer. *The Psychology of Social Norms* (New York: Harper & Row, 1936).

——. *Social Interaction: Process and Products* (Chicago: Aldine, 1967).

Smith, Christi McGuffee, and Larry Powell. "The Use of Disparaging Humor by Group Leaders," *The Southern Speech Communication Journal* 531 (1988), 279–292.

Smith, Kenwyn K., and David N. Berg. "A Paradoxical Conception of Group Dynamics," *Human Relations* 40 (1987), 633–658.

Thelen, Herbert, and Watson Dickerman. "Stereotypes and the Growth of Groups," *Educational Leadership* 6 (1949), 309–316.

Tjosvold, Dean. "Putting Conflict to Work," *Training and Development Journal* (December 1988). 61–64.

Townsend, Robert. *Further Up the Organization* (New York: Knopf, 1985).

Tubbs, Stewart L. *A Systems Approach to Small Group Interaction,* 3rd ed. (New York: Random House, 1992).

Tuckman, Bruce. "Developmental Sequence in Small Groups," *Psychological Bulletin* 63 (1965), 384–399.

Wall, Bob, et al. *The Visionary Leader* (Rocklin, CA: Prima Publishing, 1992).

Wallach, Michael A., Nathan Kogan, and Daryl J. Bem. "Group Influence on Individual Risk-Taking," *Journal of Abnormal and Social Psychology* 65 (1962), 75–86.

Wellins, Richard S., et al. *Empowered Teams* (San Francisco: Jossey-Bass, 1991).

Wheeler, Ladd. *Interpersonal Influence* (Boston: Allyn and Bacon, 1970).

Wilson, Gerald L., and Michael S. Hanna. *Groups in Context: Leadership and Participation in Small Groups,* 3rd ed. (New York: McGraw-Hill, 1993).

Chapter 10 Public Communication

Abzug, Bella S. "A New Kind of Southern Strategy," in Waldo W. Braden, ed., *Representative American Speeches: 1971–1972* (New York: Wilson, 1972), pp. 37–48.

Alexander, Benjamin. "Reflections on Education and Our Society," *Vital Speeches of the Day* 55 (1989), 563–565.

Bettinghaus, Erwin P. *Persuasive Communication* (New York: Holt, Rinehart and Winston, 1968), pp. 148–183.

Boorstin, Daniel J. "Dissent, Dissension, and the News," in Wil A. Linkugel, R. R. Allen, and Richard L. Johannesen, eds., *Contemporary American Speeches,* 2d ed. (Belmont, CA: Wadsworth, 1969), pp. 203–211.

Bowers, John Waite. "Language Intensity, Social Introversion, and Attitude Change," *Speech Monographs* 30 (1963), 345–352.

Bowers, John Waite, and Michael M. Osborn. "Attitudinal Effects of Selected Types of Concluding Metaphors in Persuasive Speech," *Speech Monographs* 33 (1966), 147–155.

Bulwer, John. *Chirologia . . . Chironomia*, 1644.

Burke, Richard E. *The Senator: My Ten Years With Ted Kennedy* (New York: St. Martin's Press, 1992).

Burke, Yvonne B. "Aspirations . . . Unrequited," in Waldo W. Braden, ed., *Representative American Speeches: 1974–1975* (New York: Wilson, 1975), pp. 143–147.

Carter, Jimmy. "Address Accepting Democratic Nomination for Presidency," *The New York Times* (July 16, 1976), A10.

Clevenger, Theodore, Jr. *Audience Analysis* (Indianapolis: Bobbs-Merrill, 1966).

Cobin, Martin. "Response to Eye Contact," *Quarterly Journal of Speech* 48 (1962), 415–418.

Collins, Rebecca, et al. "The Vividness Effect: Elusive or Illusory?" *Journal of Experimental Social Psychology* 24 (1988), 1–18.

Dabbs, J. M., Jr., and H. Leventhal. "Effects of Varying the Recommendations of a Fear-Arousing Communication," *Journal of Personality and Social Psychology* 4 (1966), 525–531.

Deutsch, Babette. *Poetry Handbook: A Dictionary of Terms* (New York: Funk & Wagnalls, 1957).

Dickson, Carolyn. "You Can't Write a Speech," *Training and Development Journal* (April 1987), 70–72.

Eakins, Barbara J. "The Relationship of Intonation to Attitude Change, Retention, and Attitude toward Source," paper delivered at the annual convention of the Speech Association of America, New York, December 1969.

Franchetti, Jack, and George McCartney. "How to Wow'em When You Speak," *Changing Times* 42 (1988), 29–32.

Gardner, John W. "People Power," in Waldo W. Braden, ed., *Representative American Speeches: 1974–1975* (New York: Wilson, 1975), pp. 158–167.

Gruner, C. R. "An Experimental Study of Satire as Persuasion," *Speech Monographs* 32 (1965), 149–153.

——. "The Effect of Humor in Dull and Interesting Informative Speeches," *Central States Speech Journal* 21 (1970), 160–166.

——. "Advice to the Beginning Speaker on Using Humor—What Research Tells Us," *Communication Education* 34 (1985), 142–147.

Haiman, Franklyn S. "The Rhetoric of 1968: A Farewell to Rational Discourse," in Wil Linkugel, R. R. Allen, and Richard L. Johannesen, eds., *Contemporary American Speeches,* 2d ed. (Belmont, CA: Wadsworth, 1969), pp. 153–167.

Hart, Roderick, Gustav Friedrich, and William Brooks. *Public Communication* (New York: Harper & Row, 1975).

Hasling, John. *The Audience, The Message, the Speaker,* 5th ed. (New York: McGraw-Hill, 1993).

Hovland, Carl, Irving Janis, and Harold Kelley. *Communication Persuasion* (New Haven, CT: Yale University Press, 1953).

Iacocca, Lee. "The Will To Take Leadership," *Vital Speeches of the Day 55* (1989), 454–458.

Janis, Irving, and Seymour Feshback. "Effect of Fear-Arousing Communications," *Journal of Abnormal and Social Psychology* 48 (1953), 78–92.

Janis, Irving, and Peter Field. "Sex Differences and Personality Factors Related to Persuasibility," in Carl Hovland and Irving Janis, eds., *Personality and Persuasibility* (New Haven, CT: Yale University Press, 1959), pp. 55–68.

Karlins, M., and H. Abelson. *Persuasion: How Opinions and Attitudes Are Changed,* 2d ed. (New York: Springer, 1970).

Kelman, H., and C. Hovland. "'Reinstatement' of the Communication in Delayed Measurement of Opinion Change," *Journal of Abnormal and Social Psychology* 48 (1953), 327–335.

Kennedy, Edward M. "La Raza and the Law," in Waldo W. Braden, ed., *Representative American Speeches: 1971–1972* (New York: Wilson, 1972), pp. 68–73.

King, Martin Luther, Jr. "I Have a Dream," in Wil Linkugel, R. R. Allen, and Richard L. Johannesen, eds., *Contemporary American Speeches,* 2d ed. (Belmont, CA: Wadsworth, 1969), pp. 290–294.

Linton, Harriet, and Elaine Graham. "Personality Correlates of Persuasibility," in Carl Hovland and Irving Janis, eds., *Personality and Persuasibility* (New Haven, CT: Yale University Press, 1959), p. 96.

Lucas, Stephen E. *The Art of Public Speaking,* 4th ed. (New York: McGraw-Hill, 1992).

Luchins, Abraham S., and Edith H. Luchins. "The Effects of Order of Presentation of Information and Explanatory Models," *Journal of Social Psychology* 80 (1970), 63–70.

Lull, P. C. "The Effectiveness of Humor in Persuasive Speeches," *Speech Monographs* 7 (1970), 26–40.

Malandro, L. A., and Larry Barker. *Nonverbal Communication* (Reading, MA: Addison-Wesley, 1982).

McCroskey, James C. "Scales for the Measurement of Ethos," *Speech Monographs* 30 (1966), 65–72.

———. "A Summary of Experimental Research on the Effects of Evidence in Persuasive Communication," *Quarterly Journal of Speech* 55 (1969), 169–176.

———. *An Introduction to Rhetorical Communication,* 3rd ed. (Englewood, Cliffs, NJ: Prentice-Hall, 1978).

McCroskey, James C., and W. Arnold. Unpublished study reported in James C. McCroskey, *An Introduction to Rhetorical Communication* (Englewood Cliffs, NJ: Prentice-Hall, 1968), p. 207.

McCroskey, James C., and R. Samuel Mehrley. "The Effects of Organization and Nonfluency on Attitude Change and Source Credibility," *Speech Monographs* 36 (1969), 13–21.

McEwen, William J., and B. S. Greenberg. "The Effects of Message Intensity on Receiver Evaluations of Source, Message, and Topic," *Journal of Communication* 20 (1970), 340–350.

McGuire, William J. "Personality and Susceptibility to Social Influence," in E. F. Borgatta and W. W. Lambert, eds., *Handbook of Personality Theory and Research* (Chicago: Rand McNally, 1968), pp. 1130–1187.

———. "The Nature of Attitude Change," in Gardner Lindzey and Elliot Aronson, eds., *The Handbook of Social Psychology,* 2d ed., Vol. III; *The Individual in a Social Context* (Reading, MA: Addison-Wesley, 1969), pp. 136–314.

———. "Attitudes and Attitude Changes" in Gardner Lindzey and Elliot Aronson, eds., *The Handbook of Social Psychology,* 3rd ed., Vol. II (New York: Random House, 1985), pp. 233–346.

Miller, Gerald R., and Murray A. Hewgill. "Some Recent Research on Fear-Arousing Message Appeals," *Speech Monographs* 33 (1966), 377–391.

Miller, Merle. *Plain Speaking: An Oral Biography of Harry S. Truman* (New York: Berkley Publishing, 1973).

Miller, N., and C. T. Campbell. "Recency and Primacy in Persuasion as a Function of the Timing of Speeches and Measurements," *Journal of Abnormal and Social Psychology* 59 (1959), 1–9.

Montgomery, C. L., and Michael Burgoon. "An Experimental Study of the Interactive Effects of Sex and Androgyny on Attitude Change," *Communication Monographs* 44 (1977), 130–135.

Noonan, Peggy. *What I Saw at the Revolution: A Political Life in the Reagan Era* (New York: Random House, 1990).

Pearson, Judy. *Gender and Communication* (Dubuque, IA: Brown, 1985).

Petrie, C. "Informative Speaking: A Summary and Bibliography of Related Research," *Speech Monographs* 20 (1963), 79–91.

Pratkanis, Anthony R., et al. "In Search of Reliable Persuasion Effects: The Sleeper Effect Is Dead, Long Live the Sleeper Effect," *Journal of Personality and Social Psychology* 54 (1988), 203–218.

Reagan, Maureen. *First Father, First Daughter: A Memoir* (Boston: Little, Brown, 1989).

Reagan, Ronald. "We The People," *Vital Speeches of the Day* 55 (1989), 10–13.

Riggio, Ronald E., et al. "Social Skills and Deception Ability," *Personality and Social Psychology Bulletin* 13 (1987), 568–577.

Rosenfeld, Lawrence, and Vickie Christie. "Sex and Persuasibility Revisited," *Western Speech* 38 (1974), 244–253.

Safire, William. *Lend Me Your Ears: Great Speeches in History* (New York: W. W. Norton, 1992).

Sharp, H., and T. McClung. "Effects of Organization on the Speaker's Ethos," *Speech Monographs* 33 (1966), 182–183.

Smith, Mary J. *Persuasion and Human Action: A Review and Critique of Social Influence Theories* (Belmont, CA: Wadsworth, 1982).

Smith, Raymond G. "An Experimental Study of the Effects of Speech Organization upon Attitudes of College Students," *Speech Monographs* 17 (1951).

Spitzberg, B. H., and W. R. Cupach. *Interpersonal Communication Competence* (Beverly Hills, CA: Sage, 1984).

Strunk, William, Jr., and E. B. White. *The Elements of Style* (New York: Macmillan, 1959).

Tedford, Thomas. *Public Speaking in a Free Society* (New York: McGraw-Hill, 1991).

Thistlethwaite, D. L., H. De Haan, and J. Kamenetzky. "The Effect of 'Directive' and 'Non-Directive' Communication Procedures on Attitudes," *Journal of Abnormal and Social Psychology* 51 (1955), 107–118.

Tubbs, Stewart. "Explicit versus Implicit Conclusions and Audience Commitment, *Speech Monographs* 35 (1968), 14–19.

Tuthill, D. M., and D. R. Forsyth. "Sex Differences in Opinion Conformity and Dissent," *Journal of Social Psychology* 116 (1982), 205–210.

Walster, E., E. Aronson, and D. Abrahams. "On Increasing the Persuasiveness of a Low Prestige Communicator," *Journal of Experimental and Social Psychology* 2 (1966), 325–342.

Chapter 11 Organizational Communication

Allport, Gordon, and Leo Postman. *The Psychology of Rumor* (New York: Holt, 1947).

Alpander, Guveng. "Planning Management Training Programs for Organizational Development," *Personnel Journal* 33 (January 1974), 15–25.

Barnard, Chester I. *The Functions of the Executive* (Cambridge, MA: Harvard University Press, 1938).

Bell, Daniel. "Welcome to the Post-Industrial Society" *Physics Today* (February 1976), 46–49.

Boyatzis, R. E. *The Competent Manager* (New York: Wiley, 1982).

Cetron, Marvin J., and Owen Davies. *Crystal Globe: The Haves and Have-Nots of the New World Order* (New York: St. Martin's Press, 1991).

Chorus, A. "The Basic Law of Rumor," *Journal of Abnormal and Social Psychology* 48 (1953), 313–314.

Conboy, William A. *Working Together . . . Communication in a Healthy Organization* (Columbus, OH: Merrill, 1976).

Conrad, C. *Strategic Organizational Communication: Cultures, Situations, and Adaption* (New York: Holt, Rinehart and Winston, 1985).

Curtin, Joseph L. "Putting Self-Esteem First," *Training and Development Journal* (October 1988), 41–44.

Dahle, Thomas. "An Objective and Comparative Study of Five Methods of Transmitting Information to Business and Industrial Employees," *Speech Monographs* 21 (1954), 21–28.

Davis, Keith. "A Method of Studying Communication Patterns in Organizations," *Personnel Psychology* 6 (1953*a*), 301–312.

———. "Management Communication and the Grapevine," *Harvard Business Review* 31 (1953*b*), 43–49.

———. *Human Behavior at Work* (New York: McGraw-Hill, 1972).

Dennis, Harry S. "The Construction of a 'Managerial Communication Climate' Inventory for Use in Complex Organizations," paper presented at the annual convention of the International Communication Association, New Orleans, April 1975.

Dennis, Harry S., Gary M. Richetto, and John M. Wiemann. "Articulating the Need for an Effective Internal Communication System: New Empirical Evidence for the Communication Specialist," paper presented at the annual convention of the International Communication Association, New Orleans, April 1974.

Downs, Cal, Michael Hazen, William Medley, and James Quiggins. "A Theoretical and Empirical Analysis of Communication Satisfaction," paper presented at the annual convention of the International Communication Association, New Orleans, April 1974.

Fisher, Kimball. *Leading Self-Directed Work Teams: A Guide to Developing New Team Leadership Skills* (New York: McGraw-Hill, 1993).

French, John R. P., and Bertram Raven. "The Bases of Social Power," in Dorwin Cartwright and Alvin Zander, eds., *Group Dynamics: Research and Theory* (Evanston, IL: Row, Peterson, 1962), pp. 607–623.

Gemmill, Gary. "Managing Upward Communication," *Personnel Journal* 49 (1970), 107–110.

Geneen, Harold, with Alvin Moscow. *Managing* (Garden City, NY: Doubleday, 1984).

General Electric Company. *The Effective Manufacturing Foreman—An Observational Study of the Job Activities of Effective and Ineffective Foremen* (New York: G. E. Public & Employee Relations Research Service, 1957).

German, Carol J., and William R. Rath. "Making Technical Communication a Real-World Experience," *Journal of Technical Writing and Communication* 14 (1987), 335–346.

Gibb, Cecil. "Leadership," in Gardner Lindzey and Elliot Aronson, eds., *Handbook of Social Psychology,* 2d ed., Vol. IV; *Group Psychology and Phenomena of Interaction* (Reading, MA: Addison-Wesley, 1968), pp. 205–282.

Goldhaber, Gerald M. *Organizational Communication* (Dubuque, IA: Brown, 1990).

Gordon, William I., and Dominic A. Infante. "Test of a Communication Model of Organization Commitment," *Communication Quarterly* 39 (1991), 144–152.

Hain, Tony, and Stewart L. Tubbs. "Organizational Development: The Role of Communication in Diagnosis, Change and Evaluation," paper presented at the annual convention of the International Communication Association, New Orleans, April 1974.

Hain, Tony, and Robin Widgery. "Organizational Diagnosis: The Significant Role of Communication." paper presented at the annual convention of the International Communication Association. Montreal, April 1973.

Halberstam, David. *The Reckoning* (New York: Morrow, 1986).

Hawes, Leonard. "Information Overload and Organization of 1984," *Western Speech* 35 (1971), 191–198.

Hendrickson, Lorraine, and John Psarouthakis. *Managing the Growing Firm* (Englewood Cliffs, NJ: Prentice-Hall, 1992).

Hoyt, D. P., and Paul Mushinsky. "Occupational Success and College Experiences of Engineering Graduates, *Engineering Education* 63 (May 1973), 622–623.

Iacocca, Lee, with William Novak. *Iacocca: An Autobiography* (New York: Bantam, 1984).

IBM chart distributed at a voice mail meeting, Eastern Michigan University, April 22, 1992.

Jain, Harish. "Supervisory Communication and Performance in Urban Hospitals," *Journal of Communication* 23 (1973), 103–117.

Jennings, Eugene E. *Routes to the Executive Suite* (New York: McGraw-Hill, 1971).

Keller, Maryann. *Rude Awakening: The Rise, Fall, and Struggle for Recovery of General Motors* (New York: Morrow, 1989).

Krone, Kathleen J. "A Comparison of Organizational, Structural, and Relationship Effects on Subordinates' Upward Influence Choices," *Communication Quarterly* 40 (1992), 1–13.

Lambert, Jack. *The Work Force Challenges of the 21st Century*. Washington, DC: National Association of Manufacturers, 1992.

Lawrence, Paul R., and Jay W. Lorsch. *Developing Organizations: Diagnosis and Action* (Reading, MA: Addison-Wesley, 1969).

Lee, Albert. *Call Me Roger* (Chicago: Conte Books, 1988).

Liden, Robert C., and Terence R. Mitchell. "In Behaviors in Organization Settings," *The Journal of Management Review* 13 (1988), 572–578.

Likert, Rensis. *New Patterns of Management* (New York: McGraw-Hill, 1961).

———. *The Human Organization* (New York: McGraw-Hill, 1967).

Lull, Paul, Frank Funk, and Darrell Piersol. "What Communication Means to the Corporation President," *Advanced Management* 20 (1955), 17–20.

Martin, Thomas. *Malice in Blunderland* (New York: McGraw-Hill, 1973).

McCormack, Mark. *What They Don't Teach You at Harvard Business School: Notes from a Street Smart Executive* (New York: Bantam, 1984).

Miller, J. G. "Psychological Aspects of Communication Overload," in R. W. Waggoner and D. J. Carek, eds., *International Psychiatric Clinics: Communication in Clinical Practice* (Boston, 1964), pp. 201–224.

Molloy, John T. "Earring Will Snag on Corporate Ladder," *Detroit Free Press* (January 22, 1989), 3C.

Mushinsky, Paul. "Performance Ratings of Engineers: Do Graduates Fit the Bill?" *Engineering Education* 65 (1974), 187–188.

Naisbitt, John. *Megatrends: Ten New Directions Transforming Our Lives* (New York: Warner, 1982).

Ouchi, William G. *Theory Z: How American Business Can Meet the Japanese Challenge* (Reading, MA: Addison-Wesley, 1981).

Pascale, Richard, and Anthony Athos. *The Art of Japanese Management: Applications for American Executives* (New York: Simon and Schuster, 1981).

Pennsylvania State University survey, personal correspondence, April 6, 1992.

Petelle, John L., Gerald Z. Slaughter, and Jerry D. Jorgensen. "New Explorations in Organizational Relationships: An Expectancy Model of Human Symbolic Activity," *Southern Journal of Speech Communication* 53 (1988), 293–306.

Pfeffer, Jeffrey. *Power in Organizations* (Marsfield, MA: Pitman, 1981).

Redding, Charles. *Communication within the Organization* (New York: Industrial Communication Council, 1972).

Reich, Theodore. *The Greening of America* (New York: Random House, 1970).

Rice, Ronald E. "Computer Mediated Communication and Organizational Innovations," *Journal of Communication* 37 (1987), 64–94.

Roach, K. David. "University Department Chairs' Use of Compliance-Gaining Strategies," *Communication Quarterly* 39 (1991), 75–88.

Rosnow, Ralph. "Rumor as Communication: A Contextualist Approach," *Journal of Communication* 38 (1988), 12–28.

Rothschild, Michael. *Bionomics: Economy as Ecosystem* (New York: Henry Holt, 1992).

Ruch, Richard S., and Ronald Goodman. *Image at the Top: Crisis and Renaissance in Corporate Leadership* (New York: Free Press, 1983).

Schein, Edgar H. *Organizational Psychology,* 2d ed. (Englewood Cliff, NJ: Prentice-Hall, 1970).

––––––. *Career Dynamics: Matching Individual and Organizational Needs* (Reading, MA: Addison-Wesley, 1978).

Scholz, William. *Communication in the Business Organization* (Englewood Cliffs, NJ: Prentice-Hall, 1962).

Sielaff, Theodore J. "Modification of Work Behavior," *Personnel Journal* 53 (1974), 513–517.

Smith, Ronald L., Gary M. Richetto, and Joseph P. Zima. "Organizational Behavior: An Approach to Human Communication," in Richard W. Budd and Brent D. Ruben, eds., *Approaches to Human Communication* (New York: Spartan Books, 1972).

Solomon, Jolie. "Firms Address Workers' Cultural Variety," *The Wall Street Journal* (February 10, 1989), B1.

Swift, Marvin H. "Clear Writing Means Clear Thinking Means . . . ," *Harvard Business Review* (January–February 1973), 59–62.

Tubbs, Stewart L. "The Importance of Watzlawick's Content and Relationship Aspects of Communication in the Classroom," paper presented at the annual convention of the Central States Speech Association, Milwaukee, April 1974.

Tubbs, Stewart L., and Tony Hain. "A Factor Analysis of Teacher Evaluations in Communication Courses," paper presented at the annual convention of the Central States Speech Association, Kansas City, April 1975.

Tubbs, Stewart L., Charles W. Oyerly, and John A. Jeffrey. *An Analysis of Communication at Packard Electric Division* (Detroit: General Motors Corporation, 1973).

Chapter 12   Mass Communication

Avery, Robert K., and Thomas A. McCain. "Interpersonal and Mediated Encounters," in Gary Gumpert and Robret Cathcart, eds., *Inter/Media: Interpersonal Communication in a Media World,* 2d ed. (New York: Oxford University Press, 1982).

Bittner, John R. *Fundamentals of Communication* (Englewood Cliffs, NJ: Prentice-Hall, 1985).

Buck, Ross. "Nonverbal Communication: Spontaneous and Symbolic Aspects," *American Behavioral Scientist* 31 (1988), 341–354.

Buxton, Rodney A. "The Late-Night Talk Show: Humor in Fringe Television," *Southern Speech Journal* 52 (1987), 377–389.

Cantor, Joanne, and Cynthia Hoffman. "Factors Affecting Children's Enjoyment of a Frightening Film Sequence," *Communication Monographs* 58 (1991), 41–59.

Cantor, Joanne, and Becky L. Omdahl. "Effects of Fictional Media Depictions of Realistic Threats on Children's Emotional Responses, Expectations, Worries, and Liking for Related Activities," *Communication Monographs* 58 (1991), 384–401.

Carter, Bill. "A Message on Drinking Is Seen and Heard," *The New York Times* (September 11, 1989), D11.

De Fleur, Melvin. "Occupational Roles as Portrayed on Television," *Public Opinion Quarterly* 28 (1964), 57–74.

Dennis, Everette. "American Media and American Values," in *Vital Speeches of the Day* 54, no. 11 (March 15, 1988), 349–352.

Deutschmann, Paul J., and Wayne A. Danielson. "Diffusion of Knowledge of the Major News Story," *Journalism Quarterly* 37 (1960), 345–355.

Dominick, Joseph R. *The Dynamics of Mass Communication,* 4th ed. (New York: McGraw-Hill, 1993).

Dominick, Joseph R., and Gail E. Rauch. "The Image of Women in Network Television Commercials," *Journal of Broadcasting* 16 (1972), 259–265.

Ellis, Donald G., and Blake Armstrong. "Class, Gender, and Code on Prime-Time Television," *Communication Quarterly* 37 (1989), 157–169.

Finnegan, Ruth. "Communication and Technology," *Language & Communication* 9, no. 2/3 (1989), 107–127.

Flay, Brian R. "Mass Media and Smoking Cessation: A Critical Review," *American Journal of Public Health* 77 (1987), 153–158.

Forester, Tom. *High-Tech Society: The Story of Information Technology Revolution* (Cambridge, MA: MIT Press, 1987).

Franzwa, Helen H. "Working Women in Fact and Fiction," *Journal of Communication* 24 (1974), 104–109.

Gagnard, Alice. "A Sociocultural Close-Up: Body Image in Advertising," in Pamela J. Creedon, ed., *Women in Mass Communication* (Newbury Park, CA: Sage, 1989), pp. 261–262.

Garnham, Nicholas. "Communication Technology and Policy," in Michael Gurevitch and Mark R. Levy, eds., *Mass Communication Review Yearbook,* Vol. 5 (Beverly Hills, CA: Sage, 1985).

Gates, Henry Louis, Jr. "TV's Black World Turns—But Stays Unreal," *The New York Times* (November 12, 1989), sec. 2, pp. 1, 40.

Gergen, David R. "The Politics of Sound Bites," *U.S. News & World Report* (September 12, 1988), 76.

Gergen, Kenneth. *The Saturated Self: Dilemmas of Identity in Contemporary Life* (New York: Basic Books, 1991).

Greenberg, Bradley S. "Person-to-Person Communication in the Diffusion of News Events," *Journalism Quarterly* 41 (1964), 489–494.

———. "Diffusion of News about the Kennedy Assassination," in Bradley S. Greenberg and Edwin B. Parker, eds., *The Kennedy Assassination and the American Public* (Stanford, CA: Stanford University Press, 1965), pp. 89–98.

Gumpert, Gary, and Robert Cathcart. "Media Grammars, Generations, and Media Gaps," *Critical Studies in Mass Communication* 2 (1985), 23–35.

Hastorf, Albert H., and Hadley Cantril. "They Saw a Game: A Case Study," *Journal of Abnormal and Social Psychology* 49 (1954), 129–134.

Henry, William A. "History as It Happens," *Time* (January 6, 1992), 24–27.

Katz, Elihu, and Jacob J. Feldman. "The Debates in the Light of Research: A Survey of Surveys," in Sidney Kraus, ed., *The Great Debates* (Bloomington: Indiana University Press, 1962), pp. 173–223.

Katz, Elihu, and Paul Lazarsfeld. *Personal Influence: The Part Played by People in the Flow of Mass Communications* (Glencoe, IL: Free Press, 1964).

Keen, Peter G. W. "Telecommunications and Choice," *Communication Research* 14 (1987), 588–606.

Kraus, Sidney, ed. *The Great Debates: Carter vs. Ford, 1976* (Bloomington: Indiana University Press, 1979).

Kunkel, Dale, and Donald Roberts. "Young Minds and Marketplace Values," *Journal of Social Issues* 47 (1991), 57–72.

Lazarsfeld, Paul, Bernard Berelson, and H. Gaudet. *The People's Choice* (New York: Columbia University Press, 1968).

Lazier-Smith, Linda. "Advertising: Women's Place and Image," in Pamela J. Creedon, ed., *Women in Mass Communication* (Newbury Park, CA: Sage, 1989), pp. 247–260.

Lichtenstein, A., and L. B. Rosenfeld. "Normative Expectations and Individual Decisions concerning Media Gratification Choices," *Communication Research* 11 (1984), 393–413.

Liebert, Robert M., and Joyce Sprafkin. *The Early Window: Effects of Television on Children and Youth,* 3rd ed. (New York: Pergamon Press, 1988).

MacArthur, John. *Second Front: Censorship and Propaganda in the Gulf War* (New York: Hill and Wang, 1992).

McGuire, William. "Attitudes and Attitude Change," in Gardner Lindzey and Elliot Aronson, eds., *Handbook of Social Psychology,* Vol. II, 3rd ed. (New York: Random House, 1985), pp. 233–346.

Markoff, John. "Here Comes the Fiber-Optic Home," *The New York Times* (November 5, 1989), sec. 3, pp. 1, 15.

Morgan, Michael, and James Shanahan. "Do VCRs Change the TV Picture?" *American Behavioral Scientist* 35 (1991), 122–135.

Redding, W. Charles. "The Enemies of Responsible Communication," in *Vital Speeches of the Day* 54, no. 22 (September 1, 1988), 702–704.

Robb, David. "FCC Reports Minority B'Cast Jobs Increasing," *Variety* 345 (October 14, 1991), 73.

Rogers, Everett M. *Diffusion of Innovations,* 3rd ed. (New York: Free Press, 1983).

Rogers, Michael. "The Literary Circuitry," *Newsweek* (June 29, 1992), 66–67.

Rubin, Alan M., and Rebecca B. Rubin. "Interface of Personal and Mediated Communication: A Research Agenda," *Critical Studies in Mass Communication* 2 (1985), 36–53.

Rubin, Rebecca B., Elizabeth M. Perse, and Carole A. Barbato. "Conceptualization and Measurement of Interpersonal Communication Motives," *Human Communication Research* 14 (1988), 602–628.

Safire, William. "Sound Bite, Define Yourself," *The New York Times Magazine* (November 13, 1988), 24 et passim.

Schramm, Wilbur. *Men, Messages, and Media: A Look at Human Communication* (New York: Harper & Row, 1973).

Schramm, Wilbur, Jack Lyle, and Edwin Parker. *Television in the Lives of Our Children* (Stanford, CA: Stanford University Press, 1961).

Schramm, Wilbur, and Donald F. Roberts, eds. *The Process and Effects of Mass Communications,* rev. ed. (Urbana: University of Illinois Press, 1971).

Schwartz, John. "The Revolution," *Newsweek* (April 6, 1992), 42–48.

Sheatsley, Paul B., and Jacob J. Feldman. "A National Survey of Public Reactions and Behaviors," in Bradley S. Greenberg and Edwin Parker, eds., *The Kennedy Assassination and the American Public* (Stanford, CA: Stanford University Press, 1965), pp. 149–177.

Sheridan, Patrick J. "Study to Show Drop in Minority Ownership," *Broadcasting* (September 23, 1991), 50.

Siegel, Alberta. "The Effects of Media Violence on Social Learning," in Wilbur Schramm and Donald F. Roberts, eds., *The Process and Effects of Mass Communication,* rev. ed. (Urbana: University of Illinois Press, 1971), pp. 612–636.

———. "Communicating with the Next Generation," *Journal of Communication* 25 (1975), 14–24.

Smith, Conrad, Eric S. Fredin, and Carroll Ann Ferguson Nardone. "Television Sex Discrimination in the TV Newsroom," in Pamela J. Creedon, ed., *Women in Mass Communication* (Newbury Park, CA: Sage, 1989), pp. 227–246.

Snow, Robert P. "Interaction with Mass Media: The Importance of Rhythm and Tempo," *Communication Quarterly* 35 (Summer 1987), 225–237.

Spitzer, Stephan P., and Nancy S. Spitzer. "Diffusion of News of Kennedy and Oswald Deaths," in Bradley S. Greenberg and Edwin B. Parker, eds., *The Kennedy Assassination and the American Public* (Stanford, CA: Stanford University Press, 1965), pp. 99–111.

Surgeon General's Scientific Advisory Committee on Television and Social Behavior. *Television and Growing Up: The Impact of Televised Violence* (Washington, DC: Government Printing Office, 1972).

U.S. Department of Health and Human Services. *Television and Behavior: Ten Years of Scientific Progress and Implications for the Eighties.* Vol. I. *Summary Report* (Washington, DC: Government Printing Office, 1982).

Wayne, Stephen J. *The Road to the White House 1992: The Politics of Presidential Elections* (New York: St. Martin's, 1992).

Williams, Frederick. *The New Communications,* 2d ed. (Belmont, CA: Wadsworth, 1989).

———. *Infrastructure for the Information Age* (New York: Free Press, 1991).

Wright, Charles R. *Mass Communication: A Sociological Perspective,* 3rd ed. (New York: Random House, 1986).

Wright, John C., Dale Kunkel, Marites Pinon, and Aletha C. Huston. "How Children Reacted to Televised Coverage of the Space Shuttle Disaster," *Journal of Communication* 39 (Spring 1989), 27–45.

Zelizer, Barbie. "CNN, the Gulf War, and Journalistic Practice," *Journal of Communication* 42 (1992), 66–82.

Ziegler, Dhyana, and Alisa White. "Women and Minorities on Network Television News," *Journal of Broadcasting and Electronic Media* 34 (1990), 215–223.

Zoglin, Richard. "How a Handful of News Executives Make Decisions Felt Round the World," *Time* (January 6, 1992), 30–32.

Chapter 13   Intercultural Communication

Althen, Gary. "The Americans Have to Say Everything," *Communication Quarterly* 40 (1992), 413–421.

Argyle, M., et al. "Cross-cultural Variations in Relationship Rules," *International Journal of Psychology* 21 (1986), 287–315.

Bateson, Mary Catherine. *Composing a Life* (New York: Plume, Penguin, 1990).

Brown, Roger. *Social Psychology,* 2d ed. (New York: Free Press, 1986).

Carlson, Jerry S., and Keith F. Widaman. "The Effects of Study Abroad during College on Attitudes toward Other Cultures," *International Journal of Intercultural Relations* 12 (1988), 1–17.

Carroll, Raymonde. *Cultural Misunderstandings: The French-American Experience,* trans. by Carol Volk (Chicago: University of Chicago Press, 1988).

Cherry, Colin. *World Communication: Threat or Promise?* (New York: Wiley, 1971).

Coleman, John R. *Blue Collar Journal: A College President's Sabbatical.* (Philadelphia: Lippincott, 1974).

Conway, Jill Ker. *The Road from Coorain* (New York: Vintage, 1990).

Cushman, D. P., and D. D. Cahn. *Communication in Interpersonal Relationships* (Albany, NY: SUNY Press, 1985).

DiMartino, Emily. "Effect of Culture on Women's Interpretations of Moral and Conventional Dilemmas," *Journal of Social Psychology* 131 (1991), 313–319.

Dominick, Joseph R. *The Dynamics of Mass Communication,* 4th ed. (New York: McGraw-Hill, 1993).

Douglis, Carole. "The Beat Goes On," *Psychology Today* 21 (November 1987), 36–42.

Driessen, Henk. "Gestured Masculinity: Body and Sociability in Rural Andalusia," in Jan Bremmer and Herman Roodenburg, eds., *A Cultural History of Gesture* (Ithaca, NY: Cornell University Press, 1992), pp. 237–252.

Ekman, P., W. V. Friesen, and J. Bear. "The International Language of Gestures," *Psychology Today* 18 (May 1984), 64–69.

Foner, Nancy, ed. *New Immigrants in New York* (New York: Columbia University Press, 1987).

Gergen, Kenneth J. *The Saturated Self: Dilemmas of Identity in Contemporary Life* (New York: Basic Books, 1991).

Goldsmith, Charles. "Look See! Anyone Do Read This And It Will Make You Laughable," *The Wall Street Journal* (November 11, 1992), B1.

Goodman, Ellen. "Americans Are Losing Regional Accents," Washington Post Writer's Group, *The Lexington Herald* (December 15, 1981).

Gudykunst, William B., and Young Yun Kim. *Communicating with Strangers: An Approach to Intercultural Communication,* 2d ed. (New York: McGraw-Hill, 1992).

Gudykunst, William B., and Stella Ting-Toomey. "Culture and Affective Communication," *American Behavioral Scientist* 31 (1988*a*), 384–400.

Gudykunst, William B., and Stella Ting-Toomey. *Culture and Interpersonal Communication* (Newbury Park, CA: Sage, 1988*b*).

Gudykunst, William B., and Stella Ting-Toomey. "Nonverbal Dimensions and Context-Regulation," in William B. Gudykunst and Young Yun Kim, eds., *Readings on Communicating with Strangers* (New York: McGraw-Hill, 1992), pp. 273–284.

Gumpert, Gary, and Robert Cathcart. "Media Stereotyping: Images of the Foreigner," in Larry A. Samovar and Richard E. Porter, eds., *Intercultural Communication: A Reader.* 4th ed. (Belmont, CA: Wadsworth, 1984), pp. 348–354.

Gumperz, John J. *Language in Social Groups* (Stanford, CA: Stanford University Press, 1971).

Hall, Edward T. *The Silent Language* (New York: Doubleday, 1959).

———. *Beyond Culture* (Garden City, NY: Doubleday, 1976).

Hall, Edward T., and William Foote Whyte. "Intercultural Communication," in

C. David Mortensen, ed., *Basic Readings in Communication Theory,* 2d ed. (New York: Harper & Row, 1979), pp. 403–419.

Hamilton, David L., Steven J. Sherman, and Catherine M. Ruyolo. "Stereotype-Based Expectancies," in William B. Gudykunst and Young Yun Kim, eds., *Readings on Communicating with Strangers* (New York: McGraw-Hill, 1992), pp. 135–158.

Healy, Barth. "Mosaic vs. Melting Pot," *The New York Times Book Review* (June 19, 1988), 22.

Hoagland, Edward. *African Calliope* (New York: Random House, 1979).

Katchian, Sonia. "Doing Business in Japan," *Barnard Alumnae Magazine* (Spring 1985), 8–9.

Kaplan, Robert. "Tales from the Bazaar," *The Atlantic* 270 (August 1992), 37–61.

Koester, J. "Communication and the Intercultural Reentry: A Course Proposal," *Communication Education* 33 (1984), 251–256.

Krauthammer Charles. "Do We Really Need a New Enemy?" *Time* 139 (March 23, 1992), 28.

Lifton, Robert Jay. "Can Images of Bosnia's Victims Change the World?" *The New York Times* (August 23, 1992), 26.

LoCastro, Virginia. "Aizuchi: A Japanese Conversational Routine," in Larry E. Smith, ed., *Discourse across Cultures: Strategies in World Englishes* (New York: Prentice-Hall, 1987), pp. 101–113.

Mahmoudi, Kooros M. "Refugee Cross-Cultural Adjustment: Tibetans in India," *International Journal of Intercultural Relations* 16 (1992), 17–32.

Mukherjee, Bharati. *The Middleman and Other Stories* (New York: Grove, 1988).

Ouchi, W. *Theory Z* (Reading, MA: Addison-Wesley, 1981).

Rohrlich, B. F. "Dual-Culture Marriage," *International Journal of Intercultural Relations* 12 (1988), 35–44.

Rohrlich, Beulah, and Judith N. Martin. "Host Country and Reentry Adjustment of Student Sojourners," *International Journal of Intercultural Relations* 15 (1991), 163–182.

Ross, Peter G., and Diane S. Krider. "Off the Plane and Into the Classroom," *International Journal of Intercultural Relations* 16 (1992), 277–293.

Samovar, Larry A., and Richard E. Porter. *Intercultural Communication: A Reader,* 6th ed. (Belmont, CA: Wadsworth, 1991*a*).

Samovar, Larry A., and Richard E. Porter. *Communication Between Cultures* (Belmont, CA: Wadsworth, 1991*b*).

Samovar, L., R. Porter, and N. Jain. *Understanding Intercultural Communication* (Belmont, CA: Wadsworth, 1984).

Sarbaugh, L. E. *Intercultural Communication* (Rochelle Park, NJ: Hayden, 1979).

Sillars, Alan L., Stephen F. Coletti, Doug Parry, and Mark A. Rogers. "Coding Verbal Conflict Tactics," *Human Communication Research* 9, no. 1 (Fall 1982), 83–95.

Sillars, Alan L., and Judith Weisberg. "Conflict as a Social Skill," in Michael E. Roloff and Gerald R. Miller, eds., *Interpersonal Processes: New Directions in Communication Research* (Newbury Park, CA: Sage, 1987), pp. 140–171.

Stephan, Cookie White, and Walter G. Stephan. "Reducing Intercultural Anxiety through Intercultural Contact," *International Journal of Intercultural Relations,* 16 (1992), 89–106.

Zikopoulos, Marianthi, ed. *Open Doors* (New York: Institute of International Education, 1992).

Chapter 14   Ethics and Communication

Abelson, Raziel. "History of Ethics," in Paul Edwards, ed., *The Encyclopedia of Philosophy,* vol. 3 (New York: Macmillan & The Free Press, 1967), pp.81–117.

Aristotle. *Introduction to Aristotle,* Richard McKeon, ed. (New York: Random House, Modern Library, 1947).

Augustine, St. *Enchiridion,* Henry Paolucci, ed. (Chicago: Regnery, 1961).

Barringer, Felicity. "*Newsday* Refuses to Reveal Source of Thomas Report," *The New York Times,* February 14, 1992, p. A20.

Bavelas, Janet Beavin, Alex Black, Nicole Chovil, and Jennifer Mullett. *Equivocal Communication* (Newbury Park, CA: Sage, 1990).

Bok, Sissela. *Lying: Moral Choice in Public and Private Life* (New York: Vintage, 1989a).

———. *Secrets: On the Ethics of Concealment and Revelation* (New York: Vintage, 1989b).

Bowie, Norman E. *Making Ethical Decisions* (New York: McGraw-Hill, 1985).

Burrough, Bryan. "Barbarians in Retreat," *Vanity Fair* (March 1993), 190–230.

Christians, Clifford G., Kim B. Rotzoll, and Mark Fackler. *Media Ethics,* 3rd ed. (New York: Longman, 1991).

Clampitt, Phillip G. *Communicating for Managerial Effectiveness* (Newbury Park, CA: Sage, 1991).

Driscoll, Lisa. "A Better Way to Handle Whistle-Blowers: Let Them Speak," *Business Week* (July 27, 1992), 34.

Ekman, Paul. *Telling Lies* (New York: Norton, 1985).

Glaberson, William. "Times Article Naming Rape Accuser Ignites Debate on Journalistic Values," *The New York Times* (April 16, 1991), A14.

Gorney, Carole. "Litigation Journalism Is a Scourge," *The New York Times* (February 15, 1993), A15.

Gray, Paul. "Lies, Lies, Lies," *Time* (October 5, 1992), 32–38.

Griffin, Em. *A First Look at Communication Theory* (New York: McGraw-Hill, 1991).

Kant, Immanuel. *Foundations of the Metaphysics of Morals,* Lewis White Beck, trans. (Indianapolis: Bobbs-Merrill, Library of Liberal Arts, 1959).

Knapp, Mark L., and Anita L. Vangelisti. *Interpersonal Communication and Human Interaction,* 2d ed. (Boston: Allyn and Bacon, 1992).

Lippard, Paula. "Ask Me No Questions, I'll Tell You No Lies," *Western Journal of Speech Communication* 52 (Winter 1988), 91–103.

Lyons, David. *Ethics and the Rule of Law* (New York: Cambridge University Press, 1984).

Mill, John Stuart. *Selected Writings of John Stuart Mill,* Maurice Cowling, ed. (New York: New American Library, 1968).

Opotow, Susan. "Moral Exclusion and Injustice," in William B. Gudykunst and Young Yun Kim, eds., *Readings on Communicating with Strangers* (New York: McGraw-Hill, 1992), pp. 420–434.

Rawls, John. *A Theory of Justice* (Cambridge, MA: Harvard University Press, 1971).

Ruby, Michael. "The Private Life of Arthur Ashe," *U.S. News & World Report* (April 20, 1992), 84.

Schuller, Robert H. *Life's Not Fair but God Is Good* (Nashville: Thomas Nelson, 1991).

Stanley, Alessandra. "Poet Told All: Therapist Provides the Record," *The New York Times* (July 15, 1991), A1.

Credits and Acknowledgments

Photo Credits

Page 2, Joel Gordon; 10, Sven Martson/Comstock; 18, AP/Wide World Photos; 19, John Coletti/ Stock, Boston; 30, Michael McGovern/Picture Cube; 45, Jim Pickerell/Stock, Boston; 51, Sven Martson/Comstock; 64, Sven Martson/Comstock; 69, Bruce Kliewe/Picture Cube; 91, Ron Chapple/FPG; 100, Rhoda Sidney/Monkmeyer; 104, Stuart Cohen/Comstock; 122, Stan Rowin/Picture Cube; 140, Sven Martson/Comstock; 146, Barbara Alper/Stock, Boston; 154, Mike Kagan/ Monkmeyer; 164, Bob Daemmrich/Stock, Boston; 167, Michael Weisbrot/Stock, Boston; 196, Richard Hutchings/Photo Researchers; 208, Richard Hutchings/Photo Researchers; 223, Ulrike Welsch; 230, Judy Gelles/Stock, Boston; 240, Joel Gordon; 248, Bob Daemmrich/Image Works; 264, Bob Kramer/Picture Cube; 267, Frank Siteman/Stock, Boston; 297, Anestis Diakopoulous/ Stock, Boston; 304, Joel Gordon; 310, Akos Svilvasi/Stock, Boston; 333, Joel Gordon; 350, Renee Lynn/Photo Researchers; 356, Gale Zucker/Stock, Boston; 371, J. Berndt/Stock, Boston; 382, Art Stein/Photo Researchers; 385, Bob Daemmrich/Stock, Boston; 408, Courtesy Aetna; 418, John Eastcott/Yva Momatiuk/Image Works; 423, J. D. Sloan/Picture Cube; 440, Gloria Karlson/Picture Cube; 450, Reuters/Bettmann; 460, AP/Wide World Photos; 464, Wide World Photos.

Figures and Tables and Text

Page 32, Figure 2.1: Drawing by Al Hirschfeld. Copyright © 1991 by Al Hirschfeld. Drawing reproduced by special arrangement with Hirschfeld's exclusive representative, The Margo Feiden Galleries Ltd., New York.

Page 81, Figure 3.2: "Abstraction Ladder" from *Language in Thought and Action,* Fourth Edition, by S. I. Hayakawa, copyright © 1978 by Harcourt Brace Jovanovich, Inc., reprinted by permission of the publisher.

Page 90, Table 3.1: From Judy Cornelia Pearson, *Gender and Communication.* Copyright © 1985 by Wm. C. Brown Communications, Inc., Dubuque, Iowa. All rights reserved. Reprinted by permission.

Page 109, Table 4.1: From *The Silent Language* by Edward T. Hall. Copyright © 1959, 1981 by Edward T. Hall. Used by permission of Doubleday, a division of Bantam Doubleday Dell Publishing Group, Inc.

Page 112, Figure 4.1: Adapted from Hargie et al., *Social Skills in Interpersonal Communication,* Cambridge, MA: Brookline Books, 1987, p. 128, Figure 2.1.

Page 115, Table 4.2: Adapted from "Judging Attraction from Non-verbal Behavior: The Gain Phenomenon," *Journal of Consulting and Clinical Psychology,* Vol. 43, 1975, pp. 491-497, The American Psychological Association. As appeared in *Nonverbal Communication in Human Interaction,* Second Edition, by Mark L. Knapp. Copyright © 1972, 1978 by Holt, Rinehart and Winston. Copyright 1975 by The American Psychological Association. Adapted by permission.

Page 120, Figure 4.3: From Barbara Madonik, "I Hear What You Say, But What Are You Telling Me?" Canadian Institute of Management, *Canadian Manager* 15 (1990), p. 19. Reprinted by permission of the author, Unicom Communication Consultants Inc., 379 Winnett Ave., Toronto, Ontario, Canada M6C 3M2.

Page 125, Figure 4.4: D. Morris, P. Collett, P. Marsh, and M. O'Shaughnessy, *Gestures,* New York: Stein and Day, 1979. Copyright © 1979 by Stein and Day, Publishers. Reprinted with permission of Stein and Day, Publishers.

Page 143, Figure 5.1: From L. Barker, R. Edwards, C. Gaines, K. Gladney, and F. Holley, "An Investigation of Proportional Time Spent in Various Communication Activities by College Students," *Journal of Applied Communication Research* 8, 1981. Reprinted by permission.

Page 177, Table 6.1: From Jack R. Gibb, "Defensive Communications," *Journal of Communication* 11 (1961): 141–148. Reprinted by permission of The International Communication Association.

Page 187, Table 6.2: From Mark L. Knapp, *Interpersonal Communication and Human Relationships* (Newton, MA: Allyn & Bacon, 1984), p. 33.

Page 198, Figure 6.1: From "Life in Hell" by Matt Groening, November 18, 1988. Published by Acme Features Syndicate. Copyright © 1988 by Matt Groening. Used by permission.

Page 220, Figure 7.1: From Joseph Luft, *Of Human Interaction,* Palo Alto, CA: National Books Press, 1969. Copyright © 1969 by National Books Press. By permission of National Books Press.

Page 221, Figure 7.2: From Joseph Luft, *Of Human Interaction,* Palo Alto, CA: National Books Press, 1969. Copyright © 1969 by National Books Press. By permission of National Books Press.

Page 229, Table 7.1: Adapted from David W. Johnson, *Reaching Out: Interpersonal Effectiveness and Self-Actualization,* 2d ed. © 1981, p. 44. Reprinted by permission of Prentice-Hall, Inc. Englewood Cliffs, NJ.

Page 247, Figure 8.1: Adapted from Thomas L. Moffat. *Selection Interviewing for Managers,* Harper & Row, Publisher, Inc., 1979. Reprinted by permission of the author.

Page 254, Table 8.3: Adapted from Cal Downs, "A Content Analysis of Twenty Interviews," *Personnel Administration and Public Review* (September 1971): 25.

Page 277, Figure 9.1: From Robert Freed Bales, *Personality and Interpersonal Behavior,* New York: Holt, Rinehart and Winston, 1970. Copyright © 1970 by Holt, Rinehart and Winston, Inc. Reprinted by permission of the author.

Page 288, Figure 9.2: From Robert Townsend, *Further Up the Organization,* New York: Knopf, 1985. Copyright © 1970, 1984 by Robert Townsend.

Page 295, Figure 9.4: From Robert Blake and Jane Mouton, "The Fifth Achievement," *Journal of Applied Behavioral Science* 6, 1970. Reprinted by permission of JAI Press, Inc.

Page 312, Table 10.1: From Lawrence B. Rosenfeld, *Analyzing Human Communication,* 2d ed., Kendall/Hunt Publishing Co., 1983.

Page 409, Table 12.1: Adapted from Frederick Williams, *The New Communications,* 2d ed. © 1989. Reprinted by permission of Wadsworth Publishing.

Page 425, Figure 13.1: From Larry A. Samovar and Richard E. Porter, *Communication Between Cultures,* Belmont, CA: Wadsworth, 1991, p. 235. Used by permission.

Name Index

Subject Index